Sufism and Saint Veneration in Contemporary Bangladesh

Focusing on the Maijbhandari movement in Chittagong, south-eastern Bangladesh, which claims the status of the only Sufi order originated in Bengal and which has gained immense popularity in recent years, this book provides a comprehensive picture of an important aspect of contemporary Bengali Islam in the South Asian context.

Expertise in South Asian languages and literatures is combined with ethnographic field work and theoretical formulations from a range of disciplines, including cultural anthropology, Islamic studies and religious studies. Analysing the Maijbhandaris tradition of Bengali spiritual songs, one of the largest popular song traditions in Bengal, the book presents an in-depth study of Bengali Sufi theology, hagiography and Maijbhandari esoteric songs, as well as a discussion of what Bengali Islam is. It is a useful contribution to South Asia Studies, as well as Islamic Studies.

Hans Harder is Professor of Modern South Asian Languages and Literatures in the South Asia Institute at Heidelberg University, Germany. His research interests include South Asian literatures and intellectual history, Bengali Islam, modern Hinduism and satirical traditions in South Asia.

Routledge Advances in South Asian Studies
Edited by Subrata K. Mitra
South Asia Institute, University of Heidelberg, Germany

South Asia, with its burgeoning, ethnically diverse population, soaring economies and nuclear weapons, is an increasingly important region in the global context. The series, which builds on this complex, dynamic and volatile area, features innovative and original research on the region as a whole or on the countries. Its scope extends to scholarly works drawing on the history, politics, development studies, sociology and economics of individual countries from the region, as well those that take an interdisciplinary and comparative approach to the area as a whole or to a comparison of two or more countries from this region. In terms of theory and method, rather than basing itself on any one orthodoxy, the series draws broadly on the insights germane to area studies, as well as the tool kit of the social sciences in general, emphasizing comparison, the analysis of the structure and processes and the application of qualitative and quantitative methods. The series welcomes submissions from established authors in the field as well as from young authors who have recently completed their doctoral dissertations.

1. **Perception, Politics and Security in South Asia**
   The compound crisis of 1990
   P. R. Chari, Pervaiz Iqbal Cheema and Stephen Philip Cohen

2. **Coalition Politics and Hindu Nationalism**
   Edited by Katharine Adeney and Lawrence Saez

3. **The Puzzle of India's Governance**
   Culture, context and comparative theory
   Subrata K. Mitra

4. **India's Nuclear Bomb and National Security**
   Karsten Frey

5. **Starvation and India's Democracy**
   Dan Banik

6. **Parliamentary Control and Government Accountability in South Asia**
   A comparative analysis of Bangladesh, India and Sri Lanka
   Taiabur Rahman

7. **Political Mobilisation and Democracy in India**
   States of emergency
   Vernon Hewitt

8. **Military Control in Pakistan**
   The parallel state
   Mazhar Aziz

9. **Sikh Nationalism and Identity in a Global Age**
   Giorgio Shani

10. **The Tibetan Government-in-Exile**
    Politics at large
    Stephanie Roemer

11. **Trade Policy, Inequality and Performance in Indian Manufacturing**
    Kunal Sen

12. **Democracy and Party Systems in Developing Countries**
    A comparative study
    Clemens Spiess

13. **War and Nationalism in South Asia**
    The Indian state and the Nagas
    Marcus Franke

14. **The Politics of Social Exclusion in India**
    Democracy at the crossroads
    Edited by Harihar Bhattacharyya, Partha Sarka and Angshuman Kar

15. **Party System Change in South India**
    Political entrepreneurs, patterns and processes
    Andrew Wyatt

16. **Dispossession and Resistance in India**
    The river and the rage
    Alf Gunvald Nilsen

17. **The Construction of History and Nationalism in India**
    Textbooks, controversies and politics
    Sylvie Guichard

18. Political Survival in Pakistan
Beyond ideology
Anas Malik

19. New Cultural Identitarian Political Movements in Developing Societies
The Bharatiya Janata Party
Sebastian Schwecke

20. Sufism and Saint Veneration in Contemporary Bangladesh
The Maijbhandaris of Chittagong
Hans Harder

Sufism and Saint Veneration in Contemporary Bangladesh

The Maijbhandaris of Chittagong

Hans Harder

Routledge
Taylor & Francis Group
LONDON AND NEW YORK

First published 2011
by Routledge
2 Park Square, Milton Park, Abingdon, Oxfordshire OX14 4RN

Simultaneously published in the USA and Canada
by Routledge
711 Third Avenue, New York NY10017

First issued in paperback 2015

Routledge is an imprint of the Taylor & Francis Group, an informa business

British Library Cataloguing in Publication Data
A catalogue record for this book is available from the British Library

Library of Congress Cataloging in Publication Data
Harder, Hans.
Sufism and saint veneration in contemporary Bangladesh : the Maijbhandaris of Chittagong / Hans Harder.
p. cm.
Includes bibliographical references and index.
(ebook) 1. Sufism—Bangladesh—Maijbhandar. 2. Sufi poetry, Bengali—Bangladesh—Maijbhandar. 3. Muslim saints—Bangladesh—Maijbhandar.—4. Sufis—Bangladesh—Maijbhandar.—I. Title.
BP188.8.B36H37 2010
297.40954'14—dc22

2010031553

ISBN 13: 978-1-138-94827-3 (pbk)
ISBN 13: 978-0-415-58170-7 (hbk)

Typeset in Times by
RefineCatch Ltd, Bungay, Suffolk

Contents

List of illustrations ix
Preface x
Transliteration and writing conventions xii
Abbreviations xiv

1 Introduction **1**

1.1 Approaching Maijbhandar 7
1.2 Shrines in Chittagong 10
1.3 Maijbhandar: a shrine complex and religious movement 14
1.4 Historical outline 20

2 Structure and religious practice **31**

2.1 Structure of the Maijbhandari movement 31
2.2 Religious practice in Maijbhandar 48

3 Theological and hagiological writings **66**

3.1 Love (ʿišq, prem) *69*
3.2 Light (nūr) *72*
3.3 Stations (maqāmāt) *76*
3.4 Manifest (ẓāhir) *and concealed* (bāṭin), šarīʿa *and* ṭarīqa *80*
3.5 Unity (tawḥīd) *84*
3.6 Spiritual sovereignty (wilāya) *88*
3.7 The Maijbhandari tarīqa *96*

4 Hagiographies **106**

4.1 Muslim hagiography in Bengal 107
4.2 Maijbhandari hagiographies 112
4.3 Hagiographies about founding Saint Ġawṯ al-Aʿẓam Ahmadullah Maijbhandari (1829–1906) 113

4.4 Hagiographies about the second great Maijbhandari saint, Gholam Rahman alias Bābā Bhāṇḍārī (1865–1937) 136
4.5 Shahanshah Ziaul Haq Maijbhandari (1928–88) 148
4.6 Syed Shafiul Bashar (1919–2001) 162
4.7 Analysis 167

5 Maijbhandari songs **172**

5.1 Origins and basic properties 173
5.2 Performance situations 175
5.3 Debates on audition (samā‘) *179*
5.4 Musical performance 183
5.5 Classifications of Maijbhandari songs 185
5.6 Language and communicative design 189
5.7 Motifs of Maijbhandari songs 195
5.8 Conclusion 270

6 Songs in contemporary Maijbhandari interpretations **272**

6.1 Boat journeys and sandhābhāṣā *274*
6.2 Lovers as Radha and Krishna 280
6.3 Symbolical changes of sex 282
6.4 The avatāra *concept 284*

7 Contextualising Maijbhandar **287**

7.1 'Syncretism', 'little tradition', 'discursive fields' 287
7.2 Correlating Maijbhandar with Islam and other religions 298
7.3 Lack of structural fixity: a sketch of the discursive field of Maijbhandar 305
7.4 How does Maijbhandar work? An interpretation 311

8 Conclusion: a note on Bengali Islam **315**

8.1 The configuration of shrine and pīr *veneration in Bengal 317*
8.2 Medieval Bengali Islamic literature: documentation rather than mediation 323
8.3 On Bengali Islam 326

Appendix I: translations of selected Maijbhandari songs 330
Appendix II: glossary of terms 343
Bibliography 347
Index 367

List of illustrations

Maps

1 Bengal 4
2 Chittagong/Maijbhandar 14

Photos

1 Saint Ahmadullah Maijbhandari's new mausoleum, Maijbhandar 35
2 Dancing at an *ʿurs* celebration in 1999, Maijbhandar 53
3 Syed Moinuddin Ahmad al-Hasani al-Maijbhandari receiving *murīds* 60
4 Prophet Muhammad's and Saint ʿAbd al-Qadir Gilani's footprints in the Qadam Mubarak Mosque, Anderkilla, Chittagong 74
5 Cover of *Jībanī o kerāmat* 126
6 Mausoleum of Saint Gholam Rahman Maijbhandari 137
7 Mausoleum of Saint Ziaul Haq Maijbhandari 157
8 Singing Maijbhandari songs at an *ʿurs* celebration in 1999, Maijbhandar 177
9 Another example of an *ʿurs* performance situation of Maijbhandari songs, Maijbhandar 1999 252
10 Bathing in the pond by the side of Saint Ahmadullah's former mausoleum; Maijbhandar 1999 299
11 The entrance to Saint Gholam Rahman's shrine, Maijbhandar 321

Preface

During my first journey to Chittagong, Bangladesh's major harbour city, in 1992, I happened to hear Maijbhandari songs played in a shop by the roadside in the city. I decided to pay a visit to the spot that is the centre of this highly popular musical tradition: the shrine complex of Maijbhandar in rural Chittagong, some forty kilometres north of the city. Talking to some visitors and shrine servants there, I was impressed by the friendly atmosphere, and managed to collect a few books and cassettes. My then Ph.D guide, Professor Rahul Peter Das, had mentioned this popular religious movement to me, and I gradually realised how interesting the Maijbhandaris were in themselves and in the context of Bengali Islam in general. I returned in 1999 and 2001 for two-month fieldwork periods and again for a short visit in 2008. The book at hand originated as a postdoctoral thesis or *Habilitation* at the Seminar for South Asian Studies at Martin Luther University, Halle-Wittenberg. It is the first comprehensive monograph on this religious movement in any European language.

A subject like Bengali Islam might seem to fall into the academic field of Islamic Studies, and someone authoring a book on this topic might thus be expected to be formally trained in that field. My academic affiliation, however, is to South Asian Studies with a focus on Bengali language and culture. Though I have tried my best to handle the Urdu and Persian sources found in Maijbhandar and to acquaint myself with Islamic culture and the research about it, I am sure that knowledge of Arabic would have opened up a number of additional perspectives on the topic. But, as things stand in the present academic landscape, no single existing discipline could claim to furnish a comprehensive basis for the study of Bengali Islam. And a South Asianist perspective on Bengali Islam has the one advantage of quite naturally granting it centre-stage.

I am grateful to a large number of persons for help, advice and assistance in many ways, and it is not possible to name them all. In Chittagong, the representatives of Ahmadiyya Manzil in Maijbhandar, especially Syed Shahidul Haq, hosted me while in Maijbhandar, and assisted me in various ways in my research work, for which I owe them my most heartfelt gratitude. The present volume, of course, deviates a lot from the way believers would portray Maijbhandar, but I have tried to do justice to Maijbhandari self-representations, and sincerely hope my hosts and interlocutors will find the result appreciable and useful. I also found an open reception at other branches of the Maijbhandari movement, and I would like to thank the late Syed Shafiul Bashar, Syed Badruddoza, Syed Muinuddin Ahmad, Syed Hasan, Syed Amirul Islam, the late Syed Abul Fazl and his sons, to name only very few, for their readiness to meet me and bear with my questioning. In particular, the songwriter Abdul Gafur Hali helped me a lot with his comments, friendship and hospitality; the same is true of Syed Badiuzzaman of Haq Manzil. I also wish to thank Syed Ahmadul Haq of the Allama Rumi Society of Chittagong for the open reception and the interest he has taken in my research. My friend Sujit Chowdhury (Göttingen/Chittagong), as well as Shishir Datta and the BITA staff in Chittagong, helped me enormously at various stages, and not in the least by providing me with accommodation and e-mail access, thus furnishing me with an infrastructure while in Chittagong. Mahabubul Haq and Shamsul Hosain, both affiliated to Chittagong University, assisted me by their hospitality and by discussing various aspects of my work. Dr Manzurul Mannan (Dhaka) has variously helped me with information and discussions about Maijbhandar. In particular, I would like to thank Mofidul Haq (Dhaka) for his friendship and long-standing interest in my research.

As regards the more narrowly academic side of this work, I wish to thank first of all my teacher and supervisor, Professor Rahul Peter Das, of Halle University, who has all along inspired and very thoroughly guided me, and without whose help this volume would never have seen the light of day. I also thank Professor Jürgen Paul (Halle University), Professor Richard Eaton (University of Arizona) and Professor Catharina Kiehnle (Leipzig University) for their readiness to act as examiners of this postdoctoral thesis. Professor Patrick Franke (Bamberg), Dr Olaf Kranz (Halle/Chemnitz), Professor Walter Beltz (Berlin), Professor Peter Bertocci (Rochester/USA), Dr Alokeranjan Dasgupta (Heidelberg), Dr Makoto Kitada (Kyoto/Tokio), Professor Michael Bergunder (Heidelberg), Keri Jones (Cork, Ireland), Ahmed Abdelsalam (Halle), Dorothea Deutler (Heidelberg) and many others have helped me at different stages of this work. I am also grateful to Professor Marcus Nüsser and Nils Harm from the geographical department of the South Asia Institute (Heidelberg) for preparing the maps included in this volume. A special thank you goes to my colleague Subrata K. Mitra (Heidelberg), editor of Routledge's Advances in South Asian Studies, for looking favourably at my work and for including this book in his series. Last but not least, I am grateful to the Routledge team (Dorothea Schaefter and Jillian Morrison), who have taken good care of this undertaking, and to Torsten Tschacher (Heidelberg) for his many last-minute corrections and comments.

Hans Harder
Heidelberg, April 2010

Transliteration and writing conventions

(a) Terms and passages

The established systems of transliteration for Arabic, Persian, Urdu, Hindi, Bengali and Sanskrit are used for rendering terms, publications and passages from these languages. With single terms, however, the problem is that they are used in more than one of these languages. Some Arabic words, for instance, have entered Bengali via Persian and Urdu. To transcribe them differently according to the language in which they occur would put a heavy strain on the reader's patience and also risk appearing obscure. I have therefore decided to use a subsidiary principle: I will give well-known Islamic terms (the bulk of the terms in this book) in Arabic, unless their specific syntactic forms require a rendering according to – in this order – Persian, Urdu or Bengali transcription. For instance, *wilāya* (Ar., 'spiritual sovereignty, sainthood') generally appears as *wilāya*, but also when required as *vilāyat* in *vilāyat-i muṭlaqa* (P.), *wilāyat* in *wilāyat kā zamāna* (U.), or *belāẏat* in *belāẏater ghaṇṭā* (Bg.). The respective languages and terms of origin are given in brackets whenever deemed necessary for transparency. Likewise with terms of Sanskrit origin for a Hindu or Buddhist background: e.g. *triveṇī* (Skt.), but *tribeṇīr ghāṭ* (Bg.).

- In transcribing the Arabic script, I have paid heed to the system proposed by the transcription commission of the German Oriental Society (Deutsche Morgenländische Gesellschaft); cf. Brockelmann et al. 1969, especially the tables for Arabic and Persian (p. 9) and for Urdu (p. 20). I deviate from that system mainly in writing out the *hamza* in Persian terms (*āʾīna*, not *āīna*) and in avoiding all *umlaut* vowels. For Arabic terms, I use the consonantal system of transcription (*nubuwwa* instead of *nubūwa*, *ġawṯiyya* instead of *ġauṯīya*). Arabic plural forms are avoided whenever they are uncommon in Bengali and unlikely to be understood by South Asian speakers (e.g. *murīd*s instead of *murīdīn* and *fatwa*s instead of *fatāwa*; but *maqāmāt* as the plural of *maqām*).
- In Persian, the Arabic *ṯ*, *ḏ*, *ḍ* and *w* are given as *s̱*, *ẕ*, *ż* and *v* respectively. Contrary to modern Persian, I retain the vocalisation as in Arabic, which is closer to subcontinental usage.
- Urdu transcription follows the Persian, with a number of additions: *t*˙, *d*˙ and *ṛ* for the retroflex consonants; *ē* and *ō* when written out as *yā* and *wāw*, but *e* and *o* when not (e.g. *woh* but *lōg*, *yeh* but *karnēwālē*); and *ṇ* for the *nūn-i ġunna*.

- Bengali is transcribed mostly according to standard Sanskrit transcription, with a few additions (I mostly follow Rahul Peter Das 1983: 66, n.2, except in his treatment of retroflex *r* and *b* as a latter part in conjuncts): I use *ṛ* for the retroflex and *r̥* for the vocalic *r*, *ẏ* for the *antastha ẏa*, ' to mark the omission of inherent *a* wherever not evident from Bengali pronunciation rules, and to represent *hasanta* (i.e. the *virāma*). Further, *b*, whenever not separately pronounced as the latter part of consonant combinations, is rendered by *v* (e.g. *tattva* instead of *tattba*). In quotations from metrical Bengali sources, especially Maijbhandari songs, I have whenever possible tried to indicate additionally pronounced inherent *a* in brackets (e.g. *āllār(a) āuliẏā yārā/duniẏāte jindā marā*).
- Notwithstanding the subsidiary principle outlined above, whole passages given in the text are transcribed consistently according to the norms for the respective language (Arabic, Persian, Urdu, Bengali, Sanskrit).
- Italics are used for non-English terms in the text (e.g. *ḥalqa-i ẕikr*, *ādhyātmik*), for transcriptions from non-Latin scripts and occasionally for emphasis.

(b) Names

Names of persons (contemporary or historical, human or non-human) and places are given in Anglicised forms (e.g. Allah, Krishna, Mecca, Vrindavan, Kashi, Muhammad, Abdul Karin Sahityavasharad). The original forms in transliteration may in some instances be given along with these if deemed necessary. Exceptions are uncommon names, epithets and titles (e.g. Ajapā, Phoẏā, Śyāmā, Ġawṯ al-Aʿẓam) and etymological arguments (e.g. *aḥad*, *Aḥmad*, *Muḥammad*) where the literal form of the name assumes meaning. In names transcribed from Arabic, Persian and Urdu, diacritics are omitted except the signs for *ʿayn* and *hamza* (e.g. Ibn ʿArabi, ʿAbd al-Qadir Gilani).

- Names of saints, prophets, venerated persons, deities, etc. are usually given in the shortest possible forms. Titles, epithets aud eulogies are mostly omitted for the sake of transparency and brevity.
- Whenever given, titles are rendered in diacritics but not italicised (e.g. Bābājān, Ġawṯ al-Aʿẓam, Ǧanāb Mawlā).
- Authors' names of publications in languages not using Roman script are given in Anglicised forms when they appear independently in the text, but in diacritics according to the respective language when they appear in bibliographic references (e.g. Wahidul Alam; but 'Cf. Ohīdul Ālam (1989: 13)').
- Names of religions and religious groups, including Sufi brotherhoods, are given in their Anglicised forms without diacritics (e.g. Maijbhandaris, Sufis, Bauls, Vaishnavism, Qadiriyya). Forms transcribed from the original languages are, if deemed necessary, given at their first occurrence in the text.
- Hybrid adjectives built from names of religious groups or religious and literary categories are written without diacritics, and they are capitalised only if derived from clearly circumscribed groups (e.g. pauranic, tantric, Sufic).

Abbreviations

ĀB — ʿ**A**bd al-Ġanī Kānčanpūrī (1914–15): *Āʾīna-i bārī*. Reprint, ed. Dilāwar Ḥusain. Čandanpūra, Islāmiyya Līt·hō ēnd· Print·ing Prēs; 2nd edn approx. 1950; 1st edn 1914–15; 3rd edn (given as 2nd edn) 2007, ed. Saiẏad Em'dādul Hak Māij'bhāṇḍārī. Maijbhandar, editor's publication.

AJ — Mo. **M**āh'bub ul Ālam (2000): *Aiśī ālor jal'sāghar*. Caṭṭagrām, Saiẏad Mohāmmad Hāsān.

ĀM — Svargīẏa **R**ameś Candra Sar'kār (Lok Kabi Kabiẏāl Rameś Śīl) (1992): *Āśek mālā: māij bhāṇḍārī mār'phatī o bicched gāner baï*. Gom'daṇḍī, Pulin Bihārī Śīl.

BB — Śāh'jādā Saiẏad **B**ad'ruddojā (1394 BE [1377 BE]): *Alīkul śiromaṇi hay'rat bābā bhāṇḍārī*. Māij'bhāṇḍār, Śāh'jādā Saiẏad Bad'ruddojā, Gāuchiẏā Rah'mān man'jel; 4th edn.

BhM — *Bhāṇḍāre māolā*. In: **R**ameś Śīl (1993): *Rameś śīl racanābalī*. Ḍhākā, Bāṃlā Ekāḍemī; pp. 117–36.

BM — Maolānā Saiẏad **D**elāor Hosāin (1980?): *Belāẏate mot·lākā*. Māij'bhāṇḍār, Gāuchiẏā Āh'madiẏā Mañjil; 4th edn.

DS — Md. **G**hulam Rasul (1994): *The Divine Spark. Shahanshah Ziaul Hoque (K.)*. Maizbhandar, Gausia Hoque Manzil; 1st edn.

ER — Maulānā Saiẏad **D**elāoẏār Hosāin (n.d.): *Elākār renesā̃ yuger ek'ṭi dik·*. Māij'bhāṇḍār, Gāuchiẏā Āh'madīẏā Mañjil.

GP — Āl-hājv Śāh'jādī Saiẏadā **L**ut·phunnechā Hosāīnī 'Suphiẏānā' (1992): *Gāuchiẏater phul: jal'oẏāẏe 'śaphi bābā'*. Caṭṭagrām, author's publication.

HB — Śāh'jādā Saiẏad **M**unirul Hak (ed.) (1988): *Hṛdaẏ bhāṇḍār*. Māij'bhāṇḍār Śarīph, editor's publication; 2nd edn.

IPS — Saiẏad **G**olām Mor'śed (1994): *Is'lāmī prabandha sambhār*. Caṭṭagrām, Saiẏadā Os'mānā Mor'śed.

JC — Śāh Chuphī Māolānā Chaiẏad Āb'duch Chālām **I**chāpurī Chāheb (ra.) (n.d.): *Hay'rat Gāuchul Ājam Māolānā āl· Chaiẏad Golāmur Rah'mān āl·-Hāsānī āl·-Māij'bhāṇḍārī (ka.) Bābājān Kveb'lā Kābār jīban carit*. Khātun'gañj, Mo. Mijānur Rah'mān/Saiẏad Śaphiul Baśar.

JH — Jāmāl Āh'mad **S**ik'dār (1987 [1982]): *Śāhān'śāh jiẏāul hak māij'bhāṇḍārī*. Māij'bhāṇḍār, Gāuchiẏā Hak Man·jil; 2nd edn.

JJ Āb'dul **G**aphur Hālī (1989): *Jñān'jyoti.* Raśidābād, Mohāmmat·Rābeẏā Khātun.

JK Maolānā Mo. Faijullāh **B**hūiẏā (1993 [1967]): *Hayarat gāuchul ājam śāh chuphī māolānā saiẏad āh'mad ullāh (ka.) māij'bhāṇḍārīr jībanī o kerāmat.* Māij'bhāṇḍār, Śāh'jādā Saiẏad Munirul Hak; 9th edn.

JK(a) Maulānā Mo. Faijullāh **B**hūiẏā (1979 [1967]): *Hay'rat gāuchul ājam śāh chuphī maulānā saiẏad āh'mad ullāh (ka.) māij'bhāṇḍārīr jībanī o kerāmat.* Māij'bhāṇḍār, Śāh'jādā Saiẏad Munirul Hak; 4th edn.

JS Svargīẏa **R**ameś Candra Sar'kār (Lok Kabi Kabiẏāl Rameś Śīl) (1992): *Jīban sāthī: māij bhāṇḍārī mār'phatī o bicched gāner baï.* Gom'daṇḍī, Pulin Bihārī Śīl.

KB Jahir Āh'mad **C**audhurī (1989): *Khat·mul belāẏat.* Caṭṭagrām, publisher unknown.

Madirā Adhyāpikā **B**ad'run·nesā Sāju (1998): *Madirā.* Dam'damā, Gāuchiẏā Rah'māniẏā Gaṇi Man·jil.

MD Svargīẏa **R**ameś Candra Sar'kār (Lok Kabi Kabiẏāl Rameś Śīl) (1992): *Muktir dar'bār: māij bhāṇḍārī mār'phatī o bicched gāner baï.* Gom'daṇḍī, Pulin Bihārī Śīl.

MŚ Miẏā **N**az'rul Is'lām (ed.) (1995): *Māij'bhāṇḍār śarīph.* Ḍhākā, Māij'bhāṇḍār Gabeṣaṇā Pariṣad.

MT Khādemul Phok'rā Maolānā Saiẏad **D**elāor Hosāin (1995): *Mūl tattva bā taj'kīẏāẏe mokh'tāchār.* Māij'bhāṇḍār, author's publication; 5th edn; 1st edn 1969.

ND *Nure duniẏā.* In: **R**ameś Śīl (1993): *Rameś śīl racanābalī*; Ḍhākā, Bāṃlā Ekāḍemī; 59–77.

PH Maolānā Mohāmmad **B**aj'lul Karim (n.d.): *Premer hem.* Ed. Maolānā Śāh'jādā Saiẏad Bad'ruddojā. Bhāṇḍār Śarīph, Gāuchiẏā Rah'mān Man'jel.

PR Mo. Āb'dul Jabbār Śāh·**M**im'nagarī (1999): *Pañcaratnagītikā.* Karim'gañj (Mymensingh), S.M. Naj'rul Is'lām; 2nd edn; 1st edn 1988.

RB Śāh'jādā Saiẏad **M**unirul Hak (1994): *Ratnabhāṇḍār*, pratham khaṇḍa. Māij'bhāṇḍār, Gāuchiẏā Āh'madiẏā Mañjil.

RS Sūphī Mau. Āb'dul **H**ādī (n.d.): *Ratna sāgar.* Ed. Pīr'jādā Saiẏad Ābu Āh'mad Miẏā. Māij'bhāṇḍār, editor's publ ication; 5th edn.

SB Śāh'jādā Saiẏad **M**unirul Hak (ed.) (1985): *Saurabh bhāṇḍār.* Māij'bhāṇḍār Śarīph, editor's publication.

ŚB Svargīẏa **R**ameś Candra Sar'kār (Lok Kabi Kabiẏāl Rameś Śīl) (1992): *Śāntibhāṇḍār: māij bhāṇḍārī mār'phatī o bicched gāner baï.* Gom'daṇḍī, Pulin Bihārī Śīl.

ŚBJ Āl·hājv Śāh·jādī Chaiẏadā **L**ut·phunnechā Hosāinī Āl·-Māij'bhāṇḍārī (1993): *Śājjādānaśīn o montājeme dar'bār, Śāh'jādāẏe Gāuchul Ājam Haj'rat Śāh'chuphī āl·-hājv Māolānā āl· Chaiẏad Śaphiul Baśar āl·-Hācānī āl·-Māij'bhāṇḍārī (mu. ā.) keb'lā kābār jībanī.* Caṭṭagrām, Suphiẏānā; 3rd edn; 1st edn 1987.

SD *Satya darpaṇ.* In: **R**ameś Śīl (1993): *Rameś śīl racanābalī.* Ḍhākā, Bāṃlā Ekāḍemī; 97–116.

ŚJ	Māolānā **B**aj'lul Karim Māndākinī (1999): *Śeṣ jīban*. Ed. Māh'bub ul Ālam. Māij'bhāṇḍār, Saiẏad Mohāmmad Hāsān.
Tāohīd	Āl·hājv Śāh·jādī Saiẏadā **L**ut·phunnechā Hosāinī 'Suphiẏānā' (1999): *Tāohīd*. Caṭṭagrām, author's publication.
TB	Āb'dul **G**aphur Hālī (1989 [1969]): *Tattvabidhi*. Raśidābād/Śobhan'daṇḍī, author's publication.
Tuḥfat	Chaiẏad **Ā**minul Hak Phar'hādābādī (1997): *Tuḥfat al-aḫyār fī daf' šarārat al-ašrār: sema' bā gān bājānā sambandhīẏa phatoẏā*. Phar'hādābād, Phar'hādābād Dar'bār Śarīph, 1st edn 1906/7; 3rd edn 1997; 2 vols.
VG	Hans Harder (2004): *Der verrückte Gofur spricht. Mystische Lieder aus Ostbengalen*. Heidelberg, Draupadi Verlag.
YB	Chaiẏad **Ś**aphiul Baśar (n.d.): *Yuger ālo o buker khun*. Bhāṇḍār Śarīph, Gāuchiẏā Rah'mān Man·jil.
ZH	Syed Mohd. **A**mirul Islam (1992): *Shahenshah Ziaul Huq Maijbhandari*; n. pl., Mirza Ali Behrouze Ispahani; 1st edn.

Other abbreviations

Ar.	Arabic
Bg.	Bengali
Eng.	English
H.	Hindi
P.	Persian
Skt.	Sanskrit
U.	Urdu

1 Introduction

> We can call the religion practised in Maijbhandar a kind of indigenous [*deśaj*] Islam.[1]
>
> Islam is one. There cannot be such a thing as indigenous Islam.[2]

What is Bengali Islam? Or, posing the question more generally, is there anything such as Bengali Islam at all? Is it reasonable to inquire into the nature of such an entity, or is 'Bengali Islam' actually a non-entity formed by an illegitimate combination of categories? Strange as it may sound, these are the crossroads anyone approaching this question is confronted with sooner rather than later. In fact, the term Bengali Islam is synthetic in character, merging, as it does, ethnic, linguistic and religious denominators in an attribute-noun construction; and thus, arguments may arise about the validity of such merging. Are not, as one type of argument would have it, both categories situated on completely different planes that prevent any interaction between them, and is their combination therefore anything but a baseless contrivance? Islam being one, a variant of this line goes, it is meaningless to speak of Bengali Islam, as this would imply that the attribute 'Bengali' modifies the meaning of the noun Islam in some way or other, which by definition of the latter cannot be the case. If at all, Islam *in* Bengal might be admitted as a sensible object of investigation, concerned with the character and effects of Islam in the region of Bengal. Historical evidence and direct perception, another type of argument holds, furnish sufficient data to disprove such contentions; distinctness of religious practice, textual traditions, cultural environment, etc. bear out the assumption that the expression 'Bengali Islam' does indeed denote something that exists and can reasonably be investigated.

The hermeneutical problem sketched out in these two extreme positions is not a mere academic preoccupation, but has been a bother to many strands of Bengali society for quite a long time. The juxtaposition of Bengaliness and Islam has caused much unease, and these terms are often conceived as competing

1 Statement by one Maijbhandari *pīr* in an interview (26 March 1999).

2 Statement by another Maijbhandari *pīr* (22 January 2001).

categories. Rather than relying on their partial overlap in order to ensure their harmonious coexistence, their inherent tensions are activated by various political and cultural agencies. Imminent solutions to this problem are not in sight at present either. Especially in the young nation-state of Bangladesh, the question whether Bengaliness or Islam should be the predominant factor has, for obvious historical reasons, again become a major preoccupation in the political and cultural domains. More than other Muslims, the Bengali Muslims are portrayed as having problems in reconciling their religious and ethnic identities, so much so that Joya Chatterjee felt prompted to ask: 'The Bengali Muslims: a Contradiction in Terms?' (Chatterjee 1998). While it would be more than misleading to insinuate that most of the *c.* 160 millions of Bengali Muslims consciously suffer from any such inherent identity conflict, the fact remains that in some quarters, especially among the political and cultural elite, the question about the relationship between Bengaliness and Islam is troublesome. This is also true of much of the academic literature on the topic.

A good example of the dilemma awaiting scholars of Bengali Islam is Md. Enamul Haq (1902–82). This renowned Bengali historian of religion grew up in Baktapur in rural Chittagong, in the direct vicinity of the shrine complex of Maijbhandar which this book is about, as the son of one Maulana Aminullah.[3] A well-known Bangladeshi historian related an anecdote to me according to which Enamul Haq in his youth once visited Maijbhandar with a co-student in order to pray for success in his examinations. During their prayer at the tomb, the servants of the shrine pushed the boys to the ground, maintaining that the right way to show obeisance to a saint was to touch the floor with one's forehead. Such behaviour, however, clashed with Haq's reformist Islamic education, according to which *sağda*, 'full prostration', was exclusively due to Allah during the ritual prayers. It was allegedly triggered by this and similar experiences that Haq later decided to single out Bengali Islam as his life-long topic of research.[4] In his *History of Sufi-ism in Bengal*, which was to appear in 1975 after being withheld from publication in the Pakistani period, he describes the doctrines and history of Indian and, subsequent to it, Bengali Islam, examines Islamic saints in Bengal, discusses the mutual influences among Sufism, Vaishnavism, Yoga and Tantra, and dedicates a separate chapter to the Bengali Bauls.[5] On the one hand, Enamul Haq narrates the independent development of Bengali Islam as a story of decay:

3 Cf. the life-sketch by Mansur Musa in Hak (1991: 719) ('Muhammad Enāmul Haker jīban o sāhitya', pp. 719–51).

4 These anecdotes have been related to me in private communication by the historian Abdul Karim (Interview February 2001).

5 The Bauls are a religious group positing themselves beyond either Islamic or Hindu traditions. We shall have occasion to refer to them many times in the following pages. For a survey about this group, which has been the subject of a huge amount of literature, cf. most expertly Openshaw (2002) and Rahul Peter Das (1992), as well as the classical study by Upendranāth Bhaṭṭācārya (2001; 1st edn 1957).

> From the seventeenth century downward, Ṣūfīism in Bengal adopted a new channel and within a century and a half, it absorbed so many indigenous elements in both beliefs and practices that it not only lost its pristine purity and individuality but also its spiritual significance, inherent strength and expansive character.
>
> (Hak 1975: 52)

In his preface, Haq feels prompted to apologise to his co-religionists that he has chosen to approach the topic with a 'dispassionate attitude', and ascertains that wherever possible he has followed the teachings of the *Qur'ān* and *Ḥadīṯ*. On the other hand, when it comes to portraying the Bengali Bauls whom Haq loosely affiliates with Sufism, the tenor of his narration changes completely:

> They dreamt the dream of a 'Natural Religion' (*Sahaj Dharma*) of men, which advocates liberality, brotherhood, universality and above all the natural right of [the] human being to aspire after unravelling divine mystery.
>
> (Hak 1975: 295)

The Bauls are the quintessence of Bengali spontaneity and sensibility: their songs 'easily penetrate a Bengali heart', and Bengal 'will never forget the songs of a real Baul' (p. 316).[6] Haq is apparently torn between his seemingly incompatible alliances to Bengal and Islam. He conceives of the latter as an essentialised entity of 'pristine purity' (Hak 1995: 52), and it is obviously this normativity that blocks a value-neutral assessment of 'Bengali Islam'.[7]

Another example of such ambivalence is Asim Roy's approach. His book on the Islamic syncretistic tradition (Roy 1983) is an impressive study of a class of medieval Bengali texts written by Bengali Muslims between the fifteenth and eighteenth centuries. The texts are, according to Roy, characterised by the integration of Hindu gods and heroes, cosmologies and mythologies into an Islamic framework. In his book and related essays (Roy 1996), Roy uses the concept of syncretism as an explanatory tool for such phenomena.[8] He portrays the writers of those texts as 'cultural mediators' operating between the distinctive social groups of immigrated, Persophone 'gentry' (Ar. *ašrāf*) and lower-ranked indigenous converts to Islam (B. *āj'lāph/āt'rāp*, from Ar. *aǧlāf*), communicating Islamic teachings to the latter in an idiom understandable to them, and with the help of familiar mythological imagery. Drawing up a historical frame of conversion to

6 The notion of some essential Bengaliness in the Bauls seems to go back to Rabindranath Tagore, most prominently his essay 'The Religion of Man' (1930: 182 ff.), and it is not unlikely that Enamul Haq's appraisal was directly influenced by this.

7 Cf. Tschacher (2009: 56) who, criticising facile scholarly distinctions between scriptural and popular Islam, writes: 'All these models are ultimately based on the assumption that what is normative and what is not in Islamic religiosity can be known beforehand, that certain aspects are identifiable as normative, while others are not.' We will have occasion to deal with this problematic at different stages of this investigation, most notably in Chapter 8.

8 We will deal with this concept extensively in Chapter 7.1.

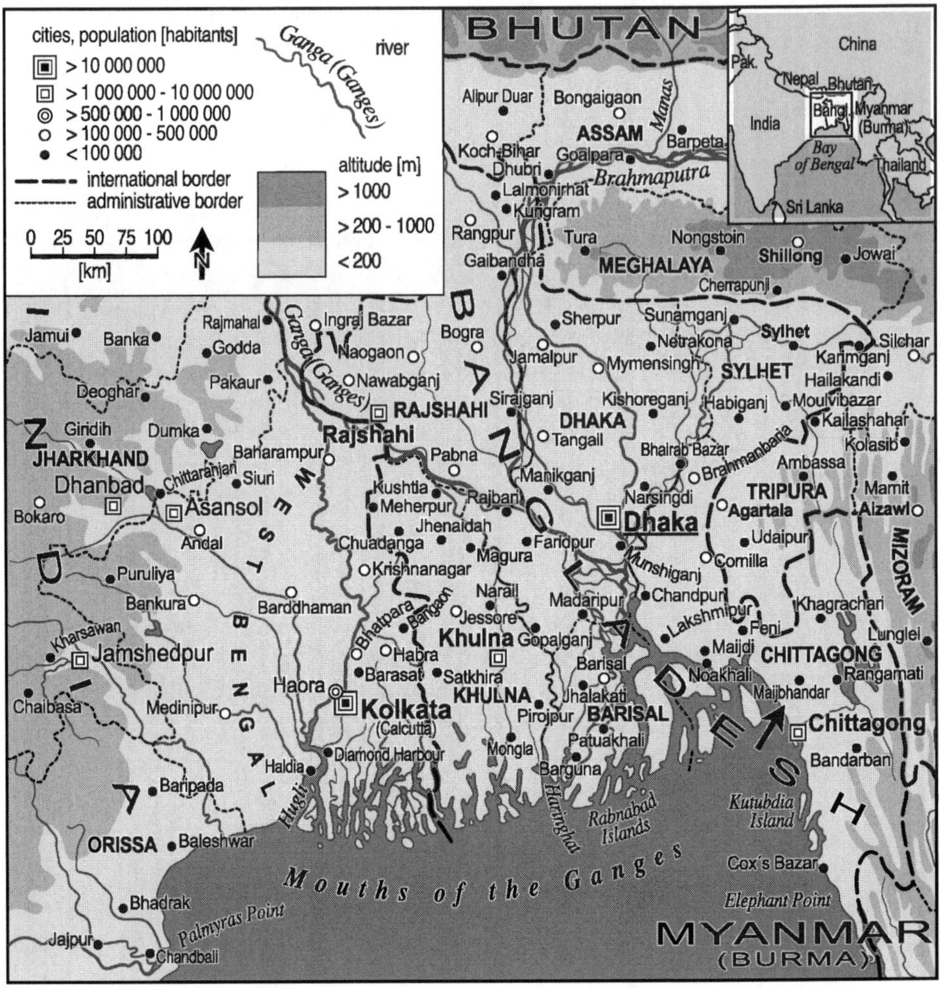

Map 1 Bengal.

Islam in the Delta, Roy distinguishes a number of overlapping but, in principle, succeeding stages: a phase of nominal group conversion in the sense of alliance shifting rather than a change of faith is followed by a 'syncretistic phase' of propagating Islam in indigenous categories, which in its turn is finally succeeded by the Islamic reformist movements of the nineteenth and twentieth centuries. Roy accuses the latter of 'widening the hiatus that already existed between the exogenous Islam and the indigenous Bengali culture and of deepening the crisis of Bengali Muslim identity' (Roy 1996: 36). Nevertheless, elsewhere, he seems to regard the purification process represented by the reformists as a necessary development, and asserts that there is continuity between the syncretist and ensuing reformist phases (Roy 1996: 114). Roy remains ambivalent in his evaluation of this Islamisation process, but his line of thought seems to come down to the following: Islam entered Bengal as an exogeneous religion; nominal converts' access remained barred due to social and linguistic boundaries; the syncretistic 'great tradition' of medieval Bengali texts and various little traditions helped indigenise Islam; but reformism, while driving the process of Islamisation further, reinscribed the gap between that exogeneous religion and indigenous culture. Roy states this uneasy tension on the object level, but it is clear that this has repercussions on the premises of his investigation and the kind of look he takes at Bengali Islam.

Similar problems pervade the studies by Rafiuddin Ahmad (1982)[9] and Razia Akter Banu (1992).[10] One may, in fact, go so far as to state that that uneasiness is inherent in the whole discussion on the topic. One reason for this is that in general perception, Bengali Islam has, at least since the nineteenth century, dwelt in the shadow of both the Islamic 'high culture' of the North-Western subcontinent and the Bengal Renaissance largely led by Hindus. It was not before the first Census in 1871 that even the numerical dominance of Muslims in Bengal was acknowledged as a puzzling surprise.[11] Thus, Bengali Islam did not assert itself as an object of scholarly attention in the first hours of Western Orientalist and indigenous academic interest in South Asia. Furthermore, it fell and continues to fall into a disciplinary gap: neither Indology nor Islamic studies, both traditional university subjects, has ever truly focused on South Asian and much less on Bengali Islam, the former with its focus on religions and traditions originated in South Asia (formerly simply India), the latter with its tendency to look at the Islamic 'homelands' of Arabia and (in a second row) Persia. It is, moreover, undeniable that Orientalist scholarship has had its share in promoting scripturalist normativity and thereby

9 This thorough, expert study has the one disadvantage of using the concept of 'Islamisation' for reformist activities and thus allowing normative notions of Islam to enter its narration through the back door. Cf. also Joya Chatterjee's criticism (Chatterjee 1998: 273).

10 Razia Akter Banu, apparently reiterating a notion popularised in South Asia by Iqbal ('The regeneration of the Muslim world lies in the strong uncompromising, ethical monotheism which was preached to the Arabs thirteen hundred years ago. Come, then, out of the fogs of Persianism and walk into the brilliant desert-sunshine of Arabia.' Muhammad Iqbal: 'Islam and Mysticism'; *New Era*, 28 July 1917, p. 83, as quoted in Sirriyeh [1999: 133] and discussed in Harder 2009), states that the Semitic religion of Islam was Aryanised in South Asia, and sees South Asian Sufism especially as a kind of 'Semitic-Aryan syncretism' full of loans from Indian traditions. 'Thus the conversion of the people of Bengal to Islam was not conversion to the pure, pristine Islam. Bengali Muslims retained some of their pre-Islamic beliefs and practices. The Sufi form of Bengal Islam made it easier for the Bengali Muslims to retain those practices' (Razia Akter Banu 1992: 17). The competition between Bengali and Islamic identity markers that runs through the introduction of this book (pp. 1–28) is an instructive illustration for the tensions we are dealing with, but is detrimental to the consistency of the text itself.

11 Cf. Eaton (1993: Chapter 5, esp. pp. 119 f.).

reifying Islam.[12] So from the angle of vision of both Indology and Islamic studies, any imprints of local culture, and thus South Asian Islam in general and Bengali Islam in particular, appeared exotic, deviative and hybrid.[13]

In such circumstances, it is of little use to put to work the demographic argument and state that Bengali Muslims number presently around 160 million, and thus at least every tenth Muslim in today's world is Bengali;[14] and speculations about a reconfiguration of traditional disciplines and a departure from the study of 'high cultures' in favour of formely neglected ones are hardly helpful. The fact is that any in-depth study of Bengali Islam is bound to be interdisciplinary in nature. Any examination of its cultural environment has to take into account the data furnished by South Asian studies and Indology, and the ideal linguistic equipment needed for a full-scale assessment would have to feature two modern Indo-Aryan languages – Bengali and Urdu – as well as Persian, Arabic and, ever since the nineteenth century, English.

It is doubtless tempting to infer from such inherent multiperspectivism the cultural hybridity of the object under discussion; but to do so prematurely would be a severe mistake, because it would mean reading the preconfigurations of one's instruments of observation into the object of study. It is desirable to treat this point with the utmost care, for while it is true that certain rifts run through Bengali Islam precisely because of the notion of hybridity in the field itself, it is equally true that academic discussions have tended to more or less directly enforce this notion. This tendency ought to be avoided at least in as much as it stems from the prefabricated perceptual predispositions developed by traditional academic disciplines. Anyone would acknowledge that it will not do to delegitimise South Asian and Bengali Islam on the simple grounds of not being Arabophone or Persophone; but other than, for example, Turcic languages in Central Asia, South Asian languages seem to be perceived as vehicles of a more penetrating set of cultural givens that interfere with Islam;[15] and hence South Asian Islam is labelled as hybrid – or at least, if we subscribe to the general

12 This point has most pungently been made by Edward Said (1979). Cf. the discussion in Marc Gaborieau (2003: 298 ff.), e.g.: 'Anything not found in this ideal type is classed as a survival of a local substratum, which is Hindu in India, according to British ethnography, and according to contemporary anthropology, tribal in Indonesia, and Berber in Morocco.' The point of reference for the latter is, of course, Clifford Geertz's *Islam Observed* (1968).

13 Cf. the normative statement in Gaeffke (1992: 80): 'Although the Muslim population of the South Asian subcontinent is by far the largest in any geographic region, the phenotypes of this religion have grown so confusingly diversified that not only in popular beliefs but also in scholarly literature a bewildering multitude of "Islamic" practices and concepts are entertained which give the term "Indian Islam" nearly a polytheistic meaning.' This notion of cultural hybridity is often conveyed by the term 'syncretism', which will be discussed at some length in Section 7.1.

14 Bangladesh, with a population nearing 160 million, has an official figure of 88% Muslim population, equalling 140 million, and the Indian state of West Bengal not less than 20 million. To these figures must be added the considerable number of Muslims among the Bengalis dwelling in the adjacent areas surrounding Bengal (Assam, Meghalaya, Tripura, etc.).

15 Cf. the debate on syncretism, Section 7.1.

hybridity of cultural formations in the wake of Homi Bhabha's theorising, as *more hybrid* than others. So it is essential to suspend any judgement regarding this alleged hybridity at the outset of this study. What is needed is an approach that can capture the current evaluations in the field of Bengali Islam *without* getting entangled in them.

1.1 Approaching Maijbhandar

Why this prolegomenon? The primary topic of the present book is not a whole-scale assessment of Islam in Bengal, nor in Bangladesh or even Chittagong, but the documentation and analysis of a prominent popular religious phenomenon in this area: the Maijbhandaris, a Sufi movement that has, since the nineteenth century, emerged from the village of Maijbhandar, situated some 40 km north of Chittagong city in Fatikchari thana, in the plain between the mountains of Sitakunda and the Chittagong Hill Tracts. When studying and assessing this movement, however, I will have to handle a number of larger contexts, in particular that of Bengali Islam, and thus cannot help venturing on the slippery academic ground sketched above. So as we focus down our optical lens and approach Maijbhandar, and even before introducing it in detail, it is necessary to address a few issues that might otherwise distort the picture we are going to contemplate. Detailed theoretical considerations are mostly reserved for the final two chapters of this book and will not be taken up here. A few rhetorical questions will sketch out the problems at hand and thus prepare the stage for the topic.

First, then, is it at all legitimate to study Maijbhandar as an *Islamic* phenomenon? The Maijbhandaris, in some contexts, as we shall see, address not only Muslims but all local religious communities. Access to the Maijbhandari saints is granted *jātidharmanirbiśeṣe*, 'irrespective of caste/class and religion', as the motto goes, and initiation of Hindu individuals into the movement is said to have taken place in a number of cases without formally converting them to Islam. Maijbhandaris thus attempt to transcend established religious boundaries through the propagation of open spirituality, and Maijbhandar might therefore seem to be at odds with the taxonomies of religions we usually put to use when classifying such movements. In brief, and without going into the discussion of the specific problems of these taxonomies of 'grand religions' as modern reifications,[16] the

16 One might point, in this connection, to Harjot Oberoi's remarks regarding the fallacies of thinking in terms of clear-set religious boundaries. Mentioning Hindus venerating Muslim shrines and Muslims following Hindu life cycles in the Punjab, and commenting upon the religious categories the first census imposed on the local population, he asks: 'How may these facts be represented and reconciled with the belief systems of the three grand religions of Punjab? Where do the boundaries of these grand religions begin and end? Is it possible that our taxonomies excluded people from their own history and prevented them making the statements they wished to make?' (Oberoi 1994: 4). Also, in this connection, Sudipta Kaviraj (1992: 20–6) for the elaboration of the difference between pre-modern 'fuzzy' and modern 'enumerated' communities; Waseem (2003: 4ff.) on the impossibility of speaking of one Islam, etc.

answer to this could be that the Maijbhandaris share most aspects of religious belief and practice with other Sufi movements on the Indian subcontinent and elsewhere, and are very solidly affiliated to Islamic lineages and Sufi spiritual genealogies. Even their attempt to transcend religious boundaries is paralleled by similar efforts in other Sufi institutions, and so this transgressive aspect can hardly be deemed sufficient to put them beyond the pale of Islam. Moreover, most importantly, they emphatically project themselves as a part of Islam, and not as some preriferal aspect of it but as its very centre. So along with William Roff (1987: 48), according to whom Muslim communities are made up of people 'to whom Muslim discourse speaks', the answer is yes: it is unproblematic and makes sense to place a study of the Maijbhandaris in the context of Islam.

But, second, if studying Maijbhandar as part of Islam, wouldn't we tend to classify all particularities of this religious formation as deviant, un-Islamic local additions? This is likely to happen if we, in a top-down fashion, apply fixed notions of what Islam means in general to the particular case of Maijbhandar. We would then assign whatever familiar features we find to Islam, and the contrastive and unfamiliar ones to local, Chittagongian or Bengali factors. Such an assignation does not yet contain any value judgement, and we may portray such a combination of 'Islamic' and 'local' features as inevitable, natural or peculiar, as desirable or undesirable, problematic or unproblematic; but it does set up a cognitive pattern with certain premises. The concept of syncretism, for instance, when used as an analytical tool, creates such a pattern.[17] The problem is, succinctly put, that in approaching the subject in this manner we pretend to know perfectly well what Islam is even before looking at the case we are going to study. We are not willing to be taught anything about Islam by the particular group we look at, but are intent on asserting our preconfigured idea of general Islam as a means of judging the particular.

Is it not more promising then, thirdly, to study the Maijbhandaris in their own right without paying attention to the overarching taxonomies that are, in other words, most prominently Islam? Such an approach, in its urge to assert the singularity of its object of observation, would risk underestimating and underplaying the impact and breadth of Islamic tradition, and missing lots of both synchronic and diachronic parallels. Further, it would not, in our case, pay sufficient attention to Maijbhandari parlance itself, which is very much about Islam as the mark of identity. So the answer is no: quite clearly, such an approach looks exclusively at the thread without examining the texture into which it is woven (and into which it weaves itself), and fails to see the decisive role of the texture in giving shape to the thread.

Should we then, fourthly, look at Maijbhandar as a micro-study of Bengali Islam? A cautious yes: it appears beyond doubt that this study will yield data that are of some significance to the wider field of Bengali Islam, and it is moreover

17 Cf. the discussion of syncretism in Section 7.1 of this book.

hardly feasible to speak about the Maijbhandari movement without discussing Bengali Islam. Characteristically, as we enter the topic of saint and shrine veneration, we shall encounter a situation in which different factions of South Asian, and in our context Bengali, Muslims compete in defining what Islam is. So we enter a complex semantic field in which the term 'Islam' itself, conceived as a target notion, means different things to different people and on different levels of observation. The Maijbhandaris are one of these contesting factions acting out their verifiable claims to 'Islamicness' in the context of what I will call (Chapter 7) an 'arena of Bengali Islam' – an arena that is, for all practical purposes, overwhelmingly Bengali in medium, and largely coincides with Bengali ethnic and political units, most prominently Bangladesh. For certain, the Maijbhandaris are not any iconic representation of Bengali Islam in general. But in as much as we contemplate this faction, the way they relate to the arena surrounding them, and interpret what Islam is, we are bound to gain some insights into that wider Bengali 'arena of Islam'. The final, eighth will take us back to our initial question about Bengali Islam in the light of the data furnished by this study.

Why not then, fifthly, look at Maijbhandar as a *local* form of Islam? Yes, indeed, the answer would go, but without imagining an all-too-neat opposition between 'local' and 'global' forms of the Islamic religion. Katy Gardner (1995 and 1999) has used this distinction in order to describe recent religious developments in Sylhet (north-eastern Bangladesh), where work migrants with newly acquired foreign notions of Mecca-centred and largely reformist Islam are causing the decline of certain types of shrine and *pīr* veneration. Gardner's analysis of this process is quite revealing, but the terms 'global' and 'local' Islam that she uses become highly problematic once stripped of their inverted commas. 'Global Islam' may be valid as a notion of the migrants themselves, and the split between 'global' and 'local' may very accurately represent their religious taxonomies. On an analytical level, however, using the concept of one (reformist) global Islam in juxtaposition to Maijbhandar would be just as misleading a short-hand as an uncritical application of the Redfieldian concept of a Great and Little Tradition.[18] Also, it should not be forgotten that Sufism commands its own globality, and many 'local' Bengali Sufis would strongly object to being classified as merely local, but align themselves with that globality. It is important for the present study to steer clear of such preconfigurations as far as possible.

How, then, to go about this study of Maijbhandar? Broadly speaking, what follows is an interpretation of a specific religious and cultural formation and its semantics. According to Clifford Geertz, culture is basically made up from interpretations of actions. In his attempt to locate ethnographic discourse, he distinguishes between a first (native) order of interpretation and second- and third-order ethnographic interpretations of a given culture, and stresses that the situation becomes much more complex in cases of scriptural cultures (Geertz 1968: 23). Along these lines, the religious culture that has evolved around the Maijbhandari

18 Cf. Robert Redfield (1955) for the first exposition of this concept.

movement would indeed seem highly complex. It has almost constantly, since its inception, been scripturalised and rationalised in reference to various traditions including Islamic scholarship, Sufic mysticism and ‘Bengali folk religion’, to name only the most obvious. This scripturalisation has, on the one hand, led to a degree of self-referentiality and, on the other, to repercussions in the spheres of religious practice and popular religiosity as expressed in the songs.

I will thus describe different semantic complexes pertaining to Maijbhandar as well as their interplay. These include ritual and religious practice; physical representation and orders of space and time; internal structure and relations to the religious surroundings; religious experience and its expression and routinisation; accommodation of saints and doctrines into more general frameworks; oral and scriptural culture and their interaction; the semantics of mysticism *vis-à-vis* structural confines; and many others. I hesitate, however, to assign the following description and analysis to any superposed order of interpretation in Geertz’s terms. In relation to Maijbhandari interpretations of Maijbhandar, I prefer to think of it as a lateral approach, with distance of perspective as its main characteristic feature. It goes extensively into the sources in order to render certain Maijbhandari interpretations transparent, but abstains from asserting or denying their truth or legitimacy, thus remaining at a pronounced distance from what one might call a believer’s perspective. It poses questions of a historical, literary, theological and sociological nature that may, at times, appear irrelevant or irreverent to a believer. In any case, I have attempted to keep my interpretation sufficiently distinct from the variety of Maijbhandari voices that it engages with, and to make the various steps of my analysis as transparent as possible.

Moving now indeed from the very general to the particular, this introduction will give an overview of shrines in Chittagong, an exposition of Maijbhandar and an outline of its history. Thereafter I will devote a number of chapters to different aspects of the movement. Chapter 2 will deal with the structure of the Maijbhandari movement and the religious practice associated with it. Chapters 3 to 5 investigate three different branches of Maijbhandari text production, the longest, and in a way the centrepiece of this study, being Chapter 5 with its extensive analysis of Maijbhandari songs. Chapter 6 builds upon the latter in examining the way in which certain types of songs – especially such as closely ressemble other Bengali mystical traditions like the Bauls and Vaishnavas – are understood and conceptualised today in a Maijbhandari Sufi environment. On the basis of the preceding chapter, Chapter 7 will take the discussion back to a rather abstract and general plane and investigate the logic and mechanisms of unitary mysticism. Chapter 8, finally, returns to the initial question of this book – What is Bengali Islam? – in an attempt to remove the tensions seemingly inherent in this term, and to secure it as an indispensable category for focusing research on the topic.

1.2 Shrines in Chittagong

Chittagong is a place with many names. In common Bengali speech today, at least three forms of the name have currency: the local Cāṭigā̃ or Cāṭ'gā̃, its purified and written variant Caṭṭagrām, and the English Chittagong. The district is also known as the *bāro āuliẏār deś*, 'the land of the twelve saints', referring to a group of medieval Muslim saints held responsible for the settlement and Islamisation of Chittagong,[19] and the widespread etymology of Cāṭigā̃ (in the local language meaning lit. 'village of the lamp') is intimately connected with these saints. According to Wahidul Alam,

> The most popular saying regarding the origin of the name Caṭṭagrām is that in ancient times, Caṭṭagrām was the dwelling place of *ǧinn* and fairies [*parī*]. Once, the twelve saints arrived in this green country. In order to drive out these fairies, they lighted a lamp, and the *ǧinn* and fairies flew from its light. Thus driving out the *ǧinn* and fairies, the saints prepared this place for human settlement.
>
> (Ohidul Ālam 1989: 1)

Another version of this story attributes the lighting of the lamp exclusively to Badr Shah, one of the twelve *awliyāʾ* and the guardian saint of Chittagong city.[20]

Many more etymologies can be found. The historian Abdul Hak Chaudhuri (1994) gives 13 more historical forms with different etymologies of the city's name,[21] the most noteworthy among them being Caṭṭalā as the form used in Pauranic and tantric scriptures, and Cit-taut-gauṃ, which is supposed to stem from the time Chittagong was ruled by the Arakanese, and mean 'do not make war' in the Arakanese language. Abdul Hak Chaudhuri (1988: 3–6) even gives 17 names, the additional ones being Jvālanˈdhārā (Tibetan sources, tenth century onwards), Sāmandar (ninth-century reference in Arabic sources), Karṇabul (tenth-century Arabic reference), Rosāṅg and Phateẏābād (medieval Bengali sources), Porto Grando [*sic*] (Portuguese) and Islamabad (name given by Aurangzeb in 1666). The English form Chittagong is current since the eighteenth

19 There seems to be some doubt as to who these twelve saints were. Enamul Hak (1995: 236) gives a list of ten saints, admitting that the remaining two are not known. Different lists (none of them complete) have been given to me during my fieldwork. The village Baro Auliya, some kilometres north of Sitakunda, has a mausoleum dedicated summarily to the *bāro āuliẏā*, but it does not furnish information about their identities. For a discussion of Islamisation theories regarding Bengal, cf., most authoritative, Richard Eaton (1993: 113 ff.).

20 Cf. Enamul Hak (1995: 243 ff.), who identifies Badr Shah with Shah Badruddin Allamah (alive in 1340) – in contrast to Latif (1993: 53 f.), who thinks that Badr Shah was 'Badruddin Badr-i Alam Zahidi'. On his *dargāh* at Bakhshi Bazar in Chittagong city, cf. Asma Serajuddin (1998).

21 These are namely: 1. Caityagrām (deemed a Buddhist appellation: 'village [with a] *caitya*'); 2. Catuḥgrām [*sic*] (a British interpretation, 'four villages'); 3. Caṭṭalā (cf. in the text), 4. Śyāt·gāṅga (supposedly derived from Ar. for 'Ganges delta'); 5. Cit-Taut-Gauṃ (cf. in the text); 6. Cāṭigrāṃ (historical appellation, fifteenth to seventeenth century); 7. Cāṭigā̃ (cf. in the text); 8. Catˈkā̃o/ Cāṭˈgā̃o (Persian form of 7.); 9. Sudˈkāoẏān (Ibn Battuta); 10. Cāṭikiẏāṃ (fifteenth-century Chinese form); 11. Śāṭˈjām (sixteenth-century Turkish form); 12. Cārṭīgān (sixteenth-century English form); 13. Jeṭiẏā (on a seventeenth-century English map – spelt here according to the form given by Abdul Hak Chaudhuri); 14. Caïṭṭegaṃ (a new Arakanese etymology, meaning 'main/superior fort').

century, and the common Bengali form (Caṭṭagrām) is supposed to stem from the nineteenth century (Hak Chaudhuri 1988: 5 f.). If not of anything else, this plurality of appellations does speak of a heterogeneous history due to the border position between what is now called South Asia and South East Asia.

The name Chittagong today refers to Chittagong City, Chittagong District and Chittagong Division simultaneously. With its roughly 2 million inhabitants, urban Chittagong is the second largest city in Bangladesh and the country's major seaport. It is located to the east of the delta of Ganges and Brahmaputra, and geographically belongs to the Burmese mainland rather than to Bengal proper. Ethnically, linguistically and culturally, Chittagong is the frontier between South Asia and Myanmar. This is felt especially by the presence of the tribal population of the Chittagong Hill Tracts, a number of ethnic groups belonging to the mongoloid group and speaking Austro-Asiatic languages. The descendants of Portuguese settlers mainly in Chittagong city further contribute to the fact that the population of Chittagong is significantly more heterogeneous than that of most parts of deltaic Bangladesh.

Among other things, this results in the conspicuous presence of four major religions side by side: Islam, Hinduism, Buddhism and Christianity. All of these possess prominent places of worship, holy places or pilgrimage sites in the Chittagong area. Sitakunda, about 30 km north of Chittagong city, has a large number of Hindu temples that are visited on foot in a traditional *parikramā*, 'circumambulation', including mounting the highest peak of the Sitakunda mountain range on which a Candranātha Śiva temple is situated.[22] Mahamuni, some 15 km west of the city, hosts a huge Buddha statue in a temple and is a pilgrimage site for Buddhists of the Chittagong plains as well as from the Hill Tracts.[23] The Christian community is, unlike the Muslims, Hindus and Buddhists, largely centred in the city (except converts due to missionary activities in the Hill Tracts mainly) and possesses a number of churches. As for the Muslim majority, Chittagong has a number of prominent mosques, some of them from the fifteenth to eighteenth centuries, e.g. the *Qadam Mubārak* (Ar., 'blessed foot'; also called Yasim Khan's) mosque in Anderkilla built in 1723.[24] The oldest mosque in the city itself is the '*Jāme Saṅgīn*' (Bg., probably for P. <*ğamʿ-i sangīn*>, 'solid assembly') mosque, dating from 1667.[25] But especially noteworthy is the huge number of saintly tombs found in almost all corners of the region.

22 Hindu ashrams at Chittagong, such as those situated at Sitakunda or Suyabil in the vicinity of Maijbhandar, have brought out various small publications with songs or ballads, e.g. *pā̃cālīs* devoted to different deities (Lakshmi, Satyanarayana, Manasa, Kartikeya, Surya, etc.).

23 For Buddhism in Bangladesh in general, see, e.g., Anjana Das (1992); on the Maghs (Arakanese in Chittagong) Khan (1999); from a historical perspective Hak Caudhurī (1994) and Sunīthānanda (1995). Some specific information on Chittagong can be found in Dipak Baṛuẏā (1998). Small-scale publications distributed at Buddhist institutions stem mostly from foreign Buddhist associations of countries such as Thailand, Sri Lanka or even the USA.

24 Cf. the picture in Ali (1985: vol. Ib, Plate LI).

25 For details on these and other prominent mosques in Chittagong, see Abdul Hak Chaudhuri (1988: 386–98).

These saints and shrines are deemed important guardian institutions in popular perception. With reference to the proverbial twelve saints it is said that 'without the *bāro āuliẏā*, Chittagong would have perished a long time ago'.[26] The city itself has a great number of shrines and related holy places, the most prominent ones being those of Amanat Shah, Bayezid Bistami,[27] Sheikh Farid al-Din Shakrganj[28] and Badr Shah.[29] As all over South Asia, the most important congregational events in these shrines are the *'urūs* (pl. of *'urs*, lit. 'wedding'), namely, the death anniversaries of the respective saints. The shrines are today partly managed by the state through so-called *waqf* boards, and are partly still in the possession of their traditional keepers. These may either be servants or the descendants of servants deriving their office from a direct contact with or order from the saint, as in the case of Muhsin Auliya (d. 1397) of Anwara Thana;[30] or the keepers may be *pīrzāda*s, descendants of the *pīr* or saint, themselves. In both cases, the keepers maintain the shrine ritual and thereby control the pilgrim's or visitor's access to the saint, and they profit from the economic income of the shrine. The activities of *pīrzāda*s may be limited to such official and liturgical functions, but they may also themselves act as full-fledged *pīr*s and bestow general religious teachings upon the circle of their *murīd*s, devotees.

In popular perception, shrines in Chittagong, as probably in other parts of South Asia, are classified as either *garam*, 'hot', or *ṭhāṇḍā*, 'cold'.[31] A hot shrine is one whose saint is active in distributing spiritual inspiration and wonder-working and consequently draws many visitors; a cold one, conversely, is marked by little activity and prosperity. The most common ratio of explaining the hotness or coldness of a specific tomb is to relate these to the spiritual status of the respective saint, although it is obvious that the popularity of a shrine may prosper or decline in time. The shrine of Badr Shah, purportedly the great Islamiser of Chittagong, is a good example of a once 'hot' venue of veneration that has presently lost out to other shrines like that of Shah Amanat. For any outside observer, the popularity of a saint is obviously linked to the way he is projected and 'launched' by his present representatives. Two such 'hot' shrines in Chittagong that have simultaneously practising *pīr*s and are centres of Sufic organisations, are Mirzakhil[32] and

26 *bāro āuliẏā nā thāk'le e deś anek din ḍube yeta*. (Popular phrase repeatedly related to me during my fieldwork).

27 It is unlikely that the great Persian Sufi Bayezid Bistami (d. 874) (on him cf., e.g., Schimmel [1995: 78–84]), locally known as Bāẏejīd Bostāmi, ever visited Chittagong, and he certainly did not die there. Cf. Enamul Hak (1995: 238 f.), who claims that his name has been confused with Shah Sultan Balkhi, a saint of Sandip island. For a recent joint hagiography of Bayezid Bistami and Shah Amanat, see K.M.G. Rah'mān (1986).

28 There is a tear basin (*caś'mā*, P. <*čašma*>) called *Śekh Pharīder caś'mā* in the north of Chittagong City that Md. Enamul Haq relates to this saint (Hak 1995: 239 ff.). Cf. M.S. Ahluwalia (1989) on Farid al-Din Shakrganj (d. 1265, or 1269 according to Enamul Haq).

29 Enāmul Hak (1995: 243 ff.), Asma Serajuddin (1998).

30 For details about this saint, cf. Enamul Hak (1995: 253–5).

31 Cf. Katy Gardner (1999: 41) with reference to the shrine of Shah Jalal of Sylhet as hot.

32 Cf. Ohīdul Ālam (1985: 33–8).

Maijbhandar.[33] While the former is a rather small convent, elitist and withdrawn from the public, the latter has during the twentieth century developed into the most highly frequented and popular shrine complex of Chittagong, well known also in other parts of the country and certainly one of the most prominent Sufi institutions in all of Bangladesh.

1.3 Maijbhandar: a shrine complex and religious movement

Scholars of South Asian Islam, confronted with a two-century-long rise of Islamic reformism, tend to view saintly shrines and Sufic practice as receding traditional modes of religious orientation, and reformists themselves have been and are still launching attacks against them for being supposedly unislamic. As a result of such projections, shrine-based religiosity is sometimes viewed as something marginal. In addition to this, as regards mysticism, marginality as a kind of 'ethos of anti-structure'[34] has for a long time been part and parcel of its self-representation.

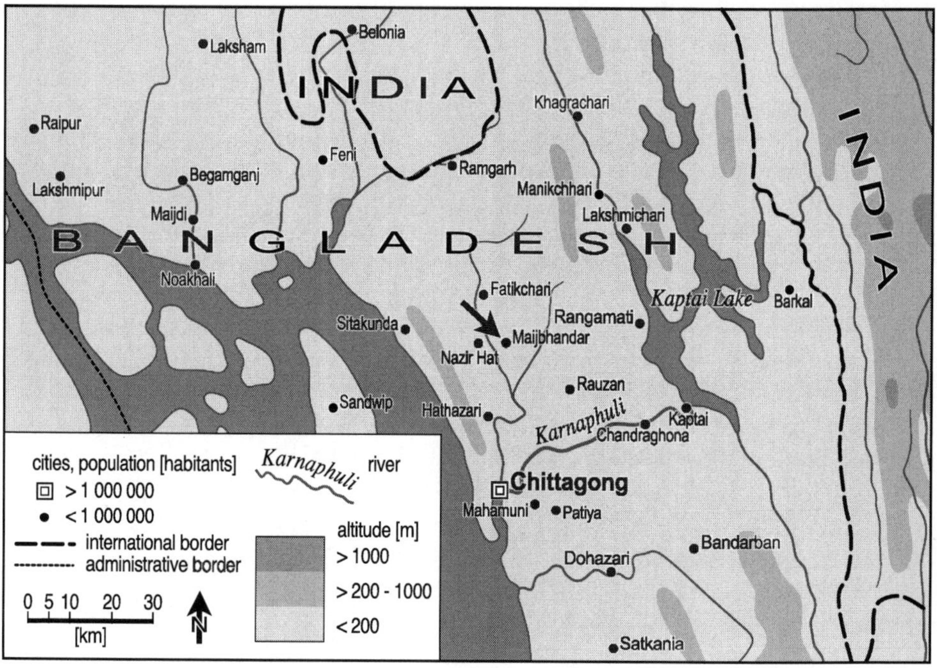

Map 2 Chittagong/Maijbhandar.

33 Beng. *māij'bhāṇḍār*. Owing to the phonetics of the Chittagong dialect, with *j* pronounced as *z*, a common anglicised form is *Maizbhandar*. I have, however, stuck to *Maijbhandar* as closer to standard Bengali pronunciation.

34 Cf. the famous distinction made by Victor Turner (1995 [1969]) between 'structure' and 'anti-structure' or 'communitas'.

It seems therefore appropriate to state right at the outset of this investigation that Maijbhandar today is a powerful religious institution whose very popularity and influence defies any notions of marginality. We shall have occasion to show that Maijbhandar and the religious movement connected with it have been able to draw adherents from all sections of society, including the urban middle class, and have managed to assert their perspective on Islam *vis-à-vis* pressure from reformist quarters while keeping in touch with the religious mainstream in Bengal.

How to measure the impact and popularity of a religious movement? We could, first, go by the number of followers and visitors; the death aniversaries (*ʿurs*) of the major Maijbhandari saints annually draw great masses to the village. Reference is usually made to hundreds of thousands of visitors at each single festival,[35] and the impression of multitude has urged a hagiographer to claim, on behalf of Maijbhandar, that '[f]rom a rough survey, it has been estimated that it ranked third in number after the Haj congression and the festival at Vetican [*sic*] city'.[36] Exact countings of the attendance of such events are not feasible, estimates are hazardous, and we may be sure that quite a few other pilgrimage spots are very likely to outnumber Maijbhandar in this respect. But Selim Jahangir is probably right when he states that these Maijbhandari festivals are the first to be mentioned in what is today the eastern part of Bangladesh.[37] The number of people formally attached to the movement is of course much smaller, but organised in a network spanning many parts of Bangladesh and beyond.

Secondly, this appeal has been long-lasting, and Maijbhandar has asserted its place as a major pilgrimage centre for more than a century now. This is also due to the fact that it has produced a chain of charismatic spiritual leaders, rather than mere teachers, who have again and again renewed the attraction of this particular centre.

Thirdly, there has been a sizeable textual output from within the movement since the beginning of the twentieth century, including hagiographies and theological treatises, in the form of monographs, leaflets and journals.[38] It is arguable to what extent this production ascertains Maijbhandar weight in the field of Islamic theology,[39] but this is a minor issue compared to another field of text production: Maijbhandari songs, numbering probably more than 10,000 at present and appearing first orally, then in print and lately mostly on cassettes, CDs and Video-CDs, are today treated and traded as a separate musical genre in Bangladesh.

Fourthly, such popularity has its economic aspects, and Maijhandar today shows many signs of a flourishing institution in this respect too. If we judge only from the display of architectural prowess, the last decade alone has seen building activities on a new scale that surpasses many similar shrines in the region.

35 Cf., e.g., Selim Jahāṅgīr (1999: 2), who speaks of a 'spontaneous assembly of hundreds of thousands [*lakṣa lakṣa*] of devotees [*āśek bhakta*]'.

36 *Shahenshah*: 92.

37 Selim Jāhāṅgīr (1999: 2 f.) ('*etadañcaler pratham ullekh'yogya mus'lim dharmīyamelā*').

38 Since 1999 there has also been a Maijbhandari homepage run by Haq Manzil organisations. The page is at present located under www.sufimaizbhandari.org/ (18 March 2010).

39 Cf. Chapter 3 of this book.

The new mausoleum of Saint Ziaul Haq (finished in the middle of the 1990s) and the replacement of Saint Ahmadullah's old tomb (the recent replacement) seem to introduce a new scale of modern mausoleum architecture in the Chittagong region.

Despite all these signs of activity and vitality, literature *about* Maijbhandar is very scarce indeed. Only very recently, a monograph by Selim Jahangir was published as the first comprehensive research work on the topic;[40] this book incurred the wrath of certain factions within the movement, and a parliamentary committee was formed which ultimately banned it as 'unislamic' from the book market one year after its publication.[41] Moreover, there is an article by the Finnish folklore researcher Lauri Harvilahti with a short general account of the Maijbhandaris.[42] Mention may also be made of a volume with translations of songs of the Maijbhandari songwriter Abdul Gafur Hali and an introduction on Maijbhandar by the present author.[43] Apart from these publications, there are only stray references in works on the history and culture of Chittagong and Sufism of Bengal.[44] As regards research works on Bengali religion, only a few published references to Maijbhandar are known to me.[45] Maijbhandari songs are given or mentioned in some anthologies or studies of Bengali mystical and folk songs,[46] and collections of them exist in various libraries,[47] but the

40 Selim Jāhāṅgīr (1999): *Māij'bhāṇḍār sandarśan*. Dhaka, Bangla Academy. This book gives a very detailed and well-researched overview of Maijbhandari institutions and personalities and has helped me immensely as a reliable source of information.

41 I have not been able to inquire into this event in any depth, but according to what I could gather from different informants, it appears that the author's affiliation as a *murīd* of one of the various factions of the Maijbhandaris was the trigger of this affair. Members of other factions felt that the account given in the book was biased to their disadvantage and, to all appearances, used their influence to have the book banned on the formal grounds of overplaying the status of his own spiritual master in a way that amounted to heresy. Mofidul Haq, in a long article in *Dainik saṃbād* (27 August 2000 – Maphidul Hak [2000]), crititicises this decision in the context of tendencies in present-day Bangladesh to replace the syncretistic (*samanvaẏ'bādī*) and tolerant tradition of Bangladesh by a one-eyed and intolerant social consciousness.

42 Harvilahti (1998). This somewhat sketchy report does not mention the existence of various factions among the Maijbhandaris and relies solely on the rare English-medium publications of the movement.

43 Hans Harder (2004): *Der verrückte Gofur spricht: mystische Lieder aus Ostbengalen von Abdul Gofur Hali* [*VG*]. Heidelberg, Draupadi Verlag.

44 Ohidul Ālam (1985: 18.33) has a chapter with Maijbhandari songs and a short introduction; Āb'dul Hak Caudhurī (1988) deals with the Maijbhandari doctrine and songs in two short sections (pp. 37 f. and 618); Sāk'lāẏen (1962: 125) introduces the Maijbhandari founding saint Ahmadullah.

45 Md. Enamul Hak (1991: 138); Peter Bertocci (2006); David Cashin (1995: 242 f.); and Rahul Peter Das (1992: 399 f.). A longer section on Maijbhandar by Md. Enamul Hak, entitled *Māij'bhāṇḍārer Maulānā Śāh Āh'madullāh o tā̃r sādhanār saṃkṣipta paricaẏ*, is quoted in a book by Selim Jahangir (Jāhāṅgīr 2000: 46 ff.) but apparently missing in his *Racanābalī*. The short remarks by David Cashin display little knowledge of Maijbhandar, as Selim Jahangir has aptly pointed out (Jāhāṅgīr 1999: 24 f.).

46 Cf. Jasīmuddīn (1977: 67–77); Tṛpti Brahma (1986: 130–2); Jāhān-Ārā Begam (1976: 79–83).

47 Selim Jahangir mentions the following: a collection of Maijbhandari songs by Ashutosh Bhattacharya on behalf of Calcutta University, in 1937; a collection of rare Maijbhandari songs by the Chittagong University Library; collections for Bangladesh radio in 1973 and 1994 (Jāhāṅgīr 1999: 3 n.11).

only extensive collection published from outside Maijbhandari circles is found in the collected works of Kabiẏāl Ramesh Shil,[48] and to some compilers of folk songs, Maijbhandar seems to be altogether unknown.[49]

Maijbhandar combines the aspect of a popular shrine complex with that of a living religious institution that has its own *ṭarīqa*, Sufi order. Often this is claimed to be the only indigenous *ṭarīqa* in Bangladesh. There are many indications that a specific Maijbhandari *ṭarīqa* did not come into being, or at any rate was not referred to by this label, before the middle of the twentieth century,[50] and the different formulations of this *ṭarīqa* shall concern us elsewhere. In any case, as the central place at which admission to the Maijbhandari *ṭarīqa* is sought and where devotees regularly congregate, Maijbhandar may also be called a large Sufi *ḫānaqāh* (P., convent), and the centre of a large number of smaller branches called *dā'ira* in various parts of Bangladesh.

With equal legitimacy, and in the light of the relatively recent formulation of a Maijbhandari *ṭarīqa*, we might characterise Maijbhandar simply as a religious movement, spanning a range from rather institutionalised aspects to quite informal fringes. Such a denomination suits best the multiple ways of referring and belonging to Maijbhandar. Depending on perspective, one can be born into an affiliation with Maijbhandar;[51] formally get initiated into the Maijbhandari 'community';[52] and also earn a reputation, and sometimes even an appellation,[53] of a Maijbhandari without any formal accession to a Maijbhandari institution.

The geographical position of Maijbhandar, I ought to stress, makes such prominence seem rather unlikely, as it lies in a very rural environment referred to by many with the Bengali expression *aja paṛāgā̃*, 'backwoods'.[54] The village of Maijbhandar is located some 40 km to the north-east of Chittagong city, in the densely populated plain between the mountains of Sitakunda in the west and the Chittagong Hill Tracts in the east. It is part of the district of Fatikchari. The nearest marketplace is Nazir Hat. Like the surrounding villages, Maijbhandar is rather 'elusive', to borrow a term from Peter Bertocci (1970) referring to the divergence

48 Rameś Śīl (1993: 1–136).

49 Such as Datta/Bhaumik (1966: [32]) who take Maijbhandar for the name of a poet; cf. Rahul Peter Das (1992: 399 n.72).

50 Cf., e.g., Syed Ahmadul Huq (1995: [9]): 'In Bangladesh Maizbhandari, Chistiya, Naqshabandia, Muizaddadia and Kaderia orders have a large following. Out of the above five orders Maizbhandari order is indigenous. [. . .] [The founding saints'] descendants and followers collected their sayings and reports about their sufistic practices. Some of them have published a number of books on Maizbhandari Tarika basing their belief on the sayings and practices of the saints.'

51 This applies, of course, mostly to the members of the Maijbhandari family proper; but I have also met families of devotees whose adult offspring had 'grown' into such an affiliation without ever formalising their relationship.

52 i.e. take a *bay'a*, 'oath of allegiance', at the hands of one of the spiritual representatives of the movement.

53 This (very rare) case has been reported to me concerning individual songwriters and interpreters of Maijbhandari songs.

54 According to local Chittagongian pronunciation; standard Bengali has *aj pāṛāgā̃* instead.

between spatial, administrative and social units in structuring the Bengali countryside. Besides the shrine complex proper, Maijbhandar *mauza*[55] has other settlements at one or two kilometres' distance divided by paddy fields; the shrine complex in its turn closely borders Azimnagar to the west, demarcated from Maijbhandar by a small canal but otherwise hardly distinguishable as a separate unit.

The increasingly large shrines, multi-storeyed living houses and guest-houses of the saintly Maijbhandari Sayyad family today occupy the very centre of this main part of Maijbhandar and are its characteristic features. Unlike many other places of saint veneration in South Asia, the *darbār* is thus not a separate locality within this main village of Maijbhandar *mauza*, but thoroughly pervades it. More than twenty mausoleums, half-a-dozen of them rather dominant architectural constructions, are built in close proximity to each other inside the village. A similar number of concrete buildings with up to six storeys of the dominant branches of that family stand in sharp contrast to the remaining one-storeyed local houses, some of which are made of clay.

Māij'bhāṇḍār literally means the 'middle storehouse', and one of the common etymologies has it that it was one of several storages of food and arms during the war between the 'Muslims and the Moghs', which refers to the Mughal annexation of Arakan in 1665.[56] But there is no archaeological or other evidence for such ancientness. It is the Maijbhandari family tradition as we find it in the hagiographies that indicates the existence of a settlement of this name before about 1800; a family of Sayyads, the predecessors of the Maijbhandari saints, had come to live in Azimnagar, the adjacent village, and the founding Saint Ahmadullah's (1829–1906)[57] father Motiullah took up the post of an Imām in Maijbhandar.[58] So, in all probability, Maijbhandar was originally an agricultural village no different from those in its present surroundings, and not one of the most ancient or prominent ones.[59]

This remote village, however, claims universal importance. In Maijbhandar, the highest rank of sainthood of a *ġawṯ al-aʿẓam* (Bg. *gāusul ājam* or *gāuchul āyam*), lit. 'Greatest Help', is claimed unanimously for the founding saint Ahmadullah and not unanimously for other saints succeeding him. The *wilāya*, sainthood, of a saint of this rank is conceived as unlimited and spanning the

55 *maujā* (Ar. <*mawḍaʿ*>, 'place, position') originally refers to a unit of tax collection dating from Muhgal times.

56 Cf., e.g., *JK*: 6. On the conquering of the Arakanese by the Mughal troups under Nawab Shaesta Khan, cf. Ohidul Ālam (1990: 46–51).

57 Usually 1826 is given as Ahmadullah's year of birth. But the earliest source on his life, *Āʾīna-i Bārī* (*ĀB*: 133), gives the year *hiğrī* 1244 which corresponds to 1829 AD. The hagiography *Jibanī o kerāmat* (*JK*: 22) is probably the source for an erroneous calendrical conversion that has become tradition. Cf. Sections 4.3.1. and 4.3.2.

58 Cf. *JK*: 19 f.

59 Cf. Enamul Haq's article 'An Account of The Jalali Family of Parganah-i-Isapur, Chittagong' (Hak 1995a), with indications that the neighbouring villages Bakhtapur and Dharmapur already existed in the seventeenth century.

whole earth. Maijbhandar may thus appear to be a rural and very local phenomenon, but to the hundreds of thousands of its devotees, it is a centre of universal importance. Apart from this spiritual significance, Maijbhandar is also the centre of an extended network of institutions in present-day Bangladesh. There is a great number of *ḫānaqāh*s, convents, of *ḫalīfa*s or spiritual deputies of Maijbhandar in Chittagong as well as in other parts (e.g. Noakhali, Kumilla) of eastern Bengal, many of whose followers adhere to Maijbhandar. In addition to this there is a structure of *dā'ira*s, 'departments' (e.g. in Dhaka, and reportedly also in foreign countries such as the Gulf States and the USA) where Maijbhandari followers congregate regularly to hold ceremonial functions and practise their faith. From these institutions people stream to Maijbhandar, especially on great festive occasions.

The confluence of the very local and rural with the urban and all-Bengali is seen in the composition of the pilgrims and devotees attached to Maijbhandar. The hagiographies of the founding saint Ahmadullah already bear witness to visitors from far-away districts and a sizeable support from *'ulamā'* also beyond the direct vicinity.[60] Today various houses (*manzil*s) in Maijbhandar[61] count among their followers local peasants as well as urban businessmen, academics and even politicians (e.g. the Minister of Education of the former Awami League government of Bangladesh from 1996 to 2001). No doubt, regional leanings are still a very strong factor among the urban classes of Bangladesh, as the persisting affiliation to one's regional origin shows;[62] and it cannot be precluded that some of the urban followers are attached to Maijbhandar as 'their' traditional, local pilgrimage centre. But in many cases no such links exist, and Maijbhandar's attempt to assert itself as a major religious site on a superior, non-local level must be called successful at least on a national Bangladeshi plane. As this also involves non-resident Bangladeshis working especially in Saudi-Arabia, the Gulf region and Canada, the Maijbhandari movement also boasts of its international impact. Some practising Maijbhandari *pīr*s have in fact travelled to various countries and 'made disciples' there. But barring very few (and very highlighted) cases, such recruitment has remained limited to persons with a Bangladeshi background.

Though not conceiving itself as a separate religious group or sect, a certain missionary impetus of the movement is undeniable. It is, however, not formalised and expresses itself in various ways. One of these is the above-mentioned active recruitment of new disciples by some of the contemporary Maijbhandari *pīr*s, another are the activities of single followers or their various organisations and institutions.

60 Cf. the volumes *Ā'īna-i bārī* (*ĀB*) and *Jībanī o kerāmat* (*JK*) and the synopses and discussions in Chapter 4 of this book.

61 Most notably Ahmadiyya, Rahmaniyya and Haq Manzils; cf. below, especially Section 2.1.2.

62 The term *deśer bāṛi*, lit. 'country home', refers especially to the provincial place of origin of city dwellers and is a very commonplace notion; usually close ties are maintained with it and some time of the year is regularly spent there.

1.4 Historical outline

External sources for the historical development of the Maijbhandari movement are rare. It is mostly from twentieth-century hagiographies and related writings from inside the movement that we learn about the family of the saints and the emergence of Maijbhandar as a popular centre of pilgrimage. According to Maijbhandari hagiographies, the Sayyad family that came to settle in this spot in the early nineteenth century are direct descendants of the Persian saint ʿAbd al-Qadir Gilani (d. 1166), founder of the Qadiriya *ṭarīqa*, who preached and was buried in Baghdad. They migrated first to Delhi, following an invitation of the rulers, and then to the ancient Bengali capital, Gaur, to serve as Imāms. Syed Hamiduddin Gaurī left Gaur during an epidemic in 1575 and migrated to Kanchanpur in Potia (Chittagong). One of his sons, called Syed Abdul Qadir, settled in Azimnagar, the village adjacent to today's Maijbhandar. His middle great-grandson, Motiullah, is said to have moved from there to Maijbhandar and fathered Ahmadullah (1829–1906), the founding saint of Maijbhandar.[63] This genealogy appears doubtful, since the five generations from Hamiduddin Gaurī to Ahmadullah have to account for the approximately 275 years separating their births.[64]

There are no scriptural, epigraphical or architectural indications regarding the history of Azimnagar or Maijbhandar that could supplement these genealogical data. But it can be deemed certain that the area of today's Fatikchari *thana* had been populated and at least partly Islamised by the seventeenth century. In 'An Account of the Jalali Family' of Baktapur and Dharmapur, two villages located a few kilometres east of Maijbhandar, Md. Enamul Haq traces the history of the descendants of Shah Jalal of Aleppo (1462–1537). This Shah set up a Muslim colony in the north of today's Chittagong city. His great-grandson Shah Hudan (1579–1662), a preacher, first settled in the Dharmapur/Baktapur area, which was then 'very thickly populated' by 'Dharampurasts' (Hak 1995: 483), that is, adherents to the *Dharma* cult.[65] The chronicles examined by Enamul Haq speak of forest clearings in the north of the villages and also mention 'a punitive "Zihad" [*ǧihād*] against the Dharampurasts' (Hak 1995: 487). Shah Hudan also commissioned eight 'missionaries' to Islamise the surroundings; two of these were Muhammad Bakhtiyar and Farhad Ali, and the above-mentioned Baktapur as well as Farhadabad, another village in the vicinity of Maijbhandar, were named after them.

63 Cf. Delawar Hosain, *JK*: 19 f. The same version is reiterated in Selim Jāhāṅgīr (1999: 136). Also Chapter 4 in this book.

64 i.e., if we estimate that Hamidullah emigrated from Gaur at the age of 25 years. This would put the average age of fathering at around 55 years, which, though not unfeasible, appears highly improbable.

65 *Dharma* is a popular deity of Bengal whose worship was widespread, especially in the middle ages; the *Dharma* cult has given rise to *Dharmamaṅgal* literature. Cf. Rahul Peter Das (1983) for a survey and a critical discussion of relevant literature up to that point, as well as, more recently, Frank J. Korom (2004).

It is tempting to try and interpret these data in the light of Richard Eaton's theses regarding the Islamisation of Eastern Bengal, the most important of which claims an intimate link between Islamisation and the establishment of agrarian culture.[66] Chittagong is not situated in the Delta, and as far as the city is concerned, can trace its contact with Islam at least back to the time of Badr Shah (14th cent.) and possibly far beyond that.[67] Among the oldest mosques in the area, constructed in the fifteenth and sixteenth centuries, three are furthermore situated in today's Hathazari *thana*, an administrational unit adjacent to Fatikchari and thus not far from the localities concerning us here.[68] But while these are certain signs of pre-Mughal moves towards Islamisation, the mention of *Dharma* worship in the Jalali family chronicle as well as their recruitment of 'missionaries' indicates that this was anything but a sudden transition. If we take the construction of the first mosque in the area (Majlis-i Ala Rastikhan, Jobra) in 1473–4 and the death of Hudan Shah (1662) as temporal confines, we may venture the supposition that the conversion of a majority of the population to Islam was a long-lasting process.[69]

Chittagong is not situated in the Delta, but the forest-clearing and new agrarian settlements – indications of which emerge from the above-mentioned family chronicle – have been under way in the northern part of Chittagong well into the twentieth century. In contrast to most parts of the delta proper, Chittagong had been settled from quite ancient times, and it offered more stable natural conditions for agriculture. But the threatening character of nature remained an important factor here, too, until at least the middle of the twentieth century. The miracles of Ahmadullah, Gholam Rahman and even Syed Ziaul Haq, three prominent Maijbhandari saints, involve rescues from, and the appeasing of, wild beasts (tigers, snakes, etc.).[70] According to oral reports collected from senior local inhabitants in the course of my fieldwork, jungle clearing around Maijbhandar has been a continuous process that has only recently come to a stop. In this sense, the role

66 Eaton (1993) refutes some of the most current Islamisation theories and argues convincingly that the success of Islam in East Bengal was connected with the fluid social conditions in the delta and the transition to wet-field cultivation, with Islam as a civilising agrarian religion.

67 Cf. Ohidul Ālam (1989: 20–3) on Muslim Arab settlements in Chittagong as early as the eighth century AD. The basis for such estimates are family traditions of a Sayyad family in Haola, as well as circumstantial evidence of Arabic settlements especially in harbour cities in other places of South Asia. Also Ābdul Hak Caudhurī (1988: 386).

68 These are the Majlis-e Ala Rastikhan mosque in Jobra, the Yusuf Shah mosque in Hathazari town, and the Nusrat Shah mosque in Fateyabad (Ābdul Hak Caudhurī 1988: 386–92).

69 Cf., in this context, Eaton's thesis regarding the gradual steps of inclusion, identification and displacement in the adoption of Islam in Bengal, and his remarks (1993: 269) on 'conversion': 'The term *conversion* is perhaps misleading when applied to this process, since it ordinarily connotes a sudden and total transformation in which a prior religious identity is wholly rejected and replaced by a new one. In reality, in Bengal, as in South Asian history generally, the process of Islamisation as a social phenomenon proceeded so gradually as to be nearly imperceptible.'

70 Cf. e.g. *Ā'īna-i Bārī*, p. 244 ff. (tiger); p. 248 ff. (snake); p. 261 (tiger, his most famous miracle; see below); p. 308 ff. (tiger); *JK*: 57, 128 (tigers); *JC*: 60 f. (tiger), 67 (snake); etc. Cf., for similar dominance over wild beasts with medieval Bengali *pīrs*, Asim Roy (1996: 110).

of the saints as protectors against natural adversities even in such recent times does hint at similar conditions to those described by Eaton.

But let us leave such speculations and return to the Maijbhandari family history. According to the hagiographies, Ahmadullah, the first and founding saint of Maijbhandar, was born in 1829 as the first son of Syed Motiullah. After finishing his primary religious education in local *madrasa*s, he was sent to Calcutta in 1844 to study at the Aliya Madrassah[71] where he stayed for eight years. He then worked as a Qadi in Jessore in 1269 *hiğrī* (1852–3) and thereupon as a teacher in a *madrasa*. It was at this time that he was initiated into the Qadiriya in Calcutta by one Shaikh Abu Shahmah.[72] The main source for this is the hagiographical description in the Urdu work *Ā'īna-i Bārī* (*AB*), the oldest extant treatise-cum-hagiography by Abdul Ghani Kanchanpuri written in 1912; later descriptions follow this one in every detail.[73] Notably, Ahmadullah did not observe the usual stages of a novice, but inherited the complete spiritual power (*wilāya*) of his master at the very first encounter.[74] In 1275 *hiğrī* (1858–9) he returned to Maijbhandar to live in a withdrawn way despite his marriages. Around the age of forty, namely in 1868, his wonder-working capacity started to show, and he began to attract visitors and followers.

The ensuing forty years saw Ahmadullah recruiting disciples from nearby and distant places; among these were many *ḫalifa*s or spiritual representatives – all of them Muslims – mostly from Chittagong, but also from Burma, Boalkhali, Noakhali, Kumilla, Faridpur and Barishal.[75] The centre of his activities, as spelt out in the *karāmat* or miracle sections of the hagiographies, was invariably his

71 The Aliya or Calcutta Madrasah was founded in 1780 by the British under Warren Hastings, and is probably the first educational institution founded by the British in India. In the beginning, only purely religious subjects were taught here. In 1854, namely a few years after Ahmadullah's attendance, the Anglo-Persian Department was opened 'where the usual subjects in a high school were taught' (*Calcutta Madrasah College. Bicentenary Celebration* 1985, article by S.A. Masud: 'Calcutta Madrasah – its Past, Present, and Future', n.p.). It was not possible to find details of Ahmadullah's studies at the Madrasah, since the older records and registration lists are not kept there any more, as the librarian and staff there told me. For a very critical evaluation of the educational performance of the Madrasah, cf. the account in W.W. Hunter(1999: 179–88). According to this, little learning and a lack of discipline had been typical of this institution, which had for decades been neglected by the English administrators. Hunter, writing originally in 1871, also reports a 'recent' scandal about courtesans taken into the Madrasah by resident students (p. 185 f.). About 80% of the students came 'from the fanatical Eastern Districts', mostly from Chittagong, Sandwip and Shahbazpur (p. 183). For further information on the Calcutta Madrasah, cf. also Mojibur Rahman (1977).

72 For detailed comments on his *šağara*, line of spiritual descent, cf. Syed Shahidul Haq's article ('Gāusul Ājam Māij'bhāṇḍārī: sajarā prasaṅga', in: Sahidul Hak (2005: 53–74).

73 Namely mainly *Jībanī o kerāmat*, the now standard Bengali hagiography of Ahmadullah. Cf. the chapter *Belāẏat arjan*, pp. 32–5.

74 Cf. *ĀB*: 117 and the more detailed summary thereof in Chapter 3 of this book.

75 Cf. the list given in *JK*: 86–9. There is another list in the pamphlet *Elākār renesā̃ yuger ek'ṭi dik* (pp. 3–7), which gives the names of 135 'eminent *murīd*s' (*biśiṣṭa muridān*), but it is not clear if 'eminent *murīd*s' and '*ḫalīfa*s' are to be taken as synonyms. Cf. Selim Jāhāṅgīr (2006: 348–52) for a compilation of the names from both lists as *ḫalīfa*s.

house in Maijbhandar; a few miracles report his appearance in far-away places, but never without stressing that at the time concerned he was *actually* staying in Maijbhandar. Not much is documented about the religious practice taught by him. Apart from a number of reported utterances of a didactic character,[76] Ahmadullah's teachings are not systematically laid down anywhere, and explicit formulations of a Maijbhandari *ṭarīqa*, some of which claim him as their architect, seem to be of a much later date. Even his title of a Ġauṯ al-Aʿẓam may have become truly current only after his death, and is later backed by one of his utterances in which he claims equal status and close communion with ʿAbd al-Qadir Gilani.[77] The language of communication at Ahmadullah's *darbār* appears to have been mainly Urdu, and it seems certain that performances of devotional music took place there very early: some of his followers are renowned songwriters.

One curious early document from outside Maijbhandari circles that speaks much of Ahmadullah's fame and reputation is the tract *Sādhur ātmabināś o janmagrahaṇ* (*SĀ*), published from Mirzakhil, another Sufi convent some 150 km south of Maijbhandar, by Abul Hasan Mostafizur Rahman Khan, a *murīd* of Shah Md. Abdul Hai, the then spiritual head of that institution. Taking down some of the utterances of his master, Khan warns his readers against the influence of the 'famous *faqīr* Shah Ahmadullah' (*SĀ*: *upakramanikā* [n.p.]). The spiritual state of saint Ahmadullah, according to this document that refers to him as Shah Sahib, had been revealed to Shah Md. Abdul Hai. On the one hand, indeed,

> The impression of the *tawağğuh* ['spiritual impact'] of the Shah Sahib was extremely intense and used to find expression with fearsome power; it has not been heard that in his time anyone else in Bengal had such an acute *tawağğuh*. By this he acquired *murīd*s and *ḫalīfa*s from many districts of Bengal, and many people started to frequent him.
>
> (*SĀ*: 18)

But Ahmadullah's *fanāʿ*, 'self-annihilation', as this author continues to report his *pīr*'s revelations, was of a *hāẏ'oẏānī* (Ar. <*ḥaywānī*>, 'animalic, bestial') nature, which resulted in the disappearance of the *šarīʿa* from Maijbhandar; and his great power of *tawağğuh* was actually *nārī* (Ar. 'fiery, hellish') and had been attained from the devil. Significant about this tract – which may be read as the hostility of a competing institution with motives not hard to guess – is the reproach of being *bīšarʿ* (P., 'without *šarīʿa*'), that is, neglecting the religious duties prescribed for every Muslim. This blemish sticks to common perceptions of Maijbhandar to this day despite the attempts of Maijbhandari representatives to

76 Which are, however, interpreted to contain all the basic features of the Maijbhandari *ṭarīqa*. For a detailed interpretation of these utterances, see Khādemul Hās'nāin (2005).

77 Cf. *JK*: 183 where Ahmadullah refers to Gilani as his elder brother.

establish the contrary. In any case, the tract bears testimony to Ahmadullah's influence and popularity during the latter part of his lifetime, starting in the last decades of the nineteenth century.

This popularity also transpires from another source from among the rare external accounts that are available, namely a description of a visit to Ahmadullah's *darbār* included in the biography of Manomohan Datta from Kumilla, which probably took place around the turn of the century. This visitor, himself a renowned Hindu *sādhu*, holy person, and writer of Maijbhandari songs, reports entering a huge courtyard in which many people had assembled. They were sitting in groups of three or four and engaging in theological discussions or humming songs in a low voice. To the side there was a long room containing the 'bed of gilded cushions and a carpet'[78] on which, Manomohan reports, Ahmadullah used to sit from time to time. After almost three hours, Ahmadullah gave the visitors the permission to come; the gifts brought by them were instantly carried off by his servants, and he was greeted by touching his feet. Ahmadullah briefly asked the visitors about their whereabouts and requests. Manomohan Datta concludingly remarks that Ahmadullah was said to perform his Friday prayers in Mecca, that many *rājā*s and *mahārājā*s were under his control, and that 'even in the provinces of Bombay and Madras his talent had come to light'.[79]

It seems hardly possible to prove whether Ahmadullah himself and his followers were *bīšar*ʿ Sufis or not. Among his *bāṇī*s, messages, as collected by Selim Jahangir, three refer to the importance of specific religious duties enjoined by the *šarīʿa*: one is the demand to his followers to perform their ritual prayers (*namāz*) and to recite the *Qurʾān*, another prescribes the avoidance of forbidden (*ḥarām*) food, and the last recommands fasting (Jāhāṅgīr 1999: 87). Md. Enamul Haq, on the basis of information gathered from his father, a follower of Ahmadullah, states that '[a]lthough at the end of his life he was not seen to strictly pay heed to all the rituals of Islam, he was, like the Sufis of the Qadiriya *ṭarīqa*, firmly established in the laws and the *šarīʿa* during all his life'.[80] The countering text from Mirzakhil cited above, however, quotes Ahmadullah as saying that 'There is no *šarīʿa* for me'.[81] Further, members of his entourage, asked by an inquirer from Mirzakhil about the laxity of certain Maijbhandari devotees in matters of the *šarīʿa*, are cited as excusing such *bīšar*ʿ followers by pointing out that due to esoteric (*bāṭin*) reasons, some are indeed exempt from the duties of the *šarīʿa*, and the usual disciples do not pray because of their

78 *hal'karā bāliś o satarañjite ek'khānā bichānā.*

79 Cf. the excerpt from Manomohan Datta's *Līlārahasya*, given under the caption of *Māij'bhāṇḍār dar'bār śarīphe Manomohan Datta* in *Jīban bāti*, 1. Māgh 1403 BE (1997), pp. [13–15] (own pagination).

80 As quoted in Selim Jāhāṅgīr (2000: 47).

81 *āmār kāche śariẏat nāi*; *SĀ*: 19.

example.[82] It also tells us that the educated among Ahmadullah's followers, upon being asked about his status in the context of the adherence to the *šarīʿa*, said that their *pīr* belonged to the categrory of *maǧḏūb sālik*, 'enraptured mystic' (*SĀ*: 18), apparently implying that due to this status he was not bound to the rules of the *šarīʿa* anymore. This status is confirmed by the tracts and hagiographies from Maijbhandar, but not its implications.[83] Today, the term *maǧḏūb*, 'enraptured', is not frequently heard in connection with Ahmadullah, but usually with his successor; and while it is still admitted that certain categories of saints are excluded from *šarīʿa* regulations, it is made clear that this does not apply to common *murīd*s.[84]

Gholam Rahman[85] (1865–1937), Ahmadullah's nephew, succeeded the latter as the second great saint of Maijbhandar. His spiritual career started a long time before Ahmadullah's demise, but there is not much information on the interrelation between these two saints. The hagiographies of Gholam Rahman stress the attachment Gholam Rahman felt towards Saint Ahmadullah already in his childhood, an attachment that increased during the years of his spiritual search when he was already in his twenties. He also took part in the guidance of *murīd*s since, according to his hagiographers, Ahmadullah used to send adepts (disciples) to him for instruction.[86] In contrast to such descriptions of 'cooperation' stand Gholam Rahman's wanderings in the woods and mountains of the larger region. These 'centrifugal' activities are indicative of a process of independent spiritual development. After 1906, these wanderings came to an

82 *ek'ṭi bātenī māmelā āche khāch khāch (biśeṣ biśeṣ) lok ukta māmelā baśataḥ nāmāj paṛe nā, kintu āoẏām murīd'gaṇ a*[. . . illegible word; possibly *ader* for *oder*, referring to *khāch khāch lok* (?)] *dekhādekhi nāmāj paṛe nā*. *SĀ*: 18. The notion that once one is beyond the *maqām* of the *šarīʿa* (cf. Section 3.3) the ritual prayers are 'no longer that important', is still widespread (interviews 3/1999 and 1/2001). Such notions are contested among Sufis here and elsewhere, and in another interview, a representative of the famous *mazār* of Nizam al-Din Auliya in Delhi dismissed such allegations as *bakwās* (U.), 'prattle' (interview H.H. 1/2001).

83 Cf. *ĀB*: 540; *BM*: 71.

84 This holds true, at least, for most of the theological and hagiographic literature from Maijbhandar. Maijbhandari songs, by contrast, may at times give quite a different impression.

85 There are different opinions regarding the correct form of this name. It is given as Gholamur Rahman by many representatives of Rahmaniyya Manzil (i.e. the 'house' of the descendants of Gholam Rahman), while namely some representatives of Ahmadiyya Manzil (descendants of Ahmadullah) insist that Gholam Rahman is the original form; and it appears that this latter form is still most widely used among the devotees. Syed Badruddoza in his hagiography of Gholam Rahman gives a facsimile of a Persian letter written by this saint which is signed *ġulām-i raḥmān*, the *iżāfa* not being marked but necessary according to Persian grammar. In Urdu, however, it can be left out. Thus, in fact, the original form of this name is either Persian or Urdu and ought to read Gholam-e Rahman or Gholam Rahman respectively. The Arabicised form *ġulām al-raḥmān* seems to be a later development in keeping with a general trend of Arabicisation of names, formula, etc. noticeable all over Bangladesh (and in fact also in the title *Ġawṯ al-Aʿẓam* common today which, in the early writings, is more often given in its Persian form *Ġawṯ-i Aʿẓam*), while *ġulām-raḥmān* would be an uncommon Persian compound and thus seems to be a misreading without *iżāfa* of the Persian original. But since the presumably original and correct form Gholam-e Rahman is hardly ever used, I have stuck to the most current form Gholam Rahman in this book.

86 Cf. Section 4.4.1 of this book, *JC*: 49–53.

end, and Gholam Rahman, alias Baba Bhandari, remained at the *darbār* until the end of his life. Around 1914, he stopped speaking except on very rare occasions, and became known as a *maǧḏūb pīr*, a spiritual master constantly in a state of meditation and rapture. In 1928, he left his father's house and moved into the newly built Gausiya Rahman Manzil. Gholam Rahman became immensely famous and popular. He did not occupy himself with administrative matters at all, and thus the *darbār* organisation was taken care of by a number of disciples and the *pīrzādas*, his four sons. Ahmadullah's son had died before Ahmadullah's death, and his grandson Syed Delawar Hosain (1893–1982) was too young for the position of a *saǧǧādanašīn*. The centre of the *darbār* thus appears to have shifted almost automatically to Gholam Rahman and his entourage.[87]

The type of spiritual mandate Gholam Rahman had received from Ahmadullah and his status as a saint are a matter of dissent to this day. Writers from Rahmaniyya Manzil, the 'house' of the descendants of Gholam Rahman, class him as a *ġawṯ al-aʿẓam*, the highest category of a *walī Allāh*, side by side with Ahmadullah, and sometimes claim that he was installed by Ahmadullah as his spiritual successor (*saǧǧādanašīn*). The position held by the descendants of Ahmadullah or Ahmadiyya Manzil, by contrast, is that he was Ahmadullah's 'main delegate' (*pradhān khaliphā*), and the title of a *ġawṯ al-aʿẓam* is usually denied to him – even if it does appear in one of Delawar Hosain's writings.[88] It is this Ahmadiyya Manzil version which seems to have most influence on outside scholarly perceptions. In writings belonging to a third 'house' called Haq Manzil, another variant occurs which grants the title of a Ġauṯ al-Aʿẓam to both of them and in addition also to Syed Ziaul Haq.[89]

Neither of these two saints has left any writings of his own, and the process of scripturalisation started only in the year of Ahmadullah's death. Hagiographers started to record *bāṇīs*, 'messages', of Ahmadullah, but those hardly fill more than two pages.[90] Writing activities are noteworthy in the decade after Ahmadullah's death;[91] they recede thereafter and reappear quite virulently after Gholam

87 Cf. Delawar Hosain's *Elākār renesā̃ yuger ekṭi dik* (*ER*: 13 ff.) for an 'opponent's view' of these developments. This tract of 58 pages is maybe the only writing by Delawar Hosain which has not been reprinted recently. This is due to its controversial character, as it contains a one-sided account of the developments at the *darbār* and very explicit accusations of fraud, commercialised religious activities, etc. against certain members of Rahmaniyya Manzil. If read cautiously, it is very valuable as a document of the formative years of the Maijbhandari movement after the demise of the great founding saints.

88 His appellation is given as *ġawṯ al-aʿẓam bi'l wirāṯa* ('Ġauṯ al-Aʿẓam in heritage') in *JK*: 89, implying that he inherted the title from Ahmadullah.

89 Cf. Amirul Islam's *Shahenshah*: 6.

90 Cf. the collection of utterances by Ahmadullah in Selim Jāhāṅgīr (1999: 86 f.); also, for some utterances not mentioned there, Syed Badruddoza's *BB*: 86 ff.

91 Three prominent books regarding the Maijbhandari movement came out during that time: *Tuḥfat* was published in 1906/07; *Premnur* in 1913; and *Āʾīna-i bārī* in 1914–15.

Rahman's death in an almost unbroken chain until today.[92] This seems in part due to a process of formalisation of charismatic religious leadership, parallels to which may be found in the history of many religious movements.[93] It is, however, just as much a result of a new constellation of competition between Rahmaniyya and Ahmadiyya Manzils. This development is closely connected with the personality of Delawar Hosain, Saint Ahmadullah's grandson.

Delawar Hosain, confronted with the growing popularity of Rahmaniyya Manzil and the decline of Ahmadullah's legacy, devoted much of his life to (re-) claiming his successorship to Ahmadullah and solidifying Ahmadiyya Manzil into an institution. Means of achieving this goal were, apart from all kinds of activities, the formalisation of the Maijbhandari *ṭarīqa* (which had until then hardly taken a fixed form) and the propagation of his ideas through a series of writings.[94] Similar efforts can be noticed simultaneously in Rahmaniyya Manzil where journals were started and hagiographies as well as expositions of Maijbhandar came to be published.[95] One specific trait of these writing activities is their shifting, for all purposes, to Bengali as the language of communication, in the place of Persian and Urdu;[96] this is indicative of a general process of vernacularisation of Islamic writing culture in Bengali, but also of a conscious effort at popularisation.

During this time, the number of annual festivities in Maijbhandar increased. Saint Ahmadullah's *ʿurs* had been established automatically after his demise; to these was added the *ḫuśrūz* (lit. 'day of joy', birthday) celebration of Gholam Rahman during this saint's lifetime. In the decades after his death, many other death anniversaries and birthdays were introduced, and the list of nine festivals given by Selim Jahangir is certainly not exhaustive.[97] While all of these celebrated personalities were or are spiritual representatives of Maijbhandar and are posited in the succession of the great founding saints, opinions regarding their saintly

92 It is hard to reconstruct the publication history of the works published in the 1930s and 40s as the original editions seem no longer extant, and the reprints do not mention any details concerning foregoing editions. They must have included Maijbhandari 'classics' such as the songs of Ramesh Shil and the works of Abdussalam Isapuri. The earliest dated documents of the time after the death of Gholam Rahman are copies of the journal *Tāohīd* from 1950.

93 In the context of Bengal, the cases of Chaitanya and Gaudiya Vaishnavism as well as that of Saint Ramakrishna may serve as classical examples here. Cf. Dimock (1989).

94 Among the ten writings Delawar Hosain authored, the most important and voluminous are the hagiography of Saint Ahmadullah *Jībanī o kerāmat* (*JK*), penned down by one of his disciples and first published in 1967, and the tract *Belāẏate motlākā* (*BM*), which apparently first appeared in 1959.

95 Noteworthy among these are the journal *Tāohīd*, brought out by two sons of Saint Gholam Rahman, Mahbubuil Bashar and Shafiul Bashar, from the early 1940s into the 50s, and the various writings by Abdussalam Isapuri, to name only the most important.

96 Cf. Chapter 4 for a discussion of this shift.

97 Jahangir lists: 10th Māgh/24 January: *ʿurs* of Saint Ahmadullah; 22nd Caitra/5 April: *ʿurs* of Saint Gholam Rahman; 27th Āśvin/12 October: *ḫuśrūz* of Saint Gholam Rahman; 10th Pauṣ/24 December: *ḫuśrūz* of Ziaul Haq; 26th Āśvin/11 October: *ʿurs* of Ziaul Haq; 7th Phālgun/29 February: *ḫuśrūz* of Shafiul Bashar; 1st Māgh/15 January: *ʿurs* of Shamsul Huda; 25th Agrahāẏan/19 December: *ʿurs* of Aminul Haq Wasil; 27th Māgh/13 February: *ḫuśrūz* of Mainuddin Ahmad (Selim Jāhāṅgīr 1999: 152).

status may vary, especially from *manzil* to *manzil*. Along with the installation of festivities in the memory of Maijbhandari *pīr*s went the construction of tombs, changing the outer aspect of Maijbhandar gradually from the normal village it used to be into a veritable shrine complex with its at present more than two dozen tombs that exceed the usual size of such edifices and are more properly termed mausoleums.

This increasing display of status triggered accusations of commercialisation that were not limited to the environment but penetrated Maijbhandari circles as a result of the factionalisation of the movement. In the beginning of the 1970s, it was Syed Delawar Hosain who recorded such reproaches in writing.[98] Such complaints have not at all disappeared, but continue to be widespread in outsiders' perceptions of Maijbhandar as well as among the followers and representatives of the movement, the tendency among the latter being to relegate such accusations to competing Maijbhandari branches while exempting one's own *manzil* or organisation. Similar complaints are today uttered with regard to the sincerity of the devotees: if in the old days 99% of them were true *bhakta*s, devotees, now this applies only to one out of a hundred.[99]

Among the spiritual leaders of Maijbhandar that emerged after Ahmadullah and Gholam Rahman, the two most popular deserve separate mention: Syed Ziaul Haq (1928–88) and Syed Shafiul Bashar (1919–2002). The former was the eldest son of Delawar Hosain and thus the great-grandson of Ahmadullah, and Sajeda Khatun, the daughter of Gholam Rahman, which, according to the genealogical arithmetics typical of Maijbhandar, makes him the recipient of an abundance of spiritual capital: first, on a general plane common to all Maijbhandaris, he received the legacies of Hasan and Husain via ʿAbd al-Qadir Gilani; and secondly, those of the two founding saints of Maijbhandar simultaneously. In comparison to other Maijbhandari spiritual personalities, Ziaul Haq's development appears particularly uneven and violent. In 1953, he sat his BA examinations, but – in parallel to Gholam Rahman – 'he handed in a white sheet of paper without anything written on it and left the examination hall' (*Jiẏāul Hak*: 66). During the following years he underwent long periods of sometimes extreme austerities, and his condition eventually became so alarming that in 1967 his family had him treated with electroshocks in Pabna Mental Hospital. Six years after this, his father formally transferred Saint Ahmadullah's *wilāya* or spiritual sovereignty[100] to him,[101] and in 1974 he was separated from his father's house and built one of his own (Haq Manzil). He earned a reputation of saintliness in these years and assembled a separate circle of *murīd*s around him; the hagiographies

98 Cf. *ER*: 32 ff. where he complains about the building of ostentatious mausoleums and the establishment of *ʿurs* celebrations for Maijbhandari personalities of (in his opinion) minor importance.

99 Interview 1/2001.

100 On *wilāya*, cf. Section 3.6 in this book.

101 But he was not made the *saǧǧādanašīn*; cf. *Jiẏāul Hak*: 102.

portray him as the ordainer behind major political events, such as the overthrow of the Shah's regime in Iran, and the killing of Indira Gandhi.[102] Haq Manzil has maintained its independence also after his death in 1988, and though its hagiological positions are quite close to those of Ahmadiyya Manzil and these two *manzil*s have a very friendly relationship, they must be regarded as two separate institutions.

Shafiul Bashar, on the other hand, has in the last decades been the main representative of Rahmaniyya Manzil. This last son of Gholam Rahman was early in his life sent to Aligarh's Muslim University in order to acquire Islamic knowledge. As a *murīd* of his father's, he wrote numerous devotional songs[103] and practised austerities. After Gholam Rahman's death, and assisted by his wife, he became active as a propagator of the Maijbhandari movement and also travelled to Britain and the USA on this mission. He became the *saǧǧādanašīn* of Rahmaniyya Manzil. During his final years, judging from the number of his disciples and the size of his *manzil*, he developed into the most popular contemporary *pīr* in Maijbhandar.

In the past there have already been other Maijbhandari spiritual leaders besides those mentioned here;[104] and today, taking into account the usual expectation that there should be one main representative of the movement, the situation has become confusing to a newcomer. There are at least a dozen persons who are practising Maijbhandari *pīr*s. Shafiul Bashar of Rahmaniyya Manzil is presently succeeded by his sons; Syed Md. Hasan is the *saǧǧādanašīn* of Haq Manzil; Syed Emdadul Haq is the spiritual successor to Syed Delawar Hosain and *saǧǧādanašīn* of Ahmadiyya Manzil;[105] in addition to these, *pīr*s have evolved or are evolving from other branches of the Maijbhandari family.[106] Many among these, and particularly the economically superior, have taken their residence in Chittagong City or Dhaka, and some very actively travel in different parts of the country and abroad to visit branches of their respective organisations and supervise their activities on the spot.

The *darbār* is to this day in the possession of the Maijbhandari family. In 1989, during Hosain Mohammad Ershad's military rule in Bangladesh, the Government attempted to transform it into a *waqf*, an Islamic religious foundation, and to put it under the control of a governmental *waqf* board. Syed Najibul Bashar, son of Syed Shafiul Bashar and a former Member of Parliament, led the campaign in opposition to this move. Meetings and demonstrations were organised in both Chittagong and Dhaka, and the case was taken to Dhaka High Court in 1991. The

102 Cf. e.g. *Jiẏāul Hak*: 122–30.
103 These are part of the Maijbhandari songs chosen for analysis in Chapter 5.
104 Notably Aminul Haq Wasil and Shamsul Huda.
105 At least until very recently (around 2005) when a friction occurred within Ahmadiyya Manzil, leading to a situation in which Syed Emdadul Haq claims to represent the spiritual tradition of Ahmadullah alone.
106 e.g. Syed Nizamuddin, Syed Muinuddin Ahmad, Syed Aminul Islam, Syed Abul Fazl, etc.

intercession of the new Prime Minister, Khaleda Zia, finally led to the abolishment of this plan and restored the prior status of legitimate proprietors to the Maijbhandari family.[107]

The history of Maijbhandar could be drawn out in much more detail, but this sketch must suffice as an orientating framework for the investigation we are about to undertake. Chapter 4 on Maijbhandari hagiographies furnishes more comprehensive information on some important Maijbhandari saints and the way they are seen by their devotees. A more meticulous documentation of some aspects of this history can be found in the monograph by Selim Jahangir.[108] The aim of the following not being an exhaustive documentation but rather an interpretation of Maijbhandar in the context of what – notwithstanding the initial reservations – I will call Bengali Islam, I wish to leave it at this outline and move on into the following chapter with its description of structure and ritual in Maijbhandar.

107 Information collected in an interview with a Maijbhandari representative (20 March 1999).

108 Cf. Selim Jāhāṅgīr (1999); historical documentation remains, however, mostly limited to data pertaining to the lives of single Maijbhandari personalities, and is not subjected to any systematic analysis or interpretation.

2 Structure and religious practice

This study as a whole focuses on Maijbhandari text production: Chapters 3 to 5 deal with different types of texts, and in a way Chapter 6 also relies on primary textual material. The present chapter, by contrast, is based on fieldwork observations. It gives an overview of the structure and religious practice of the Maijbhandari movement as observed during two stays in 1999 and 2001, using fieldwork notes, interviews and conversations with individuals on the spot.

Maijbhandar today contains quite a variety of organisations and institutions: there are various *manzil*s, societies, branches, accounts departments, spiritual guides, spiritual lineages, circles of disciples, and even forms of the Maijbhandari *ṭarīqa*. These distinctions, evolved in the course of the expansion of the movement, give Maijbhandar a polycentric character. There is not one single highest authority and no overarching organisation that unites all of those who are, or claim to be, Maijbhandaris. In this chapter, I will first describe some important categories that shape the Maijbhandari *darbār*, among them the topography of holy spaces and the nature of offices and organisations. I hope to sketch out the internal structure of this religious movement and discuss the ratio underlying this process of diversification spanning over roughly one century. Secondly, I will describe some aspects of the religious practice encountered at Maijbhandar today, including shrine pilgrimage, certain esoteric practices common in Sufism, the relationship between spiritual masters and their adepts, as well as the great festivals.

2.1 Structure of the Maijbhandari movement

There are a number of field studies on single South Asian *dargāh*s and saint and *pīr* veneration,[1] and approaches have ranged from ethnographic and sociological investigations and historical studies to phenomenological descriptions of belief systems. Some have focused on the changes brought about in single institutions during the twentieth century (Liebeskind 1998; Gardner 1995), others on the social

1 Cf. Eaton (1984); Gaborieau (1983); Einzmann (1988); Troll (1989); Gardner (1995); Liebeskind (1998), etc.

and psychological dimension of *pīr–murīd* relationships (Ewing 1993). The usual structure of South Asian shrine cults that emerges from the literature can, broadly speaking, be called twofold. On the one hand, there are the long-established *dargāh*s of mostly medieval saints. These are centred around the personalities of the deceased saints; there may or may not be legitimate spiritual successors, but these act as such rather than on their own account. Examples of this type would seem to be some of the great Chishti shrines as, for example, those of Muʿin al-Din Chishti of Ajmer and Nizam al-Din Awliya of Delhi; in Bangladesh, the shrines of Shah Jalal of Sylhet, Badr Shah of Chittagong and Khan Jahan ʿAli of Bagerhat fall into this category. On the other hand, and mostly in cases where the founding saints are not so prominent, there are spiritual successors (*saǧǧādanašīn*s) who are the heads of *ḫānaqāh* institutions and actively bestow Sufic teachings on a circle of adherents. Here, the veneration of the tombs of the predecessors also plays a role, but is certainly far less prominent than in the former case. Shrine veneration appears as only one of many aspects of their religious activities. This structure can be found, for example, at the *dargāh* of the Atrasi Pir[2] at Faridpur.

Maijbhandar, however, does not easily fit into either of these categories since it combines the veneration of the tombs of two extremely popular deceased saints with a lively religious culture centred around living spiritual guides, some of whom, though sucessors of those two founding saints, have acquired their own standing. Furthermore, spiritual succession in Maijbhandar appears multiple and is contested among many practising *pīr*s – a case which, to my knowledge, has so far not been described in the literature on South Asian shrines. I shall try to give a detailed picture of this complex structure by examining a number of institutions, offices and structure-related concepts that are current in Maijbhandar and have an effect on the course of events.

2.1.1 Holy spaces

It is the overlap of a number of different taxonomies that makes it necessary to investigate the spatial character of Maijbhandar in some detail here. Maijbhandar is simultaneously an agricultural village and a major religious site. Very obviously, these different spheres interfere and create tensions, as a *dargāh* requires one type of conduct and a peasant village quite another. A *dargāh* commands a certain spatial order. As the term *dargāh* suggests, the parallels to courtly architecture are conspicuous. Some prominent *dargāh*s on the subcontinent are surrounded by walls. In rural Bengal, this is not necessarily the case. But the *dargāh* as a demarcated space does exist here too in terms of a cognitive category. Thus, a dominant feature to mark off its holy place from the surroundings that is very commonly found in both urban and rural shrines in Chittagong is the gate, referred to by terms such as *bāb* (Ar.), *darwāza* (P.), *darǰā, toraṇ* (Bg.; the former is an old Portuguese loan word) or also *geṭ*

2 *Āṭrasī pīr*. Cf. Landell Mills (1995 and 1998).

(Eng., <*gate*>).[3] A gate may be placed at the entrance of a single shrine or of one specific shrine within a shrine complex, at the road leading to such a complex, or even at the sometimes quite remote intersection of such a road with the main road. Several shrines in Chittagong, including smaller ones, use such gates at main roads in order to draw attention from passers-by. Often, as in Maijbhandar, all three of these spatial units are marked by gates. The gates are usually recent concrete constructions in the kind of neo-saracenic style characteristic of most of the shrines themselves, and are colourfully painted. They bear the name or names and main titles of the buried saint as well as Arabic or Persian inscriptions such as the *Basmala*. In some cases, such gates are perceived as nothing but the architectural paraphernalia of shrines; in others, however, they mark the transition into the territory owned and governed by a particular saint and thus require a change of behaviour. Thus, in a place near the village of Farhadabad in the vicinity of Maijbhandar, it is customary to get off one's cycle or rickshaw and cross the local saint's shrine on foot as a matter of respect.

Within a shrine, some more spatial units are of crucial importance. One is the *ḥuğra*, the 'room' or customary dwelling place of a *pīr* or saint, namely the place where he receives or used to receive his visitors. This *ḥuğra* can be paralleled to the courtly audience hall, but also to the *basār ghar* ('sitting room') or *bāirer ghar* ('outer room'; also *baiṭhak'khānā*, 'reception room') within the traditional structure of a Bengali household. The *ḥuğra* usually faces the outer courtyard or roadside and is the first room encountered when entering a house. It is often separated from the outside by a verandah and stairs. The central item within a *ḥuğra* is the *gaddī*, the *pīr*'s 'throne', usually a wooden bed covered with costly sheets. In the case of deceased saints, the *ḥuğra*s are conserved and visited in the course of a pilgrimage, and the bedstead and other personal belongings of the saint such as his water pipe may be reverentially touched. A *pīr* would come to his *ḥuğra* at certain habitual times of the day and during festivities to communicate with his devotees, and retire from there to the rear part of his house. In Maijbhandar, the central houses are built around a small plaza with their *ḥuğra*s as the outermost units: they are places where the public sphere temporarily overlaps with the privacy of a *pīr*'s house.

Besides the *ḥuğra*s, also *čilla*s (P./U., lit. 'a forty-day period of penances') may be a part of the parcours to be performed by pilgrims. They are the places where saints retire for meditation and penances, and are usually situated outside the shrine complex. In Maijbhandar, the founding saint Ahmadullah's *čilla* is situated on the way to the adjacent village of Damdama on a spot that purportedly used to be covered by dense forest in the nineteenth century, and is now surrounded by paddy fields.

The central-most place in a *dargāh*, however, is usually one or several mausoleums of deceased saints. The term *qabr*, Ar. 'grave', is rarely used to refer to saintly tombs, and the more honorific terms *mazār* (Ar., 'tomb') or *rawḍa* (Ar., 'saintly grave') are preferred. A saintly grave differs from usual Islamic graves in

3 Also shrines in crowded places in urban environments in Chittagong invariably have more or less imposing entrance gates, such as the well-known *dargāh*s of Badr Shah and Amanat Shah, both situated in the centre of the city close to Lal Dighi, and that of Baezid Bistami (local pronunciation: Bostami), actually a *čilla* (a place where a saint has performed penances), in the northern outskirts.

being elevated usually about one meter above the ground, and of course in being the central point and sanctum of an edifice, the mausoleum. The terms *mazār* and *rawḍa* signify both the grave itself and the surrounding building. Major mausoleums in Chittagong usually have at least two concentric square or rectangular walls or archways around the grave; single-domed mausoleums are of historical importance in Bengal, but are rarely built in modern times.[4] The outermost part consists of ascending stairs or a verandah. Within the mausoleum, the centrality of the grave governs the movements of visitors, who should – again conspicuously parallel to courtly etiquette – ideally never turn their back on it. In Chittagong, this centrality of the grave in mausoleums is rarely modified by a *mihrāb*, a prayer niche facing the *qibla*, which in other places is often built into mausoleums.[5]

Since the construction of the first mausoleum after the death of Ahmadullah, numerous domed tombs have been built in Maijbhandar. In some cases this happened on the spot where the respective person used to hold *darbār*, that is, to sit and receive visitors. The transformation of formerly inhabited space into sanctified buildings has led to a backward expansion of the living quarters; notably Ahmadiyya and Rahmaniyya Manzils have grown into large building complexes.

The deceased saint, like elsewhere in South Asia and the Islamic world in general, is imagined as being present in his tomb in a very real sense, like a living person; he may act from out of his grave, appear and speak to visitors, and is therefore entitled to adequate reverence.[6] It is thus little wonder that the etiquette

4 Famous examples of single-domed mausoleums on the Indian subcontinent are those of Mu'in al-Din Chishti in Ajmer and of Bandanawaz Gisudaraz in Gulbarga. In Bengal, Khan Jahan 'Ali's mausoleum at Bagerhat is another old and well-known single-domed construction. One of the rare modern single-domed edifices is the mausoleum of Ziaul Haq in Maijbhandar, built in 1993. It relies on very different architectural concepts but shares with most of the older single-domed mausoleums the central position of the grave under one single cupola.

5 Cf. Ernst (1993: 53). For other discussions of terms like *qabr*, *dargāh*, etc. cf. also Gaborieau (1983: 293 f.). Detailed descriptions of the various localities pertaining to three Pakistani shrines are found in Einzmann (1988).

6 For a Qur'anic source taken to legitimise such a notion, see *Qur'ān* 2.154(2.149) (with reference to martyrs). For South Asia, cf. Ernst (1993: 60 f.) on two medieval sources as quoted in an eighteenth-century pilgrimage manual. Sayyid Ashraf Jahangir Simnani Chishti (d. 1425), asked by a darvesh why tombs should be venerated if the spirit is detached from the body, said that 'concentration increases', and one's 'sense-perception is engaged with the tomb'; '[the spirit] keeps an eye on the body with which it has been connected for seventy years and on its resurrection body that it will become after the resurrection, for ever and ever. Its connection is greater here than in any other place.' Deceased saints are conscious: saint Nizam al-Din went for *ziyāra* to the tomb of Khwaja Qutb al-Din, and when he wondered whether the deceased saint was aware of him, got the reply: 'Think of me as living like yourself. I will come in spirit if you come in body. Do not think me lacking in companionship, for I see you even if you don't see me.' Again Ernst (1993: 64), where the same saint admonishes a person sitting in an indecent way at his tomb. Also Desiderio Pinto (1992: 118) on contemporary accounts of Nizam al-Din 'sitting cross-legged on his tomb' and 'walking around the dargah'. Taylor (1999: 72), writing on medieval Egypt, refers to saint Ibn Khalifa al-Makhzumi who rebuked a thoughtless visitor: 'Do not sit on the grave of a man who loves and is loved by God!'; as a rule, the dead had to be greeted like the living. Such notions are, it goes without saying, anything but exclusively Islamic. For the concept of the presence of the Buddha in *stūpas* in Buddhism, cf. Schopen (1997) and Myer (1961). An impressive account of the presence of medieval Christian saints in their graves is Dinzelbacher (1990).

Photo 1 Saint Ahmadullah Maijbhandari's new mausoleum, Maijbhandar.

to be maintained at a saint's tomb bears a number of similarities to the way a living *pīr* must be approached. The spatial concept of utter centrality (resounding in the traditional term *qutb*, 'pole', for a saint of high order) on the *pīr*'s part structures the relations between him and his disciples. Numerous manuals for proper conduct furnish the details: In the presence of his spiritual preceptor, the disciple ought to keep his eyes permanently fixed on the former's, he must not turn his back on his preceptor, and he is expected to take his seat at a lower level than his *pīr*'s, usually on the ground.[7]

7 The proscription of turning one's back on the deceased saint is already mentioned in medieval Egyptian sources (Taylor 1999: 72) and in an eighteenth-century pilgrimage guide (Ernst 1993: 51). Cf. the more extensive description of etiquette *vis-à-vis* living *pīr*s in Section 2.2.3.

The concept of *wilāya*, which may mean 'territory' as well as 'spiritual sovereignty' or 'sainthood',[8] is important here. In many South Asian Sufi traditions, the *darbār* is conceived in analogy to the capital reigning over the *wilāya* as the realm, and the saints and Sufi *pīr*s divide up the country among themselves. 'Each saint had his sphere of influence in which he recognized no one besides himself. People who came from outside his spiritual kingdom were referred back to their correct saint.'[9] Of course, this horizontal structure is complemented by a classical hierarchy of saints, again in close analogy to, e.g., the taxation pyramid; and saints of higher orders command more than their direct surroundings. We shall have occasion to elaborate on these traditional concepts and their Maijbhandari adaptations in some detail in Section 3.6.

*2.1.2 Houses (*manzils*)*

We may conveniently continue our investigation by examining one of the most basic structural units that characterise Maijbhandar today: the *manzil*, 'house'. The Perso-Arabic term *manzil* is euphemistic for Bengali *bāṙi* (or *bāṙī*), meaning not necessarily one separate edifice but rather one household, with the common stove as the ultimate criterion of unity.[10] Five generations after Matiullah, the forefather of the Maijbhandari family who settled in the village some time in the beginning of the nineteenth century, the more than two hundred members of this family have spread out and come to live in about twenty-seven different houses,[11] which makes them the most populous and influential group in local village society. Living conditions being at great variance within the Maijbhandari clan, these *manzil*s are anything from small huts with thatched roofs up to multi-storeyed concrete buildings with urban commodities. Despite the great number of *manzil*s, only three are generally used to refer to the inner structure of Maijbhandar: Ahmadiyya, Rahmaniyya and Haq Manzil.[12] They are named after the prominent saints to whom the respective descendants genealogically belong: Ahmadullah, Gholam Rahman and Ziaul Haq. Two of these, Ahmadiyya and Haq Manzils, still retain the unity of a *bāṙi.* The numerous descendants of Gholam Rahman make up for a great actual number of *manzil*s that are, however, collectively referred to as Rahmaniyya Manzil; the specifications are sometimes affixed to the general denomination (e.g. Manzil-e Rahmaniyya Muiniyya). The most prominent single institution within collective Rahmaniyya Manzil has so far been Shafiul Bashar's (d. 2002) house. This last son of Gholam Rahman, himself an immensely popular saintly figure, has drawn masses of disciples and pilgrims; and his mansion,

8 Cf. Chapter 3.

9 Cf. Liebeskind (1998: 71); and, with her, Eaton (1984: 341) and Digby (1994: 62 f.).

10 For an excellent ethnographic description of social institutions, including the concept of a *bāṙi* in rural Bangladesh, see Luchesi (1983).

11 According to the calculation of a local resident.

12 Cf. Jāhāṅgīr (1999: 147) for short descriptions of these three *manzil*s, and pp. 255–92 for interviews with the representatives of each of them.

guesthouses, accountancy offices and so on are comparable in themselves to, or even exceed in size, the respective institutions in Ahmadiyya and Haq Manzils. While the *manzil*s so far mentioned are affluent and wealthy institutions today, we find extremely different degrees of economic and spiritual status in other branches of the Maijbhandari family.

These other *manzil*s with fewer direct linkages to either Ahmadullah or Gholam Rahman, but not therefore necessarily less important for the dissemination of Maijbhandari teachings, are formed, e.g., by the descendants of Syed Abdul Hamid, Ahmadullah's younger brother, among whom some are practising *pīr*s. Likewise, the descendants of the younger brothers of Gholam Rahman (Syed Md. Hashem, Abdul Wahab and Abdul Hadi) form different *manzil*s, and some of their members act as spiritual guides.

Economically speaking, these *manzil*s are the very centres of Maijbhandar. Notably Ahmadiyya and Rahmaniyya Manzils hold agrarian estates in the vicinity of the *darbār*. The trend in recent decades has been, among the affluent branches of the Maijbhandari Syed family, to acquire modern secular education and take up urban professions and residence, and consequently, since the demise of Shafiul Bashar in 2001, none of the highest representatives of the prominent *manzil*s (Ahmadiyya, Rahmaniyya, Haq) has its domicile in Maijbhandar. They are factory owners, politicians, medical doctors, etc. and visit Maijbhandar regularly on Thursdays and Fridays as well as on festive occasions. This holds true also for less prominent branches: in some cases, the younger generation has taken up urban residence, and only the older family members keep to the village; in others, part of the religious offices has been transferred to the city residences.

*2.1.3 Spiritual guides (*pīrs*)*

Who qualifies for becoming a *pīr*[13] or *muršid* (Ar. 'leader'), a spiritual preceptor?[14] There is an old discussion among Islamic theologians regarding this question, and Maijbhandari treatises also take up this issue.[15] It requires individual spiritual

13 The Persian word *pīr*, lit. 'old', but also 'spiritual preceptor', is used exclusively in the second denotation in South Asia. Cf. already Garcin de Tassy, writing in 1831 in his famous *Mémoire sur des particularités de la religion musulmane dans l'Inde, d'après les ouvrages hindoustani*: '*Pir* means literally an old man, but in this context, a person who has spiritual dignity, much like the guru of the Hindus. [...] Many of the *pirs* are venerated as saints after their death. That is why the word *wali* is synonymous with *pir*, and signifies a saint as much as the word *wali* does.' Quoted from M. Waseem's translation in Tassy (1997: 39). This is to some extent still true for the terminology used in Maijbhandar and generally in Sufic parlance in Bangladesh. But it does appear that the term *walī* is rarely used for living spiritual guides. It would seem that *pīr* has more and more become a social label for spiritual practitioners that is used by all factions regardless of their evaluation of such practice, whereas *walī* positively denotes a person the speaker deems to be a saint. For the semantic extension of the term *pīr* in Bengal, cf. Asim Roy (1996: 108), who distinguishes between fictitious, actual religious, and actual non-religious personalities. Cf. also the remarks on *pīr sāhitya* in Section 4.1.

14 The term *guru* also has wide currency in Maijbhandar, though rather in oral and informal contexts.

15 We shall have ample occasion to look at the traits of *pīr*s and saints in the following chapters.

achievements, no doubt, but these should not be all too independent; and it is agreed among all that the usual and most common and proper way of becoming a *pīr* is by spiritual succession. Rather than *silsila*, in Maijbhandar the Bengali term *ādhyātmik dhārā* is used to denote this 'stream of spirituality' emanating from the Prophet and passed via ʿAlī on through the various lines of Sufis to its present holders. There are two kinds of spiritual inheritors. The most privileged is the *saǧǧādanašīn* or *gaddīnašīn*, 'he who sits on the prayer rug' or 'cushion/throne' respectively, namely the main direct spiritual descendant of an established *pīr*: formally appointed before the latter's death, the *saǧǧādanašīn* comes to substitute him at his residence and inherits his office and followers. A second row of spiritual heirs are referred to as *ḫalīfa*s, lit. 'deputies'. These are devotees with a high degree of spiritual perfection who obtain the blessings and spiritual inspiration from the *pīr* in order to (usually) establish themselves at other places, often their native villages, and promulgate their received teachings. The impact of great saints is also measurable numerically sometimes by the number of *ḫalīfa*s they have made, and a complete graphic representation of an *ādhyātmik dhārā*, stream of spirituality, will produce regular new branches or offshoots, some of which are seen to be very productive foci while others die off.[16] Genealogical tables of spiritual descent, so-called *šaǧara*s, are, however, never given in this ramified fashion but only as one single line – possibly because the task would be much more daunting than in the case of a family tree, which in spite of the much smaller number of possible progeny soon reaches its limits. In any case, the *saǧǧādanašīn* is privileged among the *ḫalīfa*s insofar as he is the heir proper of the deceased saint's *darbār* and the recipient not only of some degree of spiritual inspiration, but also of the whole of his spiritual sovereignty or saintly power (*wilāya*).[17]

The Maijbhandaris derive their spiritual descent from ʿAbd al-Qadir Gilani[18] (d. 1166), founder of the Qadiriyya brotherhood, and down to Syed Ahmadullah Maijbhandari their *šaǧara*s are identical. It is only after him that the line of spiritual inheritance branches off in various ways; and it is here that the distinction between a *saǧǧādanašīn* and a *ḫalīfa* becomes relevant for us. For – and this is a repeated happening in Maijbhandari history – the installation of the *saǧǧādanašīn* by saint Ahmadullah (1829–1906) was not as unambiguous as the tradition would seem to require. To whom did he pass on his complete *wilāya*, to his nephew Syed Gholam Rahman (1865–1937), who in fact succeeded him as a saintly figure at the *darbār* after his demise, or to his then adolescent grandson Syed Delawar Hosain (1893–1982)? It is this question that divides the two major factions of the Maijbhandari family as it exists today. Claiming for the nephew, the representatives of

16 Shah Jalal of Sylhet, for example, is said to have had 360 *ḫalīfa*s who spread in the vicinity and helped him earn the reputation of a great Islamiser. Saint Ahmadullah of Maijbhandar supposedly, according to his grandson Syed Delawar Hosain, had 134 (or, in a more pessimistic listing, 53) such deputies (cf. Selim Jāhāṅgīr 2000: 22).

17 Cf. the discussion of *wilāya* in Section 3.6.

18 Or, according to the Arabic rendering of this Persian name, Ǧilānī; the common Bengali form is Āb'dul Kāder Jilānī. For his and the Qadiriyya's prominence in South Asia, cf., e.g., Sanyal (1996: 144).

Rahmaniyya Manzil give certain dicta of Ahmadullah in support of their contention and point to his utmost spiritual importance; claiming for the grandson, Ahmadiyya and Haq Manzils give another series of dicta. Gholam Rahman, to them, is a great saint, no doubt, but only Ahmadullah's main deputy.[19]

This point cannot be settled, because none of the factions can prove that an official installation of their respective predecessor has ever taken place. But, taking into account the fact that Gholam Rahman is regarded as a much more charismatic saint than Delawar Hosain, it is surprising that the latter position has been able to assert itself at all. The underlying factor that comes to its aid is a second kind of lineage that has, in the course of time, become another strong ingredient of a *pīr* in South Asia: the *rakter dhārā* (Bg.), 'line/stream of blood'. According to this unofficial, but very pervasive concept, spiritual *wilāya* is most conveniently passed on from father to son in patrilinear succession. Some may deplore such developments, seeing in them the deterioration of Sufism;[20] but to many adherents such reasoning seems very plausible. And it must be admitted that it does not stand in isolation but is easily connectable with other concepts such as *baraka* and the outstanding position of Sayyads. *Baraka* is the salutory effluence of everything – objects as well as persons – that has been in bodily contact with a saint, or generally a 'mode in which the divine reaches into the human' (Geertz 1968: 44), and the connection of blood is thought of as the closest possible relationship. The high status of the Sayyads, the progeny of the Prophet Muhammad, can also be accounted for by this very factor of *rakter dhārā*. In most shrines in contemporary Bangladesh – and not only there – the spiritual and genealogical lineages have in fact become coterminous.[21]

The tendency is, furthermore, to look at the spiritual heritage like any other kind of heritage; bestowing one's *wilāya* on somebody else would bring with it problems of distribution of property since the *darbār* is, in almost all cases, not easily separable from the family belongings at large. This applies especially when the respective *pīr*s are wealthy, as is the case in some Maijbhandari *manzil*s; wealth creates an overlap of functions such as head of family, spiritual preceptor and landlord within one personality, and more often than not the task of distributing these functions among the progeny is left for them to sort out.[22]

19 *pradhān khaliphā* is the wording usually employed.

20 Such polemics already occur in the Middle Ages in various *ṭarīqa*s, and they continue to this day. An Imam at the *dargāh* of Nizam al-Din Awliya of Delhi, e.g., pointed out to me that the Chishti *silsila* had been intact until about two centuries ago when it started to become hereditary.

21 e.g. in Mirzakhil, in Thakurgaon (cf. Siegfried 2001) and for the Atrasi Pir of Faridpur, not to mention all the smaller shrines in the vicinity of Maijhandar. Cf. also Sanyal (1996: 109, 148) on coinciding spiritual and genealogical succession in the context of the Ahl-i Sunnat movement, the so-called Barelwis of Northern India, in the beginning of the twentieth century.

22 An exception is the present (or at least until the rift around 2005) Ahmadiyya Manzil, which is run by four of the five sons of Delawar Hosain (exempting the eldest, Ziaul Haq, for whom a separate *manzil* was built): here the functions of spiritual preceptor, *muntaẓim* ('organiser'), etc. were distributed from the start. Quite the opposite has happened very recently after the passing away of Syed Shafiul Bashar, the youngest son of saint Gholam Rahman. At present, I am told, all his four sons act as spiritual guides, and the question of who is the *saǧǧādanašīn* has not been settled decisively.

A lack of spiritual attainment can, once a *darbār* has been established and is running well, be made good by other things. *Ādhyātmik dhārā* and *rakter dhārā* are deemed the main criteria of legitimacy for a *pīr* in Maijbhandar, and it is along these lines that disputes over legitimation are argued out. There are yet other popular classification criteria. Like *mazārs*, *pīrs* are sometimes called *garam*, 'hot', and *ṭhāṇḍā*, 'cold', which relates to their temperament and their proneness to states of trance; a *garam pīr* therefore may also be *maǧḏūb*, 'enraptured', and averse to all kinds of organisational matters (as opposed to the sober *sālik*). Gholam Rahman was such a 'hot' *pīr* who defied all established ways of recruiting disciples or installing *ḫalīfas* and a *saǧǧādanašīn*, thus leaving his succession to a process of interpretation and negotiation among his sons and followers. In interpreting his *bāṭin*, 'esoteric' or lit. 'hidden' agenda, categories such as the oath of allegiance (*bay'a*) in dreams make their way into the Maijbhandari dealings with questions of legitimacy.

The claim to have only one highest representative of the Maijbhandari movement at present seems to be most clearly articulated by the members of Ahmadiyya Manzil who rely on the combined lineages of spirituality and blood to support their argument. Other *manzils* seem to insist that plurality and, as they may put it, a 'mild competition' between the practitioners should be allowed, arguing against those formal criteria that the stream of spirituality does not necessarily move in preconceived and hereditary channels. This position is, of course, not completely sound since the *pīrs* who tend to suscribe to it do stress their affiliation to the Maijbhandari family and thus profit from those formal criteria themselves. This attitude appears to increase in reverse proportion with the closeness to the Maijbhandari establishment, namely the important and affluent *manzils*.

Another question of status is whether a *pīr* should be moving or stationary.[23] The founding saints are reported never to have left Maijbhandar once they had established themselves there as practising *pīrs*. During the last one or two decades, however, it has become customary for quite a number of Maijbhandari *pīrs* to travel in the country and even abroad to visit branches of their respective societies or organisations. In the course of the labour migration from Bangladesh into the gulf region, Europe and America, followers of Maijbhandar have spread to distant places, and the ties are thus kept in a bilateral way. What results is an interesting clash of traditional and modern concepts of authority. All over South Asia, traditionally, immobility is a privilege of the superior; in analogy to the relationship between the host and the guest, he is predestined to receive from below and give from above, and it is the duty of his followers to come to visit him. Modernity, however, has inverted this hierarchy at least in part; now certain types of movement have become a sign of prestige, and aeroplane travelling is certainly one of these. Thus today in Maijbhandar, there are travelling *pīrs* who stress the degree of their importance and influence by pointing out their international

23 Cf., in this context, Simon Digby (1994) on the way conflicts between peripatetic and sedentary holy men are depicted in hagiographical motifs.

activities,[24] while others hold up the example of the preceding saints and consider it improper for a *pīr* to travel because it contradicts his status and is a sure sign of commercialisation.[25]

Some amount of mobility, of course, has become habitual for almost all spiritual practitioners, since, as mentioned above, most have taken up permanent residences in the city. The relationship with Maijbhandar remains very tight though, as is generally the case in Bangladesh; even with second- or third-generation city dwellers, the *deśer bāṛi*, 'country home', continues to be the locality of identification. More so with Maijbhandari *pīr*s who are more than others identified with their place of origin. Thus visits tend to be very regular; on Thursday nights it is common to see their vans arrive at the *darbār*. It may be questionable whether this is mobility proper or rather the shifting between two fixed locations in the sense of a multiplication of residences. I tend to see it as the latter. However this may be, the combination of '*pīr*dom', urban residence and modern education which is happening in these families is indeed an interesting intertwining of social domains. It can be examined in the context of rural and urban in Maijbhandar, and we shall have occasion in a later chapter to return to this point.

*2.1.4 Servants (*Ḫādims*), disciples (*murīds*) and pilgrims*

A *darbār* like Maijbhandar is peopled by different classes of temporary or permanent visitors. Economically speaking, the closest relationship to the *darbār* is held by the *ḫādim*s, 'servants'. Most of these relations are contract-based and long-term, often life-long – many *ḫādim*s permanently live in and around Maijbhandar – but I have witnessed cases in which *ḫādim*s resigned from their positions to take up jobs elsewhere. The category of *ḫidma* (Bg. *<khed'mat>*, 'service') comprises quite a range of activities. To start at the uppermost position, many *manzil*s employ trained *'ulamā'*, Islamic scholars, to supervise shrine rituals. These are found in or around the mausoleums at most times of the day. They receive and instruct pilgrims who want to pray at the saints' tombs and may help them express their *mānat* ('vow'[26]) by conveying them to the deceased saint in the proper way. Their task is also to lead collective prayer sessions at the shrines in praise of the saints. The *manzil*s act as their employers and pay them for their services. Secondly, administration and especially account-keeping is usually taken care of by another type of employees also usually referred to as *ḫādim*s. The *manzil*s keep lists of their formally initiated disciples and of all the donations they

24 The ritual enacted on the spot, of course, restores the centrality of the *pīr* in placing him in symbolic immobility among his followers who still have to approach him and not vice versa.

25 This attitude, in turn, is criticised as hypocritical ('Why then are they establishing branches all over the place?' – cf. below for such expansive networking activities) and as self-conceited ('Who do they think they are that they cannot go anywhere?') by exponents of the other side.

26 Ar. *minna* is closest to it in form, but actually means 'gift, favour'; Ar. *munya*, pl. *munā* 'wishes' is not likely to be the root of Bg. *mānat*, U. *mannat*. McGregor's *Oxford Hindi-English Dictionary* suggests to derive it from H./U. *mān'nā/manānā*.

receive throughout the year;[27] the economic activities are also meticulously documented. Ahmadiyya, Rahmaniyya and Haq Manzils maintain offices of different sizes for this purpose, the largest one in Rahmaniyya Manzil being run by about five full-time clerks.

*Ḫādim*s of these higher ranks tend to be *murīd*s, disciples of the respective *manzil*s, and their engagements are in some cases rather the side-effects of their general involvement in Maijbhandari affairs. Another class of people also – sometimes euphemistically – referred to as *ḫādim*s cook and serve food or do menial work such as cleaning, household work, etc. Agricultural labour on the properties of the *manzil*s, digging of ponds, gardening, preparation of tent constructions for festivals, attending to guests and so on, may also be included in their tasks. Some of these *ḫādim*s have economic rather than spiritual client relationships with the *manzil*s they work for and might thus also be labelled *kājer lok* (Bg.) lit. 'people for work', namely agricultural and household hands.

The second and in a way most important category of persons attached to the *darbār* is that of the *murīd*s, 'disciples'.[28] The term is often loosely used in the same way as *bhakta*, 'adorer, devotee', but it carries more precise and formal connotations. A *murīd* is a disciple, male or female[29] and Muslim or non-Muslim,[30] who has formally been initiated into the Maijbhandari *ṭarīqa* by one of the Maijbhandari *pīr*s. The initiation ceremony is called *bayʿa* (Bg. <*bāyāt*>), 'oath of allegiance', and various manuals are in circulation that describe the behaviour required from a *murīd vis-à-vis* his *pīr*.[31] There is no unified fashion of performing *bayʿa* in Maijbhandar: it may be performed by touching the hands of the *pīr*, by holding a pillow or turban from opposite sides or informally by utterances of the *pīr*. Even initiations through dreams are reported; and with regard to some saints it is held that formal initiation is completely absent.[32] In principle, becoming a *murīd* is a free decision; candidates usually come into contact with Maijbhandar first and at some point aspire to formalise their relationship by undergoing initiation. This resolve, commonly communicated to the *pīr* by *ḫādim*s or other *murīd*s, has to find the consent of the latter. It is, however, also not uncommon for whole families to take *bayʿa* together, and the tendency to pass on one's spiritual affiliation to one's children is well noted.

*Murīd*s of one *pīr* are *pīr-bhāi*, '*pīr* brothers' or co-disciples, among themselves, and such relationships often extend into other spheres than the spiritual; thus *pīr-bhāi*s may also be preferred business partners, friends, etc. *Murīd*s receive

27 Receipts are issued for tax exemption.

28 This term is often employed in the Persian plural *murīdān*, besides Bengali forms denoting a plural like *murīd'gaṇ*, *murīd'dal*, *murīd'br̥nda*, etc.

29 Though it does not seem common for women to become a *murīda* ('female disciple') independently; apart from two or three cases I have heard of, women join along with the families or husbands.

30 I had occasion to talk to Hindu *murīd*s who are initiated members of the Maijbhandari *ṭarīqa*, and it was reported to me by one Maijbhandari *pīr* that a few European Christians also belong to his disciples.

31 Cf. the remarks and literature given in Section 1.3.

32 Cf. Syed Badruddoza on Gholam Rahman (*BB*: 4).

spiritual instructions from their *pīr* in closed circles, and the relationship between *pīr* and *murīd* is strictly hierarchical. Exceptions may occur if an old *pīr* passes away and is succeeded by a young *saǧǧādanašīn*; for all practical purposes, this successor appropriates the role of a *pīr* also *vis-à-vis* the former *murīd*s of his predecessor, but he will also tend to retain some of the reverential attitude towards senior *murīd*s that he had had before. In Maijbhandar there are also *murīd*s who profess an allegiance to a *pīr* deceased long ago, e.g. saint Gholam Rahman.[33] These may or may not have undergone formal initiation by one of the contemporary representatives of Maijbhandar and thus sometimes seem to by-pass the structures of legitimate succession and transmission held up by the *manzil*s. We shall deal with such ambivalent cases in Section 7.3.

Maijbhandari *murīd*s are the most regular visitors of their respective *pīr*s and the shrines. It is part of their obligations to keep a close relationship to Maijbhandar, and especially on *ʿurs* festivities they make it a point to attend. The *manzil*s act as hosts, which includes providing food and accommodation; in return, the *murīd*s give generous donations on specific occasions or in between. Among them are virtually all classes of Bangladeshi society, and the mere fact of becoming a *murīd* does not eclipse the social differences; according to my observation, urban and wealthy *murīd*s are received in a more polished fashion than the rural, poor *murīd*s from the vicinity of Maijbhandar, as is shown in the accommodation, catering and personal attention they receive from the *pīr*s.

The third class, pilgrims, are the bulk of the people encountered in Maijbhandar on festive occasions and especially on the *ʿurs* days of the most popular saints. In principle pilgrims can and do come throughout the year, and one would hardly ever find Maijbhandar completely devoid of them. Shrines such as Maijbhandar may be visited for the sake of *ziyāra* (Ar., 'shrine pilgrimage')[34] and the beneficial results obtained from it,[35] but it is equally customary to come on some special personal purpose. These purposes do not differ from those recorded at other South Asian shrines[36] and are basically the same for which living *pīr*s are approached.[37] The troubles that bring pilgrims to pray at the tombs of the great Maijbhandari saints include physical sickness, lack of progeny, crop failures, financial crises, examinations, court cases and so on – that is, basically the whole range of inconveniences and calamities daily life in Bangladesh has to offer. One

33 Cf. Gardner (1995: 264) on her fieldwork in Sylhet and the role of the medieval saint Shah Jalal: 'Although some of the most purist men in the village claimed that they did not have a living *pir*, all, without exception, told me that they were followers of Shah Jalal, whose cult is presented by many in extremely orthodox terms.' On the implications of the combination of saint veneration and orthodoxy Gardner mentions here, cf. Section 8.1 in this book.

34 The common Bengali form is *jiẏārat*.

35 Cf. Ernst (1993: 45) on the auspiciousness of *ziyāra* especially on *ʿurs* days. See Taylor (1999) for a detailed study of *ziyāra* in medieval Egypt which amply demonstrates its great popularity.

36 Cf. Desiderio Pinto (1992).

37 The *karāmāt* (plural of Ar. <*karāma*>, 'miracle'; the usual Bg. spelling is *kerāmat*) sections of Maijbhandari hagiographies convey a good picture of the inventory of wishes uttered at these occasions. Cf. Chapter 4.

might say that the pilgrims are a transitional or fringe category since whenever such pilgrimages are the starting points of more lasting relationships with the *darbār*, pilgrims may be converted into *murīd*s or eventually *ḫādim*s; most of the *murīd*s are former pilgrims.

Maijbhandar has developed into probably the most popular pilgrimage centre in Chittagong, and hence pilgrims are drawn from various places and backgrounds; they are logically just as heterogeneous as the *murīd*s. During the great festivals, it is common to form pilgrimage groups and organise the travel to Maijbhandar together and, as Selim Jahangir reports, to collect donations from the local population before departure; and so-called *māstān*s, 'crazy/intoxicated' *faqīr*s, play a special role in such fund-raising and pilgrim-recruiting activities.[38] Individualised pilgrimage is not the rule on these occasions and occurs more often in 'off-season' periods.

*2.1.5 Branches (*Dā'iras*), societies, organisations*

Maijbhandar, we have repeatedly stressed, is not only the shrine complex in northern Chittagong, but also the centre of a network of institutions spread over Bangladesh and recently also abroad. These are called *śākhā*s ('branches') or *dā'ira*s ('circles'). I do not have sufficient first-hand experience[39] of these to pass general comments on their internal structure and the way they work, and thus have to rely, in the following, on the mostly oral reports collected from members. According to representatives of different *manzil*s, such branches are quite numerous.[40] They are to some extent small replicas of Maijbhandar itself: groups of *murīd*s meet regularly for religious functions including *ḏikr* and *samā'* sessions. One of the societies to be described below, the *Āñjumāne Mottābeẏīne Gāuche Māij'bhāṇḍār* (P./U. *<anğuman-i muttaba'īn-i ġawṯ-i mā'iğbhand'ār>*, 'Society of the Followers of the *Ġawṯ* of Maijbhandar'), describes in its rules how so-called *dāẏ'rā śākhā* (Bg.), 'branch offices', may be set up in various parts of the country; they are to be composed of a chairman, deputy chairman and treasurer, etc. down to executive members; these eleven members together form the 'executive committee' of the *dāẏ'rā śākhā*.[41] Another society, the *Māij'bhāṇḍārī Pariṣad* ('Maijbhandari council'), provides for the foundation of regional committees.[42] Some *dā'ira*s develop into important institutions themselves, as for instance the

38 Cf. Selim Jāhāṅgīr (1999: 153 f.): 'Not only in different villages of Chittagong, but in many villages of Bangladesh and even urban neighbourhoods can a few such Maijbhandar-crazy *māstān*s be found.'

39 I could, however, witness a function organised by one such *śākhā* in the village Dholoi, and visit a *dā'ira* at Chittagong City.

40 I cannot give any exact figures and must limit myself to stating that they were not easily available from the *manzil*s either.

41 Cf. *Gaṭhan'tantra: āñjumāne mottābeẏīne gāuche māij'bhāṇḍār* 2.4 [n.p.].

42 Cf. *Gaṭhan'tantra: 'Māij'bhāṇḍārī Pariṣad'*: 3 f.

Dhaka branch; they run the *Māij'bhāṇḍār Gabeṣaṇā Pariṣad* ('Maijbhandar Research Council') and have published an introductory book on Maijbhandar.[43] The *dā'ira*s may be visited by Maijbhandari *pīr*s. They also function as organisation centres for collective pilgrimages as well as parallel *'urs* celebrations.

In Maijbhandar itself, ever since the passing away of the second founding saint, Gholam Rahman, there have been efforts to cast the religious life into new, modern-looking moulds and to form organisations and societies. Today, the distinctions between these societies come down to those between *manzil*s. The earliest of these societies apparently was the *Jamiẏate Māij'bhāṇḍārī*, probably founded in 1947–48 and mainly aligned with Rahmaniyya Manzil. There is an annual report of this society from the year 1952, delivered by its chairman, Mahbubul Bashar (the third son of Saint Gholam Rahman), which states that some of its goals are to provide for the legal prosecution of those who attack followers of Maijbhandar, to build a madrasa, and to found a library.[44] The *Jamiẏat* was apparently funded by fees and had a central council (*kendrīẏa pariṣad*). We do not know much about who its members were, but it almost certainly included the authors of the journal *Traimāsik tauhīd*, which was edited jointly by Mahbubul Bashar and Shafiul Bashar and was the society's mouthpiece.[45]

Another important society was founded by Syed Delawar Hosain, the grandson of Saint Ahmadullah, in 1949,[46] and continues to be an important organisation in Maijbhandar to this day. This is the *Āñjumāne Mottābeẏīne Gāuche Māij'bhāṇḍār*. This society also has its chairman and secretary and a 'central executive council' (*kendrīẏa nirbāhī pariṣad*), and in parallel to the *Jamiẏat* is mainly run by the *pīrzāda*s of Ahmadiyya Manzil. The journal issued from this society is called *Jīban bāti*, 'candle of life', and the writers are mainly *murīd*s and *'ulamā'* affiliated to Ahmadiyya Manzil.[47] The goals of this society include such things as the enhancement of the ideals of saints Ahmadullah and of Islam, promotion of the unity of Sufis, encouragement to all to pay heed to the laws of Islam, etc.; saving *Qalandar*s, *maǧḏūb*s and enraptured *faqīr*s from the violence committed by orthodox people by calling upon the legal authorities is also one of these aims.[48]

Haq Manzil also has a society called *Maramī Goṣṭhī* ('Mystical group') with a structure similar to those outlined above; among their 'executive members' are the names of two Hindus.[49] Their mouthpiece is the journal *Ālok'dhārā*.

43 Miẏā Naj'rul Is'lām (ed.) (1995): *Māij'bhāṇḍār Śarīph*. Dhaka, Māij'bhāṇḍār Gabeṣaṇa–Pariṣad.

44 Cf. *Traimāsik tauhīd* 10, 2, 1951, pp. 6–12.

45 One author who is still well-known, a *ḫalīfa* of Gholam Rahman, is Maulana Abdussalam Isapuri.

46 Cf. Delawar Hosain's controversial pamphlet *Elākār Renesā̃ yuger ek'ṭi dik·*, written after 1972 (p. 21); it is clear from this depiction that this society was established in competition to Rahmaniyya Manzil and possibly the above-mentioned *Jamiẏat*.

47 A regular contributor is Abdul Mannan Chowdhury, a professor of economics at Chittagong University; he is the translator of Delawar Hosain's seminal treatise *Belāẏate mot'lākā* into English.

48 *kalandar, maj'jub o mag·lubul-hāl bā bibhor'citta phakir'digake bibhinna ācār o dharmīẏa niẏam'mukta phakir baliẏā svīkār pūrbak ācār-dharme gõṛā lok'der julum o atyācār haïte rakṣā karā.*

49 Cf. *Maramī*: [15] (author's pagination).

Rahmaniyya Manzil today has different societies. One is the *Āñjumāne Rah'māniẏā Maïnīẏā Māij'bhāṇḍārīẏā*, headed by Syed Moinuddin Ahmad, a grandson of Saint Gholam Rahman, with the monthly journal *Nūr-e-rah'mān*. The model of establishing societies has also been taken up by the less prominent branches of the Maijbhandari family; the *Māij'bhāṇḍārī Pariṣad* has been established by Wahab Manzil, namely by the sons of Gholam Rahman's younger brother. Like the other societies mentioned, this 'Maijbhandari Council' is, according to its statutes, formed by one central committee and an open number of regional committees, and has the objects of promoting the spirit of Islam and general welfare, establishment of a library, madrassa and drugstore, as well as holding and promoting regular *milād* and *ḏikr* performances.[50]

A trend in transforming traditional structures into constituted organisations is thus widespread and was, to all appearances, not triggered by any particular outside events. I have mentioned that there were at one time efforts to declare Maijbhandar a *waqf*, an Islamic religious foundation, and thus to put it under the administration of a state-controlled board, but this happened as late as 1989 during Ershad's military rule; and I am not aware of any pressure exerted on traditional shrines at the beginning of the Pakistani era when apparently the first Maijbhandari society was founded. There are a number of internal factors that may supply plausible explanations for this trend. The passing away of Gholam Rahman in 1937 left a vacuum and may have prompted considerations about the formal framework in which the *darbār* ought to be run. Simultaneously, the antinomies between what was to become the Rahmaniyya and Ahmadiyya Manzils increased and soon became articulated: there was a court case between them concerning certain claims to property in 1939. In such circumstances, a society may have appeared as a way to integrate *murīd*s in a permanent way – they could now hold posts – and formalise their support in what is today sometimes derisively referred to as '*darbār* politics'. Furthermore, collection of fees also meant an economic rationalisation and made the financial side more predictable. And maybe most importantly, these societies give the *darbār* a democratic outlook and attenuate the connotations of hierarchy and arbitrariness in *pīr–murīd* relationships that they continue to be accused of.

2.1.5 Who is a Maijbhandari?

Maijbhandar has a multi-angular or polycentric structure, as I have stated repeatedly and demonstrated in the preceding sections. The different *manzil*s and societies stand for different leader personalities, different spiritual affiliations and different versions of the Maijbhandari *ṭarīqa*. There is no centralised authority, no overarching 'all-Maijbhandari' committee. It resembles less an autocratic institution than a democratised oligarchy. Simultaneously, and arguably more than similar religious groups, Maijbhandar appears multifunctional, covering the

50 Cf. *Gaṭhan'tantra: 'Māij'bhāṇḍārī Pariṣad'*: 8 f.

(overlapping) properties of a shrine cult, *pīr* veneration, *ṭarīqa* Sufism and popular devotional religion. What does this mean for its organisation and representation?

The most obvious result of this constellation is a deficiency of control. It is impossible for any one faction to determine, for instance, Maijbhandari song production or suppress practices on the margins of great festivities such as consumption of cannabis. Popular song culture and cannabis smoking are largely fringe phenomena, and the fringe can hardly be assigned to the authority of one or the other *manzil*. Thus a significant part of Maijbhandari culture happens on the margins – margins that can be appropriated by some *manzil*s and rejected by others, but with their existence ensured.

Decentrality also means diminished responsibility for every player on the field. We have mentioned the accusations of commercialisation that most Maijbhandari *manzil*s will not declare outright as wrong, but pass on to one or other of their competitors. Orthopraxy is treated in the same way: it may be that in some quarters the *šarīʿa* is not paid heed to in the way it should, but these are *other* quarters, *other manzil*s or *other* people on the fringes of the movement. Likewise, *g̃ãjā*, hemp, may be smoked by people who claim adherence to Maijbhandar, but they adhere to some *other* authority or stream not *really* belonging to what Maijbhandar stands for. For many insiders, then, there is a true Maijbhandar in the centre of other, wrong versions of it; and for some, it is even possible to evoke a Maijbhandar beyond the *manzil*s as a purely esoteric locus untinged by the contemporary dissent regarding representation.

In an interview a Maijbhandari *pīr* once used the Nehruvian formula 'Unity in Diversity' to describe the structure of Maijbhandar.[51] Mystifying as it is, this formula is not far in spirit from certain types of paradoxical parlance that are found in mysticism in general and also in Maijbhandar; and it may very well represent a way in which Maijbhandaris prefer to conceive of themselves. The differences in opinion between the *manzil*s and societies may trigger exclusivist evaluations for the practical exigencies of daily contacts, but on a more general level this kind of inclusivist construction seems popular.[52]

Being a Maijbhandari can therefore mean many things. So far, the representatives have not been in the position of putting a trademark on this term, and if the present structure of the movement does not change, neither will they be in the future. A member of the local Sayyad family most certainly is a Maijbhandari in the most confined sense of the term, even if he or she is a second-generation city dweller; but it does make a difference in degree whether this membership is merely genealogical or also spiritual, and as we have seen, it is from here that the conflicts regarding proper Maijbhandari *pīr*-dom and notions of true and not-so-true Maijbhandaris take their course. Beyond the confines of this family, matters become quite fuzzy. The formal *murīd*s of the various *manzil*s

51 Interview H.H. 1.4.1999.

52 For a detailed treatment of terms like 'inclusivist', 'exclusivist' etc. in the context of correlating religious groups, cf. Sections 7.1 and 7.2.

also qualify for the denomination of Maijbhandaris, although they adhere to different and sometimes contested *pīr*s with different and also contested versions of the Maijbhandari *ṭarīqa*; and in an exclusivist reading, 'Maijbhandariness' may be denied to them by adherents of competing *manzil*s. Songwriters and singers of Maijbhandari songs also tend to be seen as Maijbhandaris for their close 'professional' relations with the movement, although they may not be formally initiated *murīd*s at any of the existing *manzil*s but only profess allegiance to one of the great deceased saints. For the pilgrims, this denomination comes down to the level of self-ascription – a self-ascription not likely to be contested as it appears marginal in the perspective of those Maijbhandaris who have the say.

2.2 Religious practice in Maijbhandar

More than all others, this section relies on fieldwork observations. The written sources coming to my aid in substantiating the following are few, Selim Jahangir's monograph (Jāhāṅgīr 1999) being the most informative. In order to lend plasticity to some of the descriptions to follow, I have included slightly revised passages from my fieldwork diaries.[53] In many aspects, religious practice in Maijbhandar is very similar to other South Asian *dargāh*s, and the following sketch will be seen to reiterate certain well-known features.

2.2.1 At the shrines

> A young couple from Chittagong has come to visit the Maijbhandari shrines, apparently to pray for male progeny. It is a usual week day, and the *darbār* is relatively empty. They have a few words with the *ḫādim*s sitting at the entry of the shrine and then proceed to do their ablusions (*wuḍū'*) on the stairs of the adjacent pond. They have brought incense sticks and candles, probably acquired at one of the shops for devotional articles in the village; as they enter the mausoleum proper, they hand these over to another *ḫādim* by the entrance. The woman is led to a different side of the building reserved for females. The husband reverentially approaches the tomb and, at a small distance from it, prostrates himself completely before it, his forehead on the ground and his arms spread toward the grave. He remains in this position for several minutes, then sits up and starts praying aloud, though in a very low voice. After a few minutes, he again prostrates himself, stands up and walks backwards, his front turned toward the grave, until he reaches the door. A sum of money is inserted into the donations box, and the *ḫādim* writes out a receipt. He and his wife then proceed to another of the major Maijbhandari mausoleums to repeat their prayers.[54]

53 This procedure of self-reference is not supposed to seem self-complacent in any way, and if it does I apologise to the reader. The point of this exercise is to use the narrativisation inherent in those passages for a condensed and evocative description.

54 Written on the basis of diary notes, H.H. 2001.

A pilgrimage to a saint's shrine is known by the Arabic term *ziyāra* (Bg. <*jiẏārat*>) throughout the Islamic world. Such a pilgrimage can be performed alone or in a group, and at any time of the year. In Maijbhandar, access to the shrines is in principle free to all visitors, regardless of gender and religious affiliation. But certain rules have to be obeyed once one has reached the outer confines of the mausoleum. Anybody approaching a shrine must do so with a reverential attitude, which brings with it a number of obligatory formalities. As in a mosque, the head must be covered with a *ṭupi*,[55] a veil for women or, if nothing else is at hand, with a knotted handkerchief. The front of one's body should be facing the saint all the time, ideally also while leaving the mausoleum, though not all fully pay heed to this rule. Voices must be lowered except for liturgies during ritual functions. The tomb itself is usually not touched by visitors; in Maijbhandar, most tombs are removed from public access in an innermost sanctum, divided from the outer parts of the buildings by arched doors or glass and sometimes a threshold or stair.[56]

In all the major *mazārs*, the sanctum is under the central dome of the construction. It is abundantly illuminated by luxurious lustres and decorated by flowers in costly vessels. The tomb itself is built to about one meter's hight and covered, sometimes in multiple layers, by embroidered quilts (Bg. *cādar* from P. <*čādur*>, 'veil'), that are popular gifts to the shrines.[57] Access to the sanctum is mostly limited to the *ḫādims* of the shrine or very close *murīds*. The decoration and cleaning of the tomb is part of the *ḫādims*' duties.

When standing or kneeling down in front of the tomb, one's head must be lowered, and when sitting the feet must not point towards the grave. Commonly, *sağda* or full-body prostration is performed, but more moderate forms of bowing can also be witnessed. *Sağda* is one of the long-standing issues of dispute among the Sufi and orthodox or reformist camps.[58] Many Maijbhandari *fatwas* and tracts use the repertoire of arguments furnished by classic Sufi texts in order to justify this practice, deemed by many non-Sufis to be appropriate only during the ritual prayer in the direction of Mecca.[59] In the past, *sağda* appears to have been a *conditio sine qua non*,[60] and it is significant that today it has become optional.[61] While sitting in front

55 A small round cap of cloth.

56 This is different in other South Asian shrines; at the *dargāh* of Muʿin al-Din Chishti of Ajmer, e.g., it is customary to circambulate the tomb, touch the railing around it, and fall down at the place where the saint's feet rest.

57 As in other parts of South Asia; cf. Einzmann (1988: 16 f.) with reference to the shrine of Pir Baba in Pacha, Northern Pakistan.

58 Cf. the discussion of this topic in an eighteenth-century pilgrimage guide, in Ernst (1993: 61 f.).

59 Cf. already the earliest Maijbhandari writings, Aminul Haq Farhadabadi's *Tuḥfat* (1906/7) and Abdul Ghani Kanchanpuri's *Āʾīna-e bārī* (1914–15); most recently Gholam Khan Siraji's article in Sahidul Hak (2005: 75–91). The greater part of the hagiological and theological expositions published from Maijbhandari circles contain at least a section on the legitimacy of *sağda* to this day.

60 Cf. the anecdote about Md. Enamul Haq quoted in the beginning of Chapter 1.

61 In March 1999, I witnessed the visit of a number of VIPs from Bangladeshi public life at one of the major Maijbhandari *manzils*. They were led to the most prominent mausoleums by two *pīrzādas* and showed only the minimal signs of reverence, bowing their heads while standing before the tombs. The same could be observed, though rarely, among non-VIP visitors.

of the tomb, the visitors may hold their hands as during *du'ā* prayer, and pray they do; the hands may also at times be put together like in the Hindu *namaskār* gesture.

The access of single pilgrims may also be mediated by the *ḫādim*s, as mentioned above in Section 2.1.3; the *ḫādim*s may ask the pilgrims about the purpose of their visit and help them say their prayers or instruct them as to what prostrations or rituals they are to perform, what prayers they should recite and where they should leave their donations. It is not appropriate to approach a saintly tomb empty-handed, and some material gifts like rose water, incense sticks or candles are taken into the shrine and deposited at the *ḫādim*s' desk.[62] Money is inserted into donation boxes. These donations are usually referred to by the Urdu term *naẓrāna*, that is, a gift given when meeting someone, and thus conceived in accordance with the terms of courtly supplication.

As mentioned above, it is common to approach a shrine with a special vow (Bg. *mānat*) by promising the saint to perform specified acts as a sign of gratitude if the wish is granted by the saint. These may be donations, promises to visit the shrine at certain intervals etc. There are regular visitors to Maijbhandar who keep coming for the fulfillment of such vows. If the promises are not kept, the wrath of the saint is incurred.[63] Apart from the fulfilment of wishes, shrine visitors profit from the *baraka*, the blessing or auspiciousness of the tomb. This blessing quality is inherent in everything connected with the saint's body: his *ḥuğra* or seat, his water pipe or cigarettes, his clothes, his offspring, the *pīrzāda*s, and it is most concentrated at his tomb. *Baraka* is thought of as sticking to matter, and it is thus by bringing one's own body in contact with the shrine that one attains the effects of the saint's superior purity and spiritual power.[64]

Besides personal visits, there are religious functions held as a daily routine at the major Maijhandari shrines. These ceremonies are usually referred to as *milād* or *ḥalqa-i ẕikr* (P.), '*ḏikr* assembly'. Usually these take place after the morning and evening prayers; the most important in the week is that after the Friday prayer (around noon). These ceremonies are for the praise of the saints. In Maijbhandar, the prescribed ritual prayer (*namāz* or *ṣalāt*) is considered an integral part of *milād* and is read at the local mosque. After its completion, the assembly moves on the three major *mazār*s of Saints Ahmadullah, Gholam Rahman and Ziaul Haq where the *milād*, *qiyām*, *ḏikr* and *munāğāt* parts of the liturgy are performed. Microphones are installed in the shrines, and the main *ḫādim*s lead the function from the first row, that is, in analogy to the *imām* in the mosque, but centred on

62 Such gifts were common also in pre-modern times; cf. Ernst (1993: 49) on a pilgrimage guide of the eighteenth century mentioning offerings of sweets, roses and other flowers.

63 Cf. *ĀB*: 304 ff. for an example of such wrath by the living Saint Ahmadullah. I know of no such reports in the case of deceased saints, but as the latter are imagined as alive in their mausolea, the logic is the same.

64 As we shall see in Chapters 4 and 5, the holiness of the Maijbhandari saints reverberates on the dust of Maijbhandar, and this dust – especially that on the saint's feet – is one of the substances held precious in many Maijbhandari songs.

the tomb. The liturgy is multilingual, containing passages in Arabic, Persian, Urdu and Bengali. The *qiyām*, e.g., is read while standing up and consists of greetings of Allah, the Prophet Muhammad and a series of saints down to the respective Maijbhandari saint. These liturgies naturally differ with every saint, and there are other variations too.[65]

2.2.2 Ḏikr, Murāqaba, Samāʿ, *Dance*

> Late at night during the *ʿurs* of Saint Ahmadullah. A group of pilgrims has assembled in a hut by the side of the village entrance. The room inside is packed with people who are dancing in a frenzy. Many have joined in with the musicians, a singer with harmonium and two percussionists beating their *ḍhol* drums; the lyrics of certain well-known Maijbhandari songs are shouted rather than sung by many voices. This must have been going on for many hours now. It is very hot and sticky inside – most of the dancers are bathed in their sweat – and in this Bengali winter night, a cloud of steam comes out every time the door of the hut is opened. The dancers are of all age groups: there are quite a few over fifty, and both men and (albeit very few) women. Everybody is dancing on his own in a kind of free style; some only jump on the spot. A very condensed, very hot atmosphere; it looks as if this will continue until after dawn. On the way back to my room, I notice a man – long hair, age between fifty and sixty – by the side of the pond. He is stumbling; his eyes are rolling around, and his head moves up and down rythmically as he mutters the words *Allā-hu, Allā-hu*. The man is in a frightening state: close to utter exhaustion and completely out of his mind; he is close to falling into the pond, but completely unable to relax; in particular, he does not seem to have any power over the words that keep coming from his mouth; the *Allā-hu* seems to have developed an autodynamics he is incapable of stopping; he is run by the *Allā-hu*, not the other way round.[66]

The practice of *ḏikr* is not confined to collective assemblies, but may be performed in solitude as well. *Ḏikr* means lit. 'mentioning', 'remembering'. It is a mystico-physiological exercise that is part of Sufi practice in general and hardly needs a general exposition here.[67] I will limit myself to describing the way *ḏikr* was explained to me in Maijbhandar and its relationship with other aspects of Maijbhandari religious practice.[68]

65 Compare, e.g., the texts given for a *ḥalqa-i ẕikr* by Shafiul Bashar (Śaphiul Baśar n.d.) and Akhtar Kamal Shah. The latter is a Maijbhandari *ḫalīfa* of Nazir Bhandar Darbar Sharif in Pathantuli (Chittagong) and not from Maijbhandar proper, but he explicitly states that the liturgy follows the Maijhandari *ṭarīqa* (Ākhʾtār Kāmāl Śāh 1995: 1). Despite this, the differences between the two texts are enormous. Other, again different, liturgies are given in Nājʾmūl Hudā (2000) and Ikʾbāl Phajal (1996).

66 Diary H.H. 23.1.2001.

67 On *ḏikr*, cf., e.g., Eliade (1985: 225 ff.).

68 The basis for the following are conversations with three Maijhandaris, one of them a *pīr* himself, the other two practitioners.

The practice of *ḏikr*, first of all, must be taught by a qualified *pīr* and ought not to be attempted without training. One must learn to build it up and also to bring it down again; otherwise, as was repeatedly stated, accidents of the kind narrated in the diary note above may occur, and *ḏikr* is known to have an enormous and, if misguided, potentially very harmful impact on physis and psyche. *Ḏikr* as practised in Maijbhandar relies on the notion of the *laṭīfa*s (Ar. pl. *laṭā'if*), six energetic centres in the human body, namely the *laṭīfa-i qalb* (at the heart), *laṭīfa-i rūḥ* (symmetrically opposite the heart), *laṭīfa-i sirr* (one hand's breadth above the heart),[69] *laṭīfa-i ḫafī* (on the forehead), *laṭīfa-i aḫfā* (in the upper part of the head) and *laṭīfa-i nafs* (at the navel).[70] The two most common *ḏikr*s practised in Maijbhandar have the function of joining these locations by letting certain formula pass through the body from *laṭīfa* to *laṭīfa*. The first uses the beginning of the *fatīha*, the Islamic confession of faith: *lā ilāha illā Llāh*, 'There is no God except Allah'. This *ḏikr* joins the three *laṭīfa*s on both sides of the central axis of the body with that at the forehead. It starts at the *laṭīfa-i nafs* (the syllable *lā*) and moves on via the *laṭīfa-i rūḥ* (*-i-*) and *aḫfā* (*-lāha-*) and finally arrives at the *laṭīfa-i qalb* (*-illā Llāh-*).[71] If this *ḏikr* is continually practised, it is said to result in a sort of inner vibration and to disclose one's *kašf* (Ar. 'disclosure'), explained as 'inner sight'. To this may be added a second *ḏikr* that connects the remaining two *laṭīfa*s, the *laṭīfa-i ḫafī* and the *laṭīfa-i sirr*; this is probably the best-known one, consisting only of the name of God: *Allā-hu.* Current explanations of the use of *ḏikr* stress that the circulation of the names of God through the body has a sanctifying effect, and that *ḏikr* may indeed lead to the state of *fanā' fī Allāh*, the temporary annihilation of one's being in Allah. *Ḏikr* is said to help in bringing forth the 'meritorious faculties in men [who are] struck with sorrow and illusion',[72] and it is rewarded by the blessings and love of God.

Ḏikr practised in assemblies stands in close relation to *samā'* (Ar., 'audition'), namely listening to music. We shall have occasion to deal with *samā'* in some detail in Chapter 5 and limit ourselves here to pointing out one kind of *samā'* that evolves from the group *ḏikr* held, for example, after the Friday prayer, and according to a prominent *pīrzāda*[73] represents the ideal type of *samā'*. The liturgical prayers (*milād, qiyām, munāǧāt*) after the *maġrīb* and *'išā'* prayers and the *ǧumma namāz* include two loud (*khafī*) *ḏikr*s[74] that are recited in the prayer assembly by

69 The *pīr* I interviewed on this topic said that the *laṭīfa-i sirr* was situated in a secret place (Ar. *sirr* means 'secret'), and that it appeared only in connection (through *ḏikr*) with the other surrounding *laṭīfa*s.

70 According to Baśir'uddin (1990: 312), the Chishtiyya *ṭarīqa* lists another four *laṭīfa*s of the main elements that are dispersed all over the human body. Cf., however, also the remarks in Enāmul Hak (1995: 101 ff.); according to him, the *laṭīfa-i aḫfā* is not in the head but in the middle of the breast.

71 The assertive *illā Llāh*, the name of God, is 'thrown' into the heart, and this effect can be enhanced by beating that spot with one's fist during recitation. All this is common to many Sufi orders and is not specifically Maijbhandari.

72 *bedanā o mohaklişṭa mānuṣer pūṇyabān prabṛtti*; Ākh'tār Kāmāl Śāh (1995: 1).

73 Interview 5-3-99.

74 i.e. the name of God: *Allā-hu*, and the *kalima*: *lā ilāha illā Llāh*, both taken together connecting all six *laṭā'if* of the human body.

the *ḫādim* acting as *imām* and all the attendants, and these *ḏikr*s are to be kept in motion silently until, at the end of the prayers, the music sets in. The music, as my informant stressed, helps the *ḏikr* to acquire strength and build up long-lasting tension. Except maybe during *ʿurs* festivities, I couldnot, however, witness this type of *samāʿ* during my stays at Maijbhandar.[75]

Other than *ḏikr* and music, dance, though also a dominant feature of Maijbhandari religious practice, is hardly discussed in Maijbhandari writings. If it is ever mentioned there, it is always in connection with *samāʿ*. In the Maijbhandari songs, by contrast, dance is a very common topic.[76] In outside perception, Maijbhandar is widely renowned, and in certain quarters ill-famed for the dancing sessions that include even women. According to some of my collocutors regarding this topic, dance is conceived as entirely complementary to music. It is an expression of emotion and joy and may become an ecstatic experience. A well-known author of Maijbhandari songs reported that at his first visit to Maijhandar he fell

Photo 2 Dancing at an *ʿurs* celebration in 1999, Maijbhandar.

75 For the close relationship between *samāʿ* and 'internal' *ḏikr* ('dhikr interieur') in general, cf. also During (1996: 164).

76 An excellent example is Abdul Gafur Hali's *nāco man(a) tāle tāle māolār jikire* (*JJ*: 28); for a translation into German, see *VG*: 22.

into such a state of ecstasy that while dancing he tore his clothes into pieces and had to return naked the following day.[77] Such happenings were recorded in the medieval handbooks on Sufism; it appears that the reproduction of such phenomena today is in keeping with tradition indeed, though most probably not in direct relation to scriptural Sufi sources.[78] Dancing in Maijbhandar has no official form or style, and I lack the knowledge of indigenous dance traditions to say whether there are any similarities to existing patterns. This lack of form is recognised by some Maijbhandari writers. Syed Ahmadul Haq, for example, compares it with the dance of the Mevlevi dervishes and states:

> There are no artistic devices in Maijbhandari dance. This is a spontaneous dance; this is a dance arising from the outburst of emotions.
>
> (Āh'madul Hak 2000: 30)

Another practice of seminal importance in Maijbhandar is *murāqaba*, 'meditation'. The central notion here is the *barzaḫ*. This Sufi term, lit. 'isthm', and according to Ibn Arabi 'the in-between worlds, the domains that are neither this or that' (Chittick 1998: 113), is in common Maijbhandari parlance understood as the inner picture of one's *muršid*. The adept has to form such a picture in his mind and place it in his heart.[79] This picture is of an entirely mental and esoteric kind and is not to be confused with actual representations – in principle, it is taboo to take photographs of one's *pīr*.[80] By constant meditation on the *barzaḫ*, the adept has to relinquish his own personality and try to achieve union with his *pīr*. Such union is not usually conceived as something actively achieved by the disciple, but as an act of grace by the *pīr*; if it comes about, the adept reaches the state of *fanā' fī al-šayḫ*, 'annihilation in the spiritual master'. One notion that occurs especially in the songs is that of a movement with the *barzaḫ* as the motor;[81] and the journey thus fuelled leads through the *maqāmāt*, stations (cf. Section 3.3), and ultimately to

77 Cf. *VG*: 17.

78 Suhrawardī, e.g., in his disussion of dance, prefers silent modes of ecstasy and warns against too frequent repetition of *samā'* assemblies. He appreciates the tearing of clothes if performed with good intentions, and also quotes a Ḥadīṯ in its favour though he is not convinced of its authoritativeness: the argument would be very beautiful, he writes, 'wenn es echt wäre! Gott ist allwissend! Doch mein Inneres erfüllt (der Gedanke), daß es unecht ist. Ich finde darin nicht den Geschmack des Zusammenkommens des Propheten und seiner Genossen und dessen, was sie zu tun pflegten – wie es in diesem Ḥadīṯ auf uns gekommen ist –, und mein Herz weigert sich, es anzunehmen. Gott aber ist allweise und weiß dies am besten!' (As-Suhrawardī 25,6/188).

79 Cf. the criticism of this practice in a reformist tract of the early nineteenth century in India by Ismail Shahid (1786–?): Gaborieau (1999: 460). For an exposition of the role of the *pīr*'s picture in Naqshbandi practice, cf. Meier (1994, Chapter 4). Liebeskind (1998: 249), in a north Indian context, translates *barzaḫ* as 'the image of the pir'.

80 Although this principle in Maijbhandar today allows for many exceptions, and there are quite a few photographs of practising *pīrs* in circulation.

81 Cf., e.g., Ramesh Shil's song *Mājhi tribeṇīr ghāṭer joẏār dhaïrā bāiẏo* (*SD* No.7, full translation in Section 6.1) where the *barzaḫ* draws the boat.

fanāʾ fī Allāh, 'annihilation in God'. Constant practice of *murāqaba* is required to make the *pīr*'s presence pervasive and lasting; and, as with *ḏikr*, it is thought that *murāqaba* should be interiorised so that the *barzaḫ* is perceived at any time and during whatever activity. *Murāqaba* is basically practised alone; it may be conceptualised as an ascension through the different *maqāmāt*, and in popular practice, according to what we learn from some Maijbhandari songs, these are sometimes located in the human body.[82]

*2.2.3 Master–Disciple (***pīr–murīd***) relationships*

> In the corridor behind the reception room of one of the major *manzil*s. A little crowd has gathered without any special occasion. There are discussions and conversations; one of the *pīrzāda*s, son of the old *pīr* of this *manzil*, is present and gives advice to two men of this gathering, but he is not its centre. Food is brought in by *ḫādim*s for some new arrivals; the atmosphere is friendly, lively and relaxed. Then suddenly at one end of the corridor, the voices are brought down to excited whispering, and within a few seconds everybody has got the message: '*bābā ās'techen, bābā ās'techen*'[83] – 'Father (i.e. the old *pīr*) is coming!' The effect is like a magnetic wave or an abrupt loading of electricity. The attention of each and everyone in the room turns to the back of the corridor, all conversations come to a halt, and the former relaxation of bodily postures gives way to tense and disciplined attention. All faces turn towards the spot where the old *pīr*, aided by two attendants who hold his arms from both sides, eventually arrives. As he walks towards the reception room, some greet him, bow to him and lower their hands to the ground close to his feet. Everyone automatically readjusts his position according to his movement, thus making the *pīr* resemble a moving pole. Finally he reaches his 'throne' (*gaddī*) in the reception room: a bedstead with huge, luxurious cushions and small carpets; instead of a mosquito net there are chains of multicoloured lights hanging over it; behind it vases with plastic flowers in glass showcases and a carpet representing a prayer meeting at the Kaʿba in Mecca. While the *pīr* is taking his seat there, people are pushing and shoving at the door from the corridor, each trying to secure his place in the assembly. The *darbār* session is ready to begin.[84]

Pīr–murīd relationships are not easily observed from a researcher's perspective. There is presumably quite a range of interactions between these two that require an intimacy precluding any outsider's presence; and most *pīr*s in Maijbhandar command a lot of respect and consequently do not tend to open up their minds *vis-à-vis* a junior foreign researcher. Of course, a huge number of such interactions run through Maijbhandari hagiographies in the chapters on miracles, but those are

82 Cf., e.g., Ramesh Shil *SD* No.7. For other kinds of *murāqaba* practiced by South Asian Sufis, cf. Enāmul Hak (1995: 107 f.).

83 East Bengali form of *ās'chen*/*āsitechen* in standard *calit*/*sādhu bhāṣā*.

84 Diary H.H., 2001.

selected and canonised on grounds of their exceptionality. There is, however, a public, collective side to these relations that is more or less transparent; and there are some individual accounts from both sides that can further add to the picture.

Intimacy is characteristic of certain situations in which *pīr* and *murīd* deal with each other, but rather misleading if employed for the relationship as a whole. For, first of all, it is strictly hierarchical and ties the *murīd* up in an elaborate set of rules that seem to prevent all possible closeness. Intimacy, in this sense, is one-way only: the *pīr* is in the position to read the *murīd* like an open book and dispose of his innermost feelings as he thinks best; the person of the *muršid*, spiritual preceptor, by contrast, remains a riddle to the *murīd*. So far, at least, in theory, the main premise being the quasi-omniscience of the *pīr* in relation to the *murīd*. On the other hand, ideally, the *murīd* spends a great amount of time thinking of or meditating upon his *muršid*; he interiorises his bodily features, memorises his words and makes him the very centre of his life. This also is, in a way, utter intimacy, but an intimacy framed by tter respect and distance; and it is only when a *murīd* has attained his *pīr*'s level that mutual intimacy between the two becomes possible.[85]

We have already hinted at the etiquette governing the relationship between *pīr* and *murīd*, the *ādāb-i murīd* (P.). Akhtar Kamal Shah gives a long list of fifty rules that should be observed by the *murīd*, and here is a short paraphrased summary:

> The *murīd* should not consider any other *pīr* greater than his own *pīr*; he should constantly concentrate on him; not perform any religious practices before him without his permission; not look at any other person while the *pīr* is there; his shadow should not touch the *pīr*; he should not touch the *pīr*'s prayer carpet, bath or vessels; refrain from eating, drinking, spitting and talking; not turn his feet towards the *pīr*; not wear better clothes than the *pīr*; not convey greetings, gifts, etc. by other persons; keep the *pīr* informed about any outer or inner happenings; consider himself the lowest and humblest; not speak in a loud voice or quarrel with the *pīr*; abandon himself to his *muršid* 'like a dead person to his washer' (Śāh 1995: 9); consult the *pīr* about all he does; have the *pīr* explain visions in *murāqaba*, dreams, etc. instead of explaining them himself; honour the *pīr*'s family and relatives just like him, etc. Especially, whenever the *murīd* thinks an act prescribed by the *pīr* is wrong, he has to do it all the same and consider it right; he shall not expect miracles from the *pīr*; when he has a doubt, he should ask the *pīr*, and if he does not understand the answer or thinks it is wrong, he should attribute this to his own ignorance; he should comply with any orders received from the *pīr* and attribute all spiritual achievements to his grace.[86]
>
> (Śāh 1995: 5–12)

85 Cf. the accounts of Ahmadullah's intimate relations with his *pīr* in Calcutta (*ĀB*: 183).

86 Other similar lists of *ādāb-i murīd* are in circulation in Maijbhandar and published from different *manzils*.

Such rules have existed for a long time and are nothing specifically Maijbhandari;[87] but their wide dissemination shows that they are still regarded as valid, and they do continue to govern the *murīd*s' behaviour.

A living *pīr* is not easily approached and will hardly make fixed appointments; his physical presence is a precious good that tends to be shortened. In daily practice, therefore, the veneration of a *muršid* first and foremost means a lot of waiting for the *murīd*. Maijbhandari *pīr*s rarify the times of their public appearances in direct proportion to their fame, and the information about their whereabouts and possible times of reception gathered from *ḫādim*s of their *manzil*s is notoriously imprecise, marked by wordings expressing all shades of 'maybe' and 'perhaps'. It is up to the *pīr* to decide whether or not, and at what time he wants to receive his *murīd*s. Urgent necessities of seeing the *pīr* can be communicated to his closest *ḫādim*s who may then act as his secretaries and brief him about the day's agenda.

In principle, a *pīr* has no 'task'; there are no manuals that prescribe what a *pīr* has to do and how he has to treat his *murīd*s.[88] But empirically speaking, there are of course certain acts and occupations that keep a *pīr* busy: among these are religious instruction, guidance in life, advice in specific predicaments, etc. The establishment of a connection, the traditional *rābiṭa*,[89] is essential for the *pīr–murīd* relationship, and it is commonly expressed by reference to modern communicative devices (wire, telephone, online communication, etc.). This is no specificity of Maijbhandar but seems to have become South Asian parlance in general. Bikram N. Nanda and Mohammad Talib (1992: 131) report similar metaphors in use at the *dargāh* of Bachhraon; a *murīd* explained that 'as a television set receives the transmission, so does the spiritual set', and 'then likened the spiritual imagination of the shaikh to the structure of tuning in a television set'. The rapport between the *murīd* and *pīr* was seen as the 'finest possible tuning', and 'accurate imagination acts in the same way as an appropriate antenna, through which the spiritual messages must pass so that a proper reception is possible'. At a *ḫānaqāh* in Dhaka, a *murīd* pointed out to me that taking *bay'a* from his *pīr* was like 'going online'.[90]

The most essential thing for a *pīr* is that he must, for his *murīd*s, stand on an extraordinary spiritual level and in utter closeness to God. This may seem plausible in the case of personalities who have gone through long periods of religious exercise, penances and trials and have, after long years of internal struggle, achieved the status of saints in the eyes of their followers. But how is such a status acquired by hereditary *pīr*s who, visibly for all, have taken over a *pīr*'s office from their predecessors? How are they perceived, and – equally crucially – how do they

87 For comparison, see e.g. the *ādāb* according to Muhammad Ashraf 'Ali Thanawi as given in Mohammad Ajmal (1984: 243 f.).

88 Although there are certainly rules regarding how to recognise a true *pīr* or *walī*. Cf. Chapter 3.6 for some remarks on this topic.

89 'Relationship, connection' etc.; for an extensive discussion of the Sufic dimension of this concept, cf. Fritz Meier (1994), almost *passim*. Also Jürgen Paul (1998: 34 ff.).

90 Interview H.H. Feb. 1999.

perceive themselves? How is the spiritual capital acquired in a saint's life transferred to his successor?

I had the opportunity to interview three spiritual guides in Maijbhandar on these issues. One of them, a member of one of the central families of the Maijbhandari clan, was instructed by his father to succeed him as a *pīr-i bayʿat* (P.), namely a spiritual master bestowing initiation. He gave expression to his doubts whether he would be able to live up to this task, and agreed only on the condition that his father would remain with him. The father gave him his word and put his hand on his son's head. The *pīr* described how at that moment his father's *tawaǧǧuh*, lit. 'favour' and more specifically 'spiritual impact',[91] came upon him, creating a very intense feeling and enabling him to fulfil his father's wish.[92]

The second, rather young *pīr* was from one of the less important *manzil*s and could not point to any direct spiritual legacy; he was well read in Islamic and Sufic scriptures and himself active as an orator and author. He did not possess the self-confidence of the major Maijbhandari *saǧǧādanašīn*s and was quite obviously still striving for spiritual as well as status consolidation, as came out in the series of interviews we had. It was fascinating to witness how one night he bestowed *bayʿa* on some rural *murīd*s. Those peasants, much older than the *pīr* himself, approached him with fearful respect, and he managed the fatherly postures required by the situation without difficulties.

The third interview was the most instructive. The *pīr* in question is today perceived by some as a central figure for Maijbhandar as a whole. He stressed that he had always seen his father like 'most of the others', that is, from a distance, especially as he and his mother had lived separately from the saintly father. The father used to show his affection and love for him, but he was not as close as a usual father. The transfer of *wilāya* was described as easy and natural, and the *murīd*s and *ḫādim*s of the *darbār* proved to be a great help in this. Notwithstanding the fact that his central position had been uncontested from the beginning in this *manzil*, this *pīr* objected to being called a *pīr* and preferred to portray himself as a *golām* (Ar. <*ġulām*>, 'slave') of the *darbār*. If people venerated him it was because they saw his father in him. He also refused to admit that there were some among his followers who definitely saw something more in him than a mere representative of his father.[93] Commenting on this statement, one of his *murīd*s cited a Bengali proverb: 'the fish in the pond never considers himself a fish in the pond';[94] and humility in self-reference as opposed to glorification from the

91 See, however, Chittick (1998: 388), who gives 'attentiveness' and 'face-turning' as English renderings of *tawaǧǧuh* in Ibn ʿArabi's terminology; in our context, the attentiveness and turning of the face on the part of the *murīd* apparently are to be understood as an activity of the master (cf. Fritz Meier [1994: 42]: '[die Aufmerksamkeit kann] aber auch vom Lehrer auf den Schüler gehen'). As regards Bengali Sufi usage, according to my experiences, 'spiritual impact' comes closest to its meaning.

92 Interview H.H., 30–3–1999.

93 Interview H.H. 8–3–2001.

94 *pukurer māch nijeke kakhano pukurer māch bale mane kare nā.*

surroundings is certainly a common phenomenon with such personalities.[95] It was this very *pīr* whom I witnessed in the situation depicted in the following:

> A wedding in the city; the Maijbhandari *pīr* in question, still young, is among the invited. One of the wedding parties belongs to his *murīd*s. He is placed on a decorated seat at a distance and politely receives a number of persons. He repeatedly gets up from his seat to greet elder *murīd*s, often by shaking hands with them. A mere few fall to his feet, but this may be due to the occasion. The cordiality cannot dissimulate the formality of these encounters which have indeed the character of a reception rather than free interaction; in intervals, the *pīr* remains seated alone and immobile, with a simultaneously tranquil and keen expression on his face. I notice an acquaintance, a young man in his early twenties, from a village close to Maijbhandar, who has arrived in a group of devotees. He appears restless and distracted, and seems unable to concentrate on our conversation. His gaze is fixed on the *pīr* sitting some eight meters from where he stands. His tension increases minute by minute. He seems to be up to something and to be waiting for the right moment; at the same time he is desperately struggling to overcome his fear. The *pīr* once again gets up from his seat to greet a new arrival, and one of the sheets decorating the backrest of his chair starts to slip down from its position. In alarm and excitement, the young man makes a sudden start toward the *pīr*, stops in hesitation, then again rushes forward in a kind of suppressed haste, and finally reaches the seat where he rearranges the slipping sheet with utmost care. The *pīr* witnesses this from the corner of his eye but does not show any attention to it; he seems to conspicuously overlook the fact that this action has taken place. The young man rushes back to the group, relieved, once his performance is completed.[96]

How to interpret this scene? The *pīr* was very attentive during all the time described here and certainly noticed not only the rearrangement of the sheet, but also the intense glances and other signs of excitement of the young man. So, contrary to his statement in the interview, he definitely *knew* at that time that he had become the object of veneration. He could have dismantled the logic of the young man's action, or at least undercut it, by commenting upon it and thus transforming it into a trivial this-wordly happening; but by the way he did *not* react he enhanced

95 This is a point Rupert Snell hints at in the context of medieval Indian hagiography: 'There exists a paradox here: for whereas *bhaktas* characteristically insist on the subservience of the individual to the service of an undifferentiated supreme deity, thereby transcending the relevance of the details of individual mortal lives, the lay follower typically adopts the *bhakta*'s life as an exemplary paradigm, and thereby naturally develops a close interest in the details of his life-story. This interest grows with time, and the late hagiographical sources of a tradition are usually more detailed than the early ones' (Callewaert & Snell 1994: 3). There are Maijbhandari *pīr*s also who would refer to themselves as *murīd*s, and their sanctification, together with the elaboration of the paradigmatic aspects of their lives, rest in the hands of their entourage and of future hagiographers.

96 Diary H.H., February 2001.

the context of *bhakti*, devotion, from which the young man apparently acted. In this light, the personality we are describing is certainly a *pīr* in the making and on the rise, and his remarks in the interview are polite understatements.

The decisive point for us is that '*pīr*-dom' works as a cultural construct, and *pīr–murīd* relationships in an established *darbār* can be said to possess an automatism of *producing pīrs*. 'Father has construed a factory for the fabrication of saints', sings Abdul Gafur Hali,[97] and if we read his statement somewhat obliquely,

Photo 3 Syed Moinuddin Ahmad al-Hasani al-Maijbhandari receiving *murīds*.

97 Cf. the translation in *VG*: 30 ('Der Vater hat ein Werk gebaut zur Heiligenherstellung').

it is quite accurate. Once the saintliness of a location or family is established, the shared belief in *baraka* and the feasibility of transferring *wilāya*, 'spiritual sovereignty', work together in installing the successor in a saint's place and investing him with identical spiritual potential. Even obvious shortcomings on the *pīr*'s side do not endanger this construct as he is still conceived as the bearer of an extremely potent inherited *wilāya* and, if not himself of any merit, still the main channel to his more convincing predecessor.[98]

Pīr-dom, we have also seen, works by ascription. A *pīr* or saint does not have to be self-declared,[99] and in fact, the Sufi tradition seems to appreciate understatements and even the concealment of sainthood.[100] In Maijbhandar, too, the usual rhetoric employed by the *pīr*s themselves describes *pīr*-dom as an inherited office they execute not through any of their own achievements, but only by the grace of their predecessors.

The anthropologist Manzurul Mannan, himself a *murīd* of Haq Manzil in Maijbhandar, has tried to define *pīr*-dom in terms of a semiotic presence.[101] This approach is promising insofar as it sees the position of the *pīr* as a construct using a whole inventory of cultural signs. It is here that we can find the link between the spiritual virtuosity and idiosyncrasy of saints on the one hand and the stable routine and fixed semantics of *darbār* life on the other. Hagiography is the branch of writing that is most seminal in 'systemising' sainthood and *pīr*-dom and accommodating them in existing frames of perception. We shall see in Chapter 4 how saintly vitae are conceived in Maijbhandar and what ingredients are required for *pīr*-dom and sainthood; and we shall also have occasion to examine *pīr–murīd* relationships further on the basis of the abundant material these hagiographies furnish.

2.2.4 *Festivals (*ʿurs, ḫušrūz*)*

The 22nd of *Caitra* (beginning of April), the day Saint Gholam Rahman passed away. For a number of days, preparations for the occasion have kept

98 *Pīr*-dom, for a designated hereditary successor, is consequently easier to acquire than to relinquish. An academic in Dhaka, a descendent of an old *pīr* family in North India and a declared opponent of *pīr*-dom, told me how unhappy the people at the respective *darbār* were with his refusal to accept what they perceived as his predestined role.

99 Saint Ahmadullah is an exception here.

100 Cf. Gramlich (1987: 61): '[Es] wird immer wieder betont, daß Gottes Freunde, wenn auch nicht alle, verborgen sind. Ja es gilt als besondere Auszeichnung des Heiligen, wenn man ihm seine Heiligkeit nicht anmerkt, weil sie sich unter dem Mantel alltäglichen Verhaltens verbirgt.' Among the examples he gives are cases of saints who concealed their saintliness by openly transgressive behaviour, neglect of the ritual prayers, etc. (p. 61).

101 Cf. his article 'Pirs: The Semiotic Presence of Islamic Spiritualists', available at http://www.sufimaizbhandari.org/sufi_articles.html (accessed 18 March 2010). Cf. also Ewing (1993: 71), positing the *pīr* as a 'personal symbol' for the *murīd* that is entirely elevated from the incompleteness of the surrounding world, and relating him (by following Sudhir Kakar) to the feminine identification patterns of South Asian males (p. 72 ff.).

> the various *manzil*s busy, and flocks of pilgrims have been streaming into Maijbhandar since yesterday. This morning the flow has become so dense that it means hard work to make one's way 'upstream' toward the main road. Decorated cattle – cows, water buffaloes, goats and even a camel brought from Rajasthan – are led into the village by families and groups of pilgrims to be presented at the *manzil*s as gifts and then taken to the fields behind the village for slaughtering. In the thick crowd, with animals again and again nervously trying to break out of their course (and sometimes succeeding to do so), the *défilé* resembles a *corrida*. Among the arrivers are groups of flag-bearing members of some regional Maijbhandari branch who keep shouting slogans in praise of Saint Gholam Rahman in trance-like exhilaration. Liturgical functions are going on at the shrine of Gholam Rahman without cessation, the local music shops play Maijbhandari songs at peak volume, and pilgrims are holding musical sessions in various places. The *manzil*s bustle with people; the *pīr*s have one of the busiest times in the year, and some of them have virtually disappeared in the encirclement of their *murīd*s. In their vicinity, the situation is comparable to an unreserved second-class train wagon of South Asia: there is merciless pushing among those who want to present their *naẓrāna*s, gifts (often money), touch the *pīr*'s feet and attain his blessings. *Ḫādim*s may have to help in removing those who take more than the appropriate time and block others' access, as well as in collecting the sometimes thick bundles of currency notes that the *pīr*s receive and hand over to them. Masses assemble in and around the shrine of Saint Gholam Rahman, and the atmosphere reaches its climax in the collective *ḏikr* when the screams of *Allā-hu, Allā-hu* do their best to quieten all the other manifold sounds. The acoustic dimension of this *ʿurs*, going on incessantly for twenty-four hours or more, is awe-inspiring indeed; from some distance it sounds like a deep roaring. On the fields by the entrance to the village is the site of the Maijbhandari *melā*, fair, with its sweets and food stalls, clothes and book shops, merry-go-rounds and go-cart race courses. Fortune-tellers, vendors of amulets, travelling showmen with cobras and mongooses, traditional healers selling spectacular medicines made from reptiles and insects – intimidating not only to me but to quite a few passers-by – and many others have come for this *melā*. There is even a veritable freak-show with all kinds of bodily deformities on display, drawing much attention. Towards Azimnagar, divided from the road by a small canal, there is a special gathering of *māstān*s, literally intoxicated cannabis smokers, some of whom have already started dancing frenetically in the heat of the afternoon.[102]

The great festivals are the culmination points of the annual calendar in Maijbhandar. The most prominent among them are the *ʿurs* festivals. *ʿUrs* is lit. 'wedding', and we can quote Abdul Ghani Kanchanpuri, the Maijbhandari author

102 Diary H.H., April 1999.

of the Urdu treatise *Ā'īna-i Bārī*, for an explanation of this term: 'Know everything on earth as in sleep/He has awoken who has left the world', he states in a Persian poem; death, for a saint, is thus coterminous with awaking and finding oneself in complete union with one's beloved. The day of this union (*waṣāl*) is the day of wedding, the *'urs*.[103] *'Urs* celebrations are a specific feature of Islam in the East.[104] Besides these *'urs* or death anniversary celebrations, there are also birthday celebrations, so-called *ḫušrūz* or 'days of joy'; this type of festival is not traditional in South Asian Islam, and the Maijbhandari *ḫušrūz* celebrations have made their appearance more recently.[105]

The two main *'urs* festivals commemorate the passing away of the Maijbhandari founding saints: Ahmadullah's *'urs* is held on the 10th of the Bengali month Māgh, corresponding to 24 January, and Gholam Rahman's on the 22nd of Caitra, which falls on 5 April.[106] Other important dates are the 27th of Āśvin (12 October), the birthday of Gholam Rahman; the 10th of Pauṣ (24 December) for the birthday, and the 26th of Āśvin (11 October) for the death anniversary of Ziaul Haq; the 7th of Phālgun (20 February) for the birthday and the 21 January for the *'urs* of Shafiul Bashar (1919–2002); the 1st of Māgh (15 January), death anniversary of Shamsul Huda (1924–1979); the 25th of Agrahāẏan (10 December) for the *'urs* of Aminul Haq Wasel (?–1906); and the 27th of Māgh (10 February) for the birthday of Moinuddin Ahmad.[107] Other, minor festivals could be added to this list.

The most comprehensive and detailed description of any single Maijbhandari festival is Selim Jahangir's account of the death anniversary of Saint Ahmadullah (Jāhāṅgīr 1999: 152–75). I cannot give such a detailed picture here for lack of space, and so I will try to summarise the gist of his documentation and my own fieldwork data regarding that same festival. First of all it is important to stress that the festivals in honour of the two founding saints are not entirely the affairs of the respective *manzil*s, but involve practically every branch of the movement. The main ritual functions at the shrines of the celebrated saint are in the hands of the *manzil* representatives, but *murīd*s and pilgrims affiliated to all *manzil*s indiscriminately attend these occasions.

The rituals proper start on the day before the *'urs* with the *ġuṣal šarīf*, the 'holy bath' or washing of the tomb. During this ceremony, the old quilts (Bg. *gilāp* from

103 *ĀB*: 320; cf. also Section 4.3.1.

104 Cf. Ernst (1993: 43), who also states that the origin of the term is not clear (Schimmel 1995a: 110 explains this with reference to bride mysticism: 'Doch ist es gerade der Gedanke an die Brautseele, deren einziger Geliebter Gott ist, der dazu geführt hat, den Tod als 'urs, 'Hochzeit' zu bezeichnen – eine geistige Hochzeit, in der die Seele wieder in die ungetrennte Einheit mit dem urewigen Geliebten zurückgeführt wird.') Taylor (1999: 64) gives accounts of the *mawālid*, 'birthdays' celebrated in Egypt.

105 Birthday celebrations seem to be more common with Hindu saints, as, e.g., Dadu Dayal; cf. Thiel-Horstmann (1983: 385 ff.) on his birthday celebrations.

106 With, of course, slight alterations, as in all of the following Roman dates; but I retain the calculation of the source (Jāhāṅgīr 1999: 151 f.).

107 According to the list given in Jāhāṅgīr (1999: 151 f.).

Ar./P. <*ġilāf*>) covering the tomb are removed, and the tomb is sprinkled with the rose water and perfumes donated by pilgrims throughout the year. After this the newly gifted quilts are dressed on the tomb to be again sprinkled with rose water and perfumes and decorated with flowers. The old quilts may still be distributed among very close *murīd*s who keep them to cover their breasts with them when they are buried.[108] This ceremony is supervised by the *saǧǧādanašīn* and attended by the *pīrzāda*s and close *murīd*s.

On the day of the *ʿurs* itself, *ḥalqa-i ẕikr*, *ḏikr* assemblies, are performed by *ḫādim*s at the shrine after every ritual prayer and late into the night.[109] Simultaneously the *saǧǧādanašīn* and *pīrzāda*s are busy receiving *murīd*s and pilgrims and eventually also bestowing *bayʿa*. Late at night, a *niyāz* or 'gift ceremony' is held during which *tabarruk* in the form of food is distributed. For *murīd*s it is customary, according to Jāhāṅgīr (1999: 159), to first visit the respective shrine and then address themselves to their *manzil*s. There are special arrangements for women in the inner parts of the *manzil*s where *fātiha* readings[110] and *ḏikr* sessions are held. Along with this, there are informal music and dance sessions at the guesthouses and camp sites where the pilgrims put up for the night.[111]

Selim Jahangir estimates that the number of people coming together for the two major *ʿurs* festivals is about 200,000. Roughly 1,000 head of cattle are donated on such occasions and slaughtered, cooked and distributed on the spot; a large number of volunteers are constantly busy with these tasks on the more remote margins of the village.[112] Among these are water buffaloes, and Selim Jahangir speculates that Maijbhandar may have been path-breaking in the establishment of this dietary habit which is commonly witnessed today at *ʿurs* celebrations all over Chittagong and probably beyond it; apparently they first came as gifts of pilgrims from the Chittagong Hill Tracts (Jāhāṅgīr 1999: 164 f.).

The Maijbhandari *ʿurs* celebrations are the greatest of their kind in present Chittagong. As such, they have become models for similar celebrations at other, smaller shrines of rural Chittagong. There are again and again efforts to establish *ʿurs* festivals for new or 'rediscovered' saintly predecessors, with different

108 Cf. Selim Jāhāṅgīr (1999: 157), who describes this as a very rare happening.

109 Cf. Chapter 2.2.1 for a short description of these functions.

110 i.e. the reading of the opening sura of the *Qurʾān* on the occasion of a death commemoration.

111 For comparison, see a description of the ceremonies at the *dargāh* of Muʿin al-Din Chishti of Ajmer, in Moini (1989: 70 ff.). Also Taylor (1999: 65) who, in his description of medieval *mawālid* in Egypt, mentions features such as rhythmic dancing, processions, *ḏikr*, *Qurʾān* recitations, recitations of the saints' life stories, attractions and entertainment for the large crowds; even today the *mawālid* function as fairs, with the participation of magicians, fortune tellers, poets and street entertainers. Gaborieau (1983: 297 f.), in his depiction of *ʿurs* celebrations in Nepal, mentions processions, tomb circambulations, collective recitations, music (if allowed), and animal sacrifices, accompanied by a profane part consisting of a fair (*melā*) lasting all night and the presence of *faqīr*s, jugglers, traders, musicians, dancing girls and prostitutes.

112 Selim Jahangir has based his calculation, among other things, on information received from the 'catering department' of the *ʿurs* organisors. I cannot give any contrary evidence, but I must admit that these figures do seem very high to me.

degrees of success. The same is true for Maijbhandar itself.[113] The size of the festivities shows the acclaim of a particular saint in the eyes of the public, and just like a splendid mausoleum, hagiographies, collected sayings and songs in praise of the respective personality, a proper *ʿurs* celebration has in these parts become an obligatory condition for acclaimed sainthood. The celebration of *ḫušrūz*, birthdays, goes back, in Maijbhandar, to the time of Gholam Rahman who was an immensely popular *pīr*, and the reasons for its establishment are unclear. Ever since, however, these follow the same logic as the *ʿurs* celebrations in being indicators of a saint's popularity and a *manzil*'s standing and influence.

113 Not all efforts to establish *ʿurs* celebrations have succeeded here either, if we are to believe the account Syed Delawar Hosain gives in his controversial *Elākār renesā̃ yuger kaẏekṭi dik* (33 ff.).

3 Theological and hagiological writings

This chapter and the succeeding ones examine, in the broadest sense, different branches of textual sources pertaining to Maijbhandar. The threefold division underlying this presentation distinguishes between theological and hagiological writings, hagiographies and songs. The latter two of these categories render the classification of *gān*, songs, and *jībanī sāhitya*, hagiography, which are perceived as different branches or genres in Maijbhandar, and it is only the first category of theological and hagiological writings that may seem problematic. At the very outset, then, it is important to state that there is, in terms of a self-defined entity, no such thing as a specific 'Maijbhandari theology'. In recent times, it has become customary to speak of a certain *Māij'bhāṇḍārī darśan* ('Maijbhandari philosophy'), but this term is even now mostly used in a very confined sense, as in references to the Maijbhandari *ṭarīqa* rules, and certainly does not cover all the notions we are going to discuss in the following. Consequently, the heading of the present chapter does not claim to render any indigenous category of writings, but is a descriptive label to accommodate a variety of texts dealing with issues of a theological and hagiological nature.

I shall in the following give a survey of the works subsumed under this category and some of the issues they discuss. Such issues are also treated in the hagiographies and songs, of course, but there are some reasons why these texts ought to be treated separately. What is common to them in contrast most notably to the songs (to be discussed in Chapter 5) is that they deal with certain issues in a straightforward, fixed and 'serious' manner; nothing in them is dismissable by allusions to the poetic extravagances of the writer, as may happen with Maijbhandari songs. The texts treated here are furthermore written literature from the start, while the songs were originally oral. Due to these factors, these writings have a somewhat more official character than the songs; and we shall notice that there are significant differences between the concepts expounded in these texts and those of the songs. Further, unlike the Maijbhandari hagiographies to be treated in Chapter 4, these writings do not narrate the lives of single saints, but attempt to expound tenets and principles of Sufic Islam from different perspectives and/or in a more general way. Some of them deal with very practical and circumscribed issues such as the legitimacy of controversial practices, or try to elucidate central Islamic concepts and harmonise saint veneration as practised in Maijbhandar with them; these also occasionally digress into theological areas.

They may be long treatises, *fatwa*s or short articles (*prabandha*). One end of the scale is formed by manuals briefly exposing *darbār* etiquette, *ḏikr* rules, etc.

In view of the fact that it is not possible to speak of a separate and independent Maijbhandari theology, it is all the more important to consider the traditions of Islamic and specifically Sufic-Islamic theologies that are or have in the past been current in Bengal as possible frames within which these writings operate. A full-scale account of such developments would require expert knowledge of Islamic theology in general and a close study of regional developments and debates, and must be left to future scholarship. The contextualisation of Maijbhandari theological thought relies on the relevant secondary materials available, and pays heed to three different branches of Sufic writings.

The first of these is the medieval Muslim literature in Bengali that has been made available in editions by Abdul Karim Sahityavisharad and Ahmad Sharif, and is the object of the in-depth studies by Asim Roy (1981) and David Cashin (1995) (as well as, partly, Enāmul Hak 1995). No direct link, and certainly no tradition, can be established between those *pũthi* writings and the Maijbhandari texts we are going to discuss in this chapter – in sharp contrast to the Maijbhandari songs.[1]

The second category of texts that would need consideration are the predominantly Persian writings of medieval Sufis in the urban court environment mostly of the former capitals Gaur, Pandua and Dhaka. Unfortunately no work on these is available except the largely historical account by Latif (1993) that lacks depth in matters of theology, doctrine, etc. The historical link is even harder to establish here. Thirdly, we will take into consideration a number of 'pan-Sufic' authors, most of them Sufi classics, who have informed Maijbhandari theological thinking and served as references from its very beginning. Such frequently quoted traditional Sufi authors include Ibn ʿArabi (d. 1240), Jalal al-Din Rumi (d. 1273), Farid al-Din ʿAttar (d. 1220), Muʿin al-Din Chishti (d. 1236) and, of course, albeit with less frequency, the founder of the Qadiriyya *ṭarīqa*, ʿAbd al-Qadir Gilani (d. 1166). Other than with Maijbhandari songs, and very significantly in the context of the structure of the Maijbhandari movement, theological traditions of other religious backgrounds, such as the various streams of Hindu thought, hardly interact with Maijbhandari theological ideas.

What is noteworthy about Maijbhandari text production as a whole, and the theological and hagiological writings in particular, is its very local provenance. Translations and commentaries on the Islamic scriptures and Sufi classics such as Jalal al-Din Rumi's *Maṯnavī* are not absent, but the larger part of writings are independent works by local writers, hailing either from Chittagong proper or other parts of Eastern Bengal. There are occasional references of course to contemporary Islamic writers on the subcontinent and beyond, but there is little interlinkage with other Sufi traditions and institutions of the twentieth century.

The authors of Maijbhandari theologial tracts are generally closely affiliated to one or the other branch of the movement. Some of them are *ʿulamāʾ* and local

1 Cf., in this connection, various sections under Section 5.7, as well as Section 8.2.

religious authorities who have become disciples of Maijbhandari saints.[2] Others are themselves *pīrzāda*s or even *saǧǧādanašīns*.[3] Thirdly, there are also disciples without any formal religious education who venture into systemising their religious views.[4] It would in all of these cases be misleading to conceive of this group of writers as a separate faction within the movement. Many among them have also authored hagiographies and songs and would hardly consent to view these activities as separate in any practical sense.

What, then, is the nature of the texts we are going to examine? Here are short characterisations of the texts in chronological order.[5] The first major tract to appear from Maijbhandar is Aminul Haq Farhadabadi's (1866–1944) *Tuḥfat al-aḫyār fī dafʿ šarārat al-šarār* ('The precious gift of the good regarding the refutation of the evilness of the evil', 1906/7; *Tuḥfat*), a *fatwa* mainly on the legitimacy of *samāʿ*, listening to music, and a few other controversial topics. Originally written in a mixture of Arabic and Persian, the text was circulated as a manuscript (*pũthi*) with a Bengali translation in *paẏār* metre prepared by the author himself. Since the topics treated here are mostly of a legalist nature, this text will concern us only marginally in the present chapter.

The second treatise, and one we will have to investigate closely, is the most extensive book on Maijbhandar and runs across the genre distinctions made above: Abdul Ghani Kanchanpuri's voluminous Urdu compendium *Āʾīna-i Bārī* ('Mirror of the Lord'), written and published in 1915, is simultaneously a hagiographical account of Ahmadullah's life, a collection of more than 100 Urdu ghazals, and an exposition of the theological foundations of the movement. This work is the most comprehensive outline of Maijbhandari theology available to this day.

A more concise survey of basic theological tenets, together with the typical apparatus of *darbār* regulations, behavioural rules, etc. that also features in the above-mentioned work, is Abdussalam Isapuri's Persian tract *Fuyūżāt al-Raḥmāniyya fī ṭarīqat al-māʾiğbhandʿāriyya*. A *ḫalīfa* of Gholam Rahman, Isapuri also wrote hagiographies of both Maijbhandari founding saints; his works are not dated, but the tract in question can safely be estimated to have been written around 1950,[6] and the use of Persian in the mid twentieth century remains a striking feature of this text.[7]

2 e.g. Abdul Ghani Kanchanpuri, the author of *ĀB* (1914–15); Aminul Haq Farhadabadi, a *fatwa*-author and *ḫalīfa* of Ahmadullah's; Md. Ali Azam Rizwi, a contemporary writer affiliated to Ahmadiyya Manzil.

3 This is true of Delawar Hosain, author of *BM*; Badruddoza, writer of several expositions of Maijbhandar; and Lutfunnesa Hosaini, daughter of Shafiul Bashar and the only female who has contributed to thise category of writings.

4 A good example is Sayyad Golam Morshed, author of a collection of thoughtful articles on Islam and Maijbhandar (Mor'śed 1994).

5 For detailed biliographic references and an extensive list of the writings concerned, cf. the bibliography of primary sources (Appendix III).

6 There are references to the atom bomb and the state of Pakistan which put the possible origin after 1947.

7 It remains a matter of speculation whether this choice of language means any conscious restriction of the audience, is indicative of the privileged insularity of Isapuri's circles, or comes down to the employment of Persian as an 'Islamic language' in order to heighten the esteem and 'Islamic character' of Maijbhandar.

The writings of the second half of the twentieth century are almost exclusively in Bengali. The most influential if highly controversial writer of this period is Delawar Hosain, the grandson of Saint Ahmadullah and former *sağğādanašīn* of Ahmadiyya Manzil. Apart from a number of small tracts, Delawar Hosain authored the comprehensive *Belāẏate motlākā* (first edition in 1959, numerous revised editions), an exposition of Sufi doctrines and the significance of the founding saint of Maijbhandar. A noteworthy tract is also *Ābe hāẏāt* (P. <*āb-i ḥayāt*>, 'water of life'), written in 1951 by Abdul Jabbar Mimnagari, a disciple of Delawar Hosain and author of numerous songs. Contemporary exponents of Rahmaniyya Manzil who have contributed theological volumes are notably Syed Badruddoza and Lutfunnesa Hosaini. There remain to be added a number of authors more or less closely affiliated to the various Maijbhandari *manzil*s. These include S.M. Rahman from neighbouring Azimnagar, Syed Gholam Morshed, son of a *murīd* of Gholam Rahman, and others. Noteworthy are also collective efforts to represent aspects of Maijbhandari religiosity such as the volume *Māij'bhāṇḍār śarīph* (1995) of the *Māij'bhāṇḍār Gabeṣaṇā Pariṣad* ('Maijbhandar Research Council') in Dhaka.

From these roughly thirty tracts, two are outstanding regarding their actual size as well as their impact: Abdul Ghani Kanchanpuri's *Ā'īna-i Bārī* and Delawar Hosain's *Belāẏate mot'lākā*. The former volume in itself covers most of the topics that appear in the later writings, and usually more thoroughly too. It also anticipates much of the contents of the last-mentioned; but Delawar Hosain's book is significant for its role in developing the so-called *Māij'bhāṇḍārī darśan*, 'Maijbhandari philosophy', and for extending the interpretation of the saints' messages to a completely new level of meaning, as we shall see. If intertextuality is a criterion for determining thoroughness of approach, *Ā'īna-i Bārī* with its hundreds of quotations and references to some seventy different sources, and *Belāẏate mot'lākā* with quotations from 31 books easily beat most of the other tracts. We will therefore base our following exposition of some basic theological features in the main on these two texts.

3.1 Love (*ʿišq, prem*)

The concept of love (*ʿišq* or *prem*) is central to Sufism in general,[8] and to Maijbhandari self-representations in particular, and the tracts under discussion likewise devote much attention to this topic. *Ā'īna-i Bārī* has a chapter on the *Ḥażrat-i ʿišq*, the Lord of Love, that will serve as a suitable starting point for this discussion. Abdul Ghani allegorically describes this Lord of Love as 'a fast horse' (p. 415); the Lord of Love obeys God, but is superior to the Sir of the Intellect (*ğanāb-i aql*) whom he easily charms with a glance of his eyes. The Lord of Love is equally superior to the Master of Grace (*ṣāḥib-i nāz*) and closely allied to the Lord of Beauty (*ḥażrat-i ḥusn*) (p. 417 f.).

The concept of how love operates in the world that is expounded here uses Ibn ʿArabi's cosmological ideas, most prominently that of *tağallī* or 'self-disclosure'

8 Cf. Enāmul Hak (1995: 84–9) for an overview (with special reference to South Asia).

(cf. Chittick 1998: 52). God, Abdul Ghani argues, projects his perfections (*kamāliyyāt*) into the manifest; wishing to cover their secrets, He asks the Lord of Love to cover them with a veil. Concealing the actual non-existence of this veil, the Lord of Love then covered the perfections with the colourfulness of existence (p. 419). As emanations of God's *ḏāt*, all things in the world are 'rays of love'; and since the world originated from this essential divine beauty (*ḥusn-i ẕātī*), it ideally recognises that essential beauty as its beloved object (*ma'šūq*).

Love originates from four different entities: from the attributes (*ṣifāt*) of God, from divine beauty (*ḥusn*), from deeds (*af'āl*), and from effects (*āṯār*); among these the love born from the attributes of God is the purest, as it is without motive and completely self-contained (p. 425). The self-disclosure of God pervades the world and each and everything in it, but in them the true attributes of God are veiled. Hence the world is essentially a mirror, and on the part of the *āšiq*s it is crucial to realise that they witness 'the glory with the perfection of the divine essence' (*ğamāl bā kamāl-i ẕāt*) in the world as in a mirror only (p. 426 f.). Ultimately lover and beloved are one: 'Love says: O lover, your beloved is always with you' (p. 439);[9] but the distinctive difference between worldly and divine love is that the former must transcend the veils constituting the mirror that is the world. The state of him who sees the glory of divine truth (*ğamāl-i ḥaqq*), e.g. in women, is comparable to someone watching the reflection of the moon on the surface of a pond; a superior state is attained by him who is annihilated (*fānī*) in the essence of divine truth (*ẕāt-i ḥaqq*) and beholds Him within himself (p. 442).

Wordly love is perceived as highly ambivalent. As all things partake of the self-disclosure (Ar. *tağallī*) of God, they have an element of divine truth, and love directed to them consequently partakes in some sense of divine love. The rays of truth hit and illuminate the worldly forms like the moon lights up a cloud, and the human body is equivalent to this cloud. Such love must be purified, and only if the worldly lover starts gazing at the moon itself is the dust cleansed and true love attained (p. 444). Abdul Ghani sees the positive aspect of such worldly love in its function as a bridge leading towards true love, but he simultaneously stresses that love directed towards immature forms, unless conceived as a passing state, is bound to become illusive love (*'išq-i mağāzī*) and causes erring (P. *gumrāhī*) (p. 443). If 'the cloud of the body' covers 'the moon of the heart' and illusive love triumphs over true love, the way to spiritual progress is blocked (p. 444 f.). It is difficult to attain 'the *darbār* of true love', and it is highly advisable to keep exclusively to mature beloved objects, namely the prophets and saints (442 f.). Everything else risks becoming idol worship (P. *butparastī*):

> O dear one, do not be engrossed and drunk from the alcohol of the manifest form because that is idol worship and the fabrication of idols [P. *buttarāšī*].[10]
> (p. 445)

9 *'išq kahtā hai ki ai 'āšiq terā ma'šūq hama dam terā hamsang hai.*

10 *ai 'azīz tū us ṣūrat-i ẓāhira kī šarāb sē mast saršār na ho ğānā ki yah 'ain butparastī aur buttarāšī hai.*

Abdul Ghani distinguishes three stages of the development of true love in the concluding part of his chapter. In the initial state of confusion of love (P. *maqām-i walwalī*), man gazes at his own essence (Ar. *ḏāt*) and acts only on his own behalf; when he thus attains the beloved (*ma'šūq*) as a part of his own heart, he finds ease. This, however, is not yet love but only 'the possession of the own body' (P. *ḫwīštandārī*). The true lovers leave this stage behind and address their love to their friend (P./U. *dōst*) for whom they are ready to do everything. Proceeding from there, their gaze finally turns from the beloved to love itself, and love (*'išq*) becomes their *qibla* (p. 449 f.).[11]

Isapuri, in his Persian tract *Fuyūẓāt al-Raḥmāniyya fī ṭarīqat al-mā'iğbhandāriyya*, distinguishes three religious paths, those of the *sāleḥīn*, *abrār* and *'išq-i šatāriyya* (p. 6). The latter consists of ten components, and those following it are constantly in the *ḥālat-i ğazb*, state of rapture and need not act in any way (p. 7).

More commonplace conceptions of love in contemporary Maijbhandar can be found summarised in Abdul Jabbar Mimnagari's Bengali tract *Ābe-hāẏāt*. These concern not the psychology and classification of love, but its provenance and importance. Love is intimately connected with the creation of man. After creating the worlds and the different kinds of beings such as animals, *ğinn*, angels, etc., Allah found that love did not develop in any of these creatures. So in the end, by way of the *nūr-i muḥammadī* as the first step of all his creations,[12] he created men, made the original covenant with them (*ĀH*: 8 f.; *Qur'ān* 7.172[171]) and ordered the angels to bow before Adam. Love is the ultimate reason for this final creation:

> Man was created for love alone, otherwise the angels would not have been deficient [had it only been] for the worship of supreme Allah. It is an indispensable duty for each man to become aware of what kind of substance that *prem* or *'išq* is, how it can be attained and what its rules and manners [*rītinīti*] are.
>
> (*ĀH*: 18 f.)

The first of these rules is that love cannot be developed by oneself alone but requires a relationship between two; and Abdul Jabbar devotes many pages to the proof that the adequate object of love is the perfect *pīr*.[13] Only love is able to break the conceited feelings of self, the idea of being important and the illusion wrought by the *nafs* (p. 110). It teaches man to abandon his infatuation with worldly possessions and the self and instils in him an unparalleled capacity of sacrifice (p. 113).

Love is constituent not only of man as such, but also of the religious practice of the *aḥl-i bāṭin*, the 'people of the non-manifest', who propagate their *ṭarīqa*; that is, the search for love is what sets Sufism apart from exoteric Islam (p. 20 f.). It is connected with the religious sphere of *ma'rifa*,[14] not with the *šarī'a* (p. 114).

11 For an extensive discussion of the various meanings of *qibla*, cf. *ĀB*: 570 ff.

12 Cf. the section on *nūr* below in this chapter.

13 He uses quotations from standard sources such as the *Qur'ān*, Rumi, Hafiz, etc. Cf. p. 000 in this chapter.

14 'gnosis', 'esoteric knowledge'; cf. below in Section 3.3.

Quarrels over the legitimacy of such a practice of love are nonsensical since, following Abdul Jabbar, love annuls rules and excuses hundreds of transgressions. God's love is likened to the deepest kind of human love, that between parents and children, though much stronger: 'The man who loves God is loved by Him seventy times more than by his parents' (p. 26). The *ṭarīqa*s are the religious means devised for the acquisition of this love:

> So, ever since the generous envoy [*rasūl-i akram*] abandoned this world, the *imām*s, *walī*s, *awliyā'* [*sic*], *pīr*s and *muršid*s of the *ṭarīqa* have bestowed the education regarding the path to the *'išq* and *maḥabba* [both Ar., 'love'] of Supreme Allah by giving them, according to place, time and person, the names of different *ṭarīqa*s.
>
> (*ĀH*: 27)

It is through the *pīr* that the seeker can experience divine love. Abdul Jabbar quotes Jalal al-Din Rumi several times in order to show that remoteness from the saints is equivalent to remoteness from God; that the saints are the true representatives of the Prophet and thus of God; that, positively put, anybody seeking closeness to God should approach the saints; and that men should follow the example of the moth and immerse themselves in the divine fire of love (pp. 25–35).

Other tracts stress the role of love for the eradication of the *nafs*, lower self, or vice versa. In *Belāẏate mot'lākā*, 'holy love' (*pabitra mahabbat*) is one of two general features underlying any *ṭarīqa*, the other being *nisba*, the relationship with God (*MB*: 126). Mujibur Rahman, in his *Nurer jhalak*, claims love (*prem*) to be the very essence of the *Qur'ān*. In the 'final time' (*ākherī jamānā*, U. <*āḫirī zamāna*>), love attains its fullest development as the foremost means of attaining God, and it is the common ground of all *ṭarīqa*s. 'In order to set one's foot on this path of love, the *nafs* first has to be restrained' (*NJ*: 34); and this can only be achieved with the aid of a perfect master (*kāmel pīr*).

3.2 Light (*nūr*)

In middle Bengali Sufi literature, as we know from the editions and research volumes by Abdul Karim Sahityavisharad, Ahmad Sharif, Enamul Haq, David Cashin and Asim Roy, the concept of *nūr* or *nūr-i muḥammadī* had a prominent place. In Sufi notions, *nūr* features as the first creation of Allah from which all other beings and the material world were gradually created, and this concept was taken up in medieval South Asian Sufi traditions.[15] Like, for example, the Arabic

15 An interesting example for the adaptation of this notion is Kutuban's Sufi romance *Miragāvatī* written in 1503, according to which 'the creator first created the light of Muhammad and then for his sake manifested himself in the forms of Śiva and Śakti.' Cf. S.M. Pandey (1992: 179); also Rām'candra Śukla (1964: 94 f.) on this author, giving his name as Kut'ban. As my colleague Torsten Tschacher has pointed out to me, the early seventeenth-century Tamil *Ñāṉap pukaḻcci* of Shaykh Pirmuhammad Waliullah (Ṣeyku Pīrmuhammatu Oliyullā) has a similar introductory passage according to which the Lord made Himself 'as Śakti and Śiva' (*sattiyāyc civaññāy*) (Pīrmuhammatu Oliyullāh 1995: 1). For an introduction regarding notions of *nūr-i muḥammadī*, see also Enāmul Hak (1995: 56–62).

Kitāb aḥwāl al-qiyāma (Wolff 1872: 1–6), medieval Bengali cosmologies tended to personify this concept, but unlike that Arabic source where it is still God who creates from its sweat, they attributed parts of creation to the *Nūr Muḥammad* directly: 'Created by the lord, Nur Muhammad in his turn brought the whole world into existence from the drops of perspiration (*gharma*, *ghām*) appearing in the different parts of his body' (Roy 1983: 121). A similar passage is found in the beginning of Śekh Parāṇ's *Nūr nāmā*: 'Again Nirañjan, seeing [Himself] in one form/Emitted [from] his own part the *nūr abatār*.'[16] Having created the *nūr*, Lord Nirañjan[17] gazes at the *nūr*, on whose body drops (*bindu*) of sweat start to form and give birth to the different categories of creation, such as the prophets (Verse 10), the angels (Verse 14–16), the *kalima* (Verse 19), the Lord's throne (Verse 21), etc.

The concept of *nūr* is very commonplace in Maijbhandari writings. Especially in the songs, it is extensively used, along with the Bengali adjective *nūrī*/*nuri*, to describe the saints, their bodily features or other sensual qualities.[18] But systematic elaborations of *nūr* are rare. The only extensive cosmological description in the Maijbhandari writings known to me occurs in Lutfunnesa Hosaini's treatise *Tāohīd* (1999), in which pp. 19–24 deal with the creation of the world from the emergence of *nūr-i muḥammadī* up to the birth of Prophet Muhammad. Secondly, there is an article by Gholam Morshed that stresses the identity of *nūr* with Muhammad and discusses the consequences of this for Islamic theology. We will start with Lutfunnesa Hosaini's treatise.

In the beginning there was only Allah and nothing except Him. In order to terminate this 'emptiness' (*śūnyatā*), He created the *nūr-i muḥammadī* as the very first of his creations (*Tāohīd*: 19).[19] According to a *Ḥadīṯ* from Ibn al-ʿAbbas, however, the *nūr-i muḥammadī* is a secondary creation that was formed from one of three parts of the foregoing unspecified *nūr* (p. 20). The other two parts were used to create Muhammad's wife and his companions as well as those who love him (p. 21). This line of ideas is, however, not followed up, as Lutfunnesa Hosaini then proceeds by stating (without references) that the *nūr-i muḥammadī* was divided into *four* parts, from which emerged the *qalam* ('pen'), the *lauḥ-i maḥfūẓ* ('book of destinies') and the throne (*āraś*, Ar. <*arš*>) of God (p. 21). The fourth of these parts of *nūr* was further divided into four parts, three of which brought forth the angels holding the throne, the seat of the throne and all other angels.

16 *punnabāra nirañjana dekhi ekākāra/nija aṃśe pracārila nūr*[*a*] *abatāra* (verse 5, from the edition in Cashin [1995: 112]; my translation and addition of [*a*] in *nūr*[*a*]).

17 Lit. 'the Uncoloured', 'Stainless'; one of the most common appellations of God in medieval Bengali Sufi writings and generally in North Indian *bhakti* literature. In *Nūr nāmā* (Verse 1.3; Cashin 1995: 112) as well as in many earlier traditions, Nirañjan is the first step of shaped self-formation that emerges from the formless Divine before creation. Cf. Dasgupta (1976: 312, 314); Roy (1983: 116).

18 Cf. Ramesh Shil *ND* No.3, 33; *SD* No.3 (*nūrī caraṇ*); *ĀM* No.9 (*nūrer putulā*), 18; Farid Hosain *HB* No.15, 25; Abdul Gafur Hali *TB* No.36; *JJ* No.4 (*nūr badan*), 34 (creation from *nūr*), 56 (*nūrer putulā*); Shafiul Bashar *YB* No.3 (*nūr* = Allah), 8 (*nūrer putulī*), 15, 39, 40 (*nūrī mayʾnā*); Lutfunnesa Hosaini *GP* No.34 (*nūrī caraṇ)*; Mahbubul Alam *AJ* No.1, 9; Aliullah *PN* No.90, etc.

19 This is backed by the quotation of a *Ḥadīṯ* of Ǧabr.

Photo 4 Prophet Muhammad's and Saint Abdul Qadir Gilani's footprints in the Qadam Mubarak Mosque, Anderkilla, Chittagong.

From the last part, again divided into four, emerged the sky, the earth as well as heaven and hell; the last part was after another division used for the light of the eyes of the believers, the light of their hearts, and the light of *tawḥīd* and the *kalima* (p. 21).[20]

With reference to a certain Qur'anic commentary given as *Tafsīr-i rūḥ al-kitāb*, Lutfunnesa Hosaini opens up yet another line of argumentation. The *nūr-i muḥammadī* also served for the creation of the *nūr* of Adam, which was stored in his back. When the angels assembled behind Adam to behold the light, Adam asked the Lord to transfer it to his forehead, upon which the angels lined up in front of him. Desiring to see the light himself, Adam again asked the Lord to transfer it, and it was put onto his index finger, along with the remaining light of the *pāk pāñcātan*, the 'Holy Five',[21] on his other fingers (p. 22 f.). When Adam descended upon the earth, lights again entered his back (p. 23). From him, in due course, the *nūr* was passed on through various male backs and female wombs (*peṭ*) up to 'Abd-Allah and Amina and their son, Prophet Muhammad (p. 23 f.).[22]

20 The above-mentioned *Kitāb aḥwāl al-qiyāma* gives a more elaborate description which is similar, but not identical to Lutfunnesa Hosaini's depiction (cf. Wolff 1872: 1–8).

21 i.e., Prophet Muhammad, A'isha, 'Ali, Hasan and Husain.

22 Cf. the description in the *Bīthikā* of Shamsujjuha of Thakurgaon (Siegfried 2001: 96), where progeny are sent from the male spinal cord.

At this point, the specific discussion of *nūr* ends, but it may be inferred that the *nūr* passes on to the saints and is fully exposed in their most prominent representatives; Lutfunnesa mentions ʿAbd al-Qadir Gilani, Muʿin al-Din Chishti, Ahmadullah Maijbhandari and Gholam Rahman Maijbhandari.

Noteworthy about this account is that there are few traces of the personified concept of *nūr*. The bases for Lutfunnesa Hosaini's representation are different *Ḥadīṯ*s. She does not attempt to harmonise these somewhat contradictory accounts, but simply compiles them. This is an apt demonstration that even rather traditional Maijbhandari theological constructs cannot right away be understood as a continuation of pre-modern esoteric doctrines. A *jāri gān* by Farid Hosain has a cosmology that closely ressembles the present one: *nūr* is divided in order to form the pen, book of destinies and throne in a first step, and then the angels, sky, earth, souls, heaven, hell, *kalima*, mountains, rivers, beings, animals, corn, creepers, fish, food, *ẓāhir*, *bāṭin*, *ğinn* as well as man, the best among the beings in whom Allah takes His secret residence.[23] This may be read as an evidence that the cosmology Lutfunnesa Hosaini reports has some currency in Maijbhandar.

Gholam Morshed, in his *Islāmī prabandha sambhār* (*IP*), has a separate essay on 'The development of the *Nūr-i muḥammadī*' (*Nūre mohāmmadī (sa.) er bikāś*). The *nūr-i muḥammadī*, according to this exposition, is the moving force behind the whole creation and is not to be conceived as separate from the Prophet:

> At the background [*antarāl*] of the creation, His [Muhammad's] *nūr*, the *nūr-i muḥammadī*, is at play [*līlārata*] as the life-breath of the creation. This is the highest secret of the play of creation, full of science [*bijñānmaẏ*]. Therefore Muhammad is not any special person, nor confined to any specific country, race [*jāti*] or by any border. In the form of *nūr-i muḥammadī*, He is qualified [*guṇānvita*] by the same quality as Allah.
>
> (*IP*: 155)

Muhammad thus cannot be said to have attained prophethood at the age of forty; He had been a Prophet ever since the beginning of Creation.[24] And since there is no direct relationship [*pratyakṣa samparka*] between the Creator and His Creation, Muhammad, understood as both the person of the Prophet and His *nūr*, is the means of contact between them (*IP*: 155). Allah and Muhammad are two forms of one *nūr*; Allah is its concealed (*bāṭin*) form, Muhammad the manifest (*ẓāhir*) form, and Allah has manifested himself in the *nūr-i muḥammadī*.[25] Thus, Morshed concludes, 'it is the development of the *nūr-i muḥammadī* which really

23 Farid Hosain *HB* No.36, couplets 6–8.

24 Cf. also *IP*: 201: The Prophet 'is a Prophet from birth [*ājanma*], that is, even if He received formal prophethood at the age of forty, basically He was a prophet ever since the beginning of Creation.'

25 For this reason, Muhammad is divine and not human. Cf. also a recent Bengali treatise from Dhaka on the *nūr-i muḥammadī* in which it is explicitly stated that a prophet cannot be wrong in whatever trifling matter because of his divine nature (Majidī 1998: 71 ff.).

is the development of Allah' (*IP*: 156). But even if the *nūr-i muḥammadī* is the foundation of everything, only man is able to see it if he manages to erase his 'I-ness' (*IP*: 158). The *nūr-i muḥammadī* is in a dormant state in man, and it is through self-control and 'synthesis of the mind' (*maner samanvaẏ*) that he can succeed in removing the 'veil of duality'[26] and behold the *nūr* (*IP*: 160).

Delawar Hosain, in the theoretical opening of his hagiography of Ahmadullah (*JK [b]*), and after summarily stating the role of *nūr-i muḥammadī* as the first step in creation (*JK [a]*: 7), presents a different theory connected with *nūr*. Without giving any primary references,[27] he reports a conversation in which the Prophet relates to Abdul Mutalib that on his travels to Mecca, the light emerging from his back had the habit of splitting into two parts: one part of it illuminated Arabia, the other partly served to give him shadow and partly went off into the direction of far-away Asia.[28] By conjecture with an unspecified prophesy of Ibn ʿArabi, Delawar Hosain states that the 'sun of the Prophet which had set in Arabia would again rise in the Eastern region of Asia' (*JK [a]*: 15), and that this 'sunrise' had to be equated with the rise of Ahmadullah as a saint.[29] This argument, of course, is an isolated cross-reference serving to substantiate the prime position of Saint Ahmadullah. It defies the idea of gradually passing down the *nūr* through the generations that Lutfunnesa Hosaini elaborates, but no attempts are made to integrate it into any existing theory of *nūr*.

3.3 Stations (*maqāmāt*)

The notion of certain 'stations' (*maqāmāt*)[30] on the Sufic spiritual path is old. The first classical formulation is found in the Egyptian mystic Du al-Nun al-Misri's (Ḏu al-Nūn al-Miṣrī) works, and according to Knysh (2000: 303), it may have emerged even earlier. Al-Sarraj (d. 988) lists seven ascending stations that denote ethical and spiritual states of a seeker after God, in his *Kitāb al-lumaʿ*, starting from the station of reverting towards the Divine (*tawba*) and ending in the station of satisfaction.[31] Al-Qushayri mentions the concept in a short chapter of his *Risāla* (written before 1043) and characterises a *maqām* as a metaphorical place an adept acquires through his strivings and leaves only after having mastered it completely.[32] Ghazzali (d. 1111) takes up al-Sarraj's ascending order of

26 *duiẏer pardā*, lit. 'veil of two'.
27 His remarks rely on a work mentioned as *Maulude dil-parji* (*JK [a]*: 15).
28 The basis of this is probably a *Ḥadīṯ*, but I could not find the reference.
29 Delawar Hosain seems to refer to the prophesy in Ibn ʿArabi's *Fuṣūṣ al-hikam*, chapter 2,5 (Ibn Arabī 1997: 89 f.); cf. below in the section on *wilāya* in this chapter.
30 From Ar. *maqām*, lit. 'house', 'dwelling place', but also 'situation', 'position', 'holy place', etc. Richard Gramlich (1989) translates it as *Standplatz*, 'standing place'. In order to distinguish *maqām* from other types of levels and stages, I will stick to the somewhat uncommon 'station' as its translation.
31 Cf. al-Sarrāǧ's *Kitāb al-lumaʿ* (Richard Gramlich 1990: 87–101).
32 Cf. al-Qušayrī's *Risāla* (Richard Gramlich 1989: 109).

maqāmāt[33] and makes it the basis of chapters 31–36 of his *Iḥyā ʿulūm al-dīn*. It is equally taught briefly in ʿUmar al-Suhrawardi's *ʿAwārif al-maʿārif*.[34]

This prominent concept is also found in Bengali Sufic writings, but with significant changes that seem to be found in other parts of South Asia as well. From medieval times until the present, the category of *maqāmāt* is most commonly employed to denote no longer the stations of the seeker relative to God, but the different spheres of life, the *nāsūt* (earthly life), *malakūt* (realm of angels), *ǧabarūt* (realm of spirits and prophets) and *lāhūt* (abode of the divine) spheres, and besides *maqāmāt* they may also be referred to as *manāzil* ('abodes'). To these are usually assigned the four stages of religious life, namely *šarīʿa*, *ṭarīqa*, *maʿrifa* and *ḥaqīqa*,[35] that are to be completed by the adept or 'wayfarer' (*sālik*) on his way to ultimate union with God; the last two of these stages may also appear in interchangeable order.[36] Asim Roy discusses two medieval Bengali works on this topic, Abd al-Hakim's *Cāri makām bhed* ('The piercing of the four *maqāmāt*') and Sayyad Murtaja's *Yog kālandar*.[37] In these texts, the stations are characterised by certain predispositions and practices of the seeker and by specific apparitions. Sayyad Murtaja describes the *nāsūt maqām* as follows: It is situated at the sacrum, guarded by ʿIzrāʾīl and characterised by fire; the *mūlādhāra* is its *cakra*, the single soul (*jīvātman*) is its presiding deity, and the *kalima* is recited in it. There is a black lotus and summer in it. Then practices are described: the fire of *nāsūt maqām* should be controlled by contraction of the anus, and its light should be beheld in meditation. The signs of imminent death lead over to a depiction of *malakūt*.[38] The way in which different objects and processes are assigned to distinct parts of the body clearly stems from Tantricism, whose descriptions of the inner topography of the human body proceed in the same way and prescribe or predict corresponding visualisations during meditation.[39]

33 Cf. Ghazzali's *Iḥyā ʿulūm al-dīn* (partial translation by Richard Gramlich [1984: 351 f.]).

34 Cf. Chapter 59 (408–17) of Richard Gramlich (1978).

35 Cf. the medieval text *Jñān pradīp* (Saiẏad Sul'tān 1978: 575), in which *šarīʿa*, etc., are referred to as *manāzil* and *nāsūt*, etc., as *maqāmāt*. Hafiz Md. Tahir Ali (1989: 145) reports the same identification of *maqāmāt*, with *ṭarīqa* as *malakūt*, for the Gujerati saint Prannath (seventeenth century). Enāmul Hak (1995: 97 ff.) gives these correspondences in a matter-of-fact way in his exposition of the *maqāmāt*.

36 Cf. Asim Roy (1983: 170) (reference to Hāji Muhammad's *Nur jamāl*); also the Maijbhandari author Abdul Ghani Kanchanpuri (*ĀB*: 495). Delawar Hosain, in a short treatise, gives the more conventional order of *šarīʿa*, *ṭarīqa*, *maʿrifa* and *ḥaqīqa* and translates the latter two as 'self-acquaintance' (*nija paricaẏ*) and 'genuine knowledge' (*prakr̥ta jñān*) respectively (*MT*: [2] [my pagination]). In *Belāẏate mot'lākā*, however, he mentions them in the reverse order (*BM*: 132).

37 This title does not figure in Asim Roy's text; it is given in a translation of this work by Enamul Hak (1995: 378–96).

38 Cf. *Yoga Kālandar* in Enamul Hak (1995: 378 ff.).

39 Cf., e.g., Eliade (1985: 215 ff.). See also the remarks on the *maqāmāt* in Baul songs, where they are sometimes equated with *cakra*s, in Rahul Peter Das (1992: 402).

In Maijbhandari writings, the *maqāmāt* do not appear to be especially elaborated, but form an integral part of the ideas underlying the conceptualisation of the spiritual path. Abdul Ghani Kanchanpuri treats this topic most extensively. In *Ā'īna-i Bārī*, he mentions certain *maqāmāt* in different contexts. We first find one distinction between three *maqāmāt* that can be reached by the faithful: the *sayr ʿalā Allāh*, 'journey [on the path] of God' and said to correspond to *fanā'*; the *sayr fī Allāh* or 'journey in God', corresponding to *baqā'*; and the *sayr min Allāh*, 'journey away from God' (*ĀB*: 64). Elsewhere, Abdul Ghani uses the term *maqām* synonymously with *darğa* ('grade') and stresses that 'the grades of the perfect (*kamāl*) have neither limit nor beginning and end' (*ĀB*: 323). In a separate chapter on *maqāmāt* (*ĀB*: 356–63), then, he lists six stations that correspond to the gradual emanation and differentiation of the divine, lending this scheme aspects of a cosmology. *Hāhūt* is described as the original and highest state: 'In this *maqām*, He [God] has neither name nor qualities [*ṣifat*]; this rank [*murtaba*] is called the rank of *aḥadiyya* ['unity']' (*ĀB*: 359). It is from *hāhūt* that the emanations (*tağalliyāt*) start and that Allah, falling in love with his own sight, produced His attributes. In the second *maqām* of *bāhūt*, the divine has developed and realised its own essence, *ḏāt*, and attributes, *ṣifāt*. The third (*lāhūt*), is characterised by the knowledge of the souls. In further descending order, the *maqām* of *ğabarūt* corresponds to the *ʿālam-i miṯāl* or world of dreams;[40] that of *malakūt* is the *ʿālam-i ağsām* or world of bodies; and finally that of *nāsūt* is the *ʿālam-i insān* or world of men. The latter means humiliation, because it is a product of a long chain of emanations; but is is blessed by many revelations (*tanzīlāt*), and even if the perfect truth cannot be had in this *maqām*, it is nevertheless present in it (*ĀB*: 362 ff.). A few pages onwards, the most familiar four among these six *maqāmāt* are mentioned in isolation (with *nāsūt* featuring as *mulk*, lit. 'kingdom, country', here: earth) and reverse order: the four *maqāmāt* of *mulk*, *malakūt*, *ğabarūt* and *lāhūt* are characterised by increasing beauty and knowledge, and all the things present in one of these *maqāmāt* are known in the next higher one (*ĀB*: 368). The term *maqām*, in Abdul Ghani's usage, is not necessarily connected with the spiritual stations at all, since in the course of his discussion of music and *samāʿ*, he uses it to classify twelve different musical modes (*ĀB*: 461).

The most comprehensive depiction of the *maqāmāt* (in the sense of spiritual stations) in *Ā'īna-i bārī* is organised in a separate chapter called 'About the seven *maqāmāt* in the wayfaring [*sulūk*]' (pp. 644–58). Abdul Ghani first defines the *ḥāl* as a passing emotional state manifesting itself in the heart and the *maqām* as its steady habitude. The seven *maqāmāt* he then depicts are admittedly taken from six chapters of Rūmī's *Maṯnavī*. The first of these is the *maqām-i ṭalab*, 'station of search': the *ṭālib* or seeker cultivates hope and becomes resistant against adversities of fate as he constantly seeks his friend (*yār*) (*ĀB*: 644). The first and foremost duty of the *ṭālib* is to remain steadfast in this search and suffer any humiliation that comes his way in the course of it. He should consider himself condemned to

40 Introduced by Ibn ʿArabi, acc. to Schimmel (1995: 382).

this role just like the fallen angel Iblīs, and follow the example of Mağnūn who combed the dust in search of Layla (*ĀB*: 645–9). The second *maqām* is the *maqām-i ʿišq*, the station of love; the *sālik*, 'mystic' or 'wayfarer' of this *maqām* is drowned in the sea of love and does not care for the world. He is unconscious of the differences between blasphemy (*kufr*) and religion (*dīn*) or between good and bad, and before union he is like a fish without water. This *maqām* destroys the intellect of the intelligent (*ĀB*: 651). All is full of the wine of love, and the *sālik* has to realise that Allah is love. This *maqām* is so forceful that one may indeed lose one's life in it (*ĀB*: 652). The third is the *maqām-i maʿrifa*, the 'station of gnosis'. The sea of gnosis is described as unfathomable. There are many kinds of *ʿirfān*, mystical knowledge, and no state is as huge as the state of gnosis (*daulat-i maʿrifa*) (*ĀB*: 652 f.). The confusing secrets hit the heart and direct the *sālik* towards his beloved (*maʿšūq*). Fourthly, Abdul Ghani lists the *maqām-i istiġnāʾ*, the station of self-sufficiency; the *sālik* renounces the world and sees all things, whether huge or small, as equal (*ĀB*: 654 f.). In the fifth 'station of unity' (*maqām-i tawḥīd*), the 'colour of duality' is absent; 'the whole world sticks out its head through one collar'.[41] The *kalima*, the Islamic confession of faith, is manifest in this *maqām*, and as long as *tawḥīd* is absent, the other four pillars of Islam are useless; *tawḥīd* is the very soul of all worship (*ĀB*: 656). Another station is that of 'confusion' (*ḥaira*), characterised by pain, sorrow, weeping and burning. Everything is perceived as wounding; the *sālik*, though seeing and hearing everything, cannot perceive anything. A capable *pīr* may help him to leave this *maqām* (*ĀB*: 656 f.). Finally, the seventh *maqām-i fuqr wa fanāʾ* ('station of poverty and annihilation') is described: its dominant features are the absence of speech, muteness, oblivion and unconsciousness (*ĀB*: 657). Everything is perceived as a sea; the *sālik* takes on the attributes (*ṣifāt*) of the sea and is no longer aware of his own condition. In this *maqām* the *sālik* is no longer bound to the general religious duties such as the ritual prayer (*namāz*) (*ĀB*: 697).[42]

The divergent classifications of *maqāmāt* in *Āʾīna-i bārī* are an indication that the term *maqām* is not precisely used as a technical term throughout; its literal sense of 'station', 'abode', seems to be very present, and thus *maqām* is applicable to different theories as to what the stations of the aspirant to spiritual perfection are.

In later Maijbhandari writings, the *maqāmāt* seem to be a minor concern. When mentioned, they are often straightaway equated with the four religious spheres of *šarīʿa*, *ṭarīqa*, etc., which Abdul Jabbar Mimnagari also calls 'steps' (Bg. *sopān*) or 'levels' (Bg. *star*) (*ĀH*: 137). Of these four, only three (*šarīʿa*, *ṭarīqa*, *maʿrifa*) are discussed in detail; *ḥaqīqa* plays almost no role. One author, Mujibur Rahman in his *Nurer jhalak*, goes so far as to entirely leave out *ḥaqīqa* and devote a small chapter to the remaining three only (*NJ*: 25–7). The determination of the role of these spheres is closely connected with the fundamental distinction between *ẓāhir* and *bāṭin* and will be taken up in the following section.

41 *tamām ʿālam ek hī gariyān sē sir nikāltā hai* (*ĀB*: 656).

42 For a general account of *fanāʾ*, cf. the repeated references in ʿAbd al-Qādir al-Jīlānī (1992).

3.4 Manifest (*ẓāhir*) and concealed (*bāṭin*), *šarīʿa* and *ṭarīqa*

The terms *ẓāhir* ('manifest', 'outer') and *bāṭin* ('non-manifest', 'inner', 'concealed') are crucial to Sufi thinking in general. They appear in the *Qurʾān* several times, refering to the realms governed by Allah, and have been used as constitutive argumentative tools by many Sufi authors. Maijbhandari authors also make wide use of these terms, and Bengalified forms like *jāhirī*/*jāherī* and *bātinī*/*bātenī* are not uncommon even in general, colloquial religious discourse (and, for that matter, in Maijbhandari songs). Basically, *ẓāhir* and *bāṭin*, when applied to religious texts, practices and so on, open up a realm of interpreting, metaphor-building and contextualisation that certainly has been codified to a large extent in Sufic thought but in principle remains vital to this day. In a way this very distinction is constitutive of Sufism itself, as the transmission of 'hidden' knowledge from Muhammad via ʿAli through the various *silsila*s lies at its root.

A beautiful general description of two kinds of knowledge, the *ʿilm-i ẓāhir* and the *ʿilm-i bāṭin*, is found in *Āʾīna-i bārī*, in the form of an Urdu poem, which I want to quote here in some length as an exposition of this topic:

> Knowledge [*ʿilm*] is of two kinds, O brother/One is *bāṭin*, the other is the *ʿilm-i ẓāhir* // The *ʿilm-i bāṭin* has become the friend of the soul [*ğān*]/From which the path has certainly been established in divine truth [*Haqq*] // [But] do not give up the *ẓāhir ʿilm*/Because it is also a friend of that path of yours // These two knowledges are connected with one another/These two are like soul and body // . . . If you do not have these two knowledges/You are a loser of faith in the two worlds // He who has the *ẓāhir* and not the *bāṭin*/Where does he have the divine truth of faith [*haqq al-yaqīṇ*]? // He who has the *bāṭin* and not the *ẓāhir*/That [person's] religion [*dīn*] is not adorned // Just as the manifest brain is the skin of the hidden motive/Just so is the *ʿilm-i ẓāhir* the friend of the *ʿilm-i bāṭin* // . . . The food of your soul [*rūḥ*] is the *bāṭinī ʿilm*/ The food of your *nafs* is the *ẓāhirī ʿilm* // [etc.].[43]

The terms *ẓāhir* and *bāṭin* denote complementary aspects of reality. Applied to the religious spheres, as they usually are, they stand for the *šarīʿa* on the one hand, and the *ṭarīqa* or *maʿrifa* respectively on the other (*ĀB*: 520, 523). Just as it is one's duty to fulfil the prescriptions of the *Islām-i ẓāhir* or *šarīʿa* and *fiqh* and learn everything pertaining to these from the *ʿulamā-i ẓāhir*, likewise it is necessary that one acquires knowledge of the *Islām-i bāṭin*, *ṭarīqa* and *ṭasawwuf* (Sufism) from the *ʿulamā-i bāṭin*. Both *ẓāhir* and *bāṭin* are necessary components of Islam and of the Muslims (*ĀB*: 523).

Abdul Ghani Kanchanpuri's position in these matters is *bāšarʿ*,that is, in favour of the dual exigencies of exoteric and esoteric kinds of religious practice. In a separate chapter on *šarīʿa* and *maʿrifa*, Islam is defined as 'everything that the Prophet

43 *ĀB*: 59; *yāham* in *yah dōnōṇ mis̱l ğān wa tan haiṇ yāham* is unclear and has been left untranslated.

has brought from the holy *darbār* of God' [*ĀB*: 684], and the message of that one God that 140,000 prophets have spread in their respective regions; all these 'religions'[44] are held together by the unity (*tawḥīd*) expressed in the Islamic confession of faith. This unity has two sides: *ẓāhir* and *bāṭin*. These two aspects of Islam are also paraphrased as *ǧasdānī* ('bodily') and *rūḥānī* ('pertaining to the soul'), and they are again and again referred to as body (or flesh, as in *ĀB*: 689) and heart.[45] The first is senseless without the latter, but the latter also should not go without the former. The *ẓāhir* Islam is the protector of *bāṭin* Islam; in order to master these, man is invested with two kinds of talents, one being the capability to read the scriptures and fulfil his religious duties, the other (*aḥsān*, 'grace') to fill his heart with love of the divine and attain the sight of God (*ĀB*: 687 f.). The Qur'anic injunction to search for the knowledge that makes one a true Muslim[46] applies to both *ẓāhir* and *bāṭin* Islam, whether from thick books or from listening to the knowers of God (*ĀB*: 692). Like the former, where, for example, the rich have to give alms to the poor, the latter also has different rules for different people, and where the *nafs* is still strong, the path has to be trodden step by step; the searcher for *bāṭin* knowledge struggles away like a swimmer in the sea (*ĀB*: 695). After dealing with this path in a detailed fashion, Abdul Ghani Kanchanpuri concludes his discussion by stating that *šarī'a* and *ṭarīqa* ultimately form a unity (*ĀB*: 708).

This *bāšar'* position is typical for the later Maijbhandari authors as well.[47] The viewpoint to be established being that of *bāṭin*, however, an exoteric position often incurs their wrath for its exclusiveness;[48] the basic contention is that both belong together, and to ignore either of them is unlawful. It is furthermore true that the relationship between *šarī'a* and *ṭarīqa* is often likened to that between form and content, and while a form without a content is seen as completely senseless, content without a form may under certain circumstances be permissible.[49] So, despite the nominal unity of *ẓāhir* and *bāṭin* aspects in religious practice, the notion of an ascension from, e.g. the *šarī'a* to the *ṭarīqa* and so forth, is usually present, and there is thus a certain tacit hierarchy among these aspects, with *bāṭin*/*ṭarīqa* aspects ranging higher.[50]

The treatise by Abdul Jabbar Mimnagari is a case in point. The author discusses *ẓāhir* and *bāṭin* in connection with divine love and points out the limitations of the

44 Abdul Ghani actually uses the plural *adyān* here [*ĀB*: 685].

45 Cf. also, however, a different constellation in a song by Aliullah, the terms being *šarī'a* as the *'ilm-i ẓāhir* and *ṭarīqa* as the *'ilm-i bāṭin* (cf. below in this section): *śariẏat(a) posta jāna, gosta jāna tarikā* ('Know the *šarī'a* [as] the skin, know the *ṭarīqa* as the flesh'). *PN* No.99, p. 90.

46 A *Ḥadīṯ* from Ibn Maja [Māǧa]: *ṭalab al-'ilm farīḍa 'alā kull muslim wa muslima*.

47 Like Abdussalam Isapuri (*FR*: 3), who applies it to the interpretation of the *Qur'ān*: it can be interpreted in *ẓāhir* and *bāṭin* modes on seven distinct levels (*šarī'a*, *ṭarīqa*, *ḥaqīqa*, *ma'rifa*, *nubuwwa*, *risāla* and *wilāya*).

48 Cf. also *ĀB*: 49 ff. where Abul Ghani scolds the false *'ulamā'* who do not care for and even oppose esoteric knowledge.

49 Certain rules of the *šarī'a* do not apply once certain stages are reached; *ĀB*: 697 mentions that for a person who has attained the seventh *maqām*, the ritual prayer is not compulsory.

50 Cf. the preceding section on *maqāmāt*.

ahl-i ẓāhir when it comes to evaluating the state of a lover: they call such a person crazy (Bg. *pāgal*) because they restrict their discussions to the outer, manifest aspects.

> The object of discussion of the *ahl-i bāṭin* is spirituality,[51] by which they keep looking for the path for the attainment of closeness to Allah the Most Supreme. The original basis of both groups [*sampradāẏ*] is the *Qur'ān* and the *Ḥadīṯ*. The *ahl-i ẓāhir* accept the said *Qur'ān* and *Ḥadīṯ* in a manifest way as the path to liberation, and the *ahl-i bāṭin* search for the path to His closeness by diving into the sea of the connection [*saṃyog*] of Allah the Most Supreme's love[52] with the manifest. The question of liberation cannot arise here on behalf of the *ahl-i bāṭin*, as liberation is only the first level of the attainment of closeness. Regarding this topic there has been disagreement between the two above-mentioned groups for a lifetime [*ājīban kāl*] [up to this day].
>
> (*ĀH*: 20 f.)

As stated in the preceding section, the opposition between *ẓāhir* and *bāṭin* runs into the delimitations of the religious spheres: *šarīʿa* is equated with *ẓāhir* and either *ṭarīqa* or *maʿrifa* (or both) with *bāṭin*. Abdul Jabbar Mimnagari deals with both these oppositions. The relation of *šarīʿa* and *ṭarīqa*, is one of symbiosis, as he states illustratively in an Urdu quotation from a certain Maulana Akbar Ilahabadi that closely resembles Abdul Ghani Kanchanpuri's above characterisation of *ẓāhir* and *bāṭin*:

> Hear the secret from me in two words/The *šarīʿa* is the ritual washing, the *ṭarīqa* the ritual prayer/The *ṭarīqa* is the execution of the *šarīʿa*/The *ṭarīqa* is the perfection of worship/The *šarīʿa* is the food, the *ṭarīqa* is the medicine/ The *šarīʿa* is the garden, the *ṭarīqa* is the air.
>
> (*ĀH*: 80)

A few pages onwards, then, it is *maʿrifa* (very much like *ṭarīqa* before) which is portrayed as the path of love: a true Sufi, namely one rooted in *ṭarīqa* and *maʿrifa*, does not care for hell and heaven. The *šarīʿa* may hold out heaven as a reward and hell as a punishment, but in the sphere of *maʿrifa*, 'initiation into love' (Bg. *premer dīkṣā*) is the main thing. God can be experienced only if one is ready to 'dive into the bottomless water of *maʿrifa*' [*ĀH*: 114].

Syed Ahmadul Haq (2000), when setting out to discuss the Maijbhandari *ṭarīqa*, briefly characterises all four religious spheres (*šarīʿa*, *ṭarīqa*, *maʿrifa*, *ḥaqīqa*), but then narrows down the opposition to *šarīʿa* and *maʿrifa*. While none of the four can be omitted,

51 *rūhānīẏat bā ādhyātmikatā*. [*ĀH*: 20]

52 *eśk o mahabbat* [ibid.].

> [i]n another way, the *šarīʿa* may be compared to the outer cover of the paddy corn and the *maʿrifa* with the seed [*cāul*] that is inside it.[53] Even if the seed is the real or the essential thing of the paddy corn, the seed will not be born if the outer cover of the paddy corn does not enclose it.
>
> (Syed Ahmadul Huq 2000: 9)

If both are juxtaposed in seeming mutual dependence, the simile of cover and content nevertheless implies a certain hierarchy among them: the outer, exoteric is merely a sort of frame whereas the inner, esoteric represents the essence.

This is the usual Maijbhandari position with regard to exoteric and esoteric modes of religiosity. It comes out most clearly in a discussion by Gholam Morshed (*'Śariẏat o tarikat prasaṅge'*, *IP*: 197–216). He first compares the *šarīʿa* with the learning of the alphabet which, while being a necessary precondition to the acquisition of knowledge, does not contain every possible knowledge in itself:

> If somebody, after attending the first class in order to learn reading and writing learns the alphabet and then says that he has learnt whatever science [*elʾm*] of the world, nothing remains to be said.[54]
>
> (*IP*: 200)

But then Morshed takes up another kind of argument. Departing from the question whether the exoteric or the esoteric is to be seen as the root of Islam, he refers to the Prophet's life and argues that while Muhammad attained prophethood at the age of forty, it was only 13 years later that he promulgated the *šarīʿa* [*IP*: 201]. The meditations he used to practise in the meantime are countable among the practices connected with *ṭarīqa* and *maʿrifa*, and thus 'the birth place of the *šarīʿa* is the *maʿrifa* or *ṭarīqa*' [*IP*: 202]. To adhere exclusively to the *šarīʿa* means to neglect the attempt to come close to God, and the *ʿulamāʾ* who act thus, lie and mislead the Muslims. The story of Prophet Ḫiḏr's encounter with Moses (*Qurʾān* 18.65[64] ff.) is cited as Qurʾanic proof that esoteric knowledge is superior to the exoteric one [*IP*: 204 f.]. With reference to Sura 5,[55] Morshed establishes the existence of two different paths, one being the *šarīʿa* and the other, the *minhāǧ* (lit. also 'path'), being the *ṭarīqa* [*IP*: 206]. Followers of the *šarīʿa* perform their prayer five times a day, whereas *ṭarīqa* adepts practise the *ṣalāt al-dāʾimī* or 'constant prayer':

> Thus to remember Allah five times a day is *šarīʿa* and the remembrance or attempt to establish a relation every day or with every breath is called the

53 The distinction made here is that between *dhān*, the paddy plant on the field, and *cāl* (or dialect *cāul*), the processed rice – ready to be cooked and become *bhāt*, namely the rice served on the plate.

54 The example of primary and higher schools in order to differentiate between the different religious levels is very often used in oral explanations by adherents to the Maijbhandari movement.

55 *Qurʾān* 5.48(52) seems to be meant: 'We have a law and a path for each of you'.

> *ṣalāt al-dā'imī* or *ṭarīqa*. Consequently the readers may decide which path is [more] useful for attaining closeness to Allah.
>
> (*IP*: 206)

Qur'ān 70.23[56] is adduced in favour of such an interpretation; and the school metaphor is once again taken up in order to explain the legitimacy of certain cases in which the exoteric practice was relinquished in favour of the esoteric one. Once one has mastered the alphabet, Morshed's argument goes, it is not necessary to reiterate it like a parrot; it is so firmly established that there is no need for continuous 'rumination' (Bg. *romanthan*) anymore. In particular, saints on a high level of *ma'rifa* 'are sometimes so enmeshed in the love-relation with Allah that they do not remember the usual rules and regulations (Bg. *bidhi-bidhān*) of the *šarī'a*'. Morshed mentions Mansur al-Hallaj, Shamsher Tabrizi, Bu 'Ali Qalandar and others as examples of such a state, and complains about the *'ulamā'* bereft of *taṣawwuf*, Sufism, who persecuted them for this: 'It is because they cannot see it [i.e. the *ṣalāt al-dā'imī*, 'constant prayer'] with their outer eyes[57] that they keep levelling *fatwa*s [of being] infidels at all these great friends of God'(*IP*: 213).

3.5 Unity (*tawḥīd*)

The concept of *tawḥīd* is of very central importance to Maijbhandari theological thinking. *Tawḥīd* being conceived as a seminal term for characterising the Islamic faith as a whole, it is one of the main platforms chosen by Maijbhandari authors to argue for the Islamic credentials of the movement. It is often under this caption that the unitary mysticism of Sufism is related to the fundamentals of scriptural, Qur'anic Islam.

Tawḥīd is derived from the verb *waḥada*, 'being one' (root *w-ḥ-d*). It is intimately linked with the *kalima*, the Islamic confession of faith, which asserts God as being the one and only god; it is sometimes put forward as one of the five pillars of Islam. As a Sufi station (*maqām*), it is often more particularly the realisation of Allah's oneness as the conclusion of the mystical path (cf. Knysh 2000: 137, 303).

The *kalima*, Abdul Ghani Kanchanpuri (*ĀB*) states, is the main proof of God; as there is no duality here, there is no duality of dots (P./U. *nuqṭa*) in its written form,[58] and the positions of Allah and Muhammad are to be understood as identical [*ĀB*: 399]. The true meaning of the *kalima* is *waḥdat al-wuǧūd*, the 'unity of existence';[59] the common believers conceive of God as separate from the multiform world while forgetting that this multiformity is illusionary. Abdul Ghani describes this essential unity by referring to two animals whose blood merges in one if they are slaughtered on the same spot [*ĀB*: 401]. *Tawḥīd*, like *waḥdat*, is of two kinds: *ḏātan* ('essential') and *ṣifātan* ('by attributes'); the latter is also called

56 'Those constant/remaining [*dā'imūn*] in prayer'.
57 Bg. *carma cokh*, lit. 'skin-eye', 'eye of the skin'.
58 The origin of this idea is unknown to me.
59 The famous concept first developed by Ibn 'Arabi; for some introductory remarks about this concept, cf. Schimmel (1995: 379 f.).

tawḥīd-i asānī ('easy unity') and is attained either by imitation or by using one's intellect and texts. The former is also called *tawḥīd-i rabbānī* ('divine unity') or *tawḥīd-i ʿaiyānī* ('visual unity') and means the complete immersion in God, that is, a state of the believer in which there is nothing but God for him;[60] and 'this *tawḥīd-i rabbānī* is the truth [*ḥaqīqat*] of the religion of Islam' (*ĀB*: 388). *Tawḥīd* is covered by three veils – possession (*māl*), children (*walad*) and the body (*badan*), and Abraham's sacrifice is quoted as a test of whether the veil of parental love had been removed from his *tawḥīd.*

Apart from this twofold distinction, another scheme of subclassification is proposed according to which *tawḥīd* can appear on four levels (*murātab*) in an ascending order roughly equivalent to the religious spheres. The first level of *tauḥīd-i imān* is reached by studying the scriptures and profiting from the manifest sciences (*ʿilm-i ẓāhir*) (*ĀB*: 391). The second (*tauḥīd-i ʿilmī*) is apparently acquired by the 'hidden science' (*ʿilm-i bāṭin*) related to *ṭarīqa.* The remaining two are rather experiential than cognitive modes. *Tauḥīd-i ḥālī* is in itself twofold, one part being that of the *ʿulamā-i wuǧūdī* (characterised by a state in which nothing but Allah exists and the world is forgotten),[61] and the other that of the *ʿulamā-i šuhūdī* (in which the world is perceived as a mere shadow) (*ĀB*: 393 f.). *Tauḥīd-i ilahī,* finally, refers to an experience in which one completely merges with the essence (*ḏāt*) of Allah (*ĀB*: 395).

In the end of his book, Abdul Ghani glorifies *tawḥīd* in a way that seems to foreshadow the concept of *tauḥīd-i adyān* developed by Delawar Hosain (and treated hereafter). With reference to a *tafsīr* by Ibn ʿArabi, he stresses that all the 140,000 prophets preceding Muhammad had brought the *kalima* to their respective peoples, and it was this central message that unified their religions (*adyān*). All these religions were Islam; whatever their minor differences, all had *tawḥīd* at their base. The glory of *tawḥīd* brought light to the world, as all the texts, religions, peoples and writers testify (*ĀB*: 685 f.). Insofar as this argument refers to the line of prophets, it is clear that the Jewish and Christian religions are hereby subsumed under the label of Islam. When he writes of 'all religions' (*ǧamīʿ adyān*) as bearing this message of the *kalima*, one may even tend to go further and understand this as an inclusivistic move, also to include, for instance, Hindu and Buddhist religions; but there is no way of being certain. It is left to Delawar Hosain to draw out this point explicitly.

In his *Belāyate motʾlākā*, Delawar Hosain elaborates the concept of *tauḥīd-i adyān* so as to refer to all religions. He apparently takes the idea from a secondary source, the Urdu translation of an Egyptian work on Sufism.[62] Bu ʿAli Qalandar is cited as a follower of what Delawar Hosain calls the *maḏhab* of *tauḥīd-i adyān*, and also Ibn ʿArabi, Jalal al-Din Rumi, ʿAbd al-Qadir Gilani, Bayezid Bistami and others are mentioned as connected with this doctrine (Bg. *matabād*) (*BM*: 3). *Tauḥīd-i adyān* is characterised in the following way:

60 A state equivalent to *fanāʾ* [*ĀB*: 391].

61 iconstantly remaining in the thought of *hama ūst* ('All is He').

62 Given as *Tāchāẏophe isʾlām* by Dr Muhāmmad Mostaphā Helʾmī, Professor of the Fuwad (*Fuʾād*) University, Qairo, Urdu translation by Raīch Āhʾmad Jāpharī, Lahore: Golām Ālī and Sons.

> It is true that all the religions that exist, even if they are different according to the circumstances, are basically unseparated [Bg. *abhinna*]. Although one may not be uniform to the other in its expression,[63] this is [merely] an outer [appearance], [because] that which is called religion [Bg. *dharma*], that entity of religion [Bg. *dharmabastu*] is unseparated and one, since the goal of all religions is God, even if separate groups are connected with separate religions. This has originated from Allah's power of volition.
>
> (*BM*: 3)

Tauḥīd-i adyān is translated into Bengali as *dharma aikya, aikya* carrying no specific connotations of mystical union but simply being the general term for 'unity', 'oneness'. Delawar thus does not use the term *tawḥīd* as the experiential category it used to be for some of the early Sufi writers who posited it as the highest *maqām*, but in a generalised, and in a way secularised meaning. This is also true of another Bengali rendering Delawar Hosain proposes elsewhere in his book, *dharmasāmya*, 'equality of religions' [*BM*: 62]. As Qur'anic proof for this doctrine, he quotes *Qur'ān* 2.62(59) that anyone who believes in Allah, including the Jews and Christians, is entitled to reward. He also adduces a passage from *Qur'ān* 2.85(79), translating it as 'Do you believe in some book of the Lord and disbelieve some book?' Allah being one, this argument goes, all religious books are a part of His revelation, and consequently all religions contain some of His truth. Similarly, *Qur'ān* 2.111(105)–112(106) are adduced as a denial of exclusive claims to heaven on the part of one specific group, and as proof for the acceptability of anyone who turns his face towards Allah (understood as the One God, not as the exclusive God of the Muslims), as being worthy to receive gratifications.

> The trust [Bg. *āmānat*, from Ar. <*amāna*>] Allah the most supreme has bestowed upon mankind is *ma'rifa* and *tawḥīd*, thus everybody irrespective of religion and caste/class [Bg. *dharmma jāti nirbbiśeṣe*] bears the burden of this trust of *tawḥīd* and *ma'rifa*. If he does not repay it the trust of Allah the Most Supreme will be betrayed [*kheẏānat* (Ar. <*ḫiyāna*>) *haïbe*].
>
> (*BM*: 61)

In this passage, *tawḥīd* is used not in the technical sense outlined before, but as referring to the fundamental unity of Allah. Paraphrasing Delawar Hosain's line of thought, we might state that since there is no Divine except Allah, any manifestations of the Divine under whichever garb must necessarily pertain to Him; He is the Divine point of reference for any religion, as anything worthy of this name is defined by its search for this Divine. Thus anyone attaining true knowledge, *ma'rifa*, realises the unity of God and consequently also of the various attempts of attaining God, namely the different religions.

63 The original has *abhibyaktite ek'ṭi apar'ṭir anurūp haïleo*, which is apparently a misprint and should read . . . *nā haïleo* since the opposition to the following would otherwise make no sense. My translation follows what I think is the correct version.

This pattern of argument is inclusivist and familiar from many strands of Hinduism and particularly modern Hinduism.[64] Insofar as it relies on the *Qurʾān*, it ignores the scholastic distinction made between the *ahl al-kitāb*, 'people of the book' (usually interpreted as applying to the Jews and Christians), and the category of *kāfir*; the Qurʾanic dictum with regard to these predecessors to the Islamic faith is taken out of its specific context and generalised so as to apply to all religions. In connection with the concept of *vilāyat-i muṭlaka*, this inclusivist move serves to establish the general importance of the Maijbhandari saints, and first and foremost Ahmadullah, as we shall see in the following section.

Before proceeding, however, a third treatise deserves mention, especially as it discusses the concept of *tawḥīd* in close connection with specifically Sufic institutions of religious authority. Lutfunnesa Hosaini's book *Tāohīd* has a separate chapter (bearing again the title *Tāuhīd* [*sic*], pp. 1–18) on this topic. Lutfunnesa Hosaini translates *tawḥīd* as 'unitarianism' (Bg. *ekatvabād*; *Tāohīd*: 1), and in her introduction she explains *tawḥīd* in the following way:

> From the time the *murīd* undergoes initiation [Bg. *bāẏāt*, from Ar. <*bayʿa*>] by his *pīr*, he has to obey the instructions of the *pīr*, because *tawḥīd* means that in him by whom I have become initiated all qualities are present, and to conceive thus is a main part of faith [*īmān*].
>
> (*Tāohīd*: (3))

Such a statement requires some derivations that Lutfunnesa furnishes in a somewhat scattered manner during the following. *Tawḥīd* is the main basis [Bg. *mūl'bhitti*] of the Islamic faith; all its teachings, rituals and festivities are founded on it (*Tāohīd*: 1). *Qurʾān* 21.22 and 18.110 are quoted as assertions of this unity. This one God resides in His creation, and it is 'the essential message of *tawḥīd*' that despite His formlessness He is present everywhere (p. 3). He is at the root of the creation of everything, and it is to Him that everything returns (p. 9). The first and foremost example of living according to the principle of *tawḥīd* (which is to be read as coterminous with Islam here) is Prophet Muhammad, and to approach Him means approaching Allah (pp. 4, 13). Since the saints and *muršid*s are connected to Muhammad by the chain of spiritual transmission, Lutfunnesa Hosaini seems to argue, their status is equal to His in the sense that 'remembering them is basically remembering Allah. Committing oneself to remembering them is in no way [identical with] turning away from remembering Allah' (p. 12).[65]

64 I have dealt with this topic extensively earlier (Harder 2001). One may go so far as to say that the inclusivist assimilation of other faiths and the claim to superiority on the basis of the 'tolerance' necessary for such an assimilation has since the nineteenth century become a distinctive character trait of modern Hindu modes of thought. The term 'inclusivism' was to my knowledge first established in this particular sense by the Indologist Paul Hacker; cf. his articles (Hacker 1978 [1970] and 1978 [1971]).

65 *ihāder smaran* [sic] *mūlata āllāh'r smaran* [*sic*]. *ihāder smaraṇāpanna haoẏā kakhan'o āllāh·r smaran* [*sic*] *hate bimukh haoẏā nahe*.

What seems to happen here is a reversal of the initial argument that God is one and indivisible (Bg. *akhaṇḍa*). Like Delawar Hosain, Lutfunnesa Hosaini tends not to draw her conclusions too far,[66] but a summarising paraphrasis of her arguments would have it that Allah being all-pervasive, He must be understood as being particularly present in holy personalities; and since the concept of *tawḥīd* demands that He should never be fragmented, this presence can only be a complete one.

This argument, running in one form or the other through almost all Maijbhandari writings, is typical of Sufism in general, and almost unavoidable if it be accepted that God is not to be conceived as separate from the world. At the same time, it is the point where 'orthodox' and Sufic conceptions of *tawḥīd* clash most violently. If Allah is thought as distinct from the creation, as most 'orthodox' positions would have it, it must indeed appear that attributing any kind of divine quality to saints, etc. amounts to *širk*, 'polytheism'. But precisely the premise to this argument, namely the distinctness of God and world, is brandished as a false conception of duality, and thus a crime against *tawḥīd* and an example of *širk*, by Sufis.[67]

To sum up, *tawḥīd* is understood in various ways in the Maijbhandari writings discussed above. In accordance with Sufic thought in general, *tawḥīd* is most fundamentally interpreted as the assertion of the ultimate unity and all-pervasiveness of God. Basically a cognitive category, *tawḥīd* is also conceived as a state to be attained and experienced.[68] A peculiar concept on the basis of *tawḥīd* as a rather technical term is Delawar Hosain's *tauḥīd-i adyān.*

3.6 Spiritual sovereignty (*wilāya*)

Like *tawḥīd*, this concept is naturally a very central one to all theological thinking originating from Maijbhandar, as it concerns the very status of sainthood within Islam. The word *wilāya* is derived from *walī*, namely *walī Allāh*, 'friend of God' or 'saint', and has, apart from various secular usages,[69] become the most common expression for 'sainthood'. Explanations of *wilāya* are part and parcel of many

66 Other than *Ā'īna-i bārī*, these two writings are not very coherently argued. I cannot judge whether this is designed to attain a certain opacity of the topics exposed and thereby reduce their transparency, or whether it is due simply to a lack of experience in writing.

67 Cf. e.g. *ĀB*: 45 f. on the 'veil of duality' (*dū'ī kā parda*) that obstructs the perfect knowledge of *tawḥīd*; 70 such veils have to be overcome in order to ultimately leave the realm of duality.

68 Cf., e.g., *ĀH*: 109: Abdul Jabbar Mimnagari stresses that it does not suffice simply to accept that Allah is one, but it is necessary to constantly dedicate oneself with all one has to that oneness and completely destroy one's own being; otherwise, 'one cannot understand the genuine property/quality of *tawḥīd*' (*prakṛta tauhider dharma bujhite pāre nā*. For this use of *dharma* [to be rendered as 'property/quality' rather than 'religion' here], cf. the discussion in Harder [2001: 180–95]).

69 Thus, e.g., the provinces of the Ottoman Empire were called *wilāyet*; in modern Turkish, besides 'holiness', the term *velâyet* also means 'authority', especially in the juridical sense of guardianship. Similarly in Persian, where *vilāyat* also means 'land' or 'province', as well as the office of the ruler of a province. In Urdu and Hindi, the most common meaning is that of a 'foreign country' (particularly Great Britain) which is *bilāt*/*bilet* in Bengali.

classical Sufi expositions,[70] and the Maijbhandari elaborations of this topic rely heavily on those. The opposition of Islamic reformist movements and the wish to highlight the importance of the Maijbhandari saints, however, have led some Maijbhandari theologians (since Delawar Hosain) to go beyond the traditional parameters of this discussion and evolve some original approaches to the concept of *wilāya*.

Abdul Ghani in his *Ā'īna-i Bārī* starts the discussion of *wilāya* by introducing the traditional hierarchy of saints.[71] In every century there are 140,000 *awliyā'* in the world. Among these are 4,000 with hidden bodies who do not know one another.[72] In ascending ranks, 300 among all the *awliyā'* are called *aḥbār*, 40 *abdāl*, seven *abrār*, four *awtād*, three *atqiyā'*, and finally one *quṭb* or *ġawṯ* (*ĀB*: 17). According to another source he quotes,[73] these figures are slightly different, and instead of one *quṭb*, there are three, the highest among them being called the *quṭb al-aqtāb*. In connection with the theory of veils of the *nūr* from the creation, this hierarchy is elsewhere allocated within that concentric structure with the *ġawṯ* partaking of the centre and the others distributed between the 700 veils in greater or lesser proximity to him.[74]

Generally, *wilāya* is of two kinds: *vilāyat-i 'āmma* ('usual friendship with God') or *vilāyat-i īmān* is attributed to all believers, whereas the *vilāyat-i ḫāṣṣa*, 'special friendship with God' is reserved for those who have attained *fanā'* and *baqā'* (*ĀB*: 18 f.). A *walī* is hard to recognise and ordinary people often avoid him (p. 21); his status is beyond common perception (p. 28).[75] This applies less, however, to the category of the *mūsawī al-ṭarīqa*[76] who stay close to the *šarī'a*; but it is fully true of the *ḫiḍrawī al-ṭarīqa*[77] who are the true envoys of God on earth and derive all of their words and deeds from God's truth (*ĀB*: 253 f.). A saint can, however, be known by various signs: he should be firmly positioned within the *šarī'a*; when one sits close to him, the heart should lose its love for the world and turn to the *dargāh* instead; 'a *walī* is someone whose sight brings God to one's mind' (p. 31).

The *awliyā'* are further distinguished along the categories *ṭayāra* ('flying') and *siyāra* ('travelling'): the former have cut off their relations with the world and remain in the 'station of witnessing' (*maqām-i mušāhida*), whereas the latter are still among humans, but are 'messengers of leaving behind relations and resolved to fly' (p. 32).[78] The *quṭb-i 'ālam* or *ġawṯ al-a'ẓam* knows all the saints of all

70 e.g. Al-Qushayri's *Risāla* (Gramlich 1989, Chapter 38, pp. 358–63).

71 For a famous account of this, cf. Hujwiri's *Kašf al-Maḥǧūb* 269, 7–15. German translation in Gramlich (1985: 62).

72 Abdul Ghani gives a reference to Jami's *Nafaḥāt al-uns* for this particular figure.

73 The Urdu book *Maġaz al-madānī aur tārīḫ-i firišta*; author unknown to me.

74 *ĀB*: 44 ff.; cf. also the section on *nūr*.

75 A question of Ahmadullah (*tum lōg ham kō kis āṇkh sē dēkhtē hō?*, lit. 'By which eye do you people see me?' – *ĀB*: 67) is interpreted as an indication that this saint acknowledged that he was outside of what could be perceived by usual intellects, and that the *murīd*s should not form any conception of the saint upon anybody else's model.

76 'Moses-followers of the *ṭarīqa*'.

77 'Khidr-followers of the *ṭarīqa*'.

78 *qāṣad-i tark-i 'alā'ik aur 'ājam-i ṭairān*; *ĀB*: 32.

times; he is the porter of *nūr* and cares for all beings on earth (p. 33). One means of knowing about the rank of a saint is his own testimony, and Ahmadullah's declaration is given as proof of his being the *ġawṯ al-aʿẓam* of his times.[79]

The role of the saints is to stop the inevitable decay on earth and take the believers back to the right path. They send by God Himself to fulful their divine mission, as Abdul Ghani describes quite illustratively: when the petition of the humans reaches God, He invests one of His dearest ones with the necessary properties and commissions him to look after the well-being of His subjects.[80] They possess the power of destroying sins (p. 76). Further, the Lord acts through them. They become the centre of a circle of lovers and beloved and unite with their divine beloved. They can move around in all stations from *nāsūt* up to *lāhūt* but are essentially located in the 'sea of unity'.[81] As the saints have seen God in dreams or with their 'inner eyes' (P. *čašm-i bāṭin*, translation of Ar. *baṣr*), their status is equal to that of the companions of the Prophet. Contact with them induces contact with God, as Abdul Ghani makes clear repeatedly and expresses in the following Urdu verse: 'If you want to sit side by side with God/Sit in the presence of the *awliyā*'' (*ĀB*: 114).[82] Abdus Salam Isapuri, a disciple of Gholam Rahman, also deals with different stages of *wilāya* (*FR*: 10 f.) and the topmost position of the *ġawṯ* (*FR*: 14). The first manifestation of *wilāya* happened in ʿAli and passed from him to Hasan al-Basri and Uways al-Qarani (p. 4 f.); Gholam Rahman is called the Uways-al Karani of his times (p. 11). Isapuri stresses that the times have changed:

> The rule of the people [*sulṭanat-i ğumhūrī*] is being established in the world, and in the *dār al-ḥarb* of Hindustan, the government of Pakistan has been set up, and in this century, the telephone, radio, airplane, atom bomb etc. have been invented. And the *ṭarīqa-i vilāyat* also appeared in a new colour.[83]

Due to these exigencies of modernity, the Maijbhandari *ṭarīqa* is portrayed as a combination of three established *ṭarīqa*s, namely the Qadiriyya, Suhrawardiyya and Chishtiyya (p. 13).

If the conceptualisations examined so far are more or less in keeping with general Sufi definitions, we now move on to Delawar Hosain's *Belāẏate motl̓ākā* (cf. esp.

79 *ham ġauṣ-i zamān haiṇ. ham kō bhalā burā nēk wa bad sab kā maʿlūm hai* ('I am the *ġawṯ* of the time. I am aware of everything, whether good or bad, dutiful or evil.'). These words were uttered by Ahmadullah in the presence of a group of *murīd*s who before had been discussing his status and noted possible signs that he might indeed be a *ġawṯ al-aʿẓam* (*ĀB*: 38). The title is also most commonly used as an epithet of ʿAbd al-Qadir Gilani.

80 Cf. the similar passage in *Belāẏate motl̓ākā*, quoted below in the following chapter.

81 *yah lōg dariyā-i muḥīṭ-i waḥdat kī nahang haiṇ aur ğō kuč̌h kahtē haiṇ dariyā sē kahtē haiṇ* ('These people are whales of the sea of the sphere of unity and whatever they say they say from the sea'). *ĀB*: 537.

82 *hamnašīnī gar tū cāhē bā ẖodā/pas ḥażūr-i auliyā mēṇ baiṭʾh ğā.*

83 *sulṭanat-i ğumhūrī dar ğahān qāʾim mīšawad wa dar dār al-ḥarb-i hindūstān ḥukūmat-i pākistān qāʾim gardīd wa tʾīlīfon wa rīdʾiyo wa hawāʾī ğahāz wa etʾam bam waġaira darīn ṣadī īğād gašta ast wa ṭarīqa-i vilāyat nīz barang-i ğadīd ẓahūrpazīr gašt* (*FR*: 12).

chapters 1, 3, 6, 8 and 10) where the concept of *wilāya* undergoes a fundamental reinterpretation and universalisation. Delawar Hosain starts by introducing manifold distinctions of *wilāya*: apparently relying on Abdul Ghani, Delawar Hosain states that on a basic level, one is the *belāẏate īmān* (P. <*vilāyat-i īmān*>, explained as 'the relation with God'),[84] which is common to all *mu'minīn*, believers, and is no topic of concern;[85] the other is the *belāẏate eh'chān* (P. <*vilāyat-i aḥsān*>, 'spiritual sovereignty of grace') which is the saintly *wilāya* proper and is further classified in various ways. *Wilāya* of this second kind, Delawar Hosain elaborates, can be gained in four ways: *bi 'l-iṣāla* ('truthfully', 'enduring'; translated as 'original or natural'),[86] *bi 'l-warāṯa* ('by way of heritage'), *bi 'l-darāsa* ('by learning') and *bi 'l-malāma* ('by reproach', i.e. by restraining the *nafs*) (*BM*: 2 f.).[87] Furthermore, *wilāya* can be ascribed to different, ascending levels; a possessor of *belāẏate chog'rā* (<*vilāyat-i ṣuġrā*>) 'has obtained a place above the normal *mu'minīn*' (*BM*: 4); *belāẏate och'tā* (<*vilāyat-i wasṭā*>) leads above the angels; and *belāẏate oj'mā* (<*vilāyat-i 'uẓma*>, 'the most supreme spiritual sovereignty') enables its possessor to 'exert power and influence upon the whole creation' (*BM*: 4). Among these latter 'most perfect saints', again, two groups may be distinguished, namely those who have acquired *quṭbiyya* (rendered as 'agency in deeds') and *ġawṯiyya* ('agency in rescuing').[88]

The age of *wilāya* succeeds the age of *nubuwwa* (prophethood), but this does not mean that *wilāya* did not exist at the time of Prophet Muhammad. In fact, Muhammad was a possessor of the most supreme *wilāya* Himself, and it is in Him, through the mediation of 'Ali, that the chain of *wilāya* started (*BM*: 10). Before and in the person of Muhammad, Sufism was in a dormant state (*BM*: 21). According to Delawar Hosain, this chain is not an even flow of undiminished strength, but obeys an alternation that is detectable even in the age of *nubuwwa*. With unspecified references to Ibn 'Arabi and Ibn Khaldun, he points out:

> For the rise and fall of races by the rotation of time, and for the destruction and construction of the creation due to the reaction of the turning planets and stars coming into effect, the knowers accept a cycle of five or six centuries.
>
> (*BM*: 13)

This periodisation is substantiated by quoting the sequence of the great prophets Musa (Moses), Isa (Jesus) and Muhammad and the saints 'Abd al-Qadir Gilani and Ahmadullah Maijbhandari (*BM*: 12 ff.).[89] For the age of *wilāya*, it posits these

84 *khodār samparka*; *BM*: 2.

85 Cf. Gramlich (1987: 68), quoting Abu Bakr al-Kalabadi (Abū Bakr al-Kalābāḏī): 'Es gibt nämlich zweierlei Gottesfreundschaft: (Erstens) eine Gottesfreundschaft, die außerhalb der Gottesfeindschaft stellt. Diese ist den gewöhnlichen Muslimen eigen.'

86 *mūl'gata bā prakṛtigata*; *BM*: 2.

87 From the fourth category, Delawar Hosain derives the Malamiyya *ṭarīqa* and equates it with the Qalandariyya and Taipuri *ṭarīqa*s (*BM*: 3).

88 *karmma kartṛtva* and *trāṇ kartṛtva* respectively (*BM*: 4).

89 A much more narrativised version of this theory features in the hagiography *Jībanī o kerāmat* to be treated in the following chapter.

two saints at the very top of eminence; and in distinguishing their specific kinds of *wilāya* from one another, Delawar Hosain reaches the concept of *belāẏate mot'lākā* that constitutes the very kernel of his theological ideas. *Wilāya* first operated within the frame of Islamic scholarship and Islamic rules and was *muqayyad*, 'bound' or 'limited'.[90] It was with the breaking away of Islamic rule that another type of *wilāya* had to be developed. Referring to the British annexation of the Eastern parts of Bengal, Delawar Hosain writes:

> As a result of the establishment of English rule in the land of Bengal [*bāṃlādeśe*] on the 14th October of 1760, at the noon of the sun of the Muhammedan religion, mankind again was puzzled and became prone to the reprimands of Allah. Since the Islamic social organisation, bereft of the help of the state in social and ritualist religion, became inflexible [*acal*] and had to confront bad times [*duryog*] day by day. In this age of lifeless, weak *šarīʿa* rules, the necessity of an age of *belāẏate mot'lākāẏe āh'madī*, dominant in moral religion, became inevitable [*aparihārya*].
>
> (*BM*: 21)

The present, it is further argued, is in general characterised by the search for individual and national freedom and the matters of faith are no longer a reason for quarrels; and one of the basic claims of *vilāyat-i mutlaqa* is the removal of opposition between religions (*BM*: 138 f.). In contrast to *vilāyat-i muqayyada* and even *nubuwwa*, both of which were 'limited in terms of place, person and environment',[91] *vilāyat-i mutlaqa* is coterminous with a 'free Sufism'[92] and transcends all religious and social boundaries in extending its validity over the whole of mankind. It is portrayed as a religious power of the highest degree that combines in itself various preceding types of divine missions:

> It regards the different religious doctrines as morally equal. Because it supposes that the opinion and path of distinct doctrines, though different, all have the same goal. Due to the revolving of the religious world and social life, this power of *wilāya* [represents] an age characterised by the best natural actions or reactions, which may be called the universal power of *wilāya* or the universal peace-founding power, the eternal Islam [Bg. *sanātan is'lām*]. By the mixture of attraction [*ǧaḏb*] and wayfaring [*sulūk*], this *wilāya* is capable of bestowing upon its possessor the double development of Prophet Karim's [i.e. Muhammad's] complete *nubuwwa* and *wilāya*, and it is able to assemble along [with these] the true form of the *wilāya* [Bg. *belāẏatī svarūp*] of Hażrat Isa, the Guide of the Mahdi.
>
> (*BM*: 60)

90 *BM*: 21; for a longer exposition, see *BM*: 59.

91 *sthān, pātra o paribeṣe sīmābaddha*; *BM*: 22.

92 *mukta suphībād*; *BM*: 22.

In this way, Ġawṯ al-Aʿẓam Ahmadullah is elevated to a rank of unprecedented supremacy. He disposes of the powers of both prophethood and sainthood. Simultaneously, Islam is interpreted in a new way: its definition is dissociated from ritualist, exoteric determinators and shifted to a meta-level of divine intercession through *wilāya*. The concept corresponding to *vilāyat-i muṭlaqa* on the level of relating religions to one another is *tauḥīd-i adyān*, 'unity of religions'. The contention is that all established religions serve as different types of *šarīʿa* that fulfil the basic moral duties of exoteric religious practice; it is therefore not necessary for a non-Islamic disciple of the Maijbhandari *ṭarīqa* to convert to Islam since the message and path promulgated by the holder of *vilāyat-i mutlaqa* applies to anybody, regardless of his or her specific 'religion or caste/class' (Bg. *dharmmajātinirbiśeṣe*). Delawar Hosain takes care to adduce Qurʾanic verses to support this concept, e.g. *Qurʾān* 2,62(59), 2,85(79) and 2,111–12(105–6).

From *ĀB* to *BM*, then, we may notice a widening of the concept of *wilāya*. The assessment of present times and the resultant call for a specially powerful *wilāya* are common to all, but whereas *ĀB* still defines *wilāya* within traditional Islamic parameters, *BM* goes beyond these and inclusivistically claims that the *wilāya* proclaimed and personified by Ahmadullah is the highest step for *all* religions and simultaneously the true Islam. That is, the religions may be equivalent according to the concept of *tauḥīd-i adyān*, but the credit of developing this concept goes to Islam – an Islam which thus in a certain sense *contains* all other religions within itself. Such inclusivism can certainly be said to be commonplace in South Asian religious discourse and seems especially characteristic of modern Hinduism.[93]

Delawar Hosain's concept presents itself as ecumenical and modernist; it is consciously related to present conditions of society. The earlier descriptions by Abdul Ghani and Abdus Salam Isapuri also harmonise different religious groups in portraying the Maijbhandari *ṭarīqa* as a combination of several prominent South Asian *ṭarīqa*s; but this is hardly revolutionary as the *ṭarīqa*s were never strictly exclusive and multiple membership of various *ṭarīqa*s had been a recurring feature until the nineteenth century.[94] It is Delawar Hosain who truly generalises and freshly contextualises *wilāya*. Although he argues on the basis of Qurʾanic injunctions, he avoids the issue of *aḥl al-kitāb*, 'people of the book', with regard to Hinduism and Buddhism and tacitly assumes that these are also to be included as valuable and legitimate kinds of *šarīʿa*. Hindu devotees of the Maijbhandari saints are mentioned in *ĀB*, too, but there is no recognition of any *raison d'être* or of the validity of Hinduism. Delawar Hosain examines the moral principles of Buddhism and states that 'even if the doctrine of Ǧanāb Gautama Buddha is not completely unanimous, it does not create contradictions with *tauḥīd-i adyān* or the Sufi doctrine' (*BM*: 8).

93 Cf. Hacker (1978 [1970] and 1978 [1971]); Halbfass (1988, esp. chapters 13, 18 and 22).

94 Even Haji Shariatullah, founder of the Farāʾiżī movement, though he strongly opposed 'pirism' (Ahmed 1981: 59), is said to have belonged to more than one *ṭarīqa* by initiation.

Delawar Hosain also uses other strategies to establish Ahmadullah's greatness as a saint. He puts great stress on a prophesy of Ibn ʿArabi concerning the *Ḫātim al-awliyāʾ*, the 'Seal of Saints'.[95] In Chapter 2,9 of his *Fuṣūṣ al-hikam*, Ibn ʿArabi describes this last saint to come as born in China and speaking the local language; after him, sterility spreads among mankind, the believers die out, and society descends to a state of bestiality.[96] Delawar Hosain compares this description with the data of Ahmadullah's life and finds correspondences in nine points: like the Prophet Seth, Ahmadullah belongs to the *aḥmadī* line of prophets and saints;[97] a sister was born before him; he spoke a local language; it was during his age that birth control and sterilisation were introduced; he invited mankind to God by means of an easy *ṭarīqa*; the world has not satisfactorily responded to his call; mankind has since then been turning away from religion; Chittagong may be said to be adjacent to China, and during Ibn ʿArabi's times was under the rule of descendants of the Chinese; and his tolerance regarding religious practice (Bg. *ācār dharmma*) in various religions proves his novelty (*BM*: 29 f.). The paramount status of the Seal of Saints is established by following Ibn ʿArabi's contention that for any prophet or saint, complete knowledge is accessible only from the perspective of the respective seal; this, in Delawar Hosain's interpretation, implies the absolute superiority of the last saint, corresponding to the superiority of the last prophet, Muhammad.[98]

While the ressemblance of details may seem impressive, however, the ineffectiveness of this last saint's teachings described by Ibn ʿArabi stands in stark contrast to the supreme powers bestowed on him in the form of *vilāyat-i mutlaqa*. The prophesy further does not give any ground for the assumption that the last saint promulgated any new and easy *ṭarīqa*, as, in view of the doomed fate of humanity, the Seal of Saints must simultaneously be interpreted as a seal on all possibilities of liberation. Finally, his otherwise emancipatory and modernist views of modern times (personal and national self-assertion, democracy, religious harmony) collide with the apocalyptic design of Ibn ʿArabi's prophesy. Delawar

95 There is an extensive discussion on this concept. Cf., e.g., Tirmidhī (1996) and Chodkiewicz (1986).

96 The French translation by Charles-André Gilis (Ibn Arabī 1997: 89 f.) runs as follows: 'C'est sur les traces de Shīth que naîtra le dernier engendré du genre humain. Il sera porteur de ses secrets. Après lui, il n'y aura plus d'enfant parmi les hommes, car il est le Sceau des engendrés. Avec lui, lui naîtra une soeur. Elle viendra au monde avant lui, et lui après elle, sa tête près de ses pieds. Sa naissance aura lieu en Chine et sa langue sera celle des gens de ce pays. Ensuite, la stérilité se répandra parmi les hommes; les unions sans naissance se multiplieront. Il appelera les hommes à Allāh mais ne recevra aucune réponse. Lorsqu'Allāh le Très-Haut l'aura fait mourir, et qu'Il aura fait mourir les croyants de son temps, ceux qui resteront seront comme des bêtes, sans plus de considération pour ce qui est licite et pour ce qui ne l'est pas. Ils agiront gouvernés par la nature, en proie à une convoitise qui ne sera plus contrôlée, ni par l'Intellect, ni par la Loi. C'est sur eux que se lèvera L'Heure.'

97 For this distinction, cf. e.g. *ĀB*: 145 f.

98 Cf. Ibn ʿArabi's *Fuṣūṣ al-hikam*, Chapter 2,5 (Ibn Arabī 1997: 80 f.). I am again quoting from Gilis's translation: 'Cette science [des dons essentiels qui renferme le Secret suprême] appartient exclusivement au Sceau des envoyés et au Sceau des saints. [. . .] aucun saint ne peut la voir qu'à partir de la Niche du Saint qui scelle; au point que les envoyés ne peuvent la voir, quand ils la voient, qu'à partir de la Niche du Sceau des saints, car la mission divine et la prophétie – je veux dire la prophétie et la mission légiférantes – ont pris fin, alors que la sainteté ne cesse jamais [. . .].'

Hosain is faithful enough to his sources to quote the prophecy in full,[99] but does not discuss these problems and thus leaves a strong impression of heterogeneity in his argumentation;[100] the single point in which they meet is ultimately only their motivation of proving Ahmadullah's supremacy.

It is significant that the concept of *vilāyat-i mutlaqa* has, as far as I can see, to this day been monopolised by writers affiliated to the Ahmadiyya and Haq Manzils in Maijbhandar, and has hardly found any repercussions in Rahmaniyya Manzil publications. This is not true, however, for others among his titles. There is a writing by Jahir Ahmad Chaudhuri that claims the title of a *Ḫātim al-wilāya*, 'Seal of sainthood', along with that of *Muğaddid-i āḫirī zamāna*[101] ('Renewer of the last time') for Gholam Rahman.[102] According to this writer, and in accordance with the general opinion held in Rahmaniyya Manzil circles, Ahmadullah only prepared the ground for the Maijbhandari *ṭarīqa*, whereas it was Gholam Rahman who completed this task (*KhB*: 13). Apparently on a similar basis to Delawar Hosain, Chaudhuri argues that the last great *walī* assimilates the powers of his predecessors:

> As he is the *Ḫatm al-wilāya*,[103] the *Muğaddid-i āḫirī zamān*, the *Ġawṯ al-A'ẓam-i āḫirī zamān*, the importance and superiority of the great *ṭarīqa-i mā'ijbhand'āriyya* promulgated by him shines[104] above all the *ṭarīqa*s preceding him.
>
> (*KhB*: 14)

In this design, the *āḫirī zamāna* starts at the time Gholam Rahman acquired sainthood; Ahmadullah still belongs to the preceding age and passed his *wilāya* on to Gholam Rahman. If this argument may seem somewhat derivative and clearly modelled upon the earlier classifications made with reference to Ahmadullah, Chaudhuri goes even further and claims also Ibn 'Arabi's prophesy for Gholam Rahman:

> Certainly Haẓrat Ibn-i 'Arabī hinted at [no other than] Haẓrat Ġawṯ al-A'ẓam Māij'bhāṇḍārī Bābājān Qibla in his prophesy. Haẓrat Ġawṯ al-A'ẓam Māij'bhāṇḍārī Bābājān Qibla is the *Muğaddid-i āḫirī zamān* and therefore the *Ḫātim al-wilāya* according to the description of Ibn-i 'Arabī.
>
> (*KhB*: 10)

99 *BM*: 26 and 29; Delawar Hosain quotes from an Urdu translation, published from Mustafai Press, Lucknow (no more details given).

100 Nor do later writers who reiterate Delawar Hosain's argument, such as Md. Ghulam Rasul (1994: 39 f.).

101 This is Persianised Urdu; a correct Persian form would have to place the attribute behind the noun: *Muğaddid-i zamān-i āḫirī.*

102 As the author states in the foreword, his publisher, a *murīd* of Gholam Rahman called Abul Khair Chaudhuri, had argued with him that the appellation *Ḫātim al-wilāya* was to be used for the Mahdi only; thereupon he had a dream in which Gholam Rahman, standing inside the mausoleum of Muhammad in Medina and throwing books at him, apparently punished him for this and thus proved that it was accurate (*KhB*: n.p.).

103 *Khat·mūl belāẏat* in Bengali; the form *ḫātim*, 'terminator', would seem more probable, but *khat·m* (for Ar. <*ḫatm*>, 'end') is used consistently throughout this publication.

104 Beng. *birāj kare*.

Mujibur Rahman, another *murīd* of Gholam Rahman, even portrays his saint as the Mahdi (*NJ*: 2). In his function as *Ḫātim al-wilāya*, Gholam Rahman is the full possessor of the *nūr-i muḥammadī*; and while it is possible that other saints arise after him, their power does not directly come from the *nūr-i muḥammadī* but is mediated by him in the sense that they can become spiritual successors of various prophets and saints only through him (*NJ*: 3 f.). The tension between Ahmadiyya and Rahmaniyya versions of the kind of *wilāya* to be ascribed to the respective saints, however, is harmonised by the following statement:

> Beware! Even if Haẓrat Ġawṯ al-Aʿẓam Haẓrat [sic] Qibla Kaʿba and Haẓrat Bābājān Qibla Kaʿba ʿAzīz are two separate identities [*svatā*] from [the point of view of] their form, yet they are the truth [*hākikat*] of the *nūr-i muḥammadī*. I.e., one *nūr*, in the shape of *wilāya*, [is manifest in] two brightly shining centres.
>
> (*NJ*: 13)

With regard to Ziaul Haq, the son of Delawar Hosain and an accomplished saint himself, the hagiologists appropriate the concepts of *vilāyat-i mutlaqa* and *tauḥīd-i adyān*, and the status of a *ġawṯ al-aʿẓam* and a *muğaddid-i zamān* is conferred upon all three saints.[105] The title *Ḫātim al-wilāya*, however, is not discussed – possibly because of the contradictoriness of its multiple use and the resulting devaluation of the term.

3.7 The Maijbhandari *ṭarīqa*

Lastly in this chapter I wish to examine an issue that has already been touched upon in the preceding section but deserves detailed treatment: the Maijbhandari *ṭarīqa*. We have already mentioned repeatedly that different versions of this *ṭarīqa* are current in Maijbhandar today. This is the place to examine the textual sources chronologically in order to trace the development that this *ṭarīqa* has undergone. This topic is somewhat sensitive to Maijbhandari self-images as both Ahmadiyya and Rahmaniyya Manzils claim the Maijbhandari *ṭarīqa* to be fundamentally modelled by their respective ancestral saints.

To start with, the term *ṭarīqa* has a certain ambivalence. In Persian and Urdu, as well as to a lesser extent in Bengali, *ṭarīqa* can be used in the general sense of 'way', 'manner', 'method'.[106] When *ṭarīqa* functions as a Sufic technical term, these general denotations are not necessarily defunct, at least certainly not when

105 Cf. *Shahenshah*: 6; *Jiẏāul Hak*: 24, etc.

106 The Urdu form preferred for this is *ṭarīqa*, the Bengali form *tarīkā* (in different spellings); the Sufic term to be discussed next, by contrast, seems to be given as U. *ṭarīqat* and (at least at instances, by the side of *t[v]arīkā*) B. *t(v)arikat*. Such usage, however, does not seem to be followed very consistently (cf. e.g. Āl'hājv Śāh Chuphi Māolānā Saiẏad Maïnuddīn Āh'mad Āl-Hācānī (n.d.): *Ādābe māh'phile jikir : tarikāẏe māij'bhāṇḍārīẏā*. Māij'bhāṇḍār, 16 p.; p. 15, where both *tarikā* and *tarikat* are used side by side), so that it seems best to be prepared for all meanings in any of these forms.

it denotes a specific Sufic order. Alongside this, as we have seen, *ṭarīqa* can also denote the station (*maqām*) of spiritual searching.[107] Thus, in principle, the combination 'Maijbhandari *ṭarīqa*' can mean at least three different things: a kind of 'religious method' of that locality, a Sufic brotherhood of that name, and spiritual search as practised in that locality. Today, Maijbhandari *ṭarīqa* as a rule means a combination of the first and the second, but this does not necessarily imply that it has been so in the past.

The first written source from Maijbhandari circles is a *fatwa* by Aminul Haq Farhadabadi, entitled *Tuḥfat al-aḫyār fī dafʿ šarārat al-šarār* and published shortly after Saint Ahmadullah's death (1906/7). This examination of controversial issues such as audition (*samāʿ*), full prostration (*sağda*), *pīr–murīd* relationships, etc., contains some references and eulogies to Ġawṯ al-Aʿẓam Ahmadullah, but I could not find any mention of a Maijbhandari *ṭarīqa*. *Tuḥfat* 2,4, however, discusses the status of *taṣawwuf*, Sufism, in Islam, stating that

> The science of *taṣawwuf* is a necessary science, and searching for the *ṭarīqat* and making efforts for the attainment of the concealed perfection is compulsory for everyone among the people of faith.[108]

This mention of *ṭarīqa*, the only in Aminul Farhadabadi's introductory remarks on the topic (*Tuḥfat*: 60–63), would appear to correspond to the first meaning of *ṭarīqa*, '(religious) method'; according to the logic of such usage, the Maijbhandaris could certainly be called people of the *ṭarīqa* (in the sense of being people aspiring to master esoteric knowledge), but a separate brotherhood called Maijbhandari *ṭarīqa* is definitely not in question here.

The second-earliest written document from Maijbhandar I could find is, as it were, not a theological treatise but a collection of Maijbhandari songs: Aliullah's *Prem-nur*, kept in the British Library, which appeared in 1913, that is, seven years after the demise of Saint Ahmadullah and two years before the publication of Abdul Ghani Kanchanpuri's *Āʾīna-i bārī*. The 118 songs contained in this book can safely be considered to have been composed over a number of years, possibly after the turn of the century. The last two songs (No. 117 and 118, pp. 112–13), however, serve as a sort of index and summary to the whole book. No. 117 contains the author's remarks on his songs, apologies for possible misprints, etc., and No. 118 is a sort of final religious advice. Here, the readers/listeners are asked to stick to their spiritual master and path, to keep fighting against their *nafs*, and, saliently, to maintain peace between the four *maḏhab*s, schools of Islamic law, and four *ṭarīqa*s. These plural *ṭarīqa*s clearly denote Sufi orders, and these are then enumerated as the Chishtiyya, Qadiriyya, Naqshbandiyya and Mujaddidiyya. One might think that the Naqshbandiyya Mujaddidiyya stands for only one *ṭarīqa* here,

107 Cf. above, Section 3.4.

108 *ʿilm-i taṣawwuf ʿilm-i żarūrī ast wa ṭalab-i ṭarīqat wa saʿī kardan barāʾī taḥṣīl-i kamāl-i bāṭinī bar har yīkī az ahl-i īmān wāğib ast*. (*Tuḥfat*: 60).

the branch of the Naqshbandiyya founded by Sirhindi;[109] but since Aliullah explicitly mentions four *ṭarīqa*s and thereupon gives a list of them, it seems more likely that Naqshbandiyya and Naqshbandiyya Mujaddidiyya are listed as separate entities. Later Maijbhandari authors also give them as two distinct *ṭarīqa*s.[110] In any case, and even if the names given denote only three *ṭarīqa*s, there is no mention of a Maijbhandari *ṭarīqa* in this song; and since it serves as a kind of afterword, it is very likely to have been written directly before the publication of the volume, that is, not long before the year 1913. This is an almost certain indication that at that time nothing like a Maijbhandari *ṭarīqa* or Sufi order had as yet become an established entity, and not in any case a full-fledged *ṭarīqa* to be mentioned along with the Chishtiyya, Qadiriyya, Naqshbandiyya and Mujaddidiyya.[111]

In *Ā'īna-i bārī*, which appeared two years later, there is also no explicit mention of a Maijbhandari *ṭarīqa*, but some hints that Ġawṯ al-Aʿẓam Ahmadullah did found a new *ṭarīqa*. Abdul Ghani interprets an utterance by Ahmadullah ('Through which eye do you people see me?') as a sign of his being beyond common perception and an heir to the line of prophets. Ahmadullah attained such a station (*maqām*), the author argues, in which all *ṭarīqa*s appear as viable means for guidance;[112] and

> he also has the authority to build a mixed *ṭarīqa* by merging some *ṭarīqa*s with one another or to found a new *ṭarīqa* [. . .] and to guide the heart and soul of the sick according to it like a skilful doctor who gives an expert [or 'scientific'] medicine on the [. . . (one word illegible)] of the disease of the sick.[113]
>
> (*ĀB*: 680)

109 The respective passage reads: *cistiẏā kāderiẏā nāhi āche kona riẏā // saṅkaṭer rasi jāna ekek tarikār ekek bāni // naksebandiẏā majāddādiẏā el'me bāteni cāẏ* (*PN* No.118).

110 There is a separate listing of Naqshbandiyya and Mujaddidiyya in Delawar Hosain's *Milāde Nab'bī o tāoẏāllode gāuchiẏā* (*MN*: 1). Selim Jahangir, albeit without reference to *Prem-nur* or any other source, also mentions the Qadiriyya, Chishtiyya, Naqshbandiyya and Mujaddidiyya separately as popular *ṭarīqa*s of Bangladesh (Jāhāṅgīr 1999: 49, n. 2). The *pīr* Moinuddin Ahmad, when explaining the symbolism of the five stars on the flag of his Maijbhandari society called *Anjuman-i Muiniyya*, gives a list of five *ṭarīqa*s as one possible meaning: Qadiriyya, Chishtiyya, Naqshbandiyya, Mujaddidiyya and Maijbhandariyya (*māij'bhāṇḍārīẏā*, U. <*mā'iğbhand'āriyya*>) (cf. Āl'hājv Śāh Chuphi Māolānā Saiẏad Maïnuddīn Āh'mad Āl-Hācānī (n.d.): *Ādābe māh'phile jikir: tarikāẏe māij'bhāṇḍārīẏā*. Māij'bhāṇḍār; p. 14). Syed Ahmadul Haq of the Allama Rumi Society (Chittagong) starts a section on the 'Maizbhandari Order' by writing: 'In Bangladesh Maizbhandari, Chistiya, Naqsha bandia, Muzaddadia and Kaderia orders have large following.' (cf. Syed Ahmadul Huq 1995: [9]).

111 If Naqshbandiyya Mujaddidiyya is interpreted as refering to one *ṭarīqa* here – as may very well be the case – and the fourth (then lacking) *ṭarīqa* understood as the Maijbhandari *ṭarīqa*, the question would remain why this new upshot among the honourable company of long-standing brotherhoods is not even once mentioned, although references and glorifications of Maijbhandar in Aliullah's songs are anything but scarce.

112 Cf. also *ĀB*: 385 where the author explains that all *ṭarīqa*s are the same regarding their nature and meaning; the differences only have to do with terminology (*iṣṭilāḥāt*).

113 *yah bhī iḫtiyār hai ki čand ṭarīqōṇ kō beham milākar ēk ṭarīqa-i murakkaba banāwē yā ḫūd ēk na'ī ṭarīqa* [. . .] *apnē iğtihād sē īğād kar kē bīmārān-i qalb-o rūḥ kō uskē muṭābiq čalāwē mānand ṭabīb-i ḥāḏiq kē ki bīmār kē maraż kī* [? one word illegible] *par dawā'ī-i ʿilmī kartē haiṇ*.

Ahmadullah, we are to understand, was in possession of such a superior spiritual status that he could freely devise combined or new *ṭarīqa*s; and in the following utterance we are implicitly told that he actually did so:

> In the *ṭarīqa* of his – the means [for attaining] the state of perfection, our Ḥażrat Ġawṣ̱-i pāk [P., 'pure'], may Allah the Most Supreme be satisfied with him – [in this *ṭarīqa*] the Shaikh, connected in a relationship of love, is the leader. Through that path of love which he entertains with his *pīr*, the veritable searcher obtains his grace and blessings in an esoteric [way], and due to that relation of the intellect, he becomes similar to him.[114]
>
> (*ĀB*: 544)

There is no doubt that in these passages, *ṭarīqa* is used in the sense of Sufi order. But what, according to Abdul Ghani Kanchanpuri, are the characteristics of Ahmadullah's *ṭarīqa*? The only specific ingredient of Ahmadullah's *ṭarīqa* that Abdul Ghani Kanchanpuri mentions is the love relation between master and adept, that is a very personalised way of spiritual instruction – which, furthermore, by no means qualifies as an exclusive trait of this *ṭarīqa* alone, since, as Abdul Ghani Kanchanpuri elaborates at length again and again, this relationship is constitutive of Sufism in general.[115] How then to explain this insufficient and somewhat minimalistic delimitation?

In fact, it seems quite probable that Abdul Ghani Kanchanpuri, an expert Sufic scholar, was well aware of the practices current in various Sufi orders and noticed a certain admixture of those practices at Ahmadullah's *darbār*; especially, knowing Ahmadullah's spiritual affiliation to be to the Qadiriyya, he was conscious that Ahmadullah's teachings did not necessarily stick to the confines imposed by that tradition. On the other hand, this author possibly felt that ordered Sufi practice could not dispense with the institution of a *ṭarīqa*. So, in order to shield off criticism for such heterogeneous practice, he first established that Ahmadullah had every right to establish any method he liked. Secondly, he stressed the love relation between master and adept as the distinguishing characteristic of what he claims to be Ahmadullah's *ṭarīqa*. The outside observer feels tempted to interpret this move as making a virtue out of necessity, as this emphasis on the love relation appears to be little more than a rationalisation of the highly individual, person-bound nature of Ahmadullah's teachings.

There are, however, also indications that the Maijbhandari movement was perceived as a *ṭarīqa* by outsiders even at this early time. In the tract *Sādhur ātmabināś o janmagrahaṇ*, a *ṭarīqa* of Ahmadullah (*āhāmadollā sāheber tarikā*; *SĀ*: 19) is explicitly mentioned. Thus it is also possible that Abdul Ghani Kanchanpuri reacted to such ascriptions from the environment of the movement. In any case,

114 *waṣūl badarğa-i kamāl hamārē ḥażrat ġauṣ̱-i pāk rażī-allāh taʿālā ʿana kē ṭarīqē meṇ marbūṭ barābiṭa-i muhabbat šaiḫ muqtadā hai ṭālib-i ṣādiq usī rāh-i muhabbat sē ki apnē pīr kē sāth rakhtā hai fiyūż wa barkāt uskī bāṭin sē ḥāṣil kartā hai aur basabab-i munāsibat maʿnwiyya kē hamsang uskā hōtā hai*[.]

115 Cf., e.g., *ĀB*: 684 ff.

later authors have taken up the idea of a specific *ṭarīqa* and done their bit to enhance its profile.

The first to be mentioned among these is Abdussalam Isapuri. It is in the very title of his Persian treatise (*Fuyūḍāt al-raḥmāniyya fī ṭarīqat al-mā'iğbhand'āriyya*, *c.* 1950) that the Maijbhandari *ṭarīqa* is explicitly mentioned. This *ṭarīqa* is derived from three old *ṭarīqa*s, the Chishtiyya, Suhrawardiyya and Qadiriyya (*FR*: 13); the foundation of it was laid by Saint Ahmadullah, and it was enlarged by Gholam Rahman (*FR*: 17). The ensuing chapters deal with aspects of this *ṭarīqa*. Thus, Chapter 2 on 'necessities and obeying'[116] rules that to take *bay'a* from a Sufi master (by means of a *Čādur*) and always to obey his orders is a duty of the disciple (*FR*: 22 f.); other chapters elaborate the meaning of *bay'a* (*FR*: 27–33), *ḏikr*, *fanā'* and *murāqaba* (*FR*: 36–40) and stress the central role of the love relation with the *šayḫ*, master (*FR*: 43 f.).

This treatment of the Maijbhandari *ṭarīqa* is not yet a formula, but it certainly shows a new degree of formalisation. After the demise of Saint Gholam Rahman, his sons and close disciples, including Isapuri himself, had to look after the spiritual side of *darbār* affairs, and Isapuri's treatise is part of a process of further institutionalisation: the 'flow of spirituality', to borrow a Bengali expression often used in Maijbhandar (*ādhyātmik dhārā*), had to be channelled, and what could be better suited to this task than a 'solid' *ṭarīqa* with defined behavioural rules?[117] Around the same time, the term *ṭarīqa-i mā'iğbhand'āriyya* appears in the journal *Māsik tauhīd*, brought out by two sons of Gholam Rahman (Mahbubul Bashar and Shafiul Bashar), in which a booklet is mentioned with the title *Tvarikāẏe māij bhāṇḍārīẏār rechālā śarīph* ('The noble treatise of the Maijbhandari *ṭarīqa*').[118] The author is unfortunately not mentioned, and the booklet is to all appearances no longer extant; its title, however, suggests that it was a somewhat systematic exposition of the Maijbhandari *ṭarīqa*, and it may be taken as a further indicator of a trend towards formalisation after Gholam Rahman's demise.

In the 1960s, Delawar Hosain gave a new form to the Maijbhandari *ṭarīqa*. In the second edition of his *Belāẏate mot'lākā*, which appeared sometime between 1959 and 1969, he launched his *saptapaddhati*, 'sevenfold method'.[119] After

116 The title is: *faṣal-i dūwwum* [:] *dar bayān-i wuğūbiyyat wa aṭā'at* (*FR*: 21).

117 Isapuri's insistence on formal *bay'a* is especially noteworthy in view of the fact that Gholam Rahman, his *muršid*, is known precisely for the opposite, namely the informal recruitment of disciples through dreams, glances, etc., and the *bātenī bāẏāt* or 'concealed oath of allegiance' is still today often asserted as a valid type of initiation in connection with him.

118 See the list of publications by the 'Tauhid Book Agency' on the back cover of two issues of *Māsik tauhīd* (Pauṣ 1357 BE and Āṣāṛh 1358 BE [both 1951]).

119 Delawar Hosain refers to this second edition in another small piece of writing, *Mūl tattva*, which first appeared in 1969 (*MT*: 23). It was not possible for me to see this second edition of *Belāẏate mot'lākā*. The first edition of 1959 does not contain any reference to the *saptapaddhati*, but it is there in all the later editions I could check. – Besides *saptapaddhati*, the term *saptakarmmapaddhati* ('method of seven [kinds of] deeds') is used, and this is also refered to by the Persian *uṣūl-i sab'a*, *uṣūl* meaning 'rules, principles'. Abdul Mannan Chowdhury, the English translator of *Belāẏate mot'lākā*, renders it as 'the "Seven-Action" Principles' (Delawor Hossain 2000: 63).

treating seven kinds of *ḏikr* in his *Mūl tattva*, he introduces this concept in the following way:

> For the purification of the lower self [Bg. *taj'kīẏāẏe naph's*, P. <*tazkiyya-i nafs*>] – besides the mentioned sevenfold method of *ḏikr* and *fikr* – [and] for the opposition of the lower self [Bg. *mokhālephāte naph's*, P. <*muḫālifat-i nafs*>] or in order to finish the ill faculties of the human lower self and awaken the good faculties of the human soul, Hażrat Ġawṯ al-Aʿẓam Maij Bhandari has for the assistence of the general public [Bg. *sarbbasādhāraṇ*] given priority to the obtained and established *vusūl-i sabʿa* or *saptapaddhati* ['sevenfold method'], as an unobstructed and easily attainable means, which has been revered and accepted by all *ṭarīqa* followers. [. . .] It is to be counted as the method of the Qadiriyya Malamiyya Maijbhandari *ṭarīqa*.
>
> (*MT*: 23)

This sevenfold method consists of two groups of categories: three kinds of annihilation (*fanāʾ*) and four kinds of death (*mawt*). *Fanāʾ ʿan al-ḫalq* is 'not to have hope or wish for any help from anybody'; *fanāʾ ʿan al-hawāʾ* means to abstain from unnecessary deeds and talk, and *fanāʾ ʿan al-irāda* is 'to consider one's will or longing as dissolved in the will of Allah the Most Supreme' (*MT*: 23). As for the second group, these deaths of the 'foes' (*ripu*) of men are the white death (*maut-i abyāż*), attained by fasting and self-control;[120] the black death (*maut-i aswād*), consisting in realising one's own faults by abstaining from blaming others; the red death (*maut-i ahmar*) of (sexual) desire, and lastly the green death (*maut-i aḫzār*) which is reached by leading a life devoid of any luxury (*MT*: 24).[121]

These four kinds of death are indeed old Sufi heritage. Al-Qushayri already mentions them in his *Risāla* (1046), with white death as hunger, black death as bearing the molestation by men, red death as counteracting the *nafs* and desire (*muḫālafati n-nafsi wa-l-hawā*) and green death as 'affixing patches on one another'.[122] The most probable direct source for Delawar Hosain with regard to this concept is Abdul Ghani Kanchanpuri,[123] who describes the four kinds of death as those which have to be endured by anyone who aspires after death in life (*ĀB*: 318).

Delawar qualifies this path (*panthā*) as 'absolutely free from trouble, encouraging, joygiving, non-violent and achieving progress in both worlds': '[It is] advice and a provision of easily achievable rules for everybody – for

120 In *BM*, Mahatma Gandhi, whenever facing difficult situations, is quoted as having said: 'I obtain light from fasting' (*BM*: 77).

121 Cf. the very similar description in the fourth edition of *Belāẏate mot'lākā* (*BM*: 77).

122 Cf. Al-Qushayri, tr. by Richard Gramlich (1989: 57). The four deaths are given in a quotation from one Ḫātim and introduced by a threefold *isnād*.

123 Delawar Hosain himself had Abdul Ghani Kanchanpuri's *Āʾīna-i Bārī* reprinted, probably in the 1950s.

countries, races, whites, blacks, householders and non-householders'.[125] In *Belāẏate mot'lākā*, Delawar Hosain states that

> This sevenfold method of Qur'anic guidance is a stainless, easy, simple, natural path which brings freedom [*svācchandya*] into the method of life [*jīban paddhati*]. It is easier, simpler and more natural than the eightfold principle [*aṣṭaśīl nīti*] of Ǧanāb Gautama Buddha.
>
> (*BM*: 77 f.)

It is important to stress that Delawar Hosain does not claim the ingredients of what he defines as the sevenfold method constituting the Maijbhandari *ṭarīqa* to be new inventions by Saint Ahmadullah. Ahmadullah has only 'given priority'[126] to these 'obtained and established' methods for the benefit of mankind. The method is also not exclusively Maijbhandari but belongs to the 'Qadiriyya Malamiyya Maijbhandari *ṭarīqa*' – which may be read as an indication that Delawar Hosain saw the Maijbhandari *ṭarīqa* as a kind of sub-branch of the Qadiriyya rather than a completely independent institution. Elsewhere, however, he describes it as a combination of all *ṭarīqa*s: 'The Qadiriyya, Chishtiyya, Naqshbandiyya, Mujaddidiyya, Qalandariyya, Suhrawardiyya, Taifuriyya, Junaidiyya and other *ṭarīqa*s are included in it [the Maijbhandari *ṭarīqa*].'[127]

It is this sevenfold method which has since Delawar Hosain's presentation become canonical and coterminous with the Maijbhandari *ṭarīqa* in most of the expositions connected with the Ahmadiyya and Haq Manzils. In Delawar's *Belāẏate mot'lākā*, however, this method is only one part of what constitutes the Maijbhandari *ṭarīqa*. In a separate chapter on this topic (*Māij'bhāṇḍārī tvarīkā*, *BM*: 128–34), he does not even mention this method again but deals with certain other categories which he sees as characteristic of the Maijbhandari *ṭarīqa*: namely treating one's *muršid-i kāmil* as not separate from Allah and the Prophet, and practising music and dancing as a way of diving into the sea of love. In the beginning of this chapter, Delawar Hosain gives a definition of the Maijbhandari *ṭarīqa* and in short describes the Maijbhandaris from an outsider's perspective:

> This *vilāyat-e muṭlaqa* [P.] or unrestricted flow of *wilāya* is known as the Maijbhandari *ṭarīqa* in society. The people invested with an outer sight see

124 *MT*: 24: *deś, jāti, sādā, kālo, saṃsārī o asaṃsārī sakaler janya upadeś o sahaj'sādhya bidhi byabasthā*. The term *jāti* with its fuzzy semantical extension has been translated as 'races' here. The sentence appears somewhat elliptic and if given in full would read something like *pratyek deś* (an equally fuzzy term, rendered as 'country' here) *jāti*: '[For] every country and race', which underlies my rendering. – It may be remarked in general (cf. the preceding quotation) that Delawar Hosain's Bengali *sādhu bhāṣā* prose is characterised by the attempt to create a solemn and dignified diction which sometimes renders obscure both the exact denotations and grammatical structure of his (often exceedingly long) sentences. The same can be said of many Maijbhandari writers, although in the more recent writings there is a tendency to use a more lucid and simple essay style (cf., e.g., Gholam Morshed's *IP*, 1994; Nazrul Islam, *MŚ*, 1995).

125 *prādhānya pradān kariẏāchen* (*MT*: 23).

126 Delawar Hosain, *MN*: 1; also quoted in Jāhāṅgīr (1999: 46).

> the followers of this *ṭarīqa* as only getting together and, by/along with the practice of *ḥāl* and *ğazba*, singing *mor'śedī* [Bg.] or *tauhīdī* [Bg.] songs [and], for the most part, performing '*raqs*' or dance [*nitya* (*sic*), for Bg./Skt. <*nr̥tya*>] with a mind fully absorbed with love. Some may also practise *murāqaba*, *mušāḥida* and *ḏikr*; or they practise *ğalī* or *ḫafī ḏikr*.
>
> (*BM*: 128)

It appears, then, that for Delawar Hosain the Maijbhandari *ṭarīqa* is basically coterminous with his concept of *vilāyat-e muṭlaqa*.[127] Formally, it consists of a fixed number of traditional instructions, namely the 'sevenfold method'; and along with this, it has some typical accompanying features. Ever since Delawar Hosain's propagation of the 'sevenfold method', however, writers affiliated to the Ahmadiyya and Haq Manzils have adopted it as the essence of the Maijbhandari *ṭarīqa*. Thus Md. Ghulam Rasul, hagiographer of Ziaul Haq, introduces his overview of the sevenfold method ('golden seven-paths') under the caption 'Maizbhandari Tariqa' with the following words:

> The fountain of divine spark started gushing forth. People, irrespective of creed, religion or cast [*sic*], rushed to him and he became the dispenser of every divine gift to those who love him and live in communion with his spirit. He introduced the golden seven-paths and established the doctrine of Maizbhandari Tariqa as follows[.]
>
> (*DS*: 42)

In the Ahmadiyya Manzil the sevenfold method is given as the gist of the Maijbhandari message on leaflets and even reproduced, along with sayings of Ahmadullah and genealogical tables, on the walls of the outer confines of the Ahmadiyya Manzil buildings. It has been taken up into the Maijbhandari songs of Abdul Jabbar Mimnagari, disciple of Delawar Hosain;[128] and it has also found its way to institutions set up by *ḫalīfa*s, spiritual delegates, of Ahmadullah like Amir Bhandar in Potia. In a booklet containing, among other things, a hagiography of Saint Amiruzzaman, sayings and a genealogy, the sevenfold method is enjoined upon the followers of Amir Bhandar as a 'message of liberation of universal mankind'.[129] The research volume by Selim Jahangir, too, refers to Delawar Hosain and gives the sevenfold method as the substance of the Maijbhandari *ṭarīqa* (Jāhāṅgīr 1999: 46 f.).

Theoreticians affiliated to the Rahmaniyya Manzil, however, do not subscribe to this formula. In interviews, the sevenfold method was sometimes polemically dismissed as a mere concoction of Delawar Hosain's making, having absolutely no precedents in the teachings of Ahmadullah or Gholam Rahman. It has been mentioned repeatedly that the Rahmaniyya faction claims Gholam Rahman to be the completer of the Maijbhandari *ṭarīqa*,namely the one who was sent to finish

127 Cf. the description in Section 3.6 above.

128 Cf. his *Saurabh bhāṇḍār* No.60 (and also the exposition in the foreword, pp. [1]–[3]).

129 *biśva mānabatār mukti bāṇī*; Phaujul Ājim (1999: [13]) (own pagination).

the work begun by Ahmadullah. Badruddoza, his grandson and hagiographer as well as a *pīr* in his own right, then ventures to give a different description of the Maijbhandari *ṭarīqa*. He first presents a distinction of three kinds of *ṭarīqa*s that approach Allah by fighting for Him, doing good deeds for Him, and loving Him, respectively, and counts the Maijbhandari *ṭarīqa* among the last mentioned (*BB*: 159). It is also classified as a *ṭarīqa-i ʿišqiyya-i ḫiżriyya*:[130]

> The intellect of man in the present world is advancing from the coarse towards subtleness. This is also the exigency of the age. In order to fulfill the claims of the age, Hażrat Bābā Bhāṇḍārī Qibla promulgated a *ṭarīqa-i ʿišqiyya-i ḫiżriyya* [which is] all about love and passion,[131] through a religion of love. This is well-known among the public as the *tarikāẏe māij'bhāṇḍārīẏā* (U. <*ṭarīqa-i māʾiğbhandʿāriyya*>). The basic point of this *ṭarīqa* is that if the lover has no single-mindedness towards the object of love (Allah), [that] love has no worth at all.
>
> (*BB*: 160)

Badruddoza then lists five points that are 'extremely necessary' for the 'complete development of the human soul'.[132] These are: 1. to follow without hesitation and obey Allah and the Prophet (*BB*: 165 ff.); 2. to restrain the lower self (*nafs*) (*BB*: 169 ff.); 3. to follow one's *muršid* (*BB*: 171 ff.); 4. to practise *ḏikr* (*BB*: 179 ff.)[133] and 5. *fikr* (*BB*: 193 ff.), each of which are explained in much detail.

Muinuddin Ahmad, another *pīr* of Rahmaniyya Manzil, seems to follow in Badruddoza's footprints in his short characterisation of the Maijbhandari *ṭarīqa*:

> The name of the *ṭarīqa* [which is] decorated by love and passion through a religion of love is the *ṭarīqa-i māʾiğbhandʿāriyya*, and [other ingredients of it are] to put firm belief in Allah by becoming the lover of His dear friend, and to do just deeds.[134]

Syed Ahmadul Huq of the Allama Rumi Society of Chittagong, a personality with strong affiliations to Maijbhandar but devoid of leanings towards any specific *manzil*, appears to be the first writer to stress that among the various orders extant in Bangladesh, the Maijbhandari *ṭarīqa* is the only one that is indigenous to the country, and defends it against possible reproaches of being, due to its Chittagongian provenance, provincial in character.[135] In a speech for the San Francisco Symposium on Sufism, he pointed out that

130 'love-*ṭarīqa* of Khidr [*ḫiḍr*]'.

131 *prem o ābeg sarbasva tarikā[. . .]*: lit. 'the *ṭarīqa* whose all and everything is love and passion'.

132 *BB*: 165: *mānabātmār sampūrṇa bikāś*.

133 This point also includes *samāʿ*, for which five conditions are given (*BB*: 189 ff.).

134 *prem dharmer mādhyame prem o ābeg maṇḍita tarikār nām tarikāẏe māij'bhāṇḍārīẏā o āllāh, tā̃hār priẏa hābib er premik haïẏā tāhār* [sic] *prati dr̥ṛha īmān ānā ebaṃ sat·kāj karā* (*Ādāb*: 15).

135 Syed Ahmadul Huq (1995: [10]); and Chaiẏad Āh'madul Hak (2000: 10): 'It is not possible to look at this *ṭarīqa* from a perspective of provinciality (*ā̃ñcalikatā*) because it emerged in Chittagong.'

> [t]he key note of Maizbhandari order is universal love. [. . .] Zikr, devotional songs, music, ecstatic dance, implicit obedience to Pir or the Spiritual guide are some of the features of this order.
>
> (Huq 1995: [10])

Delawar Hosain's sevenfold method (whose *Belāẏate mot'lākā* he elsewhere calls the main book of the Maijbhandaris)[136] is then given in detail, although not as the gist of the Maijbhandari *ṭarīqa*, but as 'seven stages for achieving nearness to Allah' (Ibid.).

The most interesting point here is that the Maijbhandari *ṭarīqa* is portrayed as something indigenous to Bangladesh,[137] and in fact the only *ṭarīqa* of local provenance. This latter claim is hard to substantiate since the denomination of a *ṭarīqa* is apparently claimed by many religious groups in the country,[138] but may be accurate if it signifies a formulated *ṭarīqa* of more than local importance. Selim Jahangir also stresses this point:

> [. . .] the significant independent worth of the Maijbhandari *ṭarīqa* in this region as the only *ṭarīqa* emerged and propagated on the soil of Bangladesh is always to be admitted.
>
> (Jāhāṅgīr 1999: 1)

We shall see in the following chapter on Maijbhandari hagiographies that ever since *Ā'īna-i Bārī*, the locality of these saintly happenings, Maijbhandar/Chittagong, has been sanctified or highlighted in one way or the other. The claim to the Maijbhandari *ṭarīqa* as a local, Bangladeshi institution, however, is very recent and not yet very present in Maijbhandari writings. Outside Maijbhandari circles, a pronounced consciousness of Maijbhandar as 'the Bangladeshi *ṭarīqa*' or the like is certainly absent. Selim Jahangir's book, however, surely betrays a tendency to portray Maijbhandar as an aspect of national Bangladeshi heritage, as he again and again stresses the links between Islamic and local traits that characterise Maijbhandar, and tries to integrate it into a progressive nationalist narrative.[139] The fate of that work, which was banned from publication by a Government commission in 2000, is anything but an indication that Maijbhandar is in a process of rapid nationalisation. Nevertheless, I feel, there are chances that the Maijbhandari *ṭarīqa*, in close parallel to new fashionings of the Baul Lalan Shah in Kushtia, may gradually assume a paradigmatic role for self-representations of Bangladeshi religious culture.

136 Cf. Chaiẏad Āh'madul Hak (2000: 12).

137 I.e., within the framework of a 'Bengali' brand of Bangladeshi nationalism; cf. the remarks at the end of Section 8.3 for more detailed remarks on this topic; also Section 7.4 on the prospect of a 'nationalisation' of Maijbhandar as a 'secular' pilgrimage centre.

138 I know one example of a small *dargāh* in Chittagong, close to the so-called Tank Pahar, whose caretakers claim to possess a separate *ṭarīqa*, and I am sure that one could find many similar cases in different parts of the country.

139 Cf. Jāhāṅgīr (2000: 3), in the context of the Bangladeshi liberation war and the support of Bengali nationalism from Maijbhandari quarters: 'In one word, the whole history and tradition of Maijbhandar has intermingled and blended with the Bengali tradition and rendered the one thousand years-old syncretistic Bengali tradition more dynamic [*begabān*] and significant.'

4 Hagiographies

Hagiography can be defined as ‘a branch of biography with the task of narrating the lives of the saints’ (Rühle 1958: 26). As such, and in its property as a narrative genre, it borders on other genres such as biography, mythological accounts and historiography. Scholarly perception of hagiography has often focused on the blend of ‘solid historical description’ and ‘phantasy-born legend’ (ibid.), and efforts have been made to define criteria for the isolation of historically valid information from ‘literary topoi’ (Paul 1990: 20). A high degree of stylisation and stereotyped characterisation has no doubt developed in various hagiographical traditions of different religions, and the problem of historical validity is a serious one indeed. However, it is not the only one, and hagiography can be investigated without problematising the factuality of its narrations; William Smith (2000), for example, takes a different approach and studies patterns and motifs of Indian hagiography instead of sifting facts from fables. Rupert Snell remarks that the focus in Indian studies used to be on primary texts, and hagiographies, if taken into account at all, were treated as a kind of commentary:

> Such ‘biographies’ typically contain elements of the fantastic such as miracles and a variety of chronological implausibilities offensive to the historical basis of objective research principles; such ostensibly ’biographical’ writing has often, in consequence, been dismissed out of hand as a tedious impediment to verifiable historiography. More recent research on this literature, however, sees it as addressing and revealing facets of belief and attitude which, though at some remove from historical actuality, lie at the very heart of the traditions that they represent; and indeed this literature allows us to understand more fully not only the nature of the traditions being studied but also the mechanics whereby they propagate themselves.
>
> (Callewaert & Snell 1994: 1)

In the case of the hagiography of recent saints, moreover, basic layers of factuality are self-evident and hardly contestable; and Maijbhandari hagiography, starting in 1914–15, is a very recent phenomenon. So, rather than getting entangled in the problematics of historical validation, it seems promising to adopt a different perspective on the topic of hagiography by shifting the main emphasis from the distillation of historical factuality to the perceptional patterns and presentational conventions that underlie the writing of such texts, and promise to betray something of the meaning the texts are designed to convey.

In South Asia, hagiography today as much as in earlier times is an enormous field of literary production. Its literary status, however, is not generally accepted. And while medieval Indian hagiography of *bhakti* saints and Sufi holy persons has in the preceding decades found a considerable amount of scholarly attention,[1] the same cannot be claimed for more recent and contemporary hagiography. Recent hagiography, it seems, lacks both attributes of pedigree that would make it a suitable object of research, namely age and literary merit. In this connection, it is instructive to look at the treatment of recent hagiography in histories of South Asian literatures. While medieval hagiography is perceived very naturally as part and parcel of the literary heritage of the respective language, contemporary hagiography is completely eclipsed.[2] The reason for this is probably that the turn towards new, 'modern' genres and modes of writing in the nineteenth and twentieth centuries is the marked paradigmatic orientation underlying these histories; in such a process of differentiation, modern hagiography is no longer perceived as a literary genre in its own right. As a result, recent hagiographical production, despite its massive presence, passes almost unnoticed.

4.1 Muslim hagiography in Bengal

Bengali Muslim hagiography proper, in the sense of a narration of a local saint's life in the Bengali language, is undeniably popular today,[3] but appears to be a fairly recent development. To all appearances, it does not come into being before the twentieth century. The preceding literature on Bengali Muslim saints is either of a clearly distinct nature that deviates from saintly life narration, or is written in languages other than Bengali. This literature falls mainly into two parts: one consists of hagiographical accounts (mostly compilations) of Bengali Sufis and saints mostly in Persian;[4] the other is the so-called *pīr* literature, that is, songs and ballads devoted to mythological and historical *pīr*s in Bengali.

1 Cf. W.L. Smith (2000); Callewaert and Snell (1994).

2 The basis of this contention is my experience with examples from Bengali, Hindi and Marathi literary history.

3 Cf. publications like Khān (1997); Jaẏ'nul Ābedīn (1998); Māsūm (1998); Āh'mad (1417 *hiğrī* [1996–7]); Rah'mān (1986), Rah'mān (1998), Chiddikī (1997), etc., for mostly widely available contemporary hagiographies of Bengali and 'international' saints such as ʿAbd al-Qadir Gilani, Shah Jalal of Sylhet, Khanjahan Ali of Bagerhat, Shah Amanat of Chittagong, Bayezid Bistami, Shaikh Farid al-Din Ganj-i Shakr, and others.

4 Latif (1993) mentions a number of medieval Persian hagiographical compilations devoted at least in part to Bengal, and some of them written there, e.g., *Siyyar al-ʿārifīn*, completed by Hamid bin Fazlullah alias Darvesh Jamali, *c.* 1526 (references to the early Bengali Chishti saints at Gaur and Pandua and Shah Jalal Tabrizi); *Aḫbār al-aḫyār*, completed by Shaikh Abdul Haq, 1590 (short biographies of Bengali Chishti and Qadiri saints); *Gulzār-i abrār* by Muhammad Ghausi bin Hasan bin Musa Shattari, 1613 (biographies of many Bengali Sufis, mainly Shattaris); *Miʿrat al-asrār* by Abdur

Sukumar Sen's exposition shows that the more ancient texts of this literature, which originated in the seventeenth century, contain references to historical saints, such as Ismail Ghazi of Rangpur, but do not have the depiction of their lives as their goal.[5] They are mostly devoted to the *joṛātāli* or 'composite' (Sukumār Sen 2001: 408) deities such as Satyanārāẏaṇ/Satyapīr, a combination of Allah and Hindu gods, or legendary *pīr*s revered as divine forces (e.g. Mānik'pīr). It is not their lives, however, that are the topic of these narratives, but the way in which they act as divine intermediaries in the lives of human heroes and devotees. Girindranath Das, in his monograph on Bengali *pīr* literature, dedicates one part of his book to the treatment of historical *pīr*s, but admits that most of this literature, and especially that written in prose, did not originate before the twentieth century (Girīndranāth Dās 1976: 17). One of the oldest works devoted to a historical Bengali *pīr* is the *Pīr Ek'dil Śāh kābya* on the life of Ekdil Shah of Barasat, which, in contrast to Das's debatable estimation, was probably written in the (later) nineteenth century.[6] Das shows that, like the older texts on Satyapīr or Mānik Pīr, this work bears close resemblances to *Maṅgal'kābya* literature.[7] Parts of the narration are apparently modelled on local South Asian traditions, e.g. the *kṛṣṇalīlā*[8] (cf. Girīndranāth Dās 1976: 68 ff.)

Bengali Muslim hagiography thus seems to have no direct precedent in premodern Bengali literature. All evidence suggests that the medieval literary production on Islamic topics in the broadest sense excluded saintly vitae. The Bengali manuscript collections of the Bangla Academy and Dhaka University, started by Abdul Karim Sahityavisharad and continued by Ahmad Sharif, do not contain

Rahman Chishti, 1654 (collection of biographies containing a number of Bengali Sufis). Another text containing material on Bengali Sufis is *Siyar al-awliyā'* by Saiyid Muhammad bin Mubarak Kirmani, written during the reign of Firoz Shah Tughluq (1351–88), which contains information on Akhi Siraj and Jalaluddin Tabrizi. A non-Persian, exceptional writing which must also be mentioned is *Sekaśubhodaya*, a Sanskrit text which was probably written by Halayudha Mishra, a courtier of Lakshmanasena, and which contains an account of Shah Jalal Tabrizi. Some hagiographical and epigraphical material has been published in *JASB*, e.g. Damant (1874) on Ismail Ghazi of Rangpur. An important epigraphical collection of related material is Blochmann (1968). – For a survey of Islamic hagiographical literature, cf. the *Encyclopaedia of Islam* article on *Manākib* by C. Pellat (Pellat 1991); also Mojaddedi (2001); Gramlich (1987).

5 Cf. Sukumār Sen, *BSI* 4: 396–414; esp. pp. 397, 400.

6 Das argues, on the basis of a printed fragment of the work, that the absence of English loan words hints at such an early time of writing (p. 75). But he also points out that the language of the book is the oral language of Barasat, enriched with Arabic, Persian and Hindi lexic (p. 52). The connection between the appearance of the first Bengali printed book, William Carey's *Kathopakathan*, which Das sees as an indicator of the first penetration of English words into the Bengali idiom (p. 75), and the rural language situation in Barasat is hazardous. It seems, on the basis of Das's descriptions, to be more reasonable to suppose that the text was written as a manuscript during the second half of the nineteenth century, and printed in the twentieth.

7 A genre of medieval Bengali literature, consisting of texts devoted to the glorification of mostly local Bengali deities (Chandi, Manasa, Dharma).

8 Lit. 'Krishna's play', that is, the exploits of the young shepherd Krishna particularly in connection with the *gopī*s, cowgirls, and the theatrical, narrative and poetic traditions depicting it.

hagiographies of Bengali Muslim saints. Most of the texts contain Islamic religious instruction, narratives of the founding period of Islam, adaptations of Arabic and Persian romances, *pīr* literature and mystical, cosmological and yogic teachings[9]; the latter in particular has become well-known through the writings of Enamul Hak, Asim Roy and recently David Cashin. There are of course specific Sufi topics and allusions to spiritual preceptors by the authors, but while there are even biographies of zamindars,[10] the manuscript descriptions do not point to any hagiographies, neither of Bengali saints nor of saints at all.

This situation does not seem to change much in the nineteenth century with the advent of printed books in Bengal. The British Library catalogues of Bengali books testify to an astonishing topical similarity between the manuscripts and the printed materials.[11] Excepting a certain increase in writings with contemporary political and social orientation, and the vanishing of yogic mystical literature, the inventory of topics does not change much. According to the British Library collection, the first printed hagiographies of a Bengali Muslim saint appear no earlier than 1905. They are written by two Muslim authors and deal with the life of Shah Jalal of Sylhet.[12] In 1910 and 1911, other hagiographies of Shah Paran and Shah Jalal by Hindu authors follow.[13]

It is not surprising that Shah Jalal (d. 1346) was first picked for Bengali-language hagiographical efforts, since he is, to date, considered one of the most important, if not the most important Muslim saint to be buried in Bengali soil. But the sudden appearance of four Bengali printed books about this saint and his most popular *ḫalīfa* in a span of only six years does call for an explanation. As Richard Eaton elaborates, the first source to mention Shah Jalal is the travelogue of Ibn Battuta, the Moroccan traveller, who met the saint in 1345. The first hagiography about Shah Jalal was written in the mid sixteenth century and later (1613) incorporated into the Persian hagiographic compilation *Gulzār-i abrār* (Eaton 1993: 73 ff.). In this account, Shah Jalal is portrayed as a Turkish *ġāzī*, 'fighter for the faith', whereas later hagiographies of the seventeenth and eighteenth centuries, which are lost but form the base of the mid-nineteenth century Persian *Suhail-i*

9 Cf. *Āb'dul Karim Sāhityabiśārad-saṃkalita pũthi-pariciti* (Śarīph 1985) and *Bāṃlā ekāḍemi pũthi paricaẏ-1* (Biśvās 1995). Śarīph (1985) contains more material and more elaborated descriptions of the manuscripts. Most works in Biśvās (1995) are available in Śarīph (1985) too.

10 Śarīph (1985: No.150, MS 422, p. 172 f.): The manuscript is entitled *Jor'oẏār Siṃ kīrti*. The author of this eighteenth-century work is Noẏājis Khā̃.

11 Cf. the catalogues compiled by Blumhardt (1886 and 1923).

12 These books are in the collection of the British Library: *Śrīhaṭṭa-nūr*. A brief sketch of the life of Shāh Jalāl, and other Muhammadan saints of Sylhet, by Muḥammad ʿAbd al-Raḥīm. Sylhet, 1905; and *Śrīhaṭṭe Shāh Jalāl*. An account of Shāh Jalāl, a Muhammadan saint of Sylhet, by Muḥammad ʿAbd al-Wahhāb Chaudhurī. Sylhet, 1905. References given as in Blumhardt (1923: 317).

13 *Fakīr-prasaṇga*. A biographical sketch of Parāṇ Shāh Fakir, by Rājendrakiśora Chakravartī. Dacca, 1910; *Shāh Jalāl*. The Life of Shāh Jalāl, a famous Muhammadan saint of Sylhet, by Rajanīrañjana Deva. Sylhet, 1911. References given as cited in Blumhardt (1923: 91, 305).

Yaman, identify him as hailing from Yemen (Eaton 1993: 212 f.).[14] Altogether, then, there are at least four Persian hagiographies about this saint until the middle of the nineteenth century.

The typical language progression in literate Bengali Muslim society, which used to be largely coterminous with Ashraf society, has been from Persian and Urdu towards Bengali. Persian, and in religious contexts sometimes Arabic, used to be standard written languages, and Urdu the spoken idiom with an intermediate, but still high status. Bengali was regarded as a low variety, which, while also many Ashraf had it literally as their mother tongue, was considered unfit for qualified communication. The rise of Bengali and its emancipation from low vernacular status was an outcome of the Bengal Renaissance which took place mostly among Calcutta-based Hindu *bhadralok* society. With a delay of some decades, Bengali Muslims too began to profit from this enhancement of linguistic status.

Thus the shift to the Bengali language around the beginning of the twentieth century in the hagiographies about Shah Jalal is paradigmatic for the development of a new attitude towards Bengali in Muslim society in general. It is at this time that a Muslim Bengali-reading public starts to develop. The preceding use of Bengali in Muslim reformist movements such as the Farāʾiżīs for the sake of propagating their ideas among the rural Muslim population may seem to indicate that this shift had already taken place in the first half of the nineteenth century. But the Farāʾiżīs' use of Bengali had no effect on the urban, literate Ashraf population. Ashraf attitudes are mirrored by the words of the first important Bengali Muslim reformer Abdul Latif who, in a report regarding Hugli Madrassah in 1880, suggested that 'the Government should, therefore, in my humble opinion, devise such means whereby the Mahomedans may be taught at once English and Persian and Arabic'.[15] That is, while English education was perceived as crucial for the uplift of Bengali Muslim society, there was no talk of Bengali. Latif pointed out the diverging linguistic affiliations of Bengali Muslim society in his proposal to the Hunter Commission on Education (1882), demanding that a non-sanskritised Bengali be made the medium of education 'for the lower classes of people, who for the most part are ethnically allied to the Hindoos', whereas 'for

14 It is not clear which of these versions has come to be accepted today. There seem to be traces of both: according to a modern Bengali hagiography sold at Shah Jalal's shrine in Sylhet (K.M.G. Rahʹmān [1986]: *Hayʹrat Śāhʹjālāl o Śāhʹprāṇ*. Ḍhākā, Rahʹmāniẏā Lāibrerī), Shah Jalal was born in Konya. A *jāri gān* recording of the contemporary singer (and songwriter?) Solemān (*Śāh Jālāler jāri*. Binimaẏ Ṣṭor, Chittagong), by contrast, mentions Yemen as his birthplace. It is interesting to observe how Shah Jalal's image is developed in contemporary songwriting: in a song by Yunus Bangali (Iunuch Bāṅgālī) (*Āmi nūr bāgicāẏ*; recorded on Śiulī: *Hayʹrat Śāh Jālāl, hayʹrat Śāh Parāṇ*. Binimaẏ Kyāseṭ Bājār, Chittagong. Side A, Song No.3), Shah Jalal and Shah Paran are quite typically treated as a couple throughout the song. In another song by M.N. Ākʹtār (*Bāra āuliẏār deś*; recorded on Śimul Śīl: *Bābā Śāh Jālāl*. Āmin Ṣṭors, Chittagong. Side A, Song No.2), Shah Jalal is classified as one of the twelve *awliyāʾ* of Chittagong!

15 Quoted from Oẏākil Āhʹmad (1997: 505); the source given there is Enamul Haque (1968): *Nawab Bahadur Abdul Latif: His Writings and related Documents*. Dacca, Samudra Prakashani, p. 23.

the middle and upper classes of Mahomedans, the Urdoo should be recognised as the vernacular'.[16]

From the last decade of the nineteenth century onwards, however, a growing number of Muslim newspapers and journals in Bengali (Oẏākil Āh'mad 1997: 510) came into being. The output of books by Muslim authors, albeit still confined to Islamic topics, also increased.[17] The question regarding the proper language for Bengali Muslims gave rise to a long debate well into the 1920s in the new journals. The Ashrafs' claim to their alien descent and mastery of Urdu became a topic of scornful polemics.[18] While in the Bengali-medium press, taking sides with Bengali appears to have been somewhat self-evidently the rule, a controversial discussion evolved regarding the Bengali style that should be promoted, and whether the sanskritised Bengali of 'Hindu' nineteenth-century literature should be used, or rather a Perso-Arabised variant (Oẏākil Āh'mad 1997: 512 ff.)

Simultaneously, and certainly partly as an effect of this new consciousness, the general adherence of the Ashraf population to Persian and Urdu started to decline. The developments in Calcutta did not, to all appearances, take long to make their effects felt in the countryside. Some remarks in one of the first treatises on Maijbhandar, Abdul Ghani's *Ā'īna-i Bārī*, an Urdu work written in 1333 *hiğrī* (1914–15), can be taken as symptomatic of this process:

> It is a matter of great sorrow that the sun of the Arabic and the moon of the Persian have set. The Urdu that remains is still with us as a sun. In a short time, this story too will be over.
>
> (*ĀB*: 48)

The shift from Persian/Urdu to Bengali in Bengali Ashraf society has nevertheless, of course, been a slow and gradual process which took most of the twentieth century to be completed.[19] The decisive political happenings that ultimately led to the identification of the Bengali Muslim population in general with the Bengali

16 Quoted from ibid., p. 507; source ibid., p. 225.

17 Cf. Blumhardt (1886 and 1923).

18 Oẏākil Āh'mad (1997: 508 ff.). Cf. also Rokeya Begum, the famous Bengali educationist and feminist, writing in 1926: '[. . .] the Muslims of this place [Bengal] are motherless – that is, we do not have a mother-tongue. They do indeed claim Urdu as their mother-tongue, but they speak such distorted Urdu that one's ear is severely wounded if listening to it!' (Rokeẏā Sākhāoẏāt Hosen 1991: 258) Abdul Karim Sāhityabiśārad, writing in 1918, equally deplores the pernicious effects of a situation in which the language of the people is declared a Hindu idiom, and cites medieval Muslim poets in order to establish that Bengali could also claim the status of a traditional Muslim language (cf. Āb'dul Karim Sāhityabiśārad 1997, vol. 1: 166 ff.).

19 There are indications that the process is not perfectly completed even at present. In the course of my fieldwork in Chittagong, I met two aged Bengali men with formal Islamic learning who insisted on speaking Urdu in conversation. Their knowledge of spoken idioms included the Chittagong Bengali dialect, Urdu, some Persian and, in one case, English; standard Bengali seemed to be absent from the repertoire of these otherwise very educated men (or, at least, they consistently declined to use it in front of me). I am, however, convinced that such cases are today very rare.

language, the language movement of 1952 and the liberation war and establishment of Bangladesh in 1971–2, are well known. But it is in the first decades of the twentieth century that this linguistic transition also starts to gain momentum in provincial, mofussil towns such as Sylhet. The appearance of Bengali-medium hagiographies on Shah Jalal can be interpreted as an early mark of this process.

We find this process mirrored also in Maijbhandari hagiography, which sets in in the second decade of the twentieth century. The progression, in fact, does not stop at the Bengali stage, but lately has started to move on to English as the latest prestige language. Maijbhandari hagiographies, it must be stressed, occupy quite a central place in the movement's output of publications. The life accounts of the most popular Maijbhandari saints are constantly being reprinted. They are standard items for sale at the *darbār* stores in Maijbhandar and the outposts of the movement all over Bangladesh. In the present context, it is important to emphasise that this multilingual outlook of Maijbhandari hagiography (and theology likewise) is only partly due to shifts in targeted readership, but must mainly be viewed as a symptom of the linguistic transition that Bengali Muslim society underwent in the twentieth century.

4.2 Maijbhandari hagiographies

The earliest extant exposition of Maijbhandar, Abdul Ghani's *Ā'īna-i Bārī* (*ĀB*) from 1914 to 1915, is a compendium in Urdu with Persian and Arabic interspersions. It contains many hagiographical details about the founding-saint Ahmadullah's life, and therefore is the first important source we need to examine closely below. Nevertheless, it is by no means first and foremost a hagiography, but rather a treatise on Sufism with special reference to Maijbhandar and its great first saint; in this combination of biography and manual features, it somewhat resembles Qushayri's *Risāla*.[20] The first hagiographies in a narrow, biographical sense to appear from Maijbhandar are Maolana Isapuri's *Jīban carit* (*JC*) on Gholam Rahman (early 1940s?) and *Jibanī o kerāmat* (*JK*) about Ahmadullah (1967), written by Maulana Md. Faizullah Bhuiya on the basis of material compiled by Delawar Hosain.[21] These Bengali writings differ from *Ā'īna-i Bārī* in their emphasis on the saint's life as the organising principle of their narration. Other important books follow in this same vein, for example Syed Badruddoza's *Hay'rat Bābā Bhāṇḍārī* (*BB*, 1970), Jamal Ahmad Sikdar's *Śāhān'śāh Jiỳāul Hak Māij'bhāṇḍārī*

20 Cf. Mojaddedi (2001: 100 f.) ('The *Risāla* is a combination of the two main genres of Sufi literature, namely the *ṭabaqāt* and manual genres').

21 There is mention in this book of another hagiography of Ġawṯ al-A'ẓam Ahmadullah by the same Maulana Isapuri, entitled *Hay'rat Śāh Māij'bhāṇḍārī*; its 'first volume had appeared in an incomplete form' and, like *Ā'īna-i Bārī*, it 'lacked the simplicity of a biography (*jībanī*) because of an abundance of examples' (*JK*: 222). According to my research, this book is no longer available. Delawar Hossain's criticism of this book, in an afterword to *JK* authored by himself, is nevertheless telling and will be discussed below.

(*JH*, 1982) and Lutfunnesa Hosaini's *Jībanī* of Shafiul Bashar (*ŚBJ*, 1987), the latter two, however, with the unprecedented property of being ante-mortem hagiographies at the time of their first appearence. There remain to be added two recent English post-mortem hagiographies on Ziaul Haq, *Shahenshah Ziaul Huq Maijbhandari* (Islam 1987 [1982]) and *The Divine Spark* (Rasul 1994). The latest, rather academic life narration of Saint Ahmadullah is Selim Jahangir's *Gāusul'ājam Māij'bhāṇḍārī śata barṣer āloke* (2007). In addition to these books, there are many shorter hagiographic accounts of Maijbhandari saints and their *ḫalīfas* published in journals and leaflets.

The following detailed overview of this literature is designed to serve a double purpose: on the one hand, it furnishes summaries and descriptions of the individual hagiographies, depicting thus the developments in almost one century of hagiographical writing in Maijbhandar, which will be analysed in the end of this chapter; on the other, it provides detailed accounts of the life histories of a few important Maijbhandari saints as portrayed in this literature. The life narrations to follow are a main feature of the Maijbhandari tradition and a treasury of information on saintly lives and the conventions of telling them. Therefore there is no alternative to giving detailed accounts of them even at the risk of appearing cumbersomely outdrawn; I am nevertheless sure that an attentive reading will be rewarded by a thorough insight into what sainthood means in Bengali Islam. As in most cases there is more than one hagiography narrating a single Miajbhandari saint's life; second or third hagiographies shall be summarised by focusing on the salient features in which they deviate from their predecessors.

4.3 Hagiographies about founding Saint Ġawṯ al-Aʿẓam Ahmadullah Maijbhandari (1829–1906)[22]

Abdul Ghani Kanchanpuri (1914–15): Ā'īna-i Bārī *(*ĀB*) ('The Mirror of the Lord', U./P.)*[23]

Ā'īna-i Bārī was first published in 1333 *hiğrī* (1914–15); it was written in 1330 *hiğrī* (1911–12) by Abdul Ghani, a devotee of Saint Ahmadullah.[24] It is one of the oldest written sources from within the movement which is still well known.[25] The book, lithographed and republished in the 1950s on the initiative of Syed Delawar

22 For a discussion of Saint Ahmadullah's year of birth, cf. note 37 for this section.

23 For complete titles and bibliographical details of this and the following hagiographies in this chapter, see the list of abbreviations at the beginning or the bibliography at the end of this book.

24 According to the remarks in Syed Badruddoza's *Bābā Bhāṇḍārī* (cf. below in this chapter), p. 113.

25 The song collection *Prem-nur* ('The Light of Love'), compiled by Ali Allah from Tripura and printed in Noakhali, appeared two years before in 1913. Contrary to *Ā'īna-i Bārī*, this book is today unknown in Maijbhandar and is missing from the bibliography in Selim Jāhāṅgīr (1999). A copy of it is kept in the British Library. The earliest book from the circle of Maijhandari authors is a lengthy *fatwa* from 1906/7 that will be treated in the following chapter, namely Sayyid Aminul Haq Phar'hādābādī's *Tuḥfat al-aḫyār* (reprint 1997).

Hosain,[26] was brought out again in 2007 by the latter's son, Syed Emdadul Haq. A voluminous book of 720 pages in the old and 480 in the latest edition, *Ā'īna-i Bārī* is conceived as a thorough guide to the importance of Maijbhandar and an exposition of basic tenets of Sufism in one. The Urdu prose of the book is very frequently interspersed with poetry (*ġazal*, *bait*, *qiṭ'a*, etc.) in Urdu and Persian which is usually dedicated to Saint Ahmadullah and of a glorifying nature.

Ā'īna-i Bārī consists of an introduction (*ĀB*: 15–86) and two chapters called *ǧalwa*s, 'radiances': the *Ǧalwa-i awwal* ('First Radiance', *ĀB*: 87–356) that contains the life-narration proper, and the *Ǧalwa-i duwwum* ('Second Radiance', *ĀB*: 356–720), each of them subdivided into seven *partau* or 'light rays'.

The introduction furnishes an exposition of a number of topics connected with sainthood and Sufism (*ĀB*: 15–86), and deserves our attention as framing the biographical narration to follow. Its first 'light ray' (pp. 15–20) describes the traditional Islamic hierarchy of saints and the leading position of the *quṭb* ('pole') and *ġawṯ* ('help') in it. Two kinds of sainthood are introduced, the general *vilāyat-i īmān* (sainthood of faith) and the special *vilāyat-i aḥsān* (sainthood of sentiment), the latter being conceived as the truly mystical one. *Fanā'* and *baqā'* are attributes of a saint of sentiment; they are not attained by a saint of faith.[27] 'Light ray' two (*ĀB*: 20–40) is on the great difference between the saints and common men: as sunlight is unbearable for night eyes, the status of a saint is beyond the conception of common man (*ĀB*: 29). 'A saint [*walī*] is such a one, beholding whom one is reminded of God' (*ĀB*: 31), and all beings are busy performing his praise (*ĀB*: 37). The function of the saints (*awliyā'*) is the topic of the third 'light ray' (*ĀB*: 40–8): their mission, bestowed on them by God in reaction to mankind's petition, is to restore religion. The question of prophethood and sainthood is briefly dealt with, as well as the function of the *ġawṯ* within the saintly hierarchy. Another topic taken up here is connected with divine light and the veils separating creation from God: the different ranks of saints are separated from Allah by a proportionate number of veils (*ĀB*: 41–6). Full exposure to divine light would be unbearable for common people and saints of lower ranks; but it is necessary for the highest saints, since only the passing of all veils grants the emergence from all duality (*dū'ī*) and the attainment of the stage of *imāma*. A leading saint of his times (*ġauṣ-i zamān*) is described as 'the heart and life of the world' (*ĀB*: 48). The fourth 'light ray' (*ĀB*: 48–59) denounces, in short, the ignorance of the contemporary *'ulamā'* who rely only on exoteric knowledge, and stresses that both exoteric and esoteric (*ẓāhir* and *bāṭin*) knowledge are compulsory for a saint. The true *'ulamā'* (*Partau* five, pp. 59–74) attain *baqā' bi-Llāh* or 'abiding in Allah', which makes them heirs to and equals of all preceding prophets and saints. From this they derive the authority to promulgate mixed spiritual paths (*ṭarīqa-i murakkaba*) in order to help 'sick' mankind (*ĀB*: 68). 'Light rays' six and and seven (*ĀB*: 75–80 and 80–5) denounce

26 It was no easy task to find the book in 1999. I thank Syed Badruddoza for furnishing me with a photocopy.

27 Cf. the discussion of *wilāya* in the preceding chapter.

false claims to sainthood and the contemporary age of erring (*zamāna-i gumrāhī*), and conclude with a ghazal on the joy of becoming a *murīd*.[28]

In this way, Abdul Ghani prepares the ground for the life narration of Ahmadullah. The common perception of saints has it that their advent is a called-for, long-awaited happening. They have an important role to play in divine predestination, and the opening chapter of *Āʾīna-i Bārī* expounds this framework on a general level. It thereby establishes the field on which the following vita is supposed to assume meaning; it contextualises Ahmadullah's life story. It was pointed out that the structure of *Āʾīna-i Bārī* differs from that of the following Bengali hagiographic writings from Maijbhandar, but this framing of the life story proper remains a standard feature all through.

Ahmadullah's life story is set into a *Ǧalwa* ('Radiance') again divided into seven *Partaus* or light rays. The first of these (*ĀB*: 87–123) mainly deals with a dream announcing Ahmadullah's advent to his father Motiullah. This latter used to narrate the following story: one evening after the last prayer, he was in a state of relaxation and 'took a walk in *malakūt*', when suddenly the door to the world of dreams opened itself to him (*ĀB*: 89). He saw three burning candles, and the third and brightest was like sunlight:

> From its light, Allah's throne and the ground, the sky and the earth, the land and the *malakūt*, all became light. After waking up from this auspicious dream,[29] such happiness and joy filled my heart, and such bliss took my senses, that I was close to the joy of death.
>
> (*ĀB*: 90)

Motiullah then went to see Maulawi Abdul Hadi, a person familiar with secret knowledge, who explained that three pearls like three lamps would come into being in Motiullah's family, namely three sons. Two of them would become good Sufis; but

> One unique, hidden pearl of the ocean of your descendency will be such a society-pleasing scholar that through the reflexion of his face he will render the whole land and *malakūt* bright and lighted. And from the sky of your descendency [one] will be such a world-wide society-pleasing [person] that his divine light-rays will enlighten the whole world, and prove God to them.
>
> (*ĀB*: 92)

The rest of this section elaborates the background deemed necessary to fully understand the significance of that dream: ten types of dreams are enumerated, the last of which is the vision of saints (*ĀB*: 96). Thereupon, the cosmic process is described as a play of light. Light is manifested in the world by the prophets and, after Muhammad, the seal of prophethood, by the saints (*ĀB*: 103 f.). *Qurʾān*

28 A number of these topics have been dealt with in more detail in the preceding chapter.
29 *khvāb-i daulat maʿāb* [?].

quotations are used to distinguish *nūr* and *ḍiyā* (*Qur'ān* 10.5), to identify moonlight with *nūr* and sunlight with the light of the lamp (*Qur'ān* 71.16[15]), and the lamp (*sirāğ*) with Muhammad (*Qur'ān* 33.46[45]; *ĀB*: 106 f.),[30] the pun being that 'although the sun is brighter than the lamp, the important point here is that from the sun, no second sun emerges, but from a lamp, hundreds of thousands of other lamps can be ignited' (*ĀB*: 112). So it is the task of the lamp of *ġawṯiyya* to multiply itself and light up the hearts of believers. Abdul Ghani thus establishes the significance of Motiullah's dream and interprets it as a sign of the coming of a saint of the highest order into his family.

Next comes Ahmadullah's birth (*Partau-i duwwum*, pp. 124–40). A ghazal describes the joy and exaltation of the angels on hearing Ahmadullah's name (*ĀB*: 124), and four pages are dedicated to the glorification of Chittagong and Maijbhandar, the scenery in which the saint's advent is to take place. Ahmadullah is born in the province of Bengal close to Islamabad or Chatgam (Chittagong), in the village of Maijbhandar, 'the envy of a fine garden', situated in the Fatikchari Thana:

> Chittagong is the excellent city in which thousands of saints, thanks to the blessings of highest sainthood, have become masters of blessing, and in which thousands of lovers of God and *muğāhidīn* have followed the green path [. . .].
>
> (*ĀB*: 125)

Chittagong is further described by a long list of epithets, e.g. as 'the place of knowing *'ulamā'*', 'the mine of the astute', 'the storehouse of writers', 'the refuge for thinkers' and 'strangers', 'the keenness of the garden of paradise', 'the envy of societies', 'the garden of gardens' (ibid.). A poem (*qiṭ'a*) states that it is a vain effort on the author's part to describe Chittagong, since its praise requires 100,000 voices. A ghazal emphasises Chittagong's connection with the saints (cf. the expression *bāro āuliẏār deś*, the 'land of twelve *awliyā'*'): God's blessings rest on Chittagong, and it is firmly established in righteousness[31] (*ĀB*: 126). It is even compared to Kashmir and the Garden of Iram,[32] both equal to paradise on earth, and its waters are like *Salsabīl*, the fountain of paradise (*ĀB*: 127).

30 A comparison of the quoted *āyas* shows that the two Arabic terms for light, *nūr* and *ḍiyā*, are not consistently distinguished so as to refer to either moonlight or sunlight; nor is one consistently brighter or more powerful than the other or one a derivation (as moonlight) of the other. Abdul Ghani's rationalisations cannot be grounded in the Quranic words quoted by him.

31 The term used is *dharam*, skt. *dharma*. The Bengali term *dharma* is today usually used in the sense of 'religion' by Hindus as well as Muslims, Buddhists and Christians, and expressions like *islām dharma* are very common. This usage originates in the nineteenth century, but it is hard to estimate whether this neologism for the concept of religion had made its way into the Urdu prose of a writer in rural Chittagong. Thinking that this is rather unlikely, I chose to translate as 'righteousness', which conveys more of the traditional meanings of *dharma*. For a detailed discussion of the concept of *dharma*, see the respective chapter in Halbfass (1988); also my examination of Bankimchandra Chattopadhyay's use of the term (Harder 2001: 180–95).

32 P. *bāġ-i iram*, the Garden of Paradise.

Within Chittagong, again, Maijbhandar is of paramount importance. It is described in the following terms:

> In particular, the fame of the pure earth of Maijbhandar Sharif is evident. Its virtue is beyond description and praise. If there is any medicine for the pain of a wounded heart, it is indeed the dust of Maijbhandar. For him whose eye of the heart is blind to the lights of gnosis, the dust of Maijbhandar Sharif is a kind of collyrium of inspiring shining [*tağallī*].
>
> (*ĀB*: 127)

Abdul Ghani also alludes to the literal meaning of *bhāṇḍār*, 'storehouse', in a series of comparisons, by using words such as *ḫazīna, dafīna* or *maḫzan*: the dust of Maijbhandar is 'the treasure chamber of divine lights', 'the step to the divine throne of gnosis (*ʿarš-i ʿirfān*)', 'the truth of the mysteries of Mecca and Medina', 'the treasure of *kuntu nakiran maḫfiyyan*',[33] as well as the 'mine', 'storehouse' or 'gathering' of the three upper *maqāmāt*, that is, *malakūt, ğabarūt* and *lāhūt* (*ĀB*: 127). Maijbhandar is further 'the moon of all beings and hearts', 'the chemistry of all water and flowers', 'the mystery of the truth of prophethood', 'the place of unity [*nuqṭa-i waḥdat*]' and so on:

> In relation to the virtue of Maijbhandar Sharif, the language of the pen is a step in the desert of non-being [*ʿadam*]. If there is anybody at home, these indications will suffice for him.[34]
>
> (*ĀB*: 128)

Abdul Ghani proceeds by briefly introducing Ahmadullah's parents, Motiullah and Khairunnesa. It is pointed out that Ġawṯ al-Aʿẓam ʿAbd al-Qadir Gilani's mother had the same name. Ahmadullah's fathering – a pearl from the spine of the father threw its radiance into the womb of the mother[35] – is described as a much-celebrated event of truly cosmic dimensions: natural and supernatural beings, animals, men and angels joined in praise and congratulations, the sphere of the sky came to meet the ground, and different supernatural sounds and lights occurred. It was heard everywhere that the divine beloved (*maʿšūq-i ilahī*) had arrived; plants, stones and animals uttered this news in their own enraptured tongues; the assembly of the saints started to investigate the news, etc. (*ĀB*: 130 f.).

The actual birth of Ahmadullah took place 'in the year 1244 *hiğrī* [. . . or] respectively the year 1188 *maghī*,[36] on the first date of the month of Māgh, on the

33 Ar., 'I was unknown and hidden'; probably a *Ḥadīṯ qudsī*.

34 *agar ghar mēṇ kas hai, us kō yih išāra bas hai.*

35 The notion of sperma being stored in the spine (*ṣolb*) seems to be ancient. The Persian and Urdu adjective *ṣulbī* refer to offspring. A common translation of *ṣulb* found in Urdu dictionaries is 'loins', which seems to be an indication that the original notion has been superseded by a more modern, Western body concept. For Indian medical theories regarding the location of semen in the body, see Rahul Peter Das (2003, Index).

36 Local era of the Maghs in Chittagong.

day of Wednesday after the noon prayer' (*ĀB*: 133), and it is interesting to note that Abdul Ghani combines the Islamic, Maghī and Bengali calenders in this dating. This date in 1244 *hiğrī* corresponds to 1235 BE (*baṅgābda*) and – contrary to the current opinion in Maijbhandar – 1829 AD.[37]

The third 'light ray' (pp. 141–66) is entitled 'On to the mention of the blessed name and the description of the infancy of His Highness'. A praise of the names of Allah precedes the discussion of the prophet's two names, Muḥammad and Aḥmad (*ĀB*: 145 f.). Muḥammad is explained as representing a mixture of *maḥbūbiyya*[38] ('passive love') and *muḥibbiyya*[39] ('active love'), whereas Aḥmad represents only the first. It is argued that *maḥbūbiyya* comes closer to the loved object than *muḥibbiyya* and is thus dearer to it, namely to God. Aḥmad is further described as stemming or 'being mixed' from the holy word *aḥad*, 'divine unity', and the Arabic letter *mīm*, which 'stands for the complexities of divine secrets' (*ĀB*: 146). It is in this sense that Abdul Ghani also uses the conventional metaphor of the 'veil of the *mīm*' in a ghazal (*ĀB*: 143). Further, the name Aḥmad existed before the general creation and is connected with 'complete radiance' (*ĀB*: 148 f.). The fact that Ahmadullah received this name and no other is thus interpreted as a sign, and the author proceeds to build an analogy to prove the supremacy of Ahmadullah among the saints. Conjuring up a parallelism between the ages of prophethood and sainthood, he argues that each saint's sainthood is to be assigned to the prophethood of one specific prophet. On this basis, Ahmadullah is subordinated to Muhammad and becomes the 'seal' and 'sultan of saints':

> His Form is the cover (*ġalāf*) of God the Worshipped, and he is the flower [and] object [of worship] of the whole world of water and earth, as if all is the divine body and he is the soul and the spirit of the divine.
>
> (*ĀB*: 151)

Another point elaborated in the following is the indeclinable nature of the name Aḥmad, which is interpreted as a sign of straightness; further grammatical and etymological arguments ensue (*ĀB*: 156–62). The final passages and ghazals of this chapter describe Ahmadullah's mother Khairunessa and the way she cared for her infant; her praise includes her breast-feeding, by which she instilled in him 'the musk of divine love' (*ĀB*: 165).

The fourth 'light ray' (pp. 166–89) is dedicated to Ahmadullah's education, both wordly and spiritual. His school life started in 1248 *hiğrī* (1832–33), when he was four years and four months old. He was an excellent pupil and gained leadership among his classmates (*ĀB*: 168). In 1260 *hiğrī* (1844–45), he was sent

37 Many hagiographies and other publications give 1826 as Ahmadullah's year of birth. The root of this error appears to be *JK*: 22 where 1244 *hiğrī* is equated with 1826 AD; later hagiographies such as *DS*: 41 seem to quote from there. Today 1826 is generally recognised in Maijbhandar as the saint's year of birth, but I have given 1829 throughout as I believe that this explanation is valid and 1244 *hiğrī* is correct.

38 Abstract noun of *maḥbūb*, 'being loved, beloved'; 1. stem, passive participle of Ar. *ḥabba*.

39 Abstract noun of *muḥibb*, 'loving'; 4. stem, active participle of Ar. *ḥabba*.

to the Aliya Madrassah of Calcutta (Madrasa al-ʿĀliyya, Calcutta Madrasah; today known as the Calcutta Madrasah College),[40] where he mastered all fields of exoteric knowledge. According to the hagiographer, he was a first-class student throughout his studies and never missed any awards (p. 169). Among the skills he acquired were also calligraphy and oration. He worked as a *qāḏī* for a year in 1269 *hiğrī* (1852–53), and in the following year joined a madrassa in Calcutta as a teacher. Ahmadullah gained fame as an orator and preacher and was often called to preach to congregations (*waʿẓ maḥfil*) (*ĀB*: 169–72).

It was on the way to one of these congregations that Ahmadullah first encountered his spiritual master. Ahmadullah was called into the house and offered food by his *šayḫ*. Ahmadullah ate for four or five persons and still asked for more food. The *šayḫ* answered:

> Brother, all the food (*ḫāṣā*) that was there in my kitchen has been put before you. Cook the remaining food by your own hands and eat it.
>
> (*ĀB*: 177)

Šayḫ Abu Shahmah Muhammad Saleh Lahori, a Qadiri Sufi (1208–75 *hiğrī* [1793/4–1858/9 AD]), then put his hand on Ahmadullah, an action he had so far never performed on anybody. Abdul Ghani, our hagiographer, explains the meaning of these words and events: he equates the kitchen with the heart of the mystic, and the longing for food with the wish for the secret gift; the secret gifts stored in the *šayḫ*'s heart have become Ahmadullah's favour or grace. By this spiritual transfer, Ahmadullah and his *šayḫ* have become one and of the same rank; Ahmadullah would have to find the path to higher states (*maqāmāt*) by himself (*ĀB*: 178).

In the following time, Ahmadullah often came to talk to his *pīr*. He used to serve him, and they shared their states of spiritual exaltation (*ḥāl*). They also took part in *mağālis-i samāʿ*, sessions of 'audition', together (*ĀB*: 183). Around the time of Šayḫ Abu Shahma's death, Ahmadullah fell sick, was taken back to Maijbhandar by his middle brother, and recovered (p. 185). In 1276 *hiğrī* (1859–60), he was married to Musammat Alfunnesa, the daughter of Munshi Afazuddin from Azimnagar.[41] Alfunnesa soon died, and he married her younger sister Lutfunnesa (p. 185 f.). A daughter (Musammat Badiunnesa) born from this marriage died in 1286 *hiğrī* (1869–70) from smallpox, and a son died as an infant. Soon after, their son Faizul Haq was born, and in 1289 (1872–73) their daughter Musammat Anwarunnesa.

Another section (pp. 189–200) treats the properties and habits of the *Ġawṯ*. His physical appearance is described in much detail: he was neither weak nor fat, had white, long eyebrows and white hair; his face equalled the full moon, and his breast was rather large with little hair. His abdomen was completely flat; he had long hands, smooth fingers and short-cut nails. He was modest in his dress and

40 Cf. Chapter 1 for information on this institution.

41 A village directly neighbouring Maijbhandar to the West.

avoided all comfort: he did not sleep in a bed and never used a mosquito net. His food habits are described accordingly: he ate whatever was there, preferably grain and vegetables; when gifts were brought to him, the first share would go to the bringer. He is portrayed as a friendly and polite person. His states of *ğalāl*, 'awesome glory', during which nobody dared to come close to him, were followed by states of *ğamāl*, 'divine beauty', and he used to show benevolence and compassion then. People who served him even for only one day would never forget his kindness in their whole lifetime. His *ḫādims* considered him the dearest in their lives and were anxious when he was absent even for an hour or two. He never ate or drank before they did, and treated rich and poor alike, while preferring poverty (*ĀB*: 189–94). His words of advice and admonition were 'divine beauty', and even his curses had 'sweetness'. His appearance was proud and awe-inspiring; his hands never touched money and whoever came into his service, even for a short while, lost the taste for mundane things. Finally, he never bowed before the mighty, but all noblemen (U. *umrāw*) and politicians came to him in a spirit of subservience (*ĀB*: 197–200).

The following section (*Partau-e šešum*, pp. 201–313), by far the longest in *Ā'īna-i Bārī*, deals with Ahmadullah's miracles and starts off with a general examination of the concept of *karāma*. Abdul Ghani distinguishes between the common categories of *mu'ğiza* and *karāma*, the former applicable to miracles of prophets and the latter to those of saints. This classical distinction, part of a tripartite classification formulated already by Shal b. ʿAbdallah al-Tustari (d. 896) that also features *āyāt*, the Quranic verses, as God's miracles,[42] does not seem to be observed in common Bengali parlance, but is quite established in Maijbhandari publications.[43] The author explains that the remains of prophethood are transferred to the saints. It is thus seen as a Muslim's religious duty (*farḍ*) to believe in saintly miracles, and to negate *karāmāt* is equivalent to negating *mu'ğizāt* (*ĀB*: 201 f.).

But whereas prophets need miracles to legitimise their prophethood, sainthood (*wilāya*) needs no such proofs, and saints are to keep their miracles secret (*ĀB*: 202). The main point regarding the saints, as opposed to the *'ulamā'* and jurists, is that they command prayers to both the exoteric and the esoteric, and no miracles are required for this function. The common people may believe that reviving the dead is what counts, but the aristocrats (*ḫawāṣ*) know that the main thing is about reviving hearts and souls. The saints themselves are well aware that miracles must be kept secret and hide them 'like women their sanitary towels' (*ĀB*: 203). The true devotee's attitude is described in a poem in Persian, directed to the preceptor: 'As long as I live in the world/Be the life [*ğān*] of my life./Oh great divine *Ġawṯ*, you know all the other things [i.e. miracles, etc.]' (*ĀB*: 205). And it

42 Gramlich (1987: 16); cf., however, the critique of the distinction between *karāmāt* and *mu'ğizāt* of some Sunni and particularly Shii authors (Ibid.: 38 f.).

43 Cf. in this connection Sayyad Mustafa Siraj's novel *Alīk mānuṣ* (Sirāj 1988) about a Farā'iżī leader who is revered like a *pīr*; his miraculous deeds are referred to by the term *mu'ğiza*, e.g. *bujurger mojejā* (p. 20), but side by side, the term *karāmat* is also used (*hujurer kerāmati*, p. 21.).

is further elaborated that '[t]he tearing apart of habits, and miracles are neither parts of *wilāya*, nor [are they] among its conditions, nor is the practice of such tearing apart and miracles a cause of excellence and rank' (*ĀB*: 205 f.). Ġawt̠ al-Aʿẓam Ahmadullah, too, ordered his disciples to keep his miracles secret, but they came to light all the same as 'miracles which are here confided to the pen as a reminder' (*ĀB*: 206).

Then follow narrations of about twenty miracles performed by the Ġawt̠ al-Aʿẓam, interspersed with poetry and illustrative stories from different sources.[44] The single narrations begin with the introduction of the narrator who orally informed Abdul Ghani, and in some cases chains of two or three narrators are enlisted in a manner ressembling the *isnād*, the documentation of transmission in *Ḥadīt̠* literature. The stories are usually narrated in reported speech.

The greatest number of Ahmadullah's miracles as recounted in *Āʾīna-i Bārī* are cases of healing diseases and saving people from certain death.[45] Next are rescues of disciples from attacks by wild animals (tigers and snakes).[46] Two of his reported deeds are the punishment of contemporary other saints who have shown respectless behaviour towards him (*ĀB*: 239 ff. and 293 ff., cf. below). Other miracles include Ahmadullah's conquering of *ğinn* (*ĀB*: 230 ff.), his multiplication of food (*ĀB*: 299), the overcoming of natural forces in changing the course of a river (*ĀB*: 250), as well as the punishment conferred upon a farmer who out of avarice curtailed the amount of the gift he had promised to bring in exchange for the *Ġawt̠*'s help (*ĀB*: 304 ff.), and a prophecy concerning food to be brought in time to feed workers at his house (*ĀB*: 258 ff.).

The most famous of these is the story of how he rescued an inhabitant of Rangunia from a tiger's attack (*ĀB*: 261–7). While performing ritual ablutions at the central pond of Maijbhandar, Ahmadullah entered a *ğalāl* state and suddenly shouted: 'Bastard, you still haven't run away from here'.[47] Thereupon he threw his water vessel into the pond. The people of his *darbār* searched the pond in vain for the vessel. Two days later, however, the vessel reappeared, and the *Ġawt̠*'s first grandson latter narrated that an inhabitant of Rangunia[48] had wanted to prepare a dish for the *Ġawt̠* and therefore went into the jungle in order to collect wood. There, he was attacked by a tiger. At the moment the tiger was about to jump, a vessel flew 'through the veil of the hidden' (*parda-i ġaib*) and hit the tiger on the nose. While the tiger fled, the man lost consciousness. After awaking, he took the vessel and the wood, prepared the food and took it to Maijbhandar where

44 e.g. from Hāfiz, Saʿadī (p. 254), the Arabian Nights (p. 279).

45 Cf. *ĀB*: 215 ff. In this episode, Ahmadullah confronts the death angel and orders him to recede; also p. 267 ff.; p. 274 ff.; p. 291 ff. (where he appears to a *murīd* who has fallen sick in Rangoon and gone for treatment to a Hindu doctor; cf. below, p. 123); p. 301 ff.; and p. 311 ff.

46 Cf. *ĀB*: 244 ff. (tiger); p. 248 ff. (snake); p. 261 (tiger, his most famous miracle; see below on this page); p. 308 ff. (tiger).

47 *harāmzāda, tum ab tak yahāṇ sē nahīṇ bhāgā* (*ĀB*: 261).

48 A district about 30 km southeast of Maijbhandar, adjacent to the Rangamati district of the Chittagong Hill Tracts.

he narrated his story. The episode is concluded by a ghazal celebrating the *Ġawṯ*'s all-embracing protective powers.

The dented vessel is today one of the paraphernalia of the *Ġawṯ* and kept in his sitting room (*ḥuğra šarīf*) in Ahmadiyya Manzil. The somewhat rustic flavour of this story is paralleled by the other two narrations of tiger attacks. In one of these, another vessel is thrown at the tiger (*ĀB*: 245); in the other, it is sufficient to scold the beast.[49] In both, the attacked went into the jungle for the 'removal of a requirement' (*raf*ʿ*-i ḥāğat*, *ĀB*: 308), that is, to defecate, and were attacked while squatting behind bushes.

Ahmadullah's benevolence and protectiveness, illustrated by most of his miracles, are complemented by his power to administer severe punishments if his authority is not respected. Thus Baharullah Shah, a contemporary saint from Fatikchari who was regarded by some as the greatest saint in the region, is reported to have incurred Ahmadullah's wrath (*ĀB*: 239 ff.). A person had gone to the market and bought mutton which he was going to take to Ahmadullah's *darbār*. On the way, he found Baharullah sitting by the road, and when the latter learnt that the gift (*ḥadīya*) was not for him, he proclaimed that nobody was to receive greater gifts than he himself. Thereupon Baharullah put his finger into the pot, ate some of the contents and then spat into the food. Ahmadullah had foreseen the event and warned his disciples not to let any pot enter his *darbār*, scolding the 'bastard' (*ḥarāmzāda*) Baharullah. On the same day that Baharullah ate from Ahmadullah's *ḥadīya*, it is reported, he lost his *wilāya*. Wherever he went from there on, he encountered nothing but 'misery and shame' (*ĀB*: 241), and died soon after.

A similar fate hit a dervish from Bogura. Maulana Yusuf Ahmad, a *madrasa* teacher from Chittagong and disciple of Ġawṯ al-Aʿẓam Ahmadullah, was transferred to a College in Bogura, where people claimed absolute spiritual supremacy for a local dervish. The Maulana contested their claims by saying that there were saints in every place, but the *Ġawṯ* of Maijbhandar knew no second. On hearing this, the dervish cursed Maijbhandar and even beat the Maulana with his sword. That night, the Maulana slept with his head facing Maijbhandar, and dreamt that Ahmadullah showed him the dervish in the form of a dog, saying that he had no reason to be afraid and could beat him in his turn with a stick. The next morning upon waking up, he found a dog at his place, whom he accordingly beat with a stick. Instantly the dervish lost his *wilāya* and all his power to perform miracles (*ĀB*: 293 ff.). A ghazal following the narration describes all saints as the *Ġawṯ*'s servants and, in reference to the story, stresses everybody's wish to be allowed to lie under his feet in a state of self-destruction (*ĀB*: 298).

Non-Muslims feature in only two of the stories. One is about the death of a Hindu from Kanchannagar[50] who had been Ahmadullah's disciple. At the time of death, instead of *rām rām*, he uttered the words of the *kalima*, the Islamic proclamation of faith. His family members took him out of the house and tried to silence him without

49 *arē bēʾadab tū kahāṇ ğātā hai?* ('Hey insolent one, where are you going?' *ĀB*: 309).

50 A village in northern Fatikchari district, some 12 km from Maijbhandar.

success. When after his death they tried to burn his body, the flames proved to have no effect on it.[51] The '*kāfir*' family members then decided to throw the body into the river. Again, the corpse did not putrefy. It got stuck at the shore, and then was buried either by the people of the adjacent village whom the *Ġawṯ* had instructed to do so, or, according to another report, by the police (*ĀB*: 234–6).

The other story is about the healing of Maulawi Rahimullah from Maijbhandar who fell sick while staying in Rangoon. The local saint Shah Muhammad Nurul Haq, the nephew of Ahmadullah's *pīr* Muhammad Saleh Lahori, advised him to take a Hindu doctor's treatment. One day, in a state of pain, but lucid, he noticed that Ahmadullah came to his bed, inquired about his sickness and stroked his breast. Then he said: 'I have come to see you. Go back to your house. Absolutely abstain from using the treatment of the non-pure [*nāpāk*]', and disappeared.[52] Rahimullah discontinued the treatment by that Hindu doctor, recovered completely within one week and came back to Maijbhandar.

The miracle section concludes with a ghazal apothesising the *Ġawṯ* and emphasising the impossibility of describing his greatness:

> The divine ranks and degrees of the Highness of *ġauṯiyya* (R.) are so many that even if all trees were pens, and their leaves paper, and the totality of waters ink, and if all living beings were writers, going on to write from the first day of creation to the last, they could not write down even one part of a thousand [of his ranks].
>
> (*ĀB*: 313)

The last and seventh section (*Partau-i haftum*, pp. 314–52) of Ahmadullah's vita is about his physical death and starts with a scholarly exposition of the meaning of death. First, two Islamic concepts of death are juxtaposed: the *maut-i insānī*, meaning the separation of the soul from the body, namely physical death, and the *maut-i iḫtiyārī*, 'voluntary death', being the successful fight against the *nafs-i ammāra*. The latter is also called *fanā'-i nafs* or *ğihād-i akbar*; one who has mastered this *ğihād* is called a *šahīd*, martyr. This *ğihād* takes place before the physical death and ensures *ḥayāt-i ḥaqīqī*, 'true life', which lasts eternally (*ĀB*: 314 f.). Next, the four deaths of Sufi doctrine are put forward as compulsory for one who wants to reach death in life: *maut-i abyaż* or *safīd* ('white death': fasting), *maut-i asvad* or *siyāh* ('black death': abstaining from reprimands), *maut-i aḥmar* or *surḫ* ('red death': conquering the *nafs-i ammāra* and the devil), and *maut-i aḫżar* or *sabz* ('green death': renouncing pomp) (*ĀB*: 318).

The saints are not changed by physical death, their body is not 'eaten by the earth'; and their wonder-working capacity also does not disappear. Their *wilāya*, being an attribute of their immortal soul, does not end with their death, and they must be revered after death just as during their lifetime. During their presence on

51 In this connection, Abdul Ghani quotes *Qur'ān* 21,69: 'Fire, be cool and a peace on Abraham.'

52 *ham āpkō dēkhnē ā'ē haiṇ [.] āp apnē makān kō čalā ğā'ēgā aur nāpākōṇ kā 'ilāğ hargiz ista'māl na kīğī'ēgā.* (*ĀB*: 292 f.)

earth, they are with God like a sleeper who is with his beloved; but with their death they reach full union. For them, life is like sleep and death like waking, and their death is like finding one's beloved by one's side upon waking up (*ĀB*: 319 f.). Abdul Ghani resumes in a Persian poem (*bait*):

> Know everything on earth as in sleep/He has awoken who has left the world. (*ĀB*: 320)

The term *ʿurs* is explained in this connection as the union of the saint with God.[53] Saints after their death are compared to strongly shining lamps inside a room with windows which emit light to those outside.

Then the author turns to Ġawṯ al-Aʿẓam Ahmadullah. Four or five years before his death, he had become famous even in far-off countries. Everybody had heard of him, and there had also been speculations about the time of his death. He himself knew the time exactly. When the moment approached, many people gathered at Maijbhandar. Three days before his death, Ahmadullah entered an 'overshadowed' (*ṭārī*) state, and someone reported that he could not see him with his eyesight. On a Friday, it became clear that he would die in five days, and '. . . on the fifth day, a Tuesday, his Highness the *Ġauṣ-i pāk* left this mortal world for the eternal world' (p. 325).

What ensues is a very detailed description of his last days and his death.[54] Sixteen days before his death, two pillars of fire were seen from Maijbhandar.[55] They vanished when the *Ġawṯ* left the chair in the court where he used to receive visitors in those days. The smoke emitted triggers the author's comparison to *Qurʾān* 44,10(9) with its allusion to the day of *qiyāma*:[56] death being the departure of the bird of life (*murġ-i ǧān*) from the cage of the body, and the *Ġawṯ* being the soul of the world, his departure must be interpreted as the death of the world, and the appearance of smoke as one of the signs of *qiyāma* is seen as significant (*ĀB*: 331 f.). Further, Md. Hashem, Ahmadullah's nephew, dreamt that Ahmadullah was sitting on a throne, flanked by Gholam Rahman to his right and the *muntaẓam* Aminul Haq to his left, and announcing that he would go to the 'holy dwelling place of his divine friend'. The dream ends before he can specify the time, but in precaution, a shroud, rose water and other things are thereupon bought from Chittagong and kept in a secret place (*ĀB*: 335 f.).

Ahmadullah, seated on a chair in the courtyard, received between one and two thousand visitors on each of these days, held assemblies and sometimes stayed up all night. He had all the treasury boxes (P./U. *ṣandūqča*) of the *darbār* inspected

53 Cf. Section 2.2.4.

54 This short summary provides clues that towards the end of Ahmadullah's life, a veritable *darbār* had come into being, attracting a lot of visitors and rather permanent servants, and that routines such as *ḫādim*s helping Ahmadullah to wash, receiving pilgrims and retiring into the harem, etc. had been established.

55 In the villages of Nishchintapur and Farhadabad, both a few kilometres from Maijbhandar.

56 'Beware of the day when the sky vanishes in conspicuous smoke.'

and distributed the rings promised earlier to specific persons (*ĀB*: 336). His activities and words are described in minute detail. A number of miraculous happenings are recorded (e.g. a lantern splitting and reintegrating its light about fifteen times, three days before his death), especially on the day of his death. Thus, he forbade his *ḫādim*s to touch him during his last ablution. When after the *maġrib* prayer he became anxious, he had three water vessels used for ablutions brought to him and smashed. In the evening, two stars merged into one. It was windy and exceptionally warm after a series of cold days. The sun was 'completely black'.[57] Late at night, the *Ġawṯ* became quiet, and Qur᾽anic recitations were held. The position in which he was lying on his bedstead is described in detail and called *muḥammadī* form, probably comparing the shape of his limbs to the *nastalīq* stroke of the prophet's name. Unable to move his lips and mouth, he finally 'reached the holy bird's nest' on the 10th of Māgh, 1323 *hiǧrī* or 30 January 1906 AD (*ĀB*: 341). The whole universe reacted to this event: the moon was stained, the stars took the form of tears, the night wore its mourning dress; all that crawls and flies wept; the trees and stones became cold upon receipt of the news; every particle of dust shed tears out of sorrow about the departure of this 'sun of *wilāya*'; even the drops of water shed 'tears of blood' (ibid.), etc.

After a section of poetry (*ĀB*: 341–8), the hagiographic portion proper is brought to an end by the description of Ahmadullah's burial celebrations. A huge mass of people came to attend the burial, and it is described in some detail how the major *ḫādim*s of the *darbār* divided their labour in order to manage affairs. Miraculous visions were reported; in one, the prophet and ʿAbd al-Qadir Gilani were seen to prepare a bed by their side for the *Ġawṯ*, and angels brought personal items for his use (*ĀB*: 350). The corpse was washed on the spot in the court where he used to sit, and according to a procedure which one Abdul Rahim had received through a dream sent from the *Ġawṯ* (p. 351 f.). When the shroud was lifted from the body, Ahmadullah's face appeared alive and not at all marked with age. Around the bier, such jostling occurred that some fell to the ground. When the death prayers (U. *ǧanāza namāz*) were held on a lawn, everybody was so eager to keep his position that it was impossible to build rows, 'so that in the end, the death prayer was read in the same fashion as the prayers at the Kaʿba' (*ĀB*: 354).

The author then describes how, due to the crush, he was unable to either keep hold of the bier or reach the *rawḍa*, the tomb; when he went there later to light a candle, he saw people lying unconscious in prostration. The chain of *ʿāšiq*s coming to the tomb continued 'and will *inšāʿ Allāh* continue until doomsday [*qiyāma*]' (*ĀB*: 355). A poem and an Arabic prayer finish this chapter and the hagiographic account in *Ā᾽īna-i Bārī*.

57 This is compared to the death of Imām Husain, by reference to Ibn Jattan (Ǧattān), when three days of darkness hit the earth.

Faizullah Bhuiyan (1967):* Jībanī o kerāmat *(JK) ('Biography and Miracles', Bg.)

Jībanī o kerāmat appeared in completely different circumstances from *Ā'īna-i Bārī*. After Ahmadullah's death, his nephew Gholam Rahman came to live permanently in Maijbhandar, and gradually the focus of veneration and pilgrimage appears to have shifted towards him. Ahmadullah had not formally installed Gholam Rahman as his *sağğādanašīn*, and his own sons had died. So genealogically his succession went to his grandson Delawar Hosain, who was still a young boy of thirteen years when Ahmadullah died in 1906. Delawar grew into an able

Photo 5 Cover of *Jībanī o kerāmat.*

writer and administrator and at some point endeavoured to assert his own succession to Ġawṯ al-Aʿẓam Ahmadullah and reclaim centrality for what had become Ahmadiyya Manzil. His achievements in both *darbār* organisation and the movement's theological foundation are emphasised by his successors.[58]

Delawar Hosain's writings in general, and the publication of *Jībanī o kerāmat* in particular, must be seen in the context of his efforts to reassert the legacy of Ahmadullah *vis-à-vis* the strong position of Gholam Rahman's family and followers. Written half a century after the *Ġawṯ*'s death, and in the presence of an existing major hagiography (i.e. *Āʾīna-i Bārī*, which, as was stated, Delawar Hosain had reprinted in the 1950s), a certain revivalist and self-assertive quality about *Jībanī o kerāmat* is not unlikely.

The book was written by a *murīd* of Delawar Hosain, Maulana Md. Faizullah Bhuiyan, on the basis of material collected by the former. It uses very formal, somewhat archaically styled *sādhu bhāṣā*.[59] In a foreword (*JK*: i–iii), the author dedicates the book to Delawar Hosain, his *muršid-i kāmil*, who had ordered him 'by providence' (Bg. *daibayoge*) as well as openly to perform this task. He mentions the existence of several books, which are, however, not available at the time he writes:

> In order to make known this great *wali Allāh*, many theologians, knowers of language, disciples and followers have brought introductory books in different ways and verses, in the languages of Arabic, Urdu, Persian and Bengali, before the eyes of the world.
>
> (*JK*: ii)

The only titles he gives from among these books are *Āʾīna-i Bārī* and a short biography (*jībanī*) by Maulana Abdussalam Isapuri. The latter being out of print and unavailable, *Jībanī o kerāmat* is launched as a long-needed informative book for the Bengali-reading disciples and public. In an afterword that will be dealt with in detail below (*JK*: 222–32), Delawar Hosain himself adds that Isapuri's book had been edited only incompletely: only the first volume had come out. Furthermore, 'it lacked the simplicity of a biography because it had, in imitation of *Āʾīna-i Bārī*, an excessive number of topics (Bg. *machāẏel*, from Ar. <*maṯāʾil*>)' (*JK*: 222).

The book, thus, professes to be a biography (*jībanī*) and to concentrate on a chronological account of Ġawṯ al-Aʿẓam Ahmadullah's life. Its 32 chapters are organised accordingly: in short, the first three chapters (pp. 1–14) furnish a

58 Selim Jāhāṅgīr, the author of *Māij'bhāṇḍārī sandarśan*, has published a monograph, *Māij'bhāṇḍārī tarikār tāttvik bisleṣak Saiẏad Delāor Hosāin Māij'bhāṇḍārī* (Selim Jāhāṅgīr 2000), which brings out well this reverential attitude towards Delawar Hosain. A pamphlet in which Delawar himself documents his endeavours and, in a number of instances, harshly denounces certain actions of the family and disciples of Gholam Rahman, bears the title *Elākār renesā̃ yuger ek'ṭi dik*, 'An Aspect of the Renaissance Age of the Region' (Maulānā Saiẏad Delāoẏār Hosāin n.d.). Considered very controversial, this book has not seen any recent reprints.

59 *Sādhu bhāṣā* is the formal, written variety of the Bengali language, which was in general use as such until around the third or fourth decade of the twentieth century, and may still be used in written discourse today.

concise introduction of Sufism, the concept of *wilāya*, the *Ġawṯ*'s historical importance as well as a glorification of Chittagong and Maijbhandar. Chapters 4 and 5 (pp. 15–20) discuss foreshadowings of his birth, and his genealogy. In chapters 6–11, his childhood, education, professional career and spiritual development are dealt with. Most of the remaining part of the book is dedicated to a description of his miracles (chapters 12–26, pp. 40–165), the only interruption being chapter 19 (pp. 86–89) which contains a list of his spiritual deputies (*ḫalīfa*). Chapter 27 (pp. 166–76) describes Ahmadullah's qualities and behaviour; chapter 28 his arrangements regarding his succession; and chapter 29 his contributions for mankind. The remaining three chapters (pp. 198–219) are dedicated to his death, post-mortem miracles, festivities at the *darbār* as well as the *tarīqa* promulgated by him.

The first chapters contain short references to some of the concepts elaborated in Delawar Hosain's *Belāẏate motlākā*. The most interesting among these is the historical scheme of an alternation of light and darkness which has characterised the history of Islam. The greatest era of light is brought about by the Prophet Muhammad, 'the beginning [. . .] and the end of the creation', 'the only worthy representative of the whole creation'. Ever since mankind had descended into the world of *nāsūt*, divine vision had been obstructed; his arrival marked 'the first unobstructed divine vision (P. *dīdār*) and union with God (Bg. *prabhu-milan*)' (*JK*: 11). The problems started when, after his death, Islam split into different *maḏhab*s and even different faiths. Mankind, overcome by its interior enemies and devilish influence, succumbed to darkness. At that time, Allah felt that a reformer (*muğāddid*) had to be sent in order to give new life to religion by the infusion of spiritual light, and applied Ġawṯ al-Aʿẓam ʿAbd al-Qadir Gilani (founder of the Qadiriyya, d. 1166) to this task. Five centuries after this, however, spiritual inspiration was found lacking again. The Muslims lost political power and fell deeper than ever before; the darkness that came from this enwrapped not only them but all of mankind (*JK*: 13). In these circumstances, mankind prayed at the holy court of Muhammad, claiming that 'Man, created from your light, is on his way to hell today. The sun of your Islam has almost sunken' (*JK*: 14). Muhammad answered:

> O my servants all over the world! [. . .] The time has come. I am coming again with the ever-unwrapped sword in my hand, to save my obedient earth-dwellers from the grasp of the misleading enemy. [. . .] I will humiliate the non-religious unfavourable power forever and promulgate a spiritual world religion [Bg. *biśvadharma*].
>
> (*JK*: 14)

The saint to come had to be such that he could overcome all hindrances and boundaries and infuse spiritual renewal into men 'irrespective of religion and caste/class, by keeping them each in his *ṭarīqa*, each in his own religion' (*JK*: 14.).

Chapter 5, 'Signs of [his] birth' (pp. 15–19), features a prophesy and his father's and mother's dreams. The prophesy is the one Delawar Hosain propounds also in *Belāẏate mot'lākā*. According to certain utterances of Ibn ʿArabi and one unspecified Abdullah, the *nūr-i muḥammadī*[60] would split; one part of it would illuminate the world from Mecca, whereas the other would 'rise in the eastern region of Asia, the greatest land, and remove the darkness of the whole world' (*JK*: 15). The dream of Ahmadullah's father Motiullah, in which three lights are seen, is narrated almost in the same terms as in *Āʾīna-i Bārī*; the re-occurrence of the expression 'he took a walk in *malakūt*',[61] a rather uncommon metaphor for 'dreaming' in the Bengali language, is a strong indication that this passage has been taken from *Āʾīna-i Bārī*. The mother's dream, however, is newly added: Khayrunnesa dreamt that she stood by the seaside with her husband. Seeing that other people were diving for pearls, they too joined them and found pearls, one being so radiant that their boat was illuminated by it. Her husband explains the dream as referring to her future son Ahmadullah (*JK*: 17 f.).

Chapter 5 derives Ahmadullah's genealogy from ʿAbd al-Qadir Gilani, who was a product of the two lines of Hasan and Husain. The migration to India, and ultimately to Bengal, of ʿAbd al-Qadir Gilani's descendants is described. They settled in Gaur, the ancient Bengali capital, and worked as *qāḍī*s and *imām*s until a severe epidemic in 1575 prompted Qadi Sayyad Hamiduddin Gauri to leave and settle in Potia, Chittagong. One of his sons, Sayyad Abdul Qadir, came to Azimnagar, the village adjacent to Maijbhandar, in order to work as an *imām*. His great grandson Motiullah, Ahmadullah's father, became *imām* in Maijbhandar (*JK*: 19 f.).[62] As in *Āʾīna-i Bārī*, Ahmadullah's fathering is a celebrated event of cosmic dimensions. It is interesting to note that traditional body concepts are at work here: 'Once, in an auspicious moment, the Ġawṯ al-Aʿẓam [came] from the head of Sayyad Motiullah Sahib and took his position in the holy womb of his mother, Bibi Khairunnesa Sahiba.'[63] His birth in 1244 *hiğrī*, 1235 *baṅgābda*, '1826' AD [*sic*!] is celebrated by all men and nature; and the erroneous conversion of *hiğrī* 1244 into 1826 AD that we have here becomes the model for many future Maijbhandari writers as argued above – the correct year, however, is 1829 (Chapter 6, *JK*: 21 f.). The night before his name-giving, his father was instructed by the Prophet in a dream to call him Ahmadullah. The name is explained as the combination of God's and the Prophet's names, the 'veil of *mīm*' is discussed, and the Arabic letters of Aḥmad Allāh are interpreted as the different bodily positions during the ritual prayer (chapter 7, pp. 23–5).

Ahmadullah grew into an earnest boy with a philosophical bent of mind. He was an excellent pupil who was always top of the class. He never argued with

60 The divine light issuing from Muhammad, which plays an important part especially in Sufi cosmology. Cf. above Chapter 3.

61 *ālame māl'kute phereś'tā jagate bhramaṇ karilen* (*JK*: 16).

62 The period of 250 years (from 1575 until 1829, the birth of Ahmadullah) for five generations is a rather long time, considering that the sixth generation after Ahmadullah is under way in present Maijhandar only approx. 175 years after his birth, but not impossible.

63 The position of semen in the head (*mastak*) is in accordance with the yogico-tantric body concept. Cf. also the sections on 'boat journeys' and the 'body' in Chapter 5. In Indian medicine, by contrast, the notion that the semen is spread in all parts of the body is dominant.

anyone, avoided unnecessary talk, loved loneliness and read the *Qur'ān* and books on religious topics at an early age. Local educative facilities could not satisfy his eagerness for knowledge and religious expertise, so in 1260 *hiğrī* (1844–45) he was sent to the Aliya Madrasah in Calcutta (cf. above). While studying there, he was extremely zealous in the preformance of his religious duties. He slept and talked little, and when walking outside, he held his eyes lowered in front of himself. He loved to hear Islamic sermons (*wa'ẓ*) and visit the tombs of *awliyā Allāh*, and he became a true expert in all things Islamic (chapter 8, pp. 26–9). His professional career – *qāḍī* in Jessore (1269–70), *madrasa*-teacher in Calcutta, and simultaneously a training as a munsiff – is dealt with in another short chapter, and it is stressed that he gained a good name in Calcutta and used to be invited for preaching.

His initiation by the Qadiri Sufi Sayyad Abu Shahma Muhammad Saleh al-Qadiri Lahori (1270) is described almost as in *Ā'īna-i Bārī*. Two years later, his father Motiullah's death took him back to Maijbhandar. His mother got him married in order to turn his attention to wordly life, but his spiritual and ascetic lifestyle persisted.[64] His brothers, annoyed by his behaviour, separated their household from his in 1282 (1864); he had them cultivate his land according to the *bargā* system, thus getting one sixth of the family's income, and still did not make any efforts to earn a livelihood, which brought his family close to real poverty (*JK*: 37–9).

At this point, probably around 1870,[65] his sainthood (*wilāya*) first manifested itself (Chapter 12). His first miracle also features in *Ā'īna-i Bārī* (*JK*: 258 ff.), but not as his first; and the events are somewhat dramatised in the narration presented in *Jībanī o kerāmat*. His mother had contracted roofers in order to repair the roof of their house, and part of the contract was that they had to be given a meal. On the appointed day, however, no food was in the house. His mother and wife repeatedly asked him to make some arrangement, and he sent them away, saying that everything would be fine. Virtually in the last minute, when the roofers had already sat down to eat, carriers arrived with ready-cooked food and presented it to him as a *hadīya*.[66] From there on, God no longer being 'willing to keep him concealed' (*JK*: 42), his miracle-working power and *wilāya* developed fully, and the commotion at what now had become his *darbār* started.

The miracles recounted in *Jībanī o kerāmat* (pp. 40–165) are much more numerous then those in *Ā'īna-i Bārī*. This multiplication seems to be due to the compiler Delawar Hosain's efforts. About ninety single events from

64 Marriage as a means of preventing what may be perceived as ill-guided otherworldliness reoccurs in the hagiographies of Ziaul Haq (cf. below in this chapter), but also elsewhere. The famous Shakta saint of Dakshineshvar, 23-year-old Ramakrishna, was married to Sarada Devi for the same purpose. Without feeling much need of explanation, an English hagiography laconically states: 'He was as indifferent as ever to all worldly matters. His mother and his brother began to search for a suitable bride for Ramakrishna' (Pranab Bandyopadhyay 1990: 13).

65 The text mentions that Ahmadullah's age was beyond forty.

66 Lit. 'gift' (Ar.), the term *hādiyā* in Bengali is used in the sense of an offering to a *pīr* or religious person, and also as the substitute for *mūlya* or *dām* ('price') in religious publications.

Ahmadullah's lifetime are narrated. Seven of the twenty stories from *Ā'īna-i Bārī* are taken up, the rest is new. The denunciation of miracle-induced belief that precedes the accounts in *Ā'īna-i Bārī* is lacking here, and the stories are not only examples, but also truly a compilation. One criterion of their inclusion was apparently the reliability Delawar Hosain attested to them,[67] apart from other possible motivations to be dealt with below.

Barring very few 'purpose-free' demonstrations of power over nature and natural phenomena, as, for example, the attraction of peaceful tigers and other wild beasts to the *darbār* at night (*JK*: 116) or the emission of light during a meditation at the mosque (*JK*: 57), Ahmadullah's miracles as recounted in *Jībanī o kerāmat* are directed to specific persons mentioned by name and address, and usually of a beneficial nature. Most of them are about healing diseases, usually by the prescription or bestowal of specific food items (a boil is healed with pepper [*JK*: 64], and the 'biting disease'[68] with bananas and milk), but sometimes also by beating the 'patient' with a stick (e.g. lepra, *JK*: 117). In three cases, Ahmadullah appears to dying disciples to assure their peaceful death (*JK*: 147 ff.); he also revives dead people (*JK*: 129, 130) and saves people from certain, imminent death by confronting the death angel ʿIzrāʾīl and sending him back (*JK*: 144–6). Miraculous multiplications of food are reported (*JK*: 149–51).

Ahmadullah helps people in various ways: by sending them dreams with instructions (e.g. *JK*: 60, 84); by bestowing *kašf*, 'inspiration' upon them, often through the intermediation of food given by him (e.g. *JK*: 66, 101, 118, 134); by granting them *fayḍ*, 'favour', much in the same way (*JK*: 123 f.); by helping them to pass examinations (*JK*: 91 f., 160) and obtain success in their wordly life and career (*JK*: 134, 151, 161). He helps the childless to get offspring (*JK*: 83, 93), for instance by giving a man three flowers for the three sons he is going to have (*JK*: 95). Ahmadullah also wards off danger from beasts and natural calamities: The story of the tiger chased away by the thrown water vessel (*JK*: 128) has served as the book's cover illustration for a number of editions[69]; he is also reported to have made rain (*JK*: 139). He gives powers to men, e.g. the gift of oration to a preacher (*JK*: 81) or the ability to become a doctor to an ignorant man (*JK*: 100). Ġawṯ al-Aʿẓam Ahmadullah possesses true insight into the most insignificant happenings in the lives of his disciples (*JK*: 80, 157 f.), and his prophecies are numerous and unfailing.[70] He is especially aware of vows to bring specific presents in case one's wish is fulfilled, and does not tolerate any breaches of such vows or the curtailing of promised *hadīya*s (*JK*: 131, 13, 159).

67 If the sheer abundance of miracles had been the driving force, it could not be explained why not all of the miracles featuring in *Ā'īna-i Bārī* have found inclusion.

68 *kām'ṛi rog*: probably a chronic stomach disease is meant here.

69 Cf. above (p. 121 f.) for the description of the story in *Ā'īna-i Bārī*. Another story about a rescue from a tiger's attack that is narrated in *Ā'īna-i Bārī* features also here (*JK*: 126), as well as the changing of the course of a river (*JK*: 103; *Ā'īna-i Bārī*: 250).

70 Seven single prophesies on individual lives, the founding of madrassahs, etc. are mentioned (cf. *Jībanī o kerāmat*: 40; 48 ff.; 71; 156; 164).

Ahmadullah also possesses powers to make saints (*JK*: 67) and to convert saint-hating *'ulamā'* into Sufis and his disciples (*JK*: 58). He asserts his authority over the Sufi convent of Mirzakhil in Southern Chittagong by spiritually satisfying a disappointed Mirzakhil disciple (*JK*: 61). He can directly communicate with the dead, and is reported to have done so while sitting at night in the cemetery of Damdama, the northern neighbouring village of Maijbhandar (*JK*: 96). Furthermore, he has the capacity to display distant places, holy people and the dead at his will: when Gholam Rahman once read the prayer too early, he showed him the Ka'ba between his arm and thigh, thus demonstrating that at Mecca, the prayer was just about to begin (*JK*: 162). When his wife desired to see the Prophet Khidr (Ḫiḍr), he had him come instantaneously to his courtyard (*JK*: 163), and he showed the father of a dead child that it was safe in paradise (*JK*: 85). His powers are also reported to reside in objects of his personal use, especially in his shoes, to which beneficiary effects are attested (*JK*: 91, 133).[71]

Other than in *Ā'īna-i Bārī*, no severe punishments are narrated; the sometimes harsh behaviour of the Ġawṯ al-A'ẓam always leads to a favourable ending. The one exception is the narration in which he instructs someone to cut a certain tree; the son of a neighbour of Ahmadullah's protests by saying: 'Why did the *faqīr*-hood[72] of the Maulavi[73] come on my tree?' Hearing this, an enraged Ahmadullah revealed that the tree-cutting was to save his father from imminent death. When thereupon his father did fall sick, the son came to Ahmadullah to ask his pardon, but the latter replied: 'Once the arrow is released, it cannot be taken back', and the father died (*JK*: 96 f.).

Ahmadullah's utterances are usually quoted in Urdu, and in fact, the *darbār* language at his time was Urdu, not Bengali. The few exceptions include his remarks towards his daughter Sayyada Rabeya Khatun, in a funny episode. She asks him what she should say after her death, when the angels Munkar and Nakīr ask her about her deeds, and he tells her to remember the *ḏikr* given to her. When she says that she will not be able to do so, he tells her to remember him. Hearing that this, too, would be too much for her, he laughs and says: 'Well, my dear, you won't have to do anything. I will do it all' (*JK*: 85). This is an indication that he used to speak Bengali with women.

Lastly, there is one type of miracle completely absent from *Ā'īna-i Bārī*, namely miraculous deeds in connection with *ḥağğ*, the Mecca pilgrimage. In one case, Ahmadullah was seen as a fellow *ḥāğğī* by a pilgrim from Chittagong at Medina and Mecca; but after returning home, the pilgrim learnt that he had not moved from Maijbhandar at the respective time (*JK*: 111). In two others, he appeared to pilgrims unable to return from Mecca and arranged for their return by supernatural means (*JK*: 107 ff., 111 ff.). In two more cases, Ahmadullah asked Mecca pilgrims to give small amounts of money to a person they would meet at

71 A connection may be drawn here to the veneration of the saint's feet. Cf. the remarks in the section on the 'attributes of the saints' (Section 5.7.5).

72 *phakiri* is the term employed.

73 Ahmadullah used to be addressed as *Phakir Maulabhī*.

Mecca; the respective, mysterious person invariably singled them out and asked for precisely the amount of money Ahmadullah had given.

Chapter 27 assembles incidents and utterances of Ahmadullah that depict his character traits, behaviour and position in matters of religion. He used to receive singers at his *darbār* and listen to songs; the singers mentioned are Md. Eshaq, Gurudas Faqir, Aftabuddin, Alauddin, Asad Ali, Amiruzzaman and Abdul Hadi (*JK*: 166 f.). His visitors included members of the Chakmas, Maghs, Kukis and other ethnic groups from the Chittagong Hill Tracts (*JK*: 167). Further sections record his utterances regarding problems of religious practice (e.g. *sağda*, *JK*: 169),[74] his personal observance of the *šarīʿa* (*JK*: 171) and his compassionate and polite nature (*JK*: 172 ff.). Two pages are devoted to his *dharmanirapekṣatā* (Bg.), 'non-favouring of [one specific] religion'.[75] A Buddhist disciple from Nishchintapur[76] repeatedly asked Ahmadullah to make him a Muslim. He answered: '*Miñā*! Stay in your religion. I have made you a Muslim.' A *ḫādim* then took the disciple aside and explained that he had truly become a Muslim. After his death, his body was not cremated but buried, in the same way as a number of Hindu disciples whose corpses would not catch fire (*JK*: 175 f.). A Hindu who was eager to adopt Islam was told to eat his own food and keep a constant fast. He understood that there was 'no need for him to formally become a Muslim', and that 'abstaining from sin, as intended by fasting and praying, and depending on one's own intellect was genuine Islam' (*JK*: 176).

The following chapter (chapter 28, pp. 177–90) discusses a variety of interesting topics. First, it tries to prove the strong connection between Ahmadullah and Delawar Hosain. Ahmadullah refused to eat in Delawar's absence (*JK*: 178); he called him his Nawab[77] and Sultan;[78] he even said that Delawar's elder brother Mir Hasan was 'immature' (*nābāliġ*), whereas Delawar was 'mature' (*bāliġ*) and worthy to sit on his throne (*gaddī*). Ahmadullah is further said to have established a parallel between the Prophet's grandsons Hasan and Husayn and his own grandchildren.[79] Right after this, it is narrated that Gholam Rahman once held Ahmadullah's feet so firmly that Ahmadullah started beating him until he was bleeding all over; explaining this to his wife, he said that he had given Gholam Rahman one of his eyes already, and could not give away the second as Gholam Rahman desired. In further paragraphs, Ahmadullah's own statements regarding his spiritual status are quoted: He once entered the Kaʿba with his 'brother' Ġawṯ al-Aʿẓam ʿAbd

74 Ahmadullah legitimises *sağda* in front of five persons: father, mother, *pīr*, *ustād*, righteous king. He refers to a *fatwa* (*khājikhān phatoẏā* [?]). *Jībanī o kerāmat*: 169.

75 *dharmanirapekṣatā*, literally 'non-partiality regarding religion', is today, in Bengali and other modern Indo-Aryan languages, usually the equivalent of 'secularism'.

76 A village situated a few miles south-west of Maijbhandar and adjacent to Nazirhat.

77 *nabāb hāmārā delā maẏ'nā hyāẏ* (<*nawāb hamārā dēlā mainā hai*>; Urdu in Bengali script in the original); *JK*: 179.

78 *sul'tān hāmārā delā maẏ'nā hyāẏ* (<*sulṭān hamārā dēlā mainā hai*>; Urdu in Bengali script); *JK*: 179.

79 When Ahmadullah once saw his nephew Md. Hasan wake his grandson Mir Hasan somewhat rudely, he scolded him, asking him whether he had not heard of the Ḥasanayn, and that they had to be treated with respect (*JK*: 181).

al-Qadir Gilani and saw that the breast of Muhammad was an endless sea, into which they both jumped; and the Prophet had two *ṭupīs*[80] to hand over, one for him and one for his 'elder brother *Pīrān-i Pīr*' (ʿAbd al-Qadir Gilani) (*JK*: 183). His own explanation for his *ǧalālī* states of mind (accompanied by severe cursing) is given,[81] and some of his teachings and frequent instructions are mentioned, too.[82]

Both in his physical appearence and his character traits, Ahmadullah had the 'form' (Bg. *abaẏab*) of Prophet Muhammad. His soft manner of speaking and the way in which divine love found expression in his behaviour testify to this. And 'even if he was not illiterate', his love of Allah was so deep that his education and skills did not help him in any way (*JK*: 185 f.). He was Muhammad's 'representative' (Bg. *pratinidhi*) on earth, and in analogy to the last prophet, he was the last saint (*walī*); likewise, his grandchildren, as he had said himself, were similar to Hasan and Husain (*JK*: 186).[83] The chapter concludes by stressing the general nature of his sainthood (*JK*: 187) and his efforts to keep his miracles, induced by Allah, secret; it was due to Allah's will that they came to light to reveal his sainthood (*JK*: 190).

In the following chapter (*JK*: 191–8), Ġawṯ al-Aʿẓam Ahmadullah's contributions to mankind are summarised: other than the saints before him, he opened the door to liberation 'irrespective of religion and caste/class, by abolition of the conflicts between religious doctrines' (*JK*: 191). Simultaneously, he inspired spirituality through his *wilāya* and became the cause for 'the arising and development of many powerful saints' (*JK*: 193). His encouragement of a simple lifestyle, the revival of saint worship 'at all mausolea of the eastern part of Asia' initiated by him, and his inspiration and support for a new song tradition in Bengali, tasteful, motivated by divine love and free from obscenity, are listed as further contributions (*JK*: 193–7).

The remaining chapters feature descriptions of Ahmadullah's demise and a number of his post-mortem miracles, among them the following story: During World War II and after Chittagong had been hit by bombs in 1942, Ahmadullah, wearing a coat and pants, appeared to a postman in a dream saying that he had chased the enemies away; the postman concluded from Ahmadullah's dress that he was on the side of the English, who would consequently win the war (*JK*: 207 ff.). These accounts are to demonstrate that Ahmadullah is still present 'through the effect of his imperishable, highly forceful soul-power (Bg. *rūhānī śakti*)' and

80 i.e. caps worn on many occasions, especially for prayers.

81 Cf. *JK*: 183: he compares himself to a pot on the stove and his fits of anger to the clattering of its lid; when the fire of divine love heats the human body, the lid of knowledge (Bg. *elemer ḍhāk'ni*) is incapable of holding it tight.

82 'Become "angel-bodied" ', interpreted as an instruction to perform Allah's praise in the same purity as the angels; 'eat choosily like the pigeons', that is, avoid everything *ḥarām* and keep praising Allah; 'recite Allah's name sitting at your place like the *kun'jās·k* bird' [?; Bg. *cāl'caṛā*]; 'recite the *Qur'ān*'; fasting and praying (*JK*: 184).

83 Cf. Siegfried (2000: 81 ff., Section 6.3) on the parallel constrution of the *ḥilya*s, 'descriptions of good qualities', of Prophet Muhammad and the self-proclaimed eleventh Caliph Shamsujjuha of Thakurgaon in northern Bangladesh.

always ready to assist his disciples and fulfil their heart's desires (*JK*: 216). The book ends in chapter 32 (*JK*: 217–21) with a description of the annual *ʿurs* on the 10th of Māgh and the complete *silsila*, spiritual line, of Ahmadullah, to which Delawar Hossain is added as the last entry.

A short comparison of these two main hagiographies of Ġawṯ al-Aʿẓam Ahmadullah, *Āʾīna-i Bārī* and *Jībanī o kerāmat*, reveals a number of important points. The first of these is a new self-assertive tendency in *JK* which is absent from *ĀB*. Delawar Hosain, the *spiritus rector* behind *JK*, uses the depiction of Ahmadullah's life to assert his own position as his only legitimate successor. Chapter 28 in particular can be read as an attempt to settle the latent controversy between the Ahmadiyya and Rahmaniyya Manzils; here it is made explicit that Delawar was destined to be Ahmadullah's *gaddīnašīn*, direct successor, whereas Gholam Rahman, even if Delawar does grant him the title of a *Ġawṯ al-Aʿẓam bi'l-wirāṣat*, 'in succession',[84] is portrayed as his main *ḫalīfa* or spiritual envoy. The afterword by Delawar Hosain makes this tendency additionally clear.

Secondly, it seems significant that the rough and punishing aspects of Ahmadullah's personality and actions are somewhat downplayed in *Jībanī o kerāmat*. In *Āʾīna-i Bārī*, besides the benevolent and mighty protector, we also notice a severe punisher who does not hesitate when it comes to reducing his counterplayers to humiliated insignificance. The respective episodes are lacking in *Jībanī o kerāmat*; here his *ǧalālī* states of mind, barring one single case,[85] do not lead to anybody's destruction, but ultimately result in the respective person's elevation, be it spiritual or otherwise.

Third, the approach to miracles is different. *ĀB* is vociferous in its condemnation of belief motivated by miracles, and goes to some length in stressing that like every true saint, Ahmadullah did his best to keep his superhuman deeds concealed. In *JK*, the former point is absent, and the latter plays only an occasional role. *ĀB* hardly resolves the discrepancy between its decided contempt for the superstitious base of miracle-induced belief and the fact that it gives almost two hundred pages to the description of miracles. *JK*, on the other hand, boldly bridges this gap by claiming that it was God's will that Ahmadullah's deeds came to daylight, in order to legitimise his sainthood (*wilāya*).

The fourth and arguably most significant point is that in *JK*, a new ideology enters the scene, an ideology which has today become emblematic for Maijbhandar and many other shrine cults in Chittagong. Two of the twenty miracles narrated in *ĀB* feature Hindus, for whom the term *kāfir*, 'infidel', is used, and is even reported to have been used by Ahmadullah himself; in one of these, the treatment by a *kāfir* Hindu doctor is shown as unfavourable to the healing process, and in the other, the *kāfir* Hindus are depicted as a somewhat superstitious lot, unable to react in a 'civilised' way to the events. It is mentioned that Ahmadullah had disciples from different religious communities, but not emphasised as anything

84 Cf. *JK*: 89.
85 Cf. *JK*: 96 f.

noteworthy. In *JK*, this changes completely. The incidents narrated in *ĀB* are downplayed in it; by contrast, two others are included which testify that Ahmadullah did not require or even appreciate formal conversion to Islam. The expression *dharmajātinirbiśeṣe*, 'irrespective of religion and caste/class', appears a number of times, and is celebrated as the very essence of Ahmadullah's sainthood which sets him off from former saints, that is, the very constituent feature of his greatness. This argument will be taken further at the end of this chapter.

4.4 Hagiographies about the second great Maijbhandari saint, Gholam Rahman alias Bābā Bhāṇḍārī (1865–1937)

Abdus Salam Isapuri (n.d.): Jīban carit *[JC], ('Life account'), c. 1940*

The author of this hagiography, Maulana Abdussalam Isapuri, was one of the main *ḫalifa*s of Gholam Rahman. His *mazār* is situated at Isapur close to Maijbhandar. He wrote vitae of both Ahmadullah and Gholam Rahman, but the former is no longer extant.[86] Isapuri authored a number of other books mostly of a theological nature, among them a *tafsīr* or commentary on the *Qur'ān*[87] and a fragmentary translation of Jalal al-Din Rumi's *Masnavī*.[88] None of Isapuri's writings are dated, and his long life (*c.* 1890–1990) leaves all options open. His hagiographies, however, seem to have been written before his theological tracts and shortly after Gholam Rahman's death,[89] and the one on Ahmadullah was written first.[90] Isapuri's *Jīban carit* can thus roughly be dated around 1940. It is the first book devoted to Gholam Rahman's life and has apparently seen a number of new editions; perceived as a standard hagiography, it is easily available at the *darbār* today.[91] In comparison to the other major Maijbhandari hagiographies, *Jīban carit* is exceptionally concise. Isapuri limits himself to furnishing

86 Cf. *Jībanī o kerāmat*, *JK*: 222 ff., where Delawar Hossain criticises Isapuri's hagiography on Ahmadullah, alleging that Isapuri downplays Ahmadullah's status; *Toh·phāẏe jaśane mauled*, p. ṣola.

87 *Jal'oẏā-e-nūre mohāmmadī*, on Sura 94.

88 *Mach'nabī Śarīpher baṅgānubād o biśad byākhyā.*

89 Maulavi Abdur Rahman, in an article on Isapuri's achievements, (*Haj'rat Maulānā Īchāpurī (ka) er sādhanā o karmajībaner kaẏek'ṭi dik*; in *Toh·phāẏe jaśane mauled*, pp. sāt-āṭāś), mentions the hagiographies first in a chronological account of Isapuri's life: in 1917, on Gholam Rahman's 'sign', he joined the New Scheme Madrassa at Maijbhandar; when this Madrassa was translocated 'after some years', he quit and 'after this' set to writing the two hagiographies (p. ṣola). These 'some years', considering that Gholam Rahman died in 1937, cannot be fewer then twenty. In spite of the indeterminate nature of these indications, it does seem likely that Isapuri wrote Gholam Rahman's vita not long after the latter's death. Another possible indication that Isapuri wrote his hagiographies before his other tracts is in *Jīban carit* where he announces that he will elaborate a certain theological point elsewhere.

90 Cf., e.g., *Jīban carit*, p. 79, where he refers his readers to that book.

91 The present edition is unfortunately undated. The fact that it is 'computer-composed', however, indicates that it is hardly older than five years.

Gholam Rahman's life narration and explicitly desists from elaborating the theological dimension.[92] Wherever he does add comments on the theological purport of Gholam Rahman's life and deeds, these are given in footnotes.

Jīban carit is divided into two parts, the first (pp. 5–53) dealing with Gholam Rahman's life before the attainment of full saintly status, the second (pp. 54–108) with his travels, miracles, etc. The book starts *in medias res* with a chapter called *janmabr̥ttānta*, 'birth narration' (pp. 5–8). A *Maṣnavī* quotation on the constant reappearance of radiance opens the chapter, and following it, five such radiant Sufis are mentioned: ʿAbd al-Qadir Gilani, Muʿin al-Din Chishti, Jalal al-Din Rumi, Hafiz of Shiraz and Gholam Rahman Maijbhandari. Gholam Rahman is thus from the very start identified as a saint of the highest order, and by his arrival, the 'superstitious Bengalis [. . .] began to rise to the same prominence that had been attained by the inhabitants of Bagdad, Ajmer', etc.; 'another miraculous light' was lit in Badr Shah's Chittagong (*JC*: 6). After Gholam Rahman's birth in 1284 *hiğrī* (1867–68), everybody was amazed by his beauty. When the praise of Allah was recited, the infant opened his eyes.

The second chapter (pp. 9–11) is devoted to the praise of Chittagong and Gholam Rahman's family history. Sanctified by the advent of twelve saints, the status of Chittagong, the *bāro āuliẏār deś*, was doubled by Gholam Rahman's

Photo 6 Mausoleum of Saint Gholam Rahman Maijbhandari.

92 Cf. *JC*: 79, where he expresses the intention to discuss the status of miracles 'elsewhere' (*sthānāntare*).

appearance. Its excellence is specified in eleven points: Chittagong is strong in education and knowledge, its inhabitants are very religious, its women aspiring to *satītva*,[93] etc.; and its natural beauty and climate are such that 'even Kashmir will indeed be jealous'. In Chittagong, again, Maijbhandar is of utmost importance and glory due to the advent of this saint, and worthy of bearing the appellation *šarīf*, noble, just as Bagdad and Ajmer (*JC*: 10). The remaining part of the chapter briefly describes the migration of Gholam Rahman's predecessors from Bagdad to Delhi, Gaur, Chittagong and ultimately Maijbhandar.

Gholam Rahman's exceptional beauty is then described in some detail (Chapter 3, *JC*: 12–15), and, on his *ʿaqīqa* or name-giving ceremony, Ahmadullah is quoted as having compared him to Yusuf: 'This is the rose of my garden. The face of His Highness Yusuf has appeared in him. Take good care of him' (*JC*: 13).[94] When asked to suggest a name for the child, Ahmadullah named him Gholam Rahman. The family soon felt the auspicious effects of the infant by a general upturn in household and agricultural matters; Gholam Rahman, from the age of two onwards, in his turn, showed the utmost attraction towards his saintly uncle Ahmadullah.

Chapter 4 (pp. 16–28) describes Gholam Rahman's school life and marriage. At the age of four and a half, he was sent to the local *maktab*, and was instructed in *namāz* at seven. By the age of ten, he had become a very concentrated, quiet and obedient pupil in Islamic teachings, taking all ritual instructions highly seriously, the only thing ranging higher still being his daily visits to Ahmadullah (*JC*: 17). He attended with care to the household duties assigned to him, always attempting to get them done fast so as to enable him to see Ahmadullah. When asked to herd the cattle, he instructed the animals not to harm the harvest and settled to other work while the cows kept to the grass between the fields (*JC*: 18). When 15 years old, Gholam Rahman was sent to *madrasa*s in Chittagong and Fatikchari; after five years, he entered the Chittagong Sarkari Madrasa. He spoke little and always the truth, was polite, modest and ate little, and he began to observe the Islamic fast throughout the year. He kept his eyes downwards and used to meditate for long periods (*JC*: 19 f.). His parents, worried about his lack of interest in wordly matters, had him married in 1307 *hiǧrī* (1889–90), which, however, had no effect on his lifestyle.

At the age of 25, Gholam Rahman's final examinations were due, but he hesitated to ask for Ahmadullah's permission to leave Maijbhandar. When his brother took him with him and asked on his behalf, Ahmadullah first said that 'his exam is over', and on his repeated request had his silken robe put on Gholam Rahman's shoulders (*JC*: 24 f.). The latter then went to Chittagong to give his examinations, but on the third day, Ahmadullah said to one of his disciples he had not found a flower in his garden; at the same time, Gholam Rahman suddenly stood up from his desk, threw his pen and paper away and began to sing a Persian ghazal about the arrival of the beloved. In a state of trance, he said, apparently addressing

93 i.e. the ideal of true, devoted womanhood.

94 The Urdu quotation reads: *yah hamārē bāġ kī gul gulāb hai. hażrat yūṣuf (ʿa.) kā čihra is mēṇ āyā hai. is kō ʿazīz rakhō.*

distant Ahmadullah: 'You have come! Why did you take such trouble to come? I will walk on my head to come to your service!' He thereupon fainted and was taken back to Maijbhandar, his examination unfinished. Whenever after this incident he was asked about learning, he used to denounce book knowledge in an Arabic phrase and add the following instruction in Persian: 'Put all books and manuscripts into the fire. Turn your face towards the beloved' (*JC*: 28).[95]

In the following years (chapter 5, pp. 29–39), Gholam Rahman lived ascetically[96] and devoted all possible concentration and time to Ahmadullah, to the extent that he largely kept away from his family. At times his attachment to Ahmadullah became so intense that he held his feet clasped and had to be forcefully separated (*JC*: 35).[97] Chapter 6 (pp. 40–6) contains Gholam Rahmans *silsila*, arranged in reverse order, that is, going backwards from him to the prophet; the *silsila* is equal to Ahmadullah's, who precedes him in the list.

A separate chapter called *Beśārate Haj'rate Āk·dach (ka.)* (from P. <*bašārat-i hażrat-i aqdas*>, chapter 7, pp. 47–53) is interspersed here; it contains utterances and prophesies of Ahmadullah regarding Gholam Rahman. In one, Gholam Rahman is identified with Shah Jalal.[98] Isapuri explains this by reference to Shah Jalal of Sylhet, the great Islamiser of Bengal and Assam: just like Shah Jalal, Gholam Rahman had 'more than ten lakhs [one million] of disciples' in Bengal and Assam (*JC*: 48 f. n). Another parallel is established with Jalal al-Din Rumi, 'a dervish of world fame' (*JC*: 49n), and indeed with Uways al-Qaranī of Yemen, who started the *ṭarīqa* that Gholam Rahman further developed (*JC*: 53n). A second statement of Ahmadullah's is quoted as proof that he sent some of his disciples to Gholam Rahman for their spiritual progress,[99] and a third one, narrated in great detail, which concerns Isapuri himself rather than Gholam Rahman (*JC*: 49–53). Thus ends the first part of the book.

The bulk of the second part consists of the descriptions of Gholam Rahman's travels in the hilly regions surrounding northern Chittagong (*JC*: 54–74) and the accounts of his miracles ever since he had been formally installed at Maijbhandar

95 *ṣad kitāb va raqhā dar nār kūn/rū-i ḫūdrā ğānib-i dildār kūn.*

96 He prayed extensively; never laid down to sleep, but slept in sitting; slept as little as possible; and kept his severe fast (*JC*: 29 f., 34).

97 On seeing Gholam Rahman's state, a Hindustani dervish commented that his thirst for love was extremely powerful, and that both complete exposure and complete separation from Ahmadullah would make him a *šahīd*, and that thus he had to be allowed to see Ahmadullah only sometimes. The dervish also prophesied that if long age was granted to Gholam Rahman, he would become 'unique in the world' (*jagate advitīẏa*) (*JC*: 35 ff.).

98 The Urdu quotation reads: *wah šāh ğalāl hai. mulk-i yaman kā rahnēwālā hai [,] unkī adab karō! tum lōgōṇ kī ibtidā aur intihā unhīṇ kē hāth mēṇ hai.* ('He is Shah Jalal. He is an inhabitant of Yemen, pay respect to him! Your beginning and end is in his hand.')

99 The Urdu quotation reads: *tumhārē niʿabat pīrān-i pīr ṣāḥib kē hāth mēṇ hai [,] tum unkē pās ğāo!* ('Your spiritual perfection is in the hand of *Pīrān-i Pīr Ṣāḥib* [i.e. Gholam Rahman], go to him!'). For the appellation *Pīrān-i Pīr*, cf. *JC*: 8n: 'Haj'rat Āk·dach (ka.) had once addressed Sayyada Mosharrafjan Bibi (Gholam Rahman's mother) as "the mother of *Pīrān-i Pīr Ṣāḥib*".' Having been uttered before Gholam Rahman's birth, this statement is treated as a fulfilled prophesy.

(*JC*: 75–97). According to Isapuri's representation, Gholam Rahman's four travels, most of them lasting unspecified periods of time and all taking place before Ahmadullah's death in 1906, came close to temporary escapes from the *darbār*. He usually set out alone with nothing but a lungi and a *čādur* ('wrapper'), and even if a few disciples accompanied him, his wandering motion proved to be uncontrollable: although it seemed that he was moving slowly, they would have to run behind him with all their power, and some were still not able to keep pace.[100] He rarely accepted invitations to stay with hosts, and if so never longer than one or two nights.

During these travels, Gholam Rahman performed a number of miracles, witnessed by his disciples or the local population. When wandering in the Chittagong Hill Tracts, he moved through the jungle in utter darkness, led by a *khodāi cerāg*, divine lamp; he used short-cuts incongruent with the topography of the Hill Tracts (*JC*: 56), and reached a summit in an incredibly short time (*JC*: 58); he talked in some unintelligible language with a group of white-clad people who came to him during the night to pay their respects to him, and whom he later identified *vis-à-vis* a disciple as *khodā tāālār laskar*, the army of God (*JC*: 56 f.); the poisonous fruits he gave to that disciple to quench his hunger turned out to be edible and tasty (*JC*: 57); he healed a Hill Tracts person by spreading water on his navel, and received the adoration of Hill Tracts people, who called him *nara-rūpī nārāẏaṇ*, Narayana in human shape (*JC*: 59 f.).[101] When tigers were heard approaching, he prevented his disciples and the Hill Tracts people from warding them off, stating that 'they want to come to me', and in fact he was, later that night, seen surrounded by tigers waving their tails and licking his feet (*JC*: 60 f.). A ghazal-chanting group of disciples, who had been searching for Gholam Rahman all this time, finally arrived at that place and took him back to Maijbhandar.

Other such wanderings took him to a hilly region in southern Chittagong (*Deẏāṅger Pāhāṛ*, *JC*: 64–66), northern Chittagong (*Uttar Pāhāṛ*, *JC*: 67–69) and the mountains of Sitakunda (*JC*: 70–74). He healed a person from his obsession with alchemical gold-making by demonstrating that the production of gold was possible only through divine grace as mediated by him, not by any sort of recipe (*JC*: 64 ff.); a python snake was seen fanning his body to cool him in the heat (*JC*: 67); his return from northern Chittagong was symbolically prophesied by Ahmadullah (*JC*: 68);[102] ants built a wall to protect him at night in the jungle (*JC*: 70); he sat on

100 This is mentioned in the first chapter, *Pūrba-pārbbatya caṭṭagrām bhramaṇ-bṛttānta* ('The eastern Chittagong Hill Tracts travel account', pp. 54–63). During this first journey, many disciples started with him, 'but not all could stay with him' (*JC*: 55).

101 It is not clear which of the ethnic groups inhabiting the Chittagong Hill Tracts is meant here. Isapuri states, however, that they are *jumiẏā* <*jhumiẏā*>, the local term for shifting cultivators (*JC*: 59). Shifting cultivation by burning plots of soil is indeed the typical traditional cultivation method in the Hill Tracts.

102 Ahmadullah had said to some disciples: 'My *Miẏā* is wandering in the jungles, take these five sweets (*bātāsā*) with you. When he comes home, he will sweeten his mouth by eating these', and given them eleven; the meaning of this action became clear to everybody when Gholam Rahman returned after eleven days from then.

a rail track and forced a train to stop in order to prevent a disaster (*JC*: 71); he was seen at three different places at the same time (*JC*: 72); he also visited a number of famous *mazārs* (Amanat Shah, Badr Shah, Bayezid Bistami)[103] and religious sites in Chittagong city, and revived the formerly dormant religious and pilgrimage activities at the *mazārs* of Amanat Shah and Bayezid Bistami (*JC*: 73 f.).

After these travels, and apparently shortly after the death of Ahmadullah, Gholam Rahman came to settle permanently in Maijbhandar (chapter 5, *Gośānaśīnī*, pp. 75–7). Two years later, and for the last 23 years of his life, he relinquished talking almost completely, except in cases of utter necessity (*JC*: 77).[104]

Chapter 6 (pp. 78–97) contains accounts of approximately thirty miracles wrought by Gholam Rahman, and a further 22 names of witnesses of miracles (*JC*: 96 f.). Isapuri begins by explaining that *muʿǧazāt* and *karāmāt*, prophetly and saintly miracles, are not against nature. Like electric current, the power of a perfect soul (Bg. *kāmel ruher śakti*) is not disproved by its mere invisibility, and it is a Muslim's *farḍ*, religious duty, to believe in miracles (*JC*: 78 f.).

Many of these miracles happen in dreams of devotees.[105] Gholam Rahman appears in a student's dream as a mathematics teacher who teaches the student a certain calculation by beating him; following this, the student passes his examination (*JC*: 92). Gholam Rahman also heals illnesses and bestows initiation (*bayʿa*) in dreams (*JC*: 95, 96). He rescues his devotees from dangerous situations and heals them from diseases;[106] sitting on the water, he saves a shipwrecked, drowning man (*JC*: 83 f.); he appears before, and pulls away, a man who is about to be overrun by a train (*JC*: 84). His prophesies come true (*JC*: 91), and also animals show spontaneous devotion to him, as a camel bowing before him demonstrates (*JC*: 93). He is seen in Dhaka (*JC*: 80 f.), where he has reportedly never been, and on a *ḥaǧǧ* at the *Kaʿba* (*JC*: 81 f.); he helps a devotee to find the ship tickets for his *ḥaǧǧ* (*JC*: 85 f.). Gholam Rahman also prevented devotees from going astray to holy places other than Maijbhandar: a pilgrim who applied for a ticket to Ajmer instead of Maijbhandar fell instantly ill and recovered only after seeing Gholam Rahman in a dream (*JC*: 91); likewise, a person who wanted to take *bayʿa* from a *pīr* in Dhaka and set out to it even after Gholam Rahman had appeared in a dream, was hit by a disease and could not reach his destination (*JC*: 92). Likewise, a student who disobeyed a dream order to come to Maijbhandar in order to finish his examinations first fell sick and recovered only after reaching Maijbhandar (*JC*: 95). During his travels, Gholam Rahman once sat in front of the residence of the British owner of the Udaliya tea gardens and refused to leave; when the Sahib started shooting at him and his followers, Gholam Rahman only laughed, and

103 i.e., Bayezid Bistami, the famous early Persian Sufi. His *dargāh* at Chittagong is actually a *čilla*, but is even today commonly believed to be his real grave.

104 According to Isapuri's calculation, Gholam Rahman permanently settled in Maijbhandar 25 years before his death, namely in 1910, and two years after Ahmadullah's decease. It seems likely, but is in no way explicitly stated in the text, that Ahmadullah first had to 'make way' for his successor.

105 *JC*: 90, 92, 94, 95, 96.

106 *JC*: 79 f., 83 f., 84, 94 f., 95.

none of the bullets could do any harm to anybody. The Sahib grew afraid and, 'together with his Memsahib', apologised and tried to invite everybody to have food; Gholam Rahman declined and moved away from there (*JC*: 91).

One of Gholam Rahman's most famous miracles is about his resolution of an argument between Maijbhandaris and a number of *ʿulamāʾ*. The event took place probably before his permanently settling down in Maijbhandar after 1906, close to the Subregistrery's Office in Isapur. This location used to be frequented by Sufis, and practices such as *samāʿ*, audition, and *raqs*, dance, used to be performed 'all the time'. Once, while a number of acclaimed Maijbhandari *ʿulamāʾ* were present there, *mawlawī*s from outside came to argue and accused the Maijbhandari *murīd*s of *bidʿa*, *širk* and *kufr* (*JC*: 87 f.). When Gholam Rahman was called for help in the argument,

> Roaring like a lion, he went fast to the stairs and, standing there, three times made the sound of *Ḥaqq!! Ḥaqq!! Ḥaqq!!*, waving his blessed head along with it and making tremble all sides by this thunder. In all my life I have never heard such a loud sound by a man. As if thunder was following upon thunder. Right upon [hearing] that sound, hundreds and hundreds of people, making sky and underworld tremble, started making the sound of *Ḥaqq Ḥaqq* and began jumping around as if intoxicated. By the sound of their *Ḥaqq Ḥaqq* and the beating sound of their feet, the whole village started to tremble. (*JC*: 88)

The quarreling *mawlawī*s and many members of the opposite party either fled or joined, and the power of *wağd* set into motion grew so strong that people succumbed to it even against their will. A group of Hindus also fled from there, saying: 'Run! Run! The *Faqir Sahib* has set Mecca in motion. Whoever stays here will have to jump.' The frenzy stopped when Gholam Rahman asked Isapuri (the author) to prepare his water pipe and covered himself entirely in a *čādur* (*JC*: 89). From there onwards, Isapuri concludes, *samāʿ*, *ḥalqa* and *wağd* took place wherever Gholam Rahman went.

Chapter 7 (pp. 98–101) deals with Gholam Rahman's physical appearance. Two things standing out from the detailed description of his beautiful features – head, fingers, chest, hair, etc. – are the remarks regarding his skin, which used to change colour and thereby generate very different emotions in the persons approaching him (*JC*: 98), and his scent, to be found in his presence, clothes, etc., which was superior in its excellence to any other scent or perfume (*JC*: 99).

The remaining part of the book, entitled *Mṛtyu rahasya* (pp. 102–8), is devoted to the meaning of dying for saints and Gholam Rahman's actual death. On the basis of a Qurʾanic verse, Isapuri explains the difference between the two bodies one has, the *bhautik sthūl deha* (outer body) and the *sūkṣma deha* or *miṣālī ṣūrat* (subtle body). The human soul's (*rūḥ-i insānī*) relationship with the subtle body, prevailing, for example, in sleep and death, is closer than that with the outer body, and especially strong in the case of saints. In this sense, they are living dead, and their death is celebrated as their reunion, actually their *ʿurs*, wedding, with God

(*JC*: 102–4).[107] Still, the saints do keep contact with their outer bodies, and the bodies of some 'remain like fresh corpses until doomsday [*qiyāma*]'. The soul, situated in the *ʿālam-i barzaḫ* in union with God, can return at times from there into the subtle body, the grave or the hearts of their successors or *ḫalīfa*s (*JC*: 105). On the *murīd*'s part, however, a *muršid*'s death means the end of open vision and grace (*fayẓ*, Ar.) and is thus a deplorable event, and 'even if some *murīd*s have attained vision (*darśan*) and grace after the demise of the *muršid*, that is extremely negligible in comparison to the vision and grace attained in a manifest [*ẓāhirī*] fashion' (*JC*: 106).

After alluding to the usual and not very favourable competition succeeding a *muršid*'s death, Isapuri narrates a dream seen by Khayrul Bashar, Gholam Rahman's eldest son, which foreshadowed his death (*JC*: 107). Gholam Rahman, after having promulgated the *ṭarīqa-i māʾiğbhandʿāriyya*, died on the 22nd Caitra/5 April 1937, after lying down completely for the first time since his childhood, with his face turned towards the *qibla* (*JC*: 108).

Syed Badruddoza (1971): **Bābā Bhāṇḍārī** *(***BB***), Bg.*

Syed Badruddoza, the author of this second life account of Gholam Rahman, is a grandson of the latter and one of the contemporary exponents of the Rahmaniyya Manzil. Like Isapuri's *Jīban carit*, *Bābā Bhāṇḍārī* is a standard hagiography which saw its fourth edition in 1987, and has recently been reprinted again. The book bears a close relationship with Isapuri's *Jīban carit* in that its strictly hagiographic portions are mostly, almost literally taken from there, except for minor changes in the order of narration and the occasional transformation of Isapuri's very formal Bengali *sādhu bhāṣā* into a somewhat less formal, but still *sādhu bhāṣā* style, apparently in order to facilitate reading. *Bābā Bhāṇḍārī* is an extended version of *Jīban carit*. What is new in it is the extended discussion of the Maijhandari *ṭarīqa*, of the general status of saints in Islam and of Gholam Rahman's spiritual inheritance and rank. Isapuri's life narration is thus set into an elaborated frame and in a way recontextualised.

It is not far-fetched to suppose that the authoring of this book has to be assessed against the background of the second hagiography about Ahmadullah, *Jībanī o kerāmat*, which appeared only four years before it. As we must remember here, *Jībanī o kerāmat* establishes Delawar Hossain as the legitimate spiritual successor to Ġawṯ al-Aʿẓam Ahmadullah, assigning to Gholam Rahman the rank of a *pradhān khaliphā*, foremost deputy, and thereby contesting his Ġawṯ al-Aʿẓam-ship – which, for instance, is still uncontroversially asserted in Isapuri's hagiography.[108] *Bābā Bhāṇḍārī* re-establishes the claim to Gholam Rahman's Ġawṯ

107 Cf. Section 2.2.4.

108 Cf. already the full title of the book (*Hay'rat Gāuchul Ājam Māolānā āl·Chaiyad Golāmur Rah'mān āl·-Hāsānī āl·-Māij'bhāṇḍārī (Ka.) Bābājān Kveb'lā Kābār jīban carit*); the fact that Isapuri does not feel prompted to give reasons for Gholam Rahman's inheritance of this title of highest sainthood is a strong indication that this claim was uncontested before Delawar Hossain started to assert his own position.

al-Aʿẓam-ship. Another recurrent and interesting feature of this book is the allocation of sainthood in an ambiguously viewed 'age of science'.[109]

The fourth edition of *Bābā Bhāṇḍārī* has three prefaces. One is the original foreword by Abul Fazl, a famous intellectual of Chittagong, who was the Vice Chancellor of Chittagong University and, by the time of the book's first edition, the 'Minister of Education, Bangladesh Government' (*BB*: iii–v, own pag.).[110] Abul Fazl stresses the very special significance of Maijbhandar as an all-encompassing pilgrimage centre 'irrespective of sex, caste/class and religion', and praises the 'young author' Badruddoza for his efforts in writing the book. The second is the author's own preface to the fourth edition (*BB*: vi–xv, own pag.). Badruddoza describes the present age as one of so-called freedom and lacking spirituality; Gholam Rahman is set up as an example of a truly Islamic lifestyle in accordance with the teachings of the *Qur'ān* and the *Ḥadīṯ* (*BB*: xv). The third, short preface is that to the first edition (pp. xvi–xvii, own pag.); it introduces Gholam Rahman as the founder of the Maijbhandari *ṭarīqa*.

The text proper starts with an introduction (*Abataraṇikā*, pp. 1–8). The initial praise of Allah and the Prophet is followed by a general praise of the *awliyāʾ* and that of Gholam Rahman, the 'crown jewel of the family of saints' and 'the bright light of *wilāya* and *ġauṯiyya*' (*BB*: 1). Human life is obstructed by the effects of the six enemies;[111] the clear concept it takes to tackle with life is bestowed upon the world by the *awliyāʾ* of each age, such as Gholam Rahman, the *muǧāddid* of the present (*BB*: 2 f.). An account of his life, Badruddoza stresses, cannot possibly be accurate due to the limitations of language. No *pīri-murīdī* is practised at this saint's *darbār* (*BB*: 4);[112] characteristic rather is the free flow of love to members of all religious groups.

> As in this age of the highest progress of science the objects and the outer world abandon the coarse and are inclined towards subtlety, likewise with regard to the spiritual world, this age is one of music and love.
>
> (*BB*: 5)

Through such love, Gholam Rahman has inspired everybody 'irrespective of caste/class and religion': 'Hindus and Muslims, Shiyas and Sunnis, Hanafis and Wahhabis, rich and poor, English and Bengali (. . .)' (*BB*: 6). He did so not by leaving any verbal testimony or instruction, but by the pure effect of his being. Merely getting into contact with him made many sinners repent (*BB*: 7).

The next chapter (*2, Māij'bhāṇḍār Śarīph*, pp. 9–14), again starting with the praise of Allah, is devoted to the glorification of Maijbhandar. Chittagong, the dwelling place of 'Chinese, Burmese, Moghs, Chakmas, Hindus, Buddhists,

109 Cf., e.g., *BB*: 5.

110 This is astonishing since Bangladesh came into existence only in December 1971.

111 Lust, anger, greed, infatuation, vanity and envy.

112 Badruddozā explains: *hāte hāte kiṃbā pāg'ṛī dvārā bāẏ'āter byabasthā nāi* ('There is no arrangement for initiation from hand to hand or by a turban') (*BB*: 4).

Muslims, Christians, etc.', has been adorned by Allah with all the natural splendour for the arrival of His 'dearest friend' (*BB*: 9). The different past names of Chittagong are evoked, and uncountable 'ascetics, *awliyā'*, *muni*s and *ṛṣi*s'[113] have since long populated this *bāra āuliẏār deś* to prepare the ground for this great saint (*BB*: 10). The natural beauty of Maijbhandar, its streams and woods, is indicative of its special role (*BB*: 12). Since all names on earth are descended from the sky, they bear a secret, and the name Maijbhandar can be written and interpreted in different ways. Badruddoza accordingly presents a list of combinations of the 'Arabic' first syllables with the 'Persian' second part *bhand'ār* and translates *mā'īğ-bhand'ār* = 'precious treasury', *ma'āğ-bhand'ār* = 'refuge', *ma'az-bhand'ār* = 'praised treasury', *ma'iğ-bhand'ār* = 'suckling treasury', and *ma'aḍ-bhand'ār* = 'treasury hard to understand'.[114]

Chapter 3 (pp. 15–23) deals with Gholam Rahman's genealogy, birth and childhood. Isapuri's account (*JC*: 5–15) is generally followed, though supplied with more detail. A genealogical table is given (*BB*: 19), and it is mentioned that the baby Gholam Rahman was never a bed-wetter; also, his cradle once kept moving even after his mother had inadvertently gone to sleep (*BB*: 22 f.). Most of the following life account, as stated above, closely corresponds or is even identical with *Jīban carit*; but some of the added information deserves mention. In the following chapter (pp. 24–42), Badruddoza translates a Persian poem of Gholam Rahman's, reproduced on p. xx (own pagination), which the latter had written during his time of studying in Chittagong.[115] Chapter 5 (pp. 43–50) starts with the statements that Gholam Rahman was, by virtue of his severe outer and inner *sādhanā* (esoteric practice), 'led to the highest step of the spiritual world', and 'therefore, any of the spiritual powers [Bg. *ādhyātmik śakti*] of his *pīr*'s [i.e. Ahmadullah's] soul were infused in his soul [Bg. *ātmā*].' (*BB*: 43). Then we find a list of Ahmadullah's utterances regarding

113 The terms *muni* and *ṛṣi* were originally used for the ancient receivers of the *Veda*s in Hinduism, and today signify more broadly 'wise', 'seer', etc.

114 *Bhan'ḍār* is certainly not Persian, but Indo-Aryan; and from among the forms and translations given in *BB*, none seems to exist in Arabic. The only similar forms I could trace (with the help of a native speaker of Arabic) are *ma'āḏ*, 'refuge', and *ma'ğūn*, meaning among other things 'sweets'; so there is reason to suppose that the etymologies given by Badruddoza are fairly impressionistic.

115 The poem is actually a personal prayer by Gholam Rahman, beseeching Allah to reveal Himself, to pardon his sins and grant him a place in heaven. This being the only available detailed utterance of Gholam Rahman, I am giving a translation below of the Bengali version prepared by Badruddoza (the Persian facsimile is not at all easily decipherable in places): 'For many years I have been searching for you/You are still not fulfilling what is due to me/I have learnt through a divine saying (Bg. *daibabāṇī*)/That nobody has returned disappointed from your door/Whoever has appeared at your door/Has never returned with a heart's desire unfulfilled/Whoever has appeared at your door with the light of hope/Will certainly attain his *manzil-i maqsūd*./Oh Lord, through the means of Haórat Muhammad Mustafa (da.) and his Dear Ones, I pray to you: Forgive all my sins/And on doomsday, give me a place with the descendants of the Messenger of God (da.), and accept my prayer by the means of those who have attained your vicinity./The end/ Writer: the sinful servant/The dedicated Gholam-i Rahman (he may be forgiven)/Ğamā'at-i Siyām ['brotherhood of fasting'].' *BB*: 35 f.

Gholam Rahman, including those already quoted by Isapuri, and of instances in which Ahmadullah delegated the reception of *murīd*s to Gholam Rahman. This is to prove that Gholam Rahman was equal to Ahmadullah in spiritual rank, and was his legitimate and regularly installed successor.

Chapter 6 (pp. 51–61) is a digression on the role and status of a Ġawṯ al-Aʿẓam in the *āḫirī zamāna* (U.), the 'last time/age'. This last age, starting around 1300 *hiǧrī* (1882–83), is characterised by the perversion of Islam through *kufr* and *širk*; material science (Bg. *jaṛa bijñān*) deludes mankind with its manifold discoveries and entangles men in wordly illusions, and the *ǧāhil*, ignorant, destroy Islam from within (*BB*: 51 f.). Seeing this state of mankind, Allah sent Ahmadullah and Gholam Rahman. The construction of a new *ṭarīqa* that Ahmadullah, as a representative of the messenger of Allah, had begun had to be completed by another saint, Gholam Rahman, who discovered a new spiritual practice adjusted to the times and 'solemnly exists as an incarnation of love through a universal religion of love' (*BB*: 53). His name, Rahman (<*raḥmān*>, 'merciful'), is significant in this connection, for it is explained as 'he who guards the good and the bad, the meritorious and the sinful – everybody, irrespective of caste/class and religion.' (*BB*: 54). Like Yusuf, Gholam Rahman was of supernatural beauty; and he was the 'incarnate manifestation of Allah's merciful property [Bg. *guṇ*] (*BB*: 55). The testimonies of hundreds of thousands of disciples, Badruddoza argues, are sufficient proof for the Ġawṯ al-Aʿẓam status of the two great Maijbhandari saints, Ahmadullah and Gholam Rahman. Badruddoza further explains, quoting authorities like Dehlawī, that the superiority Abd al-Qadir Gilani had asserted by claiming that status only for himself has to be applied to his contemporary situation, not afterwards, and does in no way obstruct the appearance of other Ġawṯ al-Aʿẓams at later points of time (*BB*: 57 ff.).

The following, short chapter (chapter 7, pp. 62–4) deals with miracles. Besides *karāma* and *muʿǧaza*, there are miracles performed without the proper faith by *yogī*s and *sannyāsī*s, which are called *istidrāǧ* ('gradual elevation'; *BB*: 62). Today, on the one hand, those adhering to a scientific world view deny the possibility of supernatural happenings that go against the laws of nature, and on the other, many miracles are reported that go against Islamic convictions. Saints are today judged, and their powers estimated, by their miracles, whereas the true standard should be their spiritual attainments and unshakable devotion to truth (*BB*: 63 f.).

This chapter introduces the succeeding accounts of Gholam Rahman's wanderings in the mountains (chapter 8–11, pp. 65–98) and his settling at Maijbhandar (chapter 12, pp. 99–103), which are almost identical in structure and content with the respective portion of *Jīban carit*. Between these and chapter 15 on Gholam Rahman's miracles (pp. 115–43, again mostly identical with *Jīban carit*), two additional chapters are interspersed. Chapter 13 (pp. 104–6) is entitled *Hij'rat*; it rationalises the fact that in 1928, Gholam Rahman left his father's house and moved into the newly constructed Gausiyya Rahman Manzil on the northern side of the central pond of Maijhandar, as a *hiǧra* performed in accordance with the prophetic example. Chapter 14 (pp. 107–14) treats the installation of festivities, namely *ʿurs*-celebrations and birthdays (*ḫušrūz*), in Maijbhandar. While in Ahmadullah's times, no such celebrations were held, Gholam Rahman initiated both Ahmadullah's *ʿurs* and his own *ḫušrūz* celebrations. In connection with the latter, the first Maijbhandari Bengali journal, *Khośroj saogāt*, started to appear; Gholam Rahman also commissioned Abdul Ghani's writing of *Āʾīna-i Bārī*. On the occasion of Ahmadullah's *ʿurs*, the first books with Maijbhandari songs by Mosahebuddin Ahmad Sahapuri and Ramesh Shil appeared (*BB*: 111 f.).[116]

What follows the accounts of Gholam Rahman's miracles may in a way be considered the centrepiece of Badruddoza's book; the long chapter (chapter 16, pp. 144–98), entitled *Māij'bhāṇḍārīẏā tarīkā*, is probably the most extensive written contribution on the Maijbhandari *ṭarīqa* from the Rahmaniyya branch of the movement. The five points making up this version of the Maijbhandari *ṭarīqa* have been treated in detail before.[117] Badruddoza's point of including it here seems to be that this *ṭarīqa*, in its fully fledged form, is portrayed as a contribution from Gholam Rahman. Badruddoza thus concludes his chapter as follows:

> So it can be understood that Hazrat Shah Syed Ahmadullah opened the door to the *Māij'bhāṇḍārīẏā tarīkā*, and that through Hażrat Shah Syed Gholamur Rahman Bābā Bhāṇḍārī Qibla Kaʿba, its utmost development was attained.
> (*BB*: 198)

Chapters 17–19, again, are similar to Isapuri's account of Gholam Rahman's physical features, the foreshadowings of his death and his passing away. Chapter 20 enumerates ten post-mortem miracles of Gholam Rahman, most of the events being cases of healing and rescuing. The book ends with tables of Gholam Rahman's spiritual genealogy (*BB*: 220 ff.), his main *ḫalīfa*s (*BB*: 222 ff.), and his special *ḫādim*s (*BB*: 226), as well as a hymn (*Chālāme gāuchiẏā māij bhāṇḍārīẏā*, *BB*: 227 f.) and a bibliography (*BB*: 229 f.).

Notwithstanding the considerable differences between the four hagiographies discussed so far, a certain pattern seems to develop here. *Āʾīna-i Bārī* and *Jīban carit* are texts written by close disciples shortly after the death of the respective saints. *Jībanī o kerāmat* and *Bābā Bhāṇḍārī*, by contrast, are written decades later by *pīrzāda*s and exponents of the respective saints' *manzil*s. While the earlier texts are satisfied with uncontroversially proclaiming the spiritual status of their saints, the later ones do so in a sometimes apologetical way. All possible hints to the saints' ordained succession, formerly neglected, are now highlighted and scrutinised. The exponents of the Maijbhandari families themselves seem to feel called upon to 'set things straight' in the later texts, and the one mild apologetical bias common to all of the texts, that *vis-à-vis* reformist Islamic orthodoxy, is in the later texts complemented by inter-*manzil* apologetics.

116 Rajapuri, the author of the first traceable Maijbhandari song publication (1913), is not mentioned.

117 Cf. Chapter 3.7.

It should be said here that the rift between the two main branches of the Maijbhandari family tree must, however, not be overestimated. Despite certain tensions, the movement continues to represent itself, and to be perceived from outside, as one. The point is that under this overarching label of Maijbhandari Sufism, there is some competition regarding the legitimate succession and representation, and hagiography becomes one of the media through which controversial claims are asserted and positions articulated. Simultaneously, Maijbhandari hagiographies more and more become themselves paraphernalia of sainthood, or one of the items of an inventory which symbolises and legitimises saintly status – in a way just like a *silsila*, a *mazār*, songs, the installation of a new *ṭarīqa*, *ʿurs*-celebrations and so on. To the degree that this perception of hagiography as a powerful medium of 'launching' a saint gains ground in Maijbhandar, the production of hagiographies increases. The most obvious sign of this tendency is the fact that in 1982 for the first time a hagiography is written about a living Maijbhandari saint, as we shall see now.

4.5 Shahanshah Ziaul Haq Maijbhandari (1928–88)

Jamal Ahmad Sikdar (1982):* Jiẏāul Hak *[JH], Bg.

The author of this book, Jamal Ahmad Sikdar, is a prominent member and one of the main organisers of Haq Manzil. A *murīd* of Ziaul Haq, Sikdar was the editor of that manzil's monthly journal *Ālok'dhārā*. He is one of the advisors of the *Māij'bhāṇḍārī Maramī Goṣṭhī*. The first edition of his book was published in two parts, entitled *Phit'rāt* and *Siphat*, which were united in one volume in the second edition in 1987 and have been published in this way ever since.[118]

What is striking about *Jiẏāul Hak*, and unprecedented in the present series of hagiographies, is the fact that it appeared *before* the saint's demise; and we learn in the beginning (author's preface [pp. vi–viii]) how the writing of the book was sanctioned by Ziaul Haq: instead of answering directly to Sikdar's request, Ziaul Haq told him to repair his electric torch. Putting that on his bed frame with its light upwards, 'he shed his mercy [consisting in] the collection and development of knowledge into the empty vessel of the author', and uttered a line from the *Qur'ān*: *fa-ḏkurūnī aḏkurum* ('Remember me, I shall also remember you.' *Qur'ān* 2.152[147]). Thus commissioned, Sikdar set to work (*JH*: [vii]). Other short prescripts include a poem by Delawar Hosain (grandson of Ahmadullah and Ziaul Haq's father), a note to the second edition by the latter's son Mohammad Hasan, a table of contents and a genealogical table.

As already indicated, the book falls into two parts. The first, *Phit'rāt* <*fiṭra*> ('nature, disposition'; pp. 1–98), is equivalent to the narration of Ziaul Haq's life until the attainment of his full spiritual development, and the second, *Siphat*

118 Cf. *JH*: [v], foreword to the second edition by Syed Mohammad Hasan.

<*ṣifa*> ('attribute, property'; pp. 99–304) to the account of his sayings, deeds and miracles. *Phit'rāt* starts very topically with a discussion of human nature: 'Man is the representative of the Creator in the world. Thus he is the most excellent of creation. This superiority is due to his nature (*fiṭra*)' (*JH*: 1). This nature is constituted by a number of *guṇ* or qualities, all of which – even the negative ones like avarice, greed, violence, etc., if properly cultivated – are necessary and vital for existence.[119] Among these qualities, morality and spirituality set man apart from the rest of creation (*JH*: 1 f.). Allah's main quality is *rabūbiyya*, 'divinity', consisting in creation, maintenance and evolution (Bg. *bibartan*). His nature is complete and unlimited. Man's task is to master, in the course of his life, the qualities of Allah; and the saints are those 'who are fully established in Allah's nature'.

The following chapter (*Cirasthāẏī supath*, 'The eternal good path', pp. 6–11) furnishes a sketch of basic Islamic historical concepts: the age of *ğāhiliyya*, 'ignorance', the coming of the Prophet Muhammad and his *mi'rāğ*, journey to heaven, which 'opened the door of union between the Creator and created man' (*JH*: 11); thus, *nubuwwa* or prophethood came to its end; *wilāya* or sainthood remained as the 'path of union', and the 'all-conquering power of sainthood has instilled new life into religion in many ages and countries' (ibid.). Next (*Pather diśā*, 'The direction of the path', pp. 12–16), ʿAlī's position *vis-à-vis* the Prophet and his function as the *amīr al-ṭarīqa*, 'the emperor of the mystical path' are dealt with.

The succeeding chapter (*Pūrabī sūrya*, 'Eastern sun', pp. 17–39) is a most curious blend of fragments from international political history and descriptions of Maijbhandar and the Maijbhandari *ṭarīqa*. It is clear that Sikdar aims at demonstrating the universal significance of Maijbhandar by setting the advent of the Maijbhandari saints in the context of world history. The French Revolution is briefly described against the background of a preceding all-pervasive state of darkness, suppression and deprivation on earth (*JH*: 17 f.). The pseudo-religious regime of the Ottoman Empire, we learn, was terminated by Mustafa Kemal Atatürk (*JH*: 18). The British reigned over India; when the 1857 Mutiny failed, 'the death occurred of the very last attempt to seize power through religious fervour' (*JH*: 19 f.). Islamic history is made up of alternating periods of light and darkness; the deviations and ill-customs that had become established under Ummaiyad and ʿAbbasid rule were remedied by the appearance of Ġawṯ al-Aʿẓam Abd al-Qadir Gilani (*JH*: 20). Likewise, the fall of Islamic rule, lack of faith and crumbling devotion to the saints in the eighteenth and nineteenth centuries called for another great reformer of religion (Bg. *dharma saṃskārak*), and so Ġawṯ al-Aʿẓam Ahmadullah appeared in beautiful Chittagong:

119 This theory bears similarities with the famous Bengali novelist and intellectual Bankimchandra Chattopadhyay's *anuśīlan'tattva* (Bg.) or 'theory of cultivation' as laid out in his *Dharmmatattva* (1888) and other religious writings and essays. Bankimchandra's concept of faculties (Bg. *bṛtti*, from Skt. <*vṛtti*> a term Sikdar uses only once, otherwise prefering Bg. *guṇ*, from Skt. <*guṇa*>) is adapted from Utilitarian and Positivist ethics, especially John Stuart Mill and Auguste Comte. For a sketch of this concept and the related discussion, cf. Harder (2001, Section 2.2.2, esp. pp. 189–92).

> Cāṭ'gā̃ [Chittagong] is the fair of the light from the lamp (Bg. *cā̃ṭi*) of Badr Šāh. East of the equinox of the earth, it is the meeting place of Hindus, Muslims, Buddhists and Christians – of all races (Bg. *jāti*).[120] An unequalled alliance between sea, mountains and green nature. The place of austerities (Bg. *sādhanā*) and burial of uncounted ascetics, great men and *awliyā'-Allah*. A welcoming assemblage designed by the Great Lord for His dear friend. Just as before the emergence of the World Prophet, many prophets had arrived in Arabia.
>
> (*JH*: 21)

The *awliyā'* are the Prophet's representatives, and they themselves declare their status; therefore, Abd al-Qadir Gilani and Ahmadullah are the only legitimate bearers of the title Ġawṯ al-Aʿẓam; other claims are void and 'exaggerations' (*JH*: 22 f.).[121] His task is the promulgation of the doctrine of *tauhīd-i adyān*, 'unity of religions' (*JH*: 24), and the proclamation of the Maijbhandari *ṭarīqa*, whose seven-point version (accessible 'irrespective of caste/class and religion') is then shortly exposed (*JH*: 25–7). Further historical excursions ensue: on slavery and Abraham Lincoln (*JH*: 28 f.), the development of socialism and the labour movement (*JH*: 30), and the founding of the Red Cross and the United Nations (*JH*: 31). Sikdar continues by depicting the ambivalent role music has had in Bengali culture; though it had found very frivolous expression in the nautch sessions at the Zamindars' residences, music as such is seen as a spontaneous impulse of man. Ahmadullah had understood this and given music its place in Maijbhandari religious practice (*JH*: 33). The *ʿulamā'* arguing against music as being un-Islamic are wrong, because that applies only to music which evokes base instincts, not to spiritual music; and, moreover, music too is God's creation. *Samāʿ* is further deeply connected with *ḏikr* and helps activate the six *laṭā'if* (*JH*: 34 f.). After this, three pages are devoted to the nineteenth century: 'There is no century during which so many great minds (Bg. *manīṣī*) emerged on earth in all fields' (*JH*: 36), and a long list of international politicians, scientists, artists, etc. is added as proof to this point. Finally, two statements about Ahmadullah's status and Delawar Hosain as his rightful successor conclude this chapter (*JH*: 39).

Sikdar proceeds by furnishing portraits of Gholam Rahman (*JH*: 40–4) and Delawar Hosain (*JH*: 45–51). Gholam Rahman is described as an exceptional *walī*, but his title and status are not discussed. A short sketch of his life includes a comparison between his wanderings in the woods and the Prophet's stay in a cave on Mount Hira [*ḥirā'*] (*JH*: 41). One miracle, not included in the earlier hagiographies about Gholam Rahman, is also narrated (*JH*: 43 f.). Delawar Hosain is

120 The Modern Indo-Aryan term *jāti*, derived from Skt. *jan* 'to be born' and thus denoting origin, is a very fuzzy term that can be used in a multitude of ways. Although in the formula *jātidharmanirbiśeṣe*, I translate – in accordance with what I found to be the common understanding in Chittagong – as caste/class, 'race' seems more appropriate in this case. Of course, it may in this instance also be rendered as 'religious group'.

121 Ibn ʿArabi's prophesy (cf. Section 3.6) is quoted as further evidence of Ahmadullah's status (*JH*: 23).

introduced as the writer and theoretician of the Maijbhandari movement, its 'treasure of knowledge' (Bg. *jñān-bhāṇḍār*, the title of the chapter). His Islamic learning and teaching abilities are emphasised (*JH*: 45). In relation to Ahmadullah's *wilāya*, Delawar Hosain's position is determined as that of a *waṣī*, 'protector';[122] he is his grandfather Ahmadullah's legitimate successor. Delawar Hosain's writings are treated in some detail (*JH*: 47 f.), and his pro-Bangladesh stance is illustrated by a statement uttered as early as 1946,[123] and his blessings for Sheikh Mujibur Rahman.[124] His denial of having a *mazār* constructed for himself after his death is favourably mentioned.

After thus introducing some of the preceding Maijbhandari saints, the narration turns to Ziaul Haq. He was auspiciously born in Rağab, the month when Noah mounted the ark, Muhammad received his first revelation (*waḥy*), performed his *miʿrāğ*, and Jesus was born (*JH*: 52–4). His parents were the grandson of Ahmadullah, Delawar Hosain, and the second daughter of Gholam Rahman, Sajeda Khatun, and 'this unprecedented confluence of the sacred blood stream of two *awliyāʾ-Allah* of such great status is a rare happening in the history of world Sufi society' (*JH*: 55). Upon Ahmadullah's dream order to Delawar Hosain, the name of the child was changed from Badiur Rahman to Ziaul Haq (*JH*: 56). At the age of 21 days, the infant was very sick and close to death. His father did not want to take him to Gholam Rahman, but his maternal aunt, that is Gholam Rahman's first daughter Rabeya Khatun, claimed the child's life as a recompense for her service to Gholam Rahman; the child was then healed by two or three drops of water from Gholam Rahman's hands (*JH*: 57 f.).

At the age of five, Ziaul Haq 'left his mother's *ā̃cal*'[125] and received his first lesson from his father. He was educated at the Maijbhandar Ahmadiyya Madrassah, the Fatikchari Corporation High School and the Abu Sobhan High School (*JH*: 59 f.). His circumcision ceremony took place when he was seven years old, and is described as a prince's accession to the throne (*JH*: 61 f.). Some playful events of his childhood are mentioned, e.g. fish-catching competitions (during which he did not care about winning or losing), his insistence on having a suit tailored for him, and his early fondness for tea and confidences with his *Bubu* ('elder sister/cousin'; apparently the latter) (*JH*: 63 f.). Ziaul Haq continued his education from class nine onwards at the Chittagong Collegiate Highschool and, at the age of twenty, joined the Chittagong Government College and passed his IA

122 The term *achi* <*waṣī*> is, however, translated as *uttar'sūrī*, 'successor', by Sikdar (*JH*: 46), and it seems that it is usually used in this sense in Maijbhandar.

123 The statement reads: 'In a country which does not recognise Bengal even in its name, the self-interest of the Bengali race will not be safeguarded.' The allusion is to the acronym Pakistan (p for Punjab, a for Afghani, k for Kashmir, i for Sindh, stan for Baluchistan), which does not contain Bengal in it.

124 In 1952, Mujibur Rahman visited Maijbhandar and asked for Delawar Hosain's blessings. Delawar Hosain conferred them even after he was told that Shaikh Mujib was ready to resort to militancy (*JH*: 49).

125 The *ā̃cal* is the end of a sari and symbolises the close relationship between mother and child.

(Intermediate Arts) examinations in 1951. Thereafter, he went to the Kanungopara Sir Ashutosh College to sit his BA, but:

> On the third day of the B.A. test examinations of 1953, he became distracted and just remained seated; he handed in a white sheet of paper without anything written on it and left the examination hall. Just like his maternal grandfather [Gholam Rahman]. Like this, he came to the benevolent spiritual notice of Baba Bhandari (ka.).
>
> (*JH*: 66)

Thus was Ziaul Haq's formal education ended, and the event simultaneously marked the beginning of his spiritual search.

After sketching Ziaul Haq's very cordial relations with his elder cousin and his younger brothers (*JH*: 68 f.),[126] Sikdar now deals with the saint's spiritual development. Delawar Hosain, apparently reluctant to bestow *bay'a* on his eldest son himself, had him formally initiated into the *ṭarīqa* by Mawlānā Shafiur Rahman, the Imām of the Shahi Jame Masjid in Anderkilla/Chittagong, saying that he would take care of all the ritual requirements except the *sabaq* or instruction. Sikdar calls Delawar Hosain Ziaul Haq's *pīr-i ṭarīqat* and Gholam Rahman his *pīr-i tafwīż* ('*pīr* of delegation').[127] This double guidance, combined with the benevolence of Ahmadullah which rested upon him, made Ziaul Haq attain *vilāyat-i u'ẓma* or highest *wilāya* in a very short time (*JH*: 70 f.).

What Sikdar describes as Ziaul Haq's *riyāẓa*, austerities, were perceived as simple madness by many, a point this hagiography mentions several times. Ziaul Haq, a heavy smoker, chain-smoked on a train journey to Dhaka, ignoring the protests of his co-passengers. He ordered sweets only to look at them, or bought cinema tickets and then did not attend the show – 'In this way he started to subdue the demands born from bodily impulses' (*JH*: 73). Delawar Hosain, worried by his behaviour, was in a dream instructed by Ahmadullah to put his robe on Ziaul Haq's shoulders, which made him quiet for some days. When the latter started to beat up members of an assembly, criticising them for dancing and performing *sağda* instead of their daily prayers, Delawar Hosain called his son in. Ziaul Haq asked more than once who Ahmadullah, Gholam Rahman and Delawar Hosain were, until the latter angrily shouted: 'Have you not yet known me? Do you want to see who I am?' After this, Ziaul Haq was seen with his face on his two hands and saliva coming out of his mouth, and his father sent him to sleep. Delawar Hosain mentioned to his disciples that his state was due to the power he had transferred to him – such power as would easily have crushed even mountains. It was only because Zia was his son and successor that he had been able to somehow bear it (*JH*: 75 f.). The pain in his breast about which Ziaul Haq used to complain is explained as coming from this transfer, and compared to the pain the Prophet

126 The details mentioned here were confirmed to me in interviews with Didarul Haq and Shahidul Haq (Ahmadiyya Manzil), two of Ziaul Haq's brothers.

127 The Bengali spelling is *taphāẏyuj* (*JH*: 71).

experienced when he received the Qur'anic revelations. Ziaul Haq continued to perform austerities like standing in cold water for hours, wandering without food for days until he was picked up and brought back by somebody (*JH*: 76 f.), staring into the sun for hours and not sleeping at night (*JH*: 76–81). In 1954, Ziaul Haq was married to Monwara Begum, daughter of one of Delawar Hosain's disciples; in the first two years of their married life, he showed no interest in his wife, but later they had six children, five daughters and one son.

Despite his marriage, Ziaul Haq's austerities continued unabated. As a *ḫādim* reports, his body was virtually loaded with current; he kept severe fasts, once for as long as eighteen days, and stood on one leg for hours; he put burning cigarettes on his ears; he excreted blood; he burnt all things around him, including his clothes, and beat up anybody who tried to approach him. 'He had drunken such [a kind of] alcohol of Allah whose effect and intoxication was never-ending', and he became so uncontrollable that he had to be bound to wooden blocks (*JH*: 88–91).

Even his family took him for insane, and in 1967 he was taken to the mental Hospital in Pabna, as described in the chapter *Madhu milan* ('Sweet union', pp. 92–7). Vivid examples of the kinds of illnesses to be met with in such a place are presented (*JH*: 93). The medication Ziaul Haq was given did not prevent him from running away, and he was given tranquillising injections and finally a series of ten electric shocks. After about five months, he had become 'almost healthy' and got temporary release to attend Gholam Rahman's birthday celebrations; after this his father kept him at home. 'Through ten electric shocks, he scorched his body as if baking it in the fire' (*JH*: 97). Still, his austerities were not finished, but continued: he kept on waking at night and wandering around different parts of the region, 'and even at present, he [sometimes] does not eat for eight to ten days'. In this way, he elevated his soul from one level to the other and attained union with Allah (*madhu milan* and *fanā' fī-l-ḥaqīqa*) and finally *baqā' bi-Llah*.

The second part of the book, *Siphat*, mainly contains accounts of Ziaul Haq's miraculous deeds and utterances, but the first three chapters deal with his spiritual inheritance and status. In 1973, in the presence of a great number of *murīd*s, Delawar Hosain formally transferred Ahmadullah's *wilāya* to Ziaul Haq by putting a *čādur* (P.) on him and saying: 'I am today conferring upon you the sacred great deposit [Ar. *amāna*] of Ḥażrat Ġawt̠ al-A'ẓam Maijbhandari (ka.) which was in my guardance; guard it [well].' (*JH*: 101) In 1980, Ziaul Haq himself declared: 'I am Hazrat Sahib Kebla (<*ḥażrat ṣāhib qibla*>, i.e. Ahmadullah)', and 'Do not consider me less then Hazrat' (*JH*: 102). If in this way Ziaul Haq bore the spiritual inheritance of Ahmadullah, he was not, however, his *sağğādanašīn* or formal successor in Ahmadiyya Manzil. In 1974, Delawar Hosain had decided to bestow this responsibility on one of his younger sons and provide for separate accommodation for Ziaul Haq (*JH*: 104 ff.), thus laying the foundation of the later Haq Manzil and ramifying the *silsila* within his progeny. Ziaul Haq perceived this arrangement as a liberation. A short chapter (pp. 108–12) on the Maijbhandari *ṭarīqa*, Ziaul Haq's insistence on performing the Islamic prayers and fast, and general remarks on the role of the saints as a means, *waṣīla*, in attaining God, leads over to the accounts of Ziaul Haq's miracles and utterances.

The large number of reported events in this part, about 150, are not arranged either chronologically or thematically. Some of the accounts, and especially longer digressions on Bangladeshi and international history and politics, are by Sikdar himself, others are assembled from different witnesses. They can be grouped together in a number of categories. The most spectacular of these contains cases in which Ziaul Haq is seen as the driving force behind historical events, or 'the backstage controller of the flow of events', as a chapter on post-independence Bangladesh is headed (pp. 122–30). These events include the death of Shaikh Mujibur Rahman, the first Prime Minister of Bangladesh, the 1982 Israeli invasion of Lebanon, the demise and death of Reza Shah of Persia, the assassination attempt on US President Ronald Reagan's life, and the assassination of Indira Gandhi. In all of these cases, Ziaul Haq, in performing symbolic actions or uttering death sentences, or both, is portrayed as the foreteller or executor of fate.

Three years before Shah Reza Pahlavi's death in Egypt (1980), Ziaul Haq sat on a lawn, smoked a cigarette in fast drags and said to himself in English: 'Shah of Iran, Shah of Iran, I murder you. I murder you. Do you know me?' (*JH*: 135) It thus happened that after the Islamic Revolution in Iran in 1979, Reza Shah had to flee to 'the friends from [his] good times'; and 'not through the threats of Khomeini, but through the bullets from the invisible rifle of the Maijhbhandari Shah of Shahs,[128] the very mighty Reza Shah Pahlavi of Iran was finally lying [dead] on the earth.' (*JH*: 137) In 1982, during the Israeli occupation of Southern Lebanon, he was seen playing with toy weapons in a trance (*ǧazba ḥāl*) (*JH*: 131). One day before Indira Gandhi was assassinated on October 31, 1984, he was heard uttering: 'I shall kill [you] through the guard [Bg. *dārogā*], and I shall also kill the guard. Do you know me?', and seen playing with a toy rifle – mysterious actions to his disciples at the time, which were to become clear soon after. Likewise, President Reagan, ruler of an America which is portrayed as a dangerous, belligerent and destructive superpower, becomes his victim. A week before the attempt on Reagan's life in 1985, he told a *murīd*: 'I will burst open President Reagan's stomach. Does he know me?' (*JH*: 262 ff.)

The most interesting and ambivalent of these 'events' is the assassination of Shaikh Mujibur Rahman. After describing the shortcomings of the latter's post-independence governance, Sikdar narrates that in February 1975, Ziaul Haq, in a state of trance, said that the Government were acting against national interests, and that he would punish them; in this way, Sikdar comments, 'Allah's decision' was revealed 'through the mouth of a *walī-Allah*'. A few days before the assassination, he also warned an Awami League worker not to stay at Shaikh Mujib's house. On the 14th of August, he himself – originally a supporter of the Awami League and Sheikh Mujib, put up a black flag as a sign of grieving, and expressed his sorrow about how such a great man as Mujibur Rahman could fall like this

128 The Shah of Shahs, *šāhanšāh*, is a title commonly used for Ziaul Haq by his disciples, and here of course employed on purpose in connection with the 'Shah of Iran'.

(*JH*: 124 f.). It is also in other, more local circumstances that Ziaul Haq is portrayed as someone commissioned to know and decide about life and death, both as a life-saver (e.g. *JH*: 249 f.) and a foreteller of certain death (*JH*: 211 f.).

Another group of reported deeds consists of his handling of money. He would at times take large sums from rich men and throw them away or redistribute them among the poor, or declare money to be bad.[129] Famous, also, are his car journeys over long distances such as from Maijbhandar to Cox's Bazar and back, without fuel, using sometimes water instead of gasoline, sometimes nothing at all.[130] Many instances of healing, usually by simply bestowing blessings or uttering that things would be all right, are reported,[131] as well as cases of rescuing people from dangerous situations (such as shipwrecking or abduction),[132] and numerous examples of help in obtaining posts, running businesses and passing exams.[133] Like his Maijbhandari predecessors, Ziaul Haq could multiply his presence, and three cases of simultaneously dwelling at Mecca and Maijbhandar or Ajmer and Maijbhandar are narrated.[134] He also dominated gravity: he once threw an apple up and ordered it in Urdu to stop, whereupon the apple remained immobile in the air. This is explained with a reference to 'what the scientists call "no time and space" ', that is, probably the Theory of Relativity, and the sphere of *lā makān* (most probably erroneous for *lā-maqām*, 'without station/position'). According to a *Ḥadīṯ*, time was not in force during Muhammad's *mi'rāǧ*, and the *awliyā'-Allah* are 'able to control the whole creation' (*JH*: 220 f.). Hindus were treated no differently from Muslims by Ziaul Haq, and he stated clearly that in Maijbhandar, no such distinction existed (*JH*: 236 f.). He once advised a Hindu pilgrim to perform his *pūjā*s in order to attain the creator (*JH*: 274 f.)

One well-known and somewhat typical deed of Ziaul Haq described in *Jiẏāul Hak* is the following. Together with a companion, Ziaul Haq went to Chittagong and acquired a watch which he wore on his ankle; he took 25,000 Taka from a person in the shop, another person brought a lungi, a kurta and a vest for him, and he ordered a towel and a 'Lux' brand of soap too. He and his companion got on a rickshaw. Close to the *mazār* of Amanat Shah, they stopped: an old, emaciated sweeper was walking with two vessels full of excrement. Ziaul Haq said to that man: 'Throw all the filth into the ditch', showed him a water faucet and told him to wash himself with the soap. A young man passing by who wanted to fall to Ziaul Haq's feet was instructed to dry the sweeper with the towel. Then the latter was given the clothes Ziaul Haq had brought; when he hesitated to take Ziaul

129 Cf. *JH*: 113 ff., 173 ff., 176 f., 177 ff., 219 f., 230 f.

130 Cf. *JH*: 194 ff. 241 ff.

131 Cf. *JH*: 143 f., 144 ff.187 f., 212 f., 218 f., 222 f., 233 f., 234 f., 239 ff., 251 f., 274 f., 302 f.

132 Cf. *JH*: 150 f. (storm), 171 f. (shipwrecking), 185 f. (car accident, during which the invocation of his name by a disciple was more effective than the invocation of Allah by other passengers), 223 ff. (abduction).

133 Cf. 172 f., 192 ff., 209 f., 228 f., 237 ff., 243 ff., 246 ff., 253 f., 255 f., 256 ff., 272 f.

134 Cf. *JH*: 170 (Mecca), 206 ff. (Ajmer twice).

Haq's own sandals, the latter gave him threats. Finally, he gave him the watch and the 25,000 Taka, and instructed the sweeper:

> 'Sit at home and say Allah Allah; Do not continue all that filthy work.' The sweeper could not say anything. He kept looking without winking from eyes filled with tears; his lips were quivering to say something.
>
> (*JH*: 149)

Jiẏāul Hak ends with a short summary, pointing at his never-ending miraculous words and deeds and praising the saint as a 'personality great like an ocean', with all its superficial turbulences and unfathomable depth (*JH*: 303–4).

The Bengali of *Jiẏāul Hak* is significantly different from the preceding hagiographies. It is *calit bhāṣā*, the colloquial style and common medium of Bengali literature since the middle of the twentieth century. Sikdar often, and especially in his *Siphat* section, uses a form of report resembling both diary writing and short fiction with a journalistic touch. The events in the miracles section are mostly dated and timed in an exact manner at the beginning of their narration, and the mention of the originator is set separately from the texts. The cosmic dimension of events like a saint's conception or birth that was so characteristic of *Ā'īna-i Bārī* and still present in decreasing degrees in the following texts, is absent here – in its stead, there is a lyrical passage on the scenery of a winter morning which reads like any scenic description in a realistic Bengali novel (*JH*: 52).

Saintly life is placed much more consistently than before in a scientific world of linear time; precision in the determination of time and place actually appears to become one of the criteria that assure credibility. Connected with this, on a different level, spiritual significance continues to be expressed in the traditional idiom, but simultaneously translates into historical significance. This latter point, however, derives to a large degree from the substance of Ziaul Haq's life and can thus not be reduced to a mere change in hagiographical conventions. It applies equally to the other two English hagiographies about this saint, which are to be treated hereafter.

Syed Mohd. Amirul Islam (1992): **Shahenshah Ziaul Huq Maijbhandari** *[ZH], E.*

Syed Mohammad Amirul Islam, the author of this book, is a *murīd* of Ziaul Haq, and he started working on Ziaul Haq's life narration when the latter was still alive. In 1985, he announced his desire to write this book to Ziaul Haq, and obtained the permission ('This is necessary to write it in English' – *ZH*: xi). Explaining his reasons for using English, Amirul Islam explains that, on the one hand, the highly educated have not understood 'Maijbhandari Philosophy' sufficiently, and '[. . .] if something could be presented in English, this might attract the attention of those who are yet to come to the track, being boast of their socalled knowledge' (*ZH*: xi). On the other hand, foreigners interested in Maijbhandar could thus be supplied with proper information. The structure of *Shahenshah* conforms to the

Photo 7 Mausoleum of Saint Ziaul Haq Maijbhandari.

common pattern: preliminary questions first, then the life narration, and following these, a chapter on miracles. As far as the latter two are concerned, *Shahenshah* is closely related to *Jiŷāul Hak*, and in a number of instances, in fact, hardly more than its English translation. But some of the basic conceptualisations, dealt with mostly in the first eight pages, are different, and relevant here.

After the opening *basmala*, Amirul Islam describes the aim of his book as 'bringing to light some salient features of the most eventful life and keramat of Babajan Hazrat Ghausul Azam Shahanshah Syed Ziaul Hoq Maijbhandari (K.S.A.)'. That Ziaul Haq is a saint of the highest rank is proven by his miracles:

'From his innumerable, mysterious and wonderful deeds and utterances, it has now been proven beyond any doubt that in the presentday world of known Auliyas, he is by far the brightest star in the galaxy' (*ZH*: 1). In contrast to other saints, Ziaul Haq's works are not limited to the spiritual sphere, but extend to the 'political, social and cultural arena' (*ZH*: 1). Miracles (*muʿǧizāt* and *karāmāt*) are a common attribute of both prophets and saints. After deploring the state of those who do not believe in the saints, such as Wahhabis, Amirul Islam points out the places in the *Qurʾān* where the *awliyāʾ* are mentioned (*ZH*: 4), and introduces a hierarchy of humans according to their respective closeness to God. After the prophets and the followers and direct successors of Prophet Muhammad, the highest position in this hierarchy is held by the Ġawṯ al-Aʿẓam,namely the uppermost status that can be achieved after the initial time of Islam (*ZH*: 5). Contrary to common perception, the title Ġawṯ al-Aʿẓam is not exclusively used for Abd al-Qadir Gilani, but is a rank denomination that can be attained at different times, an 'identifying mark for such rare and extraordinary spiritual giants' (*ZH*: 6). Three Maijbhandari saints are considered Ġawṯ al-Aʿẓams: Ahmadullah, Gholam Rahman, and Ziaul Haq. Likewise, all three also possess the title of *Muǧaddid-i zamān*, 'Reformer of the Times', and their respective times are given as the twelfth, thirteenth and fourteenth centuries *hiǧrī*.

After briefly mentioning Ziaul Haq's day of birth, Amirul Islam describes Maijbhandar,[135] and goes on to praise Chittagong and Fatikchari. Maijbhandar is a pilgrimage centre for millions of people, 'male and female, Muslim and Hindu, Buddhist and Christian alike. [. . .] From a rough survey, it has been estimated that it ranked third in number after the Haj congression and the festival at Vetican [*sic*] city' (*ZH*: 9). Following this, Amirul Islam gives a long list of 58 *ḫalīfa*s of Ziaul Haq (*ZH*: 10–12) and his *šaǧara*, spiritual lineage. This latter deviates from Sikdar and from the common version current in Haq Manzil: it includes, in the following order, Ġawṯ al-Aʿẓam Ahmadullah, Ġawṯ al-Aʿẓam Gholam Rahman, Hazrat Maulana Shah Sufi Delawar Hosain, and Ġawṯ al-Aʿẓam Ziaul Haq. The advent of these saints entitles the 'erstwhile dormant village Maijbhandar' to the appellation Maijbhandar Sharif (*ZH*: 17). The 'celebrated school of KHIJRI', that is, the *ṭarīqa* founded by Ḫiḍr, 'has been introduced at the Darbar', which accounts for the fact that 'it is far beyond the capacity of followers of Musabi Branch of Shariat to grasp the far reaching acts and omissions, dos and donts [*sic*] of Babajan in particular' (*ZH*: 18).

The following accounts, starting with Ziaul Haq's forefathers and ending with his miracles (*ZH*: 18–103), closely ressemble those given by Sikdar in *Jiẏāul Hak*, and the minor deviations are mostly negligible. One exception to this, however, is Amirul Islam's way of dealing with Ziaul Haq's alledged madness. He introduces different, ascending categories of mental disturbances according to psychiatric terminology, namely hallucinations, schizophrenia, lunacy and madness, and describes the symptoms of each, pointing out that hallucinations can have very positive, creative aspects (*ZH*: 39 f.). Thereupon, he castigates the way society treats mental disturbances:

135 By using Badruddoza's etymology (cf. above).

> But the shocking news is that as and when a person is seen to behave a little bit abnormally or in terms of random thoughts, he is instantly branded to be mad. This is not only very dangerous but unwanted too. Such a naming may change the whole lifecycle of a man.
>
> (*ZH*: 40)

This criticism also implicitly strikes Ziaul Haq's family who thought that he was mentally disturbed, and in a way, Ziaul Haq's father Delawar Hosain is not completely exempted from this either, since he 'yielded to the [family's] pressure' and sent Ziaul Haq to Pabna.

The miracles recounted in *Shahenshah* (*ZH*: 72–103) are fewer than those of *Jiẏāul Hak*, being limited to such happenings as were witnessed by the author. One additional chapter describes the 'Historic last few Days of Ziababa' (*ZH*: 103–10). In a very feeble condition, Ziaul Haq, in the company of some *murīd*s, visited Rangamati in the Chittagong Hill Tracts. His vital functions were almost absent after 'severe convulsions' (*ZH*: 103), but he recovered and went to Chittagong, twice visiting the *mazār* of Shah Amanat and Patenga sea beach:

> Alighting from the car he went near to the water and exchanged views with water (as we observed) in a language audible but not understood by anybody accompanying him.
>
> (*ZH*: 104)

His ECG was taken, and the doctors present there were amazed at how somebody with almost no signs of a living being could still walk and behave as a normal man. He was taken to hospital against his will, and insisted on going to Cox's Bazar the day after. On his way back, he collapsed and was again taken into Chittagong Port Hospital. On 12 September 1988, shortly before midnight, he announced that 'My time is over. I am going' (*ZH*: 107). Between 6,000 and 7,000 disciples had by then gathered at and around the hospital and, asked about what they should do after his death, he replied: 'Go on saying Allah Allah with me' and started to perform a *ḏikr*. Everybody joined in this *ḏikr*, and finally at 12.27 a.m. (13 September), he breathed his last. Ziaul Haq's corpse was taken to Maijbhandar, and 'not less than 10 lac people' (i.e. one million) offered their burial prayers (*ğanāza*) in three phases (*ZH*: 108). Amirul Islam resumes this chapter by emphasising Ziaul Haq's spiritual legacy and his installation of his son, Syed Hasan, through several utterances,[136] and, summarising his account, states about Ziaul Haq: 'He is a history, he is an institution that has been imprinted in the souls of millions of us' (*ZH*: 110). The book closes with a compilation of 21 aphoristic sayings of Ziaul Haq (*ZH*: 111), a 'Poetry Chapter' (pp. 112–29, containing poems by the author glorifying Ziaul Haq) and a bibliography (*ZH*: 130).

136 He called his son a *walī-Allāh* twice, and also his life-saver (*ZH*: 109).

Md. Ghulam Rasul (1994):* The Divine Spark *[DS]; E.

As in *Shahenshah*, the substance of *The Divine Spark*, written by Ziaul Haq's *murīd* Md. Ghulam Rasul in 1994, is largely covered in *Jiỳāul Hak*. The basic structure (preliminaries, life narration, miracles) is equally present – if in different chapters – and the order of narration is mostly the same. As before, then, we will concentrate on the preliminaries and the specific way of presentation, asking how Ziaul Haq's life is contextualised and his significance elaborated. A discussion of why *The Divine Spark* is written in English is absent in the book, and *Shahenshah*, published two years before it, is mentioned neither in the text nor in the attached bibliography. The relationship between the two texts is not clear. It appears that both manuscripts took about four years to be published, so Ghulam Rasul did not have the printed version of *Shahenshah* when finishing his manuscript in 1990. The books were also commissioned by different persons, that is, by Ziaul Haq and Syed Hasan respectively, so it may be that the two writers' efforts were not coordinated. Today, both are for sale side by side at Haq Manzil in Maijbhandar.

The cover of *The Divine Spark* shows a graphical representation of Ziaul Haq's *rawḍa* (mausoleum) in front of a globe, symbolising the global importance of this saint. *The Divine Spark* contains three forewords or 'Messages' by Syed Md. Hasan, by an English professor, and by the Secretary of the Chittagong Port Authorities. In his following *Preface* (pp. 16–2), the author compares the life of a great man to 'the fathomless sea':[137]

> The biography of the Mystic Saints is not a series of events, nor mere [*sic*] a list of miracles and oracles. Also it is not a series of debates with which people now-a-days quarrel. It is, in the truest sense of the term, a matter of respect, reverence, honour, wonder, dignity, quality and achievements.
>
> (p. 16)

Ghulam Rasul has read the *Qur'ān* and *Sunna*, books on Sufism and biographies of other Maijbhandari saints in order to master this task (*DS*: 16), and views Ziaul Haq 'in the light of scientific and philosophial analysis based on Islamic principles, Hadiths and Qur'anic revelations' (*DS*: 17). After stressing the importance of self-knowledge and striving in the cause of Allah,[138] he presents Ziaul Haq as one who 'could establish himself on the Straight Path of Allah' (*DS*: 18). Dwelling upon the literal meaning of *Islām*, Ghulam Rasul insists on the importance of complete surrender to Allah, and quotes Ḫwāğa Mu'in al-Din Chishti on the mystic's constant concentration on God (*DS*: 20 f.). The scope of the book is to help readers gain an understanding of mysticism and sainthood (*DS*: 23).

The book proper, divided into eight chapters, starts with a *tasmiya* (invocation of the names of God) and the *fātiha* (*DS*: 25). This is paralleled by the very first pages of the book which contain illustrations of holy Meccan and Medinian places and

137 A direct rendering of the Bengali phrases *athaï* or *agādh samudra* which is often used for the saints or Maijbhandar as a whole.

138 Argued on the basis of *Qur'ān* 41.53 and 29.69 (*DS*: 18 f.).

objects. *Chapter II* (pp. 26–38) then gives a general outline of Sufism. The *Qur'ān* contains the seeds of divine unity (*tawḥīd*), and the Sufis' attempt is to go beyond its 'meaning in letter' (*ẓāhir*), 'meant for general people', towards its 'meaning of spirit' (*bāṭin*), perceiving Allah to be 'All-pervading' (*DS*: 26). After dealing with the etymology of the term *ṣūfī*, Abdul Rasul presents a number of *Qur'ān* quotations in order to show that 'Surely the seeds of mysticism are there' (*DS*: 27). *Nubuwwa* and *wilāya* are shortly exposed along the lines of Delawar Hosain's book *Belāẏate mot'lākā* (*DS*: 28 f.).[139] What ensues is a short historical sketch of the development of Sufism, starting with the woman mystic Rabiʿa of Basra (d. 801) and her example of the 'ecstatic contemplation of the Beloved' (*DS*: 30). The next to be mentioned are Harith al-Mahusibi (Ḥāriṯ al-Muḥāsibī) of Basra (d. 857) and his treatise on *maqāmāt* and *aḥwāl* (Ar. pl. of *ḥāl*, 'state' – *DS*: 30 f.) and Abu Hamid Ghazzali's (d. 1111) realisation that books are futile for the attainment of the peculiar goals of the Sufis, and his utter surrender to Allah (*DS*: 31). Hereafter, Bayezid Bistami (inventor of the 'doctrine of fana'), Mansur al-Hallaj and his martyrdom, and Ibn ʿArabi (inventor of the doctrine of *waḥdat al-wuǧūd* and the concept of *insān al-kāmil*) are summarily dealt with (*DS*: 30–2). Next comes an appraising account of Jalal al-Din Rumi, with emphasis on the anti-ritualistic stance expressed in his *Maṯnavī* (*DS*: 33 f.). After mentioning the names of a few more prominent Sufis, Ghulam Rasul narrates in some detail the story of Muʿin al-Din Chishti (d. 1190) and the tremendous influence of his *ṭarīqa* in India, and makes a connection with the Maijbhandari *ṭarīqa*:

> It is reliably believed that Maizbhandari Philosophy at Chittagong, Bangladesh is the part and parcel of the doctrine of Khaja (R) [i.e. Ḫwāǧa Muʿin al-Din Chishti] as stated many times by Hazrat Shahanshah Ziaul Hoque Maizbhandari.
>
> (*DS*: 37)

In *Chapter III* (pp. 38–48), Ziaul Haq is portrayed as a confluence of the three great preceding saints of Maijbhandar, and short biographies of the latter, including an account of the seven-point version of the Maijbhandari *ṭarīqa*, are given. The life account in the following chapters is quite similar to the other hagiographies. The stories regarding Ziaul Haq's favourite pastimes as a child are left out (*DS*: 50 f.), and no explanation is given for his electro-shocks other than that they somehow constitute a part of his *sādhanā* (Bg.), austerities (*DS*: 66 ff.). In the account of Sheikh Mujibur Rahman's assassination, Ziaul Haq's agency is asserted more unambiguously than in *Jiẏāul Hak* and *Shahenshah*. His killing from the hands of Bangladesh army people is commented upon in the following terms:

> Thus Shahanshah Ziaul Hoque (K) used to exercise direct moral control over the Government of the country in order to maintain the welfare of the subjects in general.
>
> (*DS*: 86)

139 Cf. above, Chapter 3.

More than the other hagiographers of Ziaul Haq, Ghulam Rasul, in accordance with his above-quoted statement, works Qur'anic quotations into his narration. Thus, when treating Ziaul Haq's *riyāẓāt* or penances, he states that 'The whole universe is a School of learning', and paraphrases the final passages of Sura 25 to the effect that 'All things in nature are symbols, and point to the law Divine and the destiny, good or ill, of man' (*DS*: 52 f.). Altogether, there are more than twenty detailed Qur'anic quotations and paraphrases in this book.

After the account of Ziaul Haq's demise (*Chapter VIII*, pp. 130–41), Ghulam Rasul summarises what Ziaul Haq stood for: a man of 'outstanding personality' and 'blessed with the gift of miraculous powers', his 'doctrine centred in the quest of the soul for Allah, which found its fulfilment in the breaking down of the barriers that divide man from him' (*DS*: 141). Such was Ziaul Haq's love for Allah that he abandoned all love for humans, his family and relatives (*DS*: 142). A bibliography (*DS*: 143–4) concludes the book.

4.6 Syed Shafiul Bashar (1919–2001)

Syeda Lutfunnesa Hosaini (1987): Śaphiul Baśar jībanī */*ŚBJ*/; Bg.*[140]

One final Maijbhandari hagiography deserves our attention before we move on to an overarching analysis of these works: the vita of Syed Shafiul Bashar written by his daughter Lutfunnesa Hosaini. Like *Jiỳāul Hak*, this book was also published before the death of the saint described in it; it first appeared in 1987. It is divided into a number of chapters that follow the predominant structure of Maijbhandari hagiographies: the actual life narration is preceded by remarks on the position and status of saints in the framework of Islam and, in this case, an introduction to the genealogy and history of the Maijbhandari saints (*Māij'bhāṇḍāre āolāde rāsul*, 'Progeny of the Prophet in Maijbhandar', pp. 1–6). The next five chapters depict the events in Shafiul Bashar's life in chronological succession, followed by two chapters on the saint's physical features and one containing an evaluative synopsis. A discussion of 'The miracles of the saints in the light of the *Qur'ān*' leads over to the concluding chapter on Shafiul Bashar's *karāmāt*.

In a foreword, Lutfunnesa Hosaini clarifies her own relationship with Shafiul Bashar: 'For my whole life I have not regarded Bābājān as a father but in the form of a *muršid* Qibla Ka'ba' (*ŚBJ*: cha), and equates his character, appearance and lifestyle with the Prophet's. The first chapter starts with an Arabic prayer, the *Basmala* and a eulogy of the Prophet (*ŚBJ*: 1 f.). After the end of prophethood, the task of protecting mankind passes to the saints and foremost among them to the *Ġawṯ al-A'ẓam* who necessarily belongs to the line of the Prophet (*ŚBJ*: 2). Maijbhandar possesses two *Ġawṯs*, Ahmadullah and Gholam Rahman, who belong

140 The datings in this book betray the fact that it has undergone revisions since its first publication. The first edition not being available to me, I have based the following on the revised edition of 1993.

to the spiritual line of ʿAbd al-Qadir Gilani. Lutfunnesa sketches the migration history of the family from Arabia to Chittagong and the achievements of Ahmadullah (who 'planted the first seed' of the Maijbhandari *ṭarīqa*) and Gholam Rahman (who 'inaugurated' it) (*ŚBJ*: 4); references and eulogies dedicated to the latter are more frequent and detailed. The names of the offspring of Gholam Rahman are given in a list. Shafiul Bashar, the youngest of his four sons, is referred to as 'the central jewel of the Maijbhandari *ṭarīqa*' and its *karṇadhār*, 'helmsman', and it is emphasised that it was he who first introduced the *ṭarīqa* abroad: 'He accepted boundless labour and promulgated the Maijbhandai *ṭarīqa* in far-away London, Washington and the Middle East' (*ŚBJ*: 6). The names of his five sons and six daughters conclude this chapter. Next, in answer to 'the need [. . .] of a third great man after the pair of *Ġawṯ al-Aʿẓam*s', Shafiul Bashar was nominated for this task by Allah. His birth on 20 February 1919 is accompanied by phenomena such as a blossoming nature and general happiness at the *darbār* (*ŚBJ*: 7 f.). The infant Shafi was not a bed-wetter, and he did not have to be weaned but stopped demanding his mother's breast at the age of two, 'sitting behind the curtain of nature and obeying the order of the *Qurʾān*' (*ŚBJ*: 8). His mother died when he was only two and a half, and his eldest brother Khayrul Bashar took care of him.

Shafiul Bashar's education ('Shafiul Bashar as a student', pp. 9–10) started at home, where a teacher was employed to teach him Urdu, Arabic and Persian, and another for Bengali and English. At the age of six, he entered a local madrassa: 'In matters of frequenting the madrassa, there was no carelessness on his part, and he was very eager in his learning' (*ŚBJ*: 9). Shafiul Bashar furthermore was a friendly boy who 'did not boast in any way of his family's nobility'. When certain fundamental questions about life started to rise in his mind, his father Gholam Rahman would answer them through various signs. Shafiul Bashar continued his education at Collegiate School in Chittagong, showing astonishing proficiency especially in Islamic scriptures. In 1932, his brothers, in keeping with the intention of Gholam Rahman, sent him to the famous Muslim university of Aligarh 'in order to edify him as a worthy successor of the Maijbhandari *ṭarīqa*' (*ŚBJ*: 10). There, he gained 'unfathomable knowledge' in religious matters and experience of people and languages, especially Urdu and English; after the conclusion of his studies, the love for Gholam Rahman brought him back to Maijbhandar.

Spiritually, Shafiul Bashar's development ('Shafi Baba in the world of *sādhanā*', pp. 11–17) is portrayed by this hagiographer as tempered by experiences of loss and utmost devotion to Gholam Rahman whom he accepted as his *muršid* as soon as his knowledge started to unfold. He was singleminded in his observance of Islamic duties, and his love for his master found expression in his composition of ghazals from the young age of eleven onwards. 'After returning from Aligarh University, Shafi Bābā used to either stand for whole days and nights with folded hands in front of the *huğra*, or sit silently, or sometimes remain in prostration for long times on the ground facing the *huğra*' (*ŚBJ*: 13). Observing such averseness to worldly matters, his brother decided to take him back into 'a natural state in the world', and thus in 1937, a few months after Gholam Rahman's demise, his marriage with the daughter of a zamindar and Maijbhandari disciple from Barishal took place. Khayrul Bashar died shortly after, and the loss of both his father and preceptor and his caring brother only strengthened Shafiul Bashar's pursuit of the spiritual path. His penances became more and more extreme; he observed a partial fast (Bg. *rojā*) lasting for four years and once remained in meditation and prostration for two and a half days (*ŚBJ*: 14 f.). In this way, he eventually became a fully realised man (Bg. *siddha puruṣ*). On two journeys to Burma, in 1939 and 1946, he initiated the propagation of the Maijbhandari *ṭarīqa* outside Bengal. During World War II, he left Maijbhandar without giving notice to anybody and joined the British army as a store keeper. This engagement took him to Egypt, Palestine and other places in the Near East:

> 'Here too, [it is an instance of] pure Allah's boundless predestination and Baba Bhandari Qibla Kaʿba's shoreless play [that] he got the opportunity to go to the holy land of the Muslims of western Asia. Through his participation in this great war, he easily got the opportunity to see all the great holy places' (*ŚBJ*: 16), namely, Mecca, Medina, Jerusalem and Bethlehem, as well as the tombs of Abraham and Moses.

The following chapter ('Shafi Bābā's worldly life', pp. 18–22) furnishes a detailed account of Shafiul Bashar's marriage with Ashrafunnesa and pictures the initial poverty the family had to suffer due to his indifference. Gradually, however, arrangements were made to meet the exigencies of the *darbār* that continued to be frequented by pilgrims: Shafiul Bashar, advised by his wife, enhanced agricultural activities and improved the facilities for visitors and pilgrims; Lutfunnesa mentions the construction of granaries, a kitchen, a pond, guesthouses as well as a garden. Ashrafunnesa's role as a devoted and persevering wife with a marked talent for practical and organisational matters is repeatedly emphasised.[141]

The chapter on Shafiul Bashar's dissemination of the Maijbhandari *ṭarīqa* (*Śafibābār tvarikā pracār*, pp. 23–28) is designed to explain Shafiul Bashar's significance in the context of the role of the Islamic saints. It starts with a sketch of Sufi cosmology and the role of man: the creation from light (*nūr*) and the original treaty between the creator and men[142] are exposed; the fall of Iblis is cited as a proof that mankind was made for loving God (*ŚBJ*: 23). But as God is shapeless, Lutfunnesa argues, the suitable way of showing this love must be taught through the Prophets. Muhammad as the Last Prophet has for once and all communicated the right way as laid down in the *Qurʾān*, and he is simultaneously the object of

141 Cf. p. 20, in the context of the initial poverty of the family: 'Mother [Bg. *āmmājān*] assisted in father's work with boundless patience, bearing all inconveniences'; and, regarding her dedication to the pilgrims: '[. . .] Mother forgets her meals and abandons her repose and comfort in organising day and night from within the inner chambers the accommodation and catering of the *bhakta*s and *ʿāšiq*s – everything, in a most skilled and excellent way'.

142 *Qurʾān* 1.172(171).

that love, since love of the Prophet is coterminous with love of God.[143] The legacy of the Prophet passes to ʿAli and via him to the chains of spiritual succession; thus the veneration of Sayyads, *awliyā'* and *pīr*s is ordained. Shafiul Bashar, as a perfect *walī* and Sayyad in whom 'the blood of the Prophet [. . .] is flowing', and who is furthermore described as 'the most excellent personality of present Maijbhandar Sharif and the Maijbhandari *ṭarīqa*', is thus certainly entitled to veneration (*ŚBJ*: 25 f.). His special merit is the dissemination of the Maijbhandari *ṭarīqa* abroad: in Burma, western parts of undivided Bengal and Assam, Pakistan, Indonesia and Malaysia, as well as in the United States and Great Britain (London, Manchester, Birmingham). He initiated 'hundreds of thousands of disciples' and the establishment of *dā'ira*s in many of these places (*ŚBJ*: 28).

Shafiul Bashar's character traits (*Śaphi bābār caritra mādhuryya*, pp. 29–31) are 'the combination of the indispensable qualities of a great man' who has fashioned himself on the ideal of the Prophet. Shafiul Bashar excels in basic virtues like justness and peacefulness as well as in social virtues. He is a wanderer in the realm of *fanā' fī-Llāh* as well as a fighter who endorsed a *ǧihād* against superstition and bigotry (*ŚBJ*: 29). He is not conceited and treats people of high and low ranks equally; he is entertaining in conversation and a powerful preacher; his patience and power of endurance, strengthened by years of penances, are immense. Despite his tolerance and soft ways, he does not tolerate flatterers and hypocritical, false *faqīr*s, and despises any 'action contradicting Islam', as, for example, the consumption of marijuana, alcohol, *bhāṅg* (H.), etc. (*ŚBJ*: 30). His modest food and white dress are described in a separate paragraph.

Shafiul Bashar's physical beauty is the subject of an additional chapter (*Bābājāner cehārā saundaryya*, p. 32). Lutfunnesa Hosaini holds that all *awliyā'* have in common that beauty ('as it has come for one purpose and from one entity [i.e. God]') and resemble each other. Shafiul Bashar is described as tall and having long arms; the colour of his body glows reddish and 'is always bright by the light of Allah's radiance', but during his wanderings in 'the country of *fanā' fī-Llāh*', it may change to very bright, rose, golden and yellow shades. His strong forehead bears a vertical wrinkle like 'the first letter of the Arabic alphabet, the *alif*'. His body exudes a pleasant odour. Lutfunnesa in this way gives a detailed account of Shafiul Bashar's physical features; she stresses that he walks and laughs like Gholam Rahman. Altogether, Shafiul Bashar's life in its combination of reflective and active aspects, endurance, etc. is truly exemplary, and the *ṭarīqa* is the means that may produce heroic personalities in all spheres of life (*Mahat·jīban Śaphi Bābār*, pp. 33–6).

The accounts of Shafiul Bashar's miracles that conclude the book are introduced by a discussion of the nature of saintly miracles (*Kor'āner āloke kerāmate āuliẏā*, pp. 37–41). The supernatural power required for them is seen as a 'peculiarity or indicator, and a criterion' for prophets and saints (*ŚBJ*: 37). In short, Lutfunnesa Hosaini distinguishes between *mu'ǧizāt* and *karāmāt* and explains

143 I could not find a reference for this in the *Qur'ān*.

that the agency also in *karāmāt* is basically Allah's; the *wilāya* of each saint stems from a special prophet. The argument relies on references to the *Qur'ān* and *Ḥadīṯ*. The last chapter (*Bābājāner alaukik kriẏākalāp o kerāmat*, pp. 42–52) enlists 15 reports narrated by different disciples. The miracles include healings (*ŚBJ*: 44, 45 f.), the removal of diseases (*ŚBJ*: 45), help in examinations (*ŚBJ*: 46) and election campaigns (*ŚBJ*: 48 f.), banishing storms (*ŚBJ*: 45), a grant of fatherhood to an eighty-year-old Hindu (*ŚBJ*: 43) and appearances to future disciples in dreams (*ŚBJ*: 46 ff.). In two cases, Shafiul Bashar's legitimacy is confirmed by Gholam Rahman. Four-year old Shafi, playing with a toy car, told three disciples from Barishal that their wish would be fulfilled if they brought him another car. When they approached Gholam Rahman, he said: 'Why here? My Miñā has already liberated you' (*ŚBJ*: 42). In two other episodes, Shafiul Bashar is visualised floating on air. A disciple from Rangpur reports an encounter with two 'great men' (Bg. *mahāpuruṣ*) standing still and elevated from the ground in his courtyard. Upon his request, one of them descended and introduced himself as a child of Gholam Rahman from Maijbhandar, and initiated him. Some years later, the disciple came to Maijbhandar and recognised Shafiul Bashar (*ŚBJ*: 43 f.). Another noteworthy happening is narrated by disciples from Noakhali. One of them dreamt that Shafiul Bashar ordered him to mount Burraq, namely the horse of Prophet Muhammad's *mirāǧ* (journey to heaven). He was taken to a huge stretch of water and had to swim for a long time until Burraq picked him up again and took him back to the verandah of Rahman Manzil. When he asked what he had gained from this, Burraq whispered *lā ilāha illā Llāh* three times.

A short-hand analysis of this hagiography reveals some interesting features. One is the conventionality of presentation. Shafiul Bashar's life-narration is tailored upon the blueprint of preceding Maijbhandari hagiography. This shows up most conspicuously in the chapter on his penances. Compared to preceding Maijbhandari saints and other Sufi saints in general, Shafiul Bashar's austerities appear somewhat unspectacular; the specific trait in his biography is rather the development from a *bhakta*-cum-song author into a *pīr*. His song-writing is not exactly downplayed in Lutfunnesa Hosaini's representation, but in contrast to his penances it is not portrayed as a necessary part of his saintly career. A second characteristic point is the double parallelity that runs through Lutfunnesa's narration of Shafiul Bashar's life: its models are the Prophet Muhammad as well as Shafiul Bashar's father and *muršid*, Gholam Rahman. While all Maijbhandari hagiographers would probably agree with this author that the Prophet's life is a general ideal and that the saints ressemble each other, the repeated stress on the son's similarities with his father go beyond such notions. It seems that Shafiul Bashar is elevated into a double successor: on a general Islamic level, he is made to represent the Prophet, and on a local Maijbhandari level, according to Lutfunnesa's reading, the second Ġawṯ al-Aʿẓam Gholam Rahman. Lastly, in this connection, a certain downscaling of Ahmadullah in this representation is undeniable. His title of a Ġawṯ al-Aʿẓam is left untouched, but his role in the development of the Maijbhandari *ṭarīqa* is not more than 'planting the first seeds', whereas it is due to Gholam Rahman's and his successor Shafiul Bashar's meritorious deeds that the *darbār* attained the present prosperous state. We shall discuss these points on a more general level in the pages below.

4.7 Analysis

The hermeneutical problem in the diachronic analysis of these hagiographies I want to attempt now is posed by a multiple layering of event and narration as well as, in a very basic sense, the interaction of the two. It does not take much expertise to approximately locate the hagiographies in time even without knowledge of their publication history, especially since all of them betray some sense of historical taxonomies. The life dates of the saints are given with exactitude; references to historical events on the subcontinent and beyond are legion; the authors determine their relationship to the saints whose lives they narrate and often feature as actors in the hagiographies themselves. Despite these common grounds, a discerning look at these samples of almost a hundred years of twentieth-century hagiography writing reveals a number of changes, and it is tempting to think of some kind of modernisation process in the depiction of saintliness. But, on the other hand, it is perfectly possible to imagine a hagiographical tradition that keeps track of historical progression, changing living conditions, modernised material culture, etc. without deviating from its basic generic properties. The hagiographies of Ziaul Haq, for example, are bound to take the reader to the age of petrol-fuelled vehicles in rural Bangladesh and narrate electric shock treatments in Pabna Mental Hospital, but it is obviously not on these grounds – if at all – that they may qualify as 'modern hagiography'. Neither would, for that matter, Ziaul Haq qualify as a 'modern saint' because of his use of petrol-fuelled vehicles and consumption of contemporary middle-class cigarettes, or Shafiul Bashar for his travelling on aeroplanes. These are truisms, but they are suitable reminders of traps awaiting any short-hand formulas about 'traditional' and 'modern' hagiography.

In fact, the common ground shared by all these books is much more striking than their differences. Almost all Maijbhandari hagiographies share a basic tripartite structure, consisting of a preliminary positioning of sainthood within Islam, a biography, and a *karāmāt* section containing the respective saint's miraculous sayings and deeds. At least from the beginning of the twentieth century on, the Maijbhandari movement has had to confront criticism and attacks from Islamic revivalist quarters, and the preliminary chapters use traditional Sufi apologetics to ascertain the place of saints and their worship in Islamic providence. Another common feature is local patriotism: the elevation of Chittagong and Maijbhandar to holy places that have been prepared for a long time by Allah for the arrival of these saints.

Chittagong is described in Abdul Ghani's *Ā'īna-i Bārī* by a long list of epithets, such as 'the place of knowing *'ulamā'*', 'the mine of the astute', 'the storehouse of writers', 'the refuge for thinkers' and 'strangers', 'the keenness of the garden of paradise', 'the envy of societies', 'the garden of gardens' (*ĀB*: 125 f.); indeed, the 'pure earth' or 'dust' of Maijbhandar is the best medicine for any sickness (*ĀB*: 127). Isapuri, in his *Jīban carit*, stresses that Maijbhandar is of utmost importance and glory due to the advent of Gholam Rahman, and worthy of bearing the appellation *šarīf* just as Bagdad and Ajmer (*ĀB*: 10); the 'superstitious Bengalis' 'began to rise to the same prominence that had been attained by the inhabitants of Bagdad, Ajmer', and 'another miraculous light' was lit in Badr Shah's Chittagong (*ĀB*: 6). Amirul Islam, writing at a time at which statistics have become part of the general episteme, points out its importance as a centre of pilgrimage by likening it to the Vatican (*Shahenshah*: 9, see above).

Other common traits in the hagiographies are the occasional (and sometimes, as in the case of Lutfunnesa Hosaini's work, persistent) demonstration of parallels of the saint's life with that of the Prophet Muhammad, the formal mention of the witnesses of miracles in a manner ressembling the *Ḥadīṯ*, and the combination of a chronology of ascension to saintly status in the second part and a non-chronological collection of miracles in the third. All of the hagiographies discussed here further attempt to bestow meaning on saintly life by locating it within the course of mankind and defining it in relation to the present age.

The definitions of this present age, however, differ considerably. In *Ā'īna-i bārī*, the present is the 'age of erring' (U. *zamāna-i gumrāhī*, p. 85), and is characterised by the ignorance of the *'ulamā'* who rely only on exoteric knowledge, while only exoteric and esoteric (*ẓāhir* and *bāṭin*) together constitute true knowledge. Conventional Sufi concepts are used for this definition. In Delawar Hosain's *Jībanī o kerāmat* of the 1960s, Islamic history consists of alternating ages of light and darkness, and the present is a predestined era of light brought by Maijbhandar.[144] Badruddoza describes the present age as one of so-called freedom and lacking spirituality, but it is simultaneously an ambiguous 'age of science' which has its specific qualities:

> As in this age of the highest progress of science the objects and the outer world abandon the coarse and are inclined towards subtleness, likewise with regard to the spiritual world, this age is one of music and love.
>
> (*BB*: 5)

The Maijbhandari saints thus promulgate the appropriate religious practice for this time. Three of the most recent hagiographies, too, portray the present as an age of science and political emancipation. The respective Maijbhandari saint is a controller of world history who very directly influences the course of history through his ordainments; thus the deaths of Indira Gandhi, Mujibur Rahman, the Shah of Persia and others are effects of his sentences.[145]

We witness here the gradual transition from Islamic concepts of time to secular history, and we can state that the hagiographies assert the importance of the saints they describe with reference to the dominant paradigms. Time measurements in the books become more precise; 'Islamic time' is not absent, but nailed down to the linear progression of 'secular time'. The saints no longer operate

144 Cf. preceding chapter.
145 Cf. the hagiographies on Ziaul Haq.

exclusively within the frame of Islamic salutory history, but as responsible actors of world history; or, differently put, Islamic salutory history expands and comes to comprise spheres formerly not belonging to it. Likewise, Maijbhandar comes to appeal not only to Muslims but to everyone; *jātidharmanirbiśeṣe*, 'regardless of caste and religion', as the slogan goes, gets elaborated as *the* central message of the movement.

We have already noted the linguistic transition from Persian and Urdu to Bengali (first *sādhu bhāṣā*, then also *calit bhāṣā*) and finally in part also to English. Along with these linguistic codes, writing norms, too, change a great deal from the very ornate Urdu of *Ā'īna-i bārī* to a comparatively sober Bengali apparently inspired by secular Bengali biography writing. Recently, the impact of modern journalism and fiction writing is discernible. Sikdar opens the chapter on Ziaul Haq's family ties in the following manner:

> [It was] the deepest [Bg. *nijhum*] night then. Everybody was unconcious in sleep. [Only] in one room a light was lit and a becoming mother was awake with her mother and two servants.
>
> (*JH*: 68)

The mimetic quality of this depiction is achieved by the withdrawal of the narrator, and the lack of any markers of indefiniteness (such as 'once', 'one night', etc.) confront the reader more directly with the happenings to be narrated, which gives a certain fictional flavour and dramatic immediacy to this description that is absent in the earlier hagiographies. In the *karāmāt* section of this book, specifications of time, when present, are given in a stenographic way that closely ressembles diary or newspaper reports: phrases like 'Month Ramadan of the year 1981'[146] (*JH*: 204), 'The 26th of January in the year 1983, Wednesday afternoon'[147] (*JH*: 201), etc. precede the narration. This stands in strong contrast with the earlier hagiographies that avoid such conciseness and contraction of sentences.[148]

Accordingly, some hagiographical stereotypes, as in the depiction of a saint's infancy and childhood, give way to more individualistic representation. The recurrent and traditional stereotypes are that an infant saint is never a bed-wetter,[149] the young boy spontaneously turns to religious matters, and the saintly young student is adverse to play and distraction of any kind. Ahmadullah, for instance, is portrayed in *Ā'īna-i bārī* as an excellent pupil who effortlessly mastered all fields of exoteric knowledge (*ĀB*: 168 f.); according to *Jībanī o kerāmat*,

146 *ekāśi sāler ram'jān mās* (Bg.). This may also be interpreted as a nominal clause and translated as 'It was . . .', but arguably if a full sentence had been intended, a *chila* ('was') would have been added; the shortness of expression thus seems intended here.

147 *uniś śa' tirāśī sāler chābbiśe jānuẏārī, budh'bār bikele.* Cf. preceding footnote.

148 The use of extreme alternations between short and long sentences and phrasal units seems to be a distinctive feature of contemporary Bengali prose and a kind of rapprochement to oral speech; older works seem to prefer a more even and paratactic diction. But such a thesis would of course have to be verified, and certainly would have to admit many exceptions.

149 Cf. *ŚBJ*: 8, *JC*: 20.

he was an earnest and philosophical boy (*JK*: 26); and in Isapuri's *Jīban carit*, Gholam Rahman, from the age of two onwards, showed the utmost attraction towards his saintly uncle Ahmadullah (*JC*: 25). The most recent Maijhandari saint Ziaul Haq, however, is described as a playful and sometimes capricious young boy, whose longing for a suit is certainly beyond the common early signs of sainthood in this genre (cf. *JH*: 63 f.).

One more difference that evolves from the diachronic analysis of the life narrations presented here is the decrease in didacticism *vis-à-vis* their readers. Abdul Ghani, an Islamic scholar at the beginning of the twentieth century, shows little reluctance in his *Āʾīna-i bārī* to scold fools, deplore the moral state of things and pass harsh verdicts on those who go astray from the right path. His is the superior position of a privileged member of the *ʿulamāʾ* whose status and education entitle him to a somewhat condescending attitude – even if the sound reading knowledge of the Urdu language that his readers require to share his thoughts sets them apart from the great uneducated and illiterate majority of that time and may at times have made them feel invited to share the author's outlook themselves. Abdussalam Isapuri, author of *Jīban carit*, to a somewhat lesser extent shares a similar attitude, and the same is true of Delawar Hosain who, though not a formally trained *ʿālim*, possesses the authority of a practising *pīr*. The hagiographers of Ziaul Haq, by contrast, are Western-educated disciples with an urban background. Though they may be well read in Islamic topics and occasionally digress into longish expositions of Islam in general, their hagiographies do not make them appear as the notables their preceding colleagues were, but rather as members of a larger group of co-disciples (*pīr bhāi*); their didacticism, wherever noticeable, is less obvious and somewhat attenuated. This is equally true of Lutfunnesa Hosaini's work, though in her case it seems to be more a very humble devotee's attitude than the lack of traditional scholarly authority that prevents such didacticism.

These more recent authors are perceivably under the impact of modern political and intellectual currents. The first instance of such new sensibilities is maybe the hagiography by Delawar Hosain. The highlighting, and maybe even the coinage, of the phrase *jātidharmanirbiśeṣe*, is easily decipherable in the context of East Pakistan and the early years of Bangladesh, as a reaction to the privileging of Muslim identity. The 'meta-religious' discourse which makes its appearance here seems to be linked to the historical developments on the subcontinent in the twentieth century, namely the Two-Nation Theory, the Pakistan movement and the experience of partition. In this context, I argue, notions of interreligious harmony and the ultimate unity of faiths act as a counter-ideology and do not take long to become the dominant pattern of self-representation. This counter-ideology, besides all the inherent merits it may have *per se*, is advantageous on two accounts: first, it is easily tailored to rather traditional, pre-reformist forms of religion as practised in Maijbhandar and has some amount of a matter-of-fact, descriptive value; secondly, its dictum of general accessibility can easily be harmonised with democratic principles, and thus conveys to Maijbhandar a novel type of political correctness especially in the context of liberated democratic

Bangladesh. Such parallels are hardly made explicit in Delawar Hosain's writings, but they have been consciously projected in the last decades.

Sikdar in his *Jiỳāul Hak* takes the universalisation of Maijbhandar one step further in aligning the arrival of the Maijbhandari saints in one series of events with the French Revolution (*JH*: 17 f.): thereby, Maijbhandar is given importance in a world history that conspicuously, and in accordance with the meta-religious discourse, transcends Islamic history. These developments, for certain, are not peculiar to the hagiographical tradition but span Maijbhandari writings in general; and we have noticed the same shifts at work in our examination of theological writings.

Despite the changes in language and style, the decrease in some hagiographical stereotypes, the different status of the more recent authors as well as the new contextualisations of the saintly lives, we can conclude that the basic tripartite structure of Maijbhandari hagiography remains unaltered and stable.[150] They enter their topic through the 'great' door of Islam by their invocation of Allah and the Prophet and prepare the ground for their narration by explaining the relationship between prophethood and saintship. Only then follow the chronological account of the localised events that constitute the life of the respective saint, and the separate miracle section that eventually concludes the accounts.

150 This is to some extent true even of Selim Jahangir's *Gāusul'ājam Māij'bhāṇḍārī* (2007), labelled an 'academic' life narration above. A detailed discussion of this book, fascinating though it would be for the interlacing agendas of ethnography, folklore research and saint veneration informing its author, is beyond the scope of this chapter and left for separate treatment in the future.

5 Maijbhandari songs

In a broader, cultural sense, Maijbhandari songs (*māij'bhāṇḍārī gān* or *gīti*) are the centrepiece of the Maijbhandari tradition. For many years, these songs, rather than scholarly treatises and expositions, have popularised Maijbhandar as a major spiritual centre in Chittagong and beyond. Their circulation and appeal is not limited to any particular section of the populace, but spans over the urban and rural, upper and lower, educated and uneducated ranges of East Bengali society.

The sheer number of Maijbhandari songs is impressive. At present, at a conservative estimate, at least 4,000 songs have been printed,[1] and another 1,000 have been put on cassette, CD and VCD. This figure does not even include the *oeuvres* of some well-known authors,[2] and much less those of lesser-known ones of past generations.[3] It further does not take into account unpublished material, which in some cases appears to be extensive.[4] Moreover, the fast erosion of oral traditions in Chittagong also suggests that a huge number of older Maijbhandari songs have missed the step towards scripturalisation and/or recording and have thus sunk into oblivion. While it is certainly impossible to even come close to determining the number of songs ever written, we can quite safely estimate that it runs into five digits – a figure

1 Since the beginning of the twentieth century, Maijbhandari songs have appeared in small, cheap booklets with an average of around 50 pages. Publication is undertaken either by the authors or their families themselves (as in the case of e.g. Abdul Gafur Hali and Ramesh Shil) or by the Maijbhandari *manzil*s or other institutions of the movement. The latter have published both compilations of songs by different authors (as, e.g., the volume *Ratnabhāṇḍār* [*RS*] published by Ahmadiya Manzil) as well as proper monographs (e.g. Abdul Jabbar Mimnagari's *Pañcaratnagītikā* [*PR*] and Farid Hosain's *Bhāṇḍār* series; these works have been dedicated, and their rights transferred, to Rahmaniya and Ahmadiya Manzil respectively).

2 e.g., the songs of Manomohan Datta, a famous disciple of Maijbhandar in the early twentieth century, have been published by his ashram in Brahmanbaria, but are today practically unavailable.

3 Selim Jāhāṅgīr (1999: 189) gives a list of 85 authors of Maijbhandari songs. Of these, I would guess, only about half are available on the market. In a sequel to this monograph, Jāhāṅgīr (2007: 358–65) supplies an extensive list of song books and counts 4,488 printed songs (p. 357).

4 The author and singer Abdul Gaphur Hali, for instance, has, according to my calculation, published a mere 142 songs out of reportedly more than 1,000, most of which remain in manuscript form.

which is, by the way, increasing day by day through a booming contemporary production.[5]

Especially the new media of the cassette and the compact disc have in recent years contributed to the growing fame of Maijbhandar in many parts of Bangladesh. On the contemporary music market in Chittagong, Maijbhandari songs are the most important segment of a genre called *mār'phati gān*, spiritual songs, and they sell better than *Lālan gīti*, the Baul songs of Lalan Faqir, and *Hāsan Rājār gān*, the mystical songs of Hasan Raja. Numerous offsprings of Maijbhandari songs have appeared in recent years that are identical with regard to their musical properties but praise other, mostly local saints in Chittagong such as Muhsin Auliya (d. 1397), Amanat Shah, Gurudas Faqir (1816–1898), etc.[6] Even Buddhist themes have been set to music by a Buddhist singer of Maijbhandari songs in exactly the same fashion.[7] Commercialisation naturally has become a determining factor in the recent development of this tradition. Radio stations and private music companies in Chittagong have Maijbhandari songs as a fixed item in their programmes, and a group of professional and semi-professional singers and songwriters has evolved around this infrastructure. Best-selling recordings such as Abdul Mannan's *Nurer chabi* are said to have crossed the line of 100,000 copies. This of course has repercussions on the performative conventions.

5.1 Origins and basic properties

The origins of the tradition cannot be traced with precision. The first printed volume of Maijbhandari songs seems to be Aliullah Rajapuri's *Prem'nur*, 'the light of love', a compilation of 117 songs of this author from Tripura that was published

5 The figures given here are low compared to estimates by people connected with Maijbhandar. Shafiul Ghani Chowdhury, for example, holds that about 5,000 songs have been published, while the total number of songs produced in more than a century exceeds 100,000, and the number of songwriters 1,000 (Saphiul Gaṇi Caudhurī 2000: 8).

6 In particular, the cases of Muhsin Auliya and Gurudas Faqir are interesting. The tomb of Muhsin Auliya in Anwara, the district bordering on Chittagong City south of the river Karnaphuli, is maintained by an old family of *ḫādims*. A member of this family informed me that music sessions had no tradition at the tomb and were not wanted there either; whenever pilgrims wanted to play music, for example at *'urs* celebrations, they had to stay outside the gate to the *dargāh* (Interview 23 February, 1999). The songwriter Abdul Gafur Hali claims to have initiated the tradition of writing songs for Muhsin Auliya, and today quite a few recordings of songs by different authors are available. This example impressively shows that this devotional song culture can be quite independent of the respective religious establishment. Gurudas Faqir, a Hindu *sādhu* and contemporary of Ahmadullah, has equally become the subject of devotional songs that in both musical execution and lyrics exactly resemble the Maijbhandari tradition (cf. the published collection of 15 songs called *Añjali* [Svapan Kumār Dāś and Bāsudeb Khāstagīr 2001]). I heard some of these songs at Gurudas's Ashram, the Suẏābil Siddhāśram Maṭh, at the village Suyabil (western neighbourhood of Maijbhandar). The author, Svapan Kumar Das, introduced himself as a music manager from Chittagong who works for the Bangladeshi radio and TV.

7 Shakyamitra Barua has recorded a series of four cassettes on Lord Buddha's life called *Buddher mahāparinirbāṇ* (Amin Stores, Chittagong, n.d.; Singers: Shakyamitra Barua, Sanchita Barua, Phalguni Barua).

in 1913.[8] This book was followed by Abdul Ghani's long treatise *Ā'īna-i Bārī*, appearing in 1914–15, which contains a large number of Urdu ghazals dedicated to Ġawṯ al-A'ẓam Ahmadullah. These written sources, however, can be taken to testify to an oral tradition going back well into the nineteenth century, especially if one takes into consideration their already established conventionality in style and imagery. And, as a matter of fact, the first *fatwa* from Maijbhandar defending the practice of musical performance first appeared as early as 1906/7, and it mentions explicitly that Ġawṯ al-A'ẓam Ahmadullah used to listen to music; though it remains silent about the sort of music that was then heard at the *dargāh*.[9] In an interview with Selim Jahangir, the singer Tunu Qawwal mentions that his father was in contact with Ahmadullah for a period of 26 years and used to sing Persian ghazals for him (Jāhāṅgīr 1999: 200). The hagiographies also tell us that both Ahmadullah and Gholam Rahman took part in and were appreciative of audition (*samā'*) sessions,[10] and since it was common to present new compositions in the presence of the saints themselves,[11] it is likely that Maijbhandari songs originated at the *darbār* itself. Songs composed during the lifetime of Ahmadullah include those by Aliullah, Abdul Ghani, Maulana Abdul Hadi and others. The latter became a *murīd* to Gholam Rahman later on, as were Bajlul Karim Mandakini and especially the most eminent writer of Maijbhandari songs, Ramesh Shil. The first two Islamic scholars and the last a Hindu *kabiẏāl*,[12] all these personalities from the vicinity of the *darbār* were drawn to Maijbhandar by the spiritual fame of the resident saints.

Like the hagiographies, the songs, too, betray the transition from Urdu to Bengali. The early, 'classic' authors invariably have some of their songs composed in Urdu or even Persian, and it is likely that the etiquette at the *darbār* required the use of Urdu. Even Ramesh Shil, a Bengali-language contest poet, felt the urge to write a few of his songs in Urdu. As in other areas of social life, this came to a halt after independence, and Urdu has today little importance in the Maijbhandari song tradition with the exception of certain liturgical fomulae appearing sporadically in the song texts.[13]

8 This author appears to be largely forgotten at Maijbhandar today. Selim Jāhāṅgīr (1999: 189) does mention his name in his list of 85 authors, but, the list being arranged at least roughly in chronological order, it comes far too late, even after Ramesh Shil. The fact is that Aliullah's book appeared ten years before Ramesh first came into contact with Maijbhandar in 1923. It is quite possible that the copy of *Prem'nur* in the British Library, London, is the last extant one.

9 This *fatwa* is Syed Aminul Haq Farhadabadi's *Tuḥfat* (1906/7, 3rd ed. 1997); the complete title (see Abbreviations or Bibliography) translates as 'The precious gift of the good about the refutation of the evilness of the evil: a *fatwa* on *samā'* or songs and music'. The mention of Ahmadullah's fondness for music is in Vol.1, p. 102. For a further discussion, cf. below on p. 183 of this chapter.

10 Cf. *ĀB*: 183, *JC*: 87 f.

11 As in the case of Maulana Hadi. Delawar Hosain in his *Belāẏate mot'lākā* mentions that one of his songs (*RB* No. 20) was even changed upon Ahmadullah's request (p. 16). In an interview (Feb. 1999), I was told that my aged interviewee had witnessed the following scene when he visited the *darbār* as a young boy (in the 1930s): old Maulana Hadi had dressed up in a sari and presented a love song to Gholam Rahman. My interviewee, himself a very religiously minded Sufi, recalled this sight as extremely funny. Cf. Sections 5.7.10 and 6.3 for such 'feminisations' of devotees.

12 A *kabiẏāl* is a contest singer who has to defeat his opponent by improvised rhymes to a given theme. *Kabigān*, contest singing, is a traditional Bengali genre that was popular in Calcutta and other parts of Bengal in the eighteenth and nineteenth centuries.

13 For an exception, see Gholam Muhammad Khan Siraji's Urdu ghazal, written as late as 1976, in Golām Muhāmmad Khān Sirājī 1993: No. 8.

It is important to note at the outset that Maijbhandari songs are not to be confounded with North Indian and Pakistani *Qawwālī*. Both in their musical foundations and textual orientation these traditions differ considerably, and their ritualistic and social settings are not identical either. Maijbhandari songs do not have the typical alternating singing between a soloist and an echoing group. They are basically verse songs with a refrain, and are mostly performed by solo singers with accompaniment. While it is hard to purchase *Qawwālī* texts,[14] the Maijbhandari tradition clearly has become a print phenomenon. As to its musical properties, *Qawwālī* has more explicit leanings towards North Indian classical *rāga* music, whereas Maijbhandari songs are decidedly a part of Bengali folk traditions. Moreover, regulations regarding the times and manners of performance as well as etiquette rules during singing sessions are of rather marginal importance in Maijbhandar, in contrast to, for instance, the major Indian Chishti *dargāhs* where certain refined reglementations continue to govern *Qawwālī* performances despite the long-standing commercialisation of *Qawwālī* outside those circles.[15]

In their structure, Maijbhandari songs bear more similarities with the famous Baul song tradition. Although the status of those songs, being the dominant and often the only public mode of transmission of ideas among the Bauls, and the social context in which they are performed are quite distinct, contents, imagery and poetic structure are closely related. The main differences consist in the institutional establishments such as *dargāh* and *dā'ira* sessions in the case of Maijbhandari songs, which are mostly absent for Bauls,[16] and in a semantic affiliation to the Maijbhandari saints to which the Baul tradition(s) afford(s) no direct parallel.

5.2 Performance situations

What were the original performance situations of Maijbhandari songs? Following the direct presentation of songs at the *darbār*, the *'urs* and (later) *khušrūz,* celebrations, as well as the usual gatherings on Fridays, seem to have been the second and still very typical setting of musical performance. Even in the beginning of the twentieth century, these festivities appear to have drawn a large attendance from the local population as well as from neighbouring and farther-off districts. Maijbhandar, according to what is related in many of the songs themselves, was known for institutions like *ḥalqa-i samā'*, namely audition gatherings. Similar events probably took place quite early at the residences of non-local *murīds* and *dā'iras* in districts such as Tripura, Kumilla, Noakhali, etc. Gradually,

14 Cf. Burckhardt Qureshi (1993: 113), depicting *Qawwālī* as a predominantly oral tradition.

15 Cf. Regula Burckhardt Qureshi (1993: 119 f.) on the basis of material gathered at the shrine of Nizam al-Din Awliya of Delhi. In 2001 and 2002, I could witness *Qawwālī* sessions at the great Chishti *dargāhs* of Mu'in al-Din Chishti in Ajmer and Gisudaraz in Gulbarga which seemed to support such observations.

16 At the *dargāh* of Lalan Shah at Kushtia, however, similar institutional backing for the Baul tradition in Bangladesh has developed. The growing use of the harmonium for Baul songs also can be seen as an indication that in Kushtia at least, the Baul tradition has appropriated specific *dargāh* structures which originally were rather alien to it.

from about the middle of the twentieth century onwards, the music market, too, became a determining factor in the development of the Maijbhandari song tradition.

Thus, a number of historically and typologically distinct performance situations may be distinguished here in order to demonstrate the social setting of this tradition. According to my earlier contention, the oldest and most formal type probably was the presentation of songs during meetings at the *darbār* itself, in the presence of the *pīr* to whom – or to whose spiritual predecessor – the songs were dedicated. This type continues to this day, as many songwriters and singers are affiliated with one or the other *manzil* in Maijbhandar. Sometimes, prominent singers are explicitely hired to perform during audition sessions (*samā' mahfil*) presided over by the respective *pīr*. Such sessions require a certain type of etiquette. The *pīr*, *pīr*s or *pīrzāda*s are seated separately on *gaddī*s, seats adorned by carpets, cushions and the like, retaining their centrality with the singers by the side and the audience facing them. The songs are presented to them and only indirectly to the audience seated together on mats spread on the ground. The *pīr*s determine the duration of such sessions, and the audience is expected not to leave the session without the *pīr*'s permission. On the latter's part, emotional reaction to the music is restrained and remains limited to occasional appreciative exclamations and lightly ecstatic body movements to the rhythm of the music. It may happen that single members of the audience get up in order to approach the *pīr* and bow to him, and coins or notes may be donated to the performers during the sessions. In this type of performance, despite contrary accounts from the past of the movement,[17] the *pīr*'s presence prevents ecstatic dancing and other outwardly emotive behaviour, and safeguards a somewhat formal, sober and controlled atmosphere.[18] *Samā'* sessions of this kind are not necessarily convened by formal representatives of Maijbhandar such as *pīr*s and *pīrzāda*s, but may also be initiated by wealthy, religious-minded personalities or societies (as, e.g., the Allama Rumi Society of Chittagong).

Another kind of rather rare performance situation in connection with *ḏikr* has been described in Section 2.2.2.

The more frequent, informal variety of music sessions can be witnessed at the *dargāh* in Maijbhandar as well as at the various *dā'ira*s and *śākhā*s, branches, of the movement in different parts of the country. Characterised by gatherings of

17 Cf., e.g., the account of Gholam Rahman setting the whole village into frenetical dancing in Section 4.4.1 (*JC*: 88). Frequent reference in the songs to Gholam Rahman as the one who makes everybody dance is an indication that this saint favoured ecstatic emotional expression on his *murīd*s' part. The two sessions of this type I witnessed in 1999 and 2001, however, were formal in character, and this corresponds to observations of Chishti *dargāh*s in India.

18 This is in keeping with the etiquette of *samā'* sessions as propounded in medieval Sufi treatises that deal with the topic, e.g. Abu Nasr as-Sarraj's (d. 988) *Kitāb al-luma'* (Gramlich 1990): outer signs of ecstasy, such as dancing and screaming, should be subdued as far as possible, and such subduing is a sign of a 'superior listener' (101–03). Also Regula Burkhardt-Qureshi (1993: 122) on the role of the Shaikh, in contemporary South Asia, in preventing undesired effects on the listeners of this music. Cf. also below in Section 5.3.

Photo 8 Singing Maijbhandari songs at an *'urs* celebration in 1999, Maijbhandar.

crowds and much dancing, these are the events that have become closely associated with Maijbhandar in general perception.[19] During *'urs* celebrations, such sessions take place spontaneously all over the *dargāh* and in the surroundings. Musicians assemble circles of listeners around them and go on singing their repertoire of songs for hours without cessation especially during the night. The main singer usually accompanies himself (or herself) on the harmonium and is aided by a more or less ad hoc percussionist ensemble, while both men and women enter the circle dancing frenetically. Today, such sessions never go without electronic amplification, and contests between neighbouring musicians often result in a virtual cacophony, making descriptions such as the following in a song by Abdul Gaphur Hali sound quite plausible:

> Along with [screams of] *allāhu allāhu*, various kinds of music resound/The lovers loose their consciousness when hearing the words Ġawṯ al-A'ẓam/Sky and air join in the *ḏikr allāhu allāhu.*
>
> (*Tattvabidhi*, 36)

Similar, less crowded sessions of audition and dance are held in the various outposts of the Maijbhandari movement, normally on Thursday evenings. Peter

19 A proverb about Maijbhandar in Chittagongian dialect is *khāium gjā mārum phāl/gāuchul ājam māij'bhāṇḍār*, meaning: 'I shall smoke marihuana and jump [i.e. dance]/Ġawṯ al-A'ẓam [of] Maijbhandar'.

Bertocci (2006) very evocatively describes such gatherings in Comilla, and I quote him at some length here in order to convey an adequate impression:

> Abdur Rahman, the rickshaw puller, sits in the middle of the circle. A gaunt, graying man, with intense, flashing eyes, he cradles a *dotara*, the mandolin-like instrument that often accompanies performances of indigenous Bengali music. Next to him, a world-worn pushcart driver plucks his *ektara* . . . Others in the group, also nondescript urban laborers of rural vintage, provide percussion with little more than blocks of wood which, when struck, produce sharp resonating, rythmic clicks, or with palm-sized brass cymbals that, clashed together by cupped hands, sound muted, muffled clinks. This rhythmic ensemble, miraculously, does not drown out Abdur Rahman's melodic lyrics, however, as he belts out, in solo fashion, yet another in his seemingly inexhaustible repertoire of tunes, loud, clear, never missing a beat or note. . . . As his voice rises in intensity, moving from moderate to rapid tempo, others in the stuffy little room respond to the music with the chanting of the name of Allah, all in mesmerizing unison: '*Allah-hu, Allah-hu, Allah-hu* . . .' At the height of the music's intensity, some rise to sway and rock in an attempt to dance. A few teeter to a near-fall, to be caught by their fellows, themselves only slightly less enraptured, before hitting the floor.
> (p. 4 f.)

Such sessions apparently are not limited to religious institutions explicitly aligned to Maijbhandar, but may also be witnessed in places connected with other religious denominations. A case in point is a small Hindu ashram (*Bālak Sādhur āśram*) in Nandankanan, central Chittagong, where reportedly regular sessions with Maijbhandari songs used to take place until the 1990s, and occasionally even today.[20] Trance-like, ecstatic religious experience in such musical sessions, in fact, is what Maijbhandar represents for many of its adepts, and the informal, spontaneous character of this type of performance is often perceived as a prerequisite for such experiences.

Alongside these rather traditional situations, a number of new types of performance situations have developed in the course of the commercialisation of Maijbhandari songs. Among these are commercial concerts by professional singers. As it is not customary to pay royalties to authors and singers, even 'hit singers' like the above-mentioned Abdul Mannan are economically dependent on additional concerts.[21] And even those singers who are devoted disciples of Maijbhandar do not limit their repertoire exclusively to Maijbhandari songs. Consequently, Maijbhandari songs are presented among other types of basically entertaining music on privately sponsored social occasions (mainly weddings) and the like.

To these live performance situations remain to be added the multiple roles

20 Interview with inhabitants of the neighbourhood, March 2001.

21 Interviews with several singers and managers of the two main record companies in Chittagong (Binimay Cassette Bazar and Amin Stores) in 1999 and 2001.

played by ever-increasing recorded Maijbhandari music. Barring stores strictly following Islamic reformist principles in their trade policies, cassettes and compact discs with Maijbhandari songs are available practically anywhere in Chittagong. Travellers in pilgrimage buses at the time of festivities are tuned to the occasion by constant exposition to amplified Maijbhandari music. At places far from Maijbhandar, Maijbhandari songs can be heard on the road from open stores. Campaigns for the mobilisation of pilgrims also use cassette and CD recordings.[22] Furthermore, the media (radio and TV) initiate recordings of Maijbhandari songs, along with all other kinds of folk music, for their own broadcasting purposes. Even at the *dargāh* itself, at least three shops play music at most times of the day, the almost only exceptions being prayer times and other ritual functions.[23] As a consequence, the presence of recorded music today outweighs by far the cases of live performance. It seems, however, still inconceivable to dance to recorded Maijbhandari music, and rationalising this fact, it can be argued that live performance and technical reproduction of Maijbhandari music are clearly distinguished types of events that pertain to different domains of experience.

5.3 Debates on audition (*samāʿ*)

But is it at all legitimate for Sunni Muslims to sing and dance as part of their religious practice; is it sanctioned by Islamic injunctions to even listen to music? The legal status of music and dancing in Islamic law, as mentioned before, is a matter of controversy in all of Bengali Islam, and it is little wonder that Maijbhandar also has to take some part in this discussion in order to defend its musical tradition. Both the hagiographies and the Maijbhandari songs themselves repeatedly relate confrontations with orthodox *ʿulamāʾ* over the legitimacy of music and dancing in the past and the present. Most books from Maijbhandar, whether hagiographies, treatises or manuals, refer to *samāʿ*, and there are a few separate *fatwa*s and booklets by Islamic clergymen connected more or less closely with the movement that are published by the different *manzil*s and societies.

Samāʿ, as it were, is the Arabic term for 'audition' (used in the following as a technical term to denote this specific kind of listening to music) and the label under which these issues are discussed. There is a long-standing tradition of apologetics of audition in the earlier history of Sufism. Discussions of audition run through many of the great medieval expositions of Sufism, such as al-Sarraj's *Kitāb al-lumaʿ* (before 988), al-Qushayri's *Risāla* (before 1043), Hujwiri's *Kašf al-maḥǧūb* (*c.* 1050–70), Suhrawardi's *Awārif al-maʿārif* (before 1234), etc.[24] Historically, according to During (1996: 157 ff.), apologetics for audition are tightly connected with the development of the Sufi orders adopting audition as

22 I witnessed such a campaign in Chittagong City for the birthday celebration (*ḫuğrūz*) of Syed Shafiul Bashar in February 1999.

23 This, in fact, is a major difference to the more strictly organised Chishti shrines in India that I could visit, where only live performances by approved *qawwāl*s at fixed times seem to be allowed.

24 Cf. the translations edited by Richard Gramlich in the bibliography.

part of their practice, and start to be written in Bagdad in the ninth century. *Samāʿ*, the audition of spiritual music, is discussed in opposition to *ġināʾ*, profane music. The initially defensive tone of these treatises becomes more self-conscious towards the fourteenth century, after which audition, in that tradition which we might term the 'Sufi mainstream', apparently ceases to be a controversial issue (During 1996: 159).[25] A representative position is that of Hujwiri who stresses the general legitimacy of *samāʿ* but advocates that it should not be made a routine and enjoins utmost care so as to prevent pernicious effects of its misuse.[26]

In Bengal, there appear to have been no noteworthy discussions on audition before the nineteenth century; and it seems that the Farāʾiżī movement first brought up the issue. In the contemporary tensions between Sufi and reformist Islamic strands in Bengal, audition, along with shrine and *pīr* veneration, prostration, etc., continues to be one of the principal matters of dispute.

The medieval tracts on audition are to a considerable extent compilations of authoritative passages from the *Qurʾān*[27] and *Ḥadīṯ*. The same is true of the Maijbhandari treatises I now want to discuss briefly.[28] The majority of these texts limit

25 Cf., however, Knysh (2000: 324), who puts the end of virulent discussions on *samāʿ* in the sixteenth century. This delimitation nevertheless does not seem to be irreconcilable with During's position since the last relevant authors on the topic that he mentions all belong to the fourteenth century.

26 Cf. the following passages: 'The rules of audition prescribe that it should not be practised until it comes (of its own accord), and that you must not make a habit of it, but practise it seldom, in order that you may not cease to hold it in reverence. It is necessary that a spiritual director should be present during the performance, and that the place should be cleared of common people, and that the singer should be a respectable person, and that the heart should be emptied of worldly thoughts, and that the disposition should not be inclined to amusement, and that every artificial effort (*takalluf*) should be put aside. You must not exceed the proper bounds until audition manifests its power, and when it has become powerful you must not repel it but must follow it as it requires: if it agitates, you must be agitated, and if it calms, you must be calm; and you must be able to distinguish a strong natural impulse from the ardour of ecstasy (*wajd*). [. . .]' (Nicholson 1911: 418 f.). On the other hand, 'These concerts are extremely dangerous and corrupting, because women on the roofs or elsewhere look at the dervishes who are engaged in audition; and in consequence of this the auditors have great obstacles to encounter. Or it may happen that a young reprobate is one of the party, since some ignorant Ṣūfīs have made a religion (*madhhab*) of all this and have flung truth to the winds. I ask pardon of God for my sins of this kind in the past, and I implore His help, that He may preserve me both outwardly and inwardly from contamination, and I enjoin the readers of this book to hold it in due regard and to pray that the author may believe to the end and be vouchsafed the vision of God (in Paradise)' (Nicholson 1911: 420). Cf. also During (1996: 162) who refers to this second passage.

27 In the *Qurʾān* itself, *samāʿ* is not mentioned; *āyāt* discussed in connection with it are, e.g., 30.15 and 31.5.

28 Most of the major Maijbhandari texts, such as Abdul Ghani Kanchanpuri's *Āʾīna-i Bārī* (*ĀB*) and Delawar Hosain's *Belāẏate motʹlākā* (*BM*) have sections on *samāʿ*. Among the independent texts on this topic that are at present available in Chittagong are the following: Syed Aminul Haq Farhadabadi's above-mentioned *Tuḥfat* (1906/7) (in Arabic and Persian with a Bengali rendering in *paẏār* metre); Māolānā Ābu Tāher Solʹtān Āhʹmad (1993): *Phatoẏāẏe rahmāniẏā: chāmā bā gān-bādya jāẏej haïbār dalil* ('The Rahmaniya *fatwa*: documents on the legitimacy of *samāʿ* or singing and playing music'); 1st edn 1976 (compilation of authoritative quotations); Śāhājādā Maulānā Chaiẏad Ākhʹtār Kāmāl Śāhʹ (1990): *Āl-bhāṇḍārī* (manual on Sufism and the Maijbhandari *ṭarīqa* with a chapter on *samāʿ*);

themselves to listing quotations mostly from Prophetic traditions in favour of audition. A much-quoted example is a *Ḥadīṯ* received from the Prophet's wife Aʾisha, relating how the Prophet allowed her to watch a dance, and agreed to listen to a musical performance on a festive day. To such arguments, statements from famous Sufis and *ʿulamāʾ* are added as a secondary layer of authoritative tradition. Original approaches to the question are rather rare, and most of these works are hardly more than short compilations of the medieval tradition of *samāʿ* apologetics mentioned above. Interesting, however, are the few places where the writers take the liberty of going beyond legalistic argumentation and using their own words to define the role of music. The following extract from Syed Akhtar Kamal Shah's pamphlet *Āl-bhāṇḍārī* is a good example:

> The heaps of stars of the blue sky, the stars and planets, the garland of clouds – all appear, by some infinite music, to be engaged in remembering Allah. [p. 39] [. . .] Today, musical melodies manifest themselves anytime at every home, on streets and *ghāṭ*s, shops and markets, lanes and by-lanes, radios and transistors. Melody and music have today transcended the barriers of time and space, and are swinging in front of every door to the human mind. The expedition of music is conquering all and everything in the whole world. [Music] does not respect any hindrance. Today it transgresses geographical remoteness, inaccessible mountains, harbours and seas and brings stimulation to the strings of the hearts of the thirsty ones. In our religious experience, too, the effect of music has come upon us ever since original time, and the practice of music has a great and important function in every religious department. Especially if we think about the similarity between the beginnings and ends of every verse of the Holy *Qurʾān*, we clearly understand that it, too, is filled with divine melody and music.[29]

These writings do not appear to be part of any lively controversy; opponent's views are hardly ever alluded to and thus not directly refuted either. Their defence, it appears, is not directed towards the hostile outside, but rather to the inside. The adherents to Maijbhandar are to be strengthened in their pro-audition convictions and furnished with arguments in case of disputes.

Outstanding among these, however, is the *Tuḥfat·*, the longish *fatwa* written in 1906/7 by Syed Aminul Haq Farhadabadi (1866–1944). This *ḫalīfa* of Ġawṯ al-Aʿẓam Ahmadullah from Farhadabad in the vicinity of Maijbhandar, himself venerated as a saint at his small *mazār* in his native village, was a locally

Māolānā Āk'bar Ālī **R**ej'bhī (1991): *Ādillātuch' chemā* (relatively comprehensive treatise on *samāʿ* with author's commentary); Muph'tī Phar'hād **P**hārukī (n.d.): *Śarīẏater dr̥ṣṭite 'chāmā' o bādyasaha murśedī gān* (*Samāʿ* and *murśedī* songs [accompanied] with music playing in the view of the *šarīʿa*'; comprehensive compilation); Saiẏad Āb'duch· Chālām **Ī**chāpurī (1979): *Pūṇyātmā chuphīgaṇer chemā* ('*Samāʿ* of Sufis of meritorious souls') and Saiẏad Āb'duch· Chālām **Ī**chāpurī (1978): *Uchul-e-tbarikat o āch rār-e-chemā* ('The methods of the *ṭarīqa* and the secrets of *samāʿ*') (both compilations with author's commentaries). Cf. p.350 ff. in the bibliography, primary literature.

well-known Islamic scholar, who left a number of treatises on a variety of topics.[30] The *fatwa* is written in Arabic and contains long passages in Persian and Urdu, and it moreover has a rendering by the author himself in versified Bengali. Of the two volumes, the first is entirely devoted to the defence of *samāʿ*, while the second treats other issues such as prostration, *pīr* veneration, the status of *ṭarīqa* in relation to *šarīʿa*, etc. The volume on *samāʿ* begins with a kind of introduction (*Tuḥfat*: 12–26) in which Aminul Haq states his position: music helps incite the heart of the *ʿāšiq*s, and listening to it can be a form of worship (*ibāda*) to which God (Bg. *prabhu nirañjan*) responds. Those opposing this practice are devoid of *ʿišq*, love: '[With him] who acquires knowledge (Bg. *ilam*, Ar. <*ʿilm*>) without possessing love, it is just as if he put a book on the back of an ass'.[31]

Aminul Haq then proceeds to prove his point in four chapters. The first of these (pp. 27–35) assembles quotations from the *Qurʾān* and *Ḥadīṯ*. The second (pp. 36–105) examines the views on *samāʿ* of later religious authorities. The works quoted here include among many others Ghazzali's *Iḥyā ʿulūm al-dīn* (Gramlich 1984), Abdul Haq Dihlawi's *Madāriz al-nubuwwa*, Imām Abu Hanifa's *Yaḏāḥ*, Abdul Ghani Nablusi Hanafi's *Yaḏāḥ al-dalālāt*, and also quotations from Ibn ʿArabi; and Abdul Haq Farhadabadi comes to the conclusion that according to the Hanafi school of law, *samāʿ* must be deemed legal (*mubāḥ*) (p. 98 f.). At the end of this chapter, the fact that audition sessions were held at Ġawṯ al-Aʿẓam Ahmadullah's *darbār* is enlisted as a final piece of evidence for the lawfulness of music. The Persian text closes with the words that 'this proof (*dalīl*) is sufficient for the people of faith' (p. 102). The third chapter (pp. 106–22) is a refutation of the arguments put forward by the opponents of audition. It uses exclusively Ghazzali's *Iḥyā ʿulūm al-dīn* as its source. The last part quotes further authorities on the lawfulness of the side-effects of audition, such as 'dancing in trance, quivering etc.' (p. 122), among them Qazi Sanaullah Panipati's *Risāla-i samāʿ*, Sirhindi's *Maktubāt*, Kashani's *Miṣbāḥ al-Hidāya*,[32] Abdul Hai Lakhnawi's *Mağmuʿa-i fatāwa*, the *Fatāwa ʿĀlamgīrī*[33] and many others. The volume is concluded by a list of 32 Bengali *ʿulamāʾ* validating Abdul Haq Farhadabadi's *fatwa* (p. 169).

Abdul Ghani Kanchanpuri's *Āʾīna-i Bārī*, too, has a chapter on the legitimacy of *samāʿ* (ĀB 453–89). Abdul Ghani resorts to the original treaty between God and man (*Qurʾān* 7.172[171]): the words *alastu bi-rabbikum*, 'Am I your Lord?', resound continuously in the world ever since they were uttered (p. 457). They are covered by other sounds, but when during a *samāʿ* session they resound in the

29 Śāhājādā Maulānā Chaiẏad Ākh'tār Kāmāl Śāh' (1990): *Āl-bhāṇḍārī*; Caṭṭagrām, Author's publ.

30 For example, a refutation of Wahhabi doctrines, a defence of explanations in the mother tongue during the Friday prayers, treatises on marital relations and prostration (*sağda*), etc,. *Tuḥfat*: 9 (*saṃkṣipta jībanī*).

31 *ilam(a) paṛiẏā iś'k(a) nā rākhe ye jan(a)/gardhabher(a)* [*sic*] *pṣṭe* [sic] *yena kitāb(a) rākhan(a)* // *Tuḥfat*: I, 16.

32 'The Lamp of Guidance' by ʿIzz al-Dīn Maḥmūd b. ʿAlī-i Kašānī (d. 1334–35) (cf. *EI 2*: IX, 780b).

hearts of the *'āšiq*s or devotees, they have their effect. *Samā'* is thus seen as helpful in increasing the longing for union with the divine (p. 458 f.).[34]

This short exposition of the apologetics for audition must suffice here. The Maijbhandari tracts on audition are concerned with the legal status of music and dance within Islam. They do not discuss any particular song tradition, but the legitimacy of music in general. Thus, the spiritual value or the mode of religious expression of the Maijbhandari song tradition is of no concern. Their intention is merely to furnish the *placet* of orthodox Islam; they serve the purpose of accommodating spiritual music in an Islamic framework. We may summarise this much here as we move on towards some remarks on the musical performance of Maijbhandari songs.

5.4 Musical performance

Maijbhandari songs are today usually performed with at least a harmonium and percussion, the solo singer accompaning himself on the former.[35] While group chanting is common in gatherings during festivals, it is hardly ever heard during the more formal audition sessings or, for that matter, on recordings. The instrumentation with harmonium and percussion seems to date back at least to the 1920s.[36] According to Selim Jahangir (1999), the instrumentation used during the lifetime of Ahmadullah, that is, until 1906, consisted of a *khañjari* and a *juri*.[37] Harmonium and *ḍholak*, a double-covered middle-sized drum, were added during Gholam Rahman's 'reign' until 1936. Thereafter, up to the present, a number of other instruments have been added and used for Maijbhandari songs, such as *dotārā* (a plucked double-string instrument), tabla, conga, *tumba* (a stringed instrument made from a gourd), flute and mandolin, as well as keyboard, acoustic guitar, rhythm box, etc. (Selim Jāhāṅgīr 1999: 185). Among the sounds produced by the synthesiser, that of the violin appears to be a popular choice.[38]

Obviously, some of these changes are directly connected with developments in the musical market, and since in terms of both infrastructure and personnel the commercial production of Maijbhandari songs is strongly interlaced with other musical genres in Chittagong, the transition does not meet many obstacles. On some current cassette and CD versions, the opportunities offered by modern studio recording, such as echo effects, are being explored, and the borderline with modern Bangladeshi pop music is being challenged. Notions of 'pure' musical

33 A collection of Hanafi legalistic excerpts which was compiled under Aurangzeb.

34 Cf. Schimmel (1995: 47) and esp. p. 244 on the relationship between the words of the original treaty and the practice of *ḏikr*.

35 Cf. also Ohīdul Ālam (1985: 18).

36 Cf. Ramesh Shil's song 14, *Nure duniẏā*, where the harmonium is explicitly mentioned.

37 Unfortunately I could not find any details regarding these instruments.

38 Cf., e.g., Abul Sarkar's *Daẏāl bābā keb'lā kābā*. MC, Sungreen, Dhaka, n.d.; and Ferdous Hali's *Āllāh·r ali mālek'śāh*, MC, Music Tone, Chittagong, n.d. The latter is not dedicated to any Maijbhandari saint, but to Abdul Malik Muhyuddin, a *pīr* from Kutubdia, but can be seen as an offspring of the Maijbhandari tradition, especially since the singer is the daughter of the contemporary songwriter Abdul Gafur Hali, and the latter has composed most of the songs and supervised the recording of the cassette (cf. back cover of the MC).

practice are not very dominant, in sharp contrast to the controversies raging for decades around the proper instrumentation of Tagore songs (*Rabīndra-saṅgīt*) in West Bengal;[39] but nevertheless, a notion of 'original Maijbhandari songs' (*ādi māij'bhāṇḍārī gān*) has evolved in certain circles in order to separate traditional performance from what are perceived as commercialised innovations.[40]

With regard to musical structure, it is hard to determine what the changes during the last hundred years in this musical tradition may have been. It is highly debatable, in the first place, whether is it possible to speak of Maijbhandari songs as a *musical* tradition in its own right at all. Apparently, various traditions of folk music have had their influence on Maijbhandari songs (such as *kīrtan*, *bhāṭiẏālī*, etc.). Wahidul Alam certainly exaggerates in claiming that Maijbhandari songs are 'almost alike with regard to their metre', and that 'variety in melodies is seldom noticed';[41] but it is true that traditionally, Maijbhandari songs are set to a limited number of tunes. Certain *tāla*s, metres, and *ṭhāṭ*s, scales, are preferred. The most typical metre is *khem'ṭā tāl*, a simple dancing rhythm, followed by *tāla*s like *kaharvā* and *jhumur tāl*. The *ṭhāṭ*s most frequently used in Maijbhandari songs seem to be *khamāj* and *kāfī ṭhāṭ*, both very common in Bengali folk music in general. Also *bhairavī ṭhāṭ* (quite common, for example, in *bāul* songs)[42] is used. On close listening, however, alternations between *ṭhāṭ*s are found to be quite a common occurrence, and especially an alternation between *khamāj* and *kāfī ṭhāṭ* can frequently be noticed.[43] It might be possible to argue with Sukumar Ray (1988: 110) that, just as in the case of *bhāṭiẏālī*, Maijbhandari songs have certain distinctive tune patterns that do not exactly correspond to the structure of *rāga*s.[44]

A song is not necessarily transmitted through one single channel, and as there are textual variants of some songs, the same is true for the melody. An example in point is a song by Ramesh Shil (*Ār kata kā̃dābi*, *Satyadarpaṇ* No. 5) which I have heard

39 Tagore songs (*Rabīndra saṃgīt*) are sung with the accompaniment of a harmonium and light tabla percussion. The legitimacy of the latter was for a while disputed; however, it has apparently asserted itself.

40 The same distinction is made with regard to the content of the songs. The allegation is that many contemporary authors exploit the classics for their own profit and mostly lack the spiritual sentiment necessary for composing a 'true' Maijbhandari song. I encountered the same patterns of argumentation during a visit to the tomb of the famous Baul saint Lalan Faqir in Kushtia, where a group of devotees, apparently moved at the sight of a visitor who had come such a long way, consented to sing *ādi bāul gān*, original Baul songs, for me – in apparent contrast to the music that was usually performed at the tomb. Interestingly, the harmonium, which in other sessions at that tomb appears to have become quite commonplace, was banned from that performance.

41 Ohīdul Ālam (1985: 18).

42 It appears, in fact, that it is this *ṭhāṭ* which is sometimes referred to in the booklets of Maijbhandari songs as *bāul sur*. Cf. e.g. Bajlul Karim's *Premer hem* (*PH*).

43 e.g. the song *Daẏāl bābā keb'lā kābā* on Abul Sarkar's *Daẏāl bābā keb'lā kābā*. MC, n.d., Sungreen, Dhaka, for a Maijbhandari song with such an alternation, and *Khā̃cār bhitar acin pākhi* (a Baul song by Lalan Faqir) on Farida Parvin's cassette of the same name, MC, n.d., Jan-e-Alam, n.p. For a Western listener, this alternation resembles that of major to minor in a given key.

44 Being utterly inexperienced in Indian musical theory, I do not wish to venture any necessarily speculative conclusions regarding such matters.

sung in at least three different ways.[45] In the case of Ramesh Shil's songs, the *tāla*s to be employed are noted in the author's manuscripts and reprinted both in the booklets published by his son and the Bangla Academy edition; but most of the written versions of Maijbhandari songs lack such indications regarding both *tāla*s and *rāga*s/*ṭhāṭ*s. Songs often start with a short *ālāpa* by the singer-cum-harmonium player, in a sort of dialogic interplay between voice and instrument. The songs usually contain a refrain and three to five verses, and start on the refrain; the *ālāpa* may use the first line of the refrain or (rarely) add a kind of prologue.[46] When the voice takes on the song's regular tempo, the percussion sets in.

In contemporary recording sessions, it appears to be customary, in the case of newly written songs, to set the texts to music the very day that the songwriter, singer and composer meet in the studio. Thus, alongside popular tunes received from oral tradition, studio-generated ones are gaining in importance. This change in song production, it seems, is bound to alter the musical properties of the Maijbhandari song tradition, for it also implies that the musical arrangement more and more passes into the hands of studio professionals. But as studio recording goes hardly further back than to the 1970s, it seems too early, or would anyhow require a much more thorough investigation, to comment upon these developments.

Maijbhandari songs thus undeniably have a number of specific musical characteristics, but all of these are, as it were, shared by other Bengali traditions of folk music, and it would be a difficult task to define Maijbhandari songs on musical grounds alone. Their main unifying factor remains a textual one: their semantic affiliation with the *dargāh* and the saints in Maijbhandar.

5.5 Classifications of Maijbhandari songs

It has been attempted to classify Maijbhandari songs into certain sub-genres. A number of such classifications are in fact envisaged by the exponents of the tradition themselves. We have already hinted at the division between *ādi* and *ādhunik*, 'original' and 'modern' Maijbhandari songs, referring primarily to their musical execution. These categories are, however, anything but fixed, and furthermore, the distinction appears to be quite recent and usually rather polemic. It is used by critical observers of contemporary developments, and there is certainly no

45 One is Ahmad Nur Ameri: *Māij bhāṇḍārī gān – 1*, MC, Binimoy Stores, Chittagong, n.d., where *rāga bhairava* is used. Another recording on Moslem Ali Jani's *Māij bhāṇḍāre prem bāgāne*, MC, Binimoy Stores, Chittagong, n.d., uses *kāfī* and has also melodic variations. In a live performance in 1999 at a *samā' maḥfil* in Maijbhandar, the melody was set in a mixture of *bhairava* and *kāfī*.

46 This is the case in the already-quoted version of *Ār kata kā̃dābi* by Ahmad Nur Ameri, who inserts a few words before the song proper that are lacking in the other versions: 'Brother, it was in the middle of the month of *phālgun*, the day of the *ḫuśruz śarīf* of my *Bābā* Shafi [Shafiul Bashar]; by the side of the *āstāna* [Shafiul Bashar's dwelling place], a miserable faqir is saying – hear what he is saying'. These words obviously contextualise the *bhakti* song to follow, and re-direct it to Shafiul Bashar – a *pīr* who was still a small boy at the time Ramesh Shil frequented the *dargāh* – whereas it was probably meant for the latter's father Gholam Rahman. I cannot say how frequent such 'prefixing' and redirecting of songs is, but it seems that the latter is more common than the former.

self-conscious trend of writing 'modern Maijbhandari songs'. Another basic distinction is that between ghazals (*ġazal*) and *gān*, 'songs' proper. The former usually (but not necessarily)[47] denotes songs written in Urdu in the ghazal genre, and the latter Bengali songs. Today, however, it is quite a theoretical speculation whether Maijbhandari ghazals can be regarded as a sub-branch of *Māij'bhāṇḍārī gān*, because the hundreds of Maijbhandari ghazals in the Urdu language are hardly sung anymore and exist mostly only in written form, and Maijbhandari songs are generally taken to be in the Bengali language.

The other existing modes of classifying Maijbhandari songs do not rely on criteria of musical performance or linguistic media, but refer to the topics treated in the songs as texts. They are sometimes introduced by the authors or compilers in the form of headings over the texts. Syed Abdul Malek Shah divides his songs into 'spiritual' (*ādhyātmik*) and 'lamenting' (Bg. *phariẏādī*, from P./U. <*fariyād*>) songs. 'Spiritual' songs expose some doctrine, describe certain practices or allude to traditional religious examples and tend to be instructive in character; 'lamenting' songs, by contrast, focus on the plight of the disciple who cannot get hold of his master (cf. Chaiẏad Āb'dul Mālek Śāh 1989 and 1989a). Another twofold distinction that was repeatedly mentioned to me is that between songs about spiritual union (Bg. *milan'dharmī gān*) and songs about separation (Bg. *birahadharmī gān*).

More distinctions are there in Md. Tajul Islam's song collection (Mo. **T**ājal Is'lām Phakir 1998): His 66 Bengali songs fall into five categories, namely *gajal* ('ghazal'); *bicched* ('separation', equivalent to *biraha*, Skt. <*viraha*>; songs on the pangs of separation from one's beloved); *dehatattva* ('principles of the body', esoteric knowledge about the human body); *murśidi* (from Ar. <*muršid*>, 'spiritual preceptor'; directed to one's specific spiritual master); and *ātmakathā* (containing autobiographical data on the author). Of these categories, the first one, 'ghazal', remains enigmatic, for most of the songs thus designated could easily be assigned to one or other of the following categories; apart from a certain preponderance of Persian and Arabic loan words in a few of these songs,[48] no peculiarities of structure and content are visible. In Md. Mahbubul Alam's songs, the designation 'ghazal' appears alongside prescriptions of metres (*tāla*), and is thus clearly the indication of a musical genre, not a topical one.[49]

Another common way of classifying songs is by the spiritual preceptors to whom they are dedicated. Gholam Muhammad Khan Siraji, for example, divides a portion of his 31 songs according to these lines.[50] This scheme has been taken up by Selim

47 In Maulana **H**adi's *Ratna sāgar*, songs 1–9 are introduced as *hindi bhāṣā bāṃlā akṣare* ('Hindi language in Bengali letters'), and bear the title *gajal* in contrast to the following *bāṃlā gān* (No. 10) or simply *gān* (despite the fact that there is also a genre of Bengali ghazal). Syed Abdul **M**ālek Shah, however, employs the term ghazal for his entirely Bengali compositions (Chaiẏad Āb'dul Mālek **Ś**āh 1989a and 1989b: *passim*); cf. also Maolānā Kājī **S**āhāpurī (1992: passim). In Chaiẏad Ābduchchālām **B**hūj'purī (1991: *passim*), the songs are not classified by separate terms, but simply headed by either *urddu* (Urdu) or *bāṃlā* (Bengali). For other uses of the term ghazal for Maijbhandari songs, see below in this section.

48 Cf., e.g., Songs 1, 2, and 12 (Mo. **T**ājal Is'lām Phakir 1998: 7, 12).

49 Mo. **M**āh'bub ul Ālam (2000: *passim*).

50 Golām Muhāmmad Khān **S**irājī (1993, Nos. 23–29).

Jahangir, author of the monograph *Māij'bhāṇḍār sandarśan* (1999). He attempts to set up a threefold periodisation of Maijbhandari songs, consisting of (a) songs centred on Ahmadullah (roughly until 1906), (b) songs centred on Gholam Rahman (*c.* 1906–37), and (c) songs centred on Delawar Hosain, Shafiul Bashar and Ziaul Haq (roughly from 1937 onwards). By introducing main representatives among the authors of these periods, Jahangir then proceeds to isolate certain personal traits from among the *oeuvres* of these authors.[51] Such a procedure is problematic for a number of reasons. First, songs focused on one specific saint are not necessarily written during his lifetime, but often much later; until the present, the two founding saints of Maijbhandar are again and again objects of compositions by various authors.[52] Second, not all Maijbhandari songs do actually focus on a specific saint; there are frequently either very unspecific references, in the songs, to the Bhandari, *mawlā*, friend, guru, *muršid* or the like, all of which would be applicable to any of the saints; or, and this is by no means a rare occurrence, there is reference to more than one saint or no reference at all. And third, such a periodisation presupposes that the development of the Maijbhandari song tradition is to be understood in direct parallel with the Maijbhandari saints; it thus tends to deny the authors any independent agency, and negate autonomous dynamics in the evolution of this tradition.

But while it may be easy to detect weak points in existing modes of classification, it remains a tough task to devise a better solution. The Maijbhandari song tradition cannot easily be fitted into a scheme of periodisation, since no major ruptures are visible within it. A historical, evolutionary approach to it is only partly feasible, not only because information on authors of the earlier generations is relatively scarce,[53] but mainly because the tradition is characterised by durability and perpetuation rather than drastic change – all major themes and motifs that continue to be constitutive of Maijbhandari songs can be said to have existed, in more or less fully fledged form, for the last eighty years, that is, for the greater part of its span of existence.

A synchronic typology of Maijbhandari songs is also hard to achieve. On first sight, songs on such topics as love in separation, invocation of saints or spiritual boat journeys may make such a typology seem quite feasible. On closer scrutiny, however, it becomes clear that even such dominant topics are more often than not intermingled with other topics within the span of one song; and this is much more so in the case of less extensive motifs. If we envisaged a typology of songs, it would hardly seem avoidable to be pushed into construing arbitrary ideal types on the basis of criteria largely alien to the tradition; and such a set of ideal types would automatically produce an abundant mass of hybrids. The danger of getting lost in a very formal and theoretical taxonomy and falling prey to artificially imposed friction would be great.

51 Selim Jāhāṅgīr (1999: 183–5). For Maulana Hadi, this characteristic trait is separation, for Bajlul Karim complaint, and for Ramesh Shil, love (p. 185).

52 Cf., e.g., the many songs dedicated to Gholam Rahman 'Baba Bhandari' by Abdul Gafur Hali and Muhy al-Bhandari, two contemporary authors.

53 Except Ramesh Shil.

It would, lastly, also make little sense, given the present state of affairs and the object of this book, to study Maijbhandari songs in terms of their authorship. While it is no doubt possible to analyse the individual contributions to Maijbhandari songs as a literary genre, the ethos of this tradition is rather a collective one; and the most interesting question to ask about this tradition, in my view, regards not individual literary achievements, but the way in which this tradition shapes a language of collective religious expression.

In view of these difficulties, I propose, instead, to focus on an examination of motifs. Conceived as semantic units of considerable durability, it is a specific inventory of these motifs that is characteristic of the Maijbhandari song tradition. The nature and interplay of these may give us a picture of the set-up of popular religious semantics in Maijbhandar. Diachronic aspects do come under the purview of this exercise, but the basic approach is a synchronic one.

Given the limitations of space, it is not feasible to deal with over 4,000 songs at once. But in view of the large range of variation, it would be equally hazardous to try to isolate any small number of representative texts. In order to explore the basic properties of the Maijbhandari religious idiom, I have chosen a middle path that allows statements about shared characteristics without getting lost in impractical levels of detail. I have singled out the works of ten authors as the basis of this examination, some of them considered to be classics in the development of this song tradition.[54] Works of other authors are also occasionally taken into account. The authors chosen cover all periods of Maijbhandari song production, from the late nineteenth century (Aliullah, Maulana Hadi, Bajlul Karim) through the twentieth century (Ramesh Shil, Abdul Jabbar Mimnagari, Farid Hosain), until the present (Abdul Gafur Hali, Mahbubul Alam, Badrunnesa Saju, Lutfunnesa Hosaini). The number of songs thus coming into the purview of the following investigation is around 1,100. It is only rarely possible to include any complete translations of songs in this analysis; some samples of Maijbhandari songs have been given in Appendix 1.

54 Here is a list of these authors and their works; the names under which they are ordered in the Bibliography, Primary Sources, B Songs, have a bold-font first letter): **A**liullāh Rājāpurī (*Prem-nūr* [*PN*], published in 1913); Maulānā Ābdul **H**ādī (*Ratnabhāṇḍār* [*RB*] and *Ratna Sāgar* [*RS*], two partly overlapping compilations of his songs written around the turn of the nineteenth and twentieth centuries, constantly republished); **B**aj'lul Karim Mandākinī (*Śeṣ jīban* [*ŚJ*], a contemporary compilation of his songs written around the turn of the century); **R**ameś Śīl (his seven song books: *Nure duniẏā* [*ND*], *Satya darpaṇ* [*SD*], *Śānti bhāṇḍār* [*ŚB*], *Bhāṇḍāre māolā* [*BhM*], *Āśek mālā* [*ĀM*], *Muktir dar'bār* [*MD*], and *Jīban sāthī* [*JS*], all written between the 1920s and 1940s, and still in publication); **S**aphiul Baśar (*Yuger ālo o buker khun* [*YB*], originally two song books written in mid twentieth century, republished together ever since); Ābdul Jabbār Śāh **M**im'nagarī (*Pañcaratnagītikā* [*PR*], a huge compilation first published in 1988); Fakīr Md. **F**arīd Hosen (his *Bhāṇḍār* series, especially *Saurabh bhāṇḍār* [*SB*] and *Udaẏ bhāṇḍār*, written in the second half of the twentieth century, and republished ever since); Abdul Gafur Hali (*Jñān'jyoti* [*JJ*] and *Tattvabidhi* [*TB*], both written in the late twentieth century); **B**adrunnesā Sāju (a woman writer; *Madirā*, published in 1988); **L**ut·phunnesā Hosāīnī (daughter of Shafiul Bashar; her *Gāuchiẏater phul* [*GS*], published in 1992), and **M**āh'bubul Ālam (*Aiśī ālor jal'sāghar* [*AJ*], published in 2000).

5.6 Language and communicative design

Before going into our inquiry regarding the characteristics of the popular religious idiom of Maijbhandari songs, some remarks on their linguistic characteristics and formal communicative design appear necessary. Chittagong is notorious for its dialect, which is considered unintelligible by many speakers from other parts of Bengal. The language used in the songs, however, is mostly not the Chittagongian dialect, barring very few exceptions.[55] But it is not standard Bengali either; it is distinctly Eastern Bengali and bears many dialectal influences in verbal and noun forms, pronouns and participles. There are discernible differences from author to author. Some modern authors do in fact employ modern standard Bengali (*calit bhāṣā*), sometimes alternating with *sādhu bhāṣā*.[56] But the rule is *sādhu bhāṣā*-oriented language with strong dialectal traces, and this requires the following brief linguistic remarks.

Infinitives, conditional participles, future tense, past tense and the habitual past usually insert an *i* between stem and ending.[57] The future *tumi* form occasionally has the dialectal ending *-bā* instead of standard *-be*, and the Eastern alternative infinitive form *karibāre* for *kar'te* can be found, as well as the present continuous form *kar'teche* by the side of *kar'che* (*calit*) and *kariteche* (*sādhu bhāṣā*). The *sādhu bhāṣā* absolutive participle *kariẏā* is employed along with its shortened form *kari* (common in pre-modern Bengali literature and oral literature), and occasionally the forms *kaïrā* and *kariẏe* are found.[58] Certain noun and adjective endings are (as elsewhere in East Bengal) in *-ā*, not *-o*, as in *jutā* for (Calcutta standard) *juto*, *kālā* for *kālo*, etc. Personal pronouns prefer *sādhu bhāṣā* forms (e.g. *tāhā*) to *calit* forms (*tā*), and nasalisations in respectful reference (*tā̃r*, etc.) are often omitted.

Peculiarities of spelling include the use (among some Maijbhandari authors) of the letter *cha* for sharp *s* sounds, which is uncommon in standard Bengali and considered somewhat rustic, as well as the insertion of *-b* (*-v*) as the latter part of ligatures in Arabic loan words, but also elsewhere (*tvarikā* instead of simply *tarikā* for Ar. *ṭarīqa*; *dvīn* instead of *dīn*, sometimes indiscriminately for Ar. <*dīn*>, 'religion', and the tatsama *dīn*, 'miserable'). In general, ligatures in *tatsama* words are often misspelled. These features are, however, not limited to Maijbhandari songs but concern many domains of East Bengali writing habits. Some imprints of the local dialect of Chittagong can be noticed in the lexis and participles. Examples are the word *chup(h)ān*, which is used, along with common Bengali words such as *hāl*, to denote a boatman's helm, and the participle *ni* for the function of emphasising *to* in standard Bengali.

55 Ramesh Shil has written a few songs in the Chittagong dialect, e.g. *JS* No. 37.

56 Notably Mahbubul Alam (*AJ*) and Badrunnesa Suja (*Madirā*).

57 All these are features of *sādhu bhāṣā*; thus the forms are, e.g., *karite* for *kar'te*, *karile* for *kar'le*, *kariba* for *kar'ba*, *karilām* for *kar'lām* and *karitām* for *kar'tām*.

58 *kaïrā* is a dialectal form used in many parts of Bengal. *kariẏe* is more uncommon; it is identical with the *calit bhāṣā* absolutive of the causative, but used in a non-causative function, the respective causative form being *karāiẏā*, *karāẏe* or *karāiẏe*.

The linguistically most difficult Maijbhandari songs are those contained in Aliullah's book *Prem'nūr* from 1913.[59] The trend in over one century of song production in Maijbhandar, however, is certainly a decrease in dialectal impact in connection with the eclipse of Urdu as a medium of polished communication, and the development of Bengali towards a standardised, national language. If more recent Maijbhandari songs pose difficulties to a listener or reader experienced in standard *sādhu* and *calit* Bengali, those are not due to primary linguistic properties but basically to idiosyncratic terminology and metaphor-building.

With these sweeping remarks on the language employed in Maijbhandari songs, I wish to turn to an examination of their communicative design. As stated above, Maijbhandari songs usually contain a refrain and three to five verses mostly in the traditional metres of *paẏār* and *tripadī*.[60] The refrain tends to expose the theme and gist of the text, which is then elaborated or exemplified in the verses. The last verse, and within it mostly the last two lines, usually contains the colophon (*bhaṇitā*) indicating the author's name.[61] As their refrain-verse structure

59 This is due to the strong impact of the local dialect and massive irregularities of spelling. Similar difficulties are presented only by Persian songs given in Bengali script; cf. the example given in Appendix I, No. 11.

60 These two reign over almost all of pre-modern Bengali literary production (cf. Zbavitel 1976: 123). *Paẏār* has regularly fourteen syllables per line. End rhymes are not a prerequisite, but usually employed in songs. *Tripadī*, lit. 'three-liner', consists of two shorter (usually six to eight syllables, often rhymed) and one longer (eight to fourteen syllables) parts. The long verse rhymes with its following or next but one equivalent. In traditional *paẏār* and *tripadī*, all silent inherent *a* vowels are at least slightly pronounced and counted. Bengali folk traditions in general handle these rules less strictly. In Maijbhandari songs, there is much liberty with regard to such vocalisation, and the texts themselves usually require arbitrary inclusion or omission of single vowels in order to fit into the metre. In my transcriptions in the present and the following chapters as well as in Appendix I, I have given the inherent vowels in brackets – *(a)* – whenever I deemed they should be pronounced for the sake of the metre (barring only some cases in which I could not recognise the metre from the written form of the songs).

61 The *bhaṇitā* (either Skt. nom. of *bhaṇitṛ*, lit. 'speaker', or fem. of *bhaṇita*, 'spoken, related'; also called *mudrikā*, 'seal', in Hindi/Marathi) is a very common feature in song traditions all over the Indian subcontinent. Especially in *bhakti* literature, this insertion of the author's name at the end of a song is rarely omitted. In Bengali literature, the use of *bhaṇitā*s goes right back to the *Caryāpada*s, the first document claimed for this literature by literary historiography. The author's name may be syntactically integrated into the texts or, as e.g. frequently in Kabīr's *Sākhī*s, simply be inserted at the beginning of a line (cf. Vaudeville 1993: 125). Today in Chittagong, as I was repeatedly told in interviews with authors, the *bhaṇitā* is regarded both as a traditional literary device and a signature which marks intellectual property and protects songs from claims by other authors. There are, however, quite a number of Maijbhandari songs without *bhaṇitā*; in some older cases, these appear to have been lost. In more recent cases, songs were published in print first, and appeared in complete booklets bearing the name of the author; the copyright function of the *bhaṇitā* may therefore have been deemed to be dismissible. Only two contemporary authors, Badrunnesa Saju (*Madirā*) and Mahbubul Alam (*AJ*) have omitted *bhaṇitā*s throughout. Badrunnesa Saju from Chittagong City is a poet, and her Maijbhandari works are rather poems than songs, so the omission seems to betray a modernist lyrical ethos otherwise alien to the Maijbhandari tradition. A similar orientation may be supposed for Mahbubul Alam, a journalist also from Chittagong City.

and their brevity already suggest, Maijbhandari songs are rarely narrative, in the sense of possessing a proper plot and relating events that make the conclusion differ from the outset.[62] An exception to this rule are (very few) songs of a biographic or hagiographic nature.[63] There are certain standard micro-plots,for example in the depictions of the spiritual path by way of a boat journey,[64] but these hardly have any marked temporal progression and lack narrative mimesis. The same is true of songs dealing with cosmogony[65] or the guidance of men through the course of time by prophets and saints.[66] The time relations dealt with in these songs are conceived and depicted as a cosmic, divine order rather than as a historical progression. The narration of any course of events is not usually the subject of Maijbhandari songs, but the depiction of a mood or the concise communication of a message is. These two aspects, the lyrical and the proclamatory/instructive, are, of course, hardly ever found in isolation but mostly coincide in single songs to different degrees.

Maijbhandari songs use a variety of communicative patterns. The most frequent among these is the direct address to a Maijbhandari saint or *pīr*. The informal *tumi*, and less commonly the intimate *tui*[67] forms of address and various kinds of epithets are employed. The most common among these are *bandhu/bandhuŷā* (friend),[68] *murśid* (Ar. *muršid*, spiritual preceptor),[69] *bābā* (father),[70] *kāṇḍārī* (helmsman),[71] *daŷāl <guru>* (merciful <guru>),[72] as well as, at least with certain authors, *priŷā/priŷe* (Skt. nominative/vocative of 'beloved' in the female).[73] Frequently, an unspecified *tumi* is also found.[74] This direct address is

62 This stands in sharp contrast with other genres of Bengali folk literature, such as the famous *Maŷ'man'siṃher gītikā* first edited by Dineshchandra Sen in several volumes between 1923 and 1932 (cf. Zbavitel/Mode 1976; Zbavitel 1976: 196 f.) or the decidedly narrative traditions of *Jārī gān* and *Paṭuŷā gān* (cf. Hauser 1998).

63 e.g. Shafiul Bashar, *YB* No. 6 on Gholam Rahman's life; Lutfunnesa Hosaini, *GP* No. 32 on Shafiul Bashar's life; etc.

64 e.g. Ramesh Shil, *ND* No. 8, 10; *BhM* No. 7, 8; *ĀM* No. 4; *ŚB* No. 7, *SD* No. 7; Maulana Hadi, *RB* No. 15; Abdul Gafur Hali, *TB* No. 2, 8, 17, 19, 21, 29; *JJ* No. 8, 49, 53, 72; Shafiul Bashar, *YB* No. 73; Farid Hosain, *HB* No. 4.

65 e.g. Shafiul Bashar, *YB* No. 36; Farid Hosain, *HB* No. 36; Abdul Gafur Hali, *JJ* No. 23.

66 e.g. Ramesh Shil, *ND* No. 37; *ŚB* No. 2; *MD* No. 12; Abdul Gafur Hali, *TB* No. 37; Shafiul Bashar, *YB* No. 7, 19; etc.

67 e.g. in Farid Hosain, *SB* No. 72, where the *tui* is to all appearances directed to *Kānāiŷā* (traditional *tadbhava* form of *kṛṣṇa* for Lord Krishna).

68 e.g. Ramesh Shil, *ND* No. 25, 36; *SD* 13, 30, 39, etc.; Farid Hosain *SB* No. 33, 41, 43, 44, etc.; Maulana Hadi, *RS* No. 78, 90; Abdul Gafur Hali, *TB* No. 18, 19, 60, 70; etc.

69 e.g. Farid Hosain, *SB* No. 15, 42; *HB* No. 34; Ramesh Shil, *MD* No. 3; Abdul Gafur Hali, *JJ* No. 37; etc.

70 e.g. Aliullah, *PN* No. 9; Badrunnesa Saju, *Madirā* No. 11; Ramesh Shil, *BhM* No. 33; *ĀM* No. 37; *MD* 19, 25; etc. Also Shafiul Bashar (*YB* No. 20, 45, 49, 55, 56) and Lutfunnesa Hosaini (*GP* almost *passim*) use *bābā* as an address; in their case, *pīr* and father were the same person.

71 e.g. Aliullah, *PN* No. 24, Farid Hosain, *SB* No. 12, 79; Shafiul Bashar, *YB* No. 74; etc.

72 Ramesh Shil *ND* No. 29, 30; Shafiul Bashar *YB* No. 31, 72; Jahir Ahmad Chaudhuri (1989: 24); Abdul Jabbar Mimnagari *PR* No. 1; Lutfunnesa Hosaini *GP* No. 1; etc.

73 e.g. Aliullah, *PN* No. 15; Farid Hosain, *RB* No. 22, 23; Maulana Hadi, *RS* No. 17, 25, 50, 65, 83, 88, 94; Abdul Gafur Hali, *JJ* No. 30, 69; Shafiul Bashar, *YB* No. 24; etc.

74 e.g. Abdul Jabbar Mimnagari *PR* No. 2, 9, 21, 22, etc.; Farid Hosain *SB* No. 22, 69; etc.

usually connected with invocations, imploratings and prayers; it is often accompanied by imperative forms asking the saint or *pīr* to do something for the *murīd*, that is, for the author, as identified in the *bhaṇitā*, speaking in the first-person singular. Corresponding to the performance of Maijbhandari songs by solo singers, the plural form of the first person is uncommon.

Another pattern addresses the audience in *tumi* (sg.) and *tom'rā* (pl.) forms.[75] This type is usually found in pilgrimage songs relating the glory of the Maijbhandari saints and telling the audience to visit Maijbhandar in order to partake of that place's spiritual benefits. A more intimate *tumi* may also be instructed in how to tread the mystical path.[76] A second-person plural address can, however, also be directed towards a presumably absent addressee, namely the opponents of certain Sufi creeds and practices;[77] songs of this type implore those opponents to convert to what the poets see as the right path.

A further typical way of using the *tumi* address is the complaint about one's lover's behaviour *vis-á-vis* a *sakhī*, female companion; she is repeatedly addressed to share the ailings and pains of unfulfilled love.[78] This type is mostly used for bride mysticism[79] of the *viraha bhakti* (love in separation) type, and the Self of the texts is often feminine; it is closely related to the Vaishnavite *bhakti* tradition of Bengal. Complaints of another kind are also uttered in a dialogue with one's own mind (*man*, also referred to as *manā*, *manuẏā*, *manurā*, *manurāẏ*, *manirām siṃ[ha]*), thus introducing a self-referential *tumi*.[80] The mind is usually urged to abandon its infatuation with the world and concentrate on issues of real importance such as the final salvation of the soul.

Some songs do not use any kind of address and rely solely on monologuous first person narration, and a number of other songs contain only statements in the third person. But these are exceptional, the rule being communicative contextualisation of one kind or the other. Songs of this type do not constitute separate communicative patterns, since all their inventory is also found in the types of songs discussed above; all they lack is the occasional insertion of an imperative form or a vocative form or particle.

75 e.g. Aliullah *PN* No. 7; Abdul Jabbar Mimnagari *PR* No. 5, 13, 28; Shafiul Bashar *YB* No. 63; Ramesh Shil *MD* No. 18; *JS* No. 38; Farid Hosain *SB* No. 8, 13; Maulana Hadi *RS* No. 73, 97; Abdul Gafur Hali *JJ* No. 16, 24, 31; etc.

76 e.g. Ramesh Shil's *SD* No. 7, in which a boatman is instructed regarding the right path towards unity with the divine (cf. Section 6.1).

77 e.g. Ramesh Shil, *MD* No. 11, against the Faraizis (P. *Farā'iżī*).

78 Abdul Jabbar Mimnagari *PR* No. 12; Ramesh Shil *ND* No. 18; *JS* No. 36; *ĀM* No. 39; *BhM* No. 31; Farid Hosain *SB* No. 51, 52; Maulana Hadi *RS* No. 65, 71, 80; Abdul Gafur Hali *TT* No. 4, 10, 31, 40; Shafiul Bashar *YB* No. 65, 67; etc.

79 German 'Brautmystik'.

80 Ramesh Shil, *ND* No. 8 (actually *man mājhi*, 'mind-boatman'; cf. also *BhM* No. 7), 9, 32; *ŚB* No. 33; Farid Hosain, *SB* No. 24, 47; *HB* No. 31; Maulana Hadi, *RB* No. 28; *RS* No. 49, 86; Aliullah, *PN* No. 52; Abdul Gafur Hali, *TB* No. 17, 28, 73 (17 and 73: *man mājhi*); Lutfunnesa Hosaini, *GP* No. 30; etc. Cf. similar ways of conversing with one's mind very prominently in Baul songs, but also in other traditions of devotional poetry, e.g. Mirabai: *bhaja maṇ(a) caraṇ(a)* [. . .] ('Worship, [O] mind, the feet . . .'), or *rām(a) nām(a) rasa pījai manuā̃* ('Drink the juice of the name of Rāma, [O] mind' (Caturvedī 1989: 156, 158).

Like the second-person address, the first person is also often qualified by further attributes or appositions. Most of these express the devotee's meanness, humility and inferior status *vis-à-vis* the saint or *pīr*. The terms *phakir* (Ar. *<faqīr>*, 'pauper'), *pāpī* ('sinner'), *hīn*, *dīn* or *dīn-hīn* ('humble'),[81] *adham* ('mean'),[82] *bhikhārinī* ('beggar' f.),[83] and so on denote such self-negating attitudes. The devotee-authors also use terms such as *khādem* (Ar. *<ḫādim>*, 'servant'),[84] *dās* or *dāsī* ('servant' m/f),[85] or *adhīn* ('despondent')[86] to convey their submission to their master. A different, more intimate way of expressing unflinching subjugation is to imagine oneself as a saint's child, and terms like *chele*,[87] *putra* (both 'son'),[88] *śiśu* ('child')[89] or *meẏe* ('daughter') are employed. Another set of terms accentuate the devotee's state of helplessness, desperation or distress, such as *diśehārā* ('lost'),[90] *śaktihārā* or U. *bētāb* ('powerless'),[91] *etim* (Ar. *<yatīm>*) or *anāth* ('orphan'),[92] *bidhabā* ('widow'),[93] *abhāgī*[94] or *abhāginī* ('unfortunate' m/f), etc. The lack of insight and intelligence on the devotee's part may also be expressed in terms like *hatabuddhi* (a Skt. *bahuvrīhi* compound: '[he whose] intellect [has been] killed', i.e. 'stupefied'),[95] *abujh* ('lacking judgement'),[96] and *bokā* ('stupid'). With certain authors, in particular Ramesh Shil, Farid Hosain and Abdul Gafur Hali,[97] it is very popular to attach *pāgal*, 'crazy' to their names in the colophon; and the self is often described as *pāgal*/*pāg'lā* ('crazy'),[98] *deoẏānā* (P. *<dīwāna>*, 'crazy'), *ātmahārā* ('self-lost')[99] and the like. These designations may be used in pejorative as well as appreciative ways; their ambivalence will be dealt with in Section 5.7.12.

These basic communicative patterns are indicative of certain fundamental characteristics of Maijbhandari songs. The great majority of these songs depict

81 e.g. Bajlul Karim, *PH* No. 19; Lutfunnesa Hosaini, *GP* No. 22, 28; Shafiul Bashar, *YB* No. 4, 28, 32, 33, 34, etc.
82 Shafiul Bashar, *YB* No. 22, 48.
83 Badrunnesa Saju *Madirā* No. 7.
84 e.g. Ramesh Shil, *ĀM* No. 6, 8, 9; *ŚB* No. 2; *ND* No. 12; *JS* No. 17, etc.
85 e.g. Ramesh Shil *MD* No. 8; Bajlul Karim *PH* No. 4; Lutfunnesa Hosaini *GP* No. 15; Shafiul Bashar *YB* No. 8, 9, 77; Maulana Hadi *RB* No. 16, 21 (*prem dās hādī hīn*, 'humble love-servant Hadi'), 26, etc.
86 e.g. Ramesh Shil, *MD* No. 4.
87 e.g. Ramesh Shil, *ND* No. 21; *SD* No. 5, 12 (all *pāgal chele*, 'crazy son'); Bajlul Karim, *PH* No. 10 (who uses *pāg'lā khokā*, 'crazy baby of the family'; Shafiul Bashar, *YB* No. 27.
88 Shafiul Bashar, *YB* No. 29.
89 e.g. Lutfunnesa Hosaini, *GP* No. 14 (*abodh śiśu*, 'ignorant child'); Shafiul Bashar *YB* No. 64 (*adham śiśu*, 'mean child').
90 Ramesh Shil, *ĀM* No. 5; Abdul Gafur Hali *JJ* No. 9; etc.
91 Shafiul Bashar *YB* No. 11; Maulana Hadi *RB* No. 32 (Urdu song in Bengali script).
92 Cf. Farid Hosain *HB* No. 17; Abdul Gafur Hali *JJ* No. 44.
93 Farid Hosain *HB* No. 60.
94 e.g. Lutfunnesa Hosaini, *GP* No. 16.
95 Ramesh Shil, *ND* No. 27.
96 Cf. Lutfunnesa Hosaini, *GP* No. 15.
97 And also another author signing as Pagal Chaudhuri.
98 e.g. very often Ramesh Shil (cf. *ŚB* No. 10, 16, 25, 33; *ND* No. 2, etc.); Shafiul Bashar, *YB* No. 24, 47, 75; Farid Hosain *HB* No. 18, 19, 21, 23, etc.
99 Shafiul Bashar *YB* No. 42.

the saints from the inferior position of the devotee; viewed according to established categories in the discussion on primarily North Indian *bhakti*, Maijbhandari songs are composed by the *bhakta*, not by the *sant*. The authors 'gaze up' at the holy, and if they hand down anything from their position to the co-disciples and general people, they mostly do so in the garb of humility which is so evident from the first-person qualifiers discussed above. The songs do contain quite a great deal of religious instruction, but without claiming authoritativeness; the *pīr* or saint, or Maijbhandar in general as a place of spiritual centrality, are referred to as the proper loci for gaining ultimate insight. Accordingly, the most common imperative found in the songs asks the listener to take refuge at a true *pīr*'s feet and to visit Maijbhandar.[100] Where instruction is bestowed, this usually happens from the advanced seeker's position, not from the master's.

In order to make this clear, it is necessary here to elaborate the above-made (etic) distinction between lyrical and instructive-proclamatory aspects in the religious idiom found in Maijbhandari songs. The former type of expression describes a mood or state of mind, a *bhāva* according to Indian aesthetics,[101] pertaining to some particular mental or spiritual stage of a devotee. The first person of the song usually speaks from *inside* that mood or state, articulating immediate experience of suffering or (less frequently) joy. It is left to the receptivity of the listener to realise the substance of the song and thus to experience for himself the religious mood expressed in it. The language has, or at least pretends to have, a cathartic function. The latter type, by contrast, is informative; it is primarily concerned with spreading the fame of Maijbhandar or knowledge regarding the identity and power of Maijbhandari saints and the religious ideas and practice required to attain them. The authors do not speak from inside anywhere, but *about* something; and language has not a cathartic, but rather a directive function. The listener is given certain information with a purpose, and in many cases he is explicitly told what to think and what to do.[102]

While the lyrical type of expression goes well with a devotee's position, the instructive does not, since any attempt on a devotee's part to bestow instruction is potentially presumptuous. To avoid this, instruction is always construed as intermediary, and the experiences such instruction prescribes are to be made, as stated above, under the guidance of a perfect *pīr*, that is, usually a Maijbhandari *pīr*. A common way of ending such didactic songs is, for instance, by admitting one's own failure to pay heed to the matter of instruction. But this tendency cannot be generalised, and it must be stressed that a majority of the songs does not neatly

100 An abundance of examples from almost all authors of Maijbhandari songs could be quoted to illustrate this point.

101 The theory of *bhāva* and *rasa*, elaborated in Sanskrit works such as the *Nāṭyaśāstra*, was adapted to religious sentiments by theologians of Gaudiya Vaishnavism. On Vaishnava *rasa* theory (*śānta*, *dāsya*, *sākhya*, *vātsalya*, and *mādhurya* or *śṛṅgāra rasa*s) cf., e.g., Dimock (1989: 22 f.); also Klostermeier (1990: 220); etc. (T.R. Sharma [1993] attempts a psychological analysis of this theory which remains, however, quite unsatisfactory.) Bg. *bhāb* also frequently figures in the song texts.

102 The distinction roughly corresponds to that between *ādhyātmik* ('spiritual') and *phariẏādī* (P. <*fariyādī*>, 'lamenting') songs.

fall under either of these types of expression. Some of the single motifs we will analyse in the following may typically be connected with lyrical or instructive modes,[103] while others are notoriously ambiguous.[104] It appears that, especially in the course of recent developments, both types of expression are becoming more and more combinable.

5.7 Motifs of Maijbhandari songs

The Maijbhandari song tradition rests on a relatively stable inventory of motifs. Fourteen such motifs, or complexes of motifs,[105] are outlined in the following. These motifs are situated on different semantic levels. Some are old conventional metaphors that are transposed into a specific context. Others are basically religious ideas that have become standardised in the Maijbhandari tradition. Others, again, belong to the inventory of distinct religious traditions and are integrated into the Maijbhandari idiom. My contention, in brief, is that the assembly of these motifs and their specific interlinkage constitute a Maijbhandari religious idiom.

The single motifs are in the following presented in a well-considered order. Each one has a close relationship and sometimes partial overlap with the surrounding motifs, including the last and the first. The motifs are thus organised in a closed circle. This is, of course, to some extent a matter of presentation aesthetics, and to be sure, different circles and other models of abstraction would have been possible. In any case, this mode of presentation favours cohesion and conciseness, and simultaneously demonstrates the inner cohesion of these motifs.

5.7.1 The heart

> The *Qur'ān* is inside the heart.
> Behold it with your eyes and recite.[106]
> (Aliullah)

The heart is conceived as the centre of the body and the seat of the Divine inside man;[107] it can at instances be called a microcosm within the microcosm that is the human body.[108] In *ḏikr* practice it is the *laṭīfa al-qalb* into which the affirmative *illa*

103 e.g. *viraha bhakti*, love in separation, is strongly connected with the lyrical type of expression.

104 e.g. the motive of the boat journey.

105 The categories 'heart', 'man', 'bird', 'return of the same', 'merging', 'unity of religions', 'craziness', 'play' and 'journey' can be seen as motifs proper; the remaining categories of 'death', 'identity of saints', 'love', '*viraha bhakti*' and 'body' are rather topics that subordinate various separate motifs.

106 *dil(a) bhitar āche korāṇ, paṛa tumi cakṣe cāi*; Aliullah *PN* 44.

107 Cf. al-Qushayri's *Risāla* (Gramlich 1989: 144) where the heart (*qalb*) and the 'spirit' (*rūḥ*) are described as the seat of positive human properties. The Indian saint Kabir identifies the heart as the seat of God inside man: 'Why does that Mullah climb the minaret?/Allah is not outside!/Him for whom you shout the call to prayer/You should recognize in your heart.' (Vaudeville 1993: 205 f.).

108 Cf. the remarks in Rahul Peter Das (1992: 411), commenting upon a Sahajiya text. Also Rahul Peter Das (2003: 590–93) for a comprehensive survey of the complex semantics of *hṛdaya* in Indian medical and other texts; especially p. 593 on the *hṛdaya* as the seat of the intellect.

Llāh of the Islamic confession of faith has to be thrown.[109] Like the Divine itself, it is hidden by veils and has to be uncovered for any kind of religious achievement.

Maijbhandari song-authors use a variety of terms to refer to the heart. The most frequent are *hr̥d* and *hr̥daẏ*, followed by *dil* (P./U. <*dil*>), *kalab* (Ar. <*qalb*>), *kalijā* (U. <*kalēja*>), and, in very few cases, *hiẏā* (a poetic Bengali *tadbhava* form of Skt. <*hr̥daẏa*>). Also *sīnā*/*chīnā* (P./U. <*sīna*>, 'chest, breast') is occasionally employed to denote the heart. It is the holiest place in the human body and an inner temple; the term *hr̥d mandir*, heart-temple, is quite commonplace.[110] Based on the notion of the human body as a microcosm containing the macrocosm in itself, the heart is conceived as the location of the sacred places and scriptures (cf. opening quotation) in the body. It is where prayers and worship should be directed: 'Perform your ritual prayers with diligence by putting the Kaʿba of the heart in front' (Ramesh Shil).[111] The saint, too, ought to be placed in one's heart and is to be venerated there (Farid Hosain).[112] A lamp burns in that heart-temple.[113] The temple, in fact, contains the Divine itself, and often a divine personality (the friend, Lord, father, Bhandari, etc.) is asked to open and enter the heart: 'Come, Father, into the heart-temple, and blow your flute' (Shafiul Bashar).[114] As the Lord may be asked into the temple, the divine lover may likewise be invited into one's 'heart-bed' (*hr̥d pālaṅga, śayyā*),[115] or be imagined as sitting on the 'heart-throne' (*hr̥daẏ siṃhāsan*)[116] or the seat of the heart (*hr̥d āsan, hr̥daẏ āsan*).[117] Robbers, that is, all evil thoughts and sentiments, on the other hand, must be warded off from that temple.[118] The heart is also occasionally pictured as a house, a town or a garden.[119] Another common way of imagining the heart is as a cage in which the bird is locked up: 'I would catch and hold the mind-bird by tying it up in the heart' (Lutfunnesa Hosaini).[120] Ramesh Shil depicts the

109 Cf. Section 2.2.2 in this book.

110 e.g. Ramesh Shil *ŚB* No. 37; Aliullah *PN* No. 10, 43, 102; Shafiul Bashar *YB* No. 15, 49; Abdul Jabbar Mimnagari *PR* No. 20; Ramesh Shil also uses *prāṇ mandir* (*MD* No. 2).

111 *hr̥der kābā sām'ne kari namāj paṛa yatane*. Ramesh Shil *ŚB* No. 10.

112 Farid Hosain *SB* No. 28.

113 Aliullah *PN* No. 43: *hr̥d mandire cerāg jale* [sic] ('A lamp burns in the heart-temple').

114 *esa bābā hr̥d mandire, māra tomār bā̃śīr ṭān*. Shafiul Bashar *YB* No. 49. Also Ramesh Shil *MD* No. 2: *prāṇ mandirer kapāṭ khuli bā̃śī bājāo niśi dine* ('Open the door of the life-temple and play your flute day and night').

115 Ramesh Shil *MD* No. 8: *(bandhure) rākhi hr̥d pālaṅga sājāiẏā/phuler reṇur śayyā diẏā/cupe cupe āsiẏā basio* ('[O friend], let me keep the heart-bed dressed/With a bedding of pollen/Come quietly and sit down'). Also Abdul Gafur Hali *TB* No. 11: *hr̥d āsane phul'śayyā karilām* ('I made a flowerbed at the seat of the heart').

116 *JS* 29: *hr̥daẏ siṃhāsane bandhu āche sarbbadāẏ*.

117 E.g. Abdul Gafur Hali *TB* No. 11, 38 (*hr̥d āsan*); Maulana Hadi *RB* No. 23 (*hr̥daẏ āsan*); Ramesh Shil *SD* No. 23 (*hr̥dāsan*).

118 Aliullah *PN* No. 102.

119 e.g. Abdul Gafur Hali *TB* No. 7 (*hr̥daẏ pure*); Maulana Hadi *RS* No. 51 (*hr̥d bāgān*).

120 *GP* No. 4: *man pākhire rākh'tām dhare/hr̥daẏe bā̃dhiẏā*. This could, however, also be read as tying *to* the heart; the image of the cage is more explicit, e.g., in Ramesh Shil *JS* No. 22: *hr̥d piñjarer poṣā pākhi* ('the tamed bird of the heart-cage'), or in Abdul Gafur Hali *JJ* No. 61, where the bird is tied with chains inside the heart-cage (*hr̥d piñjare*). On the bird within the heart, cf. also Aliullah *PN* No. 101: *sei pakṣī chinār bhitar, kothā haïte āilare* ('That bird is inside the breast, where has it come from?'); Abdul Gafur Hali *JJ* No. 4 (*diler maẏ'nā*).

heart as a jailhouse in which the *manacor*, 'the thief which is the mind', is to be imprisoned.[121] If from the outside the heart is symbolised by such confined spaces, it simultaneously shares divine attributes in being 'unlimited' (Ramesh Shil).[122]

As we can see already, the heart as the most sacred part of the microcosmic body is ambiguously viewed as either filled with the Divine *per se*, or as an empty container waiting for it to take its due position in it. In both cases, the way to the heart has to be cleared, the veils and darkness removed, and the door opened by some divine agency. By virtue of the name of the spiritual master, 'the veils of the heart shall be cut, and darkness shall be dispelled' (Ramesh Shil).[123] The scent of the saintly flower in Maijbhandar may achieve the same: 'By the pleasant air [emitting from] that flower, the heart is opened and darkness destroyed' (Ramesh Shil);[124] and Abdul Gafur Hali argues that the heart opened by a pilgrimage to Maijbhandar is the precondition to any true worship.[125] It takes a key to open the heart; it has two locked doors, and 'the key to the heart is in the hand of the guru' (Farid Hosain).[126]

The heart, in the above-quoted songs, is conceived as a spatial unit, a sort of stage inside the human body for the appearance of the divine. But there are also other aspects to it; it is simultaneously closely related to spiritual vision, and a number of visual phenomena take place inside the heart. The first is the visualisation of one's *pīr*, called *bar'jakh* (Ar. *barzaḫ*, 'isthmus').[127] Here, the heart appears as a canvas on which that picture must be projected: 'I have painted your enchanting picture on my heart-canvas' (Ramesh Shil).[128] Secondly, in accordance with the Sufi tradition (cf., for instance, Al-Ghazzali 2001: 21 ff.), the heart is figured as a mirror linking the human to the divine; if purified, the heart can furnish man a reflection of God. 'He put a natural mirror into the heart of Adam [i.e. man]', and this mirror needs cleansing: 'The mirror of the heart will become clean by gazing at the face of light' (Abdul Gafur Hali).[129] Maulana Hadi, apparently in order to emphasise its kingly, exorbitant significance, calls it the 'Alexander-mirror'.[130]

121 Ramesh Shil *SD* No. 37 (*hṛday jel'khānā*).
122 *JS* No. 10 speaks of an *asīm sīnā*, 'unlimited breast', in which the friend (*bandhu*) resides.
123 Ramesh Shil *MD* No. 4: *diler parddā keṭe yābe ghuce yābe andhakār*.
124 Ramesh Shil *ND* No. 7: *sei phuleri subātāse dil khole ār ā̃dhār nāśe*.
125 *ebādat*; Abdul Gafur Hali *TB* No. 36: *diler parddā khule yābe ei habe tār ebādat*.
126 Farid Hosain *SB* No. 37 (*diler cābi*). For the two 'doors' (*dar'jā*) of the heart, cf. *ĀB*: 155 f.: One opens upwards towards the throne of Allah (*'arš*) and turns one's sight away from the world and on God; the other opens downwards towards hell (*dūzaḫ*) and makes one 'stuck in the world like in cowdung'.
127 Cf. Chapter 2.2.2.
128 *ND* No. 23: [. . .]/*tomār sei mohan chabi/hṛdi paṭe rekhechi ā̃kiẏā*. Cf. also Ramesh Shil *ND* No. 36: *hṛd mājhāre chabi āche ā̃kā* ('The picture is painted inside the heart'); Abdul Gafur Hali *JJ* No. 86: *hṛde ā̃ka jiẏār chabi* ('Paint Zia's picture in the heart', referring to Ziaul Haq); Shafiul Bashar *YB* No. 10: *hṛdaẏe muratī ā̃ki* ('I paint the figure in the heart' – *mūrti* being the term used for Hindu idols too); Abdul Jabbar Mimnagari *PR* No. 6: *nurī chabi hṛde ā̃kiba* ('I will paint the light-picture in the heart').
129 *JJ* No. 90: *ādamer kalabe dila kud'ruti āẏ'nā*; and *JJ* No. 4: *sāph haïbe diler āẏ'nā nūr badan heri*.
130 *RS* No. 73 (*sekāndarī āẏ'nā*).

So far, then, one gazes *into* the heart in order to gain spiritual insight and guidance. This changes when, thirdly, the heart itself is conceived not merely as the receptive medium of visualisations, but as an additional visual sense-organ. Peter Rahul Das (2003: 592) points out that the terms employed for the 'heart' may also denote the mind, and this seems to be the case here. Lying in a dormant state in usual humans, this 'eye of the heart'[131] has to be awakened in order to attain full sight: 'Upon the breaking open of the eye of the heart, he [the disciple, or man in general] sees bright light', and 'with the eye of the heart, the Mawlā beholds in his own pitcher [i.e. body or heart]' (Ramesh Shil).[132] A saint is capable of opening one's eye of the heart, as Abdul Gafur Hali states for Baba Maijbhandari (probably Gholam Rahman).[133] The heart, according to this notion, is simultaneously the locus of the act of seeing and of the projection that is beheld; the heart actively fetches its visual object and passively contains it at the same time.[134] This is well expressed in a song by Abdul Gafur Hali: 'I take a photograph with the camera of the heart [. . . of the friend and] keep it inside the heart'.[135] Subject and object of vision, we may interpret, merge in this process, and mystical union is achieved.

Finally, the heart is also conceived as an organ with great motive power and as an emotive organ of suffering. Ramesh Shil emphasises the former aspect by comparing the heart to a battery: 'The heart-battery is inside your body, the switch is in the hands of the Bhandari'.[136] Penances and unfulfilled love, on the other hand, can torture the heart and burn it: 'The heart burns in the fire of separation' (Abdul Gafur Hali),[137] and, more vividly: 'The heart has become roasted meat, the breast is burnt out' (Ramesh Shil).[138]

As we move on to the next, connected complex of motifs concerned with man, it is important to note certain patterns that will reappear in connection with other motifs. The microcosmic human heart is depicted as corresponding to the macrocosmic holy sites, personalities and scriptures. Its semantics oscillate between the most transcendental, quasi-divine part of the human being on the one hand, and

131 Cf. the Bible Eph. 1.18. The Arabic term *baṣīra* denotes the 'inner eye' or 'eye of the heart' and implies the spiritual, non-worldly perception of things. The heart does not figure as prominently in yogic ideas as in Sufic ones; it is sometimes listed as a separate *cakra*, but one of minor importance. The *trilocana* (third eye), on the other hand, is associated with the forehead and a completely different *cakra*. In the *Upaniṣad*s, however, the heart appears as the location of the *ātman* in the body (*Muṇḍaka-Upaniṣad* 2.2.7). The heart is also referred to as the *guhā*, 'cave', in the same sense (e.g. *Kaṭha-Upaniṣad* 1.2.12; 2.1.6; etc.). In these cases, the heart is the location of something to be seen, but not the organ of sight.

132 *ND* No. 33: *hṛder cakṣe āpan ghaṭe dekhe māolā*; and *ND* No. 2: *hṛdaẏer cakṣu phuṭe dekhe nur ujalā.*

133 *JJ* No. 16: (*bābā*) [. . .] *kholāẏ hṛdaẏ cakṣu*. Also Ramesh Shil *MD* No. 9.

134 Cf. Knysh (2000: 321): 'As the seat of divine knowledge, the heart is best suited of all human organs to become the arena of the "direct vision" of God (*mushāhada*).'

135 *TB* No. 30: *hṛdaẏer kyāmerā diẏā tul'chi phaṭo* [. . .] *rākh'chi tāre hṛd-mājhāre.*

136 *MD* No. 18: *hṛd beṭārī tor[a] dehe, śuc āche bhāṇḍārīr hāte.*

137 *TB* No. 39: *biraha āgune jvale hiẏā*. Cf. also Maulana Hadi *RS* No. 4 (U.): *sīna jal gayā hai* ('The heart has burnt down') or *RS* No. 71: *hiẏā dahe* ('The heart burns').

138 *BhM* No. 41: *kalijā kābāb hala, jvaliẏe gela sinā.*

the most vital and vulnerable part of the human emotive apparatus on the other. It is either seen as the true inside or self, or as the ultimate outside or other. This ambiguity is expressed in the contrasting notions of the 'full' heart as the abode of God, and the 'void' that is yet to be entered by the divine. Similar oscillation and ambiguity can be found in other mystical motifs, as we shall see.

5.7.2 Man

> Give up the worship of earthen idols and worship man.
> Seven continents and eighteen worlds are inside man.[139]
> (Ramesh Shil)

To be born as a human is considered a privilege. Maijbhandari songwriters sometimes refer to the Qur'anic accounts of the angels who had to bow before Adam (*Qur'ān* 7.11[10]; 15.29–30; 17.61[63]; 39.72–3),[140] and stress that man is the most excellent being of Allah's creation.[141] The central aspect of being a human is the notion that God dwells in the human heart; men ought to realise this and act accordingly, and beware of missing the whole point of human existence.[142] But men's nature is hybrid: *manuṣyatva*, humanness, is counteracted by *paśutva*, animality, or *jībatva*, bestiality, that equally determine human character; *nafsāniyya* is a factor just like *rūḥāniyya*.[143] Or, as Abdul Gafur Hali puts it: 'Non-man dwells in man; it takes a man to realise man.'[144] This line reveals some of the semantical diversification that this central motif has undergone in Maijbhandari ideas, and that we shall now try to unravel.

The terms used for man are *mānuṣ* and *ādam*. Adam and the true sons of Adam who are themselves Adam, writes Bajlul Karim, are not separate from God.[145] God resides within man,[146] and therefore, the authors suggest, the distinction between God and man is ultimately untenable. Abdul Gafur Hali, for example, addresses the *Mawlā* in this spirit and states: 'You are in the city of Adam'; but for a person making such statements, he hastens to add, 'there is no place in society, [and] he gets a *fatwa* for *kufr*'.[147] Man, as the container of God, has the universe inside himself,[148] and Farid Hosain goes so far as to say that *mānuṣe hay̆ āllā khodā/bicār kare sebā kara*, which probably translates as 'Man *is* Lord Allah/Consider it and

139 *JS* No. 25: *māṭir murttir pūjā chere* [*sic*] *mānuṣ pūjā kara/saptadvip āṭhāra ālam mānuṣer bhitar(a)*.
140 Ramesh Shil *ĀM* No. 23; Abdul Gafur Hali *JJ* No. 43; etc.
141 Farid Hosain *SB* No. 73 (*ei oy̆ārlḍe mānuṣ bhinna keha nāire śreṣṭha ār*: 'In this world none is superior to man'); *SB* No. 74 (*sr̥ṣṭir serā*: 'the most excellent of the creation').
142 Cf. Ramesh Shil *ĀM* 32; Abdul Gafur Hali *TB* 12; *JJ* 25; etc.
143 Cf. Ramesh Shil *ŚB* No. 23 (*paśutva*); Farid Hosain *SB* No. 30, 74 (*jībatva*); Badrunnesa Saju *Madirā* No. 9 (*naph'sāniy̆at*).
144 *TB* No. 27: *mānuṣe amānuṣ thāke mānuṣ cin'te mānuṣ lāge*.
145 *ŚJ* No. 5: *ādam'jādā ādam hale khodār theke judā nay̆*.
146 Ramesh Shil *JS* 25 (*mānuṣer bhitar nirañjan*).
147 *TB* No. 25: *ācha tumi ādam'pure*; and *samāje tār jāgā nāi/kāpheri phatoy̆ā pāy̆*.
148 Ramesh Shil *JS* 25; cf. opening quote.

render service [to him, i.e. man]'.[149] These statements, however, apply not to everybody, but to 'true' men (*āsal/khā̃ṭi mānuṣ*; *insān al-kāmil* is rarely used),[150] and such true men are rare indeed: 'One or two conscious men are found in millions' (Ramesh Shil).[151] Usual men are not conversant with their innermost essence, and the divine in them remains a dormant potentiality, whereas true men are conscious of their divine essence, and have subjugated their *nafs* completely. The Bhandari is one of these latter and a unique being, as Aliullah states: 'There are many men in the world, [but] there is nobody like Bābā'.[152] Through the contact with such men, 'men can become men', as the songs sometimes put it; that is, a true man can lead a common man towards true humanity. 'They became men by serving Bābā', relates Aliullah.[153] Bajlul Karim writes: 'If the offspring of Adam, after receiving the inspiration[154] of the *muršid*, become Adam, they sit in the form of Adam and speak by the mouth of God'.[155] Lutfunnesa Hosaini instructs her mind (*manā*) to go to her *pīr* and father Shafiul Bashar's Muʿmin Manzil in Maijbhandar in order to 'become man/human';[156] and for Ramesh Shil, becoming man means exploring oneself with the help of a perfect master (*kāmel pīr*).[157]

So far, then, there are at least two kinds of man: common, unrealised man (henceforce also 'person') on the one hand, and 'true', 'conscious', 'perfect' man on the other. In a semantical twist quite characteristic for Maijbhandari songs, however, the latter man is often referred to as a non-human or superhuman entity; though dressed in human shape, he is actually more than a mere man: 'In the disguise of man, a non-man has come into the society of man, and bestows grace inside the life breath through immateriality'[158] (Ramesh Shil). For Abdul Jabbar Mimnagari, he,

149 *SB* No. 30; *haẏ* is interpreted as the emphatic form of a nominal sentence which would read: *mānuṣe āllā khodā*; *mānuṣe* is analysed as an *e*-nominative. The sentence is, however, highly ambiguous, and a number of other translations are grammatically feasible. If we read *mānuṣe* as locative, we get: 'It is in man that Lord Allah *is* [or: comes into being]', which is another possible interpretation. *mānuṣe* could also be read as an instrumental case, and *haẏ* as 'becomes/comes into being': '*Ālla khodā* comes into being through man'; but given the context of Farid Hosain's works and Maijbhandari songs in general, this interpretation seems far-fetched. *Khodā* should be read as an apposition to *Āllā*; sentence order makes the rendering 'It is through man that Allah becomes God' seem very unlikely. It is grammatically possible, but hardly tenable in the context of Maijbhandari ideas.

150 The *pīr* is often described as *kāmel* (Ar. <*kāmil*>, 'attained, perfect'), but not man; maybe the expression *insān al-kāmil* is felt to be reserved for the Prophet. Likewise most probably for Shamsujjoha of Thakurgaon (cf. Siegfried [2001: 51n], where *kāmel* seems to be misinterpreted).

151 *JS* 25: *cetan mānuṣ koṭir madhye dui ek'jan mile* (*koṭi* lit. '10 Mio').

152 *PN* 30: *anek mānuṣ āche bhabe, bābār matan keha nāi.*

153 *PN* No. 30: *bābār khed'mat kari tārā, bani gela mānuṣ go.*

154 *taoẏājju*, Ar. <*tawağğuh*>.

155 *ŚJ* No. 5: *morśeder taoẏājju pele, ādam'jādā ādam hale, ādam(a) chūrate basi khodār mukhe kathā kaẏ.*

156 *GP* No. 30: *ore o abujh manā/abahelā ār karonā/mumin mañjil māij'bhāṇḍāre/mānuṣ hate yāonā.*

157 Ramesh Shil *SD* No. 26. The term *mānuṣ haoẏā* is primarily 'to grow up' in Bengali; in the instances discussed here, however, it is used in the sense of 'becoming a realised man/being'.

158 Ramesh Shil *MD* No. 32: *amānuṣ mānuṣer sāje, ese mānuṣer samāje/rūhānīte prāṇer mājhe, phaẏej kare dān. Prāṇ*, 'life-breath', is often rendered as 'heart' also; I will continue to differentiate the two in the present chapter, except in the compound *prāṇ bandhu*.

the saint, has merely taken on human form, but wears a divine dress; that is, he shares divine attributes and is a 'non-man'.[159] This twist can be accounted for by the semantic extension of the terms used for 'man' (*mānuṣ* and *ādam*), or, more generally, by the overarching function of the motif of 'man'. From the mundane angle, the saint represents an intrusion from another realm and is perceived as non-human, whereas from the soteriological angle, he is the one who fully lives up to the standard set for man and therefore qualifies as a 'true man'. These semantic complexities are readily taken up by song-authors in order to produce pseudo-paradoxes.[160] Both 'true man' or 'non-man', as it may be, refer mostly to the saints, and we shall discuss their identity and status in another context.[161]

If such a 'true' or 'non-man', no matter what his ultimate ontological status may be, can be conceptualised as belonging to the outer world and sharing the outer characteristics of the human species, the third type of 'man' recurring in Maijbhandari songs defies such conventionality. When terminologically marked, this third man is called *acin mānuṣ* or *maner mānuṣ* ('unknown man', 'man of the mind'), words familiar from the Baul tradition;[162] in most cases, however, simply *mānuṣ* is employed. This man is hidden inside the human body, and must be found or caught.

> First catch the man of the mind, catch the man of the mind/Throw off the burden of bestiality and take to the path of the man // Catch and worship the man/Search the man in man/There is none in this world except man/.[163]
>
> (Farid Hosain)

This man is the true object of worship. 'The man of the mind is at home', and it is of little use to look for him in mosques and temples; but also inside the body he is hard to find: 'Crazy Gafur is lost/Man is there, but cannot be caught/[And] plays hide and seek [. . .]' (Abdul Gafur Hali).[164] This interior man comes and goes on various paths, for example on the 'path of breath': 'The man always comes and goes/21,600 times /' (Ramesh Shil).[165]

159 Abdul Jabbar Mimnagari *PR* No. 10 (*khodāẏī lebāch*).

160 Cf. Abdul Gafur Hali *TB* No. 27; Bajlul Karim *ŚJ* No. 5; etc. The use of paradoxes, oxymorons and the like in mystical language is a widespread phenomenon in various traditions; for further remarks and references, see below in this chapter under 'Attributes of the Saints' (5.7.5).

161 Cf. p. 000 of this chapter under 'Attributes of the Saints' (5.7.5).

162 Cf. Rahul Peter Das (1992: 390): 'The macrocosmic principle (as a rule seemingly = life force = universal spirit/soul = creator) is present in the human body too. It is mostly described anthropomorphically, often as one of the chief male deities current in Bengal, though terms such as "man", "man of the mind", "golden man", "unobtainable man", etc. [. . .] are commoner.'

163 *SB* No. 30: *maner mānuṣ dhara āge maner mānuṣ dhara/jībatva bhār chāirā diẏā mānuṣ pathe gaman kara // mānuṣ dhaïrā mānuṣ bhaja/mānuṣe mānuṣ(a) khoja/mānuṣ chāṛā nāi ār keha e jagat mājār /.*

164 *JJ* No. 9: *maner mānuṣ gharei āche*; and: *gaphur pāg'lā diśehārā/āche mānuṣ deẏ nā dharā/kare lukocuri khelā* [. . .]. Cf. also another song by this author (*TB* No. 23): *ek mānuṣer duiṭā deha ek'ṭā yābe dharā/ār ek mānuṣ dharā kaṭhin yei mānuṣ haẏ piñjar chārā* ('One man has two bodies, one can be caught; another man is hard to catch, the man who is cageless'; the last clause may also be interpreted as 'as soon as the man leaves his cage').

165 The figure is meant per day, and Ramesh counts 15 respirations per minute.

In contrast to 'true man', this man is not resident in the human body, or at least not permanently; the man of the mind constantly moves around either inside the body or in and out of it. His relation to the person is one of non-identity and separation, and that with true man is one of union. To common man, he is something to be caught, whereas the accomplished, true man has already caught and assimilated him; it is one of the attributes of the saint that he has caught him. In fact, true man and the man of the mind can be regarded as the macrocosmic and the microcosmic aspect respectively of the same entity.

Like the motif of the heart, the motif of man is, on the one hand, a spatial category of the next-higher degree; man can be conceived as a location in which something happens. In this relation, the heart is a *pars pro toto* of man: once the divine inside the heart is constantly realised, man becomes true man and transcends personhood. The 'man of the mind', this man within man, on the other hand, seems to be of a different provenance. Rather than explaining its meaning with reference to the Baul term of *maner mānuṣ*, I propose to further examine it in the course of our discussion of some closely related motifs in the following. The first of these is that of the bird.

5.7.3 Bird

> How long have I been sitting
> Looking into your direction, O Shafi Baba,
> Had I caught the bird of the mind
> And tied it to the heart![166]
>
> (Lutfunnesa Hosaini)

The bird is a traditional metaphor for the soul. It occurs early in the Islamic tradition; a *Ḥadīṯ* speaks of 'green birds' in the sense of souls.[167] It reappears in the works of Sufi writers, namely ʿAttar, Rumi and Suhrawardi, in the same sense,[168] and runs through various Indian mystical traditions.[169] Referred to as *pākhi* (bird) and sometimes *maẏnā* (starling) in the Maijbhandari song tradition, this motif is closely related to the 'man of the mind', and it also is one more example of considerable semantic oscillation. The bird is basically an image of the innermost, essential part of human existence; like the 'true man' and the 'man of the mind', it is a link between the human and the divine, can be imagined as either present or absent and shares the intermediate position between self and other, inside and outside, that we could state for the 'man of the mind'.

166 *GP* No. 4: *katakāl(a) base āchi tomār pāne cāhiẏā – śaphibābā/man pākhīre rākh'tām dhare hṛdaye bā̃dhiẏā.*

167 A *Ḥadīṯ* related by Muslim, about the souls of the martyrs: '[. . .] Their souls are in the insides of green birds having lanterns suspended from the Throne, roaming freely in Paradise where they please, then taking shelter in those lanterns' (*Forty Hadith Qudsi*: 108). Also *ĀB*: 152 where certain sayings of Ahmadullah are set in relation to this utterance.

168 Cf. Schimmel (1995a: 71); *ER* II: 226 mentions Farid al-Din ʿAttar's use of the motive in his *Manṭiq al-ṭayr* and the commonplace Persian image of the nightingale (*bulbul*), representing the individual soul, in love with the rose (*gul*) as 'divine beauty'.

169 Cf., e.g., Edward O. Henry (1996: 236 f.) for the use of this motif in *bhajan*s of Eastern Uttar Pradesh.

First, the bird can be used in the traditional way as the soul or the mind of man. As such, it is the *prāṇ* ('life-breath') or also the *man* (Skt. <*manas*>, 'mind'). 'You are my golden[170] bird, and I am your cage/Where will you go when you leave me, O bumble-bee of my life-breath?' (Abdul Jabbar Mimnagari).[171] The human body thus is the container of the life-breath or soul. In a conflation of images, the bird can also steer the body as a boatman: 'If, O mind-bird, you see the city of light/Put the body-boat in water and pull up the anchor-stewart' (Shafiul Bashar).[172] It possesses a nature of light and, though itself of divine provenance, can suffer separation from the divine.[173] The soul's position in the body is sometimes conceived as captivity: Bajlul Karim addresses a divine *tumi* and prays: 'May Karim's bird of the life-breath/After dwelling in this cage of the body/Have the power to fly to your pair of feet //'.[174] Abdul Gafur Hali implores his bird not to build a nest in the hope of happiness: 'O bird, fly away/Spread your wings [and fly] far away/Do not be trapped/In this city of illusion //'.[175]

At the time of death, the bird is snatched from the body: 'When the time is over, *Saman*[176] will appear/[And] snatch the bird of the life-breath, the body will remain behind' (Maulana Hadi).[177] All worldly possessions must be given up: 'Car, house and beautiful woman – all will remain behind/If the bird is gone, it will not come, O mind'; and the bird is identical with *ruhu dhan*, the 'soul-treasure' (Ar. <*rūḥ*>).[178] Once the bird has broken its chains, it does not return.[179] A temporary leave takes place during sleep: '(O friend of the life-breath), when I am in sleep, I see you in my dreams/The bird of the mind does not stay in the cage' (Ramesh Shil).[180]

Secondly, the bird may stand for the (microcosmic) divine friend or lover, the saint or God. The bird plays inside the human body, comes and goes as it likes, and,

170 The text has *soẏā*, in all likelihood a misprint for *sonā*.

171 *PR* No. 7: *tuire āmār soẏā pākhi, āmire to'r piñjirā/āmāẏ cheṛe yābe kothā, ohe prāṇ(a) bhamarā.*

172 *YB* No. 44: *dekh'bi yadi man pākhī tui nūrer nagar/deha tarī dāo bhāsāẏe tule phel nāẏeb noṅgar.* Usually, it is the *man(a)mājhi* or 'mind-helmsman' who steers this 'body-boat'. Cf. below in this chapter.

173 Shafiul Bashar *YB* No. 40.

174 *ŚJ* No. 34: *karimer(a) prāṇ(a) pākhi/e dehapiñjare thāki/uṛe yete pāẏ(a) yena tomār caraṇ'dvaẏ(a).*

175 *JJ* 98: *ore pākhi yāre uṛe/ḍānā mele bahu dūre/ei māẏā nagare – phānde paṛis nā.* The structure of this verse is a rather long *tripadī*: 8 – 8 – 13; the dash after *nagare* seems to indicate a missing syllable. – The old image of bird and cage is commonplace in various *bhakti* traditions. It can also be encoded differently, as we see in the following verse by Kabir (the 'you' referring to Rām, i.e. here the highest divinity): 'You are the cage and I your parrot –/And that cat, Death, can do nothing to me.' Vaudeville (1993: 271).

176 For *Śaman*, the messenger of death; cf. below (p. 000) 5.7.4.

177 *RB* No. 8: *samaẏ yakhan phurāibe saman āsi dekhā dibe/kāṛi nibe prāṇa pākhi paṛi rabe tan(a).*

178 Abdul Gafur Hali *JJ* No. 100: *gāṛi, bāṛi, sundar nārī – sakal kichu raïbe paṛi –/gele pākhī āibanā phiriẏā re manoẏā.* The initial words could of course also be translated in the plural.

179 Cf. Abdul Gafur Hali *JJ* No. 99 (*śikal kāṭi gele pākhi*).

180 *MD* No. 26: *(prāṇ bandhure) yakhan āmi ghume thāki, svapane tomāre dekhi/man(a) pākhī thāke nā piñjare.* Cf. Chapter 3 (sleep as 'little death'). The notion that the soul leaves the body during sleep is old and widespread; for graphical representations from different cultures (European, Indian, Chinese) cf. Coxhead/Hiller 1976.

like the 'man of the mind', must be caught. 'O gold-coloured bird of light! How, O bird, do you come and go?/Living in the house of earth, you hide and engage me in play' (Farid Hosain).[181] Later in this song, the bird is identified as a *maẏ'nā* (parakeet) which is, in this case, an indication that Farid Hosain's *muršid* Delawar Hosain is meant.[182] The bird may hide or disappear altogether, and its vanishing is often deplored in the songs: 'To which wood has my tamed bird escaped? It was in the cage in the evening, but I do not see it in the morning' (Abdul Gafur Hali);[183] 'I gave my heart to it/[But] at the time of leaving the cruel bird/Did not think of me';[184] and Farid Hosain gazes into the 'empty vessel' of his body and complains:

> When I do not find you at home/I am no longer myself/The empty vessel lies on the ground/[I] cannot carry on without you/You are my parrot-parakeet/ Always stay voluntarily.[185]

Hunters everywhere try to get hold of that bird: 'I have not seen a beautiful bird like you in the world/All hunters wander around in order to catch you'.[186] It is essential to catch the bird before death: 'Catch the bird before leaving, for otherwise there is no rescue this time' (Abdul Gafur Hali).[187] Once caught, the bird is to be locked up inside the body or, preferably, the heart; but even this is not safe, and at the time of need, it may be found lacking: 'The Mawlā is the bird of my life-breath/I keep him in the cage of my heart/He betrayed me in time of need' (Ramesh Shil).[188]

In another variant by Abdul Gafur Hali, by contrast, the bird must be set free, and the theme of captivity reappears; but in contrast to the examples mentioned above, the bird leaving the cage is not equated with death, but rather conceived as a temporary condition. The bird as the mind has to sit in the 'room of *yoga*' with a female beloved (*priẏā*) and achieve sexual union. This necessitates the release of the bird: 'I will set free the mind-bird/Let me play a game with the female beloved/It will come back if it knows its home'.[189] The idea here seems to be that the captivity of the bird limits human opportunities to interact with the (divine?) opposite; the release of the bird may be interpreted as a temporary abandonment of personhood necessary for spiritual union.

181 *SB* No. 48: *sonār baran nūrer pākhīre – pākhī kemane āsa yāo/māṭir ghare bās kariẏā lukiẏā khelāo re*.

182 Cf. also Abdul Gafur Hali *JJ* No. 82, in which the bird is identified with Ziaul Haq.

183 *JJ* No. 87: *kon bane palāiẏā gela āmār poṣā pākhī/sandhyāẏ(a) piñjare chila sakāle nā dekhi*.

184 *idem*, No. 61: *tāre dilām hṛdaẏ'khāni go/yāibār kāle niṭhur pākhī –/āmār kathā nā bhābila*.

185 *SB* No. 66: *ghare yakhan tomāẏ pāi nā/āmi ār āmār thāki nā/khālī bhāṇḍa thāke māṭhe pare* [i.e. *paṛe*]/*tomāẏ chāṛā calā yāẏ nā/tumi āmār totā maẏ'nā/thāka sadāẏ āpan icchā bale //*.

186 Farid Hosain *SB* No. 48: *tomār mata sundar pākhī dekhinā saṃsāre/sab śikārī ghure beṛāẏ dharite tomāre*.

187 *JJ* No. 92: *yāibār āge dhara pākhī/naïle eibār rakṣā nāi*. 'This time' (*eibār*) probably indicates the belief in rebirth.

188 *BhM* No. 38: *māolā āmār prāṇ(a) pākhi/hṛdaẏ(a) piñjare rākhi/asamaẏe dila phā̃ki* [. . .].

189 *JJ* No. 69: *man pākhire diba chāṛi/kheli khelā priẏār sane*. A full translation of this song is given in Appendix 1.

Like the motif of man, the bird too does not strictly stick to the singular, and it may occasionally multiply. Aliullah, in a song on the intoxicating effects of the fire of love, states: 'Two birds of the cage went away, what will you understand if the life-breath dies/Try as long as there is time, do not move carelessly'.[190] The two birds possibly denote two Maijbhandari saints: the deceased Ahmadullah and Gholam Rahman who wandered in the forests; but there is no way to be certain. Abdul Gafur Hali addresses the 'bird of the life-breath' (*prāṇ pākhī*) and deplores its vanishing from the cage of the heart. 'O bird, crazy Gafur says after considering/This bird is not that bird/Those who know this bird are supremely happy'.[191] Here, the non-identity of two birds is asserted, and this may refer to the bird as 'merely' the human life-breath ('that bird') on the one hand, and the bird as the Divine inside man ('this bird') on the other. But again, the text remains enigmatic.

Without solving such riddles, we can nonetheless venture to state that the motifs of man and the bird have undergone similar processes of semiosis. In both cases, a denominator (man = mere human) or conventional metaphor (bird = human soul) are transposed to new levels of meaning (man = perfect man or divine/beloved inside man; bird = divine/beloved inside man). Conventional and new meanings can then be contrasted and combined within the respective terms, and if set against one another, paradoxes can be produced that refer the listener to a realm of secret knowledge, instruction and experience lying *behind* the words. The Maijbhandari idiom, like mystical language in general, observes a certain ratio between information revealed and information retained, and one of the latter's functions is precisely the reference to a world behind or beyond the words.[192]

However, as we have seen, the bird, in its most traditional sense, denotes the soul or life-breath, and this basic meaning invariably runs through the semantic ramifications discussed above. The bird as one's life-breath is the essence of life; its presence or absence indicates more or less temporary states of life and death. In this sense, it is intrinsically connected with death and figures as one part of the complex of motifs we shall now investigate.

5.7.4 Death

> How many lunatics are there who die before dying?[193]
> (Abdul Gafur Hali)

Death is mostly envisaged as a passage over the river separating the earthly realm from the realm beyond. After leaving the body, the soul requires help and guidance to reach the other shore safely. A common epithet of the Maijbhandari saints is *dui kuler kāṇḍārī*, 'helmsman of the two shores'.[194] The saint is conceived as an

190 *PN* No. 23: *piñjarār pākhi duṭi gela, bujh'bi ki prāṇ maïle, din thākite ceṣṭā kara, nā calio helāẏ 2 //*

191 *JJ* No. 22: *o pākhī re – gaphur pāg'lā bhābi kaẏ/ei pākhī sei pākhī naẏ/pākhī yārā cine param sukhī.*

192 This point will be elaborated in connection with *dehatattva* texts (5.7.13 and 14; 6.1).

193 *JJ* No. 5: *marār āge mare eman pāgal kaẏ janā*. Cf. *VG*: 79 f. for a complete German translation of this song.

194 Cf. Aliullah, *PN* No. 24; Farid Hosain *HB* No. 34; etc.

intermediary between those two realms; he is at home simultaneously on both shores (has his 'feet on both sides') and is thus an apt guide at the moment of transition that is death. The saint may also be viewed as the ferryman who takes the souls over the river, and a number of songs describe the poor passenger who waits for the ferry to take him and is deeply worried whether he will be able to pay the passage: 'In the evening I sit and cry at the crossing quay/How will I go to that shore? I do not have money for the passage' (Abdul Gaphur Hali).[195] Another image that is often conflated with this passage over the river of death is that of the 'ocean of existence' (*bhabasāgar*); the saints equally offer help in crossing the perilous stretch of water that is earthly existence.[196]

ʿIzrāʾīl, the angel of death in Islamic mythology, or Yama, the Hindu god of death, called by his epithet *śaman* (Skt. *śamana*, 'the slayer'), feature especially in the songs of Maulana Hadi and Farid Hosain as the merciless executors of death.[197] 'Śamana shall come and tie (you) fast, he will not pay heed to shouts and imploratings/He will grasp the soul firmly, he will not leave it' (Farid Hosain);[198] 'When the time is consumed, Śamana will come and show himself/He will snatch away the bird of the life-breath, the body will remain behind' (Maulana Hadi).[199] But inevitable as death may seem, there is all the same a way of shielding off the God of Death: '[From him] who has a guru, Śamana flees far out of fear'; 'If he sees the shape of the *pīr* and guru, that rascal Śamana goes away' (Farid Hosain).[200] As narrated in Maijbhandari hagiographies, too,[201] the spiritual preceptor is stronger than the God of Death and capable of freeing his disciple from his hands. The concept of death, then, undergoes a distinction here; Yama/Śamana is responsible for only one kind of death, which transfers the bodiless soul to the underworld (Skt. *yamaloka*) of (Hindu) mythology; whereas 'proper' death implies the passing over to serene heavenly shores with the guidance of the *pīr*.

Another image that features in Maijbhandari songs, but especially in the songs of these two authors, is the Last Judgment on the 'field of assembly' (*hāśar maẏ'dān*, from Ar. <*mīdān al-ḥašr*>). The Qurʾanic concept is that on this final day,[202] the trombone is blown, and the souls of the deceased re-enter their former

195 *JJ* No. 12. Cf. also Abdul Jabbar Mimnagari *PR* No. 30.

196 We will deal with these topics in detail below in this chapter, in the section on boat journeys.

197 *Śamana* is often spelled as *saman*, which also represents the Bengali form of English *summons*; in a number of songs the interpretation 'call to the court of judgment' is also possible and may even be intended.

198 *SB* No. 26: *ās'be saman* [i.e. *śaman*] *bā̃dh'be kaṣe ḍāk dohāi nā mānibe se/ruhukhānāẏ dhar'be kaṣe cheṛe yābe nā.*

199 *RB* No. 8 as quoted above (5.7.3). Cf. also *RB* No. 7 (here the reference is to *yamadūt*, 'Yama's messenger'); Ramesh Shil *BhM* No. 11 (ʿIzrāʾīl); Abdul Gafur Hali *JJ* No. 11 (with reference to Munkar – Munkar and Nakīr being the helpers of death; cf. the *Encyclopedia of Islam* article on *Ḳiyāma* by L. Gardet [Gardet 1986]), and *JJ* No. 100 (Śamana).

200 *SB* No. 61 and 67: *yāhār āche gurudhan/bhaẏe dūre yāẏ saman*; and *pīr gurur churit* [Ar./P. *ṣūra*(*t*)] *dekhile saman beṭāẏ yāẏ re cale*.

201 Cf. e.g. *Āʾīna-i Bārī*: 215 ff. (Chapter 5); *Jībanī o kerāmat*: 144 ff.; etc.

202 This time is called by various names in the *Qurʾān*: *qiyāma*, *yaum al-ḥašr* ('Day of the Assembly'), *yaum al-dīn* ('Day of the Trial'), etc.; cf. Gardet (1986).

bodies to appear on the field of assembly in front of Allah's throne, and are weighed. The deeds (*ʿamal*), enlisted in individual books, are evaluated. The light ones are sent to hell (*ǧahannam*) and the heavy ones to heaven (*ǧanna*).[203] A prominent non-Qurʾanic addition to this scenario is the *ṣirāṭ*, the narrow bridge leading to heaven over the abyss of hell.[204] This scenery is elaborated upon in the songs, and the basic idea is that the saint will be present at that time to protect his disciples. The saint leads his disciples over the narrow bridge.[205] Maulana Hadi proclaims that he has no need for the joys of heaven and, when facing heaven, will not stare at the upper storeys where the heavenly virgins (*ḥūrī*) reside: 'Under your protection is the place of the servants/On the lawn of *ḥašr*, with the file in the hands/I will dance and recite ghazals, intoxicated by your trance'.[206] Dancing and singing enraptured by the saint's presence is typical for Hadi's depictions of the Day of Judgment.[207] In one of his songs, the dancers become females: 'What will we do when the day of *ḥašr* is there?/We will see the master of the three worlds sitting on the throne/Everybody will join in a session [*hāl'kā*, Ar. <*ḥalqa*>] and become female dancers while dancing/And surrounding [them] on all sides, there will be the Ġawṯ al-Aʿẓam Maijbhandar'.[208] The Mawlā, refering either the Ġawṯ or God, will grant his sight: 'In the assembly, O female companions, you will attain the Mawlā's sight',[209] and the Day of Judgment is pictured as a game of love with him: 'I will play the game of love with you in the assembly'.[210]

If a death under the protection of the saint is the aim of the bulk of Maijbhandari disciples, there is, however, still another kind of death of a completely different order. This best death of all is the one in life, the 'death before death'. This notion looms large in various ancient and contemporary religious traditions not only of South Asia, and plays a significant role in the Bengali Baul mysticism.[211] In a Sufi context, too, precedents are legion, for instance in Rumi's

203 Cf. *Qurʾān* 23.101(103)–103(105); 36.51–54.

204 According to *EI*, '*Kiyāma*' (Gardet 1986), the *ṣirāṭ* is mentioned only once in the *Qurʾān* as the *ṣirāṭ al-ǧaḥīm*; but the bridge over hell soon became a common Islamic notion. The *pul-i ṣirāṭ* in the sense of a bridge over hell is originally a Zoroastrian notion.

205 Cf. Ramesh Shil *SD* No. 9.

206 *RB* No. 17: *tomār(a) dāmān(a) tale, dāsagaṇer(a) ṭhikānā // hāśarer(a) maẏ'dānete daptar(a) laïẏā hāte/nāciba gajal(a) paṛe, tor bhābete mastānā.*

207 Cf. also *RS* No. 15, 19.

208 *RS* No. 11: *ye din(a) hāsar(a) habe, ām'rā ki kariba tabe/ārśve basi dekhi rabe trijagater karatār(a)/hāl'kā bandi kari sabe nācite nāṭakī habe/caudike beṛiẏā rabe gāūche ājam māij bhāṇḍār*. On the devotee's becoming female, cf. below (p. 251) in this chapter.

209 *RS* No. 89: *hāśarete sakhigan, pābe māolār daraśan.*

210 *RS* No. 15: *kheliba premer(a) khelā taba saṅge hāsarete*. Also *RS* No. 19.

211 Cf. Das (1992: 389); Slaje (2000) on *jīvanmukti*, liberation while living; the connection between *jīvanmukta* and *jīvanmṛta* comes out in Kabir; in Charlotte Vaudeville's paraphrase, 'he who wishes to be a *jīvanmukta*, "one liberated whilst living", must, of necessity, be a *jīvanmṛta*, "one dead while alive"' (Vaudeville 1992: 105).

Ma̱snavī.[212] The concept also appears in pre-modern Bengali Muslim literature.[213] It is considered one of the signs of saints, *awliyāʿ*, to be *jyānta marā*, 'living-dead'. As we have seen, this topic is also part of the theological elaborations of Maijbhandari doctrines, and certainly a connection can be drawn between it and the four types of death included in the Sevenfold Method (*saptapaddhati*) of the Ahmadiya and Haq Manzils.[214] In short, to be living-dead means to have completely parted with one's earthly, human impulses; to have lastingly overcome the evil influence of one's *nafs*, 'base soul'; or to have vanquished one's senses, so as to dwell constantly in divine bliss even while still on this earth. Conceived as a mark of saintly religious virtuousness, this death is, however, equally upheld as an aim for simple devotees.

The first Maijbhandari songwriter to mention this death before death is Aliullah Rajapuri: In a song describing the might of the sun, 'God's engine',[215] the devotee-listeners are asked to 'become terrific, become terrific, [and] die before death'.[216] After him, Ramesh Shil uses the concept quite frequently. 'Servant (*khādem*, Ar. <*ḫādim*>) Ramesh says, there is no death at any time for a person revering the guru/If he dies before dying, does one still call that death?'[217] Single-minded devotion to one's guru, according to this song, leads to the annihilation of the earthly ingredients of the self. And such a death defies death itself; a paradox the writers exploit again and again: 'He who has immersed himself in love, the one dead of love, has died and become deathless before [death]' (Ramesh Shil).[218] In another song, it is true love with the 'friend' that ensures death before death: 'Those who have made love with him/Die before dying/[And] go to the deathless city/Ramesh

212 Cf. *Ma̱snavī* I, 2842: *āb-i dariyā murda rā bar sar nehad/war būd zenda ze dariyā key rahad* ('The water of the sea takes the dead on its top, but if he is living, when can he escape the sea?'). Rumi explains in the following verse that a 'dead' is one who has killed his human attributes (*auṣāf-i bašar*). Schimmel (1995a: 156) mentions the notion of dying before dying in the context of the narration of Sassi in the western subcontinent: 'Schah ʿAbdul Latif lehrt seine Heldin das alte Motto der Sufis: "Sterbt, bevor ihr sterbt", denn sie muß wissen, daß "diejenigen, welche sterben, bevor sie sterben, nicht sterben, wenn sie sterben".'

213 Cf., e.g., a song by the probably eighteenth-century poet Syed Ainuddin in Abdul Karim Sahityabisharad (1997: 165): *jīban(a) thākite yadi pāra maribār(a)/tabe kāl(a) yam(a) honte bhaẏ(a) nāhi ār(a)* ('If you can die while you have this life/Then there is no fear of Kāla and Yama anymore.').

214 Cf. Chapter 3.7.

215 Cf. *PN* No. 100: *khodār iñjil*; typing error for *iñjin*.

216 Ibid: *bhaẏaṅkar hao /2/ mṛtyur āge mara*. Etymologically, 'terrific' matches *bhaẏaṅkar* well, and both, applied to humans, sound similarly unusual, too.

217 Ramesh Shil *ĀM* No. 8: *khādem rameśe bale gurubhakta loker maraṇ nāi kono kāle/mar'bār āge mariẏa gele tāre ki ār maraṇ kaẏ*.

218 *ŚB* No. 19: *ye jan preme majeche premer marā mare āge amar haẏeche*; I have understood *premer marā* an apposition to the subject, lit. 'the one dead of love'. The syntax of this verse is not clear, but the above translation is the most probable reading. Cf. also another, related song by Ramesh Shil (*JS* No. 27): 'Those who love secretly [and] die before death/Can attain [him], says Rameś, if their heart is open' (*gopan prem(a) yārā kare, maraṇer(a) āge mare/rameś kaẏ se pete pāre, hṛdaẏ thāk'le kholā*). Here, the relative pronoun *yārā* (plural) is taken up by singular *se*.

[says:] I had the inner hope of dying alive.'[219] Other than these songwriters, Abdul Gafur Hali stresses that the attainment of death before death is indeed rare and marks off the saints from common people: 'Those who are friends of Allah[220]/Are living dead in the world/They master the *yoga* by burning the soul'.[221] Full vision of the Maijbhandari saints grants such a privilege even to common devotees: 'Those who are watching the "own form" [*svarūp*] of the Mawlā/Are immortal after dying';[222] but that vision is hard to attain, and the number of the truly living-dead is very small: 'How many lunatics are there who die before dying?'[223]

Alongside such conceptual usages, the term 'dead while living' can, however, be used in a non-technical way as well. Ramesh Shil himself uses it that way on one occasion: 'Such a torture of love/[My] life has passed by crying, [now I have] death while living'. Here, 'death while living' is not more than an expression of suffering due to separation, in a typical *bhakti* context. Farid Hosain, too, conveys utter emotional fatigue when he says: 'Burning in the fire of your love, I was living dead and died'.[224] The ambivalence of death is thus not removed in the songs. Even the concept of death before death remains unfixed, being employed in its technical and common-sense meanings alike. The saints are viewed as the saviours from death; they are beyond and above death. As regards death before death, they are either its privileged possessors or its inducers and mediators. In any way, they play *the* crucial role in all of the ways Maijbhandari song-authors think about death. We shall now try to explore the attributes of these masters over death in the popular idiom of Maijbhandari songs a little further.

5.7.5 Attributes of the saints

> In severe danger, O father/Save [us], O Qibla Kaʿba.[225]
> (Bajlul Karim)

We have already noted some of the characteristics of Maijbhandari saints as conceived by the songwriters. They are frequently addressed as friend, spiritual preceptor, father, helmsman, merciful guru and beloved; they can take their abode in the disciple's heart and are implored to do so; they open the heart and the eye of the heart; they are sometimes imagined as the bird that comes and goes in the cage of the heart or body, or the man inside man that is so hard to catch; they further dwell on both sides of the line dividing this from the other world; and they have died before death and

219 *JS* No. 30: *tār sane prem kare yārā/mar'bār āge mare tārā/yāẏ* [misspelt as *ẏār*] *amarā pure/rameś jībanta maribār āśā chila antare*.

220 *JJ* No. 23: *āllār āuliẏā*.

221 ibid: *āllar(a) āuliẏā yārā/duniẏāte jindā marā/ātmā pure* [i.e. *puṛe*] *kare yog sādhan*.

222 *JJ* No. 39: *māolār svarūp dekh'che yārā/mariẏā amar(a) tārā*.

223 Cf. above (beginning of the section on death).

224 *SB* No. 7: *tomār premāgune puṛi jindā marā gelām mari*. Cf. the following sentence from the late nineteenth-century actress Binodinī's autobiography for an example of the non-technical, conversational sense of the Bengali words for 'living dead': 'That huge, cool tree was the refuge for this living-dead condition of mine' (*sei subiśāl suśītal tarui āmār ei jībanmṛta abasthār āśraẏ sthān*).

225 *ŚJ* No. 14: *biṣam(a) bipade bābā/rakṣā kara keb'lā kābā*.

thereby achieved immortality. And, as we are to see further in this chapter, the saints are also incarnations of the divine, great cosmic players, artisans inside man, bridges between different religions, and so on. The figures of the saints being of utmost centrality to Maijbhandari religious experience as its focus and object of praise and contemplation, it is little wonder that the saints appear in multiple guises and functions, and that, consequently, they reappear in almost all the motifs of Maijbhandari songs we are discussing here. Therefore, I concentrate here on such motifs connected with the saints as are not primarily dealt with in other parts of this examination; most of them are highly conventional and commonplace, so that – more than the other motifs explored – they represent the very mainstream of Maijbhandari songwriting.

Very basically, the Maijbhandari[226] is seen as the saviour (*tārak*, *paritrātā*) from all kinds of evil and danger. This includes help on the Day of Judgment, as we have seen in the preceding section, but also almost any other kind of human predicament. In the songs, this is usually expressed in very general terms; they rarely relate specific instances of saintly helpful intervention, but rather stress the general, all-encompassing nature of his capacity for rescuing. The saint can save the disciple from his inner foes;[227] he can rescue him from drowning in the 'ocean of existence' (*bhabasindhu*)[228] and save the sinners of the *kali* age.[229] His love can save one's soul.[230] He has come to the world expressly for the purpose of rescuing downfallen humanity[231] and freeing the beings of the world.[232] The saint's willingness to save can, however, not be taken for granted, and he is very commonly implored to be merciful and consider the respective author's 'case'. It is man's responsibility to call out to him,[233] and Bajlul Karim does so on behalf of mankind in times of rage and decay: 'In severe danger, O father/Save [us], O Qibla Ka'ba'.[234] Another related and very common function of the saint is that of a pathfinder and guide (*diśārī*). The disciple has lost his way (*diśehārā*) and become enmeshed in the world;[235] he asks the saint to show him the right path[236] or to take the helm for him.[237] Similarly, the disciple, lost in darkness, asks the saint to shed light so as to enable him to find the way: 'Going on an unknown path/I forget the direction and lose orientation/Show me with the lamp/The right place' (Mahbubul Alam).[238]

226 For the convenience of this section, I use this name as a collective singular here. In the songs, such unspecified reference to 'the (Maij-)Bhandari' is quite commonplace.

227 Badrunnesa Saju *Madirā* No. 23; Farid Hosain *SB* No. 11; Maulana Hadi *RB* No. 16.

228 Ramesh Shil *ŚB* No. 8.

229 Ramesh Shil *SD* No. 17; Maulana Hadi *RB* No. 38.

230 Aliullah *PN* No. 109.

231 Ramesh Shil *ĀM* No. 30; Abdul Gafur Hali *JJ* No. 13.

232 Abdul Gafur Hali *JJ* No. 46.

233 Abdul Gafur Hali *JJ* No. 72.

234 *ŚJ* No. 14: *biṣam(a) bipade bābā/rakṣā kara keb'lā kābā.*

235 Cf. Abdul Gafur Hali MS 7/2/98: *gaphur hālī diśehārā bhebe pāinā kul'kinārā* ('Gafur Hali is lost, I cannot think of a stronghold [lit. 'shore']).

236 Cf. Badrunessa Saju *Madirā* No. 21.

237 e.g. Farid Hosain *HB* No. 34.

238 *AJ* 18: *acin pathe cal'te giẏā/hārāi diśā dik bhuliẏā/dekhāo more cerāg niẏā/āsal ṭhikānā.* Cf. also Badrunnesa Saju *Madirā* No. 23; etc.

Besides evoking the Maijbhandari's personality *in toto*, certain other perceptional figures are used to refer to him. The most prevalent among these is that of the saint's feet (*pad*, *caraṇ*, *kadam*). We have noticed that the saint's feet are an object of veneration in devotional practice; it occurs in the form of (P.) *qadambūsī*, 'feet-kissing', in Sufi contexts, but is equally present in Hindu *bhakti* traditions, and notably Bengali Gaudiya Vaishnavism, where *padasevā*, the worship at the feet of the deity (or the guru), is an established observance.[239] In the songs, the feet of the Maijbhandari are sought as the ultimate refuge of the devotee and, once found, remove all worries; the devotee becomes addicted to them and cherishes them more than gems.[240] They are the touchstone that transforms the disciple's heart into gold; they show the way to the prophet and to God, etc.[241] One can secure one's salvation by tying one's boat (i.e. the body, implying of course also the mind/soul) to the saint's feet. Further, in a conflation with the notion of the saint ferrying the disciple across, the saintly feet themselves become a boat in the conventional image of the *caraṇ'tarī*, 'the boat of the feet'.[242] The dust (*dhulā*) and even the mud (*kādā*) of the saint's feet are seen as purified substances utterly beneficial for the devotee.[243]

It is also beneficial to catch the Maijbhandari's glance (*dr̥ṣṭi*, *najar* <Ar. *naẓar*>).[244] Such a glance takes only a single moment and is capable of making one forget all concerns of everyday life.[245] It is enough to take the disciple across the 'river of existence' (*bhabanadī*),[246] it tears apart the veils of his heart,[247] and it makes stones melt.[248] So the saint is frequently implored to look at the disciple, as in an Urdu song by Maulana Hadi: 'O cup-bearer (*sāqī*), give me juice to drink,

239 Cf. Klostermaier (1990: 214); Dimock (1966: 46 ff.). Sanyal (1996: 146) quotes Ahmad Riza of Bareilly who addresses 'Abd a-Qadir Gilani in a verse: 'Who is to know what your head looks like/as the eye level of other saints corresponds to the sole of your foot'. For a generalised statement on the importance of feet in the religious imagery of the Indian subcontinent, see Kripal (1995: 201): '[. . .] feet are the sacred meeting point of the human and the divine in Indian culture. They are the "bridge" that unites the world of the gods and the world of human beings. Accordingly, that which is lowest on the body of God or the guru (who embodies God for the devotee) is the very highest that humanity [. . .] can ever hope to reach: at the sacred feet, the highest of the low may touch the lowest of the high.'

240 Cf. already Aliullah *PN* No. 18 and 4.

241 Examples of this imagery in Maijbhandari songs are legion and used by all authors. I would estimate that almost half of the songs use this feet motif. Cf., for some examples: Badrunnesa Saju *Madirā* No. 13; Ramesh Shil *ĀM* No. 17: *SD* No. 3; *ŚB* No. 35; Farid Hosain *SB* No. 13; Maulana Hadi *RB* No. 26; *RS* No. 11–15, 66; Shafiul Bashar *YB* No. 9, 50; Lutfunnesa Hosaini *GP* No. 25; Aliullah *PN* almost passim, esp. No. 1, 4, 8, 9, 11, 16, 18, 54, 74, 88.

242 e.g. Abdul Jabbar Mimnagari *PR* No. 29; Maulana Hadi *RS* No. 66.

243 e.g. Aliullah *PN* No. 78; Shafiul Bashar *YB* No. 9.

244 Cf. Schimmel (1995: 412); here, however, with reference to Iran and India, *naẓar* is taken to denote the disciple's beholding the saint. In Maijbhandari songs, this is usually expressed by the term *dīdār*, not *najar*.

245 Cf. Ramesh Shil *ĀM* No. 2.

246 Cf. Abdul Jabbar Mimnagari *PR* No. 8.

247 Cf. Ramesh Shil *BhM* No. 6.

248 Abdul Jabbar Mimnagari *PR* No. 2.

please look into my direction'.[249] Gholam Rahman in particular is famous for the transforming power of his glance, and communication with his disciples takes place by the wink of an eye.[250] But rather than conceiving of the saint as the active looker, the majority of songs stress the disciple's beholding of the saint: the saint has to grant *dīdār* (P.) or *darśan*, 'sight, vision'; that is, he has to show himself (*dekhā deoẏā*) to the disciple in his true form. Such vision is hard to achieve,[251] and Maulana Hadi, in another Urdu song, modifies his metaphor to ask the saint to show himself: 'Let me drink the juice of vision'.[252] If this vision is not granted during one's lifetime, the saint is implored to appear at least at the time of death.[253] Attaining such vision can be coterminous with salvation. It is linked to meditation; concentrating on the picture of the guru reveals the hidden form: 'When you shall see the hidden form/You will become crazy by seeing [it]/Having become a perfect man/You will then understand the secret of *anā 'l-ḥaqq*'.[254]

The saint's glance and feet are full of light (*nūr*, *jyoti*, *ālo*), another general characteristic of the saints as depicted in the songs.[255] God's light, according to many Bengali Sufi cosmologies the origin of creation,[256] dwells in Maijbhandar;[257] and the Maijbhandari saints are 'puppets of light' (*nūrer putul*).[258] They dwell 'in a bed of light, in a garden of light under the moon of light' (Ramesh Shil),[259] and because of them 'the whole world is bright' (Aliullah).[260] They must enlighten the disciple's mind like the electric bulb in a dark room.[261]

249 *RS* No. 1 (Urdu in Bengali script): *śarbbat pelāde chākiẏā mere taraph'ko dekhanā <šarbat pilā dē sāqiyā, mērē taraf kō dēkh na>*. The *sāqī* is the cup-bearer and divine beloved of Persian Sufi poetry.

250 Cf. Ramesh Shil *JS* No. 38: *ālāp(a) haẏ naẏan koṇe* ('Conversation takes place at the corner of the eye').

251 Cf. Badrunnesa Saju *Madirā* No. 51.

252 *RS* No. 2 (Urdu in Bengali script): *muje sarbbate didvār pelā dao <mušhē šarbat-i dīdār pilā dō>*.

253 Cf. Abdul Gafur Hali *JJ* No. 54.

254 Abdul Gafur Hali *JJ* No. 41: *bāteni rūp dekh'bi yakhan/dekhe pāgal habi/(tui) siddha mānuṣ haïẏā takhan/ānal'haker bhed bujhibi*. Ar. *anā 'l-ḥaqq*, 'I am Divine Truth', is the famous dictum of Manṣur al-Ḥallāğ. For meditation on and visualisation of the saint/God, cf. also Ramesh Shil *ŚB* No. 15.

255 Cf. the titlepage of *Belāẏate mot'lākā* where Maijbhandar is symbolised by a candle shedding its light on the whole eastern hemisphere.

256 Cf. Chapter 3.2.

257 Aliullah *PN* No. 99 (p. 90).

258 The image was probably coined by Ramesh Shil. Cf. Ramesh Shil *ND* No. 6, 33; *ĀM* No. 9; Abdul Gafur Hali *JJ* No. 56; Shafiul Bashar *YB* No. 8; Lutfunnesa Hosaini *GP* No. 16. The ambivalence of the term *putul* reminds one of similar ambivalences in other motifs, since first and foremost, the puppets must be understood as the common men who are set into motion *ad libitum* by a divine puppet-player, namely the saint or God; and it is only on a secondary level that the saint himself may be regarded as a (completely different kind of) puppet, possibly implying that his outer form is illusionary.

259 *ĀM* No. 18 (Urdu in Bengali script): *nur'kā pālaṃ me nur'kā gālichā nur'kā cā̃doẏā tale*.

260 Aliullah *PN* No. 1 (*saẏāl saṃsār rośan*).

261 Badrunnesa Saju *Madirā* No. 23: *ā̃dhār ghare bidyut·bāti ye rūp ālo jvālāẏ/āmār mane teman suyog tomā hate cāi*. Cf. also Shafiul Bashar *YB* No. 20.

The name of the saint likewise stands for the saint's personality. This idea is closely related to the practices of *nāmasmaraṇa*, the 'remembering of the name' so prominent in *bhakti* and Sikh traditions, and *ḏikr* in the Sufi tradition. Underlying both is the notion that the divine name in itself has a salutory effectiveness. Calling it in the right way can save one from mischief and death: 'Lovingly say Ġawṯ al-Aʿẓam everybody/You will cross over by virtue of the name, Yama will disappear' (Abdul Jabbar Mimnagari).[262] Utterance of the saint's name takes that name to one's heart and creates love there, just like in a *ḏikr*;[263] the bird in one's heart starts to speak.[264] The recitation of the saint's name can function as one's *kalima*, proclamation of faith.[265] It is the disciple's only hope.[266] The name is conceived as 'enacted', that is, established and bestowed with effectivity, in Maijbhandar;[267] it should be remembered by the disciple with each breath and especially at the time of death.[268]

The saints are sometimes portrayed as omniscient and omnipotent benefactors. 'Make me float or make me drown, Bābājān knows everything' (Shafiul Bashar).[269] The saint takes care of both worlds, earthly life and the hereafter, and everything works according to his command.[270] He is the guardian of the world and the universal mover who 'can unite earth and sky in a moment' (Ramesh Shil).[271] He is even occasionally held responsible for creation: 'Ramesh says: I have understood well, you are the root of all',[272] or likewise, 'My creation [came about] from you, you are the root of everybody' (Shafiul Bashar).[273]

The holy places of various religious traditions are at times identified with the saints. In fact, appellations like *qibla kaʿba* are affixed to saints' names in other, not

262 *PR* No. 13: *prem(a) bhābe bala sabe gāuchul(a) ājam(a)/nāmer guṇe tvariẏe yābe palāẏe yābe yam(a).*

263 Cf. Ramesh Shil *ND* No. 14.

264 Abdul Gafur Hali *JJ* No. 4 (*ai nām karile japanā/kaïbe kathā diler maẏ'nā*).

265 Ramesh Shil *BhM* No. 30.

266 Ramesh Shil *ĀM* No. 16: *ek'mātra bharasā hṛde daẏāl tomār nām.*

267 Farid Hosain *SB* No. 11: *gāuch(a) nām'ṭi haïla jārī – māij bhāṇḍārī sonār purī* ('The name [of the] Ġawṯ has become enacted [in] the golden city of Maijbhandar'); one could, however, also translate *jāri haoẏā* less emphatically as 'being circulated'.

268 Abdul Gafur Hali *JJ* No. 8.

269 *YB* No. 71: *bhāsāo kiṃbā ḍubāo more, sab'i jāne bābājān.*

270 Aliullah *PN* No. 91 (Urdu in Bengali script): *āph dektā hāẏ din, duniẏā dojā̃hā̃n [. . .] āph'kā hukum'che cal'tā hāẏ* ('You look after religion [*dīn*], the world, both worlds [. . .] [it] moves by your command').

271 *JS* 33: *māolā biśva pālak sabār cālak se cālāle āmi yāi/māolā rahim rah'mān, palake ek kar'te pāre jamin ār āc'mān/pāhāṛ'ke dariẏā kare dite pāre deś ḍubāi* ('The master is the guardian of the world, the mover of everybody, I go [only] if he makes me move/The master is *raḥīm raḥmān*, he can unite earth and sky in a moment/He can make mountains into the sea, drowning the country'). Ar. *raḥīm* and *raḥmān*, 'merciful' and 'compassionate', are very common appellations of Allah which figure in the *Basmala*.

272 *MD* No. 13: *rameś bale ṭhik bujhechi tumi sabār mūl(a)re.*

273 *YB* No. 72: *sṛṣṭi āmār tomā ha'te tumi sabār mul.* Shafiul Bashar addresses Gholam Rahman, who was his natural father; but even if the first part of this line might be taken to refer to this, the second generalises it and projects Gholam Rahman as a universal creator.

only subcontinental Sufi circles, as well.[274] The saint being world-pervading, the *ḥağğ* pilgrimage becomes superfluous;[275] and the saint himself can effectuate the instantaneous pilgrimage of his devotees: 'Maijbhandari Bābājān, he upon whom you have mercy/Shall absolve his travel to Mecca and Medina in a moment' (Shafiul Bashar).[276] For Badrunnesa Saju, a pilgrimage to Maijbhandar represents a *ḥağğ* for the poor: the peace that is gained by a pilgrimage to Mecca can equally be found at the *darbār*.[277] Ramesh Shil, the writer who employs this motif most frequently, also emphasises the worthlessness of holy places like Vrindavan, Mecca, Medina, Bodh Gaya and Benaras if only the name of the Bhandari be known and his form be present before one's eyes.[278] The Kaʿba, the house of Allah, is found in Ajmer, Medina, Bagdad and Maijbhandar;[279] and the Kaʿba, Benaras and Vrindavan can be found at the feet of the Maijbhandari.[280] And the beloved friend is everything to his lover, including the holy places: 'You are my Kaʿba and Kashi [Benaras], you are my Vrindavan' (Ramesh Shil).[281] The mention of Vrindavan is particularly significant as the saint is also likened to Lord Krishna. While the name Krishna is never mentioned, epithets of Krishna such as *madan mohan* ('charmer of the god of love'), *śyām* ('[greenish] black'], *kālā cā̃d* ('black moon'), etc. are found in Maijbhandari songs of various authors in relation to the saints.[282] We shall come back to this in this chapter under the caption of *viraha bhakti*.

In fact, the saints are often portrayed as being divine in human shape. The rationale behind this includes not only the notion that, just like a guru by his *śiṣya*, a *muršid* should for all practical purposes be regarded as divine by his *murīd*, but also the more general idea that any saint, by virtue of the union with God that constitutes this very sainthood, is merged in God and therefore identical with Him.[283] The saint is simultaneously human and divine. The songs express this in

274 For a Maijbhandari example, cf. Bajlul Karim *ŚJ* No. 14 as quoted above in this section. For a nationalist use of these terms, cf. Adeeb Khalid (2004: 257).

275 Cf. Bajlul Karim *ŚJ* No. 3 (*jagajjāmī* -> *jagadyāmī*, 'world-pervading').

276 *YB* No. 28: *māij'bhāṇḍārī bābājān, yār prati hao daẏābān/palake tār chāẏer* [<P. *seyr*>] *habe makkā ār(a) madinā.*

277 *Madirā* No. 35. For the *ḥağğ* function of the *ʿurs* at Maijhandar, cf. also the poem by Maulavi Ayub Ali and the song by Abdul Gafur Hali quoted in Selim Jāhāṅgīr (1999: 163 f.). Similar conceptions asserting even the superiority of *ziyāra* over *ḥağğ* are testified also for pre-modern times in South Asia; cf. Ernst (1993: 51).

278 *ĀM* No. 29.

279 Ramesh Shil *ŚB* No. 17: *bāitullā kābā āj'mīre, madinā bog'dād bhāṇḍāre.*

280 Ramesh Shil *MD* No. 4: *ai kadam bar'kate pābi kābā kāśī br̥indāban.*

281 *SD* No. 5: *tumi āmār kābā kāśī, tumi āmār br̥ndāban.*

282 Cf., e.g., Bajlul Karim *ŚJ* No. 4 (*madan mohan*, *śyām*); Shafiul Bashar *YB* No. 18 (*nāgar kānāi*); Abdul Gafur Hali *JJ* No. 49 (*madan mohan śyām sundar*); Farid Hosain *SB* No. 72 (*kānāiẏā*); Ramesh Shil *ĀM* No. 12 (*śyām*), No. 7 (*madan mohan śyām sundar*); *kānāi/kānāiẏā* are in fact *tadbhava* variants of Krishna's name.

283 Cf. Rahul Peter Das (1992: 389) ('To many Indian religious groups the preceptor is not only often a deity, but also may be algamated with the supreme divine principle'), and (1997: 99n); also the remarks of the status of the guru in Bengali Vaishnavism ('To the orthodox Vaiṣṇavas, the guru is Kr̥ṣṇa) in Dimock (1989: 198). Also, cautiously, Klostermeier (1990: 224) on the utmost importance of the guru in various *bhakti* traditions (he is the 'personal representative of the Supreme Lord'); and Gold (1987).

various ways: 'You have put on a godly dress, having taken the form of man', says Abdul Jabbar Mimnagari, suggesting that the Ġawt̲ al-Aʿẓam who is addressed here is of divine rather than human substance.[284] For Ramesh Shil, the Ġawt̲ should not be conceived as separate from God and the Prophet;[285] and he addresses Baba Bhandari as such: 'You are my God and Prophet'.[286] He is non-man in the form of man,[287] and Rumi is cited to prove that the courts of the saints and that of Allah are one and the same thing.[288] It is the Bhandari who makes the mountain shine, and he is thus identified with Allah.[289] Farid Hosain declares that the guru is of Allah's category of being (as I would like to render the term *jāti* here),[290] and, as 'the miserable servant Hadi says, God and *muršid* are not separate'.[291] Abdul Gafur Hali points out that 'Allah, Prophet, *pīr* and *muršid* are the innumerable names of the One',[292] and Aliullah stresses that Ahmadullah has made himself God.[293]

This substantial identity of God and the saint thus recurs in a multitude of Maijbhandari songs, with a tendency to ignore the subtle distinctions made in theological elaborations. A special configuration of this relationship is the idea of incarnation, closely related to the notions treated in the preceding paragraph. We shall examine this in the following section.

5.7.6 Incarnation

> You were the primeval father, the light of the Merciful and Compassionate / Coming in different vessels you again (and again) enlightened both worlds.[294]
>
> (Shafiul Bashar)

The term *abatār* (Skt. <*avatāra*>, 'he who descends', 'incarnation') is frequently used in Maijbhandari songs. The Maijbhandari, on the one hand, is depicted as the incarnation of some abstract quality or emotion, such as premer abatār, 'incarnation of love'. On the other, he is also seen as an avatāra in the more conceptual sense of the human form of some fundamentally transcendent and non-human entity. The classical formulation of the Hindu doctrine of incarnation can, for example, be found in *Bhagavadgītā* 4.7–8 where Krishna proclaims that he brings

284 *PR* No. 10: *parecha khodāẏī lebāch mānuṣ rūp(a) dhariẏā.*

285 *ĀM* No. 26: [. . .] *gāuchul ājam khodā rasul bhinna bhābe nā* (lit.: '[those who are fortunate] do not think the Ġawt̲ al-Aʿẓam, God and the Prophet [as] separate'.

286 *ĀM* No. 33: *tumi āmār khodā rasul.*

287 *MD* No. 32 (*amānuṣ mānuṣer sāje*).

288 *MD* No. 34: *aliullār dar'bār ār(a) khodār dar'bār ek samān.*

289 Ramesh Shil *ŚB* No. 26: *tomār nūrer tajallite pāhāṛ jale, muchā muhāgata dekhe nūr ujalā.*

290 *SB* No. 18: *guru haẏ(a) āllār jātī* [*sic*].

291 *RB* No. 15: *kahe dās(a) hādī hīn(a), khodā murśīd nahe bhin(a).*

292 *JJ* No. 65: *āllā, rasul, pīr murśid eker asaṃkhya nām.*

293 *PN* No. 28: *khod khodā baniẏāchen āpe ekā eki haï* ('He [Ahmadullah is meant] became himself God, being all by himself'.

294 *YB* No. 19: *ādi pitā tumi chile, nūre rahim rahamān/nānā ghaṭe esa punaḥ ujjvalilā do-jā̃hā. esa* seems to be a misprint for *ese*, the absolutive participle, which underlies the translation.

himself into being in every age, and whenever dharma is endangered.[295] In a song by Ramesh Shil, who in all probability was well acquainted with the *Bhagavadgītā*, that formulation seems to be echoed: 'He who is not found through meditation age after age/Is so gracious to descend himself upon earth'.[296] Lutfunnesa Hosaini also writes: 'You come in every age [called] by the names of prophets and saints'.[297] In accordance with the notion that there is an *avatāra* for every age, the Maijbhandari is sometimes referred to as *kalir abatār*, the incarnation of the last of the four Hindu ages, the *kali yuga*: 'He is the *avatāra* of the *kali* [age] – the divine form in human shape' (Farid Hosain).[298]

The concept of incarnation, Ar. *ḥulūl*, has no sanction in 'orthodox' Islam, and it was this that Mansur al-Hallaj had been found guilty of when pronouncing *anā 'l-ḥaqq* ('I am Divine Truth') (cf. Schimmel 1995: 209). Interestingly, one Maijbhandari song uses exactly this reference to justify the idea that the Maijbhandari is an incarnation of divine substance: 'You make Mansur utter *anā 'l-ḥaqq* again and again' (Farid Hosain).[299] The fundamental unity of human lover and divine beloved is emphatically asserted,[300] and Farid Hosain, in an appendix to his song, quotes *Qur'ān* 19.17 in support of the possibility of divine incarnation.

In many songs, the Maijbhandari is identified with preceding saints and prophets, among them the Prophet Muhammad. 'He has come in the guise of the Prophet, he has given guidance/Lighting the light of the Bhandari, he disperses darkness' (Lutfunnesa Hosaini).[301] Bajlul Karim, alluding to the *ṭarīqa* founders 'Abd al-Qadir Gilani and Mu'in al-Din Chishti respectively, states in one of his Urdu songs that 'You wander around sometimes in Bagdad, sometimes in Ajmer and in [Maij-] Bhandar';[302] likewise Shafiul Bashar narrates that 'After coming to Baghdad in *qādirī* glory, and to Ajmer with the Ḫwāğa's [i.e. Mu'in al-Din

295 The respective verses read: *yadā yadā hi dharmasya glānir bhavati bhārata/abhyutthānam adharmasya tad ātmānaṃ sṛjāmy aham/7/paritrāṇāya sādhunāṃ vināśāya ca duṣkṛtām/ dharmasaṃsthāpanārthāya saṃbhavāmi yuge yuge/8/*('Whenever, O Bhārata, *dharma* becomes faint and *adharma* arises, I create myself. [7] I come into being age after age to safeguard the righteous, to destroy the doers of evil deeds and to establish *dharma* [8]').

296 *BhM* No. 2: *yug(a) yugāntare dhyāne yāre nāhi pāẏ/kṛpā kare svaẏaṃ abatīrṇa e dharāẏ.*

297 *GP* No. 29: *yuge yuge eso tumi nabī alī nāme.*

298 *HB* No. 37: *tini kalir haẏ abatār – mānab rūpe khodāi ākār.* Cf. also Ramesh Shil *JS* No. 38: *kali kaluṣita nare, uddhār(a) karibār tare/udaẏ hale māij'bhāṇḍāre daẏāl abatār* ('In order to rescue the men stained by the *kali* age/You arose in Maijbhandar, O merciful *avatāra*').

299 *PR* No. 14: *āinal'hak(a) bāre bāre balāo tumi mun'chure.*

300 Ibid: *tumi maj'nu tumi lāili, tumi phar'hād tumi śiri* ('You are Majnun, you are Laila, you are Farhad, you are Shirīn'); Farid Hosain identifies the divine player, the Maijbhandari, with both parts of these loving couples so famous in Sufi allegories.

301 *GP* No. 12: *rāsuler beśe esechen, dik darśan tini diẏechen/bhāṇḍārīr ālo jvele tāṛān andhakār.* Cf. also another song by Lutfunnesa Hosaini (*GP* No. 22) on her father, the Maijbhandari *pīr* Shafiul Bashar as arising anew in every age, and having proclaimed Islam in the form of Muhammad.

302 *ŚJ* No. 2: *kabhī bag'dād me ājmīr me bhāṇḍār me phera tom* (Urdu in Bengali script); cf. also *ŚJ* No. 8: *bog'dād(a) āj'mīr(a) haẏe māij'bhāṇḍāre dekhā dilā* ('Having been in Bagdad and Ajmer, he showed himself in Maijbhandar').

Chishti's] status/He again delights the spirits of the lovers in Maijbhandar',[303] and Abdul Gafur Hali seems to say that the Maijbhandari is actually Muʿin al-Din Chishti: 'Wandering through Medina and Bagdad, you arose in Maijbhandar, O *hindīwāle* Muʿin al-Din from Ajmer'.[304]

The Maijbhandari saint is depicted as taking human shape when coming into this world, but actually being of an altogether different nature.[305] Ramesh Shil equates the Maijbhandari with prophets, saints and God Himself: 'Under the cover of *aḥmad*, you play through *aḥad*'.[306] The divine One (*aḥad*) is separated only by (the veil of) the letter *mīm* from Aḥmad,namely *Muḥammad*, and it is the Divine that is the identity of the saint, behind his deceiving forms. Similarly, Abdul Jabbar Mimnagari identifies the Maijbhandari as *Muḥammad*, who in his turn stems from *aḥad*, the One.[307] In another song, he specifies the relationship between *Aḥmad* and *Muḥammad*: 'You are *Aḥmad* on the heavenly throne, and bear the name *Muḥammad* in the world'.[308] Ramesh Shil, finally, in a long series of identifications, describes his Mawlā as follows:

> You are Munkar and Nakīr,[309] you are the noble writers,[310]/The secret and the manifest are by your artifice/You are west and east, you are Medina and Vrindavan,/Kaʿba and Kashi, you are everywhere/You are *aḥad* and *Aḥmad*, you are the Great Pīr in Baghdad,/And in Ajmer they call you Cistiẏā.[311]

The tendency to efface the lines of distinction between single Maijbhandari saints, sometimes merging them into one person, thus continues at this level. Saints, prophets and the Divine are assembled in ultimate unity. They assume human shape under different names, in different times and in different capacities (such as prophets or saints), but their essence remains the same. Maijbhandari

303 *YB* No. 7: *bāg'dāde kāderī śāne āj'mīre khājārī māne/ese punaḥ māij'bhāṇḍāre āśekāner man majāẏ*.

304 *JJ* No. 13: *madinā bāg'dāde ghure udaẏ haïla māij bhāṇḍāre/hindi oẏāle maīnuddin āj'miri*. The term *hindīwāle*, used in its Urdu/Hindi form of polite reference here, means literally 'Hindi speaker'; Abdul Gafur Hali probably uses it as a geographical denomination corresponding to what would have to be *hindwāle* ('person from Hind'). Cf. the German translation of this song in *VG*: 24. For similar examples of identifying the Maijbhandari with saints and prophets in the songs of Abdul Gafur Hali, cf. *TB* No. 37 (the Maijbhandari as Adam, Muhammad, Gilani, Chishti); *JJ* No. 45 (the Ġawṯ in Medina and Maijbhandar); No. 95 (like *TB* No. 37). Cf. also Shafiul Bashar *YB* No. 7; Ramesh Shil *ŚB* No. 2 (Maijbhandari as Muhammad, Gilani, Chishti); *MD* No. 12 (the Mawlā in Medina, Baghdad, Ajmer and Chittagong).

305 Cf., e.g., Farid Hosain *SB* No. 9; Ramesh Shil *BhM* No. 25.

306 *ND* No. 37: *āh'mader ḍhākani diẏā khelā khela āhād diẏā*.

307 *PR* No. 24; *PR* No. 29.

308 *PR* No. 29: *āraśe āhāmmad tumi jagate muhammad nāmi*.

309 The angels of death.

310 Bg. *korāman'kātebin*, from Ar. <*kirāman kātibīn*> (*Qurʾān* 82.11); the angels Munkar and Nakīr who write down men's good and evil deeds.

311 BhM No. 24: man'kir(a) nakir(a) tumi, korāman-kāte bin tumi,/gupta byakta tomār kauśale/mag'rib(a) maś'rik(a) tumi, madinā bṛndāban tumi/kābā kāśī tumi sarbasthale/āhād(a) āhāmmad tumi barapīr [sic] bog'dāde tumi/āj'mire cistiẏā tomāẏ bale.

song-authors tend towards identifying all these entities with the Maijbhandari; that is, it is the Maijbhandari who first appears as Adam, then shows himself as Muhammad, ʿAbd al-Qadir Gilani and so forth. But these are not usually thought of as one-way identifications implying, for instance, that the preceding saints are *actually* or *ultimately* the Maijbhandari; the argument works also vice versa in that one could claim that, for example, the Maijbhandari is *actually* Muʿin al-Din Chishti of Ajmer. Of course, such an argument is rather rare since the usual order of reasoning is from the widely known and generally acclaimed *down* to the local manifestation; but it does occur.[312]

Such unity of the saints and God can, however, produce tensions between formed (*sākāra*) and formless (*nirākāra*) concepts of divinity. Debates on this topic are very common in South Asia and run through various traditions. Attempts have often been made to reconcile both notions: one may recall here Gaudiya Vaishnava theology according to which the *nirākāra brahman* 'unfolds' and 'descends' into *sākāra* deities.[313] Medieval Sufi cosmogonies, with the *nūr-i muḥammadī* as the entity triggering creation, propose a similar process of unfolding.[314] This issue touches upon the long-held distinction between *nirguṇa* and *saguṇa bhakti*. This distinction has given rise to some amount of theory-building.[315] On the basis of research on the Maharashtrian deity Viṭhobā, Hardy (1983) shows that the deity is regarded as containing *both* the *nirguṇa* and *saguṇa* brahman, and argues that 'a simplistic usage of terms like *nirguṇa* [. . .] creates lines of demarcation which, by using a different type of conceptual framework, reveal[s itself] as artificial' (p. 149). Maijbhandari songs, as we have seen, simultaneously assert the ultimate unity of the saint with God and the latter's descent into flesh and blood; the saint is thus at the same time limitless and confined, *nirākāra* and *sākāra*. A few songs deal with the way these notions can be reconciled.

One way of dealing with this tension is to assign both aspects to different spheres of activity. Bajlul Karim writes: 'Playful One! Who is able to understand your play?/You live in the city of non-form [*nairūp*] and are playing in many forms [*bahurūpe*]'.[316] Another strategy is to assert the validity of both aspects by creating paradoxes and oxymorons. Ramesh Shil, for example, employs the oxymoron of the 'unlimited breast/chest' in order to convey simultaneous belonging to the earthly and the divine.[317] Abdul Gafur Hali uses a similar paradox, and seems to attempt an arbitration by ultimately dismissing both *sākāra* and *nirākāra* positions:

312 Cf. the above-quoted song by Abdul Gafur Hali (*JJ* No. 13).

313 Cf. Dimock (1966: 126 ff.).

314 Cf. Section 3.2.

315 Cf. Lorenzen (1996: 13 ff.) for an attempt to read *saguṇa bhakti* as an instance of hegemonic, and *nirguṇa bhakti* as subaltern, ideology.

316 *ŚJ* No. 8: *līlāmaẏ! kār sādhya bujh'te pāre tomār līlā,/(tumi) nairūp nagare thāka bahurūpe kar'cha khelā.*

317 Cf. *JS* No. 10 (*asīm sīnā*).

> Who has the power to determine the boundaries of your form/You are endless and unlimited, in whichever vessel in that way accordingly/One thinks you are *sākāra*, another thinks you are *nirākāra*/You are in one form, helmsman of the lover's mind.[318]

We may paraphrase the first part by saying that the Divine is unlimited despite the limits of the (human) form in which it is experienced. In isolation, this statement sounds almost vedantic, but the argument then takes a turn that seems to be typical of certain trends in *bhakti* thought;[319] the Divine is neither only formed nor merely formless, but 'in one form', that is, beyond these categories of limited human perception. If we adduce the Maijbhandari tradition to *bhakti* categories, then the bulk of it would certainly have to be classed as *saguṇa bhakti* with the saints as the formed and qualified Divine; but as the above has shown, a number of songs investigate the relation between *sākāra* and *nirākāra* concepts and effectively question the ultimate validity of such a distinction.

The doctrine of incarnation, to come back to the main topic of this section, is nominally absent from theological writings in the Maijbhandari tradition, and its presence and even popularity in the songs thus stands to be explained. The term *abatār* is very common in Bengali vocabulary with semantic extensions well beyond theological confines, and it may thus seem debatable to what extent its occurrences really point at any *avatāra* doctrine. But the indications do seem very clear that such a link exists. The theological construct (in texts such as *Ā'īna-i Bārī* and *Belāẏate mot'lākā*) is that the prophets and saints are sent down with a specific mission to perform, and by way of penances, etc. do achieve union with the divine on earth. The popular idiom of the songs, by contrast, seems to make use of the commonly understood notion of *avatāra* in order to elucidate the relationship between saint and divine, giving it thus an entirely new meaning, because an *avatāra* is a manifestation of, and thus identical with, the Divine, and union does not have to be achieved, but is there from the beginning. In Section 6.3 we shall have occasion to investigate this further and probe into contemporary understandings of the *avatāra* motif. For now, we can state that according to the songs we have discussed, the Maijbhandari as *avatāra* unites diverse religious manifestations within, and potentially even beyond Islam. In the following section, we shall see that he comprises various religious traditions within himself, and can be conceived of as a sort of crystallisation point of interreligious experience.

318 *JJ* No. 59: *dite tomār rūper sīmā hena śakti āche kār/ananta asīm(a) tumi yei ghaṭe yei prakār/ keha tomāẏ bhābe sākār ār keha bhābe nairākār/tumi ācha ek ākāre āśek maner karṇadhār.*

319 The Maharashtrian poet-saint Tukaram, for instance, employs the image of the unlimited sky above every single scratch on a fruit to convey the same notion regarding the participation of the single in the general, or the many in the one, and then recommends sticking to visible saints as God is invisible in his plural or non-form. Cf. Tukārāma (1991, No. 232).

5.7.7 Unity of religions

> The Kaʿba, Kashi and Vrindavan are the living places of that man/Gafur says, recognize and catch that man as long as there is time.[320]

We have seen that the formula 'irrespective of religion and caste/class' has gained wide currency in Maijbhandar as a label of self-representation. It basically claims that one's religious group of belonging does not matter when approaching the Maijbhandari. The formula itself and statements to this effect as well as more general statements on harmony between religions are occasionally found in Maijbhandari songs; and since concepts regarding the relationship between different religious groups and doctrines are one of the focal points of interest of this book, this topic shall be examined below. It must, however, be stressed that the question of interreligious relations is not equally relevant to all the authors under discussion here, and is not dealt with at all by some of them. The two authors most intent on tackling this issue are Ramesh Shil and Abdul Gafur Hali, and the following thus relies heavily on their works.

It is possible to distinguish esoteric and social statements regarding the different religions present in Chittagong. The esoteric ones, again, fall into three categories. The first of these groups the exoteric, formalistic aspects of various religious traditions together in seeming equivalence with respect to their inefficacy in attaining the divine. 'If the Bhandari's name is known/And [his] form is the target of the eye/What do I care for Vrindavan, Mecca, Medina, [Bodh] Gaya and Kashi', asks Ramesh Shil,[321] implying that the holy places of (Hindu) Vaishnavism, Islam, Buddhism and (Hindu) Shaivism are equally ineffective and irrelevant in comparison to the direct experience bestowed by the Maijbhandari. Similarly, Abul Gafur Hali stresses the worthlessness of conventional institutions of various religious traditions when it comes to searching for God, in an impressive way worthy of a lengthy quotation:

> How many mosques, churches and Kali temples/Have I searched, O my mind/I have not left out the Kaʿba and Kashi either/Allah, God, Krishna, Hari/By how many names have I called out/I do not find his true name // Can one know his secret/By reading the *Qurʾān*, the *Gītā* and the Bible/[All of] which can be burnt if put into fire?[322]

Regular places of worship, central holy places, the current names of the divine as well as the scriptures are discarded as irrelevant; the true divine, Hali asserts in

320 *TB* No. 34: *kābā kā̃śī* [sic] *śrībr̥ndāban ai mānuṣer thākār ghar/gaphur bale din thākite ciniẏā sei mānuṣ dhar.*

321 *ĀM* No. 29: *bhāṇḍārīr nām thāk'le jānā/cakṣe thāk'le rūp niśānā/br̥ndāban makkā madinā gaẏā kāśīr ki dhār dhārī.*

322 *JJ* No. 37: *o man(a)re – mas'jid, gīrjjā, kālībāṙī – /dekh'lām kata tālās kari/kābā kāśī bākī rākhi nāi/āllā, gaḍ, kr̥ṣṇa, hari – /ḍākilām kata nām dhari/āsal nām tār khũjiẏā nā pāi // o man(a)re – korān, gītā, bāibel paṛe – /bhed ki tār jānite pāre,/āgune dile yā poṛā yāẏ/[. . .].*

another song, must be looked for in one's 'vessel' (body), as neither mosques nor churches, the Kaʿba nor Kashi are the abode of the creator.[323]

The logic of this argument that denounces the emptiness of outer religious symbols can, however, be turned upside down, and this takes us to the second category. In a twist by now familiar from motifs such as the heart, the holy places can also be imagined as 'filled', that is, as containers of the most sacred essences of the respective religious traditions. We have, – in different contexts, – already quoted a number of Maijbhandari songs that make use of this assertion. 'You are my Kaʿba and Kashi, you are my Medina', writes Ramesh Shil,[324] expressing the idea that the Maijbhandari saint is just as central to the murīd as the foremost holy places of Islam and Hinduism. 'The Kaʿba, Kashi and Vrindavan are the living place of that man', states Abdul Gafur Hali, as quoted at the beginning of this section, implying that the essences of all religions are present in that inner man who is either the Maijbhandari himself or caught with his help. Hali's statement, by the way, stands in opposition to his above-quoted contention regarding the voidness of the holy places (*JJ* No. 37). This can be read as an indication of the ambivalent and fragile nature of such utterances, and demonstrates vividly that they are not theological positions in any feasible way, but rather seem designed to refer us to an experiential realm behind the words.[325]

This variant leads to a third category of esoteric notions that do not only compare the centrality of the saint to that of the holy places, but also actually assert his (ultimate) identity with the highest deities of different traditions, as well as the ultimate identity of these deities. This has precursors in medieval *bhakti*, most famously in Kabir's poetry.[326] Again, Ramesh Shil and Abdul Gafur Hali are the major proponents of such views. 'One sees Krishna in him/Another sees God [*khodā*, P.<*ḫudā*>]',[327] claims Abdul Gafur Hali; 'he' is the one who has come to Maijbhandar 'in the form of a man in the dark age'.[328] It is understood that such seeing is not conceived as illusionary; the Maijbhandari *is* Krishna and Ḫodā. Likewise, with increased diversification, Ramesh Shil: 'If they behold him with

323 Paraphrase of *JJ* 49: *masjid, gīrjjā, kābā, kāśī/ei sab nahe śraṣṭār* [*sic*] *ghar/tāre āpan ghaṭe tālās kar*.

324 *SD* No. 5: *tumi āmār kābā kāśī tumi āmār madinā*.

325 Harmonising statements of this kind are legion in South Asia, but probably more common in the North than in the South; for a contemporary Sufi parallel from northern India, cf. Liebeskind (1998: 187) ('The same God is to be found in the mosque, the church and the pagoda [temple]', statement by Warith ʿAli Shah, *pīr* of Dewa in Uttar Pradesh, India).

326 Or, putting it more cautiously, the corpus ascribed to Kabir. Cf., e.g., the invocation *Allah Rāṃm*, 'O Allah-Rama', in one of his *Sabad* verses (Kabīr 1981: 28). It deserves mention that Aziz Ahmad (1969: 144 f.) tries to dismiss the implications of such combinations in Kabir's poetry by calling them a ' "lexique technique" of his Bhakti syncretism'; in reality, according to Ahmad, Kabir knew little of Islamic concepts, and his scope was rather the rejection than the affirmation of the formal sides of both Hinduism and Islam. 'His was a popular and revolutionary restatement of the essence of Hinduism, with a conciliatory gesture of syncretic assimilation for Islam' (Ahmad 1969: 145).

327 *JJ* No. 91: *tār mājhe keu kṛṣṇa dekhe keubā dekhe khodāre*.

328 Ibid.; the opening line of the song is *andhayuge mānab rūpe ke ela re bhāṇḍāre*.

devotion/The Christians see Jesus, the Buddhists Phaẏā[329]/The Hindus see the charmer of the god of love, the black golden one of Nanda'.[330] The Maijbhandari saint, we are to understand, is one, and the 'fact' that devotees from different religious provenances visualise their respective deities through him reveals the illusionary character of all religious distinctions.[331] Such unity, these songs claim, exists not only in theory as some fundamental analogy between all religious endeavours, but can be spiritually experienced. Maijbhandar can disclose the ultimate identity of different divinities that Ramesh Shil expresses thus: 'If you lift the veil of the *mīm*, O mind, you will see/That Rama, Rahim, Krishna and Karim are fundamentally one.'[332]

The group of statements I have termed social emphasise the desirability of harmonious relations between different religious communities and the role of Maijbhandar in bringing about such harmony. Some authors only quote the Maijbhandari motto dharmajātinirbiśeṣe or variants thereof: 'He filled the city and harbour with the light of nūr [sic]/Irrespective of caste/class and religion, by his free spiritual sovereignty' (Lutfunnesa Hosaini),[333] or – maybe the earliest occurrence of this formula in a song – 'men and spirits worship Bābā's feet/They call [him] Bābājān irrespective of [their] jāti and varṇa' (Bajlul Karim).[334] Ramesh Shil, the one author who dwells most consistently on this topic, describes the darbār as a 'meeting point of Hindus, Muslims, Christians and Buddhists'.[335] All religions are basically the same: 'Whether Hindu, Muslim, Christian or Buddhist, it is the same with all

329 A local Chittagongian appellation of the Buddha. Maijbhandari songs do not reflect upon the originally non-divine status of the historical Buddha or on subtle issues regarding the general negation of divinity in Hīnayāna Buddhism, but construe the Buddha in analogy to other religious traditions as the highest Buddhist godhead. In this respect, the songwriters are probably not far from popular Buddhist perceptions as crystallised, for instance, in the famous Buddhist pilgrimage site at Mahamuni in Chittagong.

330 *ĀM* No. 13: *tāke bhakti bhābe kar'le daraśan/yiśu dekhe khṛṣṭānerā, kaẏā* [misprint for *phaẏā*] *bauddhagaṇ/hindu dekhe madan mohan śrīnander kāla sonā*. Nanda is Krishna's mythological foster father in Vrindavan.

331 It is a common notion held by Maijbhandaris that adherents to different religions can visualise their respective deity in the Maijbhandari. Similar notions seem to exists in other South Asian Sufi traditions; cf. Liebeskind (1998: 185 f.), reporting that Warith ʿAli Shah of Dewa had been seen as Jesus by an Englishman.

332 *ND* No. 32: *mimer pardā uṭhāile dekh'bi ore man/rām(a) rahim kṛṣṇa karim mūlete ek'jan*. *Raḥīm*, 'the Merciful', and *Karīm*, 'the Gracious', are appellations of Allah. For the term *mimer pardā*, 'the veil of mīm', cf. above.

333 *GP* No. 32: *nurer āloẏ bhariẏe dilen śahar o bandar/jāti, dharma nirbiśeṣe mugdha* [*sic*] *belāẏete*. *Nurer ālo* may seem redundant, but in Bengali, *nur* is exclusively used for divine light and thus specifies the general term for light, *ālo*. *Mugdha belāẏet* would mean 'charmed' or 'spell-bound spiritual sovereignty' and is probably a misprint for *mukta belāẏet*, 'free spiritual sovereignty', a variant of which (*unmukta belāẏat*) is used in *BM*, and which underlies my translation. It is, however, also possible that Lutfunnesa Hosaini plays with assonances here.

334 *ŚJ* No. 26: *mānab(a)-dānab(a)gaṇ(a)/bhaje bābār śrīcaraṇ(a)/jāti-barṇa-nirbiśeṣe bale bābājān(a)*. *Dānab*s, Skt <*dānava*>, are evil semi-gods and counterplayers of the gods (*devas*) in Hindu mythology.

335 *MD* No. 6 (*hindu, mus'lim, khṛṣṭān, bauddha milan kendra*).

religions/There are only reshufflings of policies, [but] where are there two destinations?'[336] The unity of God similarly is asserted in the different scriptures: 'Qur᾽ān, Purāṇas, Bible and Gītā proclaim that there is no second besides the One',[337] and quarrels between the religious communities are nonsensical since all are the creation of that one God who is neither a Hindu nor a Muslim:

> Why do you struggle in vain whether this or that religion is greater?/Search for the true substance [*satya bastu*], all conflicts will dissolve/If the Lord [*īśvar*] were a Hindu, he would not have created the Muslims/If Allah were a Muslim, who then has created the Hindus?[338]

Hindus and Muslims are actually brethren, and controversies about different modes of worship are superfluous.[339] Farid Hosain joins in with Ramesh Shil by imploring the members of different communities to lay aside religious quarrels; all humans are of the same blood, 'Hindus, Muslims, Buddhists and Christians are made by one [person/being]',[340] and 'Bhagavan, Ishvara, Allah and Khoda' (Skt. <*Bhagavān, Īśvara*>, Ar. <*Allāh*>, P. <*Ḫudā*>) should not be conceived of as separate.[341]

The statements quoted in this section have in common that they parallel religious ideas. It is assumed that all the religions in question fundamentally rest upon the belief in, and experience of one God. As men are basically equal – 'the same blood runs through our veins' – and all made by God, those ideas and experiences, it is argued, must also correspond to each other. In all the traditions, this one God is hardly knowable by man, and utterly indescribable in His grandeur and glory beyond all names and descriptions. Differences in these names and descriptions share the common feature that they are fragmentary and thus indicate the limited insight of man, and it is implied that the unity of that God beyond common perception is self-evident. Consequently, the various places of worship, appellations and religious books must be equivalent.

The problem of this step towards meta-religious universality is that it renders religious traditions relative; it devalues all exclusive claims inbuilt in those single traditions. Religious idioms either come down to being man-made, imperfect representations of One principle, or, if they are asserted as revelations, stand to be harmonised in a basically historico-geographical way as utterances adapted to climes and circumstances. In either case, they cannot be entitled to absolute validity. This

336 Ramesh Shil *MD* No. 24: *hindu, much'lim, khṛṣṭān, bauddha, sakal dharmer ek'i kathā/nīti rad(a) badal mātra gantabya sthān duiṭi kothā.*

337 Ramesh Shil *SD* No. 31: *ghoṣe ek bine dvitīẏa nāsti korān purāṇ bāibel gītā.*

338 Ramesh Shil *ĀM* No. 41: *ei dharmma sei dharmma baṛa bṛthā kena dvandva kara/satya bastur sandhān dhara, sakal dvandva yābe ghuce/īśvar yadi hindu hata, much'lim sṛṣṭi ke karita/āllāh yadi much'lim hata, hindu sṛṣṭi ke kareche.*

339 Cf. Ramesh Shil *ĀM* No. 38.

340 *SB* No. 38: *hindu mus'lim bauddha khṛṣṭān ek'janār taiẏār.*

341 Ibid.

explains the ambivalence of the songs vis-à-vis established religions, which are judged as either all true or all false: true insofar as they grant experience of the Divine, and false insofar as they stand for narrow, exclusive claims to possess the true doctrine and true exoteric rituals that grant salvation almost mechanically.

The solution to this problem presented in the songs is the Maijbhandari. His *darbār* is the meeting place of all religions; he addresses men irrespective of their religious affiliation; he even contains all religions within himself in granting visions of various religious founders and deities.[342] By his glance, shape, feet, etc., he bestows the experience of the divine that, for the authors, corresponds to the true, *ādhyātmik* (spiritual) basis of all religions. He thus is the link that dissolves all religious differences into harmony and unity.

It goes without saying that the antagonism between Muslims and Hindus that came to determine the course of South Asian history in the twentieth century is part and parcel of the background of such songs. And it may also strike us that almost half of the examples quoted above, and the most impressive ones for that matter, are authored by Ramesh Shil, descendant of a rural low-caste Hindu family of the barber caste. Ramesh thus belonged to that part of the population of what was to become Pakistan and later Bangladesh, that was not in the position to resolve the sometimes difficult living conditions of being a member of a religious minority by emigrating to West Bengal. The topic of harmony between Hindus and Muslims and the emphasis on cultural unity in the independent state, rather than religious identity, run through his other writings too.[343] We must very briefly state here that it is not only, but is most decidedly the non-Muslim minorities that insist on the compatibility of various traditions, thus venting their concerns for adequate representation by appeals to equality.[344]

The Maijbhandari, then, is a merger of religious traditions. He is also connected with another kind of merging, that of I and you, or the self and God, as we shall see in the following.

5.7.8 Merging

> I ask you one alm: I say 'I' and 'I' through my 'I-ness'.
> I want you to wipe away that I and make that I you.[345]
> (Ramesh Shil)

One indigenous taxonomy of Maijbhandari songs that was suggested to me during my fieldwork is the distinction between *birahadharmī* ('having the properties of separation') and *milan'dharmī* ('having the properties of union') types. It reflects the basic conditions of the *bhakta* as theorised in Gaudiya Vaishnavism, and truly the bulk of Maijbhandari songs revolve around these categories more or less

342 For the implications of the Maijbhandari showing himself as Christ to the Christians, Muhammad to the Muslims, etc., cf. Sections 7.2–4 in this book.

343 Cf. the different song collections in his *Racanābalī*.

344 For a further discussion of these central issues, cf. Chapter 7 in this book.

345 Cf. below, p. 225 f.

explicitly; thus, the oscillation of motifs like the heart or the bird may be explained as springing from the polarity of separation and union. There are basically two ways in which separation and union are correlated. They are either conceived as alternating states of mind of the *bhakta*, in analogy to human and erotic love, with instances of union followed by long periods of separation, or with union as the final and stable goal of a life leading through various states of separation. Both can be combined by discriminating between momentary, fugitive forms of union and lasting, irreversible ones. The songs that refer to spiritual union do so in different modes and use a variety of concepts and imagery.

One mode of referring to union is to assert the ultimate unity between the human *āmi*, self ('I'), and the divine *tumi* ('you'). We find this mode in medieval *bhakti* and Sufi sources, for instance in Kabir,[346] and likewise in Maijbhandari songs. 'I am you, everybody is you', since the Bhandari is the root of the creation (Farid Hosain);[347] and 'Tell me, what is the gap between I and you?/In the Yamuna of trance [*bhāb yamunā*] we can see that we become equal through merging of the two'.[348] 'We think I and you erroneously', says Shafiul Bashar, implying that union is the one and ultimate truth; but he makes clear that the world is built on such erroneous thinking, and even heaven is no escape: 'Know, brother, that even there the difference of the two has not been removed'.[349] 'You are me, and I am you', asserts Gafur Hali, but adds that nevertheless he cannot know that 'you'.[350] Likewise, Ramesh Shil, in one of the hymns to the highest Lord that usually open his song books, and as the final one of a long series of identifications, says 'I am you, you are you',[351] and, elsewhere: 'Even my I is you, there is nothing like an I'.[352]

The illusion of separation, as Ramesh Shil hints at in the preceding quotations, stems from the false idea of a human self. *Ahaṃkār*, Skt. <*ahaṃkāra*>, literally meaning the 'I-maker' or more broadly 'egotism', and one of the *tattva*s or entities of the unfolded *prakr̥ti* (female creation) in *Sāṃkhya* philosophy, is singled out as the enemy in a song by Gafur Hali: It destroys one's faith and must be abandoned before going to Maijbhandar.[353] The self, says Shafiul Bashar, must therefore be eradicated, and he implores his *muršid* to help him in this: 'Destroy me [. . .]/Burn me [. . .]'.[354] Ramesh Shil puts it very impressively as quoted above: 'I ask you one alm: I say "I" and "I" through my "I-ness" [*āmitva*]/I want you to wipe away that

346 Cf. one of his *Sākhīs*: *tūṃ tūṃ karatā bhayā, mujha maiṃ rahī na hūṃ/vārī pherī bali gaï, jita dekhauṃ tita tūṃ* (Kabīr 1976: 21). Charlotte Vaudeville translates: 'Repeating "Thou, Thou", I became Thou,/In me, no "I" remained:/Offering myself unto thy name,/wherever I look, Thou art!' (Vaudeville 1993: 173).

347 *SB* No. 2: *āmi tumi sabāi tumi*.

348 *SB* No. 70: *āmi tumi duiẏer mājhe bala kiser byābadhān* [*sic*]/*bhāb yamunāẏ* [the original has the misprint *namunāẏ*] *dekh'te pāire duiẏe mile haï samān*.

349 *YB* No. 3: *āmi tumi bhābi miche*; and: *okhāneo jān≅be bhāire duẏer taphāt≅ miṭe nāi*.

350 *JJ* No. 25: *tumi āmi āmi tumi*.

351 *ŚB* No. 1: *āmi tumi, tumi tumi*. Cf. also Rumi's *Maṯnavī* I, 3064: 'Now that you are me, come in, O I'.

352 *ND* No. 6: *āmār āmi seota* [*sic*] *tumi āmi kichu nā*.

353 *JJ* No. 27.

354 *YB* No. 59: *āmāẏ tumi dhvaṃsa kara* [. . .]/*āmāẏ tumi dahan kara*.

I and make that I you’.[355] Such offering of the self to the saint can take the form of a sacrifice, an image that especially Maulana Hadi uses frequently; but it also appears in Adul Jabbar’s, Lutfunnesa Hosaini’s and Ramesh Shil’s songs.[356]

The Sufi concept of *fanāʾ fī-Llāh*, ‘immersion’ or more literally ‘destruction in Allah’, is often quoted in the songs. Aliullah aspires to *pānā* (Ar. <*fanāʾ*>) in Nirañjan[357] and to being immersed into Allah’s form.[358] An article on Maijbhandar claims that rhythm is a good means for acquiring *fanāʾ*,[359] and Abdul Gafur Hali takes this up in a song: ‘ “Let us enter the state of *fanāʾ fī-Llāh*!”/This is why the lovers dance/Like the moth dances and falls into the flame’.[360] *Fanāʾ* instantaneously removes the veils concealing the divine: ‘By the impact of the bullet of *fanāʾ fī-Llāh*, the 70,000 veils are torn’ (Ramesh Shil).[361] As in Rumi’s *Masnavī*,[362] dissolution in water is used to illustrate *fanāʾ*: ‘I am born like a wave in water, and I become *fanāʾ* in water’ (Mahbubul Alam),[363] or ‘I look for such union as sugar in water’ (Ramesh Shil).[364] God, in His turn, is present in the world just like water in a vessel: ‘The colour of water is not different, and it assumes the form of the vessel in which one takes it/And one can see it according to its vessel; Allah dwells like that’ (Farid Hosain).[365] The beings are thus immersed in Allah, and *fanāʾ* is the individual experience of this truth. The divine *tumi* may be implored to blend the self with it: ‘Make me yours by blending me with you’,[366] or ‘Come, merciful Maijbhandari, let us blend our life-breaths’ (Shafiul Bashar),[367] etc.

According to Sufi traditions, the concept of *baqāʾ*, ‘abiding in Allah’, denotes a state of lasting immersion, as opposed to the transitory state of *fanāʾ*. The songs, however, rarely mention *baqāʾ*, and the concept seems to be much less well-known and popular.[368] But even the notion of *fanāʾ* as the destruction of self and merging with the divine is not uncontested in that it allows an inversion quite typical of the Maijbhandari idiom. Like the heart, the holy sites, etc., the self, too, may be imag-

355 *ŚB* No. 21: *ek'ṭi bhikṣā māgi āmi āmitve kaï āmi āmi/āmiṭi ghucāẏe tumi āmire cāi tumi kara*.
356 Cf. *RS* No. 13, 16, 89; *PR* No. 11; *GP* No. 26; *MD* No. 3.
357 *PN* No. 39.
358 *PN* No. 98: *āllār saṅge diba milāi, ek churate miśāire*.
359 Saiẏad Golām Mor'śed (1994: 224).
360 *JJ* No. 28: *phānā phillāhar hālete yāi – /āsek'gane* [*sic*] *nācere tāi/pataṅga nāciẏā yeman āgune paṙe*. On the image of the moth, used already by Mansur al-Hallaj, cf. Schimmel (1995a: 114).
361 *ND* No. 32: *phānāphillā gulir coṭe sattar hājār pardā phāṭe*.
362 E.g. IV, 2616–17 and 2619.
363 *AJ* No. 11: *ḍheuẏer mata janmi jale ābār jale haï phānā*. The dissolution of the drop of water in the ocean is a common traditional image for spiritual union; Guru Nanak, for instance, describes the attainment of the *sahaj* state in these terms (cf. Niharranjan Ray 1989: 18).
364 *SD* No. 20: *āmi khũji eman milan cinir sane jal* (*milane* in the original appears to be a misprint).
365 *HB* No. 29: *pānīr raṃ nāi bhinna prakār – yei pātre laẏ sei-i ākār re/dekhā yāẏ pātra anusāre – āllāẏ raẏ teman-re*.
366 Shafiul Bashar *YB* No. 11: *āmāke tomār kara tomāte miśāi*.
367 *YB* No. 33: *daẏāl māij'bhāṇḍārī esa prāṇe prāṇ miśāi*; *miśāi* could also be read as an absolute ablative participle: ‘Come by blending’, etc.
368 Aliullah, in *PN* No. 98, employs *pānā* and *bakā* <*fanāʾ*, *baqāʾ*> as a pair of terms, but does not elaborate their specific meaning.

ined as both void and filled, and in the latter case acquires a completely different meaning than in the context of *fanā'*. 'Everybody says "I", "I", to know the I is difficult/The I is in the real form and non-form [*svarūpe nirūpe*], there are two states [*bhāb*] of the one I', says Ramesh Shil, and he explains that 'The true I is the Lord of the world, the false I is egotism'.[369] Knowledge of that true self is therefore a precondition for (cf. Shafiul Bashar),[370] or even coterminous with the knowledge of God, as Ramesh Shil expresses by way of a pun on the Persian loan words *ḫūd* and *ḫudā*: 'If one knows the self [*khod*], one knows God [*khodā*].[371] It is that self, Abdul Gafur Hali claims, that the angels were asked to bow before;[372] God is in the self,[373] and 'self [*khod*] and God [*khodā*] are not different.[374] In this sense, then, the self is indeed everywhere and indestructible: ' "I" am indivisible, where are you apart from me?'[375] From the perspective of this ultimate self, merging is not necessary, as all difference is conceived as illusionary.

Our quotations have shown that union with the divine is on one level asserted as a general truth, and on another described as a state to be achieved. This double-bound notion of union mirrors many of the semantic ambivalences we have so far discussed in this chapter. It may be generalised at this point that the erasure of time as a soteriological factor that appears so typical of mystical traditions generates simultaneous presence and non-presence of the sacred sphere. In order to tackle this incommensurability, a bifurcation of modes of reference to union emerges. The first mode or level, we may say, follows an esoteric logic of underlying truth, the second a worldly logic of spiritual pursuit.

On both levels, the song-authors usually observe a code of humility in their references to spiritual union that brings to mind the etiquette of *viraha bhakti*, 'love in separation'.[376] They do not speak from inside the states they are depicting and thus avoid posing as realised beings. Statements regarding the level of underlying truth are often counterpoised by admissions of failure to realise that truth themselves; the divine is depicted as so close and yet so far; they remind their listeners and themselves alike of that fundamental union which, though ultimately the only valid truth, is so hard to attain. On the second level, the authors avoid depicting themselves as especially sucessful wanderers on the spiritual path towards merging with the divine. They rather pose as destitute losers who have

369 *ND* No. 11: *sabāi bale āmi āmi, āmi cinā hala bhār/svarūpe nirūpe āmi ek āmir bhāb dui prakār* [. . .] and: *āsal āmi jagat'svāmī* [*sic*], *nakal āmi ahaṃkār*. For the Vaishnava understanding of *svarūpa* as the qualified Divine, cf. the remarks in Dimock (1989: 31 ff.), esp. p. 40.

370 Cf. *YB* No. 16.

371 *BhM* No. 14: *khod cinile khodā cine*.

372 *JJ* No. 57; cf. *Qur'ān* 7.11(10), 15.29 ff., 17.61(63) ff., etc.

373 Cf. *JJ* No. 18.

374 *TB* No. 6: *khode khodā nahe bhinna*. I understand the *e*-ending of *khod* as an *e*-nominative case here, since a locative or instrumental meaning seem hardly feasible.

375 *MD* No. 23: *āmi akhaṇḍa haï, āmi bine tumi kai*.

376 Cf. below, section 5.7.10 in this chapter. In *viraha* songs, union is usually referred to either as a past event or as utterly unattainable.

not profited from the chances given to them; at any rate they aspire rather than attain, and long for rather than possess.

The most basic religious sentiment in Maijbhandari religiosity, and the driving force towards spiritual union, love, will concern us in the following section.

5.7.9 Love

> The river of love has two streams.
> In one there is poisonous water, the other is filled with juice.[377]
> (Ramesh Shil)

The concept of love is of utmost centrality to various *bhakti* and Sufi traditions in general and to Maijbhandari religiosity in particular.[378] Alongside the representation of the saints, it is *the* most important topic in Maijbhandari songs. In a rough estimate, more than half of the songs in my collection explicitly refer to love. The usual term is *prem*, but other terms such as *pyār* (U./H.), *ʿišq*, *maḥabba* (Ar., in both their Urdu [*muḥabbat*] and Bengali [*mohabbat*/*mahabbat*] forms) are also occasionally found.[379] This section explores the imagery and conceptualisations surrounding the motif of love in Maijbhandari songs. In view of the centrality of love to Maijbhandari thinking, however, certain motifs substantially belonging here (*viraha*, play, craziness) have been extrapolated and are treated under separate headings afterwards.

According to popular self-representations in Maijbhandar, 'love is what Maijbhandar is all about'. Love is seen as the essence of Maijbhandari religiosity, and the 'Maijbhandari philosophy' (*māij'bhāṇḍārī darśan*) is basically a 'philosophy of love' (*prem'darśan*). The songs elaborate the idea that Maijbhandar is the true locus of love, and the Maijbhandari its incarnation. 'All of you who want to go, come to the square of love of the dearest sultan',[380] says Aliullah, and 'Father Mawlānā has built a square of love'.[381] For Ramesh Shil, Maijbhandar is the *prem dar'bār*, the 'court of love' (*ND* No. 20) where the *premer khelā*, 'play of love' can be witnessed (*MD* No. 6). It is also called a garden of love: 'In Maijbhandar in the garden of love, a flower of love blossomed'.[382] The Maijbhandari's object is to teach love: 'You came to give love-education, you took the name Ġawṯ al-Aʿẓam/An *avatāra* of love has arisen in the end time'.[383] And Farid Hosain imagines Maijbhandar as a school of love: 'The annual examinations are being held in the school of father Ġawṯ/What a beautiful school of love! Come whoever wants to have love education'.[384]

377 *JS* No. 14: *prem nadīr dui dhārā/ek dhārāte biṣer pāni ār ek dhārā rase bharā.*

378 I am keeping *bhakti* and Sufi traditions terminologically apart. But there are also instances of speaking of 'Muslim' or 'Sufi *bhakti*'. Cf. Hamid Afaq Qureshi (1989).

379 The latter (Bg. *mahabbat*) rarely; but e.g. in Farid Hosain *HB* No. 20.

380 Aliullah *PN* No. 7: *keke yābi āẏ're torā, chol'tān dhaner premer cake.*

381 *PN* No. 76: *bābā māolā premar cak basāila.*

382 Ramesh Shil *MhB* No. 39: *māij'bhāṇḍāre prem bāgāne phuṭ'la premer phul.*

383 Ramesh Shil *BhM* No. 3: *prem(a) śikṣā dite ele, gāucul ājam nām dharile/śeṣ jamānāẏ udaẏ hala premer abatār.*

384 *HB* No. 46: *gāuch bābār iskulete – cal'che bārṣik parīkṣā re/ki sundar premeri iskul – āẏ ke nibi prem śikṣā.*

The love to be experienced at Maijbhandar may be seen as a river: ‘Come on, brother, and play love in the river of love of the dearest Ġawṯ’ (Maulana Hadi),[385] or as the sea.[386] ‘There is a sea of love inside the storehouse, and in that pitcher is the city of God’, says Aliullah, playing on the assonances between *bhāṇḍār*, lit. ‘storehouse’ and of course simultaneously Maijbhandar, and *bhāṇḍa*, ‘pitcher, pot’.[387] ‘If you jump into that sea, your name and mark will not remain’,[388] that is, the individual self will be wiped out. According to Ramesh Shil, ‘if one dives into the sea of love once, the life-breath is cool [i.e. at ease] for [the rest of] the life’.[389] He elaborates that there is ebb and flow in this sea (*SD* No. 16), or rather the estuary of a huge river; the waves move upstream,[390] and a bath in the middle stream promises eternal reward. But three specific waves must be known and mastered, otherwise diving is risky (‘Various great divers have drowned’).[391] Maulana Hadi also stresses that the sea of love is anything but smooth and peaceful, and a boat and the saint’s help are needed when one ventures to such waters: ‘Set me across the sea of love in the boat of love, O dearest Ġawṯ/My naive mind is troubled from seeing the waves of the sea of love’.[392] In an Urdu song, again, he implores the Ġawṯ: ‘Put my boat into the sea of love’.[393] At this point, the imagery apparently blends with that of the ‘sea/ocean of existence’ (*bhabasāgar*, *bhabasindhu*) we have already encountered in the context of death, and the saint again becomes the helmsman or boatswain: ‘O boatswain of the river of love/Take the boat of love to the other shore fast’ (Shafiul Bashar).[394] ‘The Maijbhandari arose, bringing with him a boat of love/Take me into the boat of love’ (Abdul Jabbar Mimnagari);[395] and Maulana Hadi qualifies this boat of love further: the *muršid* is in its middle and teaches the play of love, the boat is tied to his feet, and he has installed an oar of divine light in order to take his servants across.[396]

385 *RB* No. 27: *gāuch dhaner prem nadīte, calare bhāi prem khelite*. Cf. also Ramesh Shil *BhM* No. 16, where the sound of the friend’s flute makes the boat of trance move upstream on the Yamunā of love (*śune bā̃śīr dhvani bhāb taraṇī prem yamunā ujān yāẏ*). For the possible tantric implications of such imagery, cf. below in the section on boat journeys (5.7.13).

386 Terms like the Skt. *sindhu* and *sāgara* or the Persian *dariyā* can denote both floating and still waters and thus comprise anything from huge rivers to the ocean.

387 *PN* No. 29: *bhāṇḍār bhitar prem(a) sāgar sei bhāṇḍate khodār nagar*.

388 *PN* No. 22: *sei sāgare jhā̃p dile, nām nisān rabe nā*.

389 *SD* No. 14: *ek'bār ḍub dile prem sāgare janmer tare prāṇ śītal*.

390 Ramesh Shil *SD* No. 14: *prem sāgare bhāṭi gāṅge ḍheu khele ujān*.

391 Ibid: *mahā mahā ḍuburirā ḍuibe mareche*. A tantric interpretation of this song, with the middle stream as the *suṣumnā* and the dying divers as loss of semen during ritual sexual exercises is tempting and would not seem too eccentric in a Baul context. Cf., however, the section on boat journeys below, as well as the discussion about the interpretation of *dehatattva* songs in Section 6.1.

392 *RS* No. 28: *prem tarīte pār karago prem(a) nidhi gāuch(a) dhan/prem samudrer ḍheu dekhiẏā hare gela bholā man*. Alternatively, *prem nidhi* may be read as an epithet of the Ġawṯ: ‘O dearest Ġawṯ, you sea of love’.

393 *RS* No. 2 (Urdu in Bengali script): *eskeki dariẏāme mere kisti lāgādao* [*sic*].

394 *YB* No. 73: *ore prem nadīr nāiẏā/śīghra cala prem tari opārete bāiẏā*.

395 *PR* No. 23: *saṅge laẏe premer tarī, udaẏ haïlā māij bhāṇḍārī/prem tarīte lao āmāẏ uṭhāi*.

396 *RB* No. 27: *antare murśid dhan āche – prem(a)khelā śikhāite/murśid dhaner caraṇ kāche – premer tarī bā̃dhā āche/tāte nūrī dā̃ṛ lāgāiche/dāsagaṇ(a) pār karāite*.

The saint, then, is where true love is to be found; he teaches love and leads through the sea of love that his *darbār* is; he receives love and also gives love. Mahbubul Alam expresses the latter through the image of wine: 'O storer [*bhāṇḍārī*] of the wine of love, open your tavern/For I have come, a happy-go-lucky one, a wine-drinker without measure [*be-hisābī*]'.[397] Such imagery in Maijbhandari songs consciously uses a register supplied by Persian poets from Omar Khayyam up to Khomeini,[398] but it is not altogether possible to attribute it entirely to recent reception since Ramesh Shil already mentions 'the wine of love' (though without the tavern).[399] The usual way of asking the saint to give love, however, is to pose as a beggar: 'O Baba Bhandari, I am the beggar of your mercy/I am walking around in the *darbār* because I want to get the alm of love' (Abdul Gafur Hali).[400] Shafiul Bashar approaches the saint in utter humility: 'This is my solicitation at [your] pure feet, do donate [me] the jewel of love'.[401]

On the other hand, love is situated inside the *bhakta*. Once ignited by the saint, it burns internally[402] and ravages the lover's personality. In a song by Maulana Hadi, the fire of love burns down 'the garden of the heart', including interior 'mountains, groves and woods' and even the 'three-world'; 'Hadi was reduced to ashes without the dearest Ġawt̲'.[403] Elsewhere, he describes this feeling as *madan jvālā*, 'the vexation of Madan [the god of love]', and accuses his beloved: 'Having robbed Hadi's life-breath, you sit there and watch the spectacle'.[404] Farid Hosain complains that 'Burning in your fire of love, I died a living death'.[405] Aliullah compares this love to a snake: 'The snake of love made me miserable, there is no sign of life/What do I know when he wrote my death into my fate'.[406] Farid Hosain complains: 'Under the vexation of that love I cry to death/You have gone away and disguised yourself as a cruel stone'.[407] The love described here is an excess of feeling that does not find its addressee and thus remains unreleased inside the lover. This torture of love, then, is essentially the torture of separation or unreciprocated love. Its dominant mode being that of complaint, it is nevertheless

397 *AJ* No. 28: *prem-śārāber bhāṇḍārī go sarāikhānā khol re tor/esechi ek mastānā ye be-hisābī śārāb'khor.*

398 Badrunnesa Saju, author of the song book *Madirā*, mentioned Khomeini's poetry as one of her inspirations (Interview February 2001).

399 Cf. *BhM* No. 22: *māolār premer sirāb piẏe haore dioẏānā* ('Become crazy by drinking the wine of love of the Mawlā').

400 *JJ* No. 74: *ore bābā bhāṇḍārī – āmi tomār daẏār bhikhārī/prem bhikṣā pāba bale – dar'bāre ghuri phiri.* Cf. also *JJ* No. 97.

401 *YB* No. 45: *ei minati pāk caraṇe/prem(a) ratan dān karanā.*

402 Cf. Abdul Gafur Hali *TB* No. 1; Aliullah *PN* No. 9; etc.

403 *RS* No. 51 (*hṛd bāgān, parbbat kānan ban, tribhuban*): *gāuch(a) dhan(a) bine hādī bhaṣma haẏe gela re.*

404 *RB* No. 60: *basi dekha raṅ tāmāsā hādīr hare prāṇ.*

405 *SB* No. 7: *tomār premāgune puṛi – jindā marā gelām mari.* Lit. 'I am living dead [and] died'.

406 *PN* No. 105: *premer sarpe kailya hina, haẏ'āter <hayāt> nāhi cin/kakhan jāni mṛtyu āmār tak-direte likhila.*

407 *HB* No. 54: *sei premer jvālāte pari* [*sic*] – *kā̃dākāṭi kare mari/dure* [*sic*] *giẏā sājiẏācha niṣṭhur(a) pāṣān(a)* [*sic*].

acclaimed as a necessary state in a *bhakta*'s spiritual development. This love is of utmost importance among the ways of relating to love in Maijbhandari songs and will be treated separately below under the heading of *viraha bhakti*.

Love can be true and false, and that depends on its object. Love attached to the wrong object hinders progress and ultimately leads to destruction. Such objects include the notorious *gāṛi bāṛi sundar nārī*, 'car, house and beautiful woman' (Abdul Gafur Hali), and terms like the 'sandbank of illusion'[408] or the 'sleep of illusion'[409] are employed to warn about getting entangled in worldly objects. Aliullah, for example, admonishes his mind to keep to the right path and not to hide in false love.[410] Farid Hosain distinguishes between two kinds of love, *ṣādiqī* (Ar. <*ṣādiq*>, 'right')[411] and *fāsiqī* (Ar. <*fāsiq*>, 'immoral'). The former searches union, and 'if the two merge and become one, the function of love is accomplished'.[412] The latter is bought for money 'exactly like at the butcher's on the market'.[413] Shafiul Bashar mentions the *ma'šūq*, the divine beloved in Sufi terminology, as the true object of love, and stresses that both women and men can be a *ma'šūq* if they possess the *ṣifāt*, 'qualities' of Allah. The problem is that 'Upon seeing a beautiful woman they know her as *māśukī* by mistake/Drowning in the magic of infatuation, how many connoisseurs [*rasik*] die'.[414] The root of such problems is the close relationship between *prem*, 'love', and *kām*, 'erotic love/lust/desire'.[415] For Shafiul Bashar, 'two demonesses, *kām* [lust] and *kāminī* [beautiful woman], are sitting at the mouth of the river of love',[416] and in a song by Ramesh Shil, 'The river of love has two streams/In one there is poisonous water, the other is filled with juice' (*JS* No. 14, cf. beginning of this section). Abdul Gafur Hali opens a shop on the market of the world, 'but through the influence of *kām* and *kāminī*, all including the stock capital is lost'.[417] Nevertheless, *kām* remains necessary, as he makes clear in another song: 'A power [*śakti*] makes love [*kām*] in many forms in the world/Builds itself, destroys itself, does not fulfil its heart's desire [*manaskām*]/And within that love [*kām*], the creation itself is the self'.[418] The usual notion here seems to be that *kām* should be watched closely and – in legitimate relationships between men and women

408 Cf., e.g., Ramesh Shil *ŚB* No. 7 (*māẏār car*); *ND* No. 10 (*māẏā car*); etc.

409 Cf. Abdul Gafur Hali *TB* No. 3 (*māẏā ghum*).

410 *PN* No. 52.

411 Cf. Upendranāth Bhaṭṭācārya (2001: 513), where *ṣādiqī 'išq* is translated as *mūl prem*, 'original love', with reference to a Baul song by Pāñjar.

412 *HB* No. 32: *duiẏe miśyā haïle ek'ṭi – premer kāryya haẏ're purā.*

413 Ibid: *bājārer kas'bir abikal*. Cf. also Ramesh Shil *SD* No. 34: *phāsekite narak bhaẏ*, 'through immoral [love comes about] fear of hell'.

414 *YB* No. 53: *sundarī ramaṇī dekhe/bhrame 'māśukī' jene thāke/moher(a) kuhake ḍube, kata rasik mare yāẏ.*

415 Cf. Aliullah *PN* No. 99 (p. 86).

416 *YB* No. 44: *kām kāmini dui rākṣasī prem nadīr mohanāẏ basi.*

417 *TB* No. 12: *kām, kāminīr baśe āsal saha yāẏ.*

418 *JJ* No. 55: *ek(a) śakti jagat mājhe bahurūpe kare kām/nije gaṛe nije bhāṅge purāẏ nā tār manaskām/se kāmer(a) mājhe ābār sṛṣṭi nije āpanā.*

– amalgamated to prem to find its true destination. Its disastrous effect occurs only if it is mistaken for prem and thus blocks access to true love.[419]

True love, that is love directed to the right beloved, is the most important thing and is held dearer even than life. For him who has been caught by love, 'life and death are the same',[420] and 'those who practise love with him [the true beloved] die before dying' (Ramesh Shil).[421] Aliullah points out that 'without love it is extremely hard to find God and the Prophet';[422] religion must be practised with love.[423] The intoxication of love overrides all considerations of social status: 'Ramesh says: what use are caste and family?/Will this intoxication leave me if they put a knife to my throat?',[424] or: 'Whoever has been able to understand the word "love"/And has immersed the honour of his family in the sea of love/Always swims in a relationship of love with the joy of love'.[425] And Abdul Gafur Hali refers to Islamic cosmology to stress that love is the whole scope of man: 'Lastly He [Allah] made the earthen Adam for love'.[426]

To evoke love, Maijbhandari songs often refer to model lovers mostly (but not only) from the Islamic, and more specifically Sufi tradition. The couples that are mentioned are Laila and Qais (Majnun),[427] Zulaykha and Yusuf,[428] as well as less frequently Shirin and Farhad,[429] Radha and Krishna,[430] Eve and Adam, and Fatima and ʿAli.[431] Single exemplary figures for love of the divine are Abraham, Moses and Uways al-Karani as well as the Sufis Mansur al-Hallaj, ʿAbd al-Qadir Gilani and Muʿin al-Din Chishti.[432] The couples usually illustrate the desperate condition of the lover in separation: 'As Majnun wanders around in the forests in his love for Laila/Mimnagari, having fallen into the trap of your love, always cries' (Abdul Jabbar Mimnagari).[433] 'Farhad without Shirin is like Majnun without Laila/Burnt

419 This point cannot be substantiated from the songs. But it summarises the opinions of contemporary song writers and adherents to Maijbhandar I was able to gather in various interviews. This is in close agreement with Vaishnava concepts as analysed by Dimock: *prema* is substantially a derivation of *kāma*; it must be redirected from 'women' to the self so as to achieve a 'unity of flesh and spirit, of human and divine' (Dimock 1989: 163, 153).

420 Ramesh Shil *ŚB* No. 19 (*jīban maraṇ samān kathā*).

421 *JS* No. 30: *tār sane prem kare yārā, mar'bār āge mare tārā.*

422 *PN* No. 19: *prem bine khodā nabī pāoẏā baṛā kaṭhin.*

423 Cf. *PN* No. 2.

424 Ramesh Shil *ĀM* No. 12: *rameś bale ki karibe jāte ār(a) kule/ei niśā ki chuṭ'be āmār galāẏ churi dile.*

425 *ND* No. 31: [*rameś bale*] *prem śabdaṭi ye bujh'te pereche/prem sāgare kulamān bisajjiẏā diẏāche/premānande prem sambandhe sadā santaraṇ.*

426 *JJ* No. 90: *māṭir ādam śeṣe bānāila premer lāgīẏā.*

427 E.g. Abdul Jabbar Mimnagari *PR* No. 16; Maulana Hadi *RB* No. 20, 23; *RS* No. 50; Abdul Gafur Hali *JJ* No. 55; Ramesh Shil *SD* No. 20; etc.

428 e.g. Maulana Hadi *RB* No. 20; Abdul Gafur Hali *JJ* No. 55; Ramesh Shil *SD* No. 20; *ND* No. 22, 31, 34; *MD* No. 31; etc. For a general account of this story, see, e.g., Schimmel (1995a: 58 ff.).

429 Maulana Hadi *RS* No. 50.

430 Ramesh Shil *SD* No. 20; other divine couples of the Hindu pantheon, such as Śiva and Gaurī (i.e. Pārvatī) and Indra and Shachi are also mentioned in this song.

431 Both in Abdul Gafur Hali *JJ* No. 55.

432 All of them together are found in Ramesh Shil's song *SD* No. 34 (discussed below, p. 000).

433 *PR* No. 16: *maj'nu yeman lāilī preme ghure beṛāẏ banete/mim'nagarī sadāẏ kānde paṛiẏā tor premer phānde.*

in the fire of love, he finally was reduced to ashes' (Maulana Hadi).[434] Love is portrayed as the great driving force between well-known religious events and miracles and the primary motivation of prophets and saints. Ramesh Shil describes Abraham's sacrifice, Moses' exodus, Mansur's exclamation *anā 'l-ḥaqq* on the gallows, as well as events connected with ʿAbd al-Qadir Gilani and Muʿin al-Din Chishti and Uways al-Karani's acquisition of the Prophet's robe (*jubbā*) as all directly resulting from that power of love (*ʿišq*).

Love, finally, is the main criterion of distinguishing true from false religious practice. A *faqīr*, Shafiul Bashar argues, is not determined by some dress code, but by developing one's love.[435] Normal people do not understand love, only the *ʿāšiqān*, lovers of the Mawlā, know about it. 'The lover knows the significance of love/The thief knows the thief's work', sings Farid Hosain, implying that lovers possess expert knowledge of the main substance of any religion.[436] Ramesh Shil accuses the Faraizis (Farāʾiżī) of fraud and points out, with reference to Muʿin al-Din Chisti, that music is a means to open up one's love.[437] And Maulana Hadi denounces the fraudulent Maulawi as half-educated, greedy and ignorant regarding the scriptures; but most importantly, he has no love: 'There is no desire for love in his mind, he does not know his own identity [*cin*]/He does not know himself, what should he teach others?'[438]

Let us summarise the attributes of love so far gathered from the songs before we move on to the examination of yet another specific kind of love. Love, denoted by *prem* and *ʿišq* in apparent synonymity, is the essence of Maijbhandar and the Maijbhandari. The latter is a teacher and bestower of love; and once he has infused it into his disciples he becomes its object. Such true love is held to be more important than life or death. It is the key to true religiosity and life, but it may also cause desperate suffering. True love is usually equivalent to utter self-negation, in contrast to false love which remains selfish. We will pursue our inquiry regarding the characteristics of love in the succeeding sections.

5.7.10 Love in Separation (viraha bhakti)

> By what fraud did you charm me, playing your flute?
> How shall I now bear the infamy of those blaming me?[439]
> (Lutfunnesa Hosaini)

Viraha, 'separation', is a central concept of *bhakti*, and it has come to be used as a technical term in *bhakti* studies.[440] Maijbhandari songs usually use the term

434 *RS* No. 50: *phar'hād(a) ye siri bine, maj'nun yena lāili bine/abaśeṣe premānale jvali haïla chār(a)khār.*

435 Cf. *YB* No. 52.

436 *SB* No. 45: *premik jāne premer marma/core jāne corer karma.* Cf. also Ramesh Shil *SD* No. 16: *rameś kaẏ māolār prem kemane jāne sab āsekāne.*

437 Cf. Ramesh Shil *ND* No. 15.

438 *RS* No. 72: *prem(a) sādh(a) nāhi mane, nija cin(a) nāhi cine/parere ki cināibe nā cine āpan. Cenā* is more literally 'to recognise', *cin* is 'sign, mark'.

439 *GP* No. 19: *kon chalanāẏ bholāilire, bā̃śī bājāiẏā (bābā)/ekhan āmi kem'ne saïbo, ninduker bad'nām.*

440 Cf., e.g., Vaudeville (1992: 105 f.) on the way Kabir uses the notion of *viraha*.

bicched but *biraha* also occurs. We cannot deal here in any detail with the various literary traditions connected with the *bhakti* movement all over South Asia for simple lack of space, and a few introductory remarks must suffice.[441] *Viraha bhakti* may be translated as 'devotion in separation'.[442] In *viraha bhakti* literature, the *bhakta* or devotee suffers from the absence of his venerated and beloved deity and vents his feelings of pain and despair. As a movement, *bhakti* is deemed to have gained momentum around the seventh century AD in the Krishna devotion of the Alvars of Tamil Nadu, or even earlier in Tamilian Shiva devotion, and spread from there to the north. Krishna has remained the most widely venerated deity of Hindu *bhakti* traditions, followed by Rama. In the Bengali context, the most dominant medieval *bhakti* literature are the songs of the so-called *Baiṣṇab padāvalī* ('Vaishnava verses').[443] To be sure, Bengali Vaishnavism has to a large extent always been devotion to Krishna, and that, together with the extensive literature produced from it, had a deep impact on Bengali language and culture that did not remain confined to Hindu society. This can be impressively substantiated by the sheer number of Bengali Muslim writers of Vaishnava lyrics. Writing in 1905, Abdul Karim Sahityavisharad (1997: 382) mentions 44 such writers who flourished well into the nineteenth century.[444]

The mass of that production accounts for the conventionality of the topoi used. The *Bhāgavata Purāṇa* (ninth–tenth century AD) apparently first makes these known beyond South India, but its account does not yet feature Radha and her prominent role as Krishna's main beloved;[445] that story develops later and becomes the main framework for the Bengali *Baiṣṇab padābalī* and also, as I will

441 There is extensive literature on the topic. On *bhakti* religion in general, cf. Monika Thiel-Horstmann (ed.) (1983); Karel Werner (ed.) (1993); N.N. Bhattacharyya (ed.) (1989); R.S. McGregor 1992; David N. Lorenzen (ed.) (1996); Aziz Ahmad (1999: 140–52); etc. For single traditions and *bhakti* literature, cf. Charlotte Vaudeville (1993); Milton Singer (ed.) (1966); Monika Thiel-Horstmann (1983b) and (2002); Par'śurām Caturvedī (1989) and A.J. Alston (1980) on Mirabai; Tukaram (1991) and Tukārāma (1991); etc.

442 On the different etymologies of the term *bhakti*, cf. e.g. Klostermaier (1990: 210). A derivation from the Sanskrit root *bhaj*, 'to share, partake, apportion, venerate', appears to be the most convincing.

443 For an exhaustive compilation of this literature, cf. Harekṛṣṇa Mukhopādhyāẏ (ed.) (1980). On the *Gauṛīẏa* and *Sahajiẏā* strands of Bengali Vaishavism, cf. Edward C. Dimock (1989). Rahul Peter Das, 'Recent Works On Bengali Vaiṣṇavism', in Das (1997: 39–103) gives a thorough overview of research on the topic, especially by Bengali authors.

444 Cf. also the rather concise volume *Madhyayuger bāṅ'lā gītikabitā* (ed. Muhammad Ābdul Hāi and Āh'mad Śarīph, 1998) that gives contributions by well-known Hindu Vaishnava authors side by side with works of less-known Muslim writers under headings such as *Baiṣṇab padābalī* (pp. 1–7), *Rādhānurāg* ('passion for Rādhā, pp. 55–63), *Biraha* (pp. 154–72), etc. Further, see the compilations *Bāṅgālār baiṣṇab-bhābāpanna musal'mān kabi* and its much larger sequel *Bāṅgālār baiṣṇab-bhābāpanna musal'mān kabir padamañjuṣā* by Yatīndramohan Bhaṭṭācārya (1962, 1984).

445 On the role of the *Bhāgavatapurāṇa* in disseminating the idea of *bhakti*, cf. Friedhelm Hardy (1983) and Freda Matchett (1993). Useful expositions are also found in Thomas J. Hopkins (1966), and J.A.B. van Buitenen (1966).

argue, for Maijbhandari songs. The site of this story is the village of Vrindavan on the shore of river Yamuna where Krishna, the cowherd, plays his flute and by its sound instils an indominable longing in the hearts of the *gopīs* or/and Radha. Radha, a young married woman, has a love affair with Krishna and spends long periods of time waiting and yearning for her uncontrollable beloved. In the poetry, Radha is usually the speaker, or in any case the situation is viewed from her perspective; the variety of the states of mind her love for Krishna produces in her – ailings, sexual desire, restlessness, desperation, anger, etc. – are, generally speaking, the subject matter of such poetry.

This imagery has for a long time been a part of Sufi literature in various South Asian traditions.[446] In Maijbhandari songs, Radha and Krishna are hardly ever mentioned, and, as shown above, the names of Laila and Qais/Majnun, or Zulaykha and Yusuf, are much more frequently quoted. We find different degrees of rapprochement *vis-à-vis*, in this case, the Vaishnava tradition: on the whole, references to Vaishnava imagery are usually implicit rather than explicit, and sometimes even apparently involuntary. If I then use *kr̥ṣṇabhakti* as the overarching frame of reference in this section, it is in the arbitrary conviction of an outsider-observer that the substance of these songs vindicates such a procedure. It must be stressed that in Maijbhandar multiple referentiality regarding such issues of classification predominates. The discussion of whether such motifs on the ground are regarded as loans or not, and in which way (if at all) different religious traditions are set in relation to each other, must be left to the discussion below.[447]

In order to experience the states of mind of Radha, Krishna's model lover, a *kr̥ṣṇabhakta* may have to 'become female' or, according to Dimock (1989: 158), cultivate the gopībhāva or emotional state of the gopīs. Milton Singer gives impressive examples of the important position that this concept of becoming a woman continues to hold among certain Vaishnava groups;[448] and Annemarie Schimmel stresses the great importance of the bride image in South Asian Islamic

446 Cf. one outstanding example, the eighteenth-century Panjabi Sufi Bullhe Shah with his frequent references to Krishna and Krishna's flute-playing as a symbol of *fanā'*. Denis Matringe (1992: 197) distinguishes between the rather theoretical harmonising gestures of the Persian-writing Sufi elite and the high degree of integration of such materials by those using the local languages ('[. . .] as regards popular Sufism, even if Bullhe Śāh had such predecessors as Śāh Ḥusain of Lahore (1539–93/4), no Panjabi Sūfī poet before him integrated Hindu elements to that extent in his poetry'), and states: 'Kr̥ṣṇaism and Nāth yoga provided Bullhe Śāh with an imagery from which he derived symbols to express the various states and emotions of his mystical experience: loving devotion (*'iśq, prem*) and renunciation (*zuhd, tyāga*) are as typical of Sufism as they are of Saint mysticism.'

447 For indigenous interpretations of songs falling under the category of *viraha bhakti*, cf. Section 6.2. The relationship between different traditions as defined in Maijbhandar will be discussed in Chapter 7.

448 Singer (1966: 129 ff.), especially the interviews with Tamil Vaishnavas on p. 130 ff.

mysticism.[449] Carla Petievich (2007) presents an abundance of examples from Punjabi and Urdu Sufi poetry well into the nineteenth century for what she calls 'vocal masquerade' in her impressive anthology When Men Speak as Women. In Rahul Peter Das's words, 'a notion important to this Bhakti is that the highest and most selfless love is that of a woman for a man, and that the love for the divinity can attain this perfection only if the devotee becomes a woman'.[450] In *viraha* Maijbhandari songs, too, assuming femininity on the part of male songwriters is a common feature. Abdul Jabbar Mimnagari, for example, describes how he (or, indeed, she) dresses up for the Mawlā: 'I will put collyrium [*kājal*] to my eyes, dearest Mawlā/And smear the dust of your feet on my body, I will paint my make up with collyrium [*surmā*]/And put a bindi [*tilak*] to the forehead, dearest Mawlā'.[451] Maulana Hadi, who in fact is reported to have dressed in a sari and danced in front of Gholam Rahman in already advanced age,[452] decides to give up his life: 'I cannot bear the vexation of separation, I have come to give up my life-breath/Why should I, a woman [*abalā*], bear the grief [*tāp*] you have inflicted on my mind?'[453] The image of the *yoginī*, already very common, by the way, in the poetry of the eighteenth-century Panjabi Sufi Bullhe Shah, is used: 'It was [written] on my forehead that I should give up my life-breath in separation from him/I was a wife, a woman of family, by his trance I became a *yoginī*'.[454] Abdul Jabbar Mimnagari has become *pāg'linī*, a crazy woman;[455] Ramesh Shil a

449 Schimmel (1995a: 21); she does not want to see this as a mere adaptation of the *virahinī*, but admits the parallels: 'Am deutlichsten ausgeprägt ist in der mystischen Tradition das Bild der "Brautseele" im indo-pakistanischen Bereich. Es wäre zu einfach, hier nur eine automatischen Übernahme des Begriffes der *virahini* anzunehmen, die in der indischen Tradition, vor allem in der *bhakti*-Mystik, im Mittelpunkt steht, denn nur die Frau, so heißt es, kann wirklich *prema*, "Liebe" und *viraha*, "Sehnsucht2 empfinden, und wenn ihr Geliebter, Verlobter oder Ehemann fern von ihr ist, leidet sie unsagbar unter dem Trennungsschmerz.' Again on p. 109: 'Besonders im indischen Subkontinent ist eine echte Brautmystik entstanden, in der die Seele, dem göttlichen Geliebten seit dem Ur-Vertrag (Sura 7: 172) verbunden, auf die Hochzeit wartet, die in volkstümlichen Sängen mit allen Details des Festes beschrieben wird: Decken werden ausgebreitet, köstliche Speisen bereitet, Rosenwasser wird ausgegossen.'

450 Cf. Rahul Peter Das (2003: 161 f.), with references to other relevant literature; Das stresses that this is a pan-South Asian notion.

451 *PR* No. 6: *naẏaner kājal bānāiba go māolā dhan/caraṇ dhuli gāẏe mākhiba, chur'mā kare ā̃khi sājāiba/kapāle tilak kariba go māolā dhan.* The expression *chur'mā kare* has been translated as *chur'mā diẏe/diẏā*, but is uncommon; *kare* might also be interpreted as the locative of *kar*, 'hand': 'Collyrium in the hand, I will paint/make up the eye[s].'

452 Cf. Section 5.1.

453 *RS* No. 15: *bicched jvālā saïte nāri elām ebār prāṇ tyajite/ye tāp(a) diẏācha mane abalā sahimu kene*. Cf. also *RS* No. 52, where the first person is a *duḥkhinī*, sad woman, whose youth has been stolen; *RS* No. 85 (*tāper tāpinī*: 'the agrieved from grief'.

454 *RS* No. 80: *kapāle mor ei chila tār bicchede prāṇ tyajiba/kāminī kulinī chilām, yār bhābe yoginī hailām*. The relative pronoun *yār* must be related to *tār*; the interposition of another clause makes an exact English translation difficult. On Bulhe Shah's use of this image, cf. Denis Matringe (1992: 193 f.); the seeker, suffering from the pangs of separation, takes the garb of a *yoginī* and imposes suffering upon himself (or rather herself).

455 *PR* No. 9: *āmi tomāẏ prāṇ diẏe pāg'linī haẏechi*. Also Ramesh Shil *BhM* No. 31.

kalaṅkinī, a stained woman,[456] or a *dāsī*, a female servant (*SD* No. 30), as well as a *duḥkhinī* (sad), *udāsinī* (indifferent)[457] and *kāṅgālinī* (miserable) woman (BhM No. 31); he burns 'night and day like a female deer whose wood has been burnt'.[458] The people hurl insults: 'I am an unchaste, stained woman, a whore, a black snake/Always hearing [such insults] from the mouth of the people, my head is lowered day and night'.[459] Farid Hosain, too, calls himself a *kalaṅkinī* (*SB* No. 46) and asks the flute-playing friend to make her his *saṅginī*, consort.[460] 'Alas, I am dying in this love separation from the black one', cries out Abdul Gafur Hali and calls himself a *birahinī*, a separated one, and *bairāginī*, a renouncer;[461] he is an *abhāginī*, ill-favoured, and *kalaṅkinī*, stained woman (*TB* No. 24); the people call him a wicked woman;[462] he even likens himself to a *cātakinī*, that is a female swallow always thirstily waiting for rain clouds – a common image for the bhakta.[463] And asking himself how he has deserved all this suffering of separation, Abdul Gafur Hali says: 'What is my crime? [It is] because I became a woman'.[464] Also Shafiul Bashar becomes variously a *duḥkhiẏā* (sad), *pāg'linī* (mad) and *udāsinī* (indifferent) woman (*YB* No. 34 and 54). The female authors, accordingly, usually remain female in the first person of the songs.[465]

The *viraha* songs for the most part fall under the category of bride mysticism.[466] Although the single images are found in almost any possible combination, it seems possible to isolate three distinct stages regarding the development of this love in separation and the gradual increase in distance and despair. In a first stage, the female lover, while waiting for her beloved, weaves garlands, adorns the bedstead with flowers and spends sleepless nights in attendance. Shafiul Bashar asks his beloved to 'take the garland into your hands',[467] and in another song he proclaims: 'I weave a garland with flowers of love to drape it around your neck, lord of my life'.[468] Likewise, Abdul Jabbar Mimnagari says: 'I have woven a garland of different wild flowers/Take it around your neck with a cheerful mind'.[469] Associations

456 *ND* No. 13; *SD* No. 22; *SD* No. 39; etc.

457 i.e., indifferent to everything in the world except the divine beloved; cf. *MD* No. 36 (*āmi udāsinī tomār nām niẏāre bandhu*).

458 *ŚB* No. 12: *ban poṛā hariṇīr mata jvali niśīdin.*

459 *JS* No. 31: *dvicāriṇi kalaṅkinī, kul'ṭā kāla sāpinīre/loker mukhe nitya śuni din yāmini māthā nata.*

460 *SB* No. 51 (to a *saï*, female friend): *pharid'ke saṃginī kar'te kao mane cāile* ('Tell him to make Farid his consort if he wills').

461 *TB* No. 11: *hāẏ're kālār prem bicchede marilām re.*

462 *JJ* No. 21: *loke bale duṣṭa nārī.*

463 *JJ* No. 60 (*megher āśāẏ cātakinī*).

464 *JJ* No. 88: *āmār aparādh ki haïlām bale nārī.* The somewhat topsy-turvy syntax makes other interpretations possible, but these do not significantly modify the meaning of the utterance.

465 Cf., e.g., Lutfunnesa Hosaini *GP* No. 8.

466 German 'Brautmystik'. Cf. also the remarks on this topic in Rahul Peter Das (2003a: 167) and (1997: 24).

467 *YB* No. 75: *hāte nāo mālā khāni.*

468 *YB* No. 30: *prem phuler mālā gā̃thi (go) pariẏe dite prāṇa pati tomar'i gale. Prāṇapati* simultaneously is lexicalised in the meaning of 'husband'.

469 *PR* No. 1: *nānā banaphule gāthiẏāchi mālā/laha gale tule haẏe phulla mane.*

with marriage ceremonies are part of this imagery and certainly intended. The carnal aspect of this imagery is most conspicuous in references to the bed where the lover waits for her beloved, and in the following line, Maulana Hadi also furnishes one of the rare instances in which Krishna (here Hari) is mentioned: 'Not seeing beloved Hari, I toss and turn alone on the bed'.[470] Abdul Gafur Hali's *kālā*, 'black one', also probably refers to Krishna, and he transposes the flower bed of loving union metaphorically inside the heart: 'I have given up all hope/I need the black one's love/I made a bed of flowers on the seat of my heart'.[471] Shafiul Bashar sits in attendance: 'Sitting alone on the bed in hope for you [to come]/I draw [your] figure in my heart, [but] it runs [away] in a moment'.[472] And Abdul Gafur Hali addresses Ziaul Haq as his friend: 'I prepared a bed of flowers, I made a garland in [my] hope/I do not know which co-wife bound a thread [of friendship or love to the wrist] of my friend'.[473] Ramesh Shil quite explicitly uses the image of carnal love: 'I had hoped that we two would merge in our innermost beings [*prāṇe prāṇe*] and have amorous talks/Lie on one bed, both on one mattress'.[474] Sexual union in these songs symbolises spiritual union, and is, in keeping with the motif of *viraha*, 'separation', without exception expressed as not a presence, but an absence. The closest we get to union is exemplified by the following, rather rare song by Maulana Hadi, where union is expected to happen in the near future: 'I will put you [i.e. the female beloved] on the throne, we shall embrace each other/At the dawn of love, the two of us shall merge in love and become one'.[475] Usually, however, as in the songs portrayed above, sexual union is either something awaited in vain, or it is regarded as belonging to the past and lost, as discussed below.[476]

The second stage comprises the suffering from both frustrated waiting for the beloved and from the social consequences of an illicit love affair. The female lover laments the loss of her virginity, family and honour; her 'treasure of youth' (*yauban'dhan*) is irrevocably gone. She hears the gossiping about her among the

470 *RS* No. 71: *nā heriẏe prāṇer hari, ekā śayyāẏ gaṛāgaṛi*. Cf. also No. 85: *ekelā śayyāte tyājilā more* ('He abandoned me alone on the bed').

471 *TB* No. 11: *āmi chāṛiẏāchi sakal āśā/cāi kālār bhālabāsā/āmār hṛd āsane phulaśayyā karilām re*. Cf. also Ramesh Shil *MD* No. 8 (*hṛd pālaṅga*).

472 *YB* No. 10: *bichānāte ekā base tomāri āśāẏ/hṛdaẏe muratī ā̃ki palakete dhāẏ*.

473 *JJ* No. 82: *phuler pālaṃ sājāilām āśāte mālā gā̃thilām/nā jāni bandhure āmār kon satīne dila rākhi*. Besides the Hindu festival of Rākhi (which, in fact, celebrates the ties between siblings rather than lovers), *rākhi* may of course also be read as an absolutive participle of *rākhā* and then mean 'kept'; in that case, however, one would expect a construction with *neoẏā* ('kept for herself') rather than *deoẏā*.

474 *JS* No. 29: *āśā chila prāṇe prāṇe miliba dui jan, kar'ba prem ālāpan/ek pālaṃke kar'ba śaẏan duijane ek bichānāẏ*. *Bichānā*, actually 'bed', has been rendered as 'mattress' here in order to differentiate it from *pālaṃka*, and as it is derived from the verb *bichāna*, 'to spread out'.

475 *RS* No. 26: *siṃhāsane basāiba, buke buke miśāiba/dui jane prem(a) bhore preme miśi ek(a) haba*. The sexual metaphor is obvious here; it may be interesting to note that traditionally, dawn is considered the best time for sexual intercourse (cf. Mau. Nūr Mohāmmad 1997: 144).

476 Such imagery also runs through Indian *bhakti* traditions; cf. the Maharashtrian poet-saint Tukaram using as a motif the unsatiated sexual hunger of a young woman (Tukārāma 1991, No. 387), or Kabir's quite explicit statement: 'They all say I am Your wife/but I have my doubts –/If we don't sleep together on one couch/what kind of love is that? *Re*!' (Vaudeville 1993: 270).

neighbours and scolds her lover for being a fraud. 'He robbed the treasure of youth, why did my life not end/My honour was destroyed and my family [honour] was destroyed, the clothes on my body were destroyed/The gold-coloured youth was destroyed, my beloved came not' (Maulana Hadi).[477] The friend has become adverse to her: 'The chosen friend in whose trance the status of the family was destroyed, became an enemy';[478] and the arrow of love has destroyed the status of the family (Maulana Hadi).[479] That friend, guilty of fraud (*chalanā*), has withdrawn from her:

> O friend, what is that cruel smile? You said that you love./Your and my love happened in secrecy./Now, you are acting oppositely and have retreated far./ How much the people are gazing at me from the corner of the eye.[480]
>
> (Abdul Gafur Hali)

The Bhandari seduced her to leave what is now irretrievably lost: 'In the hope of your love/I left my father and brothers and came/How many bad things the neighbours say' (Ramesh Shil).[481] Her status as a *satī*, a chaste and true woman, is also gone: 'Before I was good/Everyone said good things/The neighbours loved me/ Now they say "fie fie"/Curse [me] a lot/And call me an unchaste whore'.[482] Similarly in the following song: 'I was a woman of family, I became an unchaste [*asatī*] woman by your love' (Abdul Jabbar Mimnagari).[483] Lutfunnesa Hosaini describes this love as seduction: 'By what fraud did you charm me, playing your flute?/How shall I now bear the infamy of those blaming me?' (*GP* No. 19, as above). Badrunnesa Saju, too, accuses the Mawlā of fraud,[484] and laments: 'I am a frightened lover on my way to the beloved/Alas, I returned/Vainly from your door/With infinite pain.'[485] The beloved is described as cold and cruel: 'Would I have given him my life-breath if I had known that his mind is made of stone and full of crookedness?' (Abdul Gafur Hali).[486]

The third stage of this torture of love in separation is painful renunciation. The female lover withdraws from society to spend her life wandering through the woods as a *yoginī*, and laments the hopelessness of ever attaining her

477 *RB* No. 52: *yauban dhan luṭiẏe nila jīban kena gela nā/mān(a) gela kul(a) gela aṅger(a) basan(a) gela/sonār baran yauban gela kānta āmār āila nā.*

478 *PB* No. 80: *yār bhābe kulamān gela iṣṭa mitra bairī haïla.*

479 *RB* No. 93: *khāiẏe premer(a) bān, hārāilem kulamān.*

480 *TB* No. 24: *bandhuẏāre – sei ki niṭhur hāsi?/balechilām bhālabāsi – tomār āmār prem haïla gopane/āji tār biparīt kari tumi ācha dure sari –/āmāẏ yata loke cāhe coukher koṇe.*

481 *MD* No. 19: *tomār premer āśā pāi/cheṛe elem bāp(a) bhāi/pāṛā par'śi* [*sic*] *yata manda bale*. The last line could also be read as 'no matter how many bad things the neighbours say'.

482 *MD* No. 29: *āge āmi chilām bhāla/sakale balita bhāla/pāṛāpaṛ'śi bhālabās'ta more/ekhan bale dur(a)dur(a)* [*sic*], *gālāgāli de pracur/asit* [*sic*, misprint for *asatī*] *kulaṭā bale more.*

483 *PR* No. 16: *chilām āmi kulabatī tomār preme halem asatī.*

484 Cf. *Madirā* No. 6 (*chalanā*).

485 *Madirā* No. 5: *bhīru abhisārikā āmi/phirechi hāẏ/byartha haẏe tomār duẏār hate/ananta bedanāẏ.*

486 *TB* No. 30: *man ye tār pāṣāne gaṛā śaṭher bharā/jān'le ki prāṇ ditām tāre.*

beloved.[487] Farid Hosain thus addresses *Kānāiẏā* (Krishna): 'O Kānāiẏā, I wandered in woods and forests/In this way my life was spent/Always looking up to the sky'.[488] Maulana Hadi stresses the aspect of renunciation: 'Through love for the friend and mental grief, I have become a wood-dweller';[489] 'I, a *yoginī*, wander in the woods because of you, playing the sitar'.[490] And Abdul Gafur Hali puts it thus: 'I left my home and came out; I left the country and went to the woods/I became a renouncer at a young age'.[491]

We have said that Krishna and Radha are rarely explicitly mentioned. The very name Krishna is, as far as I can say, not mentioned in this context, but its *tadbhava* variant *kānāiẏā* is, and there are a number of epithets that also make for an almost certain conscious reference, among them those mentioned above and a few others, namely *śyām* ('the Black One'),[492] *madan mohan* ('the Charmer of the Lord of Love')[493] and, somewhat less strongly, *mohan mūrti* ('charming figure').[494] Furthermore, mention of the localities connected with *kr̥ṣṇalīlā*, such as Vrindavan and the river Yamuna, may be read as conscious allusions.[495] On such a basis, however, only very few Maijbhandari songs could be affiliated with the literary traditions of *kr̥ṣṇabhakti*. But many features of other Maijbhandari songs employing the *viraha* complex of motifs suggest at least an implicit connection with Krishnaite literature. The imagery of love in separation in the three stages outlined above is one such implicit link; others include the motifs of the flute[496] and of the bosom friend (*sakhī*).

The sound of Krishna's flute is spell-binding; it makes the lover leave her house and abandon her settled life.

> You played the flute at the wrong time, how much can a woman bear?/I became a mad woman through the songs of friend Śyāma's flute/I was the

487 Cf. two examples of medieval Vaishnava literature written by Muslim authors, in Adul Karim Shahityabisharad (1997: 168, 171) (Nasiruddin, Sirtaj).

488 *SB* No. 2: *a kānāiẏā – ghur'lām āmi ban jaṅgale/em'ni jīban gela cale/ākāś pāne cāhiẏā cāhiẏā.*

489 *RB* No. 16: *haïẏāchi bandhur bhābe manatāpe* [*sic*, misprint for *manaḥtāpe*] *bana bāsī.*

490 *RB* No. 85: *tomār kāraṇe phiri bane bane setār bājāẏe yoginī.* Cf. also No. 80 as quoted above in this section.

491 *TB* No. 11: *āmi ghar chāṛi bāhire āilām –/deś chāṛiẏā bane gelām/alpa base* [*sic*, misprint for *baẏ'se*] *bairāginī haïlām re.*

492 Cf. Ramesh Shil *BhM* No. 28, 35; *ĀM* No. 3, 12; Abdul Gafur Hali *JJ* No. 48 (although not in a *viraha bhakti* context), 56.

493 Ramesh Shil *MD* No. 37; Maulana Hadi *RS* No. 87; Abdul Gafur Hali *JJ* No. 48 (not in a *viraha bhakti* context); Shafiul Bashar *YB* No. 69, 75.

494 Ramesh Shil *BhM* No. 40; Maulana Hadi *RS* No. 10.

495 Vrindavan features, e.g., in the following songs: Maulana Hadi *RS* No. 27, 31, 39, 45, 65; Shafiul Bashar *YB* No. 18. The Yamuna appears as the site of love and flute-playing in Ramesh Shil *BhM* No. 16; *ŚB* No. 37; *MD* No. 2; Maulana Hadi *RS* No. 14, 79, 83, 91; Shafiul Bashar *YB* No. 69, 75. Nanda, Krishna's foster-father, is mentioned in Ramesh Shil *ĀM* No. 39.

496 Cf. the chapter *Baṃśī* (pp. 64–73) in Muhammad Abdul Hai and Ahmad Sharif (eds) (1997) for a collection of medieval Bengali songs featuring the motif of the flute.

bride of a householder, I set out upon hearing the flute/I lost this and that shore, all by the songs of the terrible flute.[497]

(Ramesh Shil)

Farid Hosain implores his beloved: 'Stay with me/And play the flute with peace',[498] and describes the effect of the tunes: 'Playing the charming flute/He set up a trap of love/O bosom friend, he makes me cry day and night by catching me in his devices [*pheliẏā kale*]'.[499] In a song by Maulana Hadi, the flute is heard by the river Yamuna: 'Sitting on the shore of the Yamuna, I gazed at the full moon/Through the sound of the flute, I had to cry from sorrow for the beloved'.[500] All these songs bear clear testimony of close contact with Krishnaite literature. There is, however, still another way of conceiving of the flute. Rumi's *Maṯnavī* starts with the lament of the reed-flute (P. *nay*) that has been cut off from the reed-wood,[501] and some Maijbhandari songs draw out that connection. Briefly, according to various commentators (cf. Türkmen 1999: 67 f.), the reed-flute stands for the human body; God's breath infuses the soul into it which then yearns to rejoin its divine origin, and this yearning again may be interpreted as a crucial initial stage when entering the spiritual path. Shafiul Bashar alludes to this when he inquires who is crying inside the heart-temple: 'Having fallen off into a different land, he is maddened day and night/Like the flute cries day and night in separation'.[502] Ramesh Shil also elaborates this image in the remaining part of *BhM* No. 35 (the opening of which is quoted at the start of this paragraph): 'Nine holes are in the flute, seven continents make up the earth/The flute resounds even if one does not blow, does friend Śyāma know the mantra?'[503] The nine holes refer to the nine openings of the human body,[504] and Ramesh Shil seems to blend references to Rumi and *kr̥ṣṇabhakti* here. Finally, there is one recent song by Mahbubul Alam that apparently inverts the traditional imagery altogether: 'You gave the flute, you gave the melody, but did you actually come?/Come, and let me become your flute player'.[505] Notwithstanding such exceptions, anyhow, the majority of occurrences of the flute indicate a close relationship to *kr̥ṣṇabhakti*.

Other, minor conventional tropes that often go with *viraha* songs, as well as with many branches of folk literature and also *kāvya*s, are the images of the bumble-bee and the way it is attracted by the scent of flowers, as a metaphor for

497 *BhM* No. 35: *asamaẏe bājāle bā̃śī kata saẏ abalār prāṇe/pāgalinī halem āmi śyām bandhuẏār bā̃śīr gāne/gr̥hasther(a) badhu chilām, bā̃śī śune bāhir halem/ekul okul sab hārāilām dāruṇ(a) bā̃śīr(a) gāne.*

498 *SB* No. 46: *tumi mor kāche thākiẏā/bā̃śī bājāo śānti niẏā.*

499 *SB* No. 51: *bājāiẏā mohan bā̃śī/lāgāila prem(a) phā̃si/kā̃dāẏ ga saï dibāniśi pheliẏā kale.*

500 *RS* No. 79: *yamunār kuline basi herilām pūrṇimā śaśī/bā̃śīr svare kānta śoke kā̃dite haïla re.*

501 Cf. *Maṯnavī* I, 1–13.

502 *YB* No. 16 (*hr̥d mandire ke kā̃de tor*): *khase ese bhinna deśe, dibāniśi raẏ(a) māti/birahete yeman bā̃śi, kā̃diteche dibāniśi.*

503 *BhM* No. 35: *nabachidra bā̃śīr mājhe, saptadvīp pr̥thibī sāje/bā̃śīṭī phuk nā dile tabu bāje śyām bandhu ki mantra jāne.*

504 Cf. below under the motif of 'the body'.

505 *AJ* No. 17: *dile bā̃śī, dile sur(a), tumi ele kaï/tumi esa āmi taba bā̃śuriẏā haï.*

the lover;[506] the *cātaka*, 'swallow', with its proverbial thirst for water, in the same function;[507] and the cuckoo with its sweet voice, denoting lovely scenery predestined for games of love.[508]

The bosom friend (*sakhī* or *saï*), finally, is a typical literary device in Krishnaite literature and other folk and *kāvya* traditions that is often found in Maijbhandari *viraha* songs. The delicate nature of what the female friend has to say narrows down the circle of possible interlocutors to an extreme degree; only her bosom friend is worthy of full confidence, and the intimate details of her love can be narrated to her. The bosom friend has no characteristics, no story of her own, and no messages; she does not interfere with the narration and acts solely as a receptacle and listener within the text, though she may be asked questions and requested to do things for the lover. 'Do tell me, O bosom friend, how shall I keep this life?'[509] asks Maulana Hadi. Abdul Gafur Hali has his lover confess: 'O bosom friend – the people call me stained/And even he calls me adulterous'.[510] The invocation of the bosom friend in this case and in many others happens between the lines of the song and outside the metre as an interjection. Likewise in the following song by Shafiul Bashar: 'Bosom friend O bosom friend – O father of mine, who is there/ In this world except you'.[511] The double vocative in this passage is a sure indicator of the conventionality of this device: the overarching address to the bosom friend in the whole song and the particular address to the saint-father in the present couplet directly succeed each other, and this change of address is apparently not felt to be confusing.

This double vocative shows the possible overlap of the two dominant communicative designs of *viraha* songs, namely the direct address of the beloved on the part of the female self, and the report about her feelings and his behaviour *vis-à-vis* her bosom friend. Both these types combine a monological pattern of suffering self-reference with a dialogical one, and in both the interlocutor is equally mute. Entirely monologic songs are rare; if it occurs, it is usually camouflaged by invoking the *man*, 'mind', as an interlocutor.[512] Recent songs, however, seem to show a tendency to use a purely monologic set-up more frequently, which is arguably due to the influence of modern poetry.[513]

506 Cf. Farid Hosain *SD* No. 22; Ramesh Shil *BhM* No. 39; *JS* No. 23; Aliullah *PN* No. 3, 45; Abdul Jabbar Mimnagari *PR* No. 7; Abdul Gafur Hali *TB* No. 7; *JJ* No. 25; etc.

507 Ramesh Shil *SD* No. 38; *MD* No. 36; Mahbubul Alam *AJ* No. 21; Aliullah *PN* No. 50; etc.

508 Cf. Ramesh Shil *SD* No. 22; *BhM* No. 19; *JS* No. 23; Farid Hosain *SB* No. 51; Maulana Hadi *RB* No. 23; *RS* No. 25; Abdul Gafur Hali *TB* No. 31; Aliullah *PN* No. 3; etc.

509 Maulana Hadi *RS* No. 71: *balanā sakhi kemane rākhiba ejīban.*

510 *TB* No. 4: *asakhigo* [*sic*] – *āmāẏ loke bale kalaṅkini/seo ḍāke do-cārini go. Balā* and *ḍākā* here both denote English 'call' and have not been differentiated in the translation. Vocative particles such as *a, o, ore, go, re, he,* etc. are frequent in connection with the bosom friend, but they cannot usually be translated.

511 *YB* No. 65: *(saïgo saï) tumi bine bābā āmār/ei bhabete ke āche ār.* Calls to the bosom-friend outside the metre are often given in brackets in the originals.

512 Cf., e.g., Ramesh Shil *BhM* No. 38.

513 Cf., e.g., Badrunnesa Saju *Madirā* No. 11; Mahbubul Alam *AJ* No. 11; etc.

Generally, the above sketches the inventory of single motifs and patterns that *viraha* songs use. It goes without saying that they do not usually occur in their completeness; even seemingly crucial ingredients such as the feminity of the lover may or may not be adapted to the idiom of Maijbhandari songs. It should have become clear then that the *viraha* songs bear close ressemblance to *kr̥ṣṇabhakti* as it crystallised in the Bengali genre of *Baiṣṇab padābalī*, but as the motifs in question are common property of various traditions, no monocausal links can be established.

Before we move on to other motifs, one more issue within the context of *viraha bhakti* must be mentioned that partly challenges any exclusive affiliation of these songs to the Radha–Krishna complex of motifs. One kind of symbolic change of gender, as we have seen, is that of the male *bhakta* into a female. There is, however, also another change of gender in quite a number of Maijbhandari songs: the beloved, that is, the saint or God, is portrayed as a female. And this is not a recent development; it starts exactly with Aliullah and the oldest layer of this tradition.[514] 'It weeps in the life-breath from the sound of the [female] beloved's flute', and 'the flute of the [female] beloved resounds inside the body always, day and night', says Aliullah.[515] Maulana Hadi, too, reverts the relations of sex between lover and beloved in quite a number of his songs: 'What fault have I committed, [female] beloved, tell [me at your] revered feet/Why do you chase away again and again this subordinated one?'[516] In one instance, he even attaches *priẏā*, 'female beloved', to the name of Gholam Rahman.[517] Abdul Gafur Hali asks God to show himself: 'At [my] time of leaving, show yourself once in the form of the [female] beloved';[518] and in another song, though in quite a different context, God is again identified as the *priẏā*: 'Tearing everything apart I will set free the bird of the mind/After playing a game with the [female] beloved it will return to its nest if it recognizes it'.[519] And lastly, Badrunnesa Saju, a woman writer, also transforms the sex of her beloved in a song that otherwise consistently refers to a male *muršid* and helmsman: 'Putting my two hands on your united feet, I tell you my polite request/Do not be cruel, [female] beloved, this traveller longing for a blessing is very helpless'.[520]

514 Cf. Schimmel (1995a: 97 ff.) for the woman as a manifestation of the Divine, according to Jalal al-Din Rumi and Ibn ʿArabi.

515 *PN* No. 15: *priẏār baṃksir* [*sic*] *sbare, prāne sadāẏ uhu uhu kare*; and *deher bhitar priẏār baṃsi, bāje sadāẏ dibā niśi*.

516 *RB* No. 22: *ki doṣ(a) karichi priẏā, bala taba śrī caraṇe/tāṛāiẏā deo kena, bāre bāre ei adhīne*.

517 Cf. *RS* No. 83. Other mentions of the female beloved in Maulana Hadi's songs include: *RB* No. 23; *RS* No. 17, 25, 50, 65, 88, 93.

518 *JJ* No. 30: *yābār kāle priẏā rūpe ek'bār dio daraśan*.

519 *JJ* No. 69: *sakal kichu chinna kari- man pākhīre diba chāṛi/kheli khelā priẏār sane – cin'le bāsā ās'be phire*. *kheli* is to be interpreted as an absolutive participle here, not as a first person present form.

520 *Madirā* No. 48: *joṛ kadame du'hāt rekhe binīta anurodh jānāi/niṭhur haẏonā priẏā, doẏākāmī e musāphir baṛo asahāẏ*.

These songs can only partly be derived from the tradition of Vaishnava *bhakti* songs addressed to Radha.[521] In the first song quoted, by Aliullah, the female beloved retains the flute; and Maulana Hadi explicitly addresses Gholam Rahman as his female beloved. These features reveal that there is not one single blueprint upon which Maijbhandari *viraha* songs are modelled. Rather, we find a typical ambivalence in the figure of the beloved – male or female, human or divine – that is present also in other types of religious love poetry from Vaishnava, Sufic and other provenances. We shall again touch upon this issue in Chapter 6 with the aid of interviews of song-authors. We may, however, state in summary that such a reversal of sexes, in Maijbhandari songs as well as in other traditions, seems indicative of the adaptability of various secular codes of love into religious ones.

5.7.11 Play

> What are the results of other games? The heart is satisfied by the play of love/[. . .]/If you are skilled in the play of love, you can attain the Prophet of God. [522]
>
> (Ramesh Shil)

Play, B. *khelā*, is another central complex of motifs in Maijbhandari songs that stands in close relation to love. It has been said that the ludic element is one of the fundamental determinators of humanity and a distinctively cultural phenomenon;[523] and as a very important feature common to all human cultures, play has acquired a confusing multitude of meanings. I would like to sketch out a few of them by way of an introduction to this section in the following.

Basically play, in contrast to other types of human action, does not spring from circumstantial necessities. It is action without direct constraints and free of purpose. In this sense, the relationship between play and reality is loose; play is creative in that it may simulate other realities, and it is essentially not serious, although of course one can play 'just for fun' but also 'seriously'. Play originates in pure and often joyful volition. It is spontaneous, and may thus be perceived as unpredictable, capricious and 'unruly'. Play usually has an element of acting. On the other hand, rules may be imposed on playing, reducing it, in the English lexis, to a game;[524] in its course, action is submitted to a code that differs from reality, and sets itself apart from it. However, in a game something is at stake which may or may not continue to be relevant when the game is over; it may involve competition and lead to gain or loss. As such, it may become a very concrete part of reality and even a strategic way of dealing with the latter. Games must be learnt, and so must play in general. A good player needs a whole range of different qualities, among them experience, skill, trickiness and slyness, and the dissimulation of

521 Cf. the section *Rādhānurāg* in Muhammad Adul Hai and Ahmad Sharif (eds) (1998: 55–63).

522 *ĀM* No. 36: *anya khelāẏ ki phal āche prem khelāte prāṇ juṛāẏ*/[. . .]/*prem khelāte hale nipuṇ khodār rasul pāoẏā yāẏ*.

523 Cf., for instance, Johan Huizinga's famous monograph on *homo ludens* (Huizinga 1939).

524 Many languages, among them Bengali, do not make such a distinction; Bengali *khelā* is both play and game.

one's intentions frequently is an important exigency for playing. In simplifying the rules of successful action, play affords a handy analogy to 'real life' in rendering aspects of strategic action transparent. In setting apart its own realm of play from the surrounding realm of reality, on the other hand, play lends itself equally well to an analogy of the unreal and illusionary as opposed to the real and true.

It is not my intention here to draw out any amateur, impressionist phenomenology of play, but merely to invoke some of the semantic extension of that word. And it is no doubt hazardous to use common-sense notions of central categories in one culture in order to explore their equivalent (or not-so equivalent) in another. But in this case, as we shall see, the semantics of *khelā* do seem to come quite close to those of similar categories in different European languages. And as regards Maijbhandari songs, it is more than a shallow playing with words if we state at the outset that they very much play with the complex semantics of *khelā*, play.

There are different constellations of players: the self, the self with the saint, and the saint alone. As with love, the object of play, that is, one's playing partner, decides the value of that play in Maijbhandari songs, and that object is usually the saint or God. Other involvements are deemed senseless: 'As long as there is time, crazy Gafur, forget the play of the world',[525] says Abdul Gafur Hali, or 'How much longer do you want to play the game, will you not have to die?'[526] Play is involvement with worldly affairs, and death will prove that ultimately nothing remains of it. 'Having come into this false world, what kind of spectacle are you playing, O my mind *manurā*?', asks Maulana Hadi.[527] Farid Hosain puts it similarly: 'O crazy one – born into this world/You remained charmed by merry play/What will you give on the day of the assembly [after death] if the Mawlā demands it?'[528] And Ramesh Shil, about to leave the shore of life, implores his mind: 'Now leave this deceptive play', meaning infatuation with the world.[529] For Aliullah, playing for profit, that is, gambling [B. *juẏākhelā*], leads to other modes of intoxication (smoking hemp, drinking) and is coterminous with the deceptive love for the world that hinders true love from prospering:

> If you gamble, mind, you will smoke cannabis/Cannabis smokers do not know the joy of God and the Prophet/If you smoke cannabis, mind, you will be like a drunkard/You will fall from the right path like the Pharaos.[530]

525 *JJ* No. 64: *samaẏ thāk'te gaphur pāg'lā/bhule yāo duniẏār khelā.*

526 *TB* No. 9: *ār kata din khel'bi khelā maraṇ ki tor habe nā.*

527 *RB* No. 28: *michā bhaber mājhe ese kiser raṃ khelare man manurā.*

528 *SB* No. 68: *a pāg'lāre – ei duniẏāẏ janma laïẏā/raṃ khelāẏ thāk'le bhuliẏā/ki dibāre hāsarer din cāile māolāẏ.*

529 *ĀM* No. 4: *ebe chāṛ māẏābī khelā.*

530 *PN* No. 99 [a ballad spanning 13 pages and treating a large variety of topics; p. 87]: *juẏā khelā khelāile, khābire man gā̃jā/gā̃jā khore nāhi cine, khodā nabir majā/gā̃jā khāile habi mān, māt'oālār mata/bedisāte paṛ'bi yāi, pherāuner mata*. The causative *khelāile* might be interpreted according to the old Indian model (e.g. in Sāṃkhya philosophy) according to which the *manas* coordinates the other sense organs; in this sense is has the sense organs play rather than playing itself. *Gā̃jā khāoẏā* may of course also refer to eating and drinking cannabis, but, as far as I can tell, smoking, rather than drinking it with curd (H. *bhāṃg*) is the usual way of taking cannabis in Chittagong.

In these cases, play is an analogy to infatuation with the illusionary realm of this world. It should be abandoned as false and disastrous in its consequences for the individual.

The right kind of play, on the other hand, is the play of love between *ʿāšiq* and *maʿšūq*, lover and beloved. Abdul Jabbar Mimnagari, posing as a woman, sings: 'In the garden of love, the two of us shall play love in utter secrecy'.[531] Aliullah asks his mind to engage in play: 'O mind [*manurā*], go to play love at the feet of Baba Maula'.[532] Similarly, Maulana Hadi says: 'Come on, brother, let us go to play love in the river of love of the dearest Ġawṯ/Life passes in vain, come on, let us play as long as there is time';[533] and the *muršid* is inside them to teach them the play of love.[534] Extending that play of love until the assembly on the Day of Judgment, Maulana Hadi uses his favourite imagery in imploring his beloved to kill him: 'Hold the sharp sword in your hand and cut me into a hundred pieces/I want to play the game of love with you in the assembly'.[535] Abdul Gafur Hali also invites his listeners to go to Maijbhandar in order to play the play of love, and advises: 'If you find a lover of true love, immerse yourself.'[536] As a female lover, by contrast, and reminding us of the ambivalence of love, he scolds the beloved of playing: 'O bosom friend – the friend gave me vexation without my knowledge/Had I [only] understood his deceptive playing [*māẏā khelā*]'.[537] Ramesh Shil confronts this game of love with games such as chess or cards (the latter leading to destruction): 'What are the results of other games? The heart is satisfied by the play of love/[. . .]/If you are skilled in the play of love, you can attain the Prophet of God.'[538] Farid Hosain writes: 'If you want to play the play of the lover [*ʿāšiq*] and the beloved [*maʿšūq*], come, come/Mawlā father, the golden *muršid*, has [us] always play the play of love'.[539] The game of love takes place in the secrecy of one's inner being: 'O crazy mind – the game of love happens in secrecy/Nobody sees it/The inside burns severely'.[540]

531 *PR* No. 6: *duijane premer bāgāne prem khel'ba ati gopane*.

532 *PN* No. 21: *bābā māolānār caraṇ tale, cala manurā prem khelite*.

533 *RB* No. 27: *gāuch(a) dhaner prem nadīte, calare bhāi prem khelite/bṛthā jīban yāẏ go cali, kheli cala kāl thākite*.

534 Ibid (*antare murśid dhan āche – prem(a)khelā śikhāite*).

535 *RS* No. 15: *tīkṣna kharga dhari kare śata khaṇḍa kara more/kheliba premer(a) khelā taba saṅge hāsarete*. Self-sacrifice and evocation of the assembly on the Day of Judgment are two of Maulana Hadi's preferred images. Cf. also *RS* No. 17: *prem(a) miśāmiśi khelā, khāiba hāśar(a)-belā/tomār(a) samā'te hādī, jhāmpa diba par'oẏānā*. *khāiba* makes little sense and seems to be a misprint for *khel'ba*; the resulting translation would be: 'I will play the play of mixing in love at the time of the assembly/I, Hadi, will jump into your *samāʿ* ['audition', probably 'musical session' here] [like a] moth'. One more example is *RS* No. 89, in which the assembly is equated with the Maula's 'stony play' (*pāṣāṇ khelā*; i.e. probably a 'tough play' that does not respect the feelings of the poor lover): *tāte āche hār(a) jit(a)/khelare man sacakita/jaẏa pāre* [*sic*, probably misprint for *pābe*] *jini dibe prathame parāṇ* ('There is winning and losing in it/Mind, play very attentively/He will win who gives his life-breath first').

536 *TB* No. 27: *āsal premer premik pāile nijere bisarjjan dio*.

537 *TB* No. 4: *asakhigo* [*sic*] – *bandhu ajānte karita jvālā/bujhitām tār māẏā khelā go*.

538 *ĀM* No. 36, cf. above.

539 *SB* No. 13: *āśeki māśeki khelā khel'bi yadi āẏ're āẏ/sonār murśid māolā bābā prem khelā sadāẏ khelāẏ*.

540 *SB* No. 45: *prem khelā cale gopane/dekhenāre kona jane/antar'khānā jvale yāẏ ghusiẏā*.

If play in the examples given so far is still some kind of conscious interaction between two actors, the existence of any kind of agency on the lover's part in such playing is often questioned, and the saint and God are ultimately held to be those who really conduct the game. They merely use the lovers as their pieces, as Ramesh Shil puts it: 'The game of love [*prem*] is a business of love, try and play that play/The Maijbhandari plays the game, Ramesh is like his playing piece'.[541] The Ġawṯ plays love in various forms: 'He plays love under different pretences, he hangs on a branch as a flower/He again drinks nectar from the flower as a saint [*walī*]/[. . .]/On the pretence of Hadi, stained by love, the dearest Ġawṯ [plays love]' (Maulana Hadi).[542] In a song by Abdul Gafur Hali, Ziaul Haq's play is truly cosmic: 'He used to play all over the universe/Sitting in meditation alone in solitude'.[543] The same idea is expressed by Farid Hosain in the following terms: 'Nothing in all the creations in the skies, underworlds, the [whole] world/Has been left out in your game/[Their] rise and fall depend on your volition'.[544] According to Abdul Jabbar Mimnagari, 'You [the Mawlā] are playing in the world inside all beings'.[545] The ambivalence of this play is well expressed in a song by Shafiul Bashar by reference to the veil of the *mīm*: 'It plays [*līlā kare*] incessantly in the form of *mīm*'.[546]

The passivity of the objects of play is especially conspicuous in the image of the puppet player. 'You made Farid a puppet and are having a puppet play played' (Farid Hosain);[547] and 'This world is a stage, we can behold it in a puppet play/He whose play it is plays' (Shafiul Bashar).[548] Ramesh Shil also uses this image: 'You play the puppet in the breath channel, I cannot recognize you/Making the puppet yourself, and entering yourself into it,/You laugh, sing, dance and play, [it is] your contrivance'.[549] This play inside the world involves not only humans, but all sorts of beings; it is the ultimate moving force of the world.[550]

The play of the Mawlā is especially unpredictable and beyond human understanding: 'Mawlā, [even] Yogīs and Ṛṣis cannot understand your play [*līlā*]/Some you make laugh, some you make cry, some you make into wood

541 *ND* No. 9: *prem khelā esker mām'lā, khele dekhanā ei khelāṭi/māij'bhāṇḍārī khel'che khelā rameś yena tār khelār guṭi.*

542 *RS* No. 61: *nānā chale prem(a) khele, puṣpa haẏe ḍāle dole/punaḥ ali haẏe puṣpe kare madhu pān(a)* [. . .]/*premer(a) kalaṅki hādī chale gāuch(a) dhan(a).*

543 *JJ* No. 83: *brahmāṇḍa juṛiẏā karita khelā,/dhyāne basiẏā ekā niralā.*

544 *HB* No. 13: *ākāśe pātāle yata sṛṣṭi duniẏāẏ/kona kichu bād pare* [*sic*, for *paṛe*] *nāi tomāri khelāẏ/utthān ār patan tor icchār kāraṇ.*

545 *PR* No. 20: *bhabete kar'techa khelā, sarba prāṇīr antare.*

546 *YB* No. 14: *mīm chūrate līlā kare – khele sethāẏ abirata.* The song explains the creation from the *nūr-i muḥammadī*; the Arabic letter *mīm* is all that separates *Aḥmad* (and *Muḥammad*) from *aḥad* (the One, God).

547 *HB* No. 20: *pharid'ke bānāiẏā putulā – khelāitecha put'lā khelā.*

548 *YB* No. 3: *ei bhaba ek raṅgamañca putul nāce dekh'te pāi.*

549 *ND* No. 6: *tumi damer kale putul nācāo cin'te pāri nā/nije putul taiẏār kare nije ḍhuke tār bhitare,/hāsa gāo nāca khela, tomār kār'khānā.* Cf. the translation of this song in Appendix 1.

550 Cf. Abdul Jabbar Mimnagari *PR* No. 20 as quoted above.

dwellers'.[551] The term *līlā* is common especially for the playful deeds of certain divinities such as Rama, Krishna or Durga.[552] Such play can aptly be rendered by 'divine play' since it is held impenetrable for the human mind.[553] Bengali *līlā* also has the the meanings of 'life' and 'incarnation', and in fact the imagery of playing may be found in an *avatāra* context in Maijbhandari songs. 'Having played in Arabia and Ajmer, he [now] plays [in] Maijbhandar',[554] writes Abdul Gafur Hali. Similarly Lutfunnesa Hosaini: 'You come in every age under the names of prophets and saints/[And] again you come in the form of Munis and Ṛṣis and show yourself lifelong, play lifelong'.[555]

Lastly, the play inside the beings that is attributed to the Divine or the saint has not only a general meaning of all-pervasiveness, but also a very specific one of 'bodily' presence inside the microcosmic, single body.[556] In a song by Abdul Gafur Hali, it is the presence of the man inside the body: 'Crazy Gafur is lost/The man is there, [but] he does not let himself be caught/He plays hide and seek/What do I know what he does afterwards?' (*JJ* No. 9, cf. 5.7.2). Ramesh Shil too refers to inner vision born from certain meditative practices: the Ġawṯ is visualised as playing the flute in one's heart, and 'when the sun blends with Ajapā, you shall hear the flute/You shall get to see the flute-player in play with Ajapā'.[557] Ajapā is a tantric goddess here.[558] The purport seems to be the basic tantric idea that the male and the female principles inside the body 'play', that is, approach union.[559] A similar internal phenomenon is described thus: 'There is play of divine light [in] the palace of merriment, there are eight chambers and sixteen locks/There is no means except the Maijbhandari who has the keys'.[560] This 'palace of

551 Ramesh Shil *SD* No. 4: *māolā tomār ājab līlā bujhe nāre* [*sic*] *yogī ṛṣi/kāre hāsāo kāre kā̃dāo kāre kara banabāsī. Bujhe nāre* may stand either for *bojhe nā re* ('do not understand' with a vocative particle), or as a misprint for *bujh'te nāre* (dialect for *bujh'te nā pāre*, 'cannot understand'). The contraction of *nāre* in the print might suggest the latter.

552 For the role of *līlā* in various Hindu traditions, cf. Sax (ed.) (1995), and, in a specifically Bengali context, the contributions by Malcolm McLean and Donna Wulff in this volume. In his introduction, Sax shows that divine play is a very commonplace Hindu notion (Sax 1995: 3 ff.). It is, however, not completely absent from the Islamic tradition either. Cf. Erkinov's edition and translation of a nineteenth-century poem by Shaydai lamenting the loss of the Sultanate of Khiva in Central Asia; this ill-fate is depicted as a result of heaven playing chess (Erkinov 2004: 108, Verse 160: 'Heaven played chess and lost all you had, all your mansions and palaces are destroyed, Khorezm').

553 For another instance of using *līlā*, cf. Abdul Gafur Hali *JJ* No. 30: *sabi* [*sic*] *tomār līlā khelā* ('all is your divine play'); in the compound *līlā khelā*, *līlā* appears to add the divine, impenetrable aspect of the play of the beloved.

554 *JJ* No. 39: *ārabe āj'mire kheli khele māij bhāṇḍār.*

555 *GP* No. 29: *yuge yuge eso tumi nabī ali nāme/ābār muni ṛṣi rūpe ese dekhā dāo ājīban(a) karo khelā ājīban.*

556 Cf. the remark in Rahul Peter Das (1992: 390, n. 15): 'The cosmic principle's creating the microcosm and then residing in it is often referred to as a divine 'game' (*līlā*, *khelā*, or the like) [. . .].'

557 *ŚB* No. 4: *ajapār saṅgete yadi miś kare rabi, tabe bā̃śī śunibi,/baṃśīoẏālā dekh'te pābi ajapār saṅge khelāẏ.*

558 The term may also mean the recitation of the *haṃsa mantra.*

559 We shall have occasion to examine more similar notions in the last two sections of this analysis of motifs.

560 *ŚB* No. 6: *nūrer khelā raṃmahalā, āṭ koṭharī ṣola tālā/māij'bhāṇḍārī cābioẏālā bine nāhi upāẏ.*

merriment' is the uppermost of the 'eight chambers' constituting the human body, that is, the head or a place in the head; meditative practices generate impressions of light in that part. Ramesh Shil stresses that those without trust in such a kind of play are deplorable and condemned to staying in the dark. Another song addresses the *dar'bārī bhāi*, the co-disciples at the *darbār*, and directs their attention to the hidden (*bātunī*, A. <*bāṭin*>) *darbār* inside the body: 'There are seven locks and four rooms, the unknowable Lord [*ālek sā̃i*, Skt. <*alakṣya svāmin*>] plays [his] play'.[561] Finally, Farid Hosain sings of the key to the heart which is in the hand of the guru: 'There are fourteen locks to the room, in it he has installed a fair/He plays various merry plays, if you want, join in'.[562] All these passages belong to *dehatattva*, 'the principles of the body', and this complex will be dealt with in Sections 13 and 14 below.

5.7.12 Craziness

> In the world, all are crazy, One truly, another falsely.
> [But] how many crazy ones are there who die before dying?[563]
> (Abdul Gafur Hali)

The play of love that is seen as *the* fundamental religious experience pertaining to Maijbhandar may effect a serious dislocation of one's mental state and concerns in life. The element of dislocation that constitutes craziness is very directly expressed in the German equivalent *verrückt* ('crazy', lit. 'moved from one's place'), and it is in fact such dislocation that runs through the varied ways in which the motif of craziness is used in Maijbhandari songs. A number of terms are used to convey the idea of craziness, though not all with the same semantic extension. The Hindustani loan words of Persian origin, *diwāna* and (rarely) *mastāna*, usually denote a specifically religious concept of craziness as strongly propounded in Sufi poetry. Bengali *matta*, 'intoxicated, mad, beside oneself' occurs in connection with love along with *mātoẏārā*/*mātoẏālā* ('enrapured, beside oneself'). Even the term *bāul* is found, though it is probably not used in allusion to its supposed meaning of 'crazy' (derived from Skt. <*vātula*>), but rather as the denominator of the well-known religious group of the Bauls.[564] The usual term, however, is the colloquial Bengali word *pāgal*, and it covers the whole range of meanings that craziness assumes in Maijbhandar.

561 *MD* No. 21: *sāt tālāte cāriṭi khuṭi khelā khele ālek sā̃i.*

562 *SB* No. 37: *gharer mājhe caudda tālā/tāhāte basāiche melā re/nānā raṃger kare khelā cāile hao soẏārī. Nānā raṅger khelā* is literally either 'play of different merriments' or also 'play of different colours'. *Soẏārī haoẏā* denotes 'to mount' a horse or means of transport and is here used metaphorically.

563 *JJ* No. 6: *saṃsār mājhe sabāi pāgal,/keubā āsal keubā nakal,/marār āge mare eman/pāgal kaẏ janā.* Cf. the German translation of this song in *VG*: 79 f.

564 Cf. Mahbubul Alam *AJ* No. 24: *ye bāuler nāi ṭhikānā –/sei bāuler gāner āsar māij'bhāṇḍār* ('The musical gathering of the Baul who has no dwelling place is Maijbhandar'). For a rather conventional discussion of the etymology of *bāul*, cf., e.g., Md. Enamul Haq (1975: 296 f.). A very critical assessment is contained in Rahul Pater Das (1992: 393, n.33) (also on the different words used to denote craziness).

As we stated above, craziness in Maijbhandari songs is closely related to love. Both the exhilaration and the suffering connected with it make the lover go out of his mind and experience mental dislocation. In a song by Aliullah, the 'fire of love' (*premer āgun*) makes the lover crazy, *pāgal*.[565] Yusuf and Zulaykha were affected by this state: 'Just as Yusuf was crazy by the agitation of the fairy of love/ So was Zulaykha by the striking [?] of the fairy of love'.[566] In another *viraha* song, Aliullah sings: 'The mind is mad in the trance of the [female] beloved';[567] and in an Urdu song, he proclaims being crazy for his Bābā Mawlānā: 'I am crazy for you, my life is sacrificed [for you]'.[568] Ramesh Shil uses the terms *diwāna*, *mastāna* and *pāgal* in one song to describe the effect of the love born from beholding the unspecified divine beloved.[569] Maulana Hadi, in a typical *viraha* context, describes painful separation as the root of craziness *vis-à-vis* a bosom friend: 'Making me wander from country to country, he made me crazy [*diwāna*] with love';[570] and 'I lament in every house and country in the guise of a lunatic [*pāgal*]'.[571] Elsewhere, the craziness of love is preferred to heaven: 'I have rejoiced in your love, I do not want the joy of heaven/What should I do with the joy of heaven, I am crazy in your trance'.[572] This craziness borders on intoxication: 'Hadi is intoxicated by the play, [and] with [him] the dearest Ġawṯ';[573] and, in another song, beholding the various aspects of the female beloved makes him 'intoxicated with love'.[574] Farid Hosain is also 'crazy with love',[575] and such a state is the peak of luck: 'I see no one as fortunate in this world as him/Who is crazy among the lovers of the Bhandari'.[576] Abdul Gafur Hali longs for the spiritual vision (*dīdār*) of the Prophet and proclaims: 'I am a lunatic of love for the Prophet'.[577] The craziness of love also extends to the relationships between God, the Prophet and the Maijbhandari, as Mahbubul Alam points out: 'The Prophet is crazy in his love for God, [and] God is crazy for Mustafa/The Ġawṯ of Maijbhandar became crazy in [his] love for both of them'.[578] And in another song he depicts his craziness for a friend who is later identified as the Bhandari: 'I became

565 Cf. *PN* No. 27.

566 *PN* No. 38: *iuchap pāgal chila jei, esker parir utālāẏ/jalekhā pāgal chila, esker parir yāñjanāẏ'o*. *Yāñjanā* appears to be *jhan'jhanā*, an onomatopoeic word signifying a clattering sound, clank or clap (thus 'striking' in my translation).

567 *PN* No. 15: *priẏār bhābe matta man*.

568 *PN* No. 91: *teri liẏe pāgal homāi, kor'bān hāẏ meri jān <tērē liyē pāgal hūṇ maiṇ, qurbān hai mērī ğān>*.

569 *JS* No. 39; this song is not included in the *Racanābalī* edition of Ramesh Shil's songs.

570 *RS* No. 18: *deśe deśe bhramāiẏe preme kaila deonā*.

571 *RS* No. 58: *hāẏ hāẏ kari pāgal beśe ghare ghare deśe deśe*.

572 *RS* No. 19 (also *RB* No. 17): *majechi tomāri preme svarga sukh(a) cāhinā/ki kariba svarga sukhe tor bhābete dioānā* [*sic*].

573 *RB* No. 20: *raṅge hādī mātoẏārā, saṅge gāuch(a) dhan*.

574 *RS* No. 69 (*preme mātoẏālā*).

575 *SB* No. 43 (*premete haïẏā deoẏānā*).

576 *SB* No. 77: *bhāṇḍārīr āśeke yei jan deoẏānā –/tāhār mata su-bhāgyabān ei jagate dekhi nā*.

577 *TB* No. 29: *nabīr premer pāgal āmi*.

578 *AJ* No. 5: *khodār preme nabī pāgal, khodā pāgal mostaphār/dõhār preme pāgal halen gāuche māij'bhāṇḍār*.

crazy, I became crazy for such a friend/Who has no place of his own, who has no house [*ghar-duẏār*]'.[579] Once self-realisation has been attained, such craziness can be generated by introspection too, as Ramesh Shil claims in one of the most popular and famous Maijbhandari songs: 'The heart will become lively, he will attain the spiritual vision of the object of veneration [*maʿbūd*]/Seeing his own form, he will himself become crazy'.[580]

In the *viraha* context, this craziness is often experienced by a female, and many songs adopt the perspective of a woman lover calling herself a *pāg'linī*, 'crazy woman'. 'The flute plays with a smooth sound, the cuckoos coo/I became a crazy woman through the astonishing melody of the flute' (Aliullah).[581] Abdul Jabbar Mimnagari says: 'I have become a crazy woman by giving my life [lit. life-breath] to you',[582] and equally Shafiul Bashar sings: 'By taking my mind and life(-breath), he made me a crazy woman'.[583] The 'trance', *bhāb*, induced by the lover takes away one's senses: 'Miserable Shafi, a crazy woman/Has become indifferent [to the world] by your trance/And strolls around in the world'.[584]

In the examples so far given, craziness accompanies true love; it is thus an attribute of a veritable *bhakta* and a positive quality. This is enhanced by the designation labelled on the true lover, and sometimes specifically on Maijbhandar, from the outside. Farid Hosain, for example, complains that society brands him as a lunatic: 'After entrusting my life-breath in Maijbhandar, [I have] a spear in my heart/My relatives and family curse me by calling me crazy',[585] and 'Whoever goes to the home of the [true] man/Is called crazy by the whole world'.[586] Such admonishments are turned into marks of spiritual distinction by many of the authors, and it is this very tension between reported designations from outside and self-designations that enforces the popularity of the notion of craziness. The pejorative outside designation is asserted in

579 *AJ* No. 23: *āmi pāgal halām, pāgal halām eman bandhuẏār,/nāire yāhār nij ṭhikānā, nāire ghar-duẏār.*

580 *SD* No. 18: *kalab jindā haẏe yābe, mābuder didār(a) pābe,/nijer rūp dekhiẏe habe nije dvioẏānā.* In standard Bengali, *dekhiẏe* is the absolute ablative participle of the causative *dekhāna*, 'to show'; but it seems more likely that the absolute ablative of *dekhā*, 'to see', (<*dekhe*> or *sādhu bhāṣā* <*dekhiẏā*>) is meant here, as the form occurs in both meanings in Maijbhandari songs. The song is the famous *Māij'bhāṇḍāre uṭheche tauhider niśānā*: Selim Jāhāṅgīr (1999) includes it in his sampling of eight representative Maijbhandari songs (p. 210), two major Maijbhandari representatives in the position of *sağğādanašīn* (Shafiul Bashar and Syed Hasan) single it out as one of ten major compositions (cf. the lists in the repective interviews in Jāhāṅgīr 1999: 272, 289), and it is one of five songs, three of them by Ramesh Shil, chosen for English translation on the webpage run by Haq Manzil (http://www.sufimaizbhandari.org/maizbhandari_moromi_goshti.html, accessed 26 March 2010). Cf. also my translation in Appendix 1.

581 *PN* No. 3: *bā̃si bāje cikan śvare, kokilāẏ kuhare/āmi haïlām pāg(a)lini, baṃsvir śure camat·kār.* *Camat·kār* is an attribute to *sur* and is shifted to the end position here for the sake of the end rhyme of the song.

582 *PR* No. 9: *āmi tomāẏ prāṇ diẏe pāg(a)linī haẏechi.*

583 *YB* No. 67: *āmār man(a) prāṇ(a) niẏe, kar'lā pāg(a)linī.*

584 *YB* No. 54: *hīn(a) saphi pāg(a)linī/tomār bhābe udāsinī/haẏe āji duniẏate ghuriẏa beṛāẏ go.*

585 *SB* No. 17: *māij bhāṇḍāre prāṇ sapiẏā – hṛdaẏe bedanār sul* [*sic*, <*śūl*>]/*pāg'lā bale gāli deẏ're āmāri ātmīẏa kul.*

586 *SB* No. 13: *ye bā yāẏ mānuṣer ghare/pāgal kaẏ(a) saṃsār jure* [*sic*, <*juṛe*>].

Photo 9 Another example of an *'urs* performance situation of Maijbhandari songs, Maijbhandar 1999.

the inside, and craziness thus becomes one of the dominant distinctive features of Maijbhandari self-representation in the songs. Ramesh Shil celebrates such craziness in a song in which the word *pāgal* (here rendered as 'lunatic') occurs no less than nine times, and which begins like this:

> I saw a lunatic's play/The disciples of that lunatic are all of them a clan of lunatics/Whoever stands next to someone's lunatic also becomes a lunatic afterwards/The lunatic's eyes wink and agitate the soul [lit. 'life-breath'].[587]

587 *ŚB* No. 32: *dekh'lem ek pāgaler khelā/yata sab pāgaler baṃśa ai pāgaler celā/ye yār pāgaler(a) dhāre seo pāgal haẏe paṛe/pāgaler naẏan(a) ṭhāre prāṇ(a) kare uthalā.*

The mere sight of the saint induces this craziness, as Abdul Gafur Hali points out: 'If you see the picture of Baba Maulana, you will become crazy';[588] and what is meant is his true, hidden form: 'When you see [his] hidden form/You will become crazy'.[589] Abdul Jabbar Mimnagari, too, confesses to have become crazy (*deoẏānā*) upon seeing the craftsmanship (*kārigarī*) of nature personified in the Maijbhandari (*PR* No. 5). For Farid Hosain, craziness is a way of distancing himself from the world: 'I kick the world by taking the guise of a lunatic'.[590] Mahbubul Alam states that his *muršid* has made him crazy,[591] and describes the musical sessions in Maijbhandar as the home of homeless Bauls and the flowered wedding-bed of the crazy ones (*dioẏānā*) in search of Allah (*AJ* No. 24, cf. above).

Side by side with this transvalued craziness, however, there are also instances of 'common-sense', pejorative uses of the word *pāgal*. 'Which lunatic says that the saints have died?',[592] asks Ramesh Shil, asserting the opposite to be true. Farid Hosain enjoins his 'crazy mind' not to remain asleep, letting this life pass in vain;[593] or, in another song, scolds it for not having venerated the guru.[594] And Abdul Gafur Hali distinguishes between three kinds of craziness, namely the positive and negative craziness of normal men and the accomplished craziness of the saints as a third category apart: 'In the world, all are crazy/One truly, another falsely/[But] how many crazy ones are there who die before dying?'[595]

On the whole, however, the instances of transvalued craziness by far outweigh the pejorative uses, and this runs parallel to similar notions in other religious groups of Bengal (such as the Bauls and Gaudiya Vaishnavas) as well as elsewhere in South Asia. As stated at the beginning of this chapter, the concept of inspired, spiritual craziness is so popular that some Maijbhandari authors, such as Abdul Gafur Hali and Farid Hosain, frequently prefix *pāgal* or *pāg'lā* to their names in the *bhaṇitā*s (colophons) of their songs. Two less-known authors, Pagal Chaudhuri and Mastan Md. Tajul Islam, even carry words denoting 'crazy' as a part of their name. The main point about the popularity of this motif appears to be that it marks off Maijbhandar or, more generally put, the mystic community from the rest of human society and negates mundane rules and hierarchies; '[m]adness is linked with ecstasy, but also with the attainment of hidden knowledge'.[596] In addition, such collective self-marginalisation also evokes a strong sense of 'communitas'[597] Ramesh Shil's depiction of 'contagious craziness' at the *darbār* in

588 *JJ* No. 39: *dekh'le chabi, pāgal habi, bābā māolānār.*

589 *JJ* No. 41: *bāteni rūp dekh'bi yakhan –/dekhe pāgal habi.*

590 *SB* No. 11: *duniẏāke lāthi mārī* [*sic*] *pāgal beś dhari.*

591 *AJ* No. 18: *murśid maolānā, āmāẏ tumi kar'lā dīoẏānā.*

592 *SD* No. 17: *āoliẏā mareche bale kon·pāgale kaẏ.*

593 *SB* No. 27: *ghume pare* [*sic*, <*paṛe*>] *thākis· nāre pāg'lā man – ghume ghume jīban gele bṛthāẏ yāibe ei jīban.*

594 *SB* No. 68: *guru bhajan kar'li nā tui haïbe ki upāẏ – re pāgelā* [*sic*] *manurāẏ.*

595 *JJ* No. 6, cf. p. 249 at the head of this section.

596 Cf. Rahul Peter Das (1992: 393, n. 33), pointing out that Baul use 'mad' as 'part of the name or honorific'.

597 I refer here to Victor Turner's model of structure versus communitas; cf. Turner (1995 [1969]).

Maijbhandar is an apt illustration for this (*ŚB* No. 32, quoted above). The negation of mundane logic and common-sense attitudes about life that is implied by this self-designation constitutes the distinction of belonging to a community apart.

5.7.13 Boat journeys

> Lover brother, set the sail of the name/And steer against the stream.[598]
> (Abdul Gafur Hali)

Intense love, exaltation and craziness are the attributes of one who has entered the mystical path. According to the Sufi stages of religious life, *ṭarīqa,* literally 'the path', succeeds *šarī'a*, the Islamic law, and is a necessary step on the way towards cognition of and union with the Divine. There are a huge number of Maijbhandari songs that describe journeys and map trajectories leading to the Divine. Sometimes the disciple is portrayed as a traveller[599] or a train passenger;[600] but most commonly the imagery of boat journeys is employed. Out of the 1,100 Maijbhandari songs this investigation rests upon, more than 50 use this motif, and it occurs right from the beginning in Aliullah's songs until the present (Lutfunnesa Hosaini, Abdul Gafur Hali); the songwriters using it most frequently are Ramesh Shil and Abdul Gafur Hali.

In the context of Bengali literature, a blueprint for many of these songs is found in the *Caryāpada*s, the famous collection of 50 Buddhist tantric songs in early Eastern New Indo-Aryan that Bengali historiography of literature claims as its first document and the only specimen of Old Bengali or, more accurately, Eastern Apabhraṃśa.[601] Song No. 38 by Sarahapa (Sarahapā) may be quoted here in full as it is really paradigmatic for the dominant type of such boat songs in Maijbhandar:

> The body is the boat, the mind the helmsman/Take hold of the helm upon the word of the sadguru/Make your mind steadfast and hold the boat/You cannot cross over by any other means/The boatman pulls the boat with a rope/Unite yourself with the *sahaja*, there is no other means/There is fear on the path and the robbers are strong too/All is slippery from the huge waves/Go upstream against the strong current by the shore/Saraha says, enter the sky.[602]

598 *JJ* No. 8: *āseki bhāi – nāmer bādām tuilā diẏā/ujāne cālāio.*

599 Cf. Badrunnesa Saju *Madirā* No. 26;

600 Cf. Abdul Gafur Hali *JJ* No. 62; and already Aliullah *PN* No. 33, in which life corresponds to a train journey, the *qiẏāma* is the final station (*keẏāmate ṣṭeśan*), and 'this train [i.e. the body] is a false home' (*ei gāṛite michā bāṛi*).

601 It should be mentioned here that the claim on behalf of Old Bengali is contested in the historiographies of literature of other Eastern Indo-Aryan languages such as Assamese and Oriya, and – via Maithili – even Hindi. For a survey on *Caryāpada* research, cf. Rahul Peter Das (1996).

602 Rānā (1981: 86): *kāa ṇābaṛi khāṇṭi maṇa keṛuāla/sad·gurubaane dhara patabāla/cīa thira kari dharahu re nāī/āna upāẏe pāra ṇa jāi/naubāhī naukā ṭāṇaa guṇe/meli mela sahajẽ jāu ṇa āṇe/bāṭa abhaa khāṇṭa bi balaā/bhaba ulole biṣaa boliā/kūla laï kharasontẽ ujāa/saraha bhaṇaï gaaṇẽ samāa.* Approximate translation by H. H. with the aid of Rānā's standard Bengali rendering.

A dangerous upstream journey in the boat of the body, led by the helmsman of the mind, which, if one bewares of the robbers, leads to the sky of union: these are the main ingredients of this topical genre. Similar examples can be found in medieval Bengali literature, for example in Saiẏad Sultān's *Jñān'pradīp*,[603] but also in other South Asian traditions where the boat journey is equated to the spiritual quest;[604] and the same imagery looms large in *Bhāṭiẏālī* and Baul songs. We will have occasion to give references and point out parallels in the following pages.

As hinted above, however, there are different ways in which the image of the boat is employed in Maijbhandari songs. We have come across one of these, namely the boat of the saint's feet,[605] which is probably a derivation that we shall try to explain below. More central, however, is the boat as a metaphor for the human body. A first category of songs uses this metaphor more or less in isolation. Ramesh Shil, for instance, uses it in a song that conflates motifs of *viraha bhakti* and boat journeys; the I is floating in a 'sea of separation', and cries out to a friend: 'I cannot hold the boat of the body anymore'.[606] The sea of the world should be passed without delay, the 'sea of desire' (*kām-sāgar*) is to be avoided, and the 'old woman' [i.e. the world] should be divorced.[607] 'The boat is three and a half elbows [long]',[608] says Shafiul Bashar, using this conventional measurement for the human body. Lutfunnesa Hosaini is gasping for breath in shoreless waters and implores her 'father, the Ġawṯ of Maijbhandar' to take the boat of her body across.[609] God's creation of the human body is described by Shafiul Bashar in the following terms: 'The great Lord Nirañjan designed the glorious boat/[. . .]/ He constructed it in His own form with water, fire, earth and wind'.[610] Another

603 Saiẏad Sul'tān (1978: 676).

604 Cf. the boat journey in 'Hindi' poet Kutuban's *Mirag'vatī* (1503), in which the stations on the journey correspond to the *maqāmāt*; S.M. Pandey points out that the sea journey is an early standard symbol for the spiritual path found already in Arabic Sufi literature such as the works of Niffarī (d. 956) (Pandey 1992: 185 f.).

605 Cf. Maulana Hadi *RS* No. 66 (*caraṇ'tarī*); Abdul Jabbar Mimnagari *PR* No. 29 (*caraṇ tarī*); also noteworthy in this connection Maulana Hadi *RS* No. 12, in which the boat of love is tied to the Ġawṯ's feet. A correspondence to this may be seen in the Jaina idea of the *tīrthaṅkara*, lit. 'he who makes a ford' and thus enables one to cross over. (We may also recall here the old Buddhist image of the eightfold path as a raft to be abandoned once the shore is reached.) This image seems to unite aspects of three different figures, namely the saint's feet as the disciple's refuge; the saint as the boatswain inside one's own boat = body; and also the saint as the helmsman of the boat preceding one's own boat on the path.

606 *BhM* No. 27: *ār nā rākhite pāri dehatarī*; the term for 'sea of separation' is *biccheder sāgar*.

607 *ŚB* No. 36: *buṛā nārī tālāk de bhāi māij'bhāṇḍāre giẏā*. Cf. already Ghazzali (d. 1111) (al-Ghazzali 2001: 46), where the world is equalled to an old witch that seduces and kills men. Also Schimmel (1995a: 70 f.) on the world as an old woman who keeps the bird encaged. Furthermore Liebeskind (1998: 202) on a dream of one of Warith 'Ali Shah's (Dewa, Uttar Pradesh) devotees: 'In the night I had this dream that I was dying. An old woman with dirty and smelly clothes was standing next to me. And someone said: "This is your world" '.

608 *YB* No. 41: *sāṛe tin hāt tarī khāni*.

609 *GP* No. 1: *deha tvarī* [*sic*] *āmār bābā gāuche māij'bhāṇḍār/daẏā kare daẏāl murśīd laonā kare pār*.

610 *YB* No. 42: *sājāilen mahimā tarī mahā prabhu nirañjan(a)/*[. . .]*/āb(a), ātaś, khāk(a), bāte gaṛilen āpan churate*.

term that is sometimes used for the body is *jīban'tarī* or *jīban'naukā*, the 'boat of life'. Shafiul Bashar, again, uses it thus: 'Maijbhandari, I have set afloat the boat of [my] life in your name'.[611] Abdul Gafur Hali addresses his cruel friend as 'boatswain of the boat of my body',[612] and Ramesh Shil sings: 'The helmsman of the boat of my life is a certain Ġawṯ [of] Maijbhandar/To whom should I appeal for help, at this time of death, except you?'[613]

The last two quotations bring out one deviation from the blueprint of *Caryāpada* No. 38 that is quite frequently found in Maijbhandari songs (barring the proper *dehatattva* songs we shall deal with below): the boatswain or helmsman who leads the boat is not necessarily one's own mind, but may also be the spiritual master or beloved. This is especially prevalent in connection with a motif of a second type, according to my present classification, in which the boat journey is basically the crossing of a river, sea or other stretch of water dividing two shores. This water may either symbolise the transition from this to that world, that is, from life to death, or stand for the unstable condition of earthly life – that is, the journey is either a passage from shore to shore, or a path from inside the water towards some final shore. In both cases, the saint is the boatswain or helmsman who is deemed to control the situation and implored to do so, or the ferryman who must be solicited to take one into his boat. For instance, Ramesh Shil has come to the *ghāṭ* of the world and now comes back in the evening to the river for the preordained crossing over at the age of 72 (*bāṣaṭṭi bachare pāṛi*). He asks the Maijbhandari, the 'sailor of the world' (*bhaber nābik*) to take him into his boat (*SD* No. 12). The crossing over should be arranged early, the raft for setting over should be bound in time, and when leaving the shore: 'There is no fear of waves and storm as long as the Bhandari's name is the helm in it'.[614] Abdul Gafur Hali sits crying at the *ghāṭ* in the evening: 'Take me across, boatswain of crossing the world, time is running out [lit. 'drowning']/I came to this shore for trading in the hope of profit'.[615] The notion of the world as a marketplace to be traversed is commonplace in Bengal and elsewhere,[616] and recurs in a song by Farid Hosain, addressed to his *muršid* Delawar Hosain: 'You are the helmsman of crossing/Whoever enters your boat/Will easily set across this world-market'.[617] In this imagery, the water itself becomes the world; likewise in most songs that refer to the *bhabasindhu* or *bhabasāgar* ('sea of the world'), as for example Ramesh Shil: 'There is no other friend to take me across the sea of the world',[618] or, similarly, Abdul Gafur Hali: 'O father Maijbhandari/Who except you should set across/The

611 *YB* No. 71: *tomār nāme jīban tarī, bhāsāiẏāchi – māij'bhāṇḍārī.*

612 *JJ* No. 50 (*āmār jīban naukār mājhi*).

613 *ND* No. 28: *āmār jīban tari[r] kāṇḍārī ek gāuch māij'bhāṇḍār/ei nidāne tumi bine dohai diba kār.*

614 *ĀM* No. 4: *tāte bhāṇḍārīr nām chupān thāk'te ḍeu tuphāner kiser bhaẏ.*

615 *JJ* No. 12: *āmāẏ pār karare – bhaba pārer mājhire belā ḍube yāẏ/ei pāre bāṇijye elām lābheri āśāẏ re.*

616 Cf. al-Ghazzali (2001: 43), in which the world is portrayed as a marketplace on the way towards the next world.

617 *SB* No. 12: *tumi hao pārer kāṇḍārī/ye jan caṛe tomār tarī/anāẏāse dibe pāṛi e bhaba bājār re.*

618 *ND* No. 28: *pār karite bhabasindhu bandhu nāire ār.*

broken boat in the sea of the world'.[619] In another song, Abdul Gafur Hali uses this same imagery of crossing to a different effect: the Maijbhandari is referred to as the 'boatswain of my boat of life' (cf. above):[620] 'If he sets me across, I go across/ If he drowns me, I die drowning/The father is [my] friend in happiness and sorrow/ Both this and that shore are his.'[621] In the other constellations, the saint is basically a means to acquiring something; here he himself becomes the goal, reducing everything else to minor importance.

Depictions of this crossing of either the river separating this from that world or the ocean of existence may be embellished by dramatic details such as storms, shipwrecking, etc., but the substance of the motif remains the saint's ferrying over those seeking his help. A much more complex matter is the imagery we are going to discuss next: upstream journeys. It must be conceded, however, that like so many of the other motifs discussed here, boat jouneys are 'floating imagery' rather than fixed sets of metaphorical terminology,[622] and therefore conflations of both kinds of journey are quite common in Maijbhandari songs.[623] Thus Abdul Gafur Hali, at the beginning of a song, addresses his mind: 'O boatswain of the mind, cross the river after checking the flood of the wind', but proceeds by depicting an upstream journey towards the *tribeṇir ghāṭ*, the '*ghāṭ* of three streams'. The way is obstructed by a deathly whirlpool, and there is a *lāl niśān*, 'red sign', on the southern shore of the river; a good boatman goes upstream, using the 'power of *śakti*'.[624] To be successful in this journey, it is essential not to go first but to follow the preceding boats.

This enigmatic song works on different levels of meaning. We may read it as the depiction of some actual boat journey, and perhaps as a vague analogy to life in general. On a second level, we may interpret it as an allegory for spiritual endeavours that may also be a strenuous and mentally dangerous exercise; the song then gives some amount of advice in allegorical form, for example, to desist from solitary, hazardous spiritual adventures and take the guidance of a *pīr*. On a third level, we may read it as an instance of code language and relate its contents to an altogether different plane: the inner geography of the human body. This latter level falls under the category of *dehatattva* that will concern us for the remaining part of this chapter.

The term *dehatattva* is a well-known category in Bengal. *Dehatattva* literally means 'principles/essences/mysteries of the body'. Generally speaking, it is about the role and the functioning of the human body, perceived as the dwelling place

619 *JJ* No. 53: *ore bābā māij bhāṇḍārī/bhaba sāgare bhāṅgā tarī/tumi bine ke karibe pār*.

620 *JJ* No. 17 (*āmār jīban naukār mājhi*).

621 *JJ* No. 17: *pār karile pāre yāba/ḍubāile ḍube mar'ba,/sukh(a) duḥkher bandhu bābā/eikul ai kul dui kul tāri* [*sic*, <*tār'i*>].

622 Cf. the succeeding chapter.

623 Cf. Abdul Gafur Hali *TB* No. 17, to be discussed below.

624 *TB* No. 16: *nadī pāṛi dio hāoẏār bhāo bujhiẏā man mājhire/*[. . .] *yāite tribeṇīr ghāṭ,/sām'ne āche ghūrṇipāk/*[. . .] *nadīr dakṣiṇ dhāre lāl niśān/sujan mājhi bāẏ ujān/śaktir jore yāiteche bāhiẏā*. In a *dehatattva* context, the 'flood of wind' is the translocating agent pushing the semen up along the *suṣumnā nāḍī*, as we shall elaborate below (p. 000). Cf. Rahul Pater Das (1992: 392).

of the divine,[625] in attaining spiritual salvation. Commonly symbolised by vehicles, buildings or machines, the body has to be led along a certain path towards a goal. The microcosmic body is conceived as containing the macrocosm within its bounds. The consistency and structure of the body are expounded, and *sandhābhāṣā*, intentional language,[626] is used to describe certain types of *sādhanā*.

More than Yoga or Tantra, *dehatattva*'s association with the Hindu and Buddhist traditions does not exclude Islam: *dehatattva* may undergo changes due to the impact of these traditions, but as such it is conceived as common property to all three. *Dehatattva* is furthermore very old and closely linked to Eastern South Asia and its languages; the first examples of *dehatattva* can indeed be found in the *Caryāpadas*, as we have seen above. There are specific past and present Bengali mystic communities that are especially well known for their connection with *dehatattva*: the Bauls or Phakirs, the Sahajiyas, Kartabhajas, Sahebdhanis, as well as single personalities known for their songs, like Hasan Raja.

In contrast to the bulk of Maijbhandari songs, the boat journeys under discussion here do have a certain plot, even if they are often fashioned in the form of advice. I am therefore starting this analysis with a complete translation and extensive discussion of a song by Ramesh Shil:

> Boatman, move onwards catching the flood of the quay of three streams[627]/Steer your boat slowly with the inner picture[628] of the Bhandari/The first quay is the market of *nāsūt*, be on the watch/At that quay is the fair [*melā*] of robbers, you are inclined to lose the root[629]/After that comes the city of *malakūt*, keep steady your direction/There are the moon and the sun to your right and left, go through the middle/In *ǧabarūt*, there is play of the wind, set your sails/Hold your helm[630] as you see the bent of the imperceptible/Ramesh

625 The *Progressive Bengali-English Dictionary* (Aich & Das 1991) gives this as the central meaning: 'esoteric doctrine that the human body is the seat of all truth'.

626 Cf. Bharati (1993, chapter 6) on the preferability of *sandhābhāṣā* over the also widespread form *sandhyābhāṣā*, rendered as 'twilight language'. Likewise already Eliade (1985: 258 f.), and (not so convinced) Shashibhusan Dasgupta (1976: 413 ff.), both with reference to Vidhushekhar Shastri ('Sandhābhāṣā'. *Indian Historical Quarterly* IV, 2, 1928: 287–96).

627 *tribeṇīr ghāṭer joẏār*.

628 *bar'jakh <barzaḫ>*, lit. 'isthmus', symbolises the *muršid*'s function of setting the *murīd* in connection with God, and (in Ibn ʿArabi's usage) may be applied to any 'intermediary reality' (Chittick 1998: 332); in Maijbhandar, however, the term is generally explained as the inner picture of one's *muršid*. In another song (*ND* No. 8), Ramesh Shil refers to it as a photograph: 'The photo of the guru is inside the heart' (*hr̥d mājāre gurur phaṭo*).

629 *mūle hārāibā cāio*. *Mūle* (RŚR: 100) is apparently erroneous for *mūl* (cf. *Satya darpan* [*SD*]: 4), lit. 'root'. *Mūl* may also be interpreted as eliptical for *mūl dhan*, 'stock capital' (which may refer to semen). Another possibility (which was, however, not suggested by any of the interviewees I asked to interpret this song, and thus has been discarded as unlikely here) is to read *mūle* as 'at the beginning/outset' and translate 'you are inclined to be defeated right at the outset'. The infinitive *hārāibā* is a common dialect form for *hārāite*.

630 *chupān* (Chittagongian dialect).

> says: Attain the sight of the divine at the quay of *lāhūt*/(Finally,) when *pīr* and *murīd* take on one colour, pass [your time] in joy.[631]

This song is a fine example of *sandhābhāṣā*, the codified language that underlies *dehatattva* texts: it functions coherently on different levels of meaning. Such multiple coherence is, however, not a compulsory attribute of *sandhābhāṣā*, and examples that make no sense without applying some symbolic code are legion.

The song is, formally speaking, an instruction to a boatman: he is addressed throughout the song in the *tumi* form. It describes the itinary leading to a quay characterised by proximity to the divine and union with a *pīr*. The necessary conditions for this boat journey are mentioned in the beginning: one should use the flood and concentrate on the Bhandari's picture. Then the route is outlined: three quays have to be passed until the boatman reaches the fourth, his goal, and precautions are listed for each station.

The boatman, or the one who holds the helm, is, according to the traditional imagery we have quoted in *Caryāpada* No. 38, the mind or self, and the boat the body. Lālan Phakir (Sudhīr Cakrabartī [ed.] 1990: 228 f., 231) sings of the 'broken boat' (*bhāṅā tarī*) or the 'man-boat' (*mānab-tarī*) the mind (*man*) has attained and should utilise in the right way. The motif is frequently used in more recent Maijbhandari songs, for instance those by Abdul Gafur Hali, where the equation of boat and body is made almost as explicit as in *Caryāpad* 38: *sāṛe tin hāt naukā khāni* ('The boat is three and a half cubits [long]'; *TB* No. 2).[632]

Tribeṇīr ghāṭ, 'the quay of three streams', denotes the meeting place of three *nāḍī*s, bodily channels according to yogico-tantric body concepts. The three main *nāḍī*s (Beng. *nāṛī*), *īḍā*, *piṅgalā* (left, right) and *suṣumnā* (middle), run through the human body vertically, branching off at the perineum and reuniting in the head. These meeting places are identified with the *mūlādhāra*- and *ājñā-cakra*s respectively.[633] The 'flood' (*joẏār*), together with the upward movement through ascending spheres described in the song, would seem to indicate that the lower of

631 *SD* No. 7: *mājhi tribeṇīr ghāṭer joẏār dhaïre yeio,/bhāṇḍārīr bar'jake tarī dhīre dhīre bāio/ pratham ghāṭ nāchuter bājār husiẏāre raïo/sei ghāṭe ḍākāiter melā, mūle hārāibā cāio/tār'par mal'kuter śahar diś ṭhik rākhio/ḍāne bāme candra sūrya madhye di calio/yabrute bātāser khelā bādām uṭhāi dio/nilakṣer bāk·*[=*nirlakṣer bā̃k*] *dṛṣṭi kari chupān'ṭi dhario/rameś bale lāhuter ghāṭe didāre pā̃uchio/(śeṣe) pīr muride ek raṃ dhari ānanda kāṭāio*. There is a recording of this song by the singer Kalyani Ghosh (Kalyāṇī Ghoṣ: *Māij' bhāṇḍārī gān*, side 1, first take).

632 Cf. also *JJ* No. 12, *TB* No. 17 (with the invocation *mana mājhi*, 'mind boatman') and No. 19. In *TB*: 12, however, the boatman is the Maijbhandari, the ferryman who takes one across the river to the other world at the time of death. In a song by Faqir Mohammad Farid Hosain (*HB* No. 4), the boat seems to stand for the *murīd*'s person or his life: *bhaba sāgare pāṛi diba gā̃ucha nāma laïẏā – yei namera barakate naukā yābe caliẏā* ('I will cross the ocean of existence with the name of the Ġawṯ – the name by whose blessings the boat will move on').

633 Cf. the detailed discussion of these topics in Rahul Peter Das (1992: 392 ff.) (on the *nāḍī*s) and p. 398 (on the *triveṇī*). I lack the expert knowledge required for an in-depth analysis, and cannot examine the data I have in as wide a context as would be desirable. My attempt here is thus to keep my interpretations of this difficult material sufficiently transparent for the readers and future investigators so as to allow them to draw further-reaching and possibly also deviating conclusions. In the medieval

these *triveṇī*s is meant here.[634] This would also correspond to the practice of starting meditation in the *mūlādhāra*. In any case, the occurrence of the term *triveṇī* would seem to be a strong indication that the journey described in this song is one through the interior topography of the body as conceived in yogic disciplines.

Such an interpretation, however, may seem to get entangled in contraditions: while conventionally the boat itself would denote the body, it appears to be a vehicle moving through the body here. This apparent incoherence seems, however, to be almost as old as the imagery itself, since precisely the same semantic shift is at work in the *Caryāpada* song quoted above.[635] The contradiction can be resolved by pointing to the simultaneous existence of a microcosmic and a macrocosmic yogic body; it is one of the constituent beliefs in *dehatattva* imagination that these two are mutually contingent and thus contain each other. In this sense, the apparent paradox of a body moving through a body falls back upon the most basic paradox that *dehatattva* rests upon. The imagery of the boat is unimpaired by this.

The 'flood' required to set the movement in motion is problematic and may be understood in different ways within yogico-tantric traditions. In *kuṇḍalinī* Yoga, the driving force of the internal movement is conceived in the form of the snake, rolled up in the end of the spine,[636] which must be wakened so that it frees up the *brahmadvāra*, the entrance to the *suṣumnā*, and can rise upwards through the *cakra*s aligned on the middle channel, the *suṣumnā nāṛī*.[637] Sexual excitement can function as the 'fuel' required to arouse the *kuṇḍalinī*. Other forms of Yoga do not contain the notion of this *kuṇḍalinī*, and the substance moving through the body is conceived of differently, for example often as the male semen. Stored in a place at the back of the cranium,[638] arousal of sexual desire is required to make the semen come down from there through specific *nāḍī*s. At the *triveṇī*, the semen must be retained and driven up through the middle *nāḍī*, the *suṣumnā*. In the song, the mention of sun and moon, often identified with the *iḍā* and *piṅgalā*,[639] and the

Bengali text *Yog kālandar* (Hak 1995: 378–96), the upper meeting place between the eyebrows, which would correspond to the *ājñā-cakra*, is identified as the *triveṇī*: 'Gazing at the *Trinetra*, the meeting point of two eyes and nose, steady your mind in meditation (160). Three nerves meet together on this path of eyebrow. (Hence) gnostics call it the *Ghāṭ* (quay) of *Tribeṇī* (161). Whosoever always bathe in this *Ghāṭ* of *Tribeṇī*, can evade millions of sins committed' (162). (p. 390).

634 In the macrocosm, the *triveṇī* is the holy *saṅgam* or meeting place of the rivers Ganges, Yamuna and Sarasvati; also a place in Hoogly (West Bengal) where Yamuna and Sarasvati separate. The existence of two *triveṇī*s in the body is pointed out by Upendranāth Bhaṭṭācārya (1988: 444) (the lower one is called *yukta*, the upper one *mukta*). Cf. also Rahul Peter Das (1992: 398, n.63).

635 *Caryāpada* 38 describes a similar journey towards the 'sky' (*gaaṇ* <*gagaṇa*>), presumably the *sahasrāra cakra* situated in the topmost part under the cranium.

636 Eliade (1985: 254), according to *Śāradātilakatantra* XXVI, 34: in the form of *paradevatā*, the *kuṇḍalinī* dwells in the bone which is the centre of the place from which the *nāḍī*s (i.e. the *iḍā*, *piṅgalā* and *suṣumnā*) emerge.

637 Cf. Eliade (1985: 250).

638 Cf. Rahul Peter Das (1992: 397 ff.) for many examples and a discussion of this notion. Also Dimock (1989: 157), who quotes a study by Carstairs about the notion in Rajastan that semen is located in the human head and formed from large quantities of blood.

639 Cf. Eliade (1985: 248): The most frequent names for *iḍā* and *piṅgalā* in both the Hindu and Buddhist Tantras are moon and sun; for evidence, see, e.g., his quote from the *Ṣaṭcakranirūpaṇa* (p. 247).

instruction to keep to the middle, strongly suggest that such an ascension through the *suṣumnā* is intended here. The flood, then, represents this driving force.

The guiding principle on this internal journey, a sort of map, sometimes symbolised by a sail, or conceived as a ban on evil influences, is the name[640] or the inner picture of the spiritual master. In both Sufi and Yogic meditation, this internal visualisation of the *muršid* or *guru* is of utmost importance.

The boat journey in the song leads through four distinct places: the market of *nāsūt*, the city of *malakūt*, *ǧabarūt*, and the quay of *lāhūt*. The first three are apparently conceived as aligned on the shore, while the fourth is the boat's landing place and ultimate destination. The four spheres (*maqāmāt*) common to Sufi cosmology as discussed in Section 3.3, the realms of worldly life (*nāsūt*), angels (*malakūt*), prophets (*ǧabarūt*) and the divine (*lāhūt*), are thus allocated in the human body, and vertically on the boat's trajectory along the middle path of the *suṣumnā nāḍī*. A precedent to this can be found in the medieval *Yog kālandar*, where the spheres are explicitly assigned to *cakra*s: *nāsūt* is located at the *mūlādhāra cakra*, *malakūt* at the *maṇipura cakra* (navel), *ǧabarūt* at the *ājñā cakra*, and *lāhūt* at the heart.[641] The shift of the ultimate destination or most privileged *cakra* from the *sahasrāra*[642] to the heart seems to be due to a harmonisation with the Sufi doctrine of *laṭā'if*, and the central position of the *laṭīfa al-qalb* therein as the abode of the divine. In Ramesh Shil's song, the mention of the 'bent of the imperceptible' (*nilakṣer bā̃k*) seems to be an indication that he maintains the *sahasrāra cakra* as the location of the divine, as the *nāḍī* joining the *ājñā cakra* with the *sahasrāra* leads backwards from the forehead towards the highest point of the cranium. According to the topography suggested by *Yog kālandar*, not a bent but a reversal of the upward movement would be required to reach *lāhūt*.

After this single analysis of one representative song depicting such an interior boat journey, I want to turn back to a more collective procedure and demonstrate the variation of this imagery that we encounter in Maijbhandari songs. The image of the mind as a boatswain is quite commonly used,[643] and the oscillation of the body-boat between a macrocosmic (i.e. the whole human body) and a microcosmic meaning (i.e. the vehicle of a journey *through* that body) is central to this imagery. This boatswain is admonished to hold on to the helm, which in its turn may be

640 Cf. the above-quoted song by Mohammad Faqir Hosain: *gāuchul ājam nāmer bale/naukāṭā bhāsāiba jale/nāmer niśān māstulete diẏā/dekhile naukār niśān/āj'rāil ḍākku-śay'tān/bhaẏ pāiẏā chālām diẏā yāibe pālāiẏā* ('By the force of the name Ġawṯ al-Aʿẓam/I will set the boat afloat/Putting the sign of the name to the mast/Seeing the sign of the boat/The robber-devil ʿIzrāʾīl [the angel of death]/Will be afraid, greet and flee //') (*HB* No. 4).

641 Cf. Hak (1995: 379–82); the heart is identified with the *anāhata cakra*, not with the *hṛdaya cakra* that features in some forms of Yoga (cf., e.g., Kiehnle 1997, 1: 96). The text, however, also describes the *sahasradala kamala* (thousand-petalled lotus) as the seat of the *ātman* and the Lord, and thus seems to identify the *sahasrāra cakra* with the heart (Hak 1995: 383).

642 Cf. Eliade (1985: 252): The *sahasrāra* is situated at the uppermost part of the head and described as the place where ultimate union of Shiva and Shakti takes place.

643 Cf. the cases in which the equation is explicitly made by addressing the *man mājhi*: Ramesh Shil *ND* No. 8; *BhM* No. 7; Abdul Gafur Hali *TB* No. 17; *JJ* No. 73.

identified with devotion,[644] faith,[645] the *muršid*'s name,[646] etc. Sometimes, a sail must be set,[647] or a 'mast of courage' must be put up.[648] The trajectory usually includes the wordly shore corresponding to *nāsūt*, and here referentiality may tend to switch to macrocosmic human life in some songs. The worldly shore is dangerous: 'I went to the *ghāṭ* of joy to tally my gains and losses/There I see a female snake/I am completely in its stomach' (Abdul Gafur Hali).[649] Ramesh Shil calls this shore a 'sandbank of illusion' that conceals the true shores, and the 'water of illusion' around that place tempts the boatman to cast the 'anchor of attachment'.[650] This wordly shore is also seen as a market on which there are robbers, and one's *mūl* or *puñji*, capital, can easily be lost: 'The six robbers have snatched away my all and everything/In a moment I lost the capital of this birth' (Abdul Gafur Hali);[651] and 'The plunderers have plundered the capital that was with [me]'.[652] Such mercantile imagery looms large also in Baul songs. In a *dehatattva* reading, such capital signifies the reservoir of semen as vital energy that is stored in the body, and its loss may refer to loss of semen during sexual practices, which is to be avoided since the purpose is to take it up through the *suṣumnā*. The locus would correspond to the lower *tribeṇī* at the *mūlādhāra cakra* where the semen must be prevented from ejaculation, directed upwards through the middle channel of the *suṣumnā* and led towards union of the male and female in the uppermost *cakra*.[653] Ramesh Shil's usage of *mūl* above may connote such a localisation, but there is no way of being sure.[654] The robbers are frequently mentioned in this connection; they are usually six and seem to correspond to the 'six enemies' (*ṣaḍripu*) lust, anger, greed, infatuation, vanity and envy.[655] They occur also in dissociation with the boat journey; what their significance on the level of *dehatattva* would be is unclear. In one song, Abdul Gafur Hali mentions six *dāṛi mājhi*,[656] possibly to allude to a state of fatigue

644 Ramesh Shil *ND* No. 8; *BhM* No. 8.

645 Ramesh Shil *ND* No. 10.

646 Abdul Gafur Hali *TB* No. 8.

647 e.g. Abdul Gafur Hali *JJ* No. 8.

648 Aliullah *PN* No. 19: *hīmmater mastul gāṛha.*

649 *TB* No. 21: *gechilām ānanda ghāṭe,/lābh lok'sān milāi tāte/sethāẏ dekhi bhujaṅga nāgini.*

650 *ND* No. 10: *māẏā care ṭhek'le naukā kul pābinā bāiẏā/(mājhi bhāi) māẏā jal āsaktir naṅgar diẏācha ḍubāiẏā.*

651 *JJ* No. 50: *chaẏ ḍākāte laïlare mor sakal kichu kāṛi/nimiṣe hārāilām āmi ei janamer puñji.*

652 *JJ* No. 73: *puñji yāhā saṅge chila luṭherā luṭhi niche. Niche* is interpreted as an East Bengali perfect form (= *niẏeche*) here, as opposed to present continuous *niteche* (= *nicche*).

653 Cf. Dimock (1989: 15) for Sahajiya concepts according to which both man and woman have Radha and Krishna inside themselves and must effect their union within their body.

654 *mūl* is essentially used as a mercantile term in Maijbhandari songs; a relation to *mūlādhāra* or, for instance, *mūlabandhana* (cf. White 1996: 277) is never explicitly drawn. Nevertheless, *nāsūt* is allocated in that region of the body.

655 The six enemies (*ṣaḍripu*) occur in old Indian texts already. In Maijbhandari songs, robbers (*ḍākāt*) are mentioned in Farid Hosain *SB* No. 55; Abdul Gafur Hali *TB* No. 2; *JJ* No. 50; etc. The enemies feature in Badrunnesa Saju *Madirā* No. 9; Ramesh Shil *ND* No. 40; Farid Hosain *SB* No. 11; etc. Besides *ripu, duś'man* and *śaẏ'tān* are terms used to refer to them.

656 Boatmen driving the boat forward with the help of long rods that are stabbed into the ground in shallow water.

and indifference: 'There were six *dā̃ṛi mājhi* in the boat/I did not hear from them/At the [good] time they were there, at the time of need they left'.[657] There is also one instance of five enemies: Aliullah equates them with the senses and accuses them of suffering from greed.[658] Elsewhere these are called 'the five [people] of the body' who should be sent away with a *salām*.[659]

While the lower *triveṇī* is paralleled with the world, the upper one, broadly corresponding to the *ājñā cakra*, is sometimes taken as the goal of the journey.[660] Abdul Gafur Hali describes such an upstream journey towards the *tribeṇir ghāṭ* (*TB* No. 16, cf. above). The goal of the journey is referred to by various terms such as *āhād'ganj*, the 'market of the One' (Ramesh Shil *BhM* No. 7), *niścintāpur*, 'Sanssouci' or 'city without worry', *māniker khani*, the 'quarry of jewels' (both Abdul Gafur Hali *TB* No. 21) and the like.

As in the case of union with the divine, success in attaining the goal in these boat journeys is not the rule but the exception in Maijbhandari songs. Aliullah describes a boat journey in which a storm destroys the helm and takes both the mast and the sail with it (*PN* No. 96). Abdul Gafur Hali, especially, uses such imagery frequently: he deplores the poor state of his boat that is almost taken apart by heavy sea, and mourns the loss of his capital (cf. above): 'My money-lender has cheated me by taking my capital';[661] elsewhere, he is sitting on a market in the evening and pondering over how to cross the river: 'The mast of the boat was hit by a bad wind and broken'.[662] Another danger is that of missing the flood as the best time to set to sea: 'When there was the flood in the river [*gāṅge*], the boatswain was asleep/He did not consider what would happen to him later if the low tide would come'.[663] In a *dehatattva* context, the flood might be interpreted as sexual energy and a precondition to the *sādhanā* to be performed; but again, there is no way to be sure about these details.

The above interpretations rely on the assumption that a *dehatattva* meaning is intended in the texts, as in fact most of the songwriters themselves assert; and some of the texts discussed here contain enigmatic expressions that do not yield sense on other levels of interpretation and thus suggest themselves as ingredients of *sandhābhāṣā*. The meanings produced here have been drawn out by conjecture with material from other, and mainly the Baul, traditions; material that is better

657 *TB* No. 8: *dā̃ṛi mājhi chaẏjan chila naukār bhitar/tāder nā pāilām khabar/samaẏete chila tārā, asamaẏe gela chāṛi*. Cf., however, *TB* No. 2 where only two *dā̃ṛi mājhi* are on the boat 'of three and a half ellbows'. Cf. also a medieval song by Saiẏad Sul'tān (1978: 676) which mentions only four companions: *cārijan(a) saṅge chila/sabe more chuṛi gela/naukā ṭhekila bālucare* ('Four persons were with [me]/They just left me/The boat has run aground on a sandbank').

658 Cf. *PN* No. 57. Five enemies feature also in Buddhist mythology, e.g. in the *Gaṅgotaranikāya*, where they are portrayed as crocodiles.

659 Cf. *PN* No. 111: *śarīrer(a) pañca janā, chālām ālāik dibe tānā*.

660 The *ājñā cakra* is here apparently conflated with the *sahasrāra*. For such conflations in Baul songs, cf. Rahul Peter Das (1992: 397 f.).

661 *TB* No. 17: *āmāẏ mahājane dila phā̃ki hāriẏā āsal*.

662 *JJ* No. 89: *tarīr māstul bhāṅgiẏā geche lāgi kubātās*.

663 *JJ* No. 73: *gāṅge joẏār chila yakhan, mājhi chila ghume takhan/bhābila nā bhāṭā haïle – ki habe tār pāche*.

researched than Maijbhandari songs. It must be stressed, however, that during my fieldwork stay, I could not find any traces whatsoever of any ritualised practices of the kind in Maijbhandar or any of its branches either at present or in the past. The absence of such practice would not necessarily preclude the possibility that the songs talk about it, but such a discrepancy would need to be explained.

If, then, my observations are adequate and there are indeed no such practices in Maijbhandar, my contention is that the *dehatattva* of these boat journeys is a loan from other mystical traditions of Bengal that is emptied of its former significance and, in a sort of substitution process, gradually invested with new meanings. To prove this point, it is necessary to look at the contemporary reception of Maijbhandari songs, which will concern us in some detail in Chapter 6. Maijbhandari boat journeys appear to be an instance of a code in transition, and the validity of the explanations advanced here will be reconsidered in this light, in the context of that reception.

5.7.14 The body

> Manirām Siṃha is the watchman of the room/Six thieves wander around ceaselessly in the hope of theft/The treasure of the friend's storage chamber will be ruined if the thieves get the key.[664]
>
> (Ramesh Shil)

If the *dehatattva* songs discussed above somewhat dynamically outline inner trajectories, the ones to follow now preferably draw inner maps in a rather static manner. Apart from the boat, Maijbhandari *dehatattva* imagery also uses other means of transport (steamer, car, train, etc.), machines, spatial units (sea, city, fort, yard, field, etc.) or even political units (the state), but the most common metaphor for the human body is simply the house.[665] The basic idea is, as it were, that this microcosmic body contains the Divine and the macrocosmic universe in itself. For the description of the inner topography, the writers use such images as rooms, locks, guardians, etc., and usually also number them.

Many *dehatattva* songs, to start with, express the idea that God is hiding inside the human body and must be looked for not outside, but there; some then go on to elaborate upon inner locations; however, the majority of Maijbhandari *dehatattva* songs leave it at that. 'Mind, he whom you are searching for is inside your heart', says Ramesh Shil,[666] localising the Divine in the human heart (cf. above, p. 195 ff.); the typical location, however, is elsewhere, as we shall see. 'A wondrous artisan [is] the friend, a woundrous artisan/He has constructed an office of love and is hiding in

664 *ŚB* No. 33: *manirām siṃha gharer cakidār,/chaẏ'jan core curir āśe ghure anibār/bandhur koṭhār dhan habe chār'khār core yadi cābi pāẏ.*

665 The terms *ghar* and *bāṛi* are mostly used; *ghar*, however, may also refer to single rooms within that house. Also other terms are found, e.g. *bālākhānā*, the 'upper storey [room]' (Farid Hosain *SB* No. 62), in a *pars pro toto* function; a *bālākhānā* is usually on the second floor and considered to be the privileged part of a house or mansion. Cf., e.g., Mukherjee (1993: 80) on the prestige of upper-floor residences in nineteenth-century Calcutta.

666 *BhM* No. 14: *bāhire man khõja yāre se tomār hṛdaẏ mājhāre.*

it'[667] is the beginning of another well-known song by Ramesh Shil. This presence, however, may easily pass unnoticed: '[. . .] the two live in one house/room and do not meet'.[668] Farid Hosain puts it thus in the conclusion of one of his songs: 'He, Farid, whom you are looking for far away/Is in your own house';[669] but that 'golden friend' is not easily found in the 'house of the body' (*SB* No. 62). But actually, self and Divine are united inside: 'In one room, on one bed,/We dwell day and night like husbands and wifes'.[670] And unlike the usual image of the 'man', 'bird', etc. coming and going according to his liking, Farid Hosain turns the tables by pointing at the inevitability of that presence: 'The artisan will not be able to keep fleeing by tricks' in the case of one who has realised himself.[671] Abdul Gafur Hali also takes up Ramesh Shil's image of the artisan who lives in the house he made (*JJ* No. 38); and Aliullah advises his listeners: 'Do not stand around uselessly on the path/Go home quickly'.[672]

The house of the body is further divided; the usual number of rooms is eight.[673] Those rooms are locked, and the saint is the one who has the key. 'There are eight chambers and sixteen locks that are not opened even with much effort/The Maijbhandari is the keyholder, go and catch him' (Ramesh Shil);[674] or, by way of a similar image: 'Ramesh says: The name of the Bhandari is applied [as a] seal at every room'.[675] Abdul Gafur Hali, too, mentions eight rooms: 'It [the body] has a rod in the void, it has eight chambers'.[676] These chambers correspond to different regions of the body that are nowhere specified in the songs, except one which is identified as the dwelling place of the Lord inside the body as we shall see further on. The house also has nine doors, standing for the nine openings of the human body;[677] to these sometimes a tenth, 'closed' door is added.[678] 'Nine doors are open, on one he [the divine artisan] has put a lock'.[679]

667 *JS* No. 17: *ājab kārigar bandhu ājab kārigar/prem kācāri taiẏār kari lukāẏe āche tār bhitare.*

668 *ĀM* No. 7: *ek ghare du'janer bāsā dekhā śunā nāi. Ghar* may mean 'room' as well as 'house' here, but in view of the conventional image of the body as a house with different rooms, 'house' seems to be more likely.

669 *SB* No. 57: *dure pharid khoja yāke/se ye tomār āpan ghare*. Cf. also *SB* No. 58, where 'He' must be looked for in the *deha mas'jid ghar*, the 'house of the body-mosque'.

670 *HB* No. 30: *ek gharete ek bichāne/bās kar'techi rātra dine – svāmī-strīder matan*. Here, *ghar* is preferably translated as 'room'.

671 *HB* No. 6: *palāiẏā thāk'te pār'benā kauśalete kārigar.*

672 *PN* No. 23: *nā dā̃ṛāio michā panthe, śighra* [*sic*, <*śīghra*>] *cala gharere.*

673 This notion looms large especially in Baul songs, its meaning, however, being quite enigmatic. For a discussion, cf. Rahul Peter Das (1992: 418 ff.).

674 *BhM* No. 14: *āṭ koṭarī ṣola tālā bahu kaṣṭe yāẏ nā kholā/māij'bhāṇḍārī cābioẏālā dhara giẏe tāhāre.*

675 *MD* No. 17: *rameś bale bhāṇḍārī nām prati kām'rāẏ mohar mārā.*

676 *JJ* No. 38: *śūṇye mūl tār ek'ṭi ṭhuni/koṭh(a)ri tār aṣṭakhānā*. Cf. also *JJ* No. 62 where the body is represented by a train: *gāṛīr aṣṭa koṭ(a)rī* ('the wagon has eight chambers [i.e. compartments]'. The 'rod in the void' is the spine.

677 Cf. Shafiul Bashar *YB* No. 43; Abdul Gafur Hali *JJ* No. 62; Farid Hosain *SB* No. 37; Ramesh Shil *ĀM* No. 35; *ŚB* No. 33. These nine doors (and the closed tenth one) are common ground for Bengali *dehatattva* songs of different traditions and for South Asia in general (Rahul Peter Das 1992: 422).

678 This tenth door is differently explained as the fontanel, the navel, etc.

679 *JJ* No. 38: *naẏ darajā āche kholā – ek dar'jāẏ māirāche tālā.*

The number of locks differs considerably. Shafiul Bashar and Ramesh Shil give 16 in connection with eight chambers, possibly implying that every chamber is safeguarded by two locks.[680] Elsewhere, however, Ramesh Shil speaks of seven locks.[681] Farid Hosain doubles this into fourteen in one song: 'There are fourteen locks inside the house, he [the guru] has put up a fair[682] in them',[683] but elsewhere gives only three: 'You are moving about inside the house of three locks'.[684] The locks, in any case, do not seem to have any inherent connection with the doors of that house;[685] instead of locks, the songs have watchmen guard those doors: 'There are nine watchmen standing at the nine doors' (Abdul Gafur Hali).[686] This number can be extended, however, as the same author mentions an additional four guardians in another song: 'Thirteen patrol/Nine stay at the nine doors, four more are outside'.[687] Ramesh Shil even speaks of sixteen: 'There are walls on four sides, sixteen guard [the house]/Six spend the night, [while] those ten run around during daytime/One more does the head work standing up at the leadership [post]'.[688] This combination is interesting: the familiar number of ten to all appearances relates to the senses, and the six to the enemies; the leader is the mind. A *dehatattva* song by the Baul Din Sharat (Dīn Śarat̊) also mentions ten senses and six enemies, but in a different constellation: 'The ten senses are these six foes'[689] – which is an apt demonstration of the oscillation specifically in *dehatattva* terminology that we will discuss in the next chapter.

Farid Hosain, who does not mention seven locks, enumerates seven fields and skies inside the human body; the skies are described as vertical divisions of the body (i.e. the spaces between the sole of the foot, ankle, knee, hip, navel, breast, throat and the top of the head), and the fields are hair, skin, blood, nerves, flesh, bones and brain-matter. This house made so cleverly by the Lord should be known well: 'Measuring first inside the body, and ploughing the field of the body/Acquainting yourself with the seven skies, search for the thing so hard to attain'.[690] Elsewhere, addressing the

680 Cf. Ramesh Shil *BhM* No. 14; Shafiul *YB* No. 16.

681 Cf. *MD* No. 21; *ŚB* No. 33. This could relate to the *cakra*s.

682 In the sense of 'festival', 'market' (*melā*).

683 *SB* No. 37: *gharer mājhe caudda tālā tāhāte basāiche melā re*.

684 *SB* No. 48: *tin tālār gharer mājhe calāpherā kara*. *Tālā* is occasionally also used in the sense of *talā*, 'storey', in the songs; such a reading, however, would not be any less enigmatic in this case.

685 Ramesh Shil (*ĀM* No. 35) mentions that 'all the doors' have to be closed (i.e. apparently meditative introspection together with breath control, etc. has to be practised) in order to visualise the Divine inside oneself.

686 *JJ* No. 62: *naẏ darajāẏ dā̃ṛiẏe āche naẏ'jan praharī*.

687 *JJ* No. 38: [. . .] *tera jane deẏ pāhārā/naẏ'jan thāke naẏ darajāẏ - bāire raẏ ār cār'janā*.

688 *MD* No. 17: *cār'dike cār'ṭi deẏāl ṣola jane de* [i.e. *deẏ*] *pāhārā/chaẏ(a) jane rātre kāṭe, ai daś jan(a) dine chuṭe/ār ek jan(a) māthā khuṭe sarddārite thāki khārā*. Cf. also *MD* No. 21, where he speaks of four 'lion-doors' (*siṃha dar'jā*) and 16 *keẏār*, possibly 'care-takers' (?).

689 *BDG*: 129: *daś indriẏa ei ye ripu chaẏ*.

690 *SB* No. 6: *āge dehe jarip diẏā – deha jami cāṣ kariẏā/sapta ākāś cine niẏā durlabh bastu tālāś kara*. The term *bastu*, lit. 'thing', for the Divine essence inside the body is common in other parts of South Asia too. Tulpule, writing about Maharashtrian saints' use of that term, translates it as 'reality' (Tulpule 1983). Farid Hosain uses is again in *SB* No. 26.

bird, he gives the names of the six *laṭā'if*: 'Inside the *qalb*, *rūḥ*, *sir*, *nafs*, *ḫafī* and *aḫfā*/You come and go whichever takes hold of your mind'.[691] Ramesh Shil, in a song on the body as a steamer, defines the body as the steamer, the driver as the Maijbhandari, the lightmen as the ten senses (i.e. five *jñānendriyas* and five *karmendriyas*), and 'an electric cable plays inside the *suṣumnā*'.[692] Electricity, in another song, supplies the metaphor for the nerves: 'He [the friend] has laid telegraphic cables in various places'.[693] Farid Hosain also speaks of the body as a steamer: 'My body is a steamer, the mind is its captain/There are two headlights in front, they show the way clearly';[694] the 'headlight' are the eyes. In another song, the Lord, a mechanic (*mistrī*), has constructed the human machine 'on the divine formula' (*khodāẏī phar'māte*) that is invested with various connections and can be switched on and off.[695]

The ingredients of the human body that are frequently mentioned in the songs are the four elements, fire, water, earth and wind. Usually, they are simply enumerated;[696] in a few songs, however, their respective positions inside the body are described. Abdul Gafur Hali, for instance, writes: 'Fire burns above the water, above that, the wind plays/The house is made of earth, in front there is the Yamuna of juice'.[697] That is, the earthen body is the outer frame inside which the other elements are vertically aligned. The allocation seems to correspond to traditional medical theories regarding the inner functioning of the body. Ramesh Shil, however, describes an opposite order: 'Below is wind, above it is water, above that is the mine of fire'.[698] I have no explanation for this reversal.

Other enigmatic numbers (and images) occur in Ramesh Shil's songs, for example in *MD* No. 21. There are 60,000 'pairs' (*jorā* = *joṛā*) at the 'root' (*mūl*) of the body that is described as a *darbār*.[699] 'A tree has its roots upside down', and the 'bee of the mind' is eagerly drinking the nectar from the two flowers on the

691 *SB* No. 48: *'kalab' 'rūha' 'cher(a)' 'naphas' 'khaphi' āk(a)phār bhitare/āsā yāoẏā kara tumi mane yakhan dhare*.

692 *ŚB* No. 30: *susummā nārīte* [*sic*] *khele ilek'ṭriker tār*.

693 *JS* No. 17: *sthāne sthāne basāẏeche ṭeligrāpher tār*.

694 *SB* No. 73: *āmār baḍi hoẏ iṣṭimār māiṇḍ(a) haïla sāreṃ ihār/phranṭete haẏ(a) ṭu lāiṭār rāstā dekhāẏ pariṣkār*. A stylistic speciality of this song is the excessive, playful use of English loan words. For the original and a full translation, see Appendix 1.

695 Cf. *HB* No. 5. We may recall the popularity of electric metaphors in the context of initiation also; the *muršid* sets up a direct connection with the *murīd*'s heart that is in common Sufi parlance often paralleled to switching on a light or, most recently, as going online.

696 Cf., e.g., Farid Hosain *HB* No. 5; *SB* No. 73 mentions only three (fire, water, air) as the fuel of the engine, probably implying the foregoing creation from earth that the *Qur'ān* proclaims. Also Abdul Gafur Hali *JJ* No. 62 on the 'train' of the body: *āgun, pāni, māṭi, bātās cār jiniser taiẏārī* ('It is made from four things: fire, water, earth, wind').

697 *JJ* No. 38: *pānir upar āgun jvale – tār upare hāoẏā khele/māṭi diẏe tairī ghar'khānā – sām'ne raser yamunā*.

698 *MD* No. 17: *nīce hāoẏā upare pāni, tār upar āguner khani*.

699 *MD* No. 21: *mūle ṣāiṭ hājār jorā* [<*joṛā*>]. At the end of the song, Ramesh Shil speaks of a *bātuni dar'bār*, 'hidden [Ar. <*bāṭin*>] court' which probably refers not to the whole body, but the location of the Divine in it – probably the place of the uppermost *sahasrāra cakra* directly beneath the top of the cranium.

tree's top;[700] ten million suns are glowing, and 'there are 24 and a half moon, the light is extremely pleasant and cool'.[701] The topsy-turvy tree reminds one of the tree with 4,000 branches first created by Allah (Wolff 1872 [2004]: 1), but more specifically of the '*aśvattha*-tree with its roots above and the leaves below' of the *Bhagavadgītā*;[702] according to Kiehnle, it 'is considered in *yogī* circles as a metaphor of macrocosm as well as microcosm' (Kiehnle 1997: 159). The moons and suns Ramesh Shil mentions are in all probability experiences of light during certain yogic practices.[703] The 60,000 'pairs' may refer to the branches of the tree and possibly stand for *nāḍī*s (30,000 for each side); but this is sheer guesswork.

Let us turn then to the location of the Divine inside the body. In the beginning of this analysis of motifs, the heart was identified as the *arš Allāh*, 'Allah's seat' within man. The *dehatattva* songs discussed in this section use terms like *māl'koṭhā* (which approximately translates as 'storage chamber'), *māolā dhaner ārām'khānā* ('resting place/repose of the dearest Maula') or *nūrer ghar* ('room of light') to refer to that ultimate locus. But is it the heart the authors are speaking of? Farid Hosain, as we have cited, divides the body into seven 'skies' and concludes this part of his song thus: 'If you go from the throat to the head, that is called the seventh sky/In that place the Mawlā is sitting and saying: "I am the highest Lord [*adhīśvar*]" '.[704] According to Ramesh Shil, the *āsal dhanī*, 'truly rich one', resides in a repose *above* the locations of air, water and fire (*MD* No. 17). Only Shafiul Bashar describes the 'room of light' as situated 'in the middle' and identifies it as the *arš*, 'seat' of the Divine. The other instances rather point to the human head as the location of God in man. Ramesh Shil, especially, uses the term *māl'koṭhā* several times for this location; it equally occurs in *dehatattva* traditions outside Maijbhandari songs.[705] *Māl* is literally 'wealth/goods', hence my translation as 'storage chamber'. Rahul Peter Das (1992: 399 f.) draws our attention to the possibility that it may also refer to semen which is held to be stored in the head,[706] but states that its precise meaning is unclear. Ramesh Shil uses the term in at least three songs, but unfortunately does not state the *māl'koṭhā*'s exact position either. It is only by inference from other songs by him that we could identify it, but the problem is that Ramesh – just like Farid Hosain and others – is not at all

700 Ibid.: *ek'ṭi gāche ul'ṭā mūl, pātāẏ pātāẏ candra gāthā śiker dui phul,/man bhramarā haẏ ākul sei phuler'i madhu khāi.*

701 Ibid.: *sāre cabbiś candra jyotiḥ ati suśītal*. It is also possible to treat *sāre cabbiś candra jyotiḥ* as a compound and translate lit. '24 and a half moonlights' or, better, 'the light of 24 and a half moons'.

702 *BhG* 15.1 (*ūrdhvamūlam adhaḥśākham aśvattham*).

703 There is a mention of ten million *moons*, however, in another song by Ramesh Shil *ĀM* No. 35: *kauṭi candra yini jyoti*, 'he who is the light [of] ten million moons'. This may lead to the conclusion that this too is no fixed image.

704 *HB* No. 6: *galā haïte gele māthāẏ – sapta* [*sic*, read *saptam*] *ākāś bale kathāẏ/sei khāne basiẏā māolāẏ bal'chen āmi adhiśvar* [*sic*, read *adhīśvar*].

705 Cf., e.g., an anonymous song in Cakrabartī (1990: 68).

706 We have seen in *Jībanī o kerāmat* (*JK*: 21), the hagiography on Saint Ahmadullah, that this notion does occur in Chittagong.

coherent in his allocations and sees the Divine alternately in the heart or the head.[707] '(Ramesh says:) the dearest Maijbhandari Ġawṯ is solemnly present in the storage chamber'[708] and can be seen upon the closure of 'all doors'. In another song, the dark house must be searched to find that place:

> Take out the light by rubbing the *mantra*-matchbox of your guru/You shall see how beautiful the Mawlā is/The candle is in the dark, if you light the knowledge-wick and the *bhakti*-oil then/You shall see: Madan Mohan Śyām Sundar is solemnly present in the storage chamber.[709]

This passage, however, does not solve our question either. The third mention of *māl'koṭhā* is as follows: 'Manirām Siṃha is the watchman of the room/Six thieves wander around ceaselessly in the hope of theft/The treasure of the friend's storage chamber of the friend will be ruined if the thieves get the key'.[710] Ramesh speaks of the 'treasure of the friend's storage chamber'; thus, according to the logic of the grammar here, it seems highly unlikely that that friend himself is the 'treasure' (*dhan*) himself – notwithstanding the fact that the Mawlā is often addressed as *dhan*. Consequently, something else must be stored in that chamber, and the essential quality of that thing or substance makes it the 'friend's' abode. In view of the sufficiently known tantric transformation processes of semen, it does seem, then, that the *māl'koṭhā* is in fact the container of semen as the very substance and essence of life which, according to *dehatattva* ideas, is certainly not the heart but can only be the human head.

Maybe, then, this song is a clue to understanding references to *māl* in other Maijbhandari songs by other authors also. Aliullah,[711] Abdul Gafur Hali and Farid Hosain also use it in contexts that at least do not preclude such an understanding. But again, there is no way of being sure about this. We shall have to discuss such semantic issues in a broader framework in the course of the following chapter. What is basically striking is the parallel occurrence of two distinct notions regarding the position of the Divine in the human body in Maijbhandari songs. In the doctrinal elaborations of the Maijbhandari *ṭarīqa*, the human head does not feature in this sense. One may thus wonder how such a contradiction can persist for many decades of songwriting. I think the reason for this is mainly the fact that *dehatattva* songs codify the information they convey, and not being visible as such, contradictions of this kind simply do not clash in common perception.

707 Cf. Rahul Peter Das (1992: 411).

708 *ĀM* No. 36: *(rameś kaẏ) māl koṭāte birāj kare māij'bhāṇḍārī gāoc(a) dhan*. Cf. Das (1992: 400 n. 74), who translates: 'The Māij Bhāṇḍārī is illustriously present in the chamber of goods/wealth'.

709 *ĀM* No. 7: *tor gurur mantra salaïr bāksa ghasiẏā āgun bāhir kara/dekh'te pābi māolā ki sundar/ bātti āche ā̃dhāre, jñān salitā bhakti taila jvālāle pāre* [*sic*, probably *pare*]*/dekh'bi māl koṭāte birāj kare madan mohan śyām sundar*.

710 *ŚB* No. 33 (cf. the beginning of this section). The thief or thieves are a common image; cf. Kabir's verse: 'They all went mad, none of them keeps awake,/While the thief is plundering the house!' Translation by Vaudeville (1993: 232 f.) who interprets this as a reference to death.

711 *PN* No. 22: *gharer bhitar āche māl* ('The goods are in the house/room').

On a general level, the term *dehatattva* itself, of course, creates a number of delimitation problems. In its most limited sense, it refers to ideas about the inner topography of man and the position of the Divine therein. *Dehatattva* songs in this sense may use symbolic representation to describe these notions, but it is clear all the way that it is the human body they speak about; that is, the object of reference is discernible as such. As we have seen in the section on boat journeys, however, this reference may also be optional in songs that function on different levels of meaning; *dehatattva* could then more adequately be defined as one *mode* of interpretation that exists side by side with other modes. And thirdly, if we reduce *dehatattva* to the very basic meaning that interaction between man and God takes place within the human body, the very bulk of Maijbhandari song production can in some way or other be ascribed to that category. The notion that the human body contains the Divine, and that it must be understood and cultivated in time so as to be able to properly relate to that Divine, is fundamental to the Maijbhandari understanding of religion and forms one of the premises the Maijbhandari song tradition rests upon.

5.8 Conclusion

This analysis of motifs, then, has come full circle with this discussion of the location of the Divine within the human body. To be sure, this circle is not exhaustive; other circles could be chosen, and yet other motifs and complexes of motifs could be explored. But one point has certainly become clear from the present circular investigation: all the motifs we have discussed here are strongly interrelated and combinable. Rather than going through a number of separate items, I would like to think of this exercise as orbiting a somewhat condensed semantic complex and isolating certain aspects of it, all the way noticing multiple interlinkages between them.

This cohesion goes together, as we could state again and again, with a huge amount of semantic oscillation; and it appears that in a popular idiom like Maijbhandari songs, this relation is a necessary one. The songs use material from various sources, as we have seen, but transpose those materials into the context of Maijbhandar in incessantly asserting the centrality of a few fundamental categories (such as the saints, love, merging, the body, etc.). Materials from Sufi, Baul, Vaishnava traditions, etc. are, one could say, put into service for Maijbhandar here.[712] Such a transposition, I want to argue, is not possible in an environment of utter terminological and conceptual fixity. This mystical song tradition on the one hand proclaims the ultimate unity of man, God, religions, etc.; on the other, and much more subtly, it is itself a process of semantic fusion. We may read single songs also as semantic explorations with a *reductive* purpose, in that they absorb new links into the tradition and pretend to take them *back* to Maijbhandar. In such circumstances, and in keeping with the exigencies of 'fitting things in', semantic oscillation of terms and categories seems unavoidable.

712 Very much like in the case of Baul songs; cf. Rahul Peter Das (1992: 422) ('But their [the Bauls'] syncretism allows them to take over songs of other religious groups, or even folk songs, too, if these may be interpreted to fit their tenets').

Another reason for this lack of fixity is the proximity to an oral tradition that many Maijbhandari songs originated from and whose character they still retain. If today the printing and first circulation of new songs may in some cases coincide, this certainly was not the rule even thirty years ago. The usual order of events was that songs were presented to the public at the *darbār* or elsewhere long before they were printed, and the latter only happened at all, we may suppose, if the songs had proven successful and were found irreproachable by Maijbhandari representatives. In the process of oral dissemination that followed their composition, songs were transmitted only rudimentarily[713] or with textual changes (including alterations of the addressee).[714]

It is the cohesion of Maijbhandari songs, notwithstanding the heterogeneity of the material they work with, that qualifies them for the designation of a separate *idiom*. This does not mean that the overlaps with other such idioms (as, e.g., Baul songs) disappear, but only that Maijbhandari songs are centred on Maijbhandar as a sort of integrating point of gravity. The fringes and overlaps of this idiom with its surroundings, fuzzy and undefined as they are, appear as creative zones rather than centrifugal tendencies that could threaten the tradition. In evaluating the role of the songs for Maijbhandar, one might even go so far as to claim that it is this cohesion and the resulting common idiom that is holding Maijbhandar together in the public mind despite the factionalisation into competing *manzil*s and institutions.

713 Cf. the versions of 37 Maijbhandari songs given in Ālam (1985: 18–33), some of them very short and most probably collected from oral tradition.

714 Cf. Ramesh Shil's song *Ār kata kā̃dābi* as discussed above in this chapter.

6 Songs in contemporary Maijbhandari interpretations

In the preceding chapter, I have attempted to give an overview of motifs used in Maijbhandari songs and explain them by a circular semantic analysis. And, as we have seen, several religious traditions have left their traces in Maijbhandari songs. A historical and philological approach to them shows in which way images, motifs and religious concepts from various sides have found accommodation in this open and popular tradition. It can, however, explain only in part how such conceptual permeability has come into being and is maintained. No doubt, the contemporary ethos of Maijbhandar, resumed and celebrated in the formula *dharmajātinirbiśeṣe*, 'irrespective of religion and caste/class', acts as an overarching protective ideology for this permeability. It generates a general climate of permissiveness towards a wide variety of religious expression. But no more than this – it does not supply the rationale for understanding and treating such diverse forms of expression beyond preaching a reverent and tolerant attitude towards them. Nor do Maijbhandari theological writings teach their readers how to deal with and how to understand religious concepts, present in the songs, that fall beyond the pale of a generally acclaimed Maijbhandari Sufi canon.

In order to come closer to an understanding of the way in which Maijbhandari songs have acquired such stable religious permeability, I felt it necessary to look at their reception. In a series of interviews, I asked members of the movement and persons loosely connected or acquainted with it to interpret a chosen number of Maijbhandari songs for me. In the selection of my interviewees, I attempted to achieve an acceptable degree of mean variation with regard to their religious affiliation (Muslims and Hindus), social status, gender and the closeness of their affiliation to Maijbhandar. This attempt does not, of course, in the least provide any reliable degree of representativeness, and is certainly very far from being statistically valid in any sense. But such validity was not intended. My aim was, instead, to look for patterns of reception, and in this sense the attempt has been fruitful indeed.

Twenty interviewees were questioned, in 1999 and 2001, about a total of fifteen songs by nine authors. Four of these twenty persons were Hindus. Only three were female, due in part to the communicative difficulties and restrictions resulting from my status as a male Western researcher and visitor. Except one, an urban intellectual trained in cultural studies, all interviewees were directly connected with

Maijbhandar in one way or the other. Four among them were *pīrzada*s. Several belonged to the *murīd*s affiliated to different *manzil*s. Two were themselves writers of Maijbhandari songs, another two professional or semi-professional singers. More than half of my interviewees came from a rural background, with different degrees of contact with urban life. Formal education ranked from none to Ph.D; in general, however, my collocutors had more formal education and were much older than the average person in Chittagong.

The interpretation process I asked my interviewees to go through was quite a complex sort of communication and exegesis. First of all, the authors chosen for interpretation are considered authoritative voices in Maijbhandar, and therefore no part of any song could simply be dismissed. Secondly, as much as interpretations *of* something, these were interpretations *for* an outsider in what mostly resulted in a teaching situation. The interview situations were quite varied, and took very disparate periods of time (from 40 minutes to approximately five hours). Usually, at least some of the songs chosen by me were known to the interviewee-interpreters. Younger people often declined to interpret the songs for me and referred me to 'those who know'. In one or two cases, interviewees felt that my questioning was strategic rather than truth-seeking, and refused to carry on; in other cases, in turn, my questioning became genuine rather than strategic.

The songs were selected with regard to topicality. Topics of special interest were *dehatattva* and yogic concepts, female *bhakti* and the reappearance of the same divine agent on earth. That is, I singled out songs for this 'collective interpretation' that would, according to a historical and philological perspective, appear as especially heterogeneous; or, from a purist Islamist perspective, as particularly deviant. My aim in this selection was to examine if and how boundaries between supposed traditions of belief are perceived, and how they are tackled.

I made it my principle not to interfere with the process of interpretation on the part of my interlocutors, but as the interviews often tended to develop into discussions, the distinctions and purpose underlying my choice did, in a few cases, have effects on the directions my interviewees' explanations took. I usually offered to give my literate interlocutors the texts beforehand and hold the interview in a second sitting, but almost all preferred to give ad hoc interpretations, paraphrasing the songs line after line. What most interpreted as a teaching situation has in a few cases generated forced interpretations which were upheld only for the sake of maintaining the teacher's position; such interpretations are, however, easily identifiable.

It was not possible to have all songs interpreted by all interviewees, mostly due to time limits set by them. On average, my interviewees interpreted eight songs. Altogether, then, approximately 160 interpretations of single songs were collected. In the following, thus, I want to present some salient features of these interviews. I shall first give the relevant parts of the song texts. Then I shall summarise the various interpretations and, following that, give my analysis of them with possible comments. In the first section, emphasis is on the ways that *sandhābhāṣā* is deciphered; the remaining ones deal with the conceptualisation of 'loans' from Bengali Vaishnava love poetry.

6.1 Boat journeys and *sandhābhāṣā*

One of the songs chosen from this category was *Mājhi tribeṇīr ghāṭer joẏār*, a *dehatattva* song in 'intentional language' (*sandhābhāṣā*) by Ramesh Shil (cf. my discussion of it in Section 5.7.13). The results attained from around fifteen interviews about this song seem particularly interesting, and since the song (like other boat journey songs) has a real plot, its translation is again given in full:

> Boatman, move onwards catching the flood of the quay of three streams [*tribeṇīr ghāṭ*]./Steer your boat slowly with the inner picture [Ar. *barzaḫ*] of the Bhandari./The first quay is the market of *nāsūt*, be on the watch./At that quay is the fair of robbers, you are inclined to lose the root./After that comes the city of *malakūt*, keep steady your direction./There are the moon and the sun to your right and left, go through the middle./In *ǧabarūt*, there is play of the wind, set your sails./Hold your helm as you see the bend of the imperceptible./Ramesh says: Attain the sight of the divine at the quay of *lāhūt*./(Finally,) when *pīr* and *murīd* take on one colour, pass [your time] in joy.[1]
>
> (*SD* No.7)

What is 'the flood of the three streams' (*tribeṇīr ghāṭer joẏār*)? According to the yogico-tantric body concept, as it were, the mirocosmic three streams are the meeting point of three *nāḍīs* (*iḍā, piṅgalā, suṣumnā*), thought to be situated in the human body at the perineum. 'Moon' and 'sun' refer to *iḍā* and *piṅgalā*, while the upward movement to be achieved in one's *sādhanā* has to take the middle path of the *suṣumnā*. This movement through the *cakra*s is here leading through the *maqāmāt*, which are conceived as horizontally allocated in the human body.

None of my interviewees, however, explained the song in exactly these terms. Many of the interpretations I gathered did not even concede that the song is concerned with *dehatattva*. For those who did interpret it thus, it was the term *tribeṇī* that triggered off such an interpretation. In these cases, it was stressed, preceding the explanation, that what was to follow was secret and 'tremendous' (*sāṅghātik*), and in one case a woman present during the interview was sent into another room before my interviewee consented to continue. In other cases, I was asked to turn off my tape. Altogether, I could collect nine types of explanations of this song.

(i) The 'quay of three streams' stands for *yoni*, that is, the vagina. The three streams are the parts of the body that meet at that point, namely the two legs and the trunk. The flood is explained as the right time in a man's life for having sexual intercourse, that is, mainly in young adulthood. In a kind of overarching metaphor, this sexual union is interpreted as union as such, and the fundamental synonymity of sexual union with spiritual union is asserted. The 'fair of robbers' indicates various unspecified hindrances on the way to that union, and 'moon and sun' stand for night and day. The right time, then, is interpreted as the time of twilight, meaning an auspicious time. Sexual intercourse should be well timed. If

1 For a more detailed discussion of this song and remarks on its terminology, cf. Section 5.7.13.

there are diffiulties in achieving all this, one should pray to the *barʲjakh* (Bg.), explained as the 'inner picture', of the Bhandari.[2]

In a variant of this interpretation, the 'flood' is explained as menstrual blood, which in turn is described as a metaphor for human life: without menstruation, no human life would ever be possible.

(ii) The 'quay of the three streams' is the human heart, the three streams being the three main blood vessels.[3] The flood is explained as the state of breathing in, and *barʲjakh* as the picture of the *muršid*, which is equivalent to the form of God; the purpose of the journey is to perform *ḏikr* in one's heart. The *maqāmāt* are conventionally described and interpreted as categories interior to the human body; the lower ones are distractions on the way to the heart that have to be transcended. 'Moon and sun' are the human eyes, and their middle is the eye of meditation. The interior path leads up, supported by the wind in the realm of the prophets (*ğabarūt*), until one comes face to face with Allah and is united with him.

(iii) The *tribeṇī* is explained as the meeting point of the three *nāḍī*s (*iḍā* right, *piṅgalā* left, *suṣumnā* in the middle) at the forehead, in analogy with the macrocosmic *tribeṇī* at Allahabad. The spot is identified as the point on which one locates one's concentration during meditation, and as the *trinayana*, the 'third eye', and the destination of the boatman. The 'flood' is equated with the *kuṇḍalinī*. The Bhandari stands for the internal guru, and the relation with Maijbhandar is perceived as optional; thus, another spiritual guide may take his place. The robbers of line 4 are identified with the *ṣaḍripu*, the 'six enemies'.[4] The word *nāsūt* is identified as non-Bengali and unintelligible; the *maqāmāt* are taken to be mystical names of locations inside the body, like 'sun' and 'moon'.[5] The wind that takes one up is created by *ḏikr*, which is conceived as a kind of meditation (*dhyān*) and the one-minded calling of God. *Nilakṣer bāk* is interpreted as 'the word of the imperceptable', that is the name of God. *Dīdār* (P., 'sight') is apparently understood as a location and equated with the 'quay of three streams'.[6]

(iv) The 'quay of three streams' is seen as the (unspecified) meeting point of three *maqāmāt*, which are equated with the realms of earthly life, hell and heaven. The purpose of life is to be unperturbed by hell (moon) and even heaven (sun) and move through their middle towards God himself.[7]

(v) The *tribeṇīr ghāṭ* is understood as the Hindu *tīrtha*, 'holy place' at Allahabad/Prayag in India, that is, the confluence of the rivers Ganges, Yamuna and Sarasvati; the flood is explained as the passionate state of mind of a pilgrim.

2 The *maqāmāt* were recognised as such, but not integrated into the interpretation.

3 In analogy to the hearts of cows and buffaloes, as my interlocutor pointed out.

4 Lust, anger, greed, infatuation, vanity and envy.

5 In this connection, my interlocutor mentioned the word *dehatattva*, asserting emphatically that everything in the world is also located in the human body.

6 The interviewee is a rural Hindu connected with Maijbhandar, but not a *murīd* or *ḫādim* of any of the *manzil*s.

7 This interpretation was particularly improvised. The interviewee apparently did not know the song, but did not take the time to go through it before interpreting it. He stressed that classic Maijbhandari songs were often hard to interpret because they were created in *ḥāl* or *bhāb*, both terms meaning a state of trance, and therefore beyond general intelligibility.

The remaining part of the song, the upward movement through the *maqāmāt*, is seen as the spiritual path. It is explicitly denied that *dehatattva* concepts are implied in the song. The combination of a Hindu holy place and the Sufi concept of *maqāmāt* is not perceived as incoherent or problematic in any way, and the Muslim interlocutor does not attribute the inclusion of the *tribeṇī* image to the fact that Ramesh Shil was a Hindu.

(vi) *Tribeṇī* is identified as 'a concept from Hindu mythology', but not properly understood, and it is attributed to the song-author being a Hindu.[8] *Barzaḫ* is translated as *ekāgratā*, 'concentration'. *Nāsūt* is the place of the six enemies (see above), and the Maijbhandari *ṭarīqa* is cited as a means to overcome them. 'Sun' and 'moon' are interpreted as God and the prophet; while it is impossible to look at the sun, the divine light is mediated by the moon and tolerable for the human eye.[9] One should keep in the middle, not forgetting God for the sake of one's *pīr* or the prophet, nor forsaking all human mediation. *Dīdār* is explained as the love of one's *pīr*, which, again, should not lead to his deification; it is only a valid experience if one's *pīr*'s *silsila* is sound and takes one back to the prophet. Through such legitimate mediation, it is possible to experience union with God.

(vii) *Tribeṇi* is identified as the confluence of three rivers and the *tīrtha* at Allahabad, but the Bengali *tribeṇī* at Hugli as its 'local version' is thought to be intended in a song by Ramesh Shil. The flood is what makes the way there navigable. Simultaneously, a secret meaning of *tribeṇī* is introduced: the three lower openings of the female anatomy. The 'flood', in this sense, is desire, either male sexual desire to take the 'middle path', or female desire which has to be aroused to make sexual union possible. The *maqāmāt* are the four 'main stations' on the spiritual path that takes one ultimately to God. Moon and sun are interpreted as lights in *malakūt*, the realm of angels; one should not be deluded by them but keep steady one's direction towards God.

(viii) The 'quay of three streams' is not understood. The *barzaḫ* is explained as meditation (*dhyān*). The *maqāmāt* are explained as the different types of *nafs*, thus the first *maqām*, *nāsūt*, is the *nafs-i ammāra*. 'Sun' and 'moon' are not understood, neither is the phrase *nilakṣer bāk/nirlakṣer bā̃k*.

All these interpretations were given by persons in some way or other conversant with Maijbhandar. The last, below, was given by a highly educated urban intellectual not directly in touch with Maijbhandar, but sympathetic to the various expressions of what he regards as Bangladeshi popular culture:

(ix) The *tribeṇī* is identified as a location 'in the direction of Kāśī and Gayā', but not further specified. The remaining concepts are not known to the interviewee, neither the *maqāmāt*, nor the significance of *barzaḫ*, moon and sun or the term *nilakṣa*. While before the interview proper, Maijbhandari songs were classified as vehicles of *mānuṣer dharma*, 'religion of man', designed to be easily understood by common people, it was admitted that some of the *dehatattva* song are compli-

8 The fact that the *tribeṇī* also appears in the Muslim writer Abdul Gafur Hali's songs is explained by Ramesh Shil's influence.

9 Cf. *Ā'īna-i Bārī* 45 f.

cated, because here the authors expound their own idiosyncratic doctrines. The attitude towards the songs changed considerably during the interview.[10]

Some of these nine interpretations achieve a certain amount of coherence, while others, especially the last two, fail to do so completely. It must be stressed that about half of them were collected from initiated members of one or the other branch of the Maijbhandari *ṭarīqa*. The 'inner' Maijbhandari perspective on this Maijbhandari song is thus well represented. It is furthermore unlikely that any secret readings were withheld since many interviewees did not hesitate to utter taboo concepts, as the above interpretations sufficiently demonstrate. The result is backed by similar divergence of interpretations in the case of other songs of the categories of boat journeys and *dehatattva*.

It must be emphasised that among the interviewees there were also songwriters who have continued to write *dehatattva* songs to this day, and do in fact use the *sandhābhāṣā* terms present in this song by Ramesh Shil. It can thus be clearly stated that neither the authors nor the recipients of contemporary *dehatattva* songs in Maijbhandar (most of them initiated in the Maijbhandari *ṭarīqa*) decode them in the ways which the one-century-old study of yogic and tantric literature would suggest.[11] An 'intentional' code language, it seems, has in some way been unchained from its intended contents; it has become independent from its meaning. We can state, broadly speaking, a stability of motifs combined with an instability of semantics.

How are we to understand this situation? There are a number of possible explanations: either these *dehatattva* songs are part of a tradition which is losing its base in this area and is in the process of vanishing; or what we have here is the result of active obfuscation of secrets on the part of the collocutors; or, lastly, *dehatattva* imagery is employed in a semantic environment different from the one suggested by relevant scholarship, and in a 'deviant' communicative function.

The first hypothesis would rely mostly on the mediating role and pre-eminent position of Ramesh Shil in the Maijbhandari song tradition. Ramesh Shil is not the first writer of *dehatattva* songs in the Maijbhandari genre, but he is the most popular one, and *dehatattva* is more prominent in his songs than, for instance, in those of Aliullah. Simultaneously, he is the most famous exponent of Maijbhandari songs. Ramesh Shil came to Maijbhandar first for the *'urs* in 1923, at the age of 46 years. Before that time, he is said to have had a spiritual guide called Nasu Mālum from Madarbari (*RR*: [27]). In his testament from 1948, he mentions four other spiritual preceptors, most prominently Jagadānanda Purī

10 A condescending attitude in the beginning gave way to great curiosity when my interviewee had to admit to himself that he was lacking the codes and prerequisites to understand even the basic ideas of this song. After the interview, I was thus asked to disclose my findings, and narrated some of the other explanations I had collected. These left my interlocutor clearly perplexed.

11 This is, of course, no more than a very cautious and tentative assessment by an outsider to this area of research. For some literature on this vast topic, cf. the references given in Sections 5.7.13 and 14. Add, for the *Caryāpadas*, Per Kvaerne's interpretation (Kvaerne 1977) with reference to Tibetan Mahayana texts.

from Haola to whom he professes discipleship,[12] and by his side three others to whom he pays respect: Gangagir (Gaṅgāgīr) from the Dattatraiyi Akhra (Dattatraiẏī Ākh'ṛā) in Chittagong, Balaksadhu (Bālak'sādhu, Chittagong City) and Jyotishananda (Jyotiṣānanda) from the Shankar Math (Śaṃkar Maṭh) in Sitakunda (*RR*: [28]). It seems very likely that the teachings Ramesh Shil received from these personalities included initiation into yogic and tantric traditions. The imagery he uses would also not be hard to account for in view of the long-standing popularity of *dehatattva* songs. Ramesh Shil then combined these concepts with some of the Sufi ideas he was taught, or simply picked up, in Maijbhandar; a combination, in fact, that was not new but had been documented centuries before in the medieval tradition of Muslim Bengali texts, for example in the anonymous *Yog kālandar* or Saiyad Sultan's *Jñān pradīp*.

While Ramesh Shil thus, according to this hypothesis, still understood the code language he used, his successors continued to use it without properly grasping its inner significance. His references to yogico-tantric practices were lost on them because these practices apparently never formed a part of the ritual and doctrinal inventory of Maijbhandar proper.[13] His imagery was, in a way, fetishised. This could have happened because Ramesh's songs gradually acquired cult status and were perceived as vehicles of deeper, hidden truths; that is, the songs themselves were mystified and sanctified, and utilising their imagery promised participation in the inner core of spirituality. It speaks for this explanation that loans from Maijbhandari songs perceived as 'classics' are indeed quite common in the contemporary production. Besides Ramesh Shil, other song-authors (possibly also Bauls) and oral tradition in general may have contributed to the occurrence of *dehatattva* imagery in Maijbhandari songs. Songs, ever since the *Caryāpada*s, appear to have been the major vehicle of this imagery in the Bengali language, and we can safely assume that these were usually not preserved in script but transmitted orally.

A second explanation could claim that the different and somewhat uncommon interpretations of the song given above are in fact, and in keeping with what the original intent of 'intentional language' is thought to be, due to a codex of secrecy. If, contrary to the present researcher's impressions, all the authors and other members of the Maijhandari movement among the interviewees *are* initiated members of some secret society within Maijbhandari or connected circles, they are unlikely to explain the significance of *dehatattva* songs to an uninitiated foreign researcher. If this is the case, we run into the 'torment of secrecy' extensively described in an article by Hugh B. Urban of the same title.[14] In such circumstances, mutually exclusive, contradictory statements can hardly be evaluated because there is little chance of knowing which among them is a result of active

12 His son, Pulinbihari Shil, mentioned this spiritual relationship along with Ramesh's affiliation to Maijbhandar (Interview February 1999).

13 This can of course not be said with any certainty of the 'fringes' of Maijbhandar, such as faqir visitors on *'urs* festivals, etc.

14 Hugh B. Urban (1998) on the Kartabhajas of Calcutta; cf. pp. 212–15 (n) for literature on secrecy and the ethical dilemma of the researcher attempting to divulge such secrets.

dissimulation and which is not. So we are bound to be lost in the semantic obscurities of multiple interpretations.[15] We may, of course, fall back upon the data obtained from other, more extensively researched sources such as the Bauls, but such decoding by means of inferences must remain hazardous and unsatisfying.

Thirdly, the 'fetishisation' of *sandhābhāṣā* mentioned above in connection with Ramesh Shil could provide a clue to the role of such imagery in Maijbhandar in a more general sense. In order to make this point, we must consider the basic properties of *sandhābhāṣā* as a communicative device in some detail. The only thing that can be known for certain, both from the structure of *sandhābhāṣā*[16] and from contemporary evidence,[17] is that it is symbolic rather than literal and involves a code for deciphering. This code is usually subject to secrecy and bestowed only after initiation in the course of a master's teachings to his disciple. But unlike these codes, *dehatattva* songs themselves apparently were never strictly secret, and thus their function cannot have been a merely commemorative one. As Baul and Maijbhandari practice demonstrate, they are performed in public, and in some part certainly also *designed* for such public communication. How then are we to account for the paradox that a certain code of secret knowledge is exposing itself to the non-initiated public, while insisting all the while on its marked property as a secret code? What is the significance of such truncated communication?

Sandhābhāṣā songs suggest that there is much to know beyond their literal contents without, however, divulging those secrets. This is an instance of what Luhmann and Fuchs call artificial rarification[18] and analyse as an attribute of religious communication in general: possible access to certain mystical secrets is signalled, but not granted. In other words, according to Urban (1998: 235), the secret is 'advertised' by a 'dialectic of lure and withdrawal'. The songs communicate that there is a certain inside and speak as if from this inside to the outside; but they do not disclose that inside to the outside, and confine their message to allusive, evocative images. Telling the public listener simultaneously that there is something secret and elevated to know, but that he does not know it, and that there is a way to know (e.g. by taking refuge in the Bhandari), *dehatattva* songs have a proselytising aspect.[19] Their semantic obscurity is calculated to give and hold back at the same time, and to generate a certain half-knowledge on the listener's part.

15 Cf. Urban (1998: 233 f.) who gathered eight different interpretations from *initiated* members and texts of the Kartabhaja community regarding the meaning of *hijṛā* (castrated male) in one specific Kartabhaja saying.

16 Namely, the fact that *sandhābhāṣā* poetry, in most cases, will not yield consistent sense if read literally.

17 I refer here to interviews with Bauls at Kushtia and Maijbhandaris on *dehatattva* songs; in all cases, it was made clear in the beginning that some 'secret' (*gopan*, *gupta*) meaning was intended.

18 'Künstliche Verknappung' is the German term, cf. Luhmann/Fuchs (1989: 271).

19 A famous example of a mystic prompted by *dehatattva* songs to be initiated is Lalan Shah. Cf. Jaohar (1393 [1986], III: 11 f.): Lalan used to be fascinated by *dehatattva* songs and performed them without understanding their meaning. Siraj, a bearer from his village (Harishpur), explained some of the meanings to Lalan, whereupon Lalan almost forced Siraj to accept him as his disciple. Siraj first declined ('Lalan, I am a totally worthless man, I am born in the humble cast of bearers, I am a fool lacking any learning. I am not worthy of the position of a guru', p. 12), but Lalan insisted.

There is no doubt that such an aesthetics of mysticism is highly self-mystifying. The song, its author and the spiritual preceptor recommended in the song all enter the orbit of this mystical inside. The other part of this aesthetics is the peculiar semi-participation granted to the listener: the songs are perceived as containers of spirituality; listening to them becomes equal to getting in touch with that spirituality, and the lack of understanding is attributed to the highly spiritual, divine and thus by definition unintelligible nature of the contents. My hypothesis is that the above-mentioned aesthetic dimension of *sandhābhāṣā* predestines it for use in mystic idioms, no matter whether it operates as a fixed code or only pretends to do so. *Sandhābhāṣā* indeed lures the listener into participation by telling him that there is something more to know, and that the guru or saint in question, in our case the Bhandari, is the right guide on the path towards such mystical secrets. The Bhandari being hard to grasp,[20] and knowledge being graded,[21] songwriters themselves may legitimately claim to possess not much more than the half-knowledge of their listeners, while enhancing their saint's status by their evocation of mystical secrecy.

The issue of the role of *sandhābhāṣā* in Maijbhandar cannot be settled decisively. But I would suggest a combination of the first and third hypotheses as an explanation: Ramesh Shil's impact and the intrinsic properties of this code language as sketched above appear to have interacted to keep *sandhābhāṣā* alive in an environment where it is no longer understood in the way it used to be. But it *cannot* therefore be called an empty idiom, a code without a referent, or a signifier without signified, since it saturates itself constantly with new meanings, as the interviews in this section have demonstrated.

6.2 Lovers as Radha and Krishna

Many Maijbhandari songs describe human love and yearning, and often the conventional model of the love between Radha and Krishna is explicitly or implicitly referred to. I have collected interviews on quite a few such songs by Ramesh Shil, Maulana Hadi and Bajlul Karim, and two – one implicit, the other explicit – are given here in short excerpts. The first excerpt is again by Ramesh Shil:

> My mind is indifferent because of the friend/The life passes in the irritation of separation/In my heart I want him // I made the bad [words] of the people/ My flowers and sandal, O bosom friend/In the hope of the friend's love // Sitting in Rahman Manzil/The heart's friend day and night/Blows the flute of *tawḥīd* // [. . .] Having made a bed/Of the pollen of flowers/Lying down, my body does not find rest //[22] [etc.]

20 Cf., e.g., Section 5.7.3 (the saint as a bird), etc.

21 Cf. also Urban (1998: 236), who speaks of a 'graded hierarchy of levels of "truth" '.

22 *āmār bandhur janya man udāsi go/biched jvālāẏ jīban yāẏ,/parāṇe tāhāre cāẏ // āmi loker manda puṣpa candan go sakhi/kar'lem bandhur prem āśāẏ // rah(a)mān man·jile basi,/prāṇ(a) bandhu dibā niśi/tauhider bā̃śarī phukāẏ //* [. . .] *āmi phuler reṇur śayyā kare go sakhi/śule aṅga nā juṛāẏ //* [. . .] *JS* No. 18.

The whole design and some of the details of this song are well-known from Vaishnava lyrics: the repeated address to a female bosom-friend in a tone of intimate confession; the loss of one's good name in society; the flute; the flower bed; and so on. Regarding the correlation of motifs, there are three types of interpretations of this song that can be extracted from the interviews:

(i) The friend is Gholam Rahman, as the reference to Rahman Manzil makes clear. The yearning for the saint is expressed symbolically through human love. The scene depicted is independent of the Radha–Krishna story.

(ii) Gholam Rahman is depicted with the aid of the established motif of Radha's love for Krishna. That love story may be used as a symbol for the love for the divine. The erotic implications (flower bed) highlight the acuteness of the yearning.

(iii) Gholam Rahman is imagined as Krishna with his flute and as the lover of Radha, and there is no contradiction as, on a higher mystical level, both are images of the Divine and in that sense identical.

In another Maijbhandari song by Bajlul Karim, the reference to the Radha–Krishna topos is even more explicit:

> Who was it who stole the mind of Radha, O Śyāma?/It was the connoisseur of love, Kānāi, the Maijbhandari Ġauṯ treasure // Sitting on the *kadamba* branch, watching the good development [*sugaman*] of [his] music playing/He set a trap of love, in the beginning, [by] his flute-talk //[23] [etc.]

Here, the Maijbhandari Ġauṯ is straightaway identified with Krishna, and the attributes of the *Kṛṣṇalīlā* are present (*kadamba*, trap, flute); even if the initial rhetorical question lends itself also to another reading, the use of Kānāi as an epithet of the Ġauṯ leaves no room for ambiguities.

(i) The interpretations of this type, however, deny this. Upon being explicitly asked, it is asserted that Rādhā and Śyām do not denote Rādhā and Kṛṣṇa here, but only stand for lovers. Also Kānāi is not understood as an appellation of Kṛṣṇa, but again as 'lover', and the *kadamba* tree is not interpreted as a hint of the scenery of the *Kṛṣṇalīlā.*

(ii) Corresponding to the second interpretation above, Radha–Krishna imagery is used for symbolic and literary purposes, but no identification of Krishna with the Maijbhandari is implied. It is because of the popularity of the topos that the Radha–Krishna story has found its way even into Maijbhandari songs.

(iii) Again, as above, it is asserted that the Ġauṯ is imagined in the form of Krishna; and there is nothing wrong with such a depiction since, on an elevated level of mystical vision, Krishna and the Ġauṯ are one and the same. This interpretation, in fact, appears to be the only adequate representation of Bajlul Karim's intention.

23 *kebā hari nilare, śyām(a) rādher man/premer raśik kānāi, māij'bhāṇḍārī gāuch(a)dhan // kadamberī ḍāle thāki, bādyer(a) sugaman dekhi/prem phā̃d pātila, ārambhe, bā̃śi ālapan //* [. . .] *Premāñjali* No.17.

These interpretations lead to further questions. It is not clear to which extent popular Hindu mythology (as contained in such texts as the *Mahābhārata*, *Rāmāyaṇa*, *Bhāgavatapurāṇa*, *Viṣṇupurāṇa*, etc.) is still present and well known in an environment such as Chittagong which today is predominantly Muslim. The impression from the interviews was that such themes were relatively better known to the older interviewees. A few such random inquiries are of course anything but a sufficient database, but one may speculate that the rapid decrease in the percentage of the Hindu population during the last sixty years could be a factor here, together with a process of secularisation which, in Chittagong, seems to be more profound in the Hindu middle class than in its Muslim equivalent. Another factor might be the impact of Islamic reformism, tabooing to some extent the appreciative cognition of other religious traditions.

In any case, the refusal to see some parallels at least to Vaishnava lyrics in the two songs given above was definitely not in all cases due to a lack of knowledge, but apparently motivated by a kind of pedagogical intention *vis-à-vis* myself, the interviewer. The point seemed to be that in front of a foreign researcher (or only an outsider with regard to Maijbhandar?), Maijbhandar had to be portrayed as a Sufic Islamic institution and the impression had to be avoided that there was any sort of mixture in Maijbhandari songs.

6.3 Symbolical changes of sex

We have noted that the *bhakta* or *murīd*, who usually functions as the first-person narrator in Maijbhandari songs, has in certain categories of songs, especially those discussed under the headings of 'love' and '*viraha bhakti*' in the preceding chapter,[24] the tendency to become female. A good example is the following song by Maulana Hadi, for which I have collected around ten interpretations.

> Friend, I forbid you, do not put chains to my feet./In the mind of this weak woman, the urge of love has arisen./In the evening, under the *kadamba* tree at the shore of the Yamuna,/The amorous gallant called me by the sound of the flute./The heart [*prāṇ*] is split by the melody of the flute, I could not stay at home./At noon, while I was bathing at the shore of the Yamuna,/Smiling gently, he charmed me with the play of his eyes./Since then, I cannot bear the urge of that connoisseur of love,/I implore you, O friend, let me go./I want to fall to his feet and enclose him in my heart [*hṛde miśāi*],/I will offer him my youth to drink and thus fulfil my heart's desire [*maner bāsanā*]./Hadi says: Whoever is desirous of love-play,/Serve the feet of the Ġawṯ treasure day and night./I will fulfil the heart's desire by giving the toy of love.[25]

24 Cf. 5.7.9–10.

25 *sakhī tomāre kari mānā, āmār pāẏe beṛi dionā/abalā kāminīr mane uṭ'la premer tāṛanā // sājer belā kadam talā yamunār pāṛe,/bā̃śīr svare rasik nāgar ḍākila more // bā̃śīr sure prāṇ bidare ghare raïte pārinā/dupur belā snān karite yamunār dhāre // madhu hese naẏan ṭhāre bhulāichen more/sei abadhi saïte nāri prem rasiker tāṛanā // minati kariga sakhī chāṛi deo more/tān(a) pāẏe paṛi hṛde miśāi āniba tāre // yauban dāne pān karāba miṭāi maner bāsanā/kahe hādī prem(a) khelā yār(a) sādh(a) mane // gāuch(a) dhaner caraṇ sebā kara rātra dine/miṭāba maner sādh diẏā premer khelanā // RS* No.14.

From the point of view of literary and religious history, this is of course an example of *kṛṣṇabhakti*: Radha is addressing her female friend (*sakhī*) and talks about her love of Krishna, and only Krishna's name is substituted by 'Ġawṯ treasure'. The adoption of this motif by South Asian Sufism is anything but new, though still potentially heterodox; similar texts are, for instance, found in the compositions of the eighteenth-century Panjabi Sufi Bullhe Shah. A more direct source for Maulana Hadi, however, is of course the tradition of *baiṣṇab padābalī*, namely Bengali Krishnaite lyrics. All this hardly needs elaboration. But how, we have to ask, does a movement of contemporary Sufis, taken to task at times to display its Islamic credentials, treat such a text? The interpretations I have collected fall into three types:

(i) The song is explained with reference to a general theory of sexes. The woman is seen as an inferior being and actually not even a complete human – she is not free, but confined, limited and totally dependent upon men.[26] It is precisely these limitations that make her a model of true, sincere and self-abandoning love. The *bhakta* has to become a woman in order to learn true humility and to degrade himself. Hinduism/Vaishnavism is not referred to as a possible source of reference. Some indeed lack such background information, that is, the implicit Radha in the song is not recognised, while others (when explicitly asked) refuse to resort to that complex as a model of explanation ('No, this has nothing to do with Radha and Krishna, it is only about female love towards a lover'). A variant of this type, given by a female interviewee, adds that women are the beautiful sex, and by 'becoming female', the men want to appear as beautiful as possible in front of their *pīr*s.

(ii) The song is an allegory borrowed from Vaishnavism. The background of the story of Radha and Krishna is recognised and explained as a loan ('Maulana Hadi has taken this from the Hindus'). Such loans are seen as legitimate and unproblematic. But the divine play of Krishna is dissociated from its sacred contents and merely treated as a literary import which in the process is reloaded with Sufi topics: ('We do not believe in Krishna. This is only an allegory [*rūpak*] in order to make explicit the love that the *bhakta* should experience').

(iii) In two of the ten interviews about this song, I encountered a radical position of unitary mysticism. According to this, the Maijbhandari saint *is* Krishna, and Maulana Hadi *is* Radha. The use of such motifs in Maijbhandari songs is not due to any loan, but to the 'merging' (*milan*) of different spiritual traditions. The basic claim is that all the higher mystical (*ādhyātmik*) levels of any religion lead to the same goal, and their diverse expressions and images are therefore identical in content. This position is somewhat elitist in the sense that it assigns all those who do not agree with it to inferior levels of enlightenment. In one case, this position was combined with an Islamic inclusivism: this true love was defined as the essence of true Islam, and all religions are included in this Islam.

26 This reasoning also underlies an interpretation of why Maulana Hadi, as reported, had dressed up as a woman in front of his *muršid*: he wanted to show that he had not yet become a man completely, women being weaker by nature (Interview January 2001).

If the male *bhakta* may become female when addressing his beloved, other constellations are also possible. The beloved may be perceived as female, or even the female *bhakta* may become male and the beloved female. This latter case is very rare; it does occur, however, in a song by one of the two female authors of Maijbhandari songs, Badrunessa Saju:

> O *muršid*, O gracious, do not remain silent/Do not look [at me] mutely with both eyes./O you, guardian of my world, show me the way/The lance [is in my] heart, but I say [to myself:] 'Be patient'/The inner dies in lonely pain, the two hands beg for mercy./The air of dawn flourishes into the flower of feeling at the dreary noon,/The colour of the afternoon condenses in the fragrance of night in pen and paper./Such an atmosphere, such auspicious time is the highest prayer of this life./With joint hands posed on your feet let me politely beg:/Do not be cruel, most beloved,[27] a traveller begging for grace, I am very helpless,/A flood of grace in my dry spirit is the eternal wish today.[28]

This song, devoted to Ziaul Haq, falls into three parts: in ll. 1–5 the female *bhakta* calls upon the spiritual master, ll. 6–8 are a lyrical reflection, and in ll. 9–11, it is suddenly the male lover who addresses the female beloved.

This change of the arrangement of sexes struck none of the approximately ten people I interviewed about this song as abnormal, and all basically gave the same interpretation. Earthly love between the sexes, no matter whether a man's for a woman or a woman's for a man, is in this song a metaphor for the love for the guru or the Divine, and the 'most beloved' in l. 10 is the divine *ma'šūq*. The author herself explained the change of sexes in her song as 'stylistic' (*śailīgata*): her model for this song had been modern love poetry which is, she stressed, mostly written by men.

6.4 The *avatāra* concept

In Section 5.7.6, we dealt with the topic of incarnation and noticed that the term *abatār* (Skt. <*avatāra*>) is quite commonly used in Maijbhandari songs. The following lines of a song by Ramesh Shil express this idea with regard to the Maijbhandari saints:

> (O Mawlā) you came in shape of a human, I cannot recognize you/If you have mercy, I shall set over in a moment/(O Mawlā) Having finished the

27 *priẏatamā*, namely female dearest.

28 *ogo murśid ohe daẏāl nīrab theko nā/du'cokh mele ār ceẏe theko nā // āmār bhūbaner kāṇḍārī go path nirdeś karo/bĩdhe āche hṛdaẏe śel tabu bali dhairya dharo // antar bedanāẏ gum'ṛe mare du'hāt māge karuṇā // bhorer hāoẏā udās dupure bhāber phul phoṭe/bikāler raṃ rāter subāse kāgaj kalame oṭhe // eman paribeś, susamaẏ e jībaner caram prārthanā // joṛ kadame du'hāt rekhe binīta anurodh jānāi/niṭhur haẏonā priẏā, doẏākāmī e musāphir baṛo asahāẏ // śuṣka mane meher'bānīr joẏār ye āj cirakāmanā // Madirā* No.48.

play in Medina, Bagdad and Ajmer/The Bhandari has illuminated Chittagong/[etc.][29]

This song says, in short, that the Maulā, 'Lord' (which probably refers to the Maijbhandari and simultaneously also to God) has incarnated Himself, and that the Maijbhandari has earlier appeared as Muhammad in Medina, ʿAbd al-Qadir Gilani in Baghdad and Muʿin al-Din Chishti in Ajmer. This much was understood by all the altogether ten interviewees who commented on this song, but the evaluation of it differed among them. It may be mentioned in passing that a Muslim academic from Chittagong, who was not acquainted with Maijbhandar or Sufi thought in general, became highly perplexed when confronted with this song, and kept repeating the question whether 'they' really approved of this. By people from Maijbhandari circles, the song was broadly interpreted in three slightly different ways:

(i) The unity of the divine was strongly asserted, and since all the persons implicated were prophets and saints, they were partakers of it and thus not to be thought of as separate ('All are one'). In one case, a simile was given: water is found in the sea, in rivers, canals and ponds, but it is all water; and it remains water whether drunk from a glass, a pot, or out of a river. The vessel (*pātra*) is irrelevant when it comes to the substance. Likewise, the same Divine substance descended upon earth in different personalities and places, and the difference between the latter does not in any way impinge upon its basic unity. The concept of *avatāra* was not used to explain this song.

(ii) The second explanation referred to the *avatāra* concept as the underlying idea of this song, and stressed that this was objectionable from the viewpoint of the *šarīʿa*. For someone with a higher level of cognition inspired by divine love, however, such a perception was natural and legitimate, and indeed the goal to be achieved.

(iii) In this explanation, the *avatāra* concept was spontaneously adduced for explanation. It was unproblematic and not in any way thought to be un-Islamic. The etymology of *rasūl* and references to Jalal al-Din Rumi were given to prove that it was basically the Islamic idea that something divine is sent from God to mankind. In one case, it was admitted that the *avatāra* concept stemmed from Hinduism, but did not therefore clash with Islamic beliefs.

As in the preceding section, it is striking that some of the interlocutors were to all appearances either not aware of the Hindu connotations of the *avatāra* concept or at least did not view it as exclusively Hindu. As elaborated in Section 5.7.6, the Bengali term *abatār* thus proves to be a commonly used category beyond any association with a specific religious tradition.[30] Those who were aware of the

29 *(Māulāre) mānuṣ rūp(a) dhare ele cinite nā pāri/tumi yadi daẏā kara ek palake tari // (māolāre) madinā bog'dād, āj'mirer khelā sāṅga kari/caṭṭagrām rośan karilā bhāṇḍārī //* Ramesh Shil *MD* No.12.

30 This may also call for a new assessment of medieval uses of the term for prophets. Asim Roy (1995: 104) conceives of Saiyid Sultan's replacement of the term *abatār* for the Arabic *nabī* as an instance of localisation, bracketed by the notion of syncretism. But it is equally possible that it was designed as no more than a *translation*, and that 'syncretism', in this case, takes place exclusively in the eyes of the observer.

Hindu *avatāra* concept did not therefore regard it as a loan but as something which is just as much Islamic (Sufic and even Qur᾿anic), though the term used for it may originally be Sanskrit and connected with a Hindu context.

In the following chapter, we shall have occasion to deal with these and similar conceptualisations in a more systematic fashion. But before we proceed, I would like to contextualise the results of this present chapter. We have said that it is not possible to demarcate clearly the domains of Maijbhandari theology and hagiographies on the one hand, and Maijbhandari songs on the other. Nonetheless, as the most spontaneous and lay mode of expression among these genres, the songs are the closest to popular articulations of religiosity. Their function of fusing heterogenous elements in a far more extensive fashion than the other genres has been stated; they have been what we might call a 'floating idiom', and due to the polyangular structure of the Maijbhandari movement they have retained this property to this day.

In this context, the interviews presented here were an exercise in confronting exponents and adherents of the movement with some particularly 'transgressive' aspects of this tradition; and the results show different ways of handling such transgressiveness that coincide. One trend views the song heritage exclusively in Sufi terms and interprets concepts by reference to specific theoretical elaborations from among the teachings of a particular Maijbhandari *manzil*, thus encapsulating them in a framework that did – at least for the classics chosen here for discussion – not exist at the time they were written. Another also views it as specifically Maijbhandari, but does not oppose the openness of this song tradition to other religious idioms, because the loans are perceived as symbolic. Many of the older loans, however, are no longer recognised as such but have, to these observers, become part and parcel of the Maijbhandari tradition. A third, radically unitarian trend summarily treats loans, whether recognised or not, as not only legitimate but desirable as a demonstration of the ultimate union of different religious traditions. Significantly, these trends could not be correlated with the education and social background of the interviewees but seem to cut across all such distinctions, even if in certain cases vested interests were traceable in the interpretations. It would of course take a much larger and decidedly statistical effort to substantiate this impression, but nevertheless, as a preliminary finding, it remains striking.

7 Contextualising Maijbhandar

So far, I have avoided any thorough discussion about the status of Maijbhandar. I have limited myself to calling it a religious group or religious movement. I have had occasion to state the polycentric nature of this movement, due to the factionalisations among its officiating representatives and the many ways of accessing Maijbhandar; this results in a partial absence of clear-cut borderlines and a certain structural fuzziness which can, however, be interpreted as attributes of a lively and productive religious culture. However this may be, at this point I want to discuss a number of existing classificatory models with a view to their applicability in our case. To what extent do general religious taxonomies help us reach an understanding of what Maijbhandar is? Where do Maijbhandaris position themselves in the religious landscape of Bengal and beyond? Where are we to position Maijbhandar *vis-à-vis* other religious groups and factions? And, finally, in which way does the mystical idiom of Maijbhandar promote, modify or block such positionings? The following sections will seek to answer these questions.

7.1 'Syncretism', 'little tradition', 'discursive fields'

Religious groups such as the Maijbhandaris are, in scholarly ascriptions, frequently termed syncretistic; the term syncretism is often used for cultural and religious phenomena of exchange and fusion in South Asia in general.[1] Syncretism has also made its way into the Bengali language and found favour with many

1 Cf. Claude Lévy-Strauss (1968, in his description of a Magh village in the Chittagong Hill Tracts; Hugh van Skyhawk (1992: 76) in connection with the Maharashtrian saint Eknath; Denis Matringe (1992: 198) on the 'composite and often syncretic nature of Panjabi popular culture'; Aziz Ahmad (1999: 140 ff.) on 'popular syncretism' in connection with the medieval *bhakti*-Sufi continuum; Clifford Geertz (1968: 12), drawing parallels between Indonesian and Indian Islam and calling them 'remarkably malleable, tentative, syncretistic, and, most significantly of all, multivoiced'; Razia Akter Banu (1992) speaking of 'Semitic-Aryan syncretism' in her characterisation of South Asian Sufism; Asim Roy (1983) with reference to Islam in Bengal; E. Mann (1989: 169) on South-Asian *dargāhs* as a 'syncretic force'; Marc Gaborieau (1983: 305 f.) speaking of the 'two-way syncretism on the popular level' in connection with Nepalese shrine veneration; Rahul Peter Das (1992a: 205) with reference to Islam in Bengal ('Der Islam geriet hier also in eine stark synkretistische Umgebung; er war aber selbst schon in hohem Maße synkretistisch geprägt, waren seine Hauptverbreiter in Bengalen doch höchstwahrscheinlich Mystiker, Sufis').

theorists;[2] the Bengali *samanvaẏ* is usually used for sympathetic reference to cultural and religious phenomena of merging and fusion that are sometimes deemed constitutive of South Asian cultures in general and Bengal in particular.

The ancient Greek-derived 'syncretism' has an interesting history that has more or less become textbook knowledge.[3] First used in antiquity to refer to the temporary coalitions among Cretiens against aggressive outsiders, syncretism was taken up in the age of the Reformation to characterise the merger of different Protestant groups. It is only in the late nineteenth century that it first appears in a more abstract sense, denoting the cultural fusion characteristic of Hellenic Greece; from there it was generalised and came to be used for other kinds of especially religious fusions or – pejoratively, as it was in fact often intended – 'mixtures'.

Since the second half of the twentieth century, the term has undergone much differentiation and refining in the hands of mostly German theologists who have tried to establish it as a technical term for contact phenomena between religions. On the other hand, and mainly in anglophone publications, phenomenological uses of the term as a political category in the field have also become commonplace, sometimes with a somewhat postmodernist predilection for the heterogeneous;[4] and in subcontinental cultural politics, syncretism has become a handy category to transcribe the 'Unity in Diversity' motto of Nehruvian times and to invoke cultural cohesion across religious and ethnic boundaries.[5] Such vague usage, however, has arguably little value for the classification of religious phenomena, though it may be an interesting topic itself for the study of cultural and academic politics.

In the first place, then, I wish to examine some of the 'harder' definitions of the term evolving from the mostly German debate on the topic. Here the term is

2 *Samanvaẏ* and *samanvaẏdharmī* have apparently become common renderings of 'syncretism' and 'syncretistic' respectively. I am not in a position to trace the history of this terminology in any detail, but it goes not seem to be very recent, the Skt. term *samanvaya* being semantically close to syncretism anyway. Halbfass (1988: 253 f.) shows how the neo-Hindu philosopher Radhakrishnan universalises this concept which occurs in traditional *Vedānta* sources for the harmonisation of passages from the *Upaniṣad*s ('Today the samanvaya or harmonisation has to be extended to the living faiths of mankind' – Radhakrishnan, Sarvepalli [1960]: *The Brahma Sūtra.* London, quoted in Halbfass1988). Upendranath Bhaṭṭācārya, in his monograph on the Bauls, uses combinations like *samanvaẏ-praceṣṭā* and *samanvaẏ-nīti* with reference to the religious ideas of the Mughals Akbar and Dara Shikoh (Bhaṭṭācārya 1957: 143). Bengali–English dictionaries give translations like 'synthesis', 'co-ordination' for *samanvaẏ*, and I have not been able to find 'syncretism' here. But it must be considered that 'syncretism' continues to be used as a technical term functioning mostly beyond colloquial language. *Samanvaẏ* is repeatedly used in Selim Jahangir's volume on Maijbhandar (Jāhāṅgīr 1999), its meanings ranging from 'combination' to 'synthesis' and 'syncretism' (e.g. already in the *bhūmikā*, pp. sāt-āṭ) and seems to be entering Maijbhandari self-reference as well; and educated speakers in Dhaka and Chittagong have more than once suggested it to me as the Bengali equivalent of 'syncretism'.

3 Cf. the encyclopaedia entries of Colpe (1987); Hefner (1995); Kraemer (1962); etc. that all trace the history of the term.

4 Cf. e.g. the way the term is used in Stewart/Shaw (1994).

5 The term syncretism was even used for the official self-representation of Bangladesh until recently, as could be witnessed on the homepage of the Bangladeshi embassy in Germany. I could, however, not find the respective passage on the modified latest version of that page.

mostly defined with reference to Niklas Luhmann's systems theory. Ulrich Berner, writing in 1982, has connected it closely with the notion of religious *systems*, suggesting that religions are dynamic systems whose contacts generate manifold alterations on different levels (such as adaptations or substitutions of specific elements, systemic changes, etc.). He proposes a model on three levels, and a somewhat extensive summary of his classification seems in order here.

The most general level is that of systematisation and rationalisation, triggered by the competition between religious systems; such systemisations fall into three subcategories, relating to winning over adherents of the other system for one's own ('progressive systemisation'), fortifying one's own system *vis-à-vis* a competitor ('stabilising systemisation') and modifying one's system in the face of other cognitive systems such as natural sciences ('vertical systemisation'). Analogous distinctions are introduced for the rationalisations that a religious system may undergo (Berner 1982: 95 f.).

On the second level ('processes on the level of systems'), Berner distinguishes among 'syncretism' which erases the boundary and thereby the relationship of competition between religious systems;[6] 'pseudo-synthesis' which consists in the new combination and interpretation of elements from other traditions; 'synthesis' which means the emergence of new elements from the contact with another system; 'evolution' as a creative invention of new elements; and lastly different ways of 'rationing', or rather 'correlating' (for German 'Relationierungen'[7] – Berner 1982: 98 ff.). These latter are either harmonising ('all religions lead to the same goal'), distancing ('other religions have no right to exist') or hierarchical; and the hierarchical correlatings are again differentiated into 'different evaluation', 'assortment to different levels of realisation', 'chronological' (i.e. valid only in a certain age), 'genetic' (dependent on one's own system) and 'inclusive' (already contained in one's own system).

On the level of elements, finally, the term syncretism in Berner's scheme undergoes a great amount of differentiation. In general, it denotes the integration or emergence of new elements in any given religious system due to contact with another religious system.[8] Such syncretism on the level of elements may be 'absorbing' when one element seizes the function of, and substitutes another; 'additive' when there is a combination of formerly competing elements; 'equivalating' when an element is

6 Syncretism 'bezeichnet die Prozesse, in denen die Grenze und damit das Konkurrenzverhältnis zwischen den Systemen aufgehoben wird. Diese Aufhebung kann auf verschiedene Weise geschehen; sie kann mit Relationierungen auf Elementebene oder mit Synkretismen auf Element-Ebene verbunden sein' (Berner 1982: 96).

7 'Relationierung', as a technical term in this context, denotes 'putting religions in relation to each other' in any of the manifold ways elaborated here. 'Relationing' sounds too clumsy and artificial, and 'correlating', though also not very elegant, seems to be the only viable rendering in English. I will use it in the sense of 'relationieren/Relationierung' in the present section.

8 Syncretism 'bezeichnet: solche Verbindungen verschiedener Elemente, in denen die Grenze zwischen den Elementen aufgehoben wird, so daß diese sich dem Anhänger des betreffenden Systems als Einheit darstellen; die Überlagerung eines Elementes durch andere Bedeutungen; die Entstehung eines Elementes, das ein Äquivalent zu einem konkurrierenden Element darstellt' (Berner 1982: 101).

generated to function as an equivalent of an element of another system; and 'agglomerative' when an element is superseded by new meanings. 'Agglomeration', again, can be identifying (different elements are explicitly declared identical); transforming (an element is consciously invested with a new meaning); related to change of function (an element is taken from another system into one's own without explicit change of denotation); and substitutive (an element of the other system is denied but substituted by a new element in one's own system) (Berner 1982: 101 ff.).

But from whose perspective are such correlations and classifications perceived, from the believers' or the outer observers'? Berner's model was again modifed by Feldtkeller (1992) so as to include the difference between external and self-reference, though the new terminology introduced seems to be partly redundant and partly simply too complicated to become established.[9] While, however, the above does seem to supply a differentiated taxonomy for classifying religious contact phenomena, there are two basic problems with this approach that need to be tackled if syncretism is to be established as a useful analytical category. One of them has been noticed by many authors on the topic: from a historical perspective, there is virtually no religion that can claim to be completely self-sufficient, and hence the term syncretism threatens to become a meaningless truism. Many, in fact, feel that the term is too wide to function as an analytical category.[10]

Carsten Colpe wants to avoid the problem of gradation by understanding syncretism in more radical terms as a transitory phenomenon, claiming that once the syncretistic character is stabilised it is no longer communicated; but his exclusive reliance on a self-referential level does not solve the problem, even if the contention were tenable.[11] The question of syncretistic *for whom*, the second aspect that Werblowski raises, is in no way settled beforehand, and many cases are imaginable and in fact existent where syncretism is ascribed to the meta-level of academic observation without being perceived at all within the respective religious community.

The second and major objection to syncretism as an analytical tool for describing phenomena like Maijbhandar, however, lies in the basic claim regarding the systemic nature of religious traditions. This argument is not so much about any alleged fixity and monolithic character of such systemic religious traditions: systems do not necessarily have to be imagined as fixed entities, and systems theory certainly provides the tools to analyse them diachronically and in terms of dynamic processes. But systems are necessarily seen as commanding the organ-

9 Cf. the discussion of Feldtkeller's approach in Grünschloß (1999: 54–62); Grünschloß argues that most of the new terminology proposed here is only a redundant reformulation of Berner's earlier scheme.

10 Cf. Fritz Stolz (1996: 32), who envisages a detailed terminology of processes of exchange which is to replace the concept of syncretism altogether. Also Zwi Werblowski (1987: 7), who calls for strict gradations in its use in order to avoid tautologies.

11 Cf. Colpe (1987: 221). This contention is problematic because it is easy to find 'latent' syncretisms that reappear in consciousness under changed circumstances or in new situations of contact; e.g. many aspects of traditional South Asian Islam were (implicitly) understood as syncretistic by reformist and fundamentalist Islamic strands. The example of Sikhism he quotes (p. 226) is another case in point.

isation of elements pertaining to them, and thus as having, or generating, an inside and an outside. The notion of syncretism is based on this constellation and operates by assigning the phenomena it deals with to a position *between* overarching systems. On the one hand, it appears problematic, for instance, to assert off-hand the systemic character of Hinduism, which has often been described as consisting of highly varied traditions that would actually qualify for denomination as separate religions;[12] and similar arguments can be made for other 'great taxonomies' like Islam, Christianity, etc. On the other hand, the fringe position assigned to a 'syncretistic phenomenon' is more often than not, and certainly in the case of Maijbhandar, *against* the self-understanding of the group in question.

A systems approach that buys into established taxonomies thus has a marginalising effect and is bound to impose centre–perifery hierarchies. Syncretism, a label for what is conceived as the contact zone between otherwise stable systemic entities such as Hinduism and Islam, happens on the margins of each of these systems; and such marginality, once reinscribed into the respective systems, comes to be viewed as heterodoxy. In this way, syncretism, no matter how it is evaluated, does tend to establish a distinction between homogeneity and heterogeneity. Such assignations are bound to collide with and possibly reinforce much-cherished notions of purity of belief that are operative in the field.[13]

There are attempts, to be sure, to conceive of syncretism as a positive feature of the 'core' of a religious tradition, involving the sovereignty and strength necessary to remain open to the outside and assimilate whatever seems worth such attention. This is what Carsten Colpe has in mind when he writes:

> A tolerant attitude to all that is of value in the world is thus a basic condition for the rise of any syncretism, as well as a basic virtue of the human being who is shaped by syncretism and in turn supports it.
>
> (Colpe 1987: 226)

For such an evaluation the question seems crucial whether such syncretism is self-conscious and inscribed on the object level, or only 'by default' and ascriptive, since such 'tolerance' can be deemed a virtue only if it includes the consciousness of certain separatenesses. But, as it were, even if such crossing of borders may be evaluated positively, it is usually not conceived as a core phenomenon but as something peripheral and marginal. The way things stand, syncretism is in the great majority of cases used to describe such fringe phenomena, the implication all too often being that something which is labelled syncretistic is deviant, not 'really Islamic', etc.[14]

12 Cf., e.g., Stietencron (1995).

13 Cf. Robert Hefner (1995: 149) on 'syncretistic' Islamic groups who, however, claim to fully belong to Islam; their 'syncretism' resultantly exists only from the perspective of the 'orthodoxy', appearing as heresy and pushing them to the margins of the faith.

14 Cf. Tschacher (2009: 57), who follows Barbara Metcalf (1995) in dismissing the notion of syncretism for similar reasons and suggests, instead, 'to focus on the debates surrounding such ascriptions [of normativity or derivativeness] and on the strategies actors employ to create meaningful expressions of religiosity.'

An analysis of Maijbhandar in terms of syncretism, caught up in a somewhat static systems approach, would in all likelihood result in such an assignation to the fringes of Islam and an enumeration of various elements deemed 'non-Islamic'. Such an approach would rely on a modernist, monolithic and centre-bound taxonomy of religious development that could not hold in a genuine historical perspective. Syncretism yes, if we understand Islam and Hinduism as the more or less standardised, canonised entities which have come to dominate contemporary perceptions; but such an understanding is anachronistic even for explaining a recent movement like Maijbhandar, and the exercise of imagining two such clear-cut 'systems' colliding in Bengal is more than questionable.[15]

We shall, however, keep the discussion on syncretism in mind, and eventually also try to profit from some of the differentiated terminology it has produced, as we move on. Much of it can be used also without buying into the underlying systems approach, and the terminology for correlating different traditions which it furnishes seems especially useful for our purposes. A viable model is given by Grünschloß (1999: 16 ff.) who discusses the 'classical' tripartite scheme of interreligious correlating of exlusivism, inclusivism and pluralism.[16] He reorganises this scheme according to the ratio of superiority, parity and inferiority as the underlying principles, and adds the category of 'exotism' for cases in which other religions are deemed superior to one's own religion regarding certain elements.[17] He does not share Schmidt-Leukel's conviction regarding the inevitability, on the part of religious traditions, of positioning themselves once and for all occasions as inclusivist, exlusivist, etc.,[18] but admits that different correlationgs may coexist in one tradition ('system') simultaneously. If used in such a differentiated way, this terminology can be an apt instrument for describing interreligious relations; and I will apply it when mapping Maijbhandari references to their religious surroundings in the following section.

There are many other concepts that offer themselves as possible tools for classifying religious phenomena like Maijbhandar. If one feels disinclined to share in some of the normative premises inherent in the concept of syncretism, one might think of a more sociological approach in attempting to locate

15 Cf., e.g., the discussion of current theories of Islamisation in Eastern Bengal in Eaton (1993: chapter 5), and the most relevant argument that Islam was successful especially in those areas in which the ritual carried out by the brahmans had not established a firm hold over society.

16 According to Grünschloß (1999: 4 f.), this tripartite structure was first developed in American religious studies, namely by J. Hick (1983), and systemised by his pupil A. Race (1983); 'inclusivism' was coined by the Indologist Paul Hacker to denote a specifically Indian way of coping with religious plurality (Grünschloß 1999: 5); cf. also Hacker's essays 'Inclusivism', posthumously published in Oberhammer (1983: 11 ff.), and 'Zur Geschichte und Beurteilung des Hinduismus' (1964), in Hacker (1978: 476–83).

17 Though, of course, this category would appear to be likely to feature only in the perspective of an outside observer, for most religious groups, as long as they try to assert themselves as such, would hardly openly admit any deficiencies *vis-à-vis* other religions, and if so, probably only in retrospective assessments of their own histories.

18 Cf. Schmidt-Leukel (1997: 65–97), and the other publications by this author as mentioned in Grünschloß (1999: 16n).

Maijbhandar within Islam, and try to describe it as a (Redfieldian) little Islamic tradition.[19] It is, after all, true that, seen from one particular perspective, it seems to act as a linkage between Islamic discourse and regional religious traditions, and that the saints can be seen as local messengers of a faith which is of much wider extension, and whose historical centre is geographically and culturally distant from Bengal. But on closer examination, this distinction too does not fit as neatly as it may first seem and suffers from a certain one-sidedness of perspective. Asim Roy discusses the applicability of this scheme in one article and finds it too narrow for the medieval situation:

> The Bengal phenomenon did provide an uncommon paradigm not only of two great traditions – one orthodox and exogenous, the other syncretistic and endogenous – within the corpus of one religion but also that of a strong and vital syncretistic tradition at the level of both little and great traditions.
>
> (Roy 1995: 114)

It is arguable whether the medieval Bengali Islamic writings Roy has studied should be called a great tradition; if it were so, one might have expected them to constitute more than a transitional phase towards complete Islamisation in his framework.[20] But Roy is certainly right in pointing out that the linguistic and cultural plurality tended to double the polarity between the great and little traditions in Bengal. This double character is even more obvious in contemporary Islam, with, broadly speaking, both reformist and Sufi versions functioning as scripturalist variants and 'great traditions'.

Maijbhandar, too, in order to fit into the classical formulation of a little tradition, would first of all have to be largely non-scriptural. This is clearly not the case. It would also not do to modify this statement and describe all of Maijbhandar as a scripturalised little tradition (though this may hold some truth for the Maijbhandari song tradition).[21] We have seen that both the theological and the hagiographical writings are not only a considerable body of writing in themselves, but also establish a very Islamic, 'high-cultural' realm of intertextuality. Maijbhandar, in fact, contains aspects of both and operates in highly ambivalent circumstances, with material functioning elsewhere as part of a great tradition being given as part of the little tradition, and vice versa. These allocations are largely dependent on the perspective adopted by the outside observer.

One way of interpreting Maijbhandar along these lines would be to single out the veneration of Maijbhandari saints and the song tradition with its clear family ressemblances to other Bengali and South Asian mystic idioms as the local ingredients constituting the little tradition. Parts of the theological and hagiographical

19 Cf. Robert Redfield (1955: 15) for the first elaboration of this concept.

20 Cf. Roy (1996: 114 f.).

21 But, as my discussion in Chapter 5 has shown, this no longer oral tradition also partakes of codes that may, by a slight change of perspective, happen to be the 'great tradition' of *dehatattva*, *muršid* veneration or Vaishnava poetry.

scholarship performed in Maijbhandar would then appear as the linkage between this little tradition and the great Sufic tradition – or, in fact, rather generally Islamic than only Sufic, for the integration of typically Sufic positions into an Islamic framework are part and parcel of Maijbhandar, and rather than only linking up Maijbhandar with Sufism in general, Maijbhandar presents itself as a representative of Sufism *vis-à-vis* Islam. This may seem plausible and the only adequate way of judging. But even this picture changes once the focus is shifted from the local specificities towards the linkages with greater Sufism. An anthropological and South Asianist perspective – and eventually also a nationalist Bengali/Bangladeshi reading – will naturally tend to privilege the Maijbhandari song tradition as its popular core and overlook that, for many adherents, the emphasis lies not on that 'cultural baggage' but on the Sufic/Islamic core values to which Maijbhandar connects them.

It is an interesting and also illuminating exercise to try and figure out in which way, and in what parts, Maijbhandar is amenable to the concept of a little tradition. But all the while, we have to remain aware of the arbitrariness of our perspective. The problem inherent in this approach, then, has to do again with historicity and centrality, especially if we try to avoid open disparities of our description with Maijbhandari self-demarcations.[22] Because even within an exclusively Islamic framework, Maijbhandar claims great centrality; and, like the 'border–demarcator' syncretism, the 'little tradition' approach tends to relegate Maijbhandar to the fringes.[23] Historically, middle Bengali literature gives us ample evidence that an Islam characterised by *pīr*–disciple relationships and esoteric mysticism was prevalent for several centuries in Bengal – a history far longer than that of Wahhabism, let alone Bengali reformism.[24] To work with the terms little and big tradition in this context does not seem viable, because they are quite

22 Cf. Simon Digby (1994: 99), who warns us that '[t]he terminology may reflect the moral bias of the theorists in favour of centralism and the big battalions', but decides to make use of it all the same: 'Nevertheless this crude conceptual formulation embodies the idea of a polarization and conflict of interest between the idea of a universal community of belief and an enduring loyalty to local interests. This polarization of devotion between universal and local is also found in the Indian Muslim population as it evolved through the centuries. On the one hand was the proud concept of the spiritual power of Islam unbounded by frontiers, and on the other the emotional needs of distant groups of Muslims for a sanctification of their local earth and landscape by the identification of sources of spiritual power within them.'

23 As it were, all factions agree that Ahmadullah was a *Ġawṯ al-Aʿẓam* ('greatest leader'), that is, the most important *walī* of his age; and according to the elaborations in *Belāẏate motlākā* (*BM*, see p. 000), his *wilāya* was superior to the *wilāyas* bestowed upon preceding *awliyā*. Further, a prophesy by Ibn ʿArabī is often quoted and interpreted in such a way that the light of Muhammad (*nūr-i muḥammadī*) has split in two parts and now shines on Mecca and Maijbhandar alike. In a number of songs, the pilgrimage to Maijbhandar or to one's self with the aid of Maijbhandari spiritual guidance is depicted as equivalent or superior to the *ḥağğ* (e.g. Badrunnesa Saju *Madirā* No.37; Bajlul Karim Mandakini *ŚJ* No.3). There are also instances where Chittagong is depicted as a holy place. The most conspicuous example is the illustration on the cover of *Belāẏate motlākā*: Chittagong appears as the centre of the globe and is marked by a burning candle.

24 Cf. Asim Roy (1983) and David Cashin (1995).

perspective-bound and perpetuate the very notions of historicity and centrality that are contested by the phenomena to which they would be applied.

There are still other schemes of classification that we may examine as possible taxonomies in approaching Maijbhandar. Clifford Geertz (1968) speaks, with regard to Morocco and Indonesia, of a classical and scripturalist style of Islam. The former denotes an encultured form of Islam that retains many cultural specificities of the respective region and is historically older, and the latter refers to reformist Islam putting all its emphasis on certain scriptures and originating, in the regions concerned, in the nineteenth and mainly twentieth centuries. This terminology represents more or less what we have so far referred to as traditional and reformist respectively. Geertz's proposition posits a non-textual classicism, and thus represents a very important shift in the study of religions from historical to ethnographical criteria. It gives emphasis to the cultural, 'local' parameters in demonstrating how one religion – Islam – is integrated into different cultures. Maijbhandar, according to this model, would be a representative of a Bengali (or more generally South Asian) classical style, characterised by the personalised micro-relations, mediation and esotericism that were opposed by the reformist Islam propagated first by the Farā'iżīs. There are, as far as I can see, two major problems with such an approach. First, this classical style, corresponding by and large to Sufism, has been anything but non-scripturalist; the scholarly elaborations of the Maijbhandari movement have never moved beyond the basic criteria of faithfulness to the scriptures, and the underlying controversy has never been about the validity of the scriptures but rather about their exegesis. Secondly, I fear, the formulation of dominant, classical styles cannot completely escape the danger of essentialisation, and in proclaiming one style as Bengali (or South Asian) and the other implicitly as non-Bengali it might be found to underestimate the capacity for accommodation of Bengali culture which has, after all, been a host for both for at least two centuries. Furthermore, in Bengal, the long-standing *āś'rāph - ātrāph* (Ar. <*ašrāf-aǧlāf*>) dichotomy seems to have prevented the development of any overarching style amenable to such terminology.[25] In this connection, it is also worthwhile considering Ernest Gellner's thesis, based on Algerian data, that shrine cults are basically pre-industrialist and pre-nationalist and correspond to tribal societies, whereas scripturalism is tightly interwoven with the idea of the nation.[26] Maijbhandar would seem to contradict

25 It is also questionable whether Geertz's interpretation would be compatible with indigenous notions of Islam. In Bangladesh, such a culturalist approach to religion would certainly meet resistance even in Sufi circles. In interviews with different *pīr*s in Maijbhandar, I sometimes touched upon the question whether the *māij'bhāṇḍārī darśan* ('Maijbhandari philosophy') can be called an indigenous version of Islam (*deśaj is'lām*). The answers were mostly emphatic and very decisively either affirmative or declining ('There can never be anything like indigenous Islam. Islam is one.') (cf. the beginning of Chapter 1). The argument regarding the *ašrāf–aǧlāf* divide is similar to Asim Roy's reservations regarding an adoption of the scheme of great and little traditions as quoted above in this section.

26 Cf. Ernest Gellner (1983: 73); also the other passages on Islam (cf. Index, p. 148).

this contention; by contrast, there are traces here of a nationalisation of this traditional type of religiosity by virtue of its local character.[27]

It seems even more difficult to apply Victor Turner's (1995) very general dialectical tools of structure and communitas to the conditions in Maijbhandar and Bengali Islam. Proceeding from an analysis of 'liminal' processes in rituals, Turner develops an extremely broad classificatory scheme by discriminating two states of society: one characterised by the prevalence of structure, hierarchy and fixed positions, the other by the dissolution of structure and the preponderence of spontaneous group formation, sometimes accompanied by ecstasy. These basically complementary and alternating states can occur on micro- and macro-levels, and communitas can become institutionalised and stabilised in time. If, on a general plane, mysticism usually qualifies as a communitas mode, and certainly tends to portray itself as such,[28] it cannot be overlooked that in South Asia, it has been the main proselytising force. Of course, despite its long structure-building function in these parts, Islamic mysticism has retained the code of communitas: the *ʿurs* celebrations certainly provide communitas experiences, and frequent talk of 'general access' to 'free spirituality' without 'petrified rituals' still fulfils its functions and probably will in the future. But there are similar rhetorics of communitas among those one would put on the diametrically opposed side of the spectrum, for example adherents of the Jamaʿat-i Islami.[29] To some degree, we could term Maijbhandar a structure that contains elements of communitas *within it*, and which in this respect does not differ in principle from other competing modes of religiosity. We might say then that in Bengali Sufism, the distinction between structure and communitas has for centuries moved into the social text, playing out within it in a complicated way. Thus, to see the Maijbhandaris in the same light as Turner himself has described the Bauls of Bengal (Turner 1995: 164 f.) would be an oversimplification of rather complex matters.[30]

This trial-and-error method regarding the applicability of certain existing schemes of classification may appear as carping at the absence of any descriptive model tailored specifically to the Maijbhandari case. This is not intended, and

27 There are other cases that do not fit into Gellner's scheme. Cf. the attempt by Ziya Gökalp (1876–1924) in Turkey to connect Sufism with Western philosophy and identify the nation with God (the individual had to merge in the nation by means of what he calls a 'social *fanā*') (Sirriyeh 1999: 112–20); also Muhammad Iqbal's interpretation of al-Hallaj's *anā 'l-haqq*: 'If the individual says *anā 'l-ḥaqq*, punishment is better – /If a nation says it, it is not illicit' (Sirriyeh 1999: 136) – as two examples of links between nationalism and Sufism.

28 Cf. the remarks in Section 1.3.

29 'Orthodox' Islam itself, with rituals such as *namāz*, is sometimes propagated as a communitas experience. I have a cassette play on Khan Jahan Ali, the settler-pioneer of Bagerhat, in which Hindu boys are made to comment upon the sight of a *namāz* prayer by saying: 'How beautiful! All are praying side by side, without distinctions of caste [. . .]' (*Nāṭak Khānjāhān Ālī*. Written by Śāh Ālam Nūr. Produced by Palāś Audio Video Products. Dhaka, n.d.). Such perceptions are of course reflections of one of the main hypotheses regarding Islamisation, namely the contention that Islam came as a relief to a caste-ridden society suppressed by Brahmanical domination (cf. Eaton [1993: 116 ff.] for the 'Religion of Social Liberation thesis' which he dismisses as inadequate).

30 And it is highly questionable whether the Bauls themselves are aptly described by this label.

indeed not the point of this section; by contrast, this procedure is designed to help clarify certain aspects of Maijbhandar and indeed to find a suitable way of looking at it; for such a purpose, such a 'check-up' of paradigms, pernickety as it may seem, has its justifications. It would, of course, also be unfair to expect, on the one hand, that any existing paradigm should smoothly capture all the salient features of the phenomenon we are investigating; and, on the other, it would seem more than a trifle pretentious to argue that our case is simply too singular to fit into the academic categories at hand. Neither does this mean that I want to desist from attempting to draw up a paradigmatic description of Maijbhandar altogether; it is rather an attempt to show in a transparent way why I think certain approaches are suitable for such a description and others are not.

Werner Schiffauer, in a study of the so-called Kaplan movement, an offshoot of Turkish Islamism in Germany, has devised an interesting approach that seems promising for our task of classifying Maijbhandar.[31] Combining ideas originally developed by Michel Foucault and Pierre Bourdieu, he has introduced the concept of 'discursive fields'.[32] Islam, in this reading, appears as a multitude of voices claiming to speak for Islam, arguing about its meaning and thereby constituting a discursive field.[33]

A society can be thought of as 'a discursive field made up of discursive fields', and within any one such discursive field, there is agreement regarding the validity of certain arguments – arguments that may appear irrelevant for members of other discursive fields (p. 145). The borderlines of such fields tend to be fuzzy because most actors do not participate in only one field but simultaneously in many. Discourses are targeted towards central notions, and symbolic struggles take place between different discursive fields with identical or overlapping targets.[34]

This approach has a number of advantages. First, it is safely recognisable as a meta-language and does not interfere with value-loaded categories that play out in the field. Secondly, rather than if we were to speak simply of discourses, the notion of discursive fields, in hinting at the social structuredness of certain positions, allows us to include the sphere of religious praxis. Thirdly, in defining Islam as a target rather than a given, it steers clear of getting entangled in questions of orthodoxy and heterodoxy from the start without radically compromising a believer's perspective. And lastly, in contrast to the systems approach underlying the definition of syncretism, it allows for a certain fuzziness.

31 Schiffauer, Werner (2000): *Die Gottesmänner: Türkische Islamisten in Deutschland.* Suhrkamp, Frankfurt am Main.

32 The term is also used by Terry Eagleton (1991: 29), but only in passing and without any definition.

33 'Man trifft also auf die, in der Postmoderne so nachdrücklich beschworene, Polyphonie. Aber die Stimmen stehen nicht einfach nebeneinander. Sie beziehen sich aufeinander und lassen sich nur von diesem Bezug her verstehen. Auf diese Weise stellt sich ein Diskursfeld her, eine Arena von Debatten, in der jede Position auf andere Positionen antwortet' (Schiffauer 2000: 142).

34 Cf. also Katy Gardner (1999: 38), who wants to see Islam as 'a series of discourses that seek to define (and also to control) belief and practice'. For remarks on her approach, see Section 8.1.

It is indeed possible, in a very basic manner, to think of an entity such as Maijbhandar as a discursive field, in the sense of an assemblage of voices and practices; by studying as many as possible of these voices and practices, one should be able to isolate the shared properties (positions, self-demarcations, practices) and locate the centre of gravity of what Maijbhandar is about. Proceeding from there it is possible to draw a metaphorical map of the topographical relationships of this field with other fields.

The notion of fields largely overlaps with that of traditions, a term I have often already used in this study. But it has a certain plasticity that 'tradition' lacks. Its topographical connotation may prove helpful for the mapping of a religious landscape that we will attempt in the following section. The geographical analogy it affords can account for multiple semantical layerings and explain many of the ambivalences that Maijbhandar stands for. The Maijbhandari tradition, conceived as an ongoing process of semiosis on the basis of certain binding premises passed on from the past, is of course what constitutes the discursive field of Maijbhandar. But in contrast to the mostly diachronic term tradition, 'field' stresses the synchronic aspect and thus seems more apt to capture the quasi-spatial relations between religious entities I want to model in the following.

Such an approach avoids a rash hierarchisation of religious groupings and allows us instead to take a close and unprejudiced look at the hierarchisations that take place *within* the movevents, groups or factions under discussion. It also allows us to make use of the typologies of correlating, developed by Berner and others, what we may now call religious discursive fields rather than religious systems or subsystems.

7.2 Correlating Maijbhandar with Islam and other religions

What, then, are the target notions regarding which Maijbhandar has to compete with other discursive fields to assert its own status? These would seem to be Islam and open spirituality – two entities that are often shown to be identical within Maijbhandari discourse, but appear as different from a lateral perspective and ought thus to be kept apart for the sake of analysis. As concerns Islam, there are a number of competitors in Chittagong, and Maijbhandari discourse is under pressure to legitimise itself. This has led to the construction of rather fixed boundaries. With regards to spirituality, however, Maijbhandar discourse is the most powerful in its direct environment, which may explain the absence of boundaries here and the ease with which Maijbhandar partakes of other religious codes. The main competition in this field is the internal one between the different branches of the Maijbhandari family.

In order to localise Maijbhandar as a discursive field among other such fields targeting the idealised notions of Islam and spirituality and thus trying to assert themselves in an arena of Bengali Islam, I am now going to rationalise attitudes and utterances encountered in Maijbhandar, and to distil the possible range of positions and 'correlations' that are likely to be encountered in this field. Such a procedure involves a good amount of construction and intuition. If so far this study

Photo 10 Bathing in the pond by the side of Saint Ahmadullah's former mausoleum, Maijbhandar 1999.

has mainly kept to a descriptive level, the following ventures into giving a condensed picture from a somewhat virtual 'inside' Maijbhandari perspective – virtual because the optionality it will contain does not usually feature in single voices pertaining to the discursive field itself, but represents again a polyphony. So properly speaking, the 'inside' perspective developed in this section is generated by collation of voices from an outsider's viewpoint and ought to be read as such.

The Maijbhandaris claim to represent and speak for Islam, and they know that they are not the only ones to do so. The competing groups who, according to our chosen terminology, compete to unfold and enlarge their respective discursive fields targeted on Islam, include other shrine and *pīr* cults; other *ṭarīqa*s; general Sunni Muslims; so-called *śariẏat'panthī*s, namely followers of the *šarīʿa*; and so-called *maulabādī*s, 'fundamentalists'. In delimiting their own position *vis-à-vis* these competitors, the Maijbhandaris have a repertoire of assertions and arguments that are part of the Maijbhandari discursive field. We shall see that the identification of Islam with open spirituality plays out in some of these arguments. A second row of competitors are by definition outside the confines of Sunnī Islam, but may be aspirants to open spirituality: these include Vaishnava, Tantric or more generally Hindu traditions, as well as Buddhism and Christianity.

To start with, other shrine and *pīr* cults do not figure prominently in Maijbhandari discourse. This is due to the prominent position Maijbhandar holds among these. The highest rank of sainthood is claimed for Maijbhandari saints, thus relegating other shrine and *pīr* cults to lower orders. Practice in this field, however, has pluralistic elements: deputies, *ḫalīfa*s, are part of the institution, and Maijbhandari representatives may actively promote their veneration.[35] Likewise, the veneration of important saints of the region such as Badr Shah was, according to the hagiographies, revived by Maijbhandari saints themselves. Among many adherents, it is common also to visit other shrines and to profit from *baraka* wherever it is obtainable. On closer examination, however, this pluralism tends to take on an inclusivist garb: the shrine cults in question are shown to be subordinate organisations. There are also, on rare occasions, exclusivist elements, e.g. when a *murīd* is castigated for visiting another *pīr*; but this is usually regulated by the rules of *pīr–murīd* relationships and is not specific to Maijbhandar.

A similar stance is taken towards other *ṭarīqa*s. In Maijbhandari discourse, the Maijbhandari *ṭarīqa* is usually characterised as a combination of different *ṭarīqa*s, and portrayed as an easy and therefore most appropriate version of them for the present age. In Berner's terminology, this would come close to a 'chronological hierarchising rationing' (cf. above, p. 289). As well as such inclusivist correlating, there is also the pluralist argument that all *ṭarīqa*s are legitimate methods of striving after union with the Divine. This argument is already contained in the traditional Islamic theory of sainthood.[36] The contention that the Maijbhandari *ṭarīqa* is the most suitable for Bangladesh since it originated there and is thus adapted to the local mentality is in keeping with such pluralism – unlike Delawar Hosain's theory of a general *wilāya* first and promulgated only in Maijbhandar, which is inclusivist.

In general, these relations to what are mostly other Sufi institutions are open and friendly; their respective discursive fields seem easily connectable to Maijbhandari discourse, or even appear as included from the start. The reason for this is that the Maijbhandari discursive field functions as a representative of Sufism in general, and since there are no competitors for this representation in the direct vicinity, it is easy to be sovereign and benign in this respect.[37]

Sunni Muslims, the third discursive field mentioned above, are hard to grasp as a category. As a label for a religious denomination, it applies to 99% of the Muslims in Chittagong. Sunni Muslims are those who observe the *Sunna*, the injunctions of Islam.[38] And many Maijbhandaris refer to themselves as Sunni Muslims. Simultaneously, however, 'Sunni Muslims' is at times a term used to designate a non-Maijbhandari, outside field and is quoted as support of Maijbhandar.[39] Maijbhandaris have their own ideas of what Sunni Islam means,

35 Thus an assembly to the honour of the *ḫalīfa* Abdul Ghani Chowdhury was attended by the *saǧǧādanašīn* of Haq Manzil in 2000.

36 Cf. Section 3.6.

37 This may appear very different in the case of 'inferior' organisations which have to struggle for self-assertion in the face of Maijbhandari dominance. Cf. the polemics against Saint Ahmadullah from Shah Md. Abdul Hai from Mirzakhil quoted in the introduction.

38 Cf. Sanyal (1996: 166ff.) on the way such a normative meaning of *sunna* was used by the Ahl-I Sunnat ('Barelwis') as a self-designation.

39 e.g. when certain 'Sunnī' *madrasa*s are quoted which theologically support the veneration of saints in Islam.

that is, basically inclusive of saint veneration and persuance of *ma'rifa*, and close to the stance taken, for example, by the Ahl-I Sunnat or so-called Barelwi movement of Northern India. But they are aware that this term is given different meanings in other discursive fields. Hence the tendency to use it normatively and turn it polemically against those other claims, thereby trying to deny any legitimate relationship between those discursive fields and the target notion of Sunni Islam.

A rather mild, but distancing way of referring to one of the discursive fields that claims the denomination of 'Sunni Muslims' is to speak of *śariẏat'panthī*s, 'followers of the *šarī'a*'. The boundary between the discursive fields of Maijbhandar and these *śariẏat'panthī*s is marked by controversies about the legitimacy of shrine veneration and specifically certain ritual practices such as *sağda* and *samā'*. The *śariẏat'panthī*s on their part claim orthodoxy and a firm hold on Sunni Islam for themselves and label the Maijbhandaris and other shrine cults as potentially heterodox; Maijbhandaris, in turn, usually take an inclusivist stance, contending that the *śariẏat'panthī*s care only for the ritualist part of Islam (which the Maijbhandaris, it is implied, cover anyway) and utterly neglect *ma'rifa*. In more radical formulations, this ascription may also become exclusivist: *šarī'a* and *ma'rifa*, this argument runs, belong together, and adherence to only one of them is not in keeping with the injunctions of Sunni Islam; and hence such partial observance amounts to heresy. In this way the claims for self-assertion within Sunni Islam are acted out by means of the orthodox-heterodox distinction, and may give rise to mutual indictments of heterodoxy and heresy. Debates on these points refer on both sides to the target notion of Islam and Islamic scriptures and have a long tradition.

Finally, there are the *maulabādī*s, 'fundamentalists', or *wahhābī*s. These are conceived of as the real adversaries. It is hard to determine who actually falls under this category because direct confrontations with them are few. Reference is sometimes made to certain *madrasa*s in the vicinity and to the Jamaat-e Islami, to the theology of its founder Maududi and to preachers like Maulana Delawar Hosain Saidi. The differences are like those with the *śariẏat'panthī*s, but sharper, since to Maijbhandaris, even the observance of the *šarī'a* by these groups appears only as a truncated version and does not really qualify them for the denomination of Sunni Muslims. The attitude of Maijbhandaris towards these groups is decidedly exclusivist, and vice versa.[40]

If, then, we want to sketch the outer confines of the discursive field of Maijbhandar, we get the following picture: the field is open to adjacent Sufi institutions like other shrine cults and other *ṭarīqa*s; there are hardly exclusions here, and a certain pluralism is easily turned into an inclusivist construction with the help of the traditionally established hierarchy of saints. On the other side, boundaries are set up, clearly defined by practices and theological positions, against those who pay heed to the *šarī'a* only and not to the esoteric side of Islam. The contested discursive field encompassing all of these is that of Sunni Muslims. It is noteworthy that

40 Maijbhandari positions *vis-à-vis* the Wahhābīs come close to the Ahl-i Sunnat or 'Barelwi' stance (cf. Sanyal 1996: 244ff.)

explicit referentiality is usually established upwards or horizontally, not downwards. Many smaller shrine cults are intent on holding up their links to Maijbhandar or, as the case may be, on setting themselves apart. For the Maijbhandaris, they are of little explicit concern; here it is the correlating with great 'international' saints of the past or major movements within Islam that really counts.

In the case of religious traditions and groups outside the pale of Islam, Maijbhandari correlations are less distinct. The closeness of some types of Maijbhandari songs to the 'discursive fields' of Vaishnavism and Tantrism has not given rise to any concerted effort of correlating Maijbhandar to these, as the interviews in Chapter 6 have sufficiently shown. This is not to say that referentiality to non-Islamic religions is absent; but it takes place on a different, more general level. The rationale here seems to be that the position of the generous host is preferable over that of a debtor; rather than admitting a loan, Maijbhandari discourse tends to highlight the acceptability it grants to all religious confessions. The formula *dharmajātinirbiśeṣe* expresses this attitude in a nutshell. This 'official' correlating appears to be the legacy of Delawar Hosain and his concept of *tauḥīd-i adyān*. This author also made some attempt at evaluating other religious traditions.[41] But on the whole, there is no way of speaking of anything like a developed Maijbhandari xenology. In the correlations to Hinduism that do exist, there is no differentiation between different traditions, not to speak of Buddhism and Christianity. The harmonising gesture that is preferred in Maijbhandari discourse is inclusivist: all divinities can be visualised in the person of the Maijbhandari saint, and members of all religious communities can approach the (truly Muslim) saints of Maijbhandar for spiritual fulfilment.[42]

But the matter is more complex than this. Possibly because the harmonising, inclusivist dictum does not care for details and lacks precision, the arising needs of correlating are passed down to the level of individual assessment.[43] That is, Maijbhandari devotees are left to form their own opinions on these matters. As a result, interviews with adherents of the movement reveal a truly polyphonic variety of correlations with various inferences from other discursive fields. These are sometimes established theorems, derived, for instance, from Qur'anic xenology, and sometimes also improvised correlations similar to the interpretations of songs discussed in Chapter 6. The correlations I witnessed during my fieldwork largely fall under the following categories:

Delawar Hosain's concept of *tauḥīd-i adyān* is developed on the basis, and as a generalisation of, Qur'anic statements regarding other religions, namely the

41 Namely, Buddhism; cf. *BM*: 8.

42 If this were to be interpreted as pluralistic, similar accessibility and powers would have to be reported of Hindu saints, which is not the case; and I have not heard of visits to Buddhist or Hindu shrines by Muslim visitors or adherents to Maijbhandar. For a parallel, cf. Warith 'Ali Shah of Dewa who is also reported to have bestowed *bay'a* to Hindus, and whom an Englishman visualised as Jesus (Liebeskind 1998: 196, 185f.).

43 Grünschloß (1999: 28f.) points out in passing that 'individual and collective religious systems' and 'their representation in texts' often allow many possibilities of such correlating side by side. We will come back to this later in this section.

Jewish and Christian religions (the notion of the *ahl al-kitāb*, 'people of the book'). The Qur'anic postion may be characterised as a sort of qualified, confined inclusivism. Many Maijbhandari devotees, unaware of Delawar Hosain's generalisation of this concept, quote the original *ahl al-kitāb* model, and it is an open question – a matter of opinion and discussion – whether the Buddhists and Hindus are to be regarded as *ahl al-kitāb*. (Apparently, more often than not, they *are* included, following the consideration that 'they also have their scriptures'.)

Partly connected with this correlation, there is a second type of evolutionary inclusivism. Among the religions in question, it is argued, Islam is the youngest. This implies that it is the 'most modern and therefore best'. The other religions are at best precursors, and at any rate inferior.[44]

There is also a pluralistic model that is partly backed up by the actions of Maijbhandari saints. Every religion, according to this position, has its own revelation and its own merits. There is no need to change one's religion, since the differences between them exist mainly in the realm of *šarīʿa*, understood as the outer laws of religious conduct. On the level of mystical experience, they are not relevant. Saint Ahmadullah is quoted as preventing a Buddhist devotee from converting to Islam with the words: 'Stay in your religion. I have made you a Muslim'.[45] On this basis, it is sometimes asserted that a good Hindu or Buddhist is already a good Muslim.

Another pluralistic model builds on the widespread conviction, among Sunni Muslims in Bangladesh, that the term Islam is derived from Ar. *salām*, 'peace'; the statement 'Islam is the religion of peace'[46] is very common in different discursive fields. This 'peace' is taken to mean also peace among different religions which are then understood as leading to the same goal and therefore justified. Of course this argument can also be given an inclusivist spin. Peace being the true meaning of Islam, it is argued, a Muslim is a 'peaceful person', and this equation is understood to work in the opposite direction also: any peaceful person is thus a Muslim, whether he is aware of it or not. This is not exactly as simplistic as it may sound, since it represents a pattern of argument that is anything but alien to mysticism: Islam, in this reading, is completely disjointed from its doctrinal and ritual contents and taken as a radically moral category.

One last way of juxtaposing different religions on a level of seeming synonymity occurs mostly in Maijbhandari songs. This happens either when adherence to empty rituals is condemned, or when Maijbhandar or the Maijbhandari saints are equated with the holy places of different religions.[47] But this kind of correlation is not explicit enough to enable certain classification.

44 What plays out here seems to be a paradigm of progress we can detect also in other places, for instance in Syed Badruddoza's evaluation of the 'age of science' (*BB*: 5), and which stands in striking contrast to the notion of continuous decay evoked by references to the *kali yuga*, *zamāna-i gumrāhī* or the nearness of Doomsday that are found in all the Maijbhandari scriptural traditions.

45 Cf. *JK*: 175f.

46 *is'lām śāntir dharma*.

47 An example is Ramesh Shil *SD* No.5: *tumi āmār kābā kāśī tumi āmār madinā* ('You are my Kaʿba and Kashi, you are my Medina').

We can thus state that many kinds of different and sometimes contradictory correlations occur in what we have labelled the Maijbhandari discursive field. There is nothing like a doctrinaire adherence to any specific model. The only trend that can be deciphered is that exclusivist approaches are conspicuously rare in correlations with religious traditions outside the pale of Islam; decided exclusivism is limited to certain competitors for the target notion of Islam. I have already hinted at some of the reasons for such polyphony: detailed correlations are only marginally dealt with in Maijbhandari writings, and Delawar Hosain, the only writer to be somewhat more explicit here, has been a controversial and polarising figure. Without sufficient fixation in script, the topic is left to the realm of orality, which notoriously lacks fixity; this, in our context, accounts for the polyphony and polyvalence actually encountered in the field. The question why a movement that writes an appeal to all religious groups so prominently on its flags does not invest more in a detailed xenology will be dealt with below.

Another point of interest is the multiple inferences from other discursive fields targeting the notion of Islam. When, thus, it comes to correlating Islam with modern science – a topic we have hardly mentioned so far – there is no discernible difference between Maijbhandari and other current Islamic approaches found in Bengal and in other parts of South Asia. The point of reference here is probably the brand of Islamic reformism initiated by Syed Ahmad Khan, founder of the Aligarh Muhammadan Anglo-Oriental College in 1878.[48] Islam is declared by definition as open to the acquisition of knowledge, and since the *Qur'ān* implicitly contains all knowledge, science cannot go against it. This position, given here very briefly, is shared by many discursive fields targeted on Islam. The same is true of assessments of the international position of Islam and Islamic countries. One might be tempted to think that the Maijbhandari teachings of tolerance and harmony among religious groups temper the evaluation of such issues. But political standpoints *vis-à-vis* the Palestine issue, Iraq or Iran and the accompanying trends of anti-American and anti-Israeli feelings do not seem to differ significantly from positions held in other Islamic milieus of Bangladeshi society.

It is crucial, finally, to note the ratio of representations that are operative in the Maijbhandari discursive field. Maijbhandar may stand for itself *vis-à-vis* other shrine cults and *ṭarīqa*s; for Sufi Islam *vis-à-vis* exoteric versions of Islam; and for Islam in general *vis-à-vis* other religious communities, atheism, 'modernity', etc. These latter self-identifications with Islam also obey different patterns. First, there is the (usual) position we have encountered in connection with the *śariẏatpanthī*s: Maijbhandar, along with Sufism in general, is legitimate and complete Islam, while the other discursive fields claiming that label are only empty rituals as they lack access to the inner meaning of Islam. Secondly, it is (rarely) argued that Maijbhandar is the essence of Islam and true Islam, and that it contains everything of worth within itself, thus rendering other institutions superfluous. Thirdly, and very similarly, we also occasionally find the construction of Maijbhandar as an

48 On him and his criticism of aspects of Sufism, cf., e.g., Sirriyeh (1999: 59 ff.).

Islamic microcosm that contains greater Islam as the macrocosm within itself and reproduces it in a local framework.

The disparity between all these correlations to other Islamic factions, Islam as a whole and non-Islamic religions is open to interpretation. It does show at least one thing: while one kind of correlating of religions that is promoted in certain Maijbhandari circles – a mostly inclusivist construction granting access to all religions – is one of the specificities it is known for and wants to be known for, the actual correlations encountered in the field are not systemised. Such fluidity or lack of fixity is discernible also in other contexts and will concern us in the following section.

7.3 Lack of structural fixity: a sketch of the discursive field of Maijbhandar

The Maijbhandari discursive field is characterised by a certain lack of fixedness. The multiple positions in the case of correlating to other religious fields that we have noticed in the preceding chapter are symptomatic, and a similar polyphony is present in a more general sense.[49] We can say that in Maijbhandar there is a high degree of structural and semantic fluidity. This fluidity is, however, not without its specific tensions, which stem in some part, as I will argue, from its self-positioning *vis-à-vis* a double target – Islam and open spirituality – simultaneously. The polyvalence of a number of Maijbhandari positions is due partly to its polyangular character and partly to a lack of scripturalisation and canonisation. But in another part, it also seems to be intended. In the following, I want to draw a sketch of the Maijbhandari discursive field with special reference to some of these polyvalent or fuzzy concepts and structures. I also want to try to show in which way these may be functional and productive. Along with this, I will also venture a few speculations regarding the location of these different, and sometimes contradictory, discursive patterns within the structure of Maijbhandar.

In the preceding section, we have named some of the discursive fields surrounding Maijbhandar and noted that the boundaries may in some cases be blurred or even non-existent. Despite this, Maijbhandar has a clearly defined centre to which all sections of its discursive field are related: the great Maijbhandari saints. All the areas covered by the Maijbhandari discursive field today are legitimised in reference to them, namely Maijbhandari shrine veneration, the sanctity of the location and the Maijbhandari family, the legitimacy of the practising *pīr*s and the Maijbhandari *ṭarīqa*, the devotional song culture and even the innovative impulses from certain modernist quarters. It is in granting access to these saints, in one way or the other, that all these areas are part of Maijbhandar.

We may define the most basic scope of the pilgrims and devotees as the attainment of access to the Maijbhandari saints and through them to God, whatever may be their specific reasons for visiting. This access is mediated in a particularly great

49 Cf., e.g., my analysis of the Maijbhandari song tradition as characterised by 'semantic oscillation' and the said 'lack of fixity' (esp. Section 5.8).

variety of ways; and this multiple mediation of access is the first major pattern of Maijbhandari discourse I want to discuss here. The general idea underlying this complex is that the easiest way of getting close to God is to take the help of those who are close to Him, saints and *pīr*s, and who act as intermediaries between the human and divine spheres.[50] There are different notions about how such mediation works.

According to one type of argument, a Maijbhandari *pīr* may be thought of as the link to his predecessor, a specific saint. That saint is imagined, according to Sufi doctrine, as connected through his *silsila* with other major saints and ultimately with ʿAli and Muhammad; this latter is the closest possible link with God. Figuratively speaking, this structure is comparable to a tree, with God at the root and access to Him through the branches; the devotee passes through the different orders of branches to the trunk and finally the roots, which of course are the same for all, regardless of the branch from which the journey has started. This argument relies on a graded access and has a diachronic aspect in that the way to God may be visualised as a way back in time to the Prophet and the beginnings of Islam. It can, however, equally be understood synchronically by reference, for instance, to the veil theory:[51] the prophets and saints are all present and stand in different degrees of closeness to God, located at different positions between the 700 veils separating God from the perception of the world.

Another type of argument is based on the dual notion of human/earthly and divine realms, comparable to two shores of a river (as often encountered in Maijbhandari songs).[52] The *murīd* stands on the human shore, God on the divine, and the *pīr* or saint is the intermediary between these two. From the perspective of the *murīd*, he belongs to the other, wished-for shore and thus partakes of the Divine, or is united with God. This notion is synchronic in that the divine realm is thought of as being simultaneous with earthly life. Both these types of argument may albeit acquire a timeless aspect when time is seen as an exclusive attribute of the earthly and the divine realm is declared beyond it altogether.

These two types are reconcilable as different interpretations of the *pīr*'s relevance. But both these arguments do not remove what I would like to call the *pīr*'s contingency, that is, answer the questions why this particular *pīr* should be better than another to take one to the other shore, and why he rather than his Maijbhandari cousin should be the best link to any of the deceased saints. And furthermore, is it at all necessary to approach a living *pīr* in order to set up contact with a deceased Maijbhandari saint? As it were, access to the saints is manifold; one may be the *murīd* of a living *pīr* or the *murīd* of a deceased saint via a living *pīr*, but it is equally possible, according to a third type of argument, to be the *murīd* of a dead *pīr* without any living person's mediation. The dead saint is

50 Cf. Desiderio Pinto (1992: 122) on the popular rhetorics used to legitimise such intercession: a king is not approached directly, but through his ministers, etc.; likewise God is represented by his saints. Similar similes are employed in Maijbhandar too.

51 Cf. the remarks in Section 3.6.

52 Cf. Section 5.7.13.

conceived as 'living dead',[53] that is, someone who does not die and remains approachable and fully functional in his mausoleum and even anywhere else; he may bestow *bai'a* and give orders in dreams and so on and thus directly communicate with his *murīd*.[54] Such discipleship by-passes the regular order of mediation; and the tree model, if thought of as a simultaneous realm, does not impede in any way such jumping of single branches to the next order.

The concept of spiritual succession, as probably any other kind of succession, has, certainly, a number of fragile points. The idea held in Maijbhandar is that the successor inherits the *wilāya* or entire spiritual power of his master and thereby makes the transition from the status of a *murīd* to that of a *pīr*. But in reality, such transitions are not made so smoothly, and there remains a certain continuum or overlap between *murīd* and *pīr* status. Complications may arise as many of the Maijbhandari *pīr*s are former *murīd*s of their fathers or uncles,[55] and their accession to spiritual leadership suddenly takes them out of the community of their co-disciples (*pīr-bhāi*). Such cases may help in maintaining the feasibility of direct contacts with a deceased saint, as for such *murīd*s it may seem more natural to communicate with that deceased *pīr* at his grave than with his young and possibly inexperienced successor.

Structure is further weakened in Maijbhandar by the fact that access is thought not only to be via different (deceased or living) representatives, but also in formal or informal ways. First of all, as we have stressed repeatedly, *bay'a* has not always been bestowed formally in the history of Maijbhandar; Saint Gholam Rahman is known for his refusal to bestow formal *bay'a* and reputed to have made his *murīd*s through the medium of dreams instead. Such precedents open up a whole twilight zone of interpretation and hardly verifiable claims. Secondly, there are also other ways of profiting from a saint's spirituality, such as *baraka*, 'blessing', and *fayḍ*, 'grace'; and these informal modes may substitute *bay'a* for all practical and spiritual purposes if someone can convincingly show that these have an effect on him. From all we know from the hagiographies, not only Gholam Rahman, but also Ahmadullah himself displayed a certain laxity in establishing the formal modalities of spiritual succession, heeded in most of the Sufi *ṭarīqa*s, at Maijbhandar; and some more recent saints and *pīr*s are no different in this respect.[56] As a result of this, a certain structure-proof ambivalence is noticeable in quite a number of status and succession issues.

Such polyvalence regarding the role of the practising *pīr*s in mediating access to the Maijbhandari saints may seem harmless, in terms of its structure-weakening effects, in comparison with another line of thought. We have seen, in the

53 Cf. Section 5.7.4.

54 This concept does not feature in Maijbhandari writings, but it is part of oral discourse; and Maijbhandari hagiology does not seem to have either the means or the intention to check such notions, possibly because it is sufficiently busy with other problematic aspects such as the lack of clarity on behalf of the Maijbhandari saints in unequivocably determining their successors.

55 Such as Gholam Rahman to Ahmadullah and Shafiul Bashar to Gholam Rahman.

56 Syed Shafiul Bashar, who passed away in 2002, equally appears to have abstained from installing any particular one of his sons or any other person as his *saǧǧādanašīn*.

Maijbhandari songs, that the great sacred places (Mecca, Medina, Benares, etc.) often undergo a mystical translocation and are transposed into Maijbhandar, the *muršid*, the heart, and so on. This argument may turn self-referential: according to its logic, Maijbhandar, itself a sacred place, also cannot evade such a transposition. We need only recall the popular microcosmic reading of it as the 'middle storehouse' inside man, that is, the human heart as the seat of God in the body. This microcosmic doubling procedure is potentially devaluating, as it may bring with it connotations of the outer Maijbhandar as open and exoteric (*ẓāhir*) and the inner one as concealed or esoteric (*bāṭin*). The latter would figure in such an interpretation as the 'real' (Bg. *āsal*) Maijbhandar. For such a line of thought, Maijbhandar is not primarily a place in northern Chittagong, but in reality an interior and esoteric category; and, in the most radical formulation, it may be conceived as virtually independent of its physical location altogether.[57] Such an inner Maijbhandar is accessible from anywhere by dreams, meditation, etc., and visiting the Maijbhandari *mazār*s or becoming a *murīd* of one of the Maijbhandari *pīr*s is, strictly speaking, optional.

Maijbhandari representatives would disprove such statements by insisting on the importance of legitimate spiritual succession through a *silsila* or by employing metaphors of schooling, training, etc., but, I fear, with limited success and even, if judged by their own standards, with limited legitimation because such transpositions are part and parcel of Maijbhandari discourse. The concepts of Sufi Islamic tradition, which also betray leanings to such dislocations, overlap to such an extent with our so-called target notion of open spirituality that they are not likely to solidify the representatives' arguments.

As with Maijbhandar, so with the saints. Fixity further decreases when we enter informal Maijbhandari discourse and take into account the various mystical 'shortcuts' on the way to God that open up opportunities to religious virtuosos outside any structure. God is found potentially everywhere, it can be argued, thus blaming all those who try to channel access to Him in any exclusive way (including Maijbhandari *pīr*s, preferably of other *manzil*s); furthermore, everything is already one, such arguments state, and it is to be realised only by opening one's heart to a *ma'šūq*, a beloved object, which can in principle be anything, provided it is approached with true love.[58] Maijbhandari discourse does not particularly stress such structure-dissolving notions, but cannot completely shed them either. One reason for this is the anti-structural ethos it has actively developed and has become identified with. This keeps it connected with all kinds of unitary mysticism and invites an unrefined, 'vulgar' notion of general oneness. It is in such circumstances that the targeted area of open spirituality appears to collide with that of Islam.

57 Such arguments are rare, but not completely alien to Maijbhandari oral discourse as I was able to witness in some conversations with professed Maijbhandaris.

58 Cf. *Ā'īna-i Bārī* 426 ff. on this difficult topic; Abdul Ghani discourages love of immature objects but has to admit that in principle all pictures of men (as well as all objects in general) are reflections of the divine; the difference between them is only one of grades.

The simultaneous positioning of Maijbhandar *vis-à-vis* the target notions of Islam and open spirituality also generates certain contradictions in Maijbhandari discourse when it comes to the admissability of non-Muslims to the Maijbhandari *ṭarīqa*. Such admissions create classificatory problems: non-Islamic *murīd*s are, it is true, not formally converted to Islam, but do they really still retain their former religious affiliation, or are they not somehow implicitly converted? There are examples for both these cases, and more narrowly Islamic-minded Maijbhandaris stress the cases of conversion whereas more broadly Islamic-minded ones tend towards inclusivist constructions of all religions being inherently and ultimately Islamic.[59] In the context of open spirituality, such happenings prove the legitimacy and – radically speaking – also the relativity and interchangeability of all the different religions in question, and the radical spiritualist factions in Maijbhandar would probably not hesitate to make this point. But the different interpretations can easily coexist, because in all of them Maijbhandar and Islam have the function of a host, and their status is therefore not endangered.[60]

Another ambivalence in Maijbhandari discourse, shared with Sufism in general, concerns the status of scripture. The translocation mentioned above may also be applied to scriptures: 'The *Qur'ān* is inside the heart', sings Aliullah,[61] implying that the meaning of the *Qur'ān* is discovered in one's own heart rather than by diligent exoteric memorisation. The scriptures can be generally perceived as something outer and exoteric; and even if he does work with Qur'anic quotations in his lyrics, Abdul Gafur Hali asks in one song: 'Can one know his secret/ By reading the *Qur'ān*, the *Gītā* and the Bible/Which can be burnt if put into fire?'[62] Such instances of a critical evaluation of 'bookish' knowledge of the scriptures *vis-à-vis* the vivid first-hand cognition gained on the mystical path are largely limited to Maijbhandari songs and stand in stark contrast to the hagiological and theological tracts in which the *Qur'ān* is the most important single source of reference – a contrast that may be accounted for by tensions between Islam and open spirituality. But even in those writings, occasionally, the general limitations of written language in divulging divine secrets and describing God's glories are lamented, and the reader is referred to the experience itself. Thus, Abdul Ghani Kanchanpuri writes: 'In relation to the virtue of Maijbhandar Sharif, the language of the pen is a step in the desert of non-being';[63] that is, anybody interested in Maijbhandar should not read about it in books, but go there to see for him- or herself. Similar attitudes were revealed to me in many conversations and interviews: commenting mostly upon my research work, various people said that studying Islamic, Sufi and Maijbhandari scriptures would not reveal any of the substance of Maijbhandar to me, and that I should rather go to a tomb and meditate for a few hours if I wanted to find out what it is all about. In this light,

59 Cf. Section 7.2.
60 Cf. the remarks in the preceding section.
61 *dil[a] bhitar āche korāṇ*; Aliullah *PN* 44.
62 *JJ* No.37; cf. Section 5.7.7.
63 *ĀB*: 128. Cf. Section 4.3.1.

Maijbhandari text production with all its books, journals and leaflets would appear as a sort of oxymoron, an example of 'anti-scripturalist scripturalism'. Although these attitudes are found in all Maijbhandari factions, there is a certain preponderance of the positive assertion of scriptures in the big *manzil*s which have most of the text production to their credit, and the anti-scripturalist pose is more articulated in the smaller *manzil*s and on the fringes.

A significant part of my fieldwork in Maijbhandar consisted in tracing and critically investigating such ambivalent aspects of Maijbhandari discourse. Asking interviewees about the consistency of their notions revealed another level of Maijbhandari parlance: the tensions and potential contradictions outlined above are countered in specific ways that are themselves vital parts of the Maijbhandari discursive field. I have noticed three different types of arguments that are employed when it comes to explaining apparently contradictory features that cannot easily be resolved.

In questions regarding the multiplicity of Maijbhandari saints and the multiple access to them, the answer tends to assert the ultimate unity of these saints, sometimes virtually blending them into one single personality. Similarly, inquiries into the logic of saintly deeds may be dismissed as pernickety and hushed with a general hint at the unity of the Divine. Secondly, the happenings in the saintly sphere are – predictably – assigned to a realm of miracle that is *per definitionem* beyond common perception ('We are too limited to understand this'). Thirdly, especially when things are discussed that go against certain basic injunctions of Islam, a gradation of cognition is introduced: rules are different for different positions on the mystical path, and it is impossible for a *murīd* to judge people with a higher spiritual state. Certain words or deeds are not meant for everybody but only 'for those who understand'.[64]

All these arguments are actually blockers of inquiry; things are not laid open for critical investigation, but sealed in their *a priori* inexplicable sanctity; to ask further would be impolite, disloyal or an outrage. Such impositions of limitations and hierarchies on communication are common to mystic parlance in general and have, in Sufism, been fixed theoretically by the notions of spiritual ascension through various stations (*maqāmāt*) and states (*ḥālāt*) as well as by the elaborate practical rules of behaviour for *murīd*s *vis-à-vis* their *muršid*s. These limitations appear as self-protecting measures for safeguarding the central messages and preventing the demystification of essences. At the same time, they clearly have the function of perpetuating an existing hierarchy of spiritual ranks and the offices connected therewith. In relation to Maijbhandar, such communicative closures may indeed act as stabilisers of a complex and blurred structure. But, due to the polycentric structure and especially the autonomy enjoyed by the domain of popular religion as mostly expressed in Maijbhandari songs, even these sealing mechanisms do not prevent Maijbhandari polyphony; they may, on the contrary, be found to protect it.[65]

64 This somewhat resembles the concept of *adhikārabheda* ('differentiation of qualification') in Indian philosophical traditions; cf. Halbfass (1988: 212, 533n).

65 Cf. Section 6.1 and the mystification of *dehatattva* songs.

7.4 How does Maijbhandar work? An interpretation

What Maijbhandar has come to represent today is arguably part of a modernisation process witnessed also in other discursive fields of South Asia, and namely – on a larger scale – in Hinduism. Criticism by Christian missionaries, for instance, could easily confront the 'lofty ideals' of Hindu scriptures with what was perceived as the decayed state of contemporary devotional practices; and this disparity between what was configured as 'doctrine' and 'practice' became one of the major problems of modern Hinduism at the end of the nineteenth century. Practices were, furthermore, not at all uniform but differed very considerably with regard to region, caste, *sampradāya* ('sect'), etc.[66] Modern Hindus themselves could not help seeing the present state of 'Hinduism' as an amalgam of the most variegated beliefs. But they were astute enough to make a virtue out of necessity in declaring that synonymous existence of diverse practices and beliefs is an attribute of tolerance and to find sanctions for such tolerance in seminal Hindu scriptures; multiplicity and fuzziness could in this way be transmuted into openness and tolerance, and Hinduism could be adorned with the predicate of being the most tolerant among religions.[67]

Something similar, though on a much smaller scale, seems to have happened in Maijbhandar, too. Maijbhandar as a whole today cherishes the notion of possessing a certain interreligious character. From an observer's perspective, this is true in at least two respects. First, Maijbhandar was initially a Sufi institution in keeping with similar institutions in its surroundings, though extraordinarily popular. It became, like other such institutions (and in that respect it was not uncommon), a host not only to Muslims, but also to members of different religious communities – not so much because it was a matter of doctrine or conviction, but because religious boundaries had been sufficiently permeable to allow, at least in certain circumstances, allegiances to holy sites and spiritual personalities from other religious traditions. What is special about Maijbhandar is that this hosting was not unofficially carried on, but transformed into one of the principles of the movement: the accessibility for anybody, regardless of his or her religion or social background, became its main motto. Maijbhandar thus started to assert for itself a meta-religious position. Such a construction must certainly be read as an answer to modernity, and in Section 4.7 I have interpreted it as a counter-ideology that emerged in the early days of Pakistan.

The formula *jātidharmanirbiśeṣe* is worth analysing in this context. We have noted that it has become very popular not only in Maijbhandari self-representations, but is also appropriated by other contemporary shrine cults. What is the reason for its success? *Jātidharmanirbiśeṣe* is basically a descriptive term stating that pilgrims and *murīd*s have been and are welcome at the *darbār* whatever their caste/class and religion. Once it is used as a motto, however, it changes its character and becomes a

66 Hence the claim to speak of Hindu religions in the plural only; cf., e.g., Stietencron (1995); discussion in Harder (2001: 240).

67 I have dealt with these issues in depth in my book on Bankimchandra Chattopadhyay's *Bhagavadgītā* commentary (Harder 2001). Cf. especially Sections 2.2.2 and 2.2.3 of that book.

request or invitation: people with all kinds of religious, social and ethnic background *should* come to the *darbār*. Thus anybody receiving the announcement sheets for the *ʿurs* festivities which bear this motto, is targeted. Not everybody on earth though, even if Maijbhandari aspirations may very well be international; for the time being, such announcements are printed in Bengali and disseminated in various parts of Bangladesh. For all practical purposes, those who might feel invited to the *ʿurs* at Maijbhandar are Bangladeshis (plus Bangladeshi migrants), and in this light the abstract indefiniteness of the formula may translate into a number of positive options. *Jāti* is ambivalent; in the sense of race, it comprises Bengalis and other ethnic groups mainly from the Chittagong Hill Tracts, namely Chakmas, Maghs, Kukis and so on. If it means caste or class, it includes the high and low-born, *aśrāf* and *ağlāf*, rich and poor alike. *Dharma*, 'religion',[68] comprises Islam, Hinduism, Buddhism and Christianity; that is, the religions present in contemporary Bangladesh. If the indefiniteness of the formula is thus reduced to the positive number of groups it actually addresses, we can easily see that it operates in the *national* framework of Bangladesh. We may compare to this another motto, printed during the Bangladeshi Liberation War in 1971 and reproduced by the Liberation War Museum in Dhaka: 'Hindus of Bengal, Christians of Bengal, Buddhists of Bengal, Muslims of Bengal – we are all Bengalis'.[69]

The point of this comparison is not to argue that Maijbhandar represents, or attempts to represent, any kind of Bengali national religion, which is very clearly not the case; but it shows that the motto *jātidharmanirbiśeṣe* is easily compatible with one brand of nationalism in Bangladesh.[70] To such a nationalism, Maijbhandar may seem to represent a successful answer to the issue of religious plurality. *Dharmanirbiśeṣe*, in addition, is almost coterminous with *dharmanirapekṣa*, the Bengali equivalent of 'secular', and might still pave the way to philanthropic, nationalist pilgrimages to a 'field where religions unite' (*dharmamilanʾkṣetra*), another common epithet of Maijbhandar. This is, to be sure, not yet the case on any feasible scale, but some of the recent interpretations of Maijbhandar (namely that by Selim Jahangir) lend some plausibility to such speculations;[71] and there are parallel interpretations of such phenomena in contemporary India.[72]

68 On the traditional semantics of this central and complex term, and the way in which it was appropriated as an equivalent of 'religion' in a largely neo-Hindu environment, cf. Hacker (1978: 580–608); Halbfass (1988: Chapter 17, pp. 310–33); Harder (2001: 180–95).

69 *bāṃlār hindu bāṃlār khr̥ṣṭān bāṃlār bauddha bāṃlār musalʾmān āmʾrā sabāi bāṅālī*. In the background of the poster are given the silhouettes of a Hindu temple, a mosque, a Buddhist temple and a church.

70 It is not easy to locate this nationalism with certainty in any specific political party today, but it seems to come closest to the programme and policies of the Awami League.

71 In this connection it deserves to be mentioned that the mausoleum of Saint Ziaul Haq, having the form of a water-lily or *śāpʾlā phul*, which significantly happens to be the national flower of Bangladesh, was designed in conscious deviation from the traditional architectural model in order to symbolise the meta-religious character of Maijbhandar.

72 Cf. Gaeffke (1992: 80), who stresses that the 'meeting of the oceans' (in allusion to the famous treatise *Mağmāʾ al-baḥrain* by Mughal prince Dara Shikoh) has been transported into modern Hindu ideology as a forerunner of a 'secular multireligious state' and gives quotes from Jagadish

Maijbhandar is 'interreligious' also in a second sense; as we have seen in our analysis of Maijbhandari songs, materials from distinct religious traditions (namely, Vaishnava and tantric) have found accommodation in Maijbhandar. Unlike the meta-religious motto, this aspect of Maijbhandar's interreligious character is somewhat unofficial and not acknowledged by all Maijbhandaris because, as we have argued, the material is either not perceived as being part of any distinct tradition or, if it is thus perceived, it is not avowed because Maijbhandar would then appear as a debtor rather than a host. But there is also a trend to classify such loans, in analogy to neo-Hinduism, as a mark of distinction that practically demonstrates the amount of superior tolerance displayed by Maijbhandar.

Does Maijbhandar really live up to the claim of being a meeting point for different ethnic, social and religious groups? If taken as a whole, this certainly appears to be the case. The segmentation into different *manzil*s may seem pernicious in obstructing a concerted self-presentation, but for this claim to be realised, I argue, it is on the contrary quite advantageous. The division into many factions increases the representational range that Maijbhandar covers. The *manzil*s are very different from each other in terms of wealth, power, organisation, education, urbanity and even religious outlook. Some are urban and modernist and draw significant portions of their supporters from city-dwelling professionals. Others retain a somewhat feudal outlook and thus ensure popularity among rather traditional-minded followers. Others still are rural and of modest means and tend to attract a similar clientele. In a sense, the different *manzil*s of Maijbhandar mirror different aspects of Bangladeshi society. This iconic aspect is hardly expressed and only shines through in certain (mostly cautious) indictments that are passed around among *murīd*s, of *manzil*s being too wealthy, too commercialised, too glamour-prone, too insignificant and so on, but it can be assumed that it plays a significant role for the recruitment of different classes of followers.

The linking function of Maijbhandar is also evident from the various branches of Maijbhandari text production. It is here that the scholarly meets the popular, and both modes of religiosity coexist. The *manzil* fragmentation may even here have a healthy effect because songwriting remains a domain apart. It does not directly come under the control of *manzil*-based theologians and *pīrzāda*s but retains the character of a spontaneous production. If there were one single Maijbhandari authority, pressure on the 'fringes' of the movement might increase. There could be concerted efforts at a canonisation of songs and along with it the

Narayan Sarkar and Jadunath Sarkar to support this statement. A good example for this is Saint Kabir, the 'Indian Luther' (Sushil Gupta) who presented a 'synthesis between Islam and Hinduism' (Yusuf Husain). See also the volume *Images of Kabir* (Thiel-Horstmann 2002). Cf. further E. Mann (1989: 169), quoting a Lieutenant-Governor at the *'urs* of Nizam al-Din saying 'that the Sufi saint "stood for a composite culture", and that his teachings "will remain a cementing force among different communities" for ages to come while propagating "the message of universal brotherhood, love and peace." '

exclusion of whole parts of the Maijbhandari song heritage; in the present circumstances, this does not seem possible.

Lastly, and probably mostly due to its urban links, Maijbhandar is also not isolated from a brand of Islamic modernism. The promoters are in some cases the *pīrzāda*s and representatives themselves; and there are cases in which the *pīr*s are much more influenced by rather sober and moderate notions of sainthood and their own importance than their followers. The best example of this is the former *sağğādanašīn* of Ahmadiya Manzil, Syed Delawar Hosain. Before his death, he ordered that no *mazār* should be constructed for him and no *ʿurs* should be celebrated in his honour. This explicit denial of being treated as a saint[73] has, somewhat paradoxically, given rise to a distinct kind of veneration. Selim Jahangir, former Maijbhandar researcher of the Bangla Academy in Dhaka but also *murīd* of Ahmadiya Manzil, has written a biography of Delawar Hosain that in many respects ressembles other Maijbhandari hagiographies; the veneration changes to a modernist code here in stressing the earthly achievements of this Maijbhandari personality.[74] In this way, even the negation of shrine veneration has found its place in Maijbhandari religiosity.

73 Implicitly, of course, and according to theory, all saints should keep their sainthood hidden; but no exponent of Maijbhandar except Delawar Hosain has made that rule explicit in such a manner.

74 Cf. Selim Jāhāṅgīr (2000).

8 Conclusion

A note on Bengali Islam

What, again, is Bengali Islam? This last chapter ventures back on the slippery ground we entered in the beginning of this study. Evidently, a study of Maijbhandar cannot possibly supply sufficient material for any full-scale assessment of this problematic. But it may give us some clues on how to tackle this issue, furnishing as it does a lot of data for the contemporary position of shrine and *pīr* veneration, Sufism and the constellation of Bengal and Islam *vis-à-vis* each other.

One answer to the above question can, of course, be given right away: 'Bengali Islam' is basically a meta-category which is not current in the field denoted by it. The term *bāṅālī is'lām*, 'Bengali Islam', is hardly ever used, and it is not very likely, to say the least, that a Bengali Muslim would profess himself or herself a member of 'Bengali Islam' as a separate religious confession. Even staunch supporters of the Maijbhandari *ṭarīqa* would not describe themselves as adherents to 'Bengali Islam'. As we have seen, there is some talk of 'indigenous Islam' with reference to Maijbhandar, and a very attentive analysis may reveal signs of a nationalisation of Maijbhandar as part of Bangladeshi folklore heritage; but this process is in a very initial stage, and its further course is hard to foretell. 'Bengali Islam' is thus no more than a technical term – in sharp contrast, by the way, to *bāṅālī musal'mān*, 'Bengali Muslim', which had already started to become an important category of self-reference in the nineteenth century. This state of affairs is nothing special to Bengal, but affords parallels with many other cultures. It would, for instance, make perfect sense to speak of oneself as a French Catholic or a German Protestant, but nobody would confess allegiance to 'French Catholicism' or 'German Protestantism'; the cases where such confessions are possible – for example the Anglican Church, Greek Orthodoxy, etc. – are limited to national religions and are exceptions rather than the rule. Many of the modern nation-states in the so-called Islamic World have given Islam the status of a state religion, and Bangladesh is no exception here;[1] but in none of these – with two possible exceptions[2] – is any version of Islam asserted as an exclusive national

1 Islam was declared the state religion of Bangladesh in 1988, during the military regime of Muhammad Ershad.

2 Saudi Arabia holds a special position here as the 'guardian of the holy sites'; likewise, Iran presents itself as *the* representative of the *Šīʿa*.

property, and like in Bengal, notions of 'Turkish' or 'Egyptian Islam' may be part of academic terminology, but do not reflect any usage established among believers 'on the ground'.

'Bengali Islam', however, differs from these denominations in the perceived tensions between the notions of 'Islamic' and 'Bengali', mentioned in the introduction, that can be detected in many spheres of Bengali society in past and present. These tensions, though certainly not troubling the majority of Bengali Muslims in any concrete sense, can no doubt be posited as a long-standing issue for many of those who have reflected on the topic ever since the sixteenth century. Asim Roy (1995: 11 ff.) shows that the preception of 'deviousness' and 'laxity' in the Islamic practice of Bengali Muslims existed already in the sixteenth century and continued well into the Pakistani era and the assessments of such personalities as the military ruler Ayub Khan. Elsewhere (Roy 1983: 70 ff.), he quotes a number of medieval Bengali Muslim authors stating the deplorable condition of Islam in their regions and the reluctance to use the Bengali language for Islamic instruction. Richard Eaton cites Saiyid Sultan lamenting his birth as a Bengali and the incapability of the Bengali Muslims, lacking knowledge of Arabic, to understand their own religion, and remarks:

> Such expressions of tensions between Bengali culture and the perceived 'foreignness' of Islam were typical among those who were outsiders to the rural experience – whether they were members of Bengal's premodern Muslim literati, European travelers in Bengal, or modern-day observers. But the rural masses do not appear to have been troubled by such tensions, or even to have noticed them.
>
> (Eaton 1993: 279)

Such tensions, however, came to be more accentuated and widespread in the nineteenth century with the appearance of the popular reformist movements (Ṭarīqa al-Muḥammadīya, Farā'iżīs) and their emphasis on the 'purification' of Islamic belief and practices, and it was from then on that the identity issue was filtered down to a wider public including the rural masses. As Rafiuddin Ahmed states:

> A dominant feature of the nineteenth-century campaigns of Islamization in Bengal was the attempted rejection of virtually all that was Bengali in the life of a Muslim as something incompatible with the ideas and principles of Islam. The preachers' conception of an Islamic polity was based on a vague notion of the Middle Eastern values, and it was their dream to transform the lives of the ordinary Muslims that they conformed exclusively to this trans-Indian pattern. The very nature of their propaganda emphasizing the distinctive ethos of Islam was bound to create great misgivings among the Muslim population about their association with Bengal, including its cultural past which was a part of their heritage. The new emphasis was on differentiating popular Islam in Bengal from the local cultural traditions, much of which

> now came to be closely identified with Hinduism and polytheism and therefore as anti-Islamic.
>
> (Ahmed 1981: 106)

The Ṭarīqa al-Muḥammadīya and the Farā'iżīs dissolved in the nineteenth century,[3] but they had their followers in history, and one of their most important impacts was the influence they exerted on local mullahs, creating by the debates they initiated, an interest in their version of Islam and the Islamic way of life among the divines as well as their lay following (Ahmed 1981: 74).[4] The move of an inner-Islamic mission[5] has not come to a halt. Reformist versions of Islam have found their political platform in the Jamaat-e Islami, the Bangladeshi branch of the party founded by Abul Ala Maudoodi (1903–79) in 1941, and have been backed, at least since the 1960s, by financial support from Saudi Arabia. Different versions of reformist Islam, among them Wahhabism, are taught in many *madrasas* of contemporary Bangladesh. The constellation is therefore not completely different from the picture Rafiuddin Ahmed paints for the late nineteenth and early twentieth centuries. We shall in the following try to assemble some salient points on Bengali Islam and first look at the contemporary position of shrine veneration *vis-à-vis* these reformist trends; then attempt a somewhat new interpretation of pre-modern Bengali Islamic literature in the context of this constellation; and lastly suggest that both shrine and *pīr* veneration and reformism can conveniently be captured and viewed in their mutual relationship under the label of 'Bengali Islam'.

8.1 The configuration of shrine and *pīr* veneration in Bengal

First, I want to ask what the situation outlined above means for shrine veneration, an important aspect of Bengali Islam.[6] Shrine and *pīr* veneration, very popular in pre-modern times, has from the beginning been one of the targets of these reformist trends.[7] It is intimately connected with the issue at hand, since the belief in saints

3 For the impact and history of these movements, see Rafiuddin Ahmed (1981: chapter II), as well as, earlier, W.W. Hunter (1999 [1st edn 1871]); also Qeyamuddin Ahmad (1994), Jayanta Maitra (1984: 9–32). The Farā'iżīs were more specifically Bengali among these; as a movement, they were crushed during the Mutiny of 1857, but this did not prevent their survivors and others from carrying on similar projects of religious reform in the decades to come.

4 This is a slightly altered, paraphrase of Rafiuddin Ahmed's 'a new interest in Islam and the Islamic way of life [. . .]', a statement which is problematic, however, in implying that such interest was absent earlier, and generally indicative of the problems of Rafiuddin Ahmed's approach and terminology.

5 I prefer this term over 'Islamisation' as used by Ahmed, since the latter implicitly evaluates the 'new' religion propagated in these movements as more 'Islamic' than the preceding forms.

6 An earlier version of the remarks in Section 8.1 has been published in an article titled 'Shrine Veneration versus Reformism, Bengal versus Islam: Some remarks on perceptual difficulties regarding Bengali Islam' (Harder 2008).

7 Cf. Qeyamuddin Ahmed 1994: 285 f. for the treatment of this issue in Ṭarīqa-i Muḥammadīya tracts; also Gaborieau 1999: 459 ff. Rafiuddin Ahmed (1981) is the most expert source on the Bengali tracts authored by Farā'iżīs; for their denunciation of shrine and *pīr* veneration, cf. especially pp. 59–63.

and many shrine rituals were classed as derived from Hindu influences by the reformists. Not only by them, in fact, but also by early Orientalist scholars such as Garcin de Tassy. Writing in 1831 about Indian Muslims in general, Tassy states:

> What strikes me most about the religious ceremonies of Indian Muslims is the innovations which make them appear as local phenomena. Established as they are on account of unconscious Hindu influences, there are wholly new ceremonies, which conform little to the spirit of the Quran and are sometimes even contrary to its spirit. Further, in many cases, Muslims make pilgrimages to the tombs of saints, some of whom are actually non-Muslim, and perform there semi-pagan rites.
>
> (Garcin de Tassy 1995: 32)

As a perceptional pattern, 'Hindu influences' have run in fact through both reformist and Orientalist evaluations of Islam on the Subcontinent and especially Bengali Islam.[8] As to the appropriateness of such a qualification, we should remember the very relevant statement by Gaborieau, with reference to a nineteenth-century reformist tract:

> As seen above, our text is careful not to build any direct connection between the cult of Muslim saints and Hindu idol-worship. Later Muslim authors were not so careful: many modern reformers say more clearly that such cults were borrowed from the Hindus. In this they share one of the prejudices of British colonial ethnography – which, in fact, many of them use now. The error of both, the reformers and Western ethnographers, is to consider only two forms: a rather fundamentalist conception of Islam on the one hand, and Hindu customs on the other. They ignore an important middle form, namely medieval Sufi piety, which is responsible for most of the devotions to the saints and which was imported to India from abroad.
>
> (Gaborieau 1992: 233)

Anyhow, in view of the long missionary process carried on by various groups of reformists, one might expect a slow recession of shrine and *pīr* veneration, an alleged victim of these influences, ever since the nineteenth century, and this is in fact the most common assessment.[9] Obviously, a case like Maijbhandar seems counter-indicative to such perceptions, and they require some modifications to accommodate it. If we take into consideration developments in other parts of Bengal, this picture can be adjusted and the actual pattern of religious development may be found to be much more complex. In general, to begin with, it seems mis-

8 This applies also to Enāmul Hak (1995: 323) when he views 'saint-worship' in Bengal as a debased variant of *guruvāda*; although in other cases, such as that of *Makkeśvara Śiva* (Shiva, Lord of Mecca) (Enāmul Hak 1995: 346 f.), such assessments may be to the point.

9 This picture evolves from almost all the relevant monographs on Islam in Bengal, such as Asim Roy 1983; Rafiuddin Ahmed 1981; Razia Akter Banu 1995; etc.

leading to think of the orthodox/reformist and Sufi/shrine/popular clusters as separate and always clearly distinguishable modes of religiosity. They should be thought of rather as polarities in a field of phenomena that allow for manifold intersections and discursive overlaps. The distinctions are found to be at work in the field as assignations, but closer examinations will probably dismantle them more often than not as short-hand judgements covering up more complex interactions.

There is an interesting study that will serve as my support as I try to delineate the complex relationship between these religious modes in Bengal. The British anthropologist Katy Gardner (1995, 1999) has written on Shah Jalal of Sylhet and the reformist ideas imported into Bangladesh by migrant labourers. We have already dealt with Shah Jalal in the context of Bengali Muslim hagiography and noticed a certain historicisation of his figure and a rehumanisation of his sainthood in early twentieth-century hagiographies – features I have analysed in relation to the new importance of history in Bengal at that time.[10] Katy Gardner has found that migration to Europe and the Gulf states generates notions of what she calls a 'global Islam'. This stands for scripture-based religious practice, observance of *parda*, acceptance of Mecca and very few other places as holy sites to the detriment of local shrines, and so on. The families of those migrants who are still partly settled there or maintain close ties with their homes, constitute the dominant classes in Sylhet and thus have the power of putting their notion of proper Islam in practice. In consequence, local *pīr*s and *mazār*s lose vital parts of their traditional constituencies; they are being relegated to the lower classes of society and seem to be gradually perishing. The great exception to this is Saint Shah Jalal; as an identication figure of the Islamic character of the locality also for the migrants' families, he has become possibly more popular than ever. So this shrine cult is integrated into the globalised orthodox notions of this class. Simultaneously, however, his saintly status, in close parallel to what happened in the early-twentieth-century hagiographies examined in Chapter 4, is downscaled from a superhuman wonder-worker to a heroic, but only historical human (Gardner 1995: 264), and the practice at the shrine is being purged from controversial acts such as *samā*ʿ and *sağda*.

According to this analysis, reformism is able to accommodate a part of popular practice by transforming and redefining it, and by relegating 'original' popular practice to the lower orders of Muslim society. In one sentence, what happens here to the shrine cults is a transforming adaptation of the more prestigious among them and the simultaneous marginalisation and sometimes elimination of the smaller, local, rural ones. Gardner consciously regards this as a phenomenon of interaction between two strands of Islam that are usually conceived as diametrically opposed to each other, and she aptly warns us against thinking in neat dichotomic ways:

> The danger of discussing purism and mysticism as oppositional categories is that it disguises the flexibility of pir cults. Indeed, rather than purists rejecting

10 Cf. Section 4.1.

> pirs out of hand, cults initially associated with mysticism can change within themselves.
>
> (Gardner 1995: 263)

Extending Gardner's argument, I think that this could, however, also be read vice versa as an indication of *reformist* flexibility; and there are signs that South Asian reformists have hardly ever been able to shed their Sufi allegiances completely.[11] A more general problem, moreover, may arise from another opposition Gardner draws up, namely that between global and local Islam – not if they are used as quotations from the Sylheti context, but certainly if read as residual categories. For this distinction, handy as it may sound, in its own way disguises that there are certainly *several* such global Islams, one of them being Sufism itself (as a bracket term accommodating quite a range of phenomena);[12] and we must remain aware that 'global Islam' only denotes a concept in some Sylheti migrants' imagination and actually inhabits 'the same conceptual space'[13] as other interpretations of Islam in its locality, coming down to a certain type of reformism that successfully manages to pose as 'global' Islam in Sylhet.[14]

But this is not my point here. The point is that the constellation Gardner describes certainly features a kind of interaction between popular and reformist

11 Cf. Gaborieau 1999: 452 f. (with a quote from Maudoodi brandishing such allegiances on their part) on initiation, *ḏikr* practices and – of course – *ṭarīqa* concepts among the Farā'iżīs and the Ṭarīqa-e Muḥammadīya. Also Sirriyeh on Maudoodi himself returning to Sufi practices in his later life: 'Yet neither the older Mawdūdī nor all the members of the Jamā'at totally abandoned traditional Sufism. In the 1970s towards the end of his life, Mawdūdī was ready to return to some of the Sufi devotional practices that he had previously rejected and even acted as a shaykh initiating followers into the Chishtiyya. In the 1980s and 90s the Jamā'at was prepared to make concessions to popular Sufism in Pakistan, including shrine visitation. However, further afield the anti-Sufi orientation would usually be more dominant' (Sirriyeh 1999: 164). Again Baljon (1992) on Shah Waliullah, modifying his anti-shrine veneration and anti-Sufi positions. I will hark back to this point below.

12 Cf., in this connection, Clifford Geertz (1968: 48) on the deceptiveness of this term: 'The whole process, the social and cultural stabilization of Moroccan maraboutism, is usually referred to under the rubric of "Sufism"; but like its most common gloss in English, "mysticism", this term suggests a specificity of belief and practice which dissolves when one looks at the range of phenomena to which it is actually applied. Sufism has been less a definite standpoint in Islam, a distinct conception of religiousness like Methodism or Swedenborgianism, than a diffuse expression of that necessity [. . .] for a world religion to come to terms with a variety of mentalities, a multiplicity of local forms of faith, and yet maintain the essence of its own identity. Despite the otherwordly ideas and activities so often associated with it, Sufism, as an historical reality, consists of a series of different and even contradictory experiments, most of them occurring between the ninth and nineteenth centuries, in bringing orthodox Islam (itself no seamless unity) into effective relationship with the world, rendering it accessible to its adherents and its adherents accessible to it.' I am not sure whether one must go this far in dissolving this category, and whether the functional explanation Geertz presents is in all cases accurate; but he is certainly right in pointing out that the term 'Sufism' suggests more specificity than it actually covers.

13 A phrase taken from Tschacher (2009: 58), who deconstructs the opposition of 'global' and 'local' Islam in a similar fashion for Tamil-speaking Muslims.

14 Cf. Section 1.1 where this topic was discussed.

practice, but it does nevertheless fit into the picture of a slow recess and is easily amenable to the commonplace picture of a large-scale substitution process of popular Islam by reformist Islam. Following this ratio, we might metaphorically describe reformism as a huge and still increasing tidal wave which submerges most of the landscape of popular, shrine-based religion and leaves only a few dominant landmarks as islands – islands that may or may not survive the high tide of any such wave in the future.

Photo 11 The entrance to Saint Gholam Rahman's shrine, Maijbhandar.

If there is rarification of shrine and *pīr* veneration in Sylhet, however, we find the contrary condition in rural Chittagong, or, at any rate, in the surroundings of Maijbhandar, where this type of religiosity is to all appearances stable or even on the rise. The popularity of Maijbhandar has reverberated through many other (and also some of the very old) shrines in the region. It is important to note that Maijbhandar itself hardly qualifies for the role of a 'surviver' of pre-modern Islamic practice; the accounts of the movement ever since the beginning betray an awareness of a strong opposition from orthodox and reformist quarters, and actually speak of 'conversions' of the latter's adherents to the Maijbhandari brand of Sufism. This suggests that in this local context a certain rupture with pre-modern religiosity and a shift towards more reformist orientations had already happened *before* Maijbhandar gained full momentum. On the basis of Maijbhandari hagiographies one is tempted to speak of a veritable revival of shrine veneration triggered by the Maijbhandari movement. Booming shrines in the region include those of Shah Muhsin Auliya, believed to have been an Arab companion of Badr Shah whose journey on a floating stone had come to an end at Anwara where his *mazār* is situated, as well as Shah Amanat, a petty clerk who attained sainthood in the eighteenth century and is buried in the centre of Chittagong city. In the vicinity of Maijbhandar, there are many shrines of the *ḫalīfa*s of the great Maijbhandari saints, some of them in the process of enlargement, as well as newly discovered tombs that are objects of veneration.

The most curious, and somewhat paradigmatic, case in the context of shrine veneration and reformism in Chittagong is maybe that of so-called Garam Bibi, lit. 'Hot Lady'. The only evidence of this woman saint's existence is a dream in which she instructed the superintendent of the Chittagong police to have her *mazār* built on a hillock within the police quarters of the city – a place where, according to the dream revelation, she had been practising austerities in some remote past. This shrine is today mainly visited by women, and its rules display the imprint of reformist ideas in that *sağda* in front of the grave is not tolerated.[15] This intersection of traditional and reformist practices, similar to the case of Shah Jalal, demonstrates aptly that these trends, while deemed diametrically opposed to each other, can be combined in unforeseen ways.

We have also noted the role of popular music of the Maijbhandari brand in promoting devotional shrine veneration and extending it even to shrines without any traditional connection with it.[16] Maijbhandar has indeed become a role model for many similar institutions in Chittagong, with its inventory of shrine monuments, hagiographies, songs and meta-religious messages ready for copying. And this boom in shrine culture is not a relic of the past, but of very recent making. 'Purifications' of shrine rituals from features deemed un-Islamic, as in the case of the *mazār* of Shah Jalal of Sylhet are not completely absent; we have mentioned

15 According to the information gathered from the *ḫādim* of the shrine who was, I was told, directly employed by the Chittagong police.

16 Cf. the introduction to Chapter 5.

that one particular Maijbhandari *pīr* has even explicitly forbidden his descendants to build up a shrine cult around his tomb. But such instances of purification do not prevent the traditional modes of shrine veneration from continuing.

As the comparison between Sylhet and Chittagong shows, shrine and *pīr* veneration can relate to reformist trends in a number of ways. In Sylhet it has become a recessive mode of religiosity which is undergoing concentration and reconfiguration under the impact of reformism. In Chittagong, by contrast, it is dominant at least in certain areas, and allows for diversification. In both cases, it is necessary to view shrine and *pīr* veneration not as a closed subsystem of Islam in any clearly defined opposition to other such subsystems, but as institutions controlling a specific discursive field in the sense of a polarity, as it were, and thus affording overlaps with other discursive fields. As Elisabeth Sirriyeh puts it:

> For the most part, it is the more traditional and largely indigenous thought for and against Sufism that has proved most durable, ṭarīqas, whether traditional or reformed to any extent, facing anti-Sufi organizations modelled on ideologies owing much to the Wahhābīs and Salafīs. Both Sufis and anti-Sufis have flourished in the contemporary Islamic revival and frequently continue to be embattled, although at times they may also show awareness of the need to overcome differences in order to withstand the threat to both from the creeping dangers of secularism and the attractions of the material world.
>
> (Sirriyeh 1999: 175)

Both in Chittagong and in Sylhet, there is more than one player targeting Islam, and the self-assertive powers of the different discursive fields – reformism, Sunni mainstream, Sufism, shrine veneration, etc. – differ from locality to locality. An empirical picture of Bengali Islam can only evolve from such a perspective, and a sketch of how such a picture might be organised will be given in the final Section 8.3.

8.2 Medieval Bengali Islamic literature: documentation rather than mediation

If shrine and *pīr* veneration have thus at least in part managed to assert themselves in interaction with the contemporary reformist trends in Bengali Islam, which place can we assign to the tradition of Bengali Islamic writings of mostly pre-eighteenth-century times (which was partly made available through editions by the efforts of Abdul Karim Sahityavisharad and Ahmad Sharif and further studied in the monographs by Asim Roy and David Cashin)?[17] This literature displays many elements of decidedly Sufi provenance. It is further known for its inclusion of yogic and tantric elements and the presentation of Islam by using pre-existent religious imagery, mostly from the domain that would, according to today's taxonomies, fall under the category of Hinduism. Asim Roy has presented a theory

17 Roy 1983; Cashin 1995.

that contextualises this literature as a mode of cultural mediation. According to him, authors like Saiyid Sultan acted as missionaries among nominal Muslims whom they regarded as not familiar with the contents of their religion, and these authors consciously adapted the religious concepts which they wanted to convey, to the cultural horizon of the people. Roy, in one article, calls this production a second, local and syncretistic great tradition.[18]

This tradition, or at least the part of it that contains yogic, tantric or Vaishnava traits, apparently came to a halt even before the shift towards print during the nineteenth century, and none of these writings seems to have made the transition into print at that time. The Islamic literature printed in the nineteenth century consists mainly of manuals on religious instruction, narratives of the initial phase of Islam and adaptations of Arabic and Persian romances.[19] Topics with Sufi connotations are not completely absent, but their references are to non-local, general Sufi sources. This disappearance can arguably be seen in the context of the reformist movements setting in around 1830. They seem to have brought about sharpened notions about orthodoxy and orthopraxy, and the yogico-tantric conundrum may have appeared too obviously deviative to authors of texts at that time.

But, as we have seen in Chapter 5, some of the contents and motifs of that literature is still in full sway in Maijbhandari songs and other genres of mystical songs like *bāul gān*, *Hāsan Rājār gān*, etc. It makes little sense to suppose that a scriptural tradition went into hiding by becoming oral, because this would go against the usual order of things and need an extraordinary explanation to be acceptable. It is much more likely that this worked the other way round: namely, that the manuscripts under discussion were in some part scripturalisations of ideas pertaining to a basically oral tradition that presumably pre- and also outdated these texts.

Roy's interpretation of the role of the mediators as representatives of what he calls the 'first Great Tradition', to be sure, is not developed out of the void but in close contact with the texts and on the basis of paratextual markers, that is remarks of the authors on their motivations in introdutions, forewords, etc. found in the manuscripts. This self-documentation is, however, not a feature of all the texts but rather a sporadic occurrence, and there is a degree of speculation in asserting, as Roy does, that this was the dominant self-understanding of all the authors and each and every text in this tradition.[20] What I want to suggest here, then, is that there is also another way of conceiving of the mediating position of these writers. Rather than *inventing* a cultural idiom in order to pass on Arabic and Persian-

18 Roy 1995: 114, where he speaks of two Great Traditions. Cf. the discussion in Section 7.1.

19 Cf. the detailed discussion in Section 4.1.

20 This is also what Richard Eaton suggests in his review of Roy's work (Eaton 1985). Roy, in a reaction to this review, quotes Saiyad Sultan in favour of his theory (Roy 1996: 37), but the fact remains that Saiyad Sultan is only one author out of many – and things get even more complex if one questions the face value of his statements and tries to attribute them to a kind of self-stylisation.

based source knowledge about Islam – something they did in some cases, no doubt, but probably not in all, and especially not in the mystical texts bearing heavy imprints of yogic and tantric ideas – these authors *documented* something they found in existence on the ground. This comprises the teachings of local *pīr*s (who may in some cases have been their spiritual masters) or the songs of certain popular mystical traditions. According to this line of thought, they would have been *archivists* just as much as (and maybe more than) active *mediators*.

One point in favour of this argument is that it explains the phenomenon of scripturalisation much more convincingly than Roy's thesis. What, simply put, was the need of scripturalising the tenets of Islam for a public of illiterates? If reception of these written documents was limited to the rural educated and *'ulamā'*, were these manuscripts not rather mnemetic devices for the fixing of what was basically oral teaching and statements of religious doctrines *vis-à-vis* other, similar doctrines? These questions are easily answered if we suppose that the underlying ratio of this scripturalisation was documentation rather than mediation. According to this picture, Islamic religious ideas integrating yogico-tantric pratices were the rule rather than the exception, and their scripturalisation would then account for their pervasiveness and represent a move towards codification of this tradition and an attempt to establish it as a religious high culture – one that was situated in the shadow of existing Islamic high culture, as some of the authors knew and thus felt prompted to offer apologetics for. In any case it was probably more commonplace than it is today in Maijbhandar, where some of these ideas are still extant in the popular songs, but are mostly denied entry into proper domains of scripturalisation, that is, the theological and hagiographical writings.

The picture I propose, in short, amounts to the following: various popular religious currents in Bengal have, ever since the time of the *Caryāpada*s, shown an affinity with mysticism of yogic and tantric descent. These ideas were a part of what Tarafdar calls 'folk Islam' just as much as they had belonged to certain popular strands of Buddhism centuries ago.[21] They were rather seldom fixed or even canonised, but remained mostly confined to oral culture, finding its most stable expression in songs. As a substratum, this popular religious imagery and practice could find accommodation in Buddhist, Hindu and Islamic contexts alike and sometimes found acceptance and recognition among the higher ranks of religious establishment in these traditions, for example among the Sahajiyas.[22] The Medieval Bengali Islamic literature discussed here would then be one instance of such recognition; and the number of texts dealing with this substratum would indicate its great popularity.

In the nineteenth century, conditions became unfavourable for this popular tradition, and it ceased to be a part of scriptural Islamic culture in Bengal, though

21 M.R. Tarafdar (1986: 106) distinguishes between folk Islam and the synthetic Islam emerging from these scriptures – a distinction that appears invalid if the perspective is redefined in the way I am proposing in this section.

22 Cf. Dimock 1989: 35, linking up the Sahajiya tradition with the *Caryāpada*s.

it continued to exist in the form of oral songs.[23] These, in their turn, surfaced again in script with some delay, as a second generation of print products, since the early twentieth century[24] when printing facilities had become proliferated and affordable enough to reach the rural market, and printing had become sufficiently commonplace to accommodate non-scriptural genres. This idea of a centuries-old mystical song tradition in Bengal, surfacing, in the Islamic context, first somewhat obliquely in (manu-)script and then quite directly in print, would, if the above arguments stand test, shed a different light on one current of pre-modern Bengali Islam and call for a partial revision of Asim Roy's thesis. Conscious cultural mediation would certainly still account for some of the cases, but on the whole the documentation of orally transmitted ideas would have to be highlighted much more prominently.

8.3 On Bengali Islam

Finally, I will now draw up a schematic description of how the arena of Bengali Islam could be conceived of. Let us, as it were, imagine a number of players (traditions, movements) in this arena who are endowed with a mission. These different players compete in trying to assert their respective positions, and establish their discursive fields, in the arena of Bengali Islam. What is at stake for them is what they avowedly perceive as the true version of Islam, as well as the usually concealed vested interests they have in the type of structure and discourse they stand for. Coexistence between them is not impossible, but at times they strive for enlarging their respective fields and thereby generate conflicts with the existing fields of other players. The arena itself may have different boundaries for different observers and actors (the village, the region, the country, the *umma*), but as a platform of communication, it seldom exceeds the confines of Bengal and the Bengali community. Bengal is the immediate cultural and linguistic complex and the Bengali language the medium in which this competition takes place. This space has of course been bifurcated ever since 1947 due to the political separation of West and East Bengal, which has also generated a certain communication gap within it. With this in mind, we can nevertheless, for all practical purposes, speak of an 'arena of Bengali Islam'.

What complicates the picture is, of course, that this arena is not usually marked symbolically: the players do not compete in the name of some empirical notion of Bengali Islam but in that of Islam as a normative entity. It is this target notion of Islam that plays out in this arena. This notion, as it were, is not necessarily coterminous with any cultural-geographical entity such as the 'Islamic world', but rather addressed as an essentialised entity beyond history – even though it affords

23 I regard songs as the traditionally oral domain here and not as a part of classical scripturalist culture, notwithstanding the fact that this domain has undergone scripturalisation as well during the last one hundred years or so. Cf. the following remarks.

24 At least in as far as the Maijbhandari case suggests.

manifold connections with historical constructions. There is consent among the players regarding some of the parameters of this symbolic notion, such as the authoritativeness of the *Qur'ān* and the model character of the Prophet's life; and dissent regarding others, such as the status of the Prophet (human or divine), the evaluation of other scriptures (*Ḥadīṯ*) and later traditions, the orthopraxy to be derived from the scriptures, etc. One might thus also speak of the target notion of Islam as a centre of gravity that controls the movements in the space it generates – its arena – like a pole. The players, in order to assert their position in that arena, are forced to conform to and direct their actions towards that pole; they must use certain iconic features identified with Islam for self-definition. The symbolic, idealised notion of Islam thus constitutes the outer confine of the various discursive fields; it is in their reference to this centre of gravity, or pole, that they overlap. They cannot possibly loosen their adherence to it since that would take them out of the arena governed by it.

At this point, we can reconcile the disparaging views of the two Maijbhandari *pīr*s quoted in the very beginning of this book. They speak about different *levels* of Islam: admitting the possibility of indigenous Islam refers, of course, to the arena of Bengali Islam which may bear plenty of indigenous traces, while the target notion of Islam can be conceived only as a unity. This target notion of Islam, however, also has different levels to it, as hinted above: ideally it is situated in a congealed, 'frozen' time and space far beyond geographical and historical Arabia,[25] and on this level of consideration the modern Middle East is in no way more central in it than Bengal – except, maybe, that the holy scriptures and places of Islam are linguistically and geographically more easily accessible from there.[26] On another level, however, there are links through time and space that can connect individuals or institutions to that target notion,[27] and the different players try to establish their affiliations with it in various ways. Thus, however far the idealised notion of Islam may be removed from ordinary life, it retains a certain historical and geographical accessibility. The players in the arena of Bengali Islam may display either genealogical or spiritual affiliations (mostly both together),[28] suggesting that they are themselves carriers of the undiluted substance of Islam; they may claim an extremely close acquaintance with whatever they feel authentically constitutes that centre of gravity, that is, most prominently the *Qur'ān*; or they

25 A borrowing from Benedict Anderson's *Imagined Communities* (1983).

26 Cf. the remarks in Rahul Peter Das 1997: 3 f. on Krishna's divine play as 'eternal' or 'outside time'; also Dimock 1989: 165 ff. on the Vaishnava concept of an eternal Vrindavan. Though situated in a completely different religious context, these remarks do seem to hold true equally for Islam; cf., for instance, the implications of the concept of *nūr* as elaborated in Section 3.2, and also the general timelessness of myth (cf. Rahul Peter Das 1997: 4, with reference to Mircea Eliade).

27 This again affords a parallel with Vaishnavism; on the localisation or manifestation of time- and spaceless Vrindavan in geographic space (temples, etc.), see the article by Friedhelm Hardy (1983).

28 Compare, in this connection, also the remarks in Geertz 1968: 50 on multiple ratios of legitimacy among the Marabouts of Morocco.

may do both. These ways of affiliation express a certain valorisation of cultural imports by giving higher value to that which has directly come from the historical and geographic setting where this idealised notion is historically allocated. They impose centre–fringe relationships between the 'Islamic heart-lands' – a concept very congenial to such thinking – and the Bengali periphery. The genealogical argument seems more archaic in symbolising the diffusion of Islam by the spread of body substance, whereas the scripture-based argument appears more abstract and modernist.

While both these ways of setting up links with the target notion of Islam are hierarchising, they are nevertheless different with regard to the relations their respective exotisms allow them to have with Bengal, namely the actual communicative arena in which they try to assert themselves. The former is part of the Sufi-settler paradigm developed by Richard Eaton; the migration of Saiyads to the delta took place in the Middle Ages, and they thus had sufficient time – following this type of thinking – to 'fertilise' and 'sanctify', that is, infuse with Islam, the 'Bengali soil'.[29] It is crucial to this argument that the diffusion of Islam was effected by people from the 'centre'; but it leaves enough space for the evolution of sub-centres in having some of the inherent auspiciousness of idealised Islam reverberate on Bengali ground and celebrate this, for example, in the form of shrine veneration.[30] The latter argument, by contrast, in its exclusive reliance on affiliation to the original message of Islam as laid down in the scriptures, imposes limits to such sanctifications of the locality; it also denies in great part the validity of the Islam that had been spread in the Middle Ages, viewing it as something that has to be purged of all local imprints.

Moreover, since the arena of Bengali Islam does not exist in the void, but coincides with other arenas – or in other words, since it finds itself in a cultural and political context, and must be made accessible to people living in this context in order to be functional – it is equally important that the single discursive fields establish connectivity with these other arenas. Most prominently, new modes of rationality, under the great bracket of modernity, must be tackled, and new community formations must be correlated. In the case of scientific modernity, as we have mentioned, the different fields in the arena of Bengali Islam partake of a number of shared notions, however different their ultimate evaluations may be; and it seems not possible to assign short-hand labels of 'modernity' or 'tradition-

29 Cf. Richard Eaton's analysis of the hagiographies of Shah Jalal; this saint was given a handfull of earth in Mecca and sent eastward by his master with the task of settling down wherever he would find soil matching the lump he had with him, which was in Sylhet (Eaton 1993: 212 f.)

30 With the disappearance of Persian and Urdu in present Bengal, one decisive marker of distinction is, of course, no longer existent, and there is no doubt that Bengali *pīrs* today would display allegiances to the modern nation states not only in Bangladesh but also in India. The point seems to be that they are Bangladeshis or Indians *who have once been Arabs* – in a similar way as Gellner points out for the role of Latin in Europe ('[. . .] to be a gentleman one does not need to know Latin and Greek, but one must have forgotten them'; Gellner 1983: 72).

ality' to these discursive fields.[31] As regards modern community formations, it is especially interesting to consider the connectivity to nationalism as *the* dominant community ideology of modernity, and the way the discursive fields in question relate to what is debated as 'Bengali' and 'Bangladeshi' types of nationalism. We have touched on this issue with regard to Maijbhandar in Section 7.4. Also here, generalised judgements are not feasible without much more substantial research. In principle, the discursive fields of both shrine veneration and reformism are connectable to each of these brands of nationalism and can be expected to be closely linked to the cultural and political domains. Their fate thus seems to be up for negotiation also in the symbolic arena of Bengaliness. It is tied up with the competition between a national ethos of assimilation and cultural distinctiveness on the one hand and one of cultural homogenisation, bracketed by an essentially trans-Bengali version of Islam, on the other.

But whatever route this development takes, and despite the growing impact of transnational communication flows on all the fields in this arena, the cultural and linguistic givens will most probably warrant the continuation of an empirical arena of 'Bengali Islam' as the immediate communicative context of the religious currents in question; and it would block our perceptions if we were to dismiss it. The term 'Bengali Islam', far from reifying the object it describes or denying the multiple extra-Bengali links that inform it, has the advantage of being a proper meta-category: nobody 'believes' in it in the sense of a separate faith, but nobody can disclaim its empirical existence along the lines proposed here, either. It can thus be used as an unbiased denominator and seems a viable and necessary label for focusing research on a chronically de-focused entity.

31 Common to all quarters, on the level of informal utterances, is the assertion that Islam not only supports, but actually prescribes the acquisition of knowledge, which is interpreted as a legitimisation of modern science and technology. All possible knowledge is claimed to be contained in the Qur'ān, and if science may in some cases appear to go against the Qur'anic word, this is taken to be merely a temporary condition due to the incompleteness of scientific knowledge, which will be removed gradually as the latter approaches completion. A detailed appreciation of this issue would have to take into account much scattered material. The topic is not unpopular in Bengal; I could witness a meeting with natural scientists, organised by a Sufi society in Chittagong City, in 2001, where such questions were discussed at length. Cf., in this context, publications such as *Scientific Indications in the Sunna* (Mannan 1997) which, though apparently stemming from reformist quarters, cut across different discursive fields in their effects. A similar Maijbhandari publication is the serial *Is'lām, kur'ān o bijñān* by Md. Abdul Mannan in the journal Jīban'bāti. Geertz (1968: 105) attributes such approaches to 'scripturalists', and this seems to hold for Bengal also; but we see that boundaries are permeable enough to allow them to become common property.

Appendix I

Translations of selected Maijbhandari songs

1 Aliullah Rajapuri, *PN* No.33

kire man haoc nā bedār, āilire tui kon bājār/ekhan'tak cin'li nā tui tomār āiẏur jīban jār // dauṛiteche āẏu tomār, kon gāṛite haïlā chaoār // keẏāmate ṣṭeśan, rākhiẏāche par'oār thāmenā gāṛi tor, tomār rāstār nāhi or* caileche gāṛi thāme nā, rāstā bahut dur* upar diẏā cail'che gāṛi, ei gāṛite michā bāṛī* nice diẏā cail'che gāṛi, sei gāṛite kebā kār* ei gāṛite māler bojhāi, sei gāṛite keha nāi/gāṛir nāi nirākār, ki kairāca tār jogār + gāṛi yakhan andha habe, hechāb ketāb śuru habe // sei kathāni mane āche ki ki upāẏ kailyā tār* yadi thāke mane tomār, śabda śobhā nāi ār // mārā nāhi jābe gāṛi, chālāmate habe pār* kahe hīna rājāpuri, bābār caraṇ kare dhari* tākat nāhi āche mor, ditām āmi prem sā̃tār**[1]

O mind, do you not become aware to which market you have come?
Have you not yet recognised [him] to whom the life of your life-span belongs?
Your life-span is running; on which train is it travelling?
The station is the Day of Justice, the Patron has put it there.
Your train does not halt, your path has no direction.
The train has started and does not stop, the way is very long.
[One] train is running above; this train is the wrong home.
[Another] train is running below; who has to do with whom on that train?
Goods are loaded on this [former] train; on that [latter] train there is nobody.
The leader [lit. 'boatman'] of the train is shapeless, have you secured him?
When the train becomes dark, the book of accounts shall be opened [lit. begin].
You do remember this matter; what provisions have you made for it?
If you remember, no more words are befitting.
The train will not die, it will set over safely.
Holding the Father's feet in his hands, the humble Rajapuri says:
I do not have power – [had I,] I would swim in love.

1 The somewhat idiosyncratic punctuation of the original has been retained here.

2 Ramesh Shil, *ND* No.6

tumi damer kale putul nācāo cin·te pāri nā./nije putul taiẏār kare nije ḍhuke tār bhitare,/hāsa gāo nāca khela, tomār kār'khānā // andha āmi paṅgu āmi, badhir āmi, bobā āmi,/āmār āmi seota tumi āmi kichu nā // duniẏār ghāṇīte juri [sic], pāk· ditecha māij'bhāṇḍārī,/kalur balad ghure mari cakṣu dile nā,/nācane āẏu abasān, ei nācane nāi ki phurān,/(tomār) rameś putul nāciẏe haẏ'rān, ār nācāionā //

You play the puppet in the breath channel,[2] I cannot recognize [you].
Making the puppet yourself, and entering yourself into it,
You laugh, sing, dance and play, [it is] your contrivance.
I am blind, I am lame, I am deaf, I am dumb,
My 'I' is also you, there is nothing [like an] 'I'.
You tie me to the oil-mill of the world and turn me round, O Maijbhandari,
[As the] ox of the oil-presser, I turn to death, [and] you did not even look,
In this dance, life ends, is there no end to this dance?
Your puppet Ramesh is exasperated, do not make him dance anymore.

3 Ramesh Shil, *SD* No.18

māij'bhāṇḍāre uṭheche tauhīder niśānā/ghumāionā māẏā ghume ākheri jamānā // khed'mate hale dākhil lahuni[3] *habe hāchil,/dosta dos·man samān habe kiser bhābanā // kalab jindā haẏe yābe, mābuder didār(a) pābe,/nijer rūp dekhiẏe habe nije dvioẏānā // āche māij'bhāṇḍārīr doẏā, ki sādhya āj'rāiler choẏā,/rameś bale lā paroẏā, āche māolānā //*[4]

In Maijbhandar the sign of unity has arisen.
Do not sleep the sleep of illusion, O last of times.
If you appear for service, the mystical shall be gained;
Friend and foe shall be the same, there is no worry.
The heart shall became alive, you shall attain the sight of God,
Upon seeing[5] your own form you shall become crazy.
There is the blessing of the Maijbhandari, ʿIzrāʾīl is unable to touch [you],
Ramesh says: Do not worry, the Maulānā is there.

2 *damer kale*: lit. 'in/by the machine of breath'. *Damakal*, however, also means 'pressure pump' as used for fire extinction.

3 Misprint for *laduni*, from Ar. <*ladunī*>, 'mystical', 'esoteric', which underlies my translation.

4 This song deviates from the usual *paẏār* metre in a number of instances and is sung without insertion of inherent *a* vowels.

5 *Dekhiẏe* is usually the absolutive participle of *dekhāna*, 'to show'; but it seems more likely that it is a variant of *dekhe* from *dekhā*, 'to see', and has here been translated as such.

4 Ramesh Shil, *JS* No.17

ājab kārigar bandhu ājab kārigar/prem kācāri taiẏār kari lukāẏe āche tār bhitare // gharer rage rage bān,/hāmāucer ghare āche pūrṇamāsir cā̃n,/naẏ darajā dekh'te sojā dui darajā kābār ghar // bandhu baṛa sandhāni,/jhaṛ bādale jal paṛe nā cām'ṛā di chāni,/sārā ghare ek'ṭi ṭhuni tālā baddha tār upar // bandhur buddhi camatkār,/sthāne sthāne basāẏeche ṭeligrāpher tār,/kalabete jhalak māre palake laẏ sab khabar // khādem rameś bale/bandhu saṅge dekhā habe īmān ṭhik hale,/ īmān bine pāẏ nā tāre gele ek hājār bachar //[6]

A wonderful craftsman is the friend, a wonderful craftsman.
He has completed an office of love and is hidden in it.
There is a flood in each vein of the house.
In the room of *hama ūst*[7] is the full moon.[8]
Nine doors are easy to see, two doors [lead to] the room of the Kaʿba.
The friend is very resourceful.
By giving the roof of the skin, no water comes in from storms and clouds.
There is one rod in the whole house, and its top is locked.
The friend's intellect is fantastic.
He has put telegraph wires at different places.
He throws flashes of light into the heart [and] finds out all news in a moment.
Servant Ramesh says:
[You] shall meet the friend if your faith is correct.
Without faith [you] do not find him even when a thousand years have passed.

5 Abdul Gafur Hali, *JJ* No.69

cala man(a) bhābe basi/priẏā rūpe yoger ghare/prem(a)rase duijan bhese/haẏe yāba ekākāre // chāṛi cala ripugaṇ(a)/haïbe madhur(a) milan(a)/prem(a) niśāẏ bibhor haẏe/sā̃tār diba rūp sāgare // sakal kichu chinna kari/man pākhīre diba chāṛi/kheli khelā priẏār sane/cin'le bāsā ās'be phire // dekh'ba tāre naẏan bhari/ kāndiba tār caraṇ dhari/bal'ba yata maner kathā/basāiẏā hṛd(a) mājāre // (manare) maran [*sic*] *yadi karis bhaẏ(a)/priẏā milan nāhi haẏ(a)/maran* [*sic*] *ḍare gaphur pāg'lā/amarāpur yāite nāre //*

Come on, mind, let us sit in rapture
In the form of the female beloved in the room of *yoga*.
Drifting the two [of us] in the juice of love,
We will become of one shape.
Leave behind the foes,
There will be sweet union;

6 Here, again, the metre is unclear, and the song has been given without insertion of inherent *a* vowels. There is a variant which replaces *bandhu* by *maulā*.

7 'All is He' (Persian), attributed to Jalal al-Din Rumi.

8 More lit. 'the moon of the full moon night'.

overwhelmed by the intoxication of love,
We will swim in the ocean of beauty.
Severing all and everything,
I will set free the mind-bird.
Let me play a game with the female beloved.
She will come back if she knows her home.
I will gaze at her to my eyes' content,
Grasp her feet and cry,
Tell [her] all intimate tidings
After placing her inside the heart.
(O mind) If you are afraid of death,
The union with the female beloved does not happen.
For fear of death crazy Gafur
Cannot go to the city of immortality.

6 Abdul Gafur Hali, *JJ* No.5

bhābe maj'li nā re man(a) pāg'lā haïli nā/pāg(a)lā kon bhābe thāke tāito bujh'li nā // ek(a) pāg'lā bā̃śī bājāẏ, koṭi koṭi pāgal nācāẏ,/ār ek pāgal gācher talāẏ kar'che āstānā // cām'ṛār cokhe dekhli bhūban, jānli nāre nije keman/āpan rūp(a) dekh'bi yakhan habi dioẏānā // saṃsār mājhe sabāi pāgal, keubā āsal keubā nakal,/marār āge mare eman pāgal kaẏ janā //

You did not immerse yourself in rapture, O mind, you did not go crazy.
You did not understand in which way the crazy behave [*thāke*].
One crazy person plays the flute, makes tens of millions of crazy ones dance,
Another crazy one makes his dwelling under a tree.
You saw the world with the eyes of skin, you did not learn how the self is.
When you see your own form, you will go mad.
All in the world are crazy, one truly, the other falsely.
How many crazy ones are there who die before dying?

7 Badrunnesa Saju, *Madirā* No.26

dhyānī prabhu/sādhak bābā/smaraṇer kāṇḍārī/saṅkaṭ mājhe/tomār kāche/esechi bhikhārī // phuler ghrāṇe/subātās bahe/ai dvār āji/ruddha nahe/phuler surabhi/ āne ḍāki/musāphir sāri sāri // prem ḍāke bhāṇḍārī // bhikṣā/cāi manib/śuṣkaprāṇe/ nirjīb mane/sajībatā dāo/prakhar dṛṣṭibāne // ai cāhoni/śreṣṭha madir/kebal'i jharāẏ/ā̃khi nīr;/duḥkha mocane/premik sujane.[9]

Immersed Lord, ascetic father, helmsman of recalling,
I, a beggar, have come to you in this predicament.

9 The metre of this song, or rather poem, does not correspond to the traditional metres usually used for Maijbhandari songs.

A pleasant breeze blows with the fragrance of flowers.
That door is not shut today.
The aroma of the flowers attracts rows and rows of travellers.
Love calls out for the Bhandari.
With a dry soul, O master, I ask for alms,
Instill liveliness into my lifeless mind with the sharp arrow of your glance.
The best wine only makes tears flow for the removal of sorrow, for the lover friend.

8 Maulana Abdul Hadi, *RB* No.26

cala priẏā prem bāgāne taba saṅge prem kheliba/prema raṅge raṅg [= *raṅ*] *miśāẏe kuñjabane raṅg kheliba // siṃhāsane basāiba, buke buke miśāiba/dui jane prem(a) bhore preme miśe ek(a) haba // tumi āmi ek(a) haba, ek(a) bhinna nā rahiba,/ākāś(a) pātāl(a) ādi tribhubane ek(a) raba // raṅgete kalikā haba, ek(a) raṅga*[10] *puṣpa haba,/ek(a) raṅge ali haïẏe prem(a) phuler madhu khāba // raṅge hādī duḥkhī jan(a), raṅge habe nurītan(a),/raṅge gāuch(a) dhan(a)*[11] *naẏaner(a) āñjan haba //*

Come on, beloved [lady], into the garden of love, I want to play love with you.
Mixing colour into the sports of love I want to play love in the grove.
I will put you on the throne, press you to my breast.
In the dawn of love, we two shall be united in love and become one.
I and you shall become one, we will not remain anything but united.
In the sky, the underworld and so on, in all the three worlds we will remain one.
In sport, I will be a bud, in one sport, I will be a flower.
In one [more] sport, I will be a saint and drink the honey of the flower of love.
In sport Hadi is the sad one, in sport I will acquire a body of light.
In sport I will become a stye on the eyelid of my dearest Ġawṯ.

9 Maulana Abdul Hadi, *RB* No.19

majechi tomāri preme svarga sukh(a) cāhinā/ki kariba svarga sukhe tor bhābete dioānā [*sic*] *// bālākhānā hur(a) dale, cāhibanā ākhi tule/tomār(a) dāmān(a) tale dās(a) gaṇer ṭhikānā // hāśarer(a) maẏ'dānete, daptar(a) laïẏā hāte/nāciba gajal(a) pare* [*sic*] *tor bhābete mastānā // prem(a) miśāmiśi khelā, kheliba*[12] *hāśar(a) belā/tomār(a) sāmāte hādī jhāmpa diba par'oẏānā //*

10 Read: *raṅge*.

11 Probably erroneous for *dhaner*.

12 The text has *khāiba*, 'I will eat/drink', which seems to be a misprint for *kheliba*, ' will play', as given above.

Your love is what I have immersed myself in, I do not want the joy of heaven.
What should I do with the joy of heaven, [being] crazy in your trance?
I will not lift my eyes [to] the upper rooms [and] the group of heavenly maidens.
Under your coat-tails is the place of your servants.
On the Field of Judgment, with the account-book in my hands,
I will dance and recite ghazals, mad in your trance.
At the time of the Last Judgment, I will play the game of intermingling in love.
Into your music session I, Hadi, will jump [like a] moth.

10 Bajlul Karim Mandakini, *PH* No.16

(āmi) manipurer svādhin rājā, kar dinā kāre/bhut(a) pret(a) yata āche ḍare āmāre // prabal(a) pratāpe mor(a), śatru kā̃pe thar(a) thar(a)/trijagat(a) jaẏ kariba, alpa din pare // jīb(a)jantu, mahitale, āmār(a) ādeś(a) cale/ṣolaśata gopīsenā, cale chaudhāre // kābā kā̃śī br̥ndāban(a), sarbbatra mor bicaraṇ(a)/rāj(a)dhānī, mandākinīr uttar(a) pāre // śiber bare śakti dhari bijaẏ(a) ghoṣaṇā kari/svarga-matya [*sic*, for *martya*] *kā̃pe tāi, mor(a) huṅkāre // siṃhal(a) bijaẏ(a) ha'la, padmābatī hāte ela/ nityānanda dhabjā* [*sic*, for *dhvajā*] *dhare, purir(a) dvāre // bujh'te nā pārile kathā, gurupade rākha māthā/karimer(a) saṅge cala, māij(a)bhāṇḍāre //*

I am the independent king of Maṇipur, I do not pay taxes to anybody.
All the ghosts and spirits there are fear me.
The enemies tremble, [terrified] by my strong prowess.
I will vanquish the three worlds after a few days.
The beings and animals on earth follow my orders.[13]
The army of sixteen hundred milkmaids walk on [my] four sides.
At the Ka'ba, at Kashi and Vrindavan, everywhere I move around.
The capital is on the northern side of Mandakini.
Having acquired power from Shiva's boon, I proclaim victory.
Heaven and earth tremble, therefore, before my roars.
Sinhala has been vanquished, Padmavati has been taken over,
Nityananda is holding the flag at the door of Puri.
If you cannot understand [these] words, put your head at the feet of the guru.
Come with Karim to Maijbhandar.

11 Bajlul Karim Mandakini, *Premāñjalī* No.3 (Persian in Bengali script)

jehib jame gulestānast', em'śab/nattākhā [*sic*, misprint for *naoẏākhā̃*, P. <*navāḫān*>] *bul'bule jānast' – em'śab // āruchā̃chap kasīdā, eẏāstādand'/hāmācū̃*

13 Lit.: '[On] the beings and on earth, my order is in operation.'

car'be bostānast' – em'śab // jamīāj gul-bagul hām'raṅg' gastā/baraṅge bāge rej'oẏānast'– em'śab // baraṅge jop·le āmbar chāẏ āh'bab/jaoẏāneb chombastānast' – em'śab // ba āhāṅge nāẏ'o caṅg'o majāmīr/ājab lāle ājījā nast' – em'śab // ājījā kheś·rā gom kar'd ek'char/bechāle eẏār juyyā̃nast'– em'śab // malāek tāh'niẏāt·goyyā̃ belākārab/śabe kad·re raphā kānast' – em'śab //[14]

Gold is the assembly of the flower garden this night.
The nightingale of the soul is making music this night.
The brides are standing, aligned in rows.
All is like the bounty of the garden this night.
All the different flowers have become one colour.
This night has the colour of the garden of paradise.
In the colour of a lock of amber, like the beloved, are the sides [. . .][15] this evening.
[Surrounded by] the sound of the reed flute and the harp and the incense vessels
Is the magnificient ruby of the beloved ones this night.
The female beloved have hidden themselves completely.
All the beloved of the year have appeared this night.
The angels are congratulating those standing by.
It is the night of fate of the friends, this night.

12 Abdul Ghani Kanchanpuri, *ĀB* p.111f. (Persian)

sag-i darbār-i ġauṯ-i pāk-i mā'iğbhand'ārī šav ā'ī dil/ki az šuruf-i hamīn nisbat šavat qarb-i ẖudā hāṣil // agar qarb-i ẖudā ẖvāhī baḏayl 'išq-i ū zan čang/ki az 'išq-aš šavī ā'ī dil tū dar 'išq-i ẖudā kāmil // tū yik nīm nigāh-aš-rā dilā har dam niga mīdār/ki az nīm nigāh-i ū šavī tū bā-ẖudā vāṣil // zi ğān va dīn va dil baguḏar banām o nang ẖaṭ bar kaš/zi ḏayl-i 'išq-i ū dost-i[16] *dil-at zi nihār-i bīn magusal // čū gar don pā'ī būs-i ẖāk-i kū'ī-š pāš payvasta/ki az ẖūršīd va mah ẖāk-aš fazūntar hast dar manzil // ba ta'ẓīm dar pāk-aš čirā sarhā furū nāyand/ki bar kūnayn in'ām-aš biyāmad fā'iż va šāmil // bağuz-i mihir-aš kasī kāndar dil-aš inkār-i ū bāšad/būd ṭā'āt-i ū żā'i' būd a'māl-i ū bāṭil // būd maqbūl-i dargāh-aš yaqīn-i maqbūl-i yazdānī/qabūl-i ū dalīl-i vāṯiq-i har banda'i maqbul.*

14 Reconstruction of the somewhat distorted text as it ought to read in Persian script: <*ḏahab ğam'-i gulistān ast imšab/navāẖān bulbul-i ğān ast imšab // 'arusān ṣaf kašīda istādand/hama čūn čarb-i bustān ast imšab // ğamī' az gul-bagul hamrang gašta/barang-i bāġ-i riżvān ast imšab // barang-i zulf-i anbar say aḥbāb/ğavānib* [. . . *chombastān* unidentfied] *ast imšab // ba āhang-i nay wa čang wa muğāmir/'ağab la'l-i 'azīzān ast imšab // 'azīzān ẖvīšrā gum kard yiksar/ba sāl-i yār ğūyān ast imšab // malā'īk tahniyyat gūyā bā 'l-qarab/śab-i qadr-i rafīqān ast imšab //*>.

15 The lines *baraṅge jop·le āmbar chāẏ āh'bab/jaoẏāneb chombastānast' – em'śab //* are a riddle to the present translator and the scholars of Persian he has consulted. *Jop·le* seems to stand for *zulf-i*, but no explanation for *chombastān* could be found.

16 *dast* in the original; read as an erroneous spelling of *dost* since *dast* 'hand' makes no sense here.

Become the dog of the court of the pure leader of Maijbhandar, O heart,
So that from the closeness of this relationship closeness to God may be gained.
If you want closeness to God, play the harp to His [i.e. the Ġawṯ's] love,
So that from this love you may become perfect, O heart, in the love of God.
Watch out attentively always for half a glance of His,[17]
So that through half a glance of His you may reach God.
Pass by your life, religion and heart; part with name and shame,
From the jacket seam of the love of that friend of your heart, do not be broken by fear of separation.
Like when you stay continuously with both feet kissing the dust of his lane,
For His dust at His place is more extravagant than the sun and the moon.
Why are, at the prostration to His holiness, the heads not lowered [to the ground],
So that His present may come to the two worlds plentifully and all-encompassingly?
If, devoid of His love, there is a pit in one's heart, [and] negation of Him,
One's veneration is useless, and one's deeds in vain.
[If] one has been accepted at His court, one's faith is accepted and perfect,
His acceptance is the permanent proof of every accepted disciple.

13 Shafiul Bashar, *YB* No.4

nūrī keś(a), nūrī beś(a), nūrānī badan(a)/māij'bhāṇḍārī sonār putul, nūrī bābā dhan(a) // nūrī camak tā̃hār bhāle, ā̃khite bij(a)li khele/dhanur mata nāk mubārak sundar(a) gaṭhan(a) // pūrṇa śaśadharer mata, mukh mobārak abirata/jvalite āche yena jochanār kiraṇ(a) // manohar(a) lambā galā dekhile man haẏ utalā/ palakete chuṭe yāẏ(a) cumu khete man(a) // ājab khubi sinār māje, yār(a) mājhe āllāh rāje/gupta byakta sakal elem yekhāne sr̥jan(a) // hāt du'khānā niṭol lambā raṃ tār yena phoṭā campā/jaṛiẏe dite cāẏ yena premer āliṅgan(a) // tul'tule kadam du'khāni, dekhile nā māne prāṇī/ājab(a) khob'churat yena nūrānī gaṭhan(a) // dvīn(a) śaphi śaktihīn(a), dite nāhi pāre cin(a)/kul makh'luk(a) yā̃hār nūre haẏeche sr̥jan(a) //

Hair of light, clothes of light, a face of light,
The golden puppet of Maijbhandar, the father-treasure of light.
A flash of light is on his forehead, lightning plays in his eyes.
His blessed nose is beautifully built, like a bow.
His blessed face, like the full moon, is always
Glowing like rays of moonlight.
When seeing his charming long neck, the mind becomes agitated
And runs to kiss him at the same moment.

17 *dalā/dilā* is enigmatic and could not be translated.

A magnificient beauty is in his chest, in which Allah resides.
Where every kind of knowledge, secret and manifest, is created.
His two arms are flawlessly long, their colour is like a flourishing *campā*,
As if they want to embrace you [in] an embrace of love.
His two feet are very soft, unbelievable for a being when it sees them,
Wondrously beautiful [is he], as if [he had] a structure of light.
Humble Shafi is powerless, he cannot point out him
From whose light all beings have been created.

14 Lutfunnesa Hosaini, *GP* No.4

katakāl(a) base āchi tomār(a) pāne cāhiẏā – śaphibābā/man pākhīre rākhˈtām dhare hr̥daẏe bā̃dhiẏā // pāẏe ditām śikal rūpār hāte ditām bālā sonār – śakhire/ gale ditām phuler mālā tomāẏ parāiẏā // binā tā̃rer [sic] *phon basāitām dile dile kathā kaïtām – bābāre/ejaname dulu’r kānnā yāita thāmiẏā //*[18]

How long have I been sitting, looking toward you, Shafi Baba!
Had I held tight the bird of the mind and locked it in my heart,
I would have put chains of silver to its feet, golden bangles to its hands,
  O bosom friend.
I would have dressed a garland of flowers around your neck.
I would have installed a wireless phone, I would talk from heart to heart,
  O father.
[In this way] Dulu’s crying in this life would have come to an end.

15 Farid Hosain, *SB* No.73

oẏān ḍe naṣṭa haïbe deha isṭimār/ṭāim haïle bek karibe/guchāiẏā sab kāj kārabār // 1. manˈre – āgun pāni hāoẏār bale/yata sakal iñjin cale/yemˈni ghuṛāẏ temˈni cale kāj kārˈbār sāreṃ beṭār/āmār baḍi haẏ isṭimār/māinḍ haïla sāreṃ ihār/phranṭete haẏ(a) ṭu lāiṭār rāstā dekhāẏ pariṣkār // 2. manˈre – śona tomāẏ jijñās kari/uttar dio satya kari/kata ki praphiṭ kariẏā basāilā raṅger bājār/kām ribhārer lāin dhariẏā/lāiph bharā gelā cālāiẏā/lach praphiṭ hisāb kariẏā nadīte yāoẏā beṭār // 3. manˈre – isṭimārˈṭi olḍ haïle/oẏārˈkārerā yāibe cale/ayatane rākhˈbe phele caṙˈbe nā re pecheñjār/thākˈte jāhāj calār yogya/cinnā nere hatabhāgya/muni r̥ṣi kāmel bijña sakali tār tābedār // 4. manˈre – pharid pāgˈlāẏ kaẏ bhābiẏā/svarūpe jāhāj bānāiẏā/bhabete āiḍenṭi [sic] *diẏā nirākār karˈche ākār/chaül chila ākār śūnya/ jāhāj caïrā haïla dhanya/ei oẏārlḍe mānuṣ bhinna keha nāire śreṣṭha ār //*[19]

18 The metre of this song appears to be a *tripadī* (8/8/13), and the first line has been given with the vocalisations required for that metre.

19 Except for the irregular refrain and the interjections (*manˈre*), this song is in *paẏār* verses of 16 syllables (and sometimes 15 in the concluding line); the *tripadī* form of presentation is misleading, but has been retained here as in the original (though not in the translation).

One day the body-steamer shall break down.
Take it back when the time comes, setting all work in order.
1. O mind – all the engines work by the force of fire, water and air,
As they wind around, the captain's business works out.
My body is a steamer, the mind is its captain.
In the front are two lights, they show the way clearly.
2. O mind – listen, let me ask you, [and] answer honestly:
What have you gained as profit by setting up a market of play?
Taking to the line of the river of lust, you drove onwards your whole life.
It is better to go along the river by calculating loss and profit.
3. O mind – when the steamer becomes old, the workers will go away.
They will leave [it] without care, [and] no passengers will mount it.
When the ship is still apt to move, realize, O miserable one,
The *muni*s, *ṛṣi*s, perfect ones and knowers, all are its servants.
4. O mind – crazy Farid says, pondering, by making the ship in the true form
[And] giving it an identity in the world, [he] makes the shapeless shaped.
The soul was without shape, it was gratified when mounting the ship.
In this world nobody is more superior than man.

16 Aziz, *Maẏ'nā jagat* II, No.18

tumi dāser keb'lā kābā thāka tumi hṛd'mājāre/līlā tomār raṅ'bājāre najar tomār sarbastare // ajñānatār andhakāre jvīn phereś·tār bhaẏe mari/rasik sujan pār kāṇḍārī ācha tumi dehajuṛe // sarbaghāṭe ācha tumi āmi tumi se to tumi/tumi bine se kon jāni tauhider'i prem sāgare // tomāẏ yārā smaraṇ kare jvīn phereś·tā yābe dūre/mānik jvale ādhār [*sic*] *ghare ḍubibe se jñān sāgare // ājij tomār svadeś'bāsī yāhā kara tāhā khuśī/khuśī bejār līlā tomār tumi ācha tomār ghare //*

You are the Qibla Ka'ba of the servant, you dwell in the middle of the heart.
Your play is at the market of colours,[20] your glance is on every level.
In the darkness of ignorance, I die from fear of *ğinn* and angels.
You expert, friend, ferryman, you are all over [my] body.
You are on all quays, I, you and he is [all] you.
Whom except you do I know there in the love-ocean of unity?
[For] those who remember you, the *ğinn* and angels will go away.
A jewel glows in the dark room, it will drown in the ocean of love.
Aziz, your compatriot, is happy, whatever you do.
Happy [or] sulky, [it is] your play, you are in your room.

20 *raṅ'bājār*: also a market in Dhaka.

17 Tajul Islam, *Jāloẏāẏe śaphi bhāṇḍār No.22*

torā āẏ'go āẏ gopigaṇ śīghra kare āẏ/ājab śāne khelā kare saphicānd' bābāẏ // 7i phālgun dar'bārete, kalir(a) jīb(a) tarāite/pāpī-tāpī uddhārite, esechen bābāẏ // paśu pākhī tārā sabe, ānandete mete uṭhe/hur parī pherestā sabe, jaẏ(a) dhvani gāẏ // āśek bhāirā dale dale, snān karāba golāb jale/sājāiba phule phule, ātar ḍhele gāẏ // mānab rūp calanā-kare [*sic*, *<chalanā>*], *udaẏ hale māij'bhāṇḍāre/ṭik cinechi māolā tore, ār to keha naẏ // iuchupher(a) rūp(a) dhari, trijagat'ke pāgal kari/ tājal tomār rūp(a) heri, caraṇe luṭāẏ //*

Come on, O come on, milkmaids, come fast /
In wonderful glory Shafi *cā̃d* [‘moon’] Baba plays.
Baba has come to the *darbār* on the seventh of Phālgun
To bring across the beings of the *kaliyuga* and save the sinners.
Animals and birds all are maddened with joy.
The maidens of paradise and angels all sing cries of victory.
O *ʿašīq* brothers, in groups we shall bathe him in rose water,
Adorn him with flowers, pouring perfumes on his body.
Pretending to human form, you arose in Maijbhandar.
I have recognised you correctly, O Maula, nobody else exists.
[You who are] taking the form of Yusuf and making the three worlds crazy –
Tajul beholds your form [and] rolls at your feet.

18 Abul Kasem, *Premākar No.22*

din thākite bhāba sabe gāuce māij bhāṇḍār/gāuce māij bhāṇḍārī bine upāẏ nāire ār // satya-tretā dvāparete, kali ār arāyugete,/pāpī-tāpī uddhārite sādhya āche kār // ruhānī prem pracār kari, chaẏ(a)janer bandhan tuṛi,/cin-māolār caraṇ dhari ekatva svīkār // gāphele paṛe āpanār,/nāhi yābe ye māij bhāṇḍār/nā pābe khodār didār nāhi tār nistār // dhari māolājīr caraṇ, nij'ke nije āge cin/nā haẏ dvīn-duniẏā-dhan(a) sakali asār // ataeb, bhābanā cheṛe, śīghra cala māij bhāṇḍāre,/kāsem bale upāi nāire nā haïle ār.

Think, everybody, as long as there is time, [of] the Ġauṯ of Maijbhandar.
Except the Ġawṯ of Maijbhandar, there is no other means.
In the *satya*, *tretā*, *dvāpara*, *kali* and anarchy[21] ages
Who is capable of rescuing the sinful and afflicted?
Spreading spiritual love, breaking the bondage of the six
[And] holding the feet of the known Mawlā, oneness is accepted.
He who, becoming careless of himself, will not go to Maijbhandar,
Will not attain the sight of God, and is not saved.
Holding the feet of the Mawlā, first know yourself [by] yourself.

21 *arāyug* does not exist in the Bengali lexicon; it seems to blend *arājakete*, ‘in that which is anarchic’, with *yuge*, ‘in the age’, and has thus been rendered as ‘[in the] anarchy age’ here.

If not, religion, the world, riches are all futile.
So, give up the worries and come fast to Maijbhandar.
Kasem says, otherwise there is no other means.

19 Syed Abdul Monayem, *Ākuti* No.3

prem pather diśārī moder īchāpurī māolānā/basāẏechen premer bājār īchāpure āstānā // māẏer garbhe elen yakhan tā̃r mā mani svapan dekhen/kole tā̃hār hāsitechen baṛa pīr(a) maolānā // bhāṇḍāre yān śaiśabete haj(a)rat keb'lār khed'mate/balen tini mukhe tomār hācchāner(a) namunā // kaiśore svapane tā̃hār haïla nabīr(a) dīdār(a)/takhan hate prāṇ(a) haẏ tā̃r nabī preme deoẏānā // dvīnī elam kare hāchil tvarikate halen dākhil/satya hala jībane tā̃r prabhū [*sic* for *prabhu*] *premer sādhanā // haj(a)rater se pāk bānī hala saphal likhen tini/haj(a)rater jīban bānī kar'te tā̃ri bandanā // dvīnī elem sārā kari man cāẏ'nā duniẏādārī/murśider najare halen bibhu preme mastānā // bābājāner nek najare el'meladun hāchil kare/āmale ekine tā̃hār dvidhā dandha* [*sic* for *dvandva*] *raïlanā // belāẏet khijirī sudhā miṭhālo tā̃r prāṇer kṣudhā/likhani sacal(a) sadā peẏe bibhur karuṇā // khodā premer pathik yārā nā haẏ yena path(a)hārā/tāder tare grantha śata karen tini racanā // nirabe puṛiẏā dhūp(a) gandha bilāẏ aparūp(a)/khodā premer udāsīder parāne deẏ sāntanā* [*sic* for *sāntvanā*] *// īchāpurī amūlya dhan mane prāṇe kari baraṇ/dhariẏāchi tomār caraṇ parān gele chāṛ'ba nā //*

Our guide on the path of love is Isapuri Mawlānā.
He has established a market of love, the abode in Isapur.
When he came into the mother's womb, his mother dreamt of a pearl.
On her lap was laughing the great *pīr* Mawlānā.
He went to [Maij-] Bhandar in childhood to the service of Ḥażrat Qibla.
He [the latter] said: 'Your face resembles that of Hasan'.[22]
In his youth he beheld the Prophet in a dream.
From then on his life-breath was mad in the love of the Prophet.
Having acquired the [outer] religious knowledge, he submitted himself to the *ṭarīqa*.
His perseverence for the love of the Lord came true in life.
That holy saying of the Ḥażrat bore fruit, he wrote
The life account of the Ḥażrat in order to praise him.
Having completed the religious sciences he did not feel like [taking up] wordly matters.
Through the glance of the *muršid* he became intoxicated in the love of God.
By the auspicious glance of Bābājān he acquired mystical knowledge.
In deed and faith, no hesitation or conflict remained for him.
The *wilāya*, Ḥiḍr's alcohol, quenched the thirst of his life-breath.
The pen remained always in motion, by receiving the mercy of the Lord.

22 Lit., 'in your face is a sample of Hasan'.

In order for the wanderers on [the path of] God's love not to lose track,
He composed a hundred books for them.
Burning in the quiet, the incense stick spreads a wonderful scent.
It gives consolation to the hearts [*parāṇ*] of those indifferent from the love of God.
Isapuri, the priceless treasure, I accept with mind and heart.
I have grasped your feet and will no let them go [even] if my life-breath [*prāṇ*] leaves me.

20 Abdul Jabbar Mimnagari, *PR* No.9

āmi tomāẏ prāṇ(a) diẏe pāg(a)linī haẏechi,/atiśaẏ āpan bhābiẏe, prāṇ biliẏe diẏechi // loke bale dionā prāṇ, tabu tomāẏ diẏechi,/dūre phele rākh'be āmāẏ, āge ki tāi jenechi // praṇaẏerī ye yātanā, ekhan theke śikhechi,/bā̃ci yadi bā̃cāo āmāẏ, bipadete parechi [*sic* for *paṛechi*] *// abalā se mim'nagarī, saral prāṇe dionā berī* [*sic* for *beṛī*]*/tumi āmār āmi tomār, tāi manete bhebechi //*

I have given you my heart [*prāṇ*] and become a crazy woman,
Thinking [you] excessively mine, I have given my heart gratuitously.
The people say: 'Don't give your heart', but I have given it to you.
Did I know before that you would keep me pushed into distance?
From now, I have learnt the tortures of love [*praṇaẏ*].
If I survive, save me, I have fallen into danger.
The weak woman[23] is that Mimnagari, don't put my simple heart [*prāṇ*] into chains.
You are mine and I am yours, this is what I have thought to myself.

23 *abalā*, 'the powerless' (f.), is used simply as 'woman', but has been rendered as 'weak woman' here to convey the connotations.

Appendix II

Glossary of terms

This glossary gives English equivalents or very short explanations of frequently used foreign terms. Generally the language of origin of the given form is given in brackets. The glossary is meant exclusively as a practical tool to enable quick reference and facilitate reading. For in-depth characterisations of concepts included here, please refer to the text itself or to other sources.

abatār (Bg.) incarnation
ādhyātmik dhārā (Bg.) stream of spirituality
ʿāšiq (Ar.) lover
bāra āuliẏār deś/bāro āuliẏār deś (Bg.) land of twelve saints, epithet of Chittagong
baraka (Ar.) salutary effluence, blessing
baqāʾ bi-Llah (Ar.) abidance in God, steady union with God while alive
barzaḫ (Ar.) isthmus; the in-between worlds; the inner picture of one's *muršid*
bāšarʿ (P.) (Sufism practised in keeping) with the *šarīʿa*
bāṭin (Ar.) hidden, concealed
bāul gān (Bg.) songs of the Bauls, an esoteric religious group of Bengal
bayʿa (Ar.) initiation
bhāb (Bg.) elevated emotional state, trance
bhakta (Skt.) devotee
bhakti (Skt.) (doctrine and practice of) devotion
bhaṇitā (Bg.) colophon
bhāṭiẏālī (Bg.) a genre of Bengali songs sung by boatmen
bidʿa (Ar.) illegitimate religious innovation
bīšarʿ (P.) (Sufism practised) without heeding the *šarīʿa*
cakra (Skt.) energetic nodes according to the yogico-tantric body concept
čilla (P.) place to practice austerities
darbār (P.) court (kingly and saintly)
dargāh (P.) court (kingly and saintly)
darśan (Bg.) vision

ḏāt (Ar.) essence
dehatattva (Bg.) principles of the body
dharma (Skt./Bg.) law (cosmic, social, religious); religion
dharmanirapekṣatā (Bg.) secularism
ḏikr (Ar.) remembering God's names; the associated Sufi practice
dīn, pl. *adyān* (Ar.) religion
du'ā (Ar.) personal prayer
fanā' fī al-šayḫ (Ar.) annihilation in the spiritual master
fanā' fī-Llāh (Ar.) annihilation in God
faqīr (Ar.) pauper, religious mendicant
farḍ (Ar.) religious duty
fātiha (Ar.) the first *sura* of the *Qur'ān*
fayḍ (Ar.) grace
fiqh (Ar.) Islamic jurisprudence
ğabarūt (Ar.) realm of spirits and prophets
ğāhil (Ar.) ignorant
ğāhiliyya (Ar.) pre-Muhammadian age of ignorance
Ġawṯ al-A'ẓam (Ar.) greatest help, greatest leader (highest rank of a saint)
ġauṯiyya (Ar.) sainthood of highest rank
ghāṭ (Bg.) bank, embankment, ferry-place
ğihād (Ar.) great spiritual effort of eradicating the lower self
ğinn (Ar.) a species of supernatural beings in Islamic mythology
gopī (Skt.) cow-herd girl in Krishna mythology
ğumma namāz (P.) Friday prayers
ḫādim (Ar.) servant of a Sufi master or shrine
ḥağğ (Ar.) pilgrimage to Mecca
ḥāl, pl. *aḥwāl* (Ar.) state (emotive), trance
ḫalīfa (Ar.) a saint's spiritual delegate, deputy
ḥalqa (Ar.) assembly (usually for audition or *ḏikr*)
ḥaqīqa (Ar.) lit. truth; one of the stations of the believer *vis-à-vis* God
Ḥaqq (Ar.) truth; the True God
Hāsan Rājār gān (Bg.) Bengali esoteric songs composed by Hasan Raja (1854–1922)
hiğra (Ar.) exodus, especially Muhammad's departure from Mecca to Medina
hiğrī (Ar.) of the Muhammadan era, starting in AD 622
huğra (Ar.) the 'room' or customary dwelling place of a *pīr* or saint
ḫušrūz (P.) birthday of a saint
imām (Ar.) religious leader; reader in a mosque
insān al-kāmil (Ar.) perfect man
'išq (Ar.) love
'Izrā'īl angel of death
jāti (Skt.) caste, class, gender, race
Ka'ba (Ar.) the cube-shaped building and central holy place of Islam in Mecca
kabigān (Bg.) contest singing
kabiẏāl (Bg.) contest singer

kalima (Ar.) the Islamic confession of faith
kamāliyyāt (Ar.) perfections
karāma, pl. *karāmāt* (Ar.) saintly miracle
kašf (Ar.) disclosure
khelā (Bg.) play
kr̥ṣṇabhakti (Skt.) devotion to Krishna
kr̥ṣṇalīlā (Skt.) the Divine play of Krishna, particularly his amorous affairs with the *gopīs*
kufr (Ar.) disbelief (in Islam)
kuṇḍalinī (Skt.) serpent coiled in the lowest *cakra* in yogico-tantric body concepts
lāhūt (Ar.) abode of the divine
latīfa, pl. *latā'if* (Ar.) usually six energetic plexi in the human body
līlā (Skt.) (divine) play; life, incarnation
maḏhab (Ar.) school of Islamic law
malakūt (Ar.) realm of angels
maqām, pl. *maqāmāt* (Ar.) station of believer *vis-à-vis* God; sphere of life
ma'rifa (Ar.) gnosis, experience of the Divine
ma'šūq (Ar.) beloved object
mawlā (Ar.) master
mawlawī (Ar.) a doctor of Islamic law
mazār (Ar.) saintly tomb
mi'rāğ (Ar.) Muhammad's night journey
mu'ğaza, pl. *mu'ğazāt* (Ar.) prophetic miracle
muğāddid (Ar.) reformer (of Islamic faith)
Munkar (Ar.) helper of death
murāqaba (Ar.) meditation
murīd (Ar.) disciple
muršid (Ar.) spiritual master
mušāḥida (Ar.) contemplation of the divine
nabī (Ar.) Prophet
nāḍī/nāṛī (Skt./Bg.) bodily channels according to yogico-tantric body concepts
nafs (Ar.) lower self
Nakīr (Ar.) helper of death
namāz (P.) the prescribed five daily prayers
nāsūt (Ar.) earthly life
nirguṇa bhakti (Skt.) devotion to a formless deity
nisba (Ar.) relationship with God
nubuwwa (Ar.) prophethood
nūr (Ar.) light
nūr-i muḥammadī (P.) Mohammadan light
pāgal (Bg.) crazy
parda (P./U.) purdah, seclusion
pīr (P.) spiritual master
pīri-murīdī (P.) the Sufi master–disciple relationship

prem (Bg.) love
pūjā (Skt.) worship offered to a deity
Qalandar (P.) member of the Qalandariyya *ṭarīqa*; poor, marginal and transgressive *faqīr*s
qawwāl (Ar.) singer of *qawwālī*
qawwālī (Ar.) musical tradition associated with Sufi culture in the Indian subcontinent
qibla (Ar.) Kaʿba-facing direction in which ritual prayers are to be offered
rābiṭa (Ar.) spiritual connection between Sufi master and disciple
rakter dhārā (Bg.) 'line/stream of blood', biological genealogy
raqs (Ar.) dance
rasūl (Ar.) God's envoy, prophet
rawḍa (Ar.) mausoleum
riyāẓa (Ar.) spiritual exercise, austerities
sādhanā (Skt.) spiritual exercise, austerities
šağara (Ar.) spiritual lineage
sağda (Ar.) full-body prostration
sağğādanašīn (P.) formal spiritual successor
saguṇa bhakti (Skt.) devotion to a formed deity
samāʿ (Ar.) audition, listening to music
sampradāẏ (Bg.) religious group
sandhābhāṣā (Skt.) intentional language
sannyāsī (Skt.) Hindu ascetic, monk, mendicant
ṣifa, pl. *ṣifāt* (Ar.) attribute(s) of God
silsila (Ar.) line of spiritual succession
širk (Ar.) the sin of associating partners with God
tabarruk (Ar.) blessing substance
tağallī (Ar.) self-disclosure (of the Divine), emanation
tanzīlāt (Ar.) revelations
ṭarīqa (Ar.) spiritual path; Sufi order
taṣawwuf (Ar.) Sufism
tauhīd-i adyān (P.) unity of religions
tawḥīd (Ar.) (divine) unity
tribeṇī (Bg.) (confluence of) three streams
ʿulamāʾ, sg. *ʿālim* (Ar.) Islamic scholars and clerics
ʿurs (Ar.) celebration of the reunion of a saint with his Divine beloved, deathday
viraha bhakti (Skt.) love in separation
waḥdat al-wuğūd (Ar.) the unity of being (concept attributed to Ibn ʿArabi)
waḥy (Ar.) Qurʾanic revelation
walī, pl. *awliyāʾ* (Ar.) (or *walī-Allah, awliyāʾ-Allah*) 'friends (of God)', saints
wağd (Ar.) ecstasy
wilāya (Ar.) 'friendship with God', sainthood, spiritual sovreignty
ẓāhir (Ar.) open, manifest

Bibliography

The texts are arranged alphabetically according to the names by which the authors are commonly referred to (first letter in bold print). Epithets and honorific titles, however, are given in full and keep their position if they precede the names. For a good survey of literature from Maijbhandar, see also Jāhāṅgīr (2006: 358–70).

Primary literature

A Hagiographical writings

Āb'dur Rah'mān (1984): *Maulānā Īchāpurī*. Pratham khaṇḍa. Nānupur, Āstānā-e-Īchāpurī; 108 pp.

Ābul Baśar Caudhurī et al. (ed.) (2000): *Ruhul āmin: darbāre eś'kebandīẏā*. Phaṭik'chaṛi, Pachan Bhāṇḍār Dar'bāre Eś'kebandīẏā Najir Mañjil. 31 pp.

Chaiẏad **Ā**h'madul Hak (2000): *Biśva premik Haj'rat Gāuchul Ājam Maulānā Chaiẏad Golāmur Rah'mān Māij'bhāṇḍārīr saṃkṣipta jībanālekhya*. Caṭṭagrām, author's publ., 3rd edn (1st edn, 1999); 38 pp.

Syed Mohd. **A**mirul Islam (1992): *Shahenshah Ziaul Huq Maijbhandari*. Chittagong [?], Mirza Ali Behrouze Ispahani; 1st edn, xiii, 130 pp.

Śāh'jādā Saiẏad **B**ad'ruddojā (1394 BE [1377 BE]): Alīkul Śiromaṇi Hay'rat Bābā Bhāṇḍārī. Māij'bhāṇḍār, Śāh'jādā Saiẏad Bad'ruddojā, Gāuchiẏā Rah'mān Man'jel; 4th edn, 230 pp.

Maolānā Saiẏad **B**ad'ruddojā Māij'bhāṇḍārī (2000): *Māij'bhāṇḍārī saogāt*. Bhāṇḍār Śarīph, author's publ. 2nd edn; 1st edn, 1966; 15 pp.

Maolānā Mo. Phaijullāh **B**hūiẏā (1993): *Hay'rat Gāuchul Ājam Śāh Chuphī Māolānā Saiẏad Āh'mad Ullāh (K.) Māij'bhāṇḍārīr jībanī o kerāmat*. Māij'bhāṇḍār, Śāh'jādā Saiẏad Munirul Hak; 9th edn; 1st edn 1967; 232 pp.

Md. **G**hulam Rasul (1994): *The Divine Spark. Shahanshah Ziaul Hoque (K.)*. Maizbhandar, Gausia Hoque Manzil; 1st edn 144 pp.

Śāh·jādā Mohāmmad **H**āruṇ Śāh·, Sājjādānaśīn (1997): *Sarbatvarīkā satyāẏan'kārī Samrāṭe Ali Hay'rat Gāuche Bhāṇḍār Śekh Matiur Rah'mān Śāh Bi. A (Ka.) prakāś – Śāh·Chāheb Keb'lā*. Pub. unknown; 32 pp.

Śāh Chuphī Māolānā Chaiẏad Āb'duch Chālām **I**chāpurī Chāheb (ra.) (n.d.): *Hay'rat Gāuchul Ājam Māolānā āl·Chaiẏad Golāmur Rah'mān āl·-Hāsānī āl·-Māij'bhāṇḍārī (ka.) Bābājān Kveb'lā Kābār jīban carit*. Khātun'gañj, Mo. Mijānur Rah'mān/Saiẏad Śaphiul Baśar; 108 pp.

Hājī Śekh **I**ch'hāk Āhāmad (1988): *Garībe Neoẏāj, Gauche Bhāṇḍār, Kutubul Ākh'tār, Yug'sraṣṭā Alī, Śekh Śāh Matiẏur Rah'mān Bi. A. (Ra.) ke keman dekhechi*. Abudhabi, Zainul Abedeen; 176 pp.
Selim **J**āhāṅgīr (2006): *Gāusul'ājam māijbhāṇḍārī śata barṣer āloke*. Māij'bhāṇḍār, Āñjumāne Mottābeẏīne Gāuche Māij'bhāṇḍārī; 372 pp.
Chaiẏad **L**ut·phul Hak (1987): *Gāuche Mokār'ram, Mojāddede Jamān, Ābul Oẏāk't· Āb'rār Āllāmā Śāh· Chūpī--Chaiẏad Āminul Hak Phar'hādābādī (ra.) er saṃkṣipta jībanī o tār racita toh'phātul ākh·iẏār granther 'il'me tāchāuph' o 'bāẏāt' sambandhīẏa adhyāẏer baṅgānubād*. Caṭṭagrām, Chaiẏad Lut·phul Hak; 1st edn; 42 pp.
Āl·hājv Śāh·jādī Chaiẏadā **L**ut·phunnechā Hosāinī Āl·-Māij'bhāṇḍārī (1993): *Śājjādānaśīn o montājeme dar'bār, Śāh'jādāẏe Gāuchul Ājam Haj'rat Śāh'chuphī āl·-hājv Māolānā āl· Chaiẏad Śaphiul Baśar āl·-Hācānī āl·-Māij'bhāṇḍārī (mu. ā.) keb'lā kābār jībanī*. Caṭṭagrām, Suphiẏānā; 3rd edn; 1st edn 1987; (ja), 52 pp.
Mo. **M**āh'bub'ul Ālam (ed.) (1997): *Śāhān'śāh Hay'rat Saiẏad Jiẏāul Hak Māij'bhāṇḍārī (Ka.) byakti o byaktitva*. Māij'bhāṇḍār, Śāh'jādā Hay'rat Saiẏad Mohāmmad Hāsān; 1st edn; 136 pp.
Chaiẏad **P**haujul Ājim (1999): *Āmir Bhaṇḍār Śarīph: jahure Mojeherul Hak Śāh·(Rā.)*. Pub. unknown; 14 pp., unpaginated.
Jāmāl Āh'mad **S**ik'dār (1987): *Śāhān'śāh Jiẏāul Hak Māij'bhāṇḍārī*. Māij'bhāṇḍār, Gāuchiẏā Hak Man·jil; 2nd edn (1st edn 1982); 304 pp.

B Māij'bhāṇḍārī songs

Maolānā Saiẏad Mohāmmad **Ā**b'dul Gaṇī Kāñcan'purī (1995/96): *Gol·sane os'sāk: Gāuchul Ājam Māij'bhāṇḍārīr śāne racita māij'bhāṇḍārī gāner saṃkalan*. Prakāśanā sahāẏ'tāẏ: Mohāmmad Jāmāl Uddin, Gājīpur; 1st edn 1921/22.
Āb'dur·Rah·mān (n.d.): *Śān·-e-Īchāpūrī: (mār'phatī gāner bai)*. Nānupur, Āñjoman·-e-Āstānā-e-Īchāpūrī; 8 pp.
Saiẏad **Ā**bul Baśar (2000/1): *Jhar'nā*. Māij'bhāṇḍār, Ān·jumāne Rah'māniẏā Maïnīẏā Māij'bhāṇḍārīẏā; 5th edn; 1st edn 1940 [?]. 24 pp.
Āl Āmīr (Rā.) Khed'mat Kamiṭi (ed.) (1971): *Āmirul Āuliẏā Haj'rat Śāh'chupi Chaiẏad Āmirujjamān (Rā.) Keb'lā Kābār śāne, bhaktagaṇer racita kaẏek'ṭi gān*. Paṭiẏā, Āl·Āmīr (Rā.) Khed'mat Kamiṭi; 15 pp.
Aliullāh [Rājāpurī] (1913): *Prem-nur* ('A collection of devotional songs of a class of Muhammadan ascetics called Maij-bhandar. Compiled by 'Ali Allah, of Rajapur, District Tipperah. In Muhammadan Bengali'), pp.113; 21 × 13 cm. Noakhali, 1913; British Library, V.Tr. 3383 (original title: Māij'bhāṇḍār sariph neẏāmat sāgar/ei ketāber nām Prem'nur/racak/Śrī Hin Aliullāh/Sāṃ Rājāpur Jilā Tripurā/P.O. Lāk'syām/prakāśak/ Phakir Āmir'ullāh/San 1319 bāṃlā/Noẏākhālī/Noẏākhālī-yantre Śrīśaśibhūṣaṇ Dās dvārā mudrita/mūlya/9 ānā).
Adhyāpikā **B**ad'run·nesā Sāju (1998): *Madirā*. Dam'damā, Gāuchiẏā Rah'māniẏā Gaṇi Man·jil; 1st edn; āṭ'calliś.
Sūphī Kabi Hay'rat Māolānā Muhammad **B**aj'lul Karim Mandākinī (1991): *Premāñjalī*. Ed. Pīr'jādā Saiẏad Ābu Āh'mad Miñā. Māij'bhāṇḍār, Khālek Mañjil; 23 pp.
Maolānā Mohāmmad **B**aj·lul Karim (n.d.): *Premer hem*. Ed. Maolānā Śāh'jādā Saiẏad Bad'ruddojā. Bhāṇḍār Śarīph, Gāuchiẏā Rah'mān Man·jel; 22 pp.
Māolānā **B**aj'lul Karim Mandākinī (1999): *Śeṣ jīban*. Ed. Māh'bub ul Ālam. Māij'bhāṇḍār, Saiẏad Mohāmmad Hāsān; 48 pp.

Bāh'rul Ulum Muph·tī Chaiẏad Ābduchchālām **B**hūj'purī (ra.) (1991): *Ratna bindhu (1)*. Ed. Begam Chaiẏad Jiẏāul Hak. Hāṭ'hājārī, Phar'hādābād Dar'bār Śarīph; 1st edn 1939; 13 + 3 pp.

Jahir Āh'mad **C**audhurī (1989): *Khat·mul belāẏat*. Caṭṭagrām, Pub. unknown; 25 pp.

Pāgal **C**audhurī (Hak Bhāṇḍārī) (1998/99): *Ādhyātmik ukti māij'bhāṇḍārī gajal bāul gāner baï: taraṅga*, 2ẏa khaṇḍa. Jaraïn (Kumillā), Hak Bhāṇḍār Dar'bār Śarīph; 64 pp.

Āb'dul **G**aphur Hālī (1989): *Tattvabidhi*. Raśidābād/Śobhan'daṇḍī, author's publ.; 2nd edn; 1st edn 1969; 30 pp.

Āb'dul **G**aphur Hālī (1989): *Jñān'jyoti*. Raśidābād, Mohāmmat· Rābeẏā Khātun; 100 pp. Preface by the author; foreword by Śaokat Hāphij Khān Ruś'ni.

Haj'rat Śāh·jādā **G**olām Gaṇi Caudhurī (2000): *Māij'bhāṇḍārī gītimañjarī*. Ed. Śāh·jādā Saphiul Gaṇi Caudhuri. Caṭṭagrām, author's publ.; 48 pp.

Mohāmmad **H**ābībul Hosāin (ed.) (1998): *Ke tumi he sakhā: māij'bhāṇḍārī gāner saṃkalan*, pratham khaṇḍa. Paṭiẏā, Āmir Bhāṇḍār; 29 pp.

Sūphī Āllāmā Āb'dul **H**ādī Kāñcan'purī (2000): *Ratna sāgar*. Ed. Saiẏad Ābu Āh'mad Miẏā. Māij'bhāṇḍār, editor's publ.; 6th edn; 34 pp.

Sūphī Mau. Āb'dul **H**ādī (n.d.): *Ratna sāgar*. Ed. Pīr'jādā Saiẏad Ābu Āh'mad Miẏā. Māij'bhāṇḍār, editor's publ.; 5th edn; 51 pp.

Āl-hājv Śāh'jādī Saiẏadā **L**ut·phunnechā Hosāīnī 'Suphiẏānā' (1992): *Gāuchiẏater phul: jal'oẏāẏe 'śaphi bābā'*. Caṭṭagrām, author's publ.; 20 pp.

Mo. **M**āh'bub ul Ālam (2000): *Aiśī ālor jal'sāghar*. Caṭṭagrām, Saiẏad Mohāmmad Hāsān; 60 pp.

Śāh Chuphī Chaiẏad Āb'dul **M**ālek Śāh (ra.) Āl Māij Bhāṇḍārī (1989): *Ārśīnagar*. Ed. Deloẏār Husāin Phariẏādī. Kāñcan Nagar, Mālek Bhāṇḍār; 32 pp.

Śāh Chuphī Chaiẏad Āb'dul **M**ālek Śāh (ra.) Āl Māij'bhāṇḍārī (1989a): *Belāẏeter ghaṇṭā*. Ed. Deloẏār Husāin Phariẏādī; Kāñcan Nagar, Mālek Bhāṇḍār; 32 pp.

Mo. Āb'dul Jabbār **M**im'nagarī (1998): *Gāuchiẏā saurabh*. Karim'gañj (Mymensingh), S.M. Naj'rul Is'lām; 2nd edn; 1st edn 1992; 40 pp.

Mo. Āb'dul Jabbār Śāh·**M**im'nagarī (1999): *Pañcaratnagītikā*. Karim'gañj (Mymensingh), S.M. Naj'rul Is'lām; 2nd edn; 1st edn 1988; 148 pp.

Saiẏad Āb'dul **M**onaem (1997): *Ākuti*, pratham khaṇḍa. Caṭṭagrām, Mohāmmad Mijānur Rah'mān; 44 pp.

Śāh Sul'tān Āh'mad **M**ollā Māij'bhāṇḍārī (1993): *Premer bā̃śī*. Jhalam, Kumillā [?]; 2nd edn; 1st edn 1967; 47 pp.

Śāh Sul'tān Āh'med **M**ollā Māij'bhāṇḍārī (1993): Dīner tarī. Bhāṇḍār Śarīph, Gāuchiẏā Rah'mān Mañjil; 1st edn; (52 songs).

Mo. **M**ok'sed Ālī (ed.) (1995): Khājā bābār māij bhāṇḍārī gān. Ḍhākā, Sāl'mā Buk Ḍipo; 24 pp.

Dr. Mohāmmad **M**uchā Ālam (1990 [1984]): Maẏ'nā Jagat, pratham khaṇḍa. Kāñcan Nagar [Candanāiś], Dr. M.M. Ālam; 2nd edn; 44 pp.

Dr. Mohāmmad **M**uchā Ālam (1984): Maẏ'nā Jagat, dvitīẏa khaṇḍa. Kāñcan Nagar [Candanāiś], Dr. M.M. Ālam; 48 pp.

Dr. Mohāmmad **M**uchā Ālam (1985): Maẏ'nā Jagat, tṛtīẏa khaṇḍa. Kāñcan Nagar [Candanāiś], Dr. M.M. Ālam; 40 pp.

Chaiẏad **M**ujibul Baśar (ed.) (1992): *Māij'bhāṇḍārīẏā bicched taraṅga*. Caṭṭagrām, Ālam Priṇṭiṃ Pres; 22 pp.

Śāh'jādā Saiẏad **M**unirul Hak (ed.) (1985): *Gaurab bhāṇḍār*. Bhāṇḍār Śarīph, Gāuchiẏā Āh'madiẏā Mañjil; 68 pp.

Śāh'jādā Saiẏad **M**unirul Hak (ed.) (1988): *Hṛdaẏ bhāṇḍār*. Māij'bhāṇḍār Śarīph, editor's publ.; 2nd edn; 56 pp.
Śāh'jādā Chaiẏad **M**unirul Hak (ed.) (1982): *Premākar*. Māij'bhāṇḍār, Āñjumāne Mottābeẏīne Gāuche Māij Bhāṇḍārī; 40 pp.
Śāh'jādā Saiẏad **M**unirul Hak (1994): *Ratnabhāṇḍār*, pratham khaṇḍa. Māij'bhāṇḍār, Gāuchiẏā Āh'madiẏā Mañjil; 38 pp.
Śāh'jādā Saiẏad **M**unirul Hak (1997): *Ratnabhāṇḍār*, 2ẏa khaṇḍa. Māij'bhāṇḍār, Gāuchiẏā Āh'madiẏā Mañjil; 36 pp.
Śāh'jādā Saiẏad **M**unirul Hak (ed.) (1985): *Saurabh bhāṇḍār*. Māij'bhāṇḍār Śarīph, editor; (7), 80 pp.
Miẏā **N**aj'rul Is'lām (1999): *Śān: śāśvata Gāuchul Āyam Jiẏāul Hak Māij'bhāṇḍārī*. Māij'bhāṇḍār, Āb'dul Odud. 54 pp.
Phakir Mo. **P**harid Hosen (1998): *Ālor bhāṇḍār*. Ḍhākā, author's publ.; 30 pp.
Phakir Mo. **P**harid Hosen (1983): *Udaẏ bhāṇḍār*. Bāñchārām'pur (Kumillā), author's publ.; 30 pp.
Mo. **R**ajjab Ālī Deoẏān (1996): *Jñāner pradīp: rajjab gītikā*, pratham khaṇḍa. Ḍhākā, Sadar Lāibrerī; 56 pp.
Svargīẏa **R**ameś Candra Sar'kār (Lok Kabi Kabiẏāl Rameś Śīl) (1992): *Āśek mālā: māij bhāṇḍārī mār'phatī o bicched gāner baï*. Gom'daṇḍī, Pulin Bihārī Śīl; 24 pp.
Kabiẏāl **R**ameś Śīl (1981 [1956]): *Eś·ke sirājiẏā*. Caṭṭagrām, Saiẏad Māh'mudul Hak; 43 + (8) pp.
Svargīẏa **R**ameś Candra Sar'kār (Lok Kabi Kabiẏāl Rameś Śīl) (1992): *Jīban sāthī: māij bhāṇḍārī mār'phatī o bicched gāner baï*. Gom'daṇḍī, Pulin Bihārī Śīl; 24 pp.
Svargīẏa **R**ameś Candra Sar'kār (Lok Kabi Kabiẏāl Rameś Śīl) (1992): *Muktir dar'bār: māij bhāṇḍārī mār'phatī o bicched gāner baï*. Gom'daṇḍī, Pulin Bihārī Śīl; 22 pp.
Rameś Śīl (1993): *Rameś Śīl racanābalī*. Ed. Saiẏad Mahāmmad Śāhed. Ḍhākā, Bāṃlā Ekāḍemī. Song books on pp. 1–136.
Svargīẏa **R**ameś Candra Sar'kār (Lok Kabi Kabiẏāl Rameś Śīl) (1992): *Śāntibhāṇḍār: māij bhāṇḍārī mār'phatī o bicched gāner baï*. Gom'daṇḍī, Pulin Bihārī Śīl; 22 pp.
Chaiẏad **Ś**aphiul Baśar (n.d.): *Yuger ālo o buker khun*. Bhāṇḍār Śarīph, Gāuchiẏā Rah'mān Man˙jil; (45) + (17) pp.
Āl'hājv Māolānā Golām Muhāmmad Khān **S**irājī (1993): *Naj'rānā*, 1. khaṇḍa. Place unknown, Kṛtī Proḍāk·śan's.
Mastān Mo. **T**ājal Is'lām Phakir Māij'bhāṇḍārī (1998 [1976]): *Jāloẏāẏe śaphi bhāṇḍār*. Bhāṇḍār Śarīph, Gāuchiẏā Rah'mān Mañjil; 40 pp.

C Treatises, journals and miscellaneous

ʿ**A**bd al-Ġanī Kānčanpūrī (1914–15): *Āʾīna-i Bārī*. Reprint, ed. Dilāwar Ḥusain. Čandanpūra, Islāmiyya Līt˙hō ēnd˙ Printing Prēs; 2nd edn approx. 1950; 1st edn 1914–15; 720 pp.; 3rd edn (given as 2nd edn) 2007, ed. Saiẏad Em'dādul Hak Māij'bhāṇḍārī. Maijbhandar, editor's publ. [Urdu and Persian].
Āllāmā Chaiẏad **Ā**b'dul Karim (1995): *Nāj'me dil'kośā phi milāde mostāphā (da.)*. Phar'hādābād, Caiẏad Lut˙ phul Hak; 2nd edn; 96 pp. [Arabic and Persian, Bengali transcription and title page].
Chaiẏad **Ā**h'madul Hak (1990): *Prabandha bicitrā*. Caṭṭagrām, Chaiẏad Māh'mudul Hak and Naj'rul Is'lām Caudhurī; 296 pp.
Chaiẏad **Ā**h'madul Hak (1996): *Mur'līr bilāp*. Caṭṭagrām, Āllāmā Rumī Sosāiṭi; 198 pp.

Syed **A**hmadul Huq (1995): *Sufism in Bangladesh: Lecture Paper for San Francisco Symposium on Sufism*. Chittagong, author's publ.; n.p. (16 pp.).

Syed **A**hmedul Huq (1997): *Jalajuddin Rumi and the Dancing Dervishes/Maizbhandari Order/Maizbhandari Songs*; In *Observer Magazine* (Dhaka), Friday 4.4.97; p.3.

Āl māij'bhāṇḍārī. Journal. 14 Oct 2000. Ed. Māolānā Saiẏad Āminul Baśar. Jamiẏate Rah'māniẏā Māij'bhāṇḍārīẏā, Caṭṭagrāṃ.

Āl-najīr māij'bhāṇḍārī darśan 3, 3 (1996). Journal, ed. 'Es. Em.' Baś'rat Ullāh. Caṭṭagrām, Pāṭhān'ṭulī.

Ālok'dhārā. Journal. Ed. Jāmāl Āh'mad Sik'dār; from 1996 onwards ed. Māh'bub Ul Ālam. Māij'bhāṇḍār, Hak Mañjil; publ. from 1996 by Saiẏad Mohāmmad Hāsān. Irregular appearance from 1985 to 1996, but apparently conceived as a three-monthly (*traimāsik*). From 1996 onwards as a monthly.

Saiẏad **Ā**minul Hak Phar'hādābādī (1997): *Tuḥfat al-aḥyār fī daf' śarārat al-śarār: semā' bā gān bājānā sambandhīẏa phatoẏā*. Phar'hādābād, Phar'hādābād Dar'bār Śarīph; 3rd edn 1997 (1st edn 1906/7). 2 vols; 186 and 86 pp.

Muph·tīẏe Ājam, Gāuche Jamān Chaiẏadul Munājerin, Chanadul Muhākkekin Āllāmā Chaiẏad **Ā**minul Hak Phar'hādābādī (1989): *Āt·taojihātul·bahiẏẏāh·phi-tar'dide mā-phit ·tanakihātich·chunniẏāh·j*. Phar'hādābād, Chaiẏad Phaẏ'jul Is'lām Phar'hādābādī; 2nd edn; 76 pp. [Arabic and Persian, Bengali title page].

Āñjaman·-e-Āstānā-e-Īchāpurī (1983): *Monājāt*. Nānupur, Āñjaman·-e-Āstānā-e-Īchāpurī; 6 pp.

Āñjaman-e-Āstānāẏe Īsāpurī (comp.) (n.d.): *Toh·phāẏe jaśane mauled: maulānā īsāpurī (kaddāchā chir rāhul bārī)-er janmot·saber smaraṇikā*. Āñjaman-e-Āstānāẏe Īsāpurī, Nānupur; sātānna p., āśi p.

Āñjumāne Mottābeẏīne Gāuche Māij'bhāṇḍārī (ed.) (n.d.): *Gaṭhan'tantra*. Māij'bhāṇḍār, Āñjumāne Mottābeẏīne Gāuche Māij'bhāṇḍārī Prakāśanā Pariṣad; (32 pp.)

Ān·jumāne Rah'mānīẏā Maïnīẏā Māij'bhāṇḍārīẏā (1998): *Śāj'rāẏe kāderīẏā gāuchiẏā māij'bhāṇḍārīẏā*. Māij'bhāṇḍār; 3rd edn; 1st edn 1993; āśi pp.

Maolānā Saiẏad **B**ad'ruddojā Māij'bhāṇḍārī (1995): *Āllāh·r anugraher sandhāne*. Māij'bhāṇḍār, Nāj'mum Munir; 59 pp.

Maolānā Saiẏad **B**ad'ruddojā Māij'bhāṇḍārī (1999): 'Śāne olīāllāh'. In: *Dainik ājādī*, 5 April 1999, p.3.

Adhyakṣa Āl'hājv Śāh Phiroj Ul Hak **C**audhurī Māij Bhāṇḍārī (2000): *Śreṣṭha īd: īd-e-milādunnabī*. Ḍhākā, Ḍhākā Mahānagar Āśekāne Māij Bhāṇḍārī Esosiẏeśan; 96 pp.

***D**amama* [Journal, title in Roman script]. 1, 5.4.1999. Ed. Em. Ālī Sik'dār. Caṭṭagrām, Adhyāpikā Bad'runnesā Sāju et al. (among them the Āśekāne Māij'bhāṇḍārī Lekhak Phorām).

Svapan Kumār **D**āś and Bāsudeb Khāstagīr (2001): *Añjali (bhaktimūlak gān)*. Suẏābil, Suẏābil Siddhāśram Maṭh; 24 pp.

Maolānā Śāh'chuphī Saiẏad **D**elāor Hosāin (ed.) (1994): *Milāde Nababī o tāoẏāllode gāuchiẏā*. Māij'bhāṇḍār, Saiẏad Munirul Hak; 8th edn; 21 pp. (also 10th edn 2000).

Khādemul Phok'rā Maolānā Saiẏad **D**elāor Hosāin (1995): *Mūl tattva bā taj'kīẏāẏe mokh'tāchār*. Māij'bhāṇḍār, author's publ.; 5th edn; 1st edn 1969.

Khādemul Phok'rā Maolānā Saiẏad **D**elāor Hosāin (ed.) (1990): *Mus·lim ācār dharma*. Māij'bhāṇḍār, [Āh'madīẏā Mañjel]; 3rd edn; 32 pp.

Maolānā Saiẏad **D**elāor Hosāin (1959): *Belāẏete mot·lākā bā mukta suphībād*. Māij'bhāṇḍār, author's publ.; 103 pp.

Maolānā Saiẏad **D**elāor Hosāin (1980): *Belāẏate mot·lākā*; Māij'bhāṇḍār, Gāuchiẏā Āh'madiẏā Mañjil; 4th edn; 185 pp.

Moulana Shah Sufi Syed **D**elawor Hossain Maizbhandari (R) (2000): *Belayet-e-mutlaka (The Unchained Divine Relations or Unhindered Love of God)*. Transl. Md. Abdul Mannan Chowdhury. Maizbhandar, Syed Munirul Huq; 185 pp.

Śāh Chūphī Maolānā Saiẏad **D**elāoẏār Hosāin (1974): *Biśva-mānabatāẏ belāẏater svarūp*. Māij'bhāṇḍār, Gāuchiẏā Ā'madīẏā Mañjil; 9 pp.

Maulānā Saiẏad **D**elāoẏār Hosāin (n.d.): *Elākār renesā̃ yuger ek'ṭi dik·*. Māij'bhāṇḍār, Gāuchiẏā Āh'madīẏā Mañjil; 58 pp. [written after 1972].

Maulānā Saiẏad **D**elāoẏār Hosāin (n.d.): *Mānab sabhyatā*. Māij'bhāṇḍār, Śāh·jādā Chaiẏad Em'dādul Hak; 18 pp.

Mophācchere kvor'ān Māolānā **H**āphej Āb'dul Hālim Māij'bhāṇḍārī (2000): *Āh·le kvor'ān*. Daulat'pur (Kumillā), 'Bāẏ'tul Hābib'; 16 pp.

Hāphej Ābul Kālām (2000): *Kor'ān hādīser āloke sij'dār bidhān*. Māij'bhāṇḍār, Gāuchiẏā Hak Mañjil; 47 pp.

Khādemul **H**ās'nāin (1990): *Māij'bhāṇḍār śarīph o prasaṅga kathā*; Māij'bhāṇḍār, Āñjomāne Mottābeẏīne Gāuche Māij'bhāṇḍārī; n.p. (approx. 20 pp.).

Mohāmmad Ālī **H**usāin (1993): *Chirātul Mustakīm (1)*. Ed. Muhāmmad Baśiruddīn Āh'mad Caudhurī. Caṭṭagrām, Tājul Is'lām o Āiẏub Ālī; 15 pp.

Saiẏad Āb'duch Chālām **Ī**chāpurī (1979): *Pūṇyātmā chuphīgaṇer chemā*. Nānupur, Āñjaman-e-Āstānā-e-Īchāpurī; 57 pp.

Kut·b-e Jamān Muph'tī-e-Ājam Haj'rat Maulānā Śāh·Suphī Saiẏad Āb'ducchālām **Ī**sāpurī (1978): *Uchul-e-tvarikat o āch·rār-e-chemā*. Nānupur, Āñjamane Āstānāẏe Īsāpurī; 68 pp.

Kut·be Ājam, Gāuche Mokār'ram, Muph'ti-e-Ājam Haj'rat Maulānā Śāh·Suphī Saiẏad Āb'duch Chālām **Ī**sāpurī (1983): *Āch'hābe kāhāph o gupta jñān tattva*. Nānupur, Ān·jamane Āstānā-e-Īchāpurī; 38 pp.

Kut·b·-e-Jamān, Muph'tī-e-Ājam Haj'rat Maulānā Śāh·Suphī Saiẏad Āb'ducchālām **Ī**sāpurī (n.d.): *Adhyātma samrāṭ o śān-e-gāuchul ājam*. Nānupur, Āñjaman-e-Āstānāẏe Īchāpurī; 30 pp.

Kut·b·-e-Jamān, Muph'tī-e-Ājam Haj'rat Maulānā Śāh·Suphī Saiẏad Āb'ducchālām **Ī**sāpurī (1981): *Chobolocchālām*. Nānupur, Āñjuman-e-Āstānāẏe Īsāpurī; 2nd edn; 152 pp.

Saiẏad Āb'ducchālām **Ī**chāpurī (1981): *Ich'lāmer jarurī śikṣā*, pratham bhāg. Nānupur, Āñjamane Āstānā-e-Īchāpurī; 17 pp.

Kut·b·-e-Jamān Haj'rat Maulānā Śāh suphī Saiẏad Āb'ducchālām **Ī**chāpurī (transl./ comm.) (1981): Sūphīkūl Śiromaṇi Haj'rat Maulānā Jālāl·uddīn Rūmī: *Mach'nabī Śarīpher baṅgānubād o biśad byākhyā*. Nānupur, Āstānā-e-Īchāpurī; 116 pp.

Kut·b·-e Ājam, Mochānnephe Āk·ram, Muph'tiẏe Ājam Hay'rat Māolānā Śāh·Suphī Saiẏad Āb'ducchālām **I**chāpurī (1981): *Rūhe in'chānī o ālame bar'jakh: (maraṇer par kabare mānabātmār abasthā o abasthān)*. Nānupur, Āñjamane Āstānā-e-Īchāpurī; 60 pp.

Kut·b·-e Jamān, Muph'ti-e-Ājam, Gāuch·-e-Mokar·ram Hay'rat Māolānā Śāh·Suphī Saiẏad Āb'ducchālām **I**chāpurī (n.d.): *Tā'jīm·-e-śaā'erallāh (pratham bhāg)*; Pub. unknown; 35 pp.

Maulānā Sayyid ʿAbd al-Salām Isāpūrī (*c*. 1950): *Fuyūżāt al-raḥmāniyya fī ṭarīqa al-māʾiğbhandʿāriyya* [Persian]. No details given. 44 pp.

Kut·b·-e Jamān, Muph'tīẏe-Ājam Haj'rat Maulānā Śāh Suphī Saiẏad Āb'ducchālām **Ī**sāpurī (n.d.): *Jal·oẏā-e-nūre mohāmmadī: taph'chīr churā-e-ālam naś·rāh*. Nānupur, Āñjaman·-e-āstānāẏe Īsāpurī; 116 pp.

Kut·b·-e-Jamān Muph'tī-e-Ājam Haj'rat Śāh·Suphī Saiẏad Āb'ducchālām **Ī**sāpurī (1979): *Tvarikā-e-eś·k*, pratham bhāg. Nānupur, Āñjamane Āstānāẏe Īchāpurī; 56 pp.

Pīr'jādā Māolānā Chaiẏad Ik'bāl Phajal (1996): *Maulud Śarīph o jikire māh'phil.* Māij'bhāṇḍār, author's publ.; 30 pp.

Jīban'bāti. Journal. As a monthly since 1997. Ed. Saiẏad Sahidul Hak. Māij'bhāṇḍār, Āh'madīẏā Mañjil.

Bāndāh·Kāsem (1987): *Amṛta sañjībanī.* Bhāṇḍār Śarīph, Ānjumāne Mottābeẏīne Gāuche Māij Bhāṇḍārī Kendrīẏa Kamiṭi. 42 pp.

Ābul Hāchan Mostaphijor Rah'mān Khā̃ (1979): *Sādhur ātmabināś o janmagrahaṇ.* Lohāliẏā (Paṭuẏākhālī), Kājī Naj'rul Is'lām; 1st edn 1918; 26 pp.

Khādemul Hās'nāin (2005): *Amṛtadhārā: kālām-e-Gāusul Ājam Māij'bhāṇḍārī.* Māij'bhāṇḍār, Āñjumāne Mottābeẏīne Gāuche Māij'bhāṇḍārī.

Khoś'rojer saogāt. Journal. 4th year, 27 Āśvin 1342 BE/5th year 27th Āśvin 1343 BE; Ed. Saiẏad Maulabī Khāẏ'rul Baśar. Māij'bhāṇḍār.

Ki buddhi? subuddhi. Journal. 1987; Mati Yubo Saṅgha. Published from Mati Bhandar Sharif, Nanupur, Chittagong.

Āl·hājv Śāh·jādī Saiẏadā Lut·phunnechā Hosāinī (1992): *Aiśī ālor bhūbane bhāṇḍār śarīph.* Caṭṭagrām, author's publ.; 56 pp.

Āl·hājv Śāh·jādī Saiẏadā Lut·phunnechā Hosāinī (1995): *Mānabatār tīrtha bhūmi māij'bhāṇḍār śarīph.* Caṭṭagrām, author's publ.; 2nd edn; 1st edn 1990; 12 pp.

Āl·hājv Śāh·jādī Saiẏadā Lut·phunnechā Hosāinī 'Suphiẏānā' (1999): *Tāohīd.* Caṭṭagrām, author's publ.; 76 pp.

Māij'bhāṇḍārī Pariṣad (ed.) (n.d.): *Gaṭhan'tantra.* n.p. (9 pp.).

Māij'bhāṇḍārī paẏ'gām. Journal. Ed. Chaiẏad Jāhāṅgīr Phajal. Māij'bhāṇḍār, Māij'bhāṇḍārī Pariṣad.

Māh'mud-ul-Hak (1991): *Darud o sālām.* Māij'bhāṇḍār, Māolānā Saiẏad Bad'ruddojā; 24 pp.

Āl'hājv Śāh Chuphi Māolānā Saiẏad Maïnuddīn Āh'mad Āl-Hācānī (n.d.): *Ādābe māh'phile jikir: tarikāẏe māij'bhāṇḍārīẏā.* Māij'bhāṇḍār, Pub. unknown; 16 pp.

Sākhāoẏāt Hosen Maj'nu and Marjinā Ākh'tār Mani (1997): *Suphītattver gabeṣak Chaiẏad Āh'madul Hak.* Caṭṭagrām, Sṛjanī Prakāśanī; 231 pp.

Maramī. Journal. 21 Dec. 1991. Ed. Chaiẏad Pharid Uddin Āh'mad. Māij'bhāṇḍār, Māij'bhāṇḍārī Maramī Goṣṭhī.

Mohāmmad Āb'dul Jabbār Śāh Mim Nagarī (1997): *Ābehāẏāt.* Kiśor'gañj, ?; 4th edn; 1st edn 1951; 192 pp.

Śāh·jādā Saiẏad Āb'dul Mon·ẏem (1997): *Mach'nabī śarīpher kābyānubād*, pratham bhāg. Caṭṭagrām, Mohāmmad Mijānur Rah'mān; 80 pp.

Śāh·jādā Saiẏad Āb'dul Mon'ẏem (1987): *Mīlādunnabī.* Nānupur, author's publ.; 32 pp.

Saiẏad Golām Mor'śed (1994): *Is'lāmī prabandha sambhār.* Caṭṭagrām, Saiẏadā Os'mānā Mor'śed; 231 pp.

Es. Em. [Mujibur] Rah'mān (Āl Ājīm Nagarī) (n.d.): *Ālor jhal'mal.* Ājim Nagar, Āhmadiẏā Rah'māniẏā Phor'kāniẏā Mādrāsā; 14 pp.

Es. Em. [Mujibur] Rah'mān (1996): *Jal'oẏāẏe nūre bhāṇḍārī*, 1st vol. Ājim'nagar, Āh'madiẏa Rah'māniẏā Phor'kāniẏā Mahilā Mādrāsā ebaṃ Or'śekūl Kendrīẏa Kamiṭi; 24 pp.

Mujibur Rah'mān (n.d.): *Nurer jhalak.* No details given. 42 pp.

Muktir darśan. Journal, 3, 2; 14 January 1998. Eds Maolānā Jāphar Āh'mad, Mohāmmad Nurul Is'lām. Paṭiẏā, Āmir Bhāṇḍār Śāh·Hāch'nāt Gaṇapāṭhāgār.

Śājjādānaśīn Śāh'jādā Hay'rat Śāh Chuphi Māolānā Chaiẏad Nāj'mūl Hudā (2000): *Kānune tvarikāẏe māij'bhāṇḍārīẏā: ādābe māh·phile hāl·kāẏe jikire chemā.* Bhāṇḍār Śarīph, Pub. unknown; 14 pp.

Miẏā Naj'rul Is'lām (ed.) (1995): *Māij'bhāṇḍār śarīph.* Ḍhākā, Māij'bhāṇḍār Gabeṣaṇā Pariṣad; 137 p.

Golām Churāẏe **N**ur Śāh·(2001): *Kalir rabi nūre Rah'mān mānab jātir paraś mani*. Māij'bhāṇḍār, Ān·jumāne Rah'māniẏā Maïnīẏā Māij'bhāṇḍārīẏā; 31 pp.

Nūr-e-rah'mān. Monthly journal. Eds Saiẏad Sāiphuddīn Āh'mad, Delāoẏār Hosāin (Nirbāhī sampādak). Caṭṭagrām, Saiẏad Śahīduddīn Āh'mad.

Māolānā Āk'bar Ālī **R**ej'bhī (1991): *Ādillātuch' chemā*. Caṭṭagrām/Māij'bhāṇḍār, Jamiẏate Rah'mānīẏā Māij'bhāṇḍārīẏā; 56 pp.

Mohāmmad Ālī Āyam **R**ej'bhī (2000): *Ācharut tāk·rīm bā bhaktir nidarśan*. Caṭṭagrām, Ān·jumāne Eśāẏāte Āh·le Chunnāt Oẏāl Jamāt; 38 pp.

Pratyaẏ: natun bhaban udbodhan upalakṣe smaraṇikā. 2000. Māij'bhāṇḍār, Māij'bhāṇḍār Āh'madiẏā Ucca Bidyālaẏ.

Śāhājādā Maulānā Chaiẏad Ākh'tār Kāmāl **Ś**āh' (1990): *Āl-bhāṇḍārī*. Caṭṭagrām, author's publ.; 72 pp.

Māolānā Ābu Tāher **S**ol'tān Āh'mad (1993): *Phatoẏāẏe rahmāniẏā: chāmā bā gān-bādya jāẏej haïbār dalil*. Māij'bhāṇḍār, Saiẏad Maīn Uddin Āh'mad Āl'hāchānī; 2. edn 1993; 1st edn 1976.

Muph'tī Phar'hād **P**hārukī (Noẏākhālī): *Śarīẏater dṛṣṭite 'chāmā' o bādyasaha murśedī gān*, Vol.1. Bātākāndi/Kumillā, author's publ., n.d.

Māolānā Muhāmmad Ālī Ājam **R**ej'bhī (comp./ed.) (1997): *Ohābī, Maodudī, o tab'līg jamāter saṃkṣipta khatiẏān*. Phaṭik'chaṛi, Āñjumāne Eśāẏāte Āh·le Sunnāt Oẏāl Jāmāt; 16 pp.

Śāhājādā Maulānā Chaiẏad Ākh'tār Kāmāl **Ś**āh·(1995): *Ādābe Hāl'kāẏe jikir o ādābe murid*. Caṭṭagrām, Najīr Bhāṇḍār Dar'bār Śarīph; 2nd edn; 1st edn 1992; 12 pp.

Haj'rat Śāh·suphī Āl· Hājv Māolānā Chaiẏad **Ś**aphiul Baśar (n.d.): *Ādābe hāl·kāẏe jikir: tvarikāẏe māij'bhāṇḍārīẏā*. Bhāṇḍār Śarīph; Rahmaniya Manzil [?]; 8 pp.

Saiẏad **S**ahidul Hak (ed.) (2005): *Prabandhasambhār māij'bhāṇḍār*. Māij'bhāṇḍār, Āñjumāne Mottābeẏīne Gāuche Māij'bhāṇḍār; 99 pp.

Satyānanda Brahmacārī (ed.) (1997): *Bhaktabāñchākalpataru mahāyogīrāj śrīśrīmatsbāmī Gurudās Param'haṃsa (Phakir) Bābājīr jībanī*. Suẏābil, Śrīśrī Suẏābil Siddhāśram Maṭh; 30 pp.

Professor Shahjada **S**hafiul Ghani Chowdhury (n.d.): *Origin & Development of Maizbhanderi Philosophy*. Damdama, author's publ.; 7 pp.

***T**auhīd*. Journal. 10, 1 (Pauṣ 1357 BE) and 10, 2 (Āṣāṛh 1358 BE). Eds Saiẏad Māh'bubul Baśar, Saiẏad Śaphiul Baśar. Māij'bhāṇḍār, [Rahmaniyya Manzil].

Secondary sources

'Abd al-Qādir al-Jīlānī (1992): *Revelations of the Unseen (Futūh al-Ghaib)*. Trans. Muhtar Holland. Houston, Al-Baz Publishing.

Ahluwalia, M.S. (1989): 'Baba Shaikh Farid: A Harbinger of Hindu–Muslim Unity'. In: Bhattacharyya, N.N. (ed.): *Medieval Bhakti Movements in India*. Śrī Caitanya Quincentenary Commemoration Volume. New Dehli, Munshiram Manoharlal; 74–82.

Ahmad, Aziz (1969): *Studies in Islamic Culture in the Indian Environment*. Oxford, Oxford University Press.

Āh'mad, Mājāhār Uddin (1417 *hiğrī* [1996–97]): *Hay'rat baṛa pīrer jībanī*. Ḍhākā, Sālāuddin Baïghar.

Ahmed, Rafiuddin (1981): *The Bengali Muslims 1871–1906: A Quest for Identity*. Delhi, Oxford University Press.

Ahmed, Rafiuddin (ed.) (2001): *Understanding the Bengal Muslims: Interpretative Essays*. Delhi, Oxford University Press.

Aich, Nani Gopal and Das, Sri Rishi (1991): *Progressive Bengali-English Dictionary*. Calcutta, Indian Progressive Publishing.

Ajmal, Mohammad (1984): 'A Note on *Adab* in the *Murshid–Murid* Relationship'. In: Metcalf, Barbara (ed.): *Moral Conduct and Authority. The Place of* Adab *in South Asian Islam*. Berkeley, University of California Press; 241–51.

Al-Ghazzali (2001): *The Alchemy of Happiness*. London, Octagon Press.

Ālam, Ohīdul (1989): *Caṭṭagrāmer itihās*. Caṭṭagrām, Baïghar.

idem (1985): *Caṭṭagrāmer lok'sāhitya*. Dhaka, Bangla Academy.

Ali, Muhammad Mohar (1985): *History of the Muslims of Bengal*. Vols Ia and Ib. Riadh, Imam Muhammad Ibn Sa'ūd Islamic University.

Āli, S. Oẏājed (1988): *Pīr pāẏ'gambar'der kathā*. Ḍhākā, Āh'mad Pāb'liśiṃ Hāus.

Ansari, Iqbal A. (ed.) (1989): *The Muslim Situation in India*. Dhaka, Academic Publishers.

Assayag, Jackie (1999): 'How Can One be Hindu and/or Muslim? The Resources of the Hagiographic Exemplar in South Asia'. In: Assayag (ed.): *Les ressources de l'histoire: Tradition, narration et nation en Asie du Sud*. Paris/Pondichéry, École française d'Extreme-Orient, Institut français de Pondichéry; 173–87.

Awwal, M.A. (2000): *A Glimpse on Great KhanJahan (R)*. Bagerhat, Kagaj Ghar.

Baljon, J.m.S. (1992): 'Shah Waliullah and the Dargah'. In: Troll, Christian W.: *Muslim Shrines in India: Their Character, History and Significance*. Delhi, Oxford University Press; 189–97.

Bandyopadhyay, P.K. (1992): *Nātha Cult and Mahānād: a Study in Syncretism*. Delhi, B.R. Publishing Corporation.

Bandyopadhyay, Pranab (1990): *Ramakrishna and the Divine Mother*. Calcutta, United Writers.

Baṙuẏā 'Sṛjan', Dipak (1998): *Hājār bacharer bāṅālī bauddha*. Vol.1. Paṭiẏā, Bangladesh Buddhist Welfare Association.

Baśir'uddin, Khondakār Māolānā Mo. (1990): *IlA me mārephāt bā Āllāh prāpti tattva*. Bariśāl, Korān Mañjil Lāibrerī.

Begam, Jāhān-Ārā (1976): *Bāṃlādeśer maramī sāhitya*. Ḍhākā, Bāṃlā Academy.

Berner, U. (1982): *Untersuchungen zur Verwendung des Synkretismus-Begriffes*. Göttinger Orientforschungen, Reihe Grundlagen und Ergebnisse, Bd.2. Wiesbaden, Harrassowitz.

Bertocci, Peter J. (1970): *Elusive Villages: Social Structure and Community Organization in Rural East Pakistan*. Unpublished Ph.D. dissertation. East Lansing, Michigan State University.

Bertocci, Peter J. (2006): 'A Sufi Movement in Bangladesh: The Maijbhandari tariqa and its followers.' *Contributions to Indian Sociology* 40, 1, 2006; 1–28.

Bhaṭṭācārya, Upendranāth (2001): *Bāṃlār bāul o bāul gān*. Kalikātā, Prahlād'kumār Prāmāṇik. (New edn; 1st edn 1957).

Bhaṭṭācārya, Yatīndramohan (1962): *Bāṅgālār baiṣṇab-bhābāpanna musal'mān kabi*. 2nd edn. Kalikātā, Kalikātā Biśvabidyālaẏ.

Bhaṭṭācārya, Yatīndramohan (1984): *Bāṅgālār baiṣṇab-bhābāpanna musal'mān kabir padamañjuṣā*. Kalikātā, Kalikātā Biśvabidyālaẏ.

Bhattacharya, Bhaskar (1993): *The Path of the Mystic Lover: Baul Songs of Passion and Ecstasy*. Rochester, Destiny Books.

Bhattacharya, France (2001): 'Identité et culture au Bangladesh: le rapport de la Commission Nationale sur la Culture'. In: Racine, J.-L. (ed.): *La question identitaire en Asie du Sud*. Collection Puruṣārtha. Paris, Éditions de l'École des Hautes Études en Sciences Sociales; 181–213.

Bhattacharyya, N.N. (ed.) (1989): *Medieval Bhakti Movements in India*. Śrī Caitanya Quincentenary Commemoration Volume. New Dehli, Munshiram Manoharlal.

Bhūñā, Mo. Kāmāl (1999): *Tāsāouph sañjībanī*. Ḍhākā, Āh'mad Pāb'liśiṃ Hāus.

Binodinī Dāsī (1988): *Naṭī Binodinī Dāsī racanā-samagra*. Kalikātā, Raṇadhīr Pāl.

Biśbās, Amalendu (1994/95): *Lokakabi rameś śīl*. Caṭṭagrām, Maitrī Prakāśanā; 2nd edn (1st edn 1990/91).

Biśvās, Sukumār (1995): *Bāṃlā ekāḍemi pũthi paricaẏ – 1*. Ḍhākā, Bāṃlā Ekāḍemi.

Blumhardt, J.F. (1886): *Catalogue of Bengali Printed Books in the Library of the British Museum*. London, British Museum.

Blumhardt, J.F. (1923): *Catalogue of the Library of the India Office*, Vol.II, Part IV. Supplement, 1906–20. London, Eyre and Spottiswoode.

Brahma, Tṛpti (1986): *Bāṃlār is'lāmi saṃskṛti*. Kal'kātā, Firma KLM.

Braun, E. (1978): 'Hermeneutischer Zirkel'. In: Braun and Radermacher, H.: *Wissenschafts-theoretisches Lexikon*. Graz/Wien/Köln, Styria; 236–9.

Buitenen, J.A.B. van (1966): 'On the Archaism of the *Bhāgavata Purāṇa*'; in Singer, Milton (ed.) (1966): *Krishna: Myths, Rites, and Attitudes*. The University of Chicago Press, Chicago and London; 23–40.

Burckhardt Qureshi, Regula (1993): 'Sama' in the Royal Court of Saints: The Chishtiyya of South Asia'. In: Grace Martin Smith (ed.): *Manifestations of Sainthood in Islam*. Istanbul, The Isis Press, 111–127; 113.

Cakrabartī, Sudhīr (1990): *Bāṃlā dehatattver gān*. Kal'kātā, Pustak Bipaṇi.

Cakrabartī, Sudhīr (ed.) (1999): *Bāṃlār bāul-phakir*. Kal'kātā, Pustak Bipaṇi.

Callewaert, Winand M. and Snell, Rupert (eds) (1994): *According to Tradition: Hagiographical Writing in India*. Wiesbaden, Harrassowitz Verlag.

Canda, Pulak (1978): *Gaṇakabiẏāl Rameś Śīl o tā̃r gān*. Kalikātā, Kathāśilpa.

Cashin, David (1995): *The Ocean of Love: Middle Bengali Sufi Literature and the Fakirs of Bengal*. Stockholm, Stockholm University.

Caudhurī, Śām'sur Rah'mān (2002): *Suphidarśan*. Ḍhākā, Dibyaprakāś.

Chakrabarti, Asim Pada (1993): *Muslim Identity and Community Consciousness: Bengal Lagislative Politics 1912–13*. Calcutta, Minerva.

Chatterjee, Joya (1998): 'The Bengali Muslims: A Contradiction in Terms?' In: Hasan, Mushirul (ed.): *Islam, Communities and the Nation: Muslim Identities in South Asia and Beyond*. New Delhi, Manohar; 265–82.

Chiddikī, Golām Mostaphā (1997): *Olīẏe kāmel Haẏ'rat Śekh Pharid (ra.)*. Dhaka, Sālāuddin Baïghar.

Chiddikī, Mohāmmad Muhib'ulyāh (ed.) (2000): *Ārākāner musal'mān: itihās o aitihya*. Caṭṭagrām, Ārākān Hisṭarikyāl Sosāiṭi.

Chittick, William C. (1998): *Principles of Ibn al-ʿArabī's Cosmology: The Self-Disclosure of God*. Albany, State University of New York Press.

Chodkiewicz, Michel (1986): *Le sceau des saints: prophétie et sainteté dans la doctrine d'Ibn Arabī*. Paris, Gallimard.

Colpe, Carsten (1987): 'Syncretism'. In: *Encyclopedia of Religions*, Vol.14; ed. Eliade, Mircea. NY, Macmillan; 218–27.

Colpe, Carsten (1997): 'The Phenomenon of Syncretism and the Impact of Islam'. In: Kehl-Bodrogi, Krisztina et al. (eds): *Syncretistic Religious Communities in the Near East*. Leiden/New York/Köln, Brill; 35–48.

Coxhead, David and Hiller, Susan (1976): *Dreams: Visions of the Night*. London, Thames and Hudson.

Das, Anjana (1992): 'Der Theravāda-Buddhismus als Minderheitenreligion in Bangladesh'.

In: Grünendahl, Reinhold et al. (eds): *Studien zur Indologie und Buddhismuskunde.* Festschrift Heinz Bechert. Bonn, Indica et tibetica; 65–76.

Dās, Girīndranāth (1976): *Bāṃlā pīr-sāhityer kathā.* Kājīpāṛā, Śehid Lāibrerī.

Das, Rahul Peter (1983): 'Some Remarks on the Bengali Deity Dharma: Its Cult and Study'. *Anthropos* 78, 1983, 661–700.

Das, Rahul Peter (1992): 'Problematic Aspects of the Sexual Rituals of the Bauls of Bengal'. *Journal of the American Oriental Society* 112, 3, 388–432.

Das, Rahul Peter (1992a): 'Südindien und Bengalen' [Section on Islam]. In: Tworuschka, Monika and Udo (eds): *Bertelsmann Handbuch Religionen der Welt: Grundlagen, Entwicklung und Bedeutung in der Gegenwart.* Gütersloh/München, Bertelsmann Lexikon Verlag; 205–8.

Das, Rahul Peter (1994): 'Das Verhältnis zwischen Islam und Bengalentum'. In: Conrad, Dietel and Zingel, Wolfgang-Peter (eds) (1994): *Bangladesh: Dritte Heidelberger Südasiengespräche.* Stuttgart, Franz Steiner Verlag; 7–14.

Das, Rahul Peter (1996): 'Zu einer neuen *Caryāpada*-Sammlung'. *Zeitschrift der Deutschen Morgenländischen Gesellschaft* 146, 1996; 128–38.

Das, Rahul Peter (1997): *Essays on Vaiṣṇavism in Bengal.* Calcutta, KLM.

Das, Rahul Peter (2003): *The Origin of the Life of a Human Being: Conception and the Female Acording to Ancient Indian Medical and Sexological Literature.* Delhi, Motilal Banarsidass.

Das, Rahul Peter (2003a): 'Stranger in a strange land'. In: Czekalska, Renata and Marlewicz, Halina (eds): *2nd International Conference on Indian Studies: Proceedings.* Krakow, Ksiegarnia Akademicka; 153–77.

Dasgupta, Alokeranjan and Dasgupta, Mary Ann (transl.) (1977): *Roots in the Void: Baul Songs of Bengal.* Calcutta, K.P. Bagchi & Co.

Dasgupta, Shashi Bhushan (1976): *Obscure Religious Cults.* Calcutta, Firma KLM (3rd edn).

Datta, Gurusadaẏ and Bhaumik, Nirmalendu (eds) (1966): *Śrīhaṭṭer lok'saṅgīt.* Kalikātā, Kalikātā Biśvabidyālaẏ.

Der Koran. Transl. Max Henning. Reclam, Stuttgart, 1960; revised edn 1991.

Desiderio Pinto, S.J. (1992): 'The Mystery of the Nizamuddin Dargah: The Accounts of Pilgrims'. In: Troll, Christian W.: *Muslim Shrines in India: Their Character, History and Significance.* Delhi, Oxford University Press; 112–24.

Digby, Simon (1994): 'To Ride a Tiger or a Wall? Strategies of Prestige in Indian Sufi Legend'. In: Callewaert, Winand M. and Snell, Rupert (eds): *According to Tradition: Hagiographical Writing in India.* Wiesbaden, Harrassowitz Verlag; 99–129.

Dimock, Edward C. Jr. (1989): *The Place of the Hidden Moon. Erotic Mysticism in the Vaiṣṇava-sahajiyā Cult of Bengal.* Chicago/London, Chicago University Press; 1st edn 1966.

Dimock, Edward C. Jr. (1966): 'Doctrine and Practice among the Vaiṣṇavas of Bengal'. In: Singer, Milton (ed.): *Krishna: Myths, Rites, and Attitudes.* Chicago/London, University of Chicago Press; 41–63.

Dinzelbacher, Peter (1990): 'Die "Realpräsenz" der Heiligen in ihren Reliquiaren und Gräbern nach mittelalterlichen Quellen'. In: Dinzelbacher: *Heiligenverehrung in Geschichte und Gegenwart.* Ostfildern, Schwabenverlag; 115–74.

Drehsen, Volker and Sparn, Walter (eds) (1996): *Im Schmelztiegel der Religionen: Konturen des modernen Synkretismus.* Gütersloh, Gütersloher Verlagshaus.

During, Jean (1996): 'Musique et rites: le *samā*''. In: Popovic, Alexandre et Veinstein, Gilles (eds): *Les Voies d'Allah. Les ordres Mystiques dans l'Islam des origines à aujourd'hui.* Paris, Fayard; 157–72.

Eagleton, Terry (1991): *Ideology: An Introduction*. London/New York, Verso.

Eaton, Richard (1984): 'The Political and Religious Authority of the Shrine of Baba Farid'. In: Metcalf, Barbara D. (ed.): *Moral Conduct and Authority: the Place of Adab in South Asian Islam*. Berkeley, University of California Press; 333–56.

Eaton, Richard M. (1985): 'Review of Asim Roy, The Islamic Syncretistic Tradition in Bengal'. *The Journal of Asian Studies*, 44, 2, 442–44.

Eaton, Richard (1993): *The Rise of Islam and the Bengal Frontier*. Berkeley, University of California Press.

Eaton, Richard (2000): *Essays on Islam and Indian History*. New Delhi, Oxford University Press.

Eaton, Richard (ed.) (2003): *India's Islamic Traditions, 711–1750*. New Delhi, Oxford University Press.

Einzmann, H. (1988): *Ziara und Pir-e-Muridi: Golra Sharif, Nurpur Shahan und Pir Baba: drei muslimische Wallfahrtstätten in Nordpakistan*. Wiesbaden, Steiner.

Eliade, Mircea (1985): *Yoga: Unsterblichkeit und Freiheit*. Frankfurt/Main, Suhrkamp.

Ernst, Carl W. (1993): 'An Indo-Persian Guide to Sufi Shrine Pilgrimage'. In: Martin Smith, Grace (ed.): *Manifestations of Sainthood in Islam*. Istanbul, Isis Press, 43–68.

Ewing, Katherine P. (1993): 'The Modern Businessman and the Pakistani Saint: The Interpenetration of Worlds'. In: Martin Smith, Grace (ed.): *Manifestations of Sainthood in Islam*. Istanbul, Isis Press; 69–84.

Feldtkeller, Andreas (1992): 'Der Synkretismus-Begriff im Rahmen einer Theorie von Verhältnisbestimmungen zwischen Religionen'. *Evangelische Theologie* 52 (1992), 224–45.

Forty Hadith Qudsi. Selected and transl. by Ibrahim, Ezzeddin and Johnson-Davies, Denys. Beirut/Damascus, Dar al-Koran al-Kareem, 1980.

Gaborieau, Marc (1983): 'The cult of saints among the Muslims of Nepal and northern India'. In: Wilson, Stephen (ed.): *Saints and their Cults. Studies in Religious Sociology, Folklore and History*. Cambridge, Cambridge University Press; 291–308.

Gaborieau, Marc (1992): 'A Nineteenth-Century Indian "Wahhabi" Tract Against the Cult of Muslim Saints: Al-Balagh al-Mubin'. In: Troll, Christian W.: *Muslim Shrines in India: Their Character, History and Significance*. Delhi, Oxford University Press; 198–239.

Gaborieau, Marc (1999): 'Criticizing the Sufis: The Debate in Early-Nineteenth Century India'. In: De Jong, Frederick and Radtke, Bernd (eds): *Islamic Mysticism Contested: Thirteen Centuries of Controversies and Polemics*. Leiden, Brill; 452–67.

Gaborieau, Marc (2003): 'The Ghazi Miyan Cult in Western Nepal and Northern India'. In Waseem, Muhammad (ed.): *On Becoming an Indian Muslim: French Essays on Aspects of Syncretism*. Delhi, Oxford University Press; 238–63.

Gaeffke, Peter (1992): 'How a Muslim looks at Hindu bhakti'. In: McGregor, R.S. (1992): *Devotional Literature in South Asia: Current Research, 1985–1988*; Cambridge, Cambridge University Press; 80–8.

Gardet, L. (1986): 'Kiyāma'. In: *Encyclopaedia of Islam*, Vol.V. Leiden, Brill; 235–38 (New Edition).

Gardner, Katy (1999): 'Global Migrants and Local Shrines'. In: Manger, Leif (ed.): *Muslim Diversity. Local Islam in Global Contexts*. Richmond, Curzon; 37–57.

Gardner, Katy (1995): *Global Migrants, Local Lives: Travel and Transformation in Rural Bangladesh*. Oxford, Clarendon Press.

Geertz, Clifford (1968): *Islam Observed: Religious Development in Morocco and Indonesia*. Chicago/London, University of Chicago Press.

Gellner, Ernest (1983): *Nations and Nationalism*. Ithaca, Cornell University Press.

Gold, Daniel (1987): *The Lord as Guru: Hindu* Sants *in North Indian Tradition*. New York/ Oxford, Oxford University Press.

Gramlich, Richard (transl./ed.) (1978): *Die Gaben der Erkenntnisse des 'Umar as-Suhrawardī ('Awārif al-ma'ārif)*. Freiburger Islamstudien, Band VI. Wiesbaden, Franz Steiner Verlag; 165–92.

Gramlich, Richard (1984): *Muhammad al-Gazzālīs Lehre von den Stufen zur Gottesliebe: die Bücher 31–36 seines Hauptwerkes* [*Iḥya 'ulūm al-dīn*]. Steiner, Wiesbaden.

Gramlich, Richard (1987): *Die Wunder der Freunde Gottes: Theologie und Erscheinungsformen des islamischen Heiligenwunders*. Freiburger Islamstudien, Bd. XI. Wiesbaden, Franz Steiner Verlag.

Gramlich, Richard (ed.) (1989): *Das Sendschreiben al-Qušayrīs über das Sufitum*. Freiburger Islamstudien, Band XII. Wiesbaden, Franz Steiner Verlag.

Gramlich, Richard (1990): *Schlaglichter über das Sufitum: Abū Naṣr as-Sarrāğs Kitāb al-luma'*. Freiburger Islamstudien, Band XIII. Stuttgart, Franz Steiner Verlag.

Haas, Alois M. (1996): *Mystik als Aussage: Erfahrungs-, Denk- und Redeformen christlicher Mystik*. Frankfurt/M., Suhrkamp.

Hacker, Paul (1978 [1958]): 'Der Dharma-Begriff des Neuhinduismus'. In: Hacker: *Kleine Schriften*. Ed. Schmithausen, Lambert. Wiesbaden, Harrassowitz; 580–608.

Hacker, Paul (1978 [1970]): 'Aspects of Neo-Hinduism as Contrasted with Surviving Traditional Hinduism'. In: Hacker: *Kleine Schriften*. Ed. Schmithausen, Lambert. Wiesbaden, Harrassowitz; 510–24.

Hacker, Paul (1978 [1971]): 'Der religiöse Nationalismus Vivekānandas'. In: Hacker, : *Kleine Schriften*. Ed. Schmithausen, Lambert. Wiesbaden, Harrassowitz; 565–79.

Hāi, Muhammad Āb'dul and Śarīph, Āh'mad (eds) (1998): *Madhyayuger bāṅ'lā gītikabitā*. Ḍhākā, Māolā Brothers.

Hak, Māh'bubul (ed.) (1995): *Dainik ājādī 35 barṣapūrti biśeṣ saṃkhyā: hājār bacharer caṭṭagrām*. Caṭṭagrām, Em. E. Mālek.

Hak, Maphidul (2000): 'Māij'hāṇḍār sandarśan: ek'ṭi kathā'. *Dainik saṃbād*, 27 August 2000; p.8.

Hak, Muhammad Enāmul (1991): 'Baṅge svūphī-prabhāb'. In: *Muhammad Enāmul hak racanābalī*, Vol.1. Ed. Musā, Man'sur. Ḍhākā, Bāṃlā Ekāḍemī; 39–195.

Hak, Muhammad Enāmul (1995): 'A History of Sufi-ism in Bengal'. In: *Muhammad Enāmul hak racanābalī*, Vol.4. Ed. Musā, Man'sur. Ḍhākā, Bāṃlā Ekāḍemī; 1–445.

Hak, Muhammad Enāmul (1995a): 'An Account of The Jalali Family of Parganah-i-Isapur, Chittagong'. In: *Muhammad Enāmul hak racanābalī*, Vol.4. Ed. Musā, Man'sur. Ḍhākā, Bāṃlā Ekāḍemī; 469–500.

Hak, Muhammad Enāmul (1997): 'Sufi Movement in India'. In: *Muhammad Enāmul hak racanābalī*, Vol.5. Ed. Musā, Man'sur. Ḍhākā, Bāṃlā Ekāḍemī; 447–77.

Hak, Muhammad Enāmul (1997a): 'Impact of Islām on the Gauḍian Form of Vaishṇavism'. In: *Muhammad enāmul hak racanābalī*, Vol.5. Ed. Musā, Man'sur. Ḍhākā, Bāṃlā Ekāḍemī; 447–77.

Hak Caudhurī, Āb'dul (1988): *Caṭṭagrāmer samāj o saṃskṛtir rūp'rekhā*. Ḍhākā, Bāṃlā Ekāḍemī.

Hak Caudhurī, Āb'dul (1994): *Bandar śahar caṭṭagrām*. Ḍhākā, Bāṃlā Ekāḍemī.

Hak Caudhurī, Āb'dul (1994a): *Prācīn ārākān roẏāiṅgā hindu o baṛuẏā bauddha adhibāsī*. Ḍhākā, Bāṃlā Ekāḍemi.

Halbfass, Wilhelm (1988): *India and Europe: An Essay in Understanding*. Albany, State University of New York Press.

Harder, Hans (2004): *Der verrückte Gofur spricht. Mystische Lieder aus Ostbengalen von Abdul Gofur Hali*. Heidelberg, Draupadi Verlag.

Harder, Hans (2001): *Bankimchandra Chattopadhyay's* Śrīmadbhagabadgītā. *Translation and Analysis*. Delhi, Manohar.

Harder, Hans (2008): 'Shrine Veneration vs. Reformism, Bengal vs. Islam: Some Remarks on Perceptual Difficulties Regarding Bengali Islam'. In: Hugh van Skyhawk (ed.): *Sufi Traditions and New Departures on the Subcontinent. Recent Scholarship on Continuity and Change in South Asian Sufism*. Taxila Institute, Islamabad; 181–98.

Harder, Hans (2009): ' "Hazy Aryan Mysticism and the Semitic Desert Sun": Iqbal on Arabs and Persians, Semites and Aryans'. In: Ali Usman Qasmi, Gita Dharampal-Frick and Katia Rostetter (eds): *Revisioning Iqbal as a Poet & Muslim Political Thinker*. Heidelberg, Draupadi Verlag; 163–77.

Hardy, Friedhelm (1983): '*Viraha* in Relation to Concrete Space and Time'. In: Thiel-Horstmann, Monika (ed.) (1983): *Bhakti in Current Research, 1979–1982. Proceedings of the Second International Conference on Early Devotional Literature in New Indo-Aryan Languages, St. Augustin, 19–21 March 1982*. Berlin, Dietrich Reimer Verlag; 143–56.

Hardy, P. (1972): *The Muslims of British India*. Cambridge, Cambridge University Press.

Harvilahti, Lauri (1998): 'Divine Yearning. The Folklore of Bangladesh's Mystics'. *Temenos* 34, 1998; 41–51.

Hauser, Beatrix (1998): *Mit irdischem Schaudern und göttlicher Fügung: bengalische Erzähler und ihre Bildvorführungen*. Berlin, Das Arabische Buch.

Hefner, Robert W. (1995): *Syncretism*. In: *The Oxford Encyclopedia of the Modern Islamic World*, Vol.4. Ed. Esposito, John L. New York/Oxford, Oxford University Press; 149–52.

Heissig, Werner and Klimkeit, Hans-Joachim (ed.) (1987): *Synkretismus in den Religionen Zentralasiens*. Wiesbaden, Harrassowitz.

Henry, Edward O. (1996): 'The Vitality of the *Nirguṇ* Bhajan: Sampling the Contemporary Tradition'. In: Lorenzen, David N. (ed.): *Bhakti Religion in North India: Community Identity and Political Action*. Delhi, Manohar; 231–50.

Hopkins, Thomas W. (1966): 'The Social Teaching of the *Bhāgavata Purāṇa*'. In: Singer, Milton (ed.): *Krishna: Myths, Rites, and Attitudes*. University of Chicago Press, Chicago/London; 3–22.

Hosen Caudhurī, Deoẏān Nūrul Ānoẏār (ed.) (1995): *Āmāder sūphīẏāẏe kirām*. Ḍhākā, Is'lāmik Phāuṇḍeśan Bāṃlādeś.

Huizinga, Johan (1939): *Homo ludens: Versuch einer Bestimmung des Spielelementes der Kultur*. Amsterdam, Pantheon.

Hunter, W.W. (1999): *The Indian Musulmans*. Dhaka, Khoshroz Publications. 1st edn 1871.

Ibn Arabī (1997): *Le livre des chatons des sagesses*. Vol. 1. Traduction intégrale, notes et commentaire de Charles-André Gilis. Beyrouth, Dar al-Bouraq.

Is'lām, Āj'hār (1992): *Madhyayuger bāṃlā sāhitye mus'lim kabi*. Ḍhākā, Bāṃlā Ekāḍemi.

Jāhāṅgīr, Selim (1999): *Māij'bhāṇḍār sandarśan*. Ḍhākā, Bāṃlā Ekāḍemī.

Jāhāṅgīr, Selim (2000): *Māij'bhāṇḍārī tarikār tāttvik biśleṣak Saiẏad Delāor Hosāin Māij'bhāṇḍārī (Ra.)*. Caṭṭagrām, Saiẏad Sahidul Hak.

Jāhāṅgīr, Selim (2006): *Gāusul Āzam Māij'bhāṇḍārīr śata barṣer āloke*. Māij'bhāṇḍār, Āñjumāne Mottābeẏīne Gāuche Māij'bhāṇḍārī.

Jaohar, Mobārak Karīm (1982): *Bhārater sūphī*, Vol.1. Kal'kātā, Karuṇā Prakāśanī.

Jaohar, Mobārak Karīm (1983): *Bhārater sūphī*, Vol.2. Kal'kātā, Karuṇā Prakāśanī.

Jaohar, Mobārak Karīm (1986): *Bhārater sūphī*, Vol.3. Kal'kātā, Karuṇā Prakāśanī.

Jasīmuddīn (1977): *Murśidā gān.* Ḍhākā, Bāṃlā Academy.

Jaẏ'nul Ābedīn, Ābul Phātāh Māolānā (1998): *Bāṃlār olikul śiramani* [*sic*] *mar'hum Haẏ'rat Pīr Khān'jāhān Ālī (ra.).* Khul'nā, H.M. Ādam Ālī.

Kabīr (1974): *Ramainī. Kabīr Vāṅmay* 1. Ed. Jay'dev Siṃh, Vāsudev Siṃh. Vārāṇasī, Viśvavidyālay Prakāśan.

Kabīr (1976): *Sākhī. Kabīr Vāṅmay* 3. Ed. Jay'dev Siṃh, Vāsudev Siṃh. Vārāṇasī, Viśvavidyālay Prakāśan.

Kabīr (1981): *Sabad. Kabīr Vāṅmay* 2. Ed. Jay'dev Siṃh, Vāsudev Siṃh. Vārāṇasī, Viśvavidyālay Prakāśan.

Kabiẏāl Rameś Śīl Memorial Institute, Boẏāl'khālī, Caṭṭagrām: 21tama mṛtyubārṣikī: 23 Caitra 1394, 6 Epril 1988; n.d.; printed in Caṭṭagrām.

Karim 'Sāhityabiśārad', Āb'dul (1997): *Āb'dul Karim Sāhityabiśārad racanābalī,* 3 vols. Ed. Ābul Āh'sān Caudhurī. Ḍhākā, Bāṃlā Academy.

Kaviraj, Sudipta (1992): 'The Imaginary Constitution of India'. In: Chatterjee, Partha and Pandey, Gyanendra (eds): *Subaltern Studies* VII. New Delhi, Oxford University Press; pp. 20–26.

Khalid, Adeeb (2004): 'Visions of India in Central Asian Modernism: The Work of ʿAbd ar-Raʾūf Fiṭrat'. In: Eschment, Beate and Harder, Hans (eds): *Looking at the Coloniser: Cross-Cultural Perceptions in Central Asia and the Caucasus, Bengal, and Related Areas.* Würzburg, Ergon Verlag; 253–74.

Khan, Abdul Mabud (1999): *The Maghs: A Buddhist Community in Bangladesh.* Dhaka, University Press.

Khān, Ālāuddīn (1996): *Mā'riphāt o dīdār-e-ilāhī.* Ḍhākā/Caṭṭagrām, Bangladesh Co-operative Book Society.

Khān, Āmān Uddīn Muhāmmad Ājīm (1997): *Kerāmat o Haj'rat Śāh Sūphī Āmānat Khān (rah.).* Chittagong, Khān'kāh Āmānatiẏā (1st edn 1974).

Kiehnle, Catharina (1997): *Songs on Yoga: Texts and Teachings of the Mahārāṣṭrian Nāths* and *The Conservative Vaiṣṇava: Anonymous Songs of the Jñāndev Gāthā.* Jñāndev Studies I–III. 2 vols. Stuttgart, Franz Steiner Verlag.

Klostermaier, Klaus K. (1990): *A Survey of Hinduism*; New Delhi, Munshiram Manoharlal.

Knysh, Alexander (2000): *Islamic Mysticism: A Short History.* Leiden, Brill.

Korom, Frank J. (2004): 'The Bengali Dharmarāj in Text and Context: Some Parallels'. *Journal of Indian Philosophy* 32, 5–6, 2004; 843–70.

Kraemer, H. (1962): *Synkretismus. Religion in Geschichte und Gegenwart* (3rd edn); 563–67.

Kripal, Jeffrey J. (1995): *Kālī's Child. The Mystical and the Erotic in the Life and Teachings of Ramakrishna.* Chicago/London, University of Chicago Press.

Kvaerne, Per (1977): *An Anthology of Buddhist Tantric Songs: A Study of the Caryāgīti.* Oslo, Universitetsforlaget.

Landell Mills, Samuel (1995): 'Sacred Flesh, Sacred Soil: Sufi Cults in Bangladesh'. In: *Le culte des saints dans le monde musulman.* Sous la direction de Henri Chambert-Loir et Claude Guillot. Paris, EFEO; 217–34.

Landell Mills, Samuel (1998): 'The Hardware of Sanctity: Anthropomorphic Objects in Bangladeshi Sufism'. In: Werbner, Pnina and Basu, Helene (eds): *Embodying Charisma: Modernity, Locality and the Performance of Emotion in Sufi Cults.* London/New York, Routledge; 31–54.

Latif, Sk. Abdul (1993): *The Muslim Mystic Movement in Bengal 1301–1550.* Calcutta, K.P. Bagchi.

Lévi-Strauss, Claude (1952): *Le syncrétisme religieux d'un village mog du territoire de Chittagong. Revue de l'histoire des religions* 141, 1952; 202–37.

Liebeskind, Claudia (1998): *Piety on its Knees. Three Sufi Traditions in South Asia in Modern Times.* Delhi, Oxford University Press.
Lorenzen, David N. (ed.) (1996) *Bhakti Religion in North India: Community Identity and Political Action.* Delhi, Manohar.
Luchesi, Brigitte (1983): *Familie und Verwandtschaft in einem Dorf in Bangladesch.* Berlin, Dietrich Reimer Verlag.
Luhmann, Niklas and Fuchs, Peter (1989): *Reden und Schweigen.* Frankfurt/M., Suhrkamp.
Madan, T.N. (2001): *Muslim Communities of South Asia: Culture, Society and Power.* New Delhi, Manohar (3rd enlarged edn).
Majidī, Nūr Hosen (1998): *Nūre muḥammādīr marmakathā.* Ḍhākā, Confident Publications.
Matchett, Freda (1993): 'The Pervasiveness of *Bhakti* in the Bhāgavata Purāṇa'. In: Werner, Karel (ed.): *Love Divine: Studies in* Bhakti *and Devotional Mysticism.* Durham Indological Series No.3. Richmond, Curzon Press; 95–116.
Mahaṃmad'bābā Śrīgoṃdekar, Śekh (1981): *Yog'saṃgrām.* Ed. Rām'candra Ciṃtāmaṇ Ḍhere. Puṇe, Varadā.
Māsūm, Mohāmmad Ābul Kālām (1998): *Māt̥rsebak Hay'rat Bāyejīd Bostāmī (ra.).* Ḍhākā, Sālāuddin Baïghar.
Matringe, Denis (1992): 'Kr̥ṣṇaite and Nāth elements in the poetry of the eighteenth-century Panjabi Sūfī Bullhe Śāh'. In: McGregor, R.S. (1992): 190–206.
McGregor, R.S. (1992): *Devotional Literature in South Asia: Current Research, 1985–1988*; Cambridge, Cambridge University Press.
Meier, Fritz (1994): *Zwei Abhandlungen über die Naqšbandiyya.* Istanbul, Orient-Institut der Deutschen Morgenländischen Gesellschaft/Stuttgart, Franz Steiner Verlag.
Metcalf, Barbara D. (1995): 'Presidential Address: Too Little and Too Much: Reflections on Muslims in the History of India'. *Journal of Asian Studies* 54 (4): 951–67.
Mojaddedi, Jawid A. (2001): *The Biographical Tradition in Sufism.* Richmond, Curzon Press.
Mukherjee, S.N. (1993): *Calcutta: Essays in Urban history.* Calcutta, Subarnarekha.
Myer, Prudence R. (1961): 'Stupas and Stupa-Shrines'. *Artibus Asiae* 24, 1961; 25–34.
Naj'rul Is'lām, Mo. (1999): *Gaṇa mānuṣer kabi saṃgrāmī kabiyāl Rameś Śīl. Bhorer Kāgaj* 25 Feb 1999; 15.
Nicholson, R.A. (transl.) (1911): *The Kashf al-Maḥjūb. The Oldest Persian Treatise on Śūfiism.* E.J.W. Gibb Memorial Series, Vol. XVII. Leyden, Brill/London, Luzac & Co.
Nūr Mohāmmad, Mau. (ed.) (1997): *Svāmī-strīr milan-tattva.* Ḍhākā, Bābul Lāibreri. 3rd edn; 1st edn 1993.
Oberoi, Harjot (1994): *The Construction of Religious Boundaries: Culture, Identity and Diversity in the Sikh Tradition.* Delhi, Oxford University Press.
Openshaw, Jeanne (2002): *Seeking Bāuls of Bengal.* Cambridge, Cambridge University Press.
Pandey, S.M. (1992): 'Kutuban's *Miragāvatī*: its content and interpretation'. In: McGregor, R.S. (1992): *Devotional Literature in South Asia: Current Research, 1985–1988.* Cambridge, Cambridge University Press; 179–89.
Paul, Jürgen (1990): 'Hagiographische Texte als historische Quelle'. *Saeculum* 41, 1990; 17–43.
Paul, Jürgen (1998): *Doctrine and Organization: The Khwājagān Naqshbandīya in the First Generation after Bahā'uddīn.* ANOR 1. Berlin, Das Arabische Buch.
Pellat, Ch. (1991): 'Manāib'. In: *Encyclopaedia of Islam*, Vol.VI. Leiden, Brill; 349–57 (New Edition).
Petievich, Carla (2007): *When Men Speak as Women: Vocal Masquerade in Indo-Muslim Poetry.* Oxford University Press, New Delhi.

Pīrmuhammatu Oliyullā (1995): 'Ñāṉap pukaḻcci'. In: Añcuvaṉṉam Pīrmuhammadiyyā and Muslim Acōliyēṣaṉ (eds): *Ñāṉa māmētai Ṣeyku Pīrmuhammatu Oliyullā (rali) avarkaḷiṉ eyññāṉap pāḷalkaḷ*. Takkalai; 1–109.

Pye, M. (1971): *Syncretism and Ambiguity*. *Numen* 18, 1971; 83–93.

Qureshi, Hamid Afaq (1989): 'Nature and Roots of Islamic Bhakti Movement and Syed Ashraf Jahangir Samnani'. In: Bhattacharyya, N.N. (ed.): *Medieval Bhakti Movements in India*. Śrī Caitanya Quincentenary Commemoration Volume. New Dehli, Munshiram Manoharlal; 83–96.

Qureshi, Ishtiaq Husain (1979): *Perspectives of Islam and Pakistan*. Karachi, Ma'aref Limited.

Rah'mān, K.M.G. (1986): *Hay'rat Śāh'jālāl o Śāh'prāṇ (rah.)*. Ḍhākā, Rah'mānivā Lāibrerī.

Rah'mān, K.M.G. (1998): *Hay'rat Bāẏeyīd o Śāh Āmānat*. Dhaka, Rah'mānivā Lāibrerī.

Rahman, Mojibur (1977): *History of Madrassah Education, with Special Reference to Calcutta Madrasah and W.B. Education Board*. Calcutta, Rais Anwer and Brothers.

Randeria, Shalini (1996): 'Hindu-"Fundamentalismus": Zum Verhältnis von Religion, Geschichte und Identität im modernen Indien'. In: Weiß et al. (eds): *Religion – Macht – Gewalt: Religiöser 'Fundamentalismus' und Hindu-Moslem-Konflikte in Südasien*. Frankfurt/M., IKO Verlag; 26–56.

Ray, Niharranjan (1989): 'The Concept of Sahaj in Guru Nanak's Theology and its Antecedents'. In: Bhattacharyya, N.N. (ed.): *Medieval Bhakti Movements in India*. Śrī Caitanya Quincentenary Commemoration Volume. New Dehli, Munshiram Manoharlal; 17–35.

Ray, Sukumar (1988): *Folk Music of Eastern India. With Special Reference to Bengal*. Shimla, Indian Institute of Advanced Studies.

Razia Akter Banu, U.A.B. (1992): *Islam in Bangladesh*. Leiden, etc., Brill.

Redfield, Robert (1955): 'The Social Organisation of Tradition'. *Far Eastern Quarterly* XV, 1, 1955; 13–21.

Rizvi, Saiyid Athar Abbas (1978): *A History of Sufism in India*. 2 vols. New Delhi, Manohar.

Robson, James (1938): *Tracts on Listening to Music, being* Dhamm al-malāhī *by Ibn abī'L-Dunyā and* Bawāriq al-ilmā' *by Majd al-Din al-Ṭūsī al-Ghazālī*. Oriental Translation Fund, New Series, Vol XXXIV. London, Royal Asiatic Society.

Roy, Asim (1983): *The Islamic Syncretistic Tradition in Bengal*. Princeton, Princeton University Press.

Roy, Asim (1996): *Islam in South Asia: A Regional Perspective*. New Delhi, South Asian Publishers.

Rühle, O. (1958): 'Hagiographie'. In: *Religion in Geschichte und Gegenwart*, Vol. 3, 1–6, 3rd edn Tübingen, J.C.B. Mohr; 26–8.

Śāhed, Saiẏad Mohāmmad (1987): *Rameś Śīl: 1877–1967*. Jībanī Granthamālā. Ḍhākā, Bāṃlā Ekāḍemi.

Said, Edward (1979): *Orientalism*. New York, Vintage Books.

Sāīd, Śām'sul Ālam (1992): *Caṭṭagrāmer mānas sampad*. Maitrī, Caṭṭagrām.

Sāk'lāẏen, Golām (1962): *Bāṃlādeśer sūphī sādhak*. Ḍhākā, Is'lāmik Phāuṇḍeśan Bāṃlādeś.

Sanyal, Usha (1996): *Devotional Islam and Politics in British India: Ahmed Riza Khan Barelwi and his Movement*, 1870–1920. Delhi, Oxford University Press.

Śarīph, Āh'mad (ed) (1985): *Āb'dul Karim sāhityaiśārad-saṃkalita puthi-pariciti*. Ḍhākā, Ḍhākā Biśvabidyālaẏ.

Schimmel, Annemarie (1983): *Der Islam im indischen Subkontinent*. Darmstadt, Wissenschaftliche Buchgesellschaft.

Schimmel, Annemarie (1995): *Mystische Dimensionen des Islam. Die Geschichte des Sufismus*. Frankfurt am Main, Insel Verlag.

Schimmel, Annemarie (1995a): *Meine Seele ist eine Frau. Das Weibliche im Islam.* München, Kösel-Verlag.

Schopen, Gregory (1997): 'Burial *Ad Sanctos* and the Physical Presence of the Buddha in Early Indian Buddhism. A Study in the Archaeology of Religions'. In: Schopen: *Bones, Stones, and Buddhist Monks*. Honolulu, University of Hawai'i Press; 114–47.

Sen, Sukumār (2001): *Bāṅgālā sāhityer itihās*, Vol.2. Kal'kātā, Ānanda Pāb'liśārs. 1st edn 1940.

Serajuddin, Asma (1998): 'Badr Pir and His Dargah at Chittagong: A Study in the Architectural Extension of Pirism'. In: Rahim, Enayetur and Schwarz, Henry (eds): *Contributions to Bengal Studies: And Interdisciplinary and International Approach.* Dhaka, Pustaka; 344–58.

Sharma, T.R. (1993): 'Psychological Analysis of *bhakti*'. In: Werner, Karel (ed.): *Love Divine: Studies in* Bhakti *and Devotional Mysticism*. Durham Indological Series No.3. Richmond, Curzon Press; 85–94.

Shastri, Vidhushekhar (1928): 'Sandhābhāṣā', *IHQ* IV, 2, 1928; 287–96.

Siegfried, Robert (2001): *Bengalens Elfter Kalif: Untersuchungen zur Naqšandiyya Muǧaddidiyya in Bangladesh.* Würzburg, Ergon Verlag.

Singer, Milton (1966): 'The Radha-Krishna Bhajans of Madras City.' In: Singer (ed.): *Krishna: Myths, Rites, and Attitudes*. Honolulu, East-West Center Press; 90–138.

Sirāj, Mustāphā Saiẏad (1988): *Alīk mānuṣ*. Kal'kātā, De'j Pāb'liśiṃ.

Sirriyeh, Elisabeth (1999): *Sufis and Anti-Sufis: The Defence, Rethinking and Rejection of Sufism in the Modern World.* Richmond, Curzon.

Skyhawk, H. van (1992): 'Ṣūfī influence in the *Ekanāthī-bhāgavat*: some observations on the text and its historical context'. In: McGregor, R.S. (1992): *Devotional Literature in South Asia: Current Research, 1985–1988*; Cambridge, Cambridge University Press; 67–79.

Slaje, Walter (2000): 'Liberation from Intentionality and Involvement: On the Concept of Jivanmukti according to the Mokṣopāya'. *Journal of Indian Philosophy* 28, 2, 2000; 171–94.

Smith, W.L. (2000): *Patterns in North Indian Hagiography*. Department of Indology, University of Stockholm, Stockholm.

Stewart, Charles and Shaw, Rosalind (eds) (1994): *Syncretism/Anti-syncretism*. London, Routledge.

Stietencron, Heinrich von (1995): 'Religious Configurations in Pre-Muslim India and the Modern Concept of Hinduism'. In: Dalmia, Vasudha and Stietencron (eds): *Representing Hinduism: The Construction of Religious Traditions and National Identity*. New Delhi, Manohar; 51–81.

Stolz, Fritz (1996): *Austauschprozesse zwischen religiösen Gemeinschaften und Symbolsystemen*. In: Drehsen, Volker and Sparn, Walter (ed.) (1996); 15–36.

Strauss, Anselm (1968): *Spiegel und Masken. Die Suche nach Identität.* Frankfurt/M., Suhrkamp.

Sunīthānanda, Bhikṣu (1995): *Bāṃlādeśer bauddha bihār o bhikṣu jīban*. Ḍhākā, Bāṃlā Ekāḍemi.

Tagore, Rabindranath (1930): *The Religion of Man*. London, George Allen & Unwin.

Tarafdar, M.R. (1986): 'The Bengali Muslims in the Pre-colonial Period: Problems of Conversion, Class Formation and Cultural Evolution'. In: Gaborieau, Marc (ed.): *Islam et Société en Asie du Sud*. Collection Puruṣārtha. Paris, École des Hautes Études en Sciences Sociales; 93–110.

Tassy, Garcin de (1995): *Muslim Festivals in India and Other Essays*. Transl. and ed.M. Waseem. Delhi, Oxford University Press.

Taylor, Christopher S. (1999): *In the Vicinity of the Righteous:* Ziyāra *and the Veneration of Muslim Saints in Late Medieval Egypt*. Leiden, Brill.

Thiel-Horstmann, Monika (ed.) (1983): *Bhakti in Current Research, 1979–1982. Proceedings of the Second International Conference on Early Devotional Literature in New Indo-Aryan Languages, St. Augustin, 19–21 March 1982*. Berlin, Dietrich Reimer Verlag.

Thiel-Horstmann, Monika (1983a): 'The *Bhajan* Repertoire of the Present-Day Dādūpanth'. In: Thiel-Horstmann (ed.) (1983): 385–401.

Thiel-Horstmann, Monika (1983b): *Crossing the Ocean of Existence. Braj Bhāṣā Religious Poetry from Rajasthan. A Reader.* Wiesbaden, Harrassowitz.

Thiel-Horstmann, Monika (ed.) (2002): *Images of Kabīr*. Delhi, Manohar.

Tirmidhī [Muḥammad Ibn-ʿAlī al-Ḥakīm al-Tirmidhī] (1996): *The Concept of Sainthood in Early Islamic Mysticism: Two Works by al-Ḥakīm al-Tirmidhī*. Transl. Radtke, Bernd and O'Kane, John. Richmond, Curzon Press.

Troll, C.W. (1989): *Muslim Shrines in India: Their Character, History and Significance*; Delhi, Oxford University Press.

Trottier, Anne-Hélène (2000): *Fakir: La quête d'un Bâul musulman*. Paris, L'Harmattan.

Tschacher, Torsten (2009): 'Rational Miracles, Cultural Rituals and the Fear of Syncretism: Defending Contentious Muslim Practice among Tamil-speaking Muslims'. *Asian Journal of Social Science 37 (2009)*; 55–82.

Tukaram (1991): *Says Tuka: Selected Poetry by Tukaram*. Transl. Dilip Chitre. Delhi, Penguin Books India.

Tukārāma (1991): *The Poems of Tukārāma*. Transl. and re-arranged with notes and introduction by J. Nelson Fraser and K.B. Marathe. Delhi, Motilal Banarsidass. 1st edn 1909.

Tulpule, S.G. (1983): 'The *Vastu*, or the Reality, of Medieval Indian Saints'. In: Thiel-Horstmann, Monika (ed.) (1983): *Bhakti in Current Research, 1979–1982. Proceedings of the Second International Conference on Early Devotional Literature in New Indo-Aryan Languages, St. Augustin, 19–21 March 1982*. Berlin, Dietrich Reimer Verlag; 403–11.

Türkmen, Erkan (1999): *The Essence of Rumi's Masnevi*. Lahore, Jumhoori Publications.

Turner, Victor (1995): *The Ritual Process. Structure and Anti-Structure*. New York, Aldine de Gruyter. 1st edn 1969.

Urban, Hugh B. (1998): 'The Torment of Secrecy: Ethical and Epistemological Problems in the Study of Esoteric Traditions'. *History of Religions* 37, 3, 1998; 209–48.

Urban, Hugh B. (2001): 'The Marketplace and the Temple: Economic Metaphors and Religious Meanings in the Folk Songs of Colonial Bengal'. *The Journal of Asian Studies* 60, 4, 2001; 1085–1114.

Vaudeville, Charlotte (1993): *A Weaver Named Kabir: Selected Verses With a Detailed Biographical and Historical Introduction*. Delhi, Oxford University Press.

Waseem, M. (2003): *On Becoming an Indian Muslim. French Essays on Aspects of Syncretism*. New Delhi, Oxford University Press.

Weiß, Christian (2001): 'Islam und Gesellschaft in Bangladesh'. In: Schreiner, Klaus H. (ed.): *Islam in Asien*. Bad Honnef, Horlemann; 70–85.

Werbner, Pnina and Basu, Helene (1998): *Embodying Charisma. Modernity, Locality and the Performance of Emotion in Sufi Cults*. London/New York, Routledge.

Werner, Karel (ed.) (1993): *Love Divine: Studies in* Bhakti *and Devotional Mysticism*. Durham Indological Series No. 3; Richmond, Curzon Press.

White, David Gordon (1996): *The Alchemical Body. Siddha Traditions in Medieval India.* Chicago/London, University of Chicago Press.

Wolff, Moritz (1872): *Kitāb aḥwāl al-qiyāma.* Muhammedanische Eschatologie. Leipzig, Brockhaus (Reprint Georg Olms Verlag, Hildesheim/Zürich/New York, 2004).

Zbavitel, Dušan (1976): *A History of Bengali Literature*. In: Gonda, Jan (ed.): *A History of Indian Literature*, Vol. IX, Fasc. 3. Wiesbaden, Harrassowitz.

Zbavitel, Dušan and Mode, Heinz (1976) (eds): *Bengalische Balladen.* Leipzig, Insel-Verlag.

Index

This index lists proper names, places, concepts, institutions, etc. of both local and general purport. As regards the numerous Maijbhandari personalities featuring in this book, it is not possible to index them all, and included are only the short forms of the names of the most prominent past saints and those singers and scholars that have been given particular attention in this study.

abatār / avatāra 73, 215, 216, 219, 228, 284–86

Abd al-Qadir Gilani / Jilani 20, 23, 28, 38, 67, 75, 79, 85, 90 n80, 91, 107 n3, 117, 125, 129, 134, 137, 146, 149–50, 158, 163, 211 n239, 216–18, 232–33, 285

Abdul Gafur Hali 16, 53 n76, 60, 73 n18, 172 n1, 173 n6, 183 n38, 187 n52, 188, 191 n64, 192–93, 196–99, 201, 203–06, 209–10, 212–15, 217–18, 220–21, 225–27, 230–32, 237–40, 242–43, 245–50, 253–54, 256–57, 259, 261 n643, 262–63, 265–67, 269, 276 n8, 309, 332–33

Abdul Ghani Kanchanpuri 22, 49 n59, 62, 68–71, 77 n37, 78–82, 84–85, 89–91, 93, 97–99, 101, 111–13, 115–21, 123 n51, 124, 147, 167, 170, 174, 180 n28, 182, 308 n58, 309, 352

Abdul Haq Farhadabadi 49 n59, 68, 97, 174 n9, 180 n28, 181–82

Abdul Jabbar Mimnagari 69, 71–72, 79, 81–82, 88 n69, 103, 172 n1, 188, 191 n72f., 192 n75f., 196 n110, 197 n128, 200–01, 203, 206, 211 n242, 213, 215, 217, 226, 229, 232, 236–37, 239, 242 n506, 246–47, 251, 253, 255 n605, 342

Abdul Karim Sahityavisharad 67, 72, 108, 111 n18, 234, 323

Abu Shahmah Muhammad Saleh Lahori 119, 123, 130

Adam 71, 74, 197, 199–201, 218, 232

ādhyātmik dhārā 38, 40, 100

ahl al-kitāb 87, 93, 287

Ahmad Sharif 67, 72, 108, 240 n496, 244 n521, 323

Ahmadiyya Manzil 25 n85, 26–27, 29, 39–40, 45–46, 68 n2, 69, 103, 122, 127, 152 n126, 153, 172 n1, 314

Ahmadullah Maijbhandari 16, 18–29, 33–39, 45, 50–51, 56, 61 n99, 63, 66–69, 75–76, 87, 89 n76, 90–91, 93–95, 97–100, 102–04, 112–36, 138–41, 143, 145–53, 158, 162–63, 166, 169–70, 173 n6, 174, 181–83, 187, 202, 205, 215, 268 n706, 294, 299–300, 303, 307

ʿAli (b. Abi Talib) 38, 74 n21, 80, 90–91, 149, 165, 232, 306

Aliullah Rajapuri 73 n18, 81 n46, 97–98, 173–74, 188, 190–92, 195–96, 200, 205, 208, 210 n230, 211 n240f.–213 n270, 215, 226, 228–32, 242 n506f., 243–46, 250–51, 254, 262 n648, 263, 265, 269, 277, 309, 330

Aliya Madrassah (Calcutta) 22,119, 130

Allama Rumi Society (Chittagong) xi, 98 n111, 104, 176
Amanat Shah (Chittagong) 13, 33 n3, 107 n3, 141, 155, 159, 173, 332
Amir Bhandar (Potai, Chittagong) 103
anā 'l-ḥaqq 212, 216, 233, 296 n27
Āñjumāne Rah'māniẏā Maïnīẏā Māij'bhāṇḍārīẏā / Anjuman-i Muiniyya 46, 98 n111
Anjumane Mottabeyine Gauche Maijbhandar 44–46, 98 n111
Anwara (Chittagong Division) 13, 173 n6, 322
Arabic (language) 6, 25 n85, 51, 68, 108 n6, 110–12, 127, 139, 145, 163, 186, 189, 316, 324–35
Ashraf ʿAli Thanawi 73 n87
ʿāšiq 70, 125, 164 n141, 182, 183, 233, 246, 340
Atrasi Pir (Faridpur) 32, 39 n21
avatāra see abatār

Badr Shah (Chittagong) 11, 13, 21, 32, 33 n3, 137, 141, 168, 300, 322
Badruddoza Maijbhandari 25, 68–69, 104, 112, 113 n24, 114 n26, 143–47, 158 n135, 168, 303 n44
Badrunnesa Saju 188, 190 n61, 191 n 70, 193 n83, 199 n143, 210 n227, 211 n241, 212, 251f., 214, 239, 242 n513, 243, 254 n599, 262 n655, 284, 294 n23, 333
Bagdad 137–38, 168, 180, 214, 216, 217, 285
Bajlul Karim Mandakini 174, 184 n42, 187 n51, 188, 193 n81f., 199–200, 201 n160, 203, 209–10, 214 n274f., 216, 218, 222, 280–81, 294 n23, 335
Bankimchandra Chattopadhyay 116 n31, 149 n119, 311 n67
bāra āuliẏār deś / bāro āuliẏār deś 11, 110, 116, 137, 145
baraka 39, 50, 61, 259 n632, 300, 307
baqāʾ bi-Llah 78, 89, 153, 226
barzaḫ 54, 55, 143, 197, 258 n628, 274, 276
bāšarʿ 80, 81
bāṭin 24, 40, 71, 75, 79–82, 85, 90, 97 n109, 99 n115, 114, 161, 168, 249, 267 n699, 308
Battuta, Ibn 11 n21, 109
Bauls *(bāul)* 2, 3, 10, 77 n40, 105, 173, 175, 184, 192 n80, 201, 202, 207, 229 n391, 231 n411, 249, 253, 255, 258, 262, 263, 265 n673, 266, 270, 271, 278, 279, 288, 296
Baul songs *(bāul gān)* 77 n40, 173, 175, 184, 192, 231, 255, 262, 263 n660, 265 n673, 270, 271, 324
bayʿa 17 n52, 40, 42, 57, 58, 64, 87, 100, 141, 152, 302 n42, 307
Bayezid Bistami 13, 85, 107 n3, 141, 161
Benares *see* Kashi
Bengali Islam *see* Islam
Bethlehem 164
bhāb 194 n101, 207 n206, 213 n262, 215 n285, 219 n318, 222 n350, 225, 227, 229 n385, 236 n454, 239 n478, 240 n489, 250 n567f., 251, 275 n7, 284 n28, 332–34
Bhagavadgītā 215–16, 268, 311 n67
Bhāgavatapurāṇa 234 n445, 282
bhakta 15 n35, 28, 42, 59 n95, 164 n141, 166, 194, 208 n217, 224, 225, 230, 231, 237, 243, 251, 282–84
bhakti 60, 73 n17, 107, 185 n46, 190 n61, 192, 194, 195 n103, 203 n175, 209, 211, 213, 214, 218–22, 225, 227–28, 231, 233–44, 255, 269, 273, 282, 283, 287 n1
bhaṇitā 190, 192, 253
bhāṭiẏālī 184, 255
Bible 198 n131, 220, 223, 309
bidʿa 142
bīšarʿ 23, 24
Buddha 12, 18 n34, 34 n6, 91, 102, 173 n7, 222
Buddhist(s) 11 n21, 12, 116 n31, 133, 144, 150, 160, 223, 202, 312
Buddhism 12, 18 n34, 34 n6, 85, 91, 93, 159, 220, 222, 254, 255 n605, 258, 260 n639, 263 n658, 299, 302, 312, 325

cakra 77, 198 n131, 259–63, 266–67, 274
Calcutta 16 n47, 22, 56 n85, 110, 111, 119, 130, 158 n12, 189, 264 n665, 278 n14

Caryāpadas 190 n61, 254, 256, 258–60, 277–78, 325
Chakma 133, 144, 312
Chishtiyya 32, 34 n4, 39 n20, 49 n56, 52, 64 n111, 67, 90, 97, 98, 100, 102, 107 n4, 161, 175, 176 n17, 179, 216, 320 n11
Chittagong x, xi, 2, 7, 8, 10–14, 16–22, 29, 32–34, 44, 45, 48, 51, 64, 67, 74, 94, 98 n111, 104, 105, 107 n3, 110 n14, 111 n19, 116, 117, 122, 124, 128, 129, 132–34, 137–41, 144, 145, 149–52, 155, 158–161, 163, 167, 168, 172, 173, 176–81, 189, 190 n61, 217 n304, 220, 222 n329, 245 n530, 268 n706, 273, 278, 282, 285, 288 n2, 294 n23, 298, 300, 308, 312, 322, 323, 329 n31
Chittagong Hill Tracts 7, 12, 17, 64, 121 n48, 133, 140, 159, 287 n1, 312
čilla 33, 141 n103

darbār 18, 23–24, 26, 29, 31, 34, 36–42, 44, 46, 48, 55, 58–61, 67–68, 70, 81, 99–100, 112, 121–33, 136, 140, 144, 158, 163–64, 167, 174–76, 182, 214, 222, 224, 230, 249, 253, 267, 271, 311–12, 336, 340
dargāh 11 n, 31–34, 39 n20, 48–49, 57, 64 n111, 89, 105 n139, 141 n103, 173–77, 179, 185, 287 n1, 336
darśan 143, 212
ḏāt 70, 78, 84
dehatattva 186, 205 n192, 229 n391, 249, 256–60, 262–66, 268–70, 273–79, 293 n21, 310
Delawar Hosain Maijbhandari 26–29, 38–39, 45, 64 n113, 68 n3, 69, 76, 77 n37, 85–86, 88–96, 98, 100–03, 105, 112–13, 126–28, 130–31, 133, 135–36, 143, 148, 150–53, 158–59, 161, 168, 170–71, 174, 180, 187, 204, 256, 300, 302–04, 314
Delawar Hosain Saidi 301
Dhaka 19, 29, 45, 57, 61 n98, 67, 69, 75 n25, 108, 141, 152, 288 n2, 312, 314, 339 n20
Dharma (as 'religion') 3, 86, 88 n69, 116 n31, 128, 149, 216, 276, 303 n46, 312
Dharma (deity) 20, 21, 108 n7
dharmajātinirbiśeṣe / jātidharmanirbiśeṣe ('irrespective of religion and caste / class') 7, 86, 128, 134, 144, 146, 150, 169–70, 220, 222, 224, 272, 286, 311–12
dharmanirapekṣatā 133, 312
ḏikr / jikir 44, 46, 50–53, 55, 62, 64, 67, 100–01, 103–04, 132, 150, 159, 176, 183 n34, 195, 213, 275, 320 n11
discursive field (as a notion applied to Maijbhandar) 287, 297–305, 310–11, 323, 326–29
du'ā / doẏā 50, 243 n520, 284, 331
Durga 248

Eaton, Richard 11 n19, 21–22, 31 n1, 36 n9, 109–10, 292 n15, 296 n29, 300, 324 n20, 328
Ekdil Shah (Barasat) 108
Enamul Haq, Muhammad 2–3, 11 n19f., 13 n27f., 16 n45, 18 n59, 20, 24, 49 n60, 52 n70, 55 n82, 69 n8, 72, 77 n36f., 109, 110 n15, 249 n564, 318 n8
Ershad, Hosain Mohammad 29–30, 315 n1
Eve 232

fanā' 33, 52, 54–55, 78–79, 85 n61, 89, 100–01, 114, 123, 153, 161, 165, 226–27, 235 n446, 296
faqīr 23, 44–45, 64 n111, 132, 142, 165, 185 n46, 193, 233, 278 n13
Farā'iżīs 93 n95, 110, 120 n43, 180, 192 n77, 233, 295, 316–17, 320 n11
farḍ 120, 141
Farhadabadi *see* Abdul Haq Farhadabadi
Farid al-Din 'Attar 67, 202 n168
Farid al-Din Shakrganj / Ganj-i Shakr 13, 107 n3
Farid Hosain 73 n18, 75, 172, 188, 191 n64f., 192 n75f., 193, 196–97, 199, 200 n149, 201, 204, 205 n194, 208–09, 210 n227f., 211 n241, 213 n267, 214 n282, 215–16, 217 n305, 223, 225–26, 228, 230–1, 233, 237, 240–41, 242 n506f., 245–47, 249–51, 253, 256, 259 n632, 262 n655, 264 n665, 265–69, 338–39

fātiha 52, 64, 160
fayḍ 131, 307

ǧabarūt 77, 117, 258, 261, 274–75
Gafur Hali *see* Abdul Gafur Hali
ǧāhil / ǧāhiliyya 146, 149
Gandhi, Indira 29, 154, 168
Gandhi, Mahatma 101 n121
Garam Bibi 322
Gaudiya Vaishnavism 27 n93, 194 n101, 211, 218, 224, 253
Gaur 20, 67, 107 n4, 129, 138
Ġawṯ al-A'ẓam / ġauṯiyya (except where used as a mere title) 18, 25 n85, 26, 89–91, 95–96, 114, 116–17, 122–25, 128, 133–35, 143, 146, 149–50, 153, 158, 162–63, 166, 177, 207, 213, 215, 228, 247–48, 250, 255, 259 n632, 269, 283, 294, 334, 337, 340
Geertz, Clifford 6 n12, 9–10, 39, 287 n1, 295, 320 n12, 327 n28, 329 n31
ghazal 68, 115–16, 118, 122–23, 138, 140, 163, 174, 186, 207, 335
Ghazzali, Abu Hamid 76, 77 n33, 161, 182, 197, 255 n607, 256 n616
Gholam Rahman Maijbhandari 21, 25–29, 36–40, 42 n32, 43, 45–46, 50, 61–63, 65, 68–69, 75, 90, 95–96, 100, 103, 112, 124, 126–27, 132–33, 135–47, 150–53, 158–59, 163, 165–66, 168, 170, 174, 176 n17, 183, 185 n46, 187, 191 n63, 198, 205, 212, 213 n273, 236, 243–44, 283, 307, 321
ǧihād 20, 123, 165
ǧinn 11, 71, 75, 121, 339
Gisudaraz, Bandanawaz (of Gulbarga, India) 34 n4, 175 n15
gopī 108 n8, 235, 335, 340
ǧumma namāz 52
Gurudas Faqir 133, 173

Hadi, Maulana Abdul 133, 174 n11, 186 n47, 187 n51, 188, 191 n64f., 192 n75, 193 n85f., 196 n117f., 197, 198 n137, 203, 206–07, 210 n227f., 211–12, 226, 229–30, 232 n427f., 233, 236, 238–47, 250, 255 n605, 280, 282–84, 286 n47, 287 n51, 334–35
ḫādim 41–42, 44, 48–50, 53, 55, 57–58, 62, 120, 124 n54, 125, 133, 147, 153, 173 n6, 193, 208, 275 n6, 322 n15
Ḥadīṯ 2, 54 n78, 73, 76, 81 n47, 82, 117 n33, 121, 144, 155, 160, 166, 168, 180–82, 202, 327
ḥaǧǧ 132, 143, 214, 294 n23
ḥāl, pl. *aḥwāl* 45 n48, 71 (*ḥālat-i ǧazb*), 78, 85 (*tauḥīd-i ḥālī*), 103, 119, 154, 161, 189, 275 n7
ḫalīfa / khaliphā 19, 22–23, 26, 38–40, 45 n45, 51 n65, 68, 103, 109, 113, 128, 135–36, 143, 147, 158, 183, 300, 322
Hallaj *see* Mansur al-Hallaj
ḥalqa (*-i ḏikr, -i samā'*) 50, 51 n65, 64, 142, 175, 191
Haq, Muhammad Enamul *see* Enamul Haq, Muhammad
Haq Manzil 15 n38, 19 n61, 26, 28–29, 36–37, 39, 42, 45, 61, 95, 102–03, 148, 153, 158, 160, 208, 251 n580, 300 n35
ḥaqīqa / hākikat 77, 79, 81–82, 85, 96, 153
Ḥaqq 70, 80, 142, 212, 216, 233, 296
Hasan al-Basri 90
Hasan Maijbhandari, Syed 159–60, 251 n580
Hāsan Rājār gān 173, 258, 324
Ḫiḏr 83, 89, 104 n131, 158, 341
hiğra 146
Hindu (concepts, practices, deities, institutions) 3, 6 n12, 37 n13, 50, 63 n105, 67, 108, 116 n31, 145 n113, 178, 197 n128, 206, 211, 215–16, 220, 234, 235 n446, 228 n473, 248 n552, 258, 260, 275–76, 282, 285–86, 318, 325
Hinduism 2 n5, 12, 85, 87, 93, 221, 283, 285, 291–92, 296 n29, 299, 302, 311–13, 317–18, 323, 325
Hindus 5, 7, 12, 24, 42, 45, 93, 109–11, 121 n45, 122–23, 133, 135, 142, 144, 150, 155, 158, 166, 173–74, 222–24, 232, 272, 276, 303, 311–12
huǧra 33, 50, 122, 163
ḫušrūz 27, 61, 63, 147, 175, 179, 185 n46

Ibn 'Arabi 54, 58 n91, 67, 69, 76, 78 n41, 84 n60, 85, 91, 94–95, 129, 150 n121,

161, 182, 243 n514, 258 n628, 294 n23
inclusivism (cf. also under Islam and Maijbhandar) 87 n65, 292
insān al-kāmil 161, 200
Iqbal, Muhammad 5 n10, 296
Islam: as religion of peace 92, 303; Bengali 1–3, 5–10, 30, 113, 179, 293, 296, 298, 315–18, 323, 325–29; inclusivist 85–87, 93, 283, 303, 305, 309; reformist / reformism 2, 4–5, 14–15, 49, 54 n79, 89, 110, 147, 170, 179–80, 282, 290 n11, 293–95, 304, 316–24, 329; Sunni 144, 179, 315–17, 319
Islamisation of East Bengal 5, 11, 21, 292 n15, 293, 296 n29, 317 n5
ʿišq 69–72, 79, 104, 182, 228, 231 n411, 233, 235 n446, 336
ʿIzrāʾīl 77, 131, 206, 261 n640, 331

Jahangir, Selim 15–16, 20 n63, 22 n75, 24, 26 n90, 27, 30, 36 n12, 38 n16, 44, 48, 63–64, 98 n111, 102 n127, 103, 105, 113, 129, 171 n150, 172 n3, 174, 183, 187, 214, 251 n580, 288 n2, 312, 314
Jalal al-Din Rumi 67, 71 n13, 72, 78, 85, 136–37, 139, 161, 202, 207–08, 215, 225 n351, 226, 241, 243 n514, 285, 332 n7
Jamaat-e Islami 301
Jamiẏate Māij'bhāṇḍārī 45
jāti 75, 102 n125, 150, 215, 222, 312
jātidharmanirbiśeṣe see dharmajātinirbiśeṣe
Jerusalem 164
Jesus Christ 91, 151, 222, 224 n342, 302

Kaʿba (except when used as honorific) 55, 125, 132, 133, 141, 196, 213–14, 217, 220–21, 303 n47, 332, 335, 339
kabigān / kabiẏāl 174
Kabir 190 n61, 195 n107, 203 n175, 207 n211, 221, 225, 233 n440, 238 n476, 269 n710, 313 n72
Kali (goddess) 220
kali yuga 210, 216, 303 n44, 340
kalima 52 n74, 73,–75, 77, 79, 84–85, 122, 213
kamāliyyāt 70
Kanchanpuri *see* Abdul Ghani Kanchanpuri
karāma, pl. *karāmāt* 22, 43 n37, 120, 141, 146, 158, 162, 165–67, 169
Kashi / Benares 214, 217, 220, 221, 303 n47, 308, 335
Khan, Syed Ahmad 304
Khan Jahan ʿAli 32, 34 n4, 296 n29
Khelā 201n, 204n, 207n, 217n, 218n, 228–29, 243–49, 252n, 282n, 285n, 331–32, 334, 340
kr̥ṣṇabhakti 235, 240–41, 243, 283
kr̥ṣṇalīlā 108, 240, 281
kufr 79, 142, 146, 199
Kuki 133, 312
Kumilla 19, 22, 24, 175
kuṇḍalinī 260, 275

lāhūt 77–78, 90, 117, 259, 261, 274
Lalan Faqir (or Shah) 105, 173, 175 n16, 184, 249, 279 n19
laṭīfa, pl. *laṭāʾif* 52, 195, 261
Liberation War (of Bangladesh) 105 n140, 112, 312
līlā 75, 108, 218 n316, 240, 247–48, 281, 339
Little Tradition (Redfield) 5, 9, 293–94, 295 n25
Lutfunnesa Hosaini 68 n3, 69, 73–76, 87–88, 113, 162, 165–66, 168, 170, 188, 191, 192 n80, 193 n81f., 196, 200, 202, 211, 212 n258, 216, 218, 222 n333, 226, 233, 237 n465, 239, 248, 254–55, 338

maḏhab 85, 97, 128
Maghs / Moghs 12, 18, 117 n36, 118, 133, 144, 287 n1, 296
Mahamuni 12, 222 n329
Mahbubul Alam 57 n18, 186, 188 n54, 189 n56, 190 n61, 210, 226, 230, 241, 242 n507f., 249 n564, 250, 253
Maijbhandar: discursive field 298–310; in secondary literature 16–17;

inclusivist 47, 93, 300–03, 305; *māij'bhāṇḍārī darśan*, 'Maijbhandari philosophy' 66, 69, 156, 161, 228, 295 n25; Maijbhandari songs (*gān*) 10, 15–16, 17 n53, 24, 25 n84, 29 n103, 47–48, 50 n64, 51, 53, 55, 62, 66–67, 80, 97, 103, 147, 188–286, 293–94, 302–03, 305 n49, 306, 308–10, 313–14, 324, 330–42; nationalisation of 105, 296, 312, 315; on Bangladeshi national plane 19, 105, 294, 312, 315; outline 14–30; polycentric structure 31, 46, 289, 310; praised in hagiographical accounts 116–17, 138, 144–45, 158, 167–69
Maijbhandari *ṭarīqa* 17, 23, 27, 31, 42, 46, 48, 51 n65, 66, 93–105, 128, 139, 143–44, 146–50, 153, 161, 163–66, 180 n28, 269, 276–77, 299–300, 305, 309, 315
Māij'bhāṇḍārī Gabeṣaṇā Pariṣad 45
Māij'bhāṇḍārī Pariṣad 44
malakūt 77–78, 115, 117, 129, 258, 261, 274, 276
Manasa (*manasā*, deity) 12 n22, 108 n7
Mandakini *see* Bajlul Karim Mandakini
Mānik'pīr 108
Mansur al-Hallaj 84, 161, 212 n254, 216, 226 n360, 232–33
maqām, pl. *maqāmāt* 25 n82, 54–55, 71, 76–79, 81, 84, 86, 89, 97–98, 117, 155, 161, 255, 261, 274–76, 310
Maramī Goṣṭhī 45, 164
ma'rifa 71, 77, 79–84, 86, 301
mastāna 207 n206, 230 n397, 249–50, 334, 341
ma'šūq 70–71, 79, 117, 231, 246, 284, 308
*maulabādī*s / 'fundamentalists'
mawlā 187, 198–99, 204, 207, 209, 217, 228, 230, 233, 236, 239, 245–47, 268–69, 284, 340, 341
mazār 25 n82, 33–34, 40, 49–50, 136, 141, 148, 151, 155, 159, 181, 308, 314, 319, 322
Mecca 9, 24, 49, 55, 76, 117, 129, 132–33, 142, 155, 160, 164, 214, 220, 294, 308, 318–19, 328
Medina 95 n103, 117, 132, 164, 214, 217, 220–21, 285, 303 n47, 308
Mimnagari *see* Abdul Jabbar Mimnagari
Mirabai 192 n80, 234 n441
mi'rāğ 149, 151, 155
Mirzakhil 13, 23–24, 39 n21, 132, 300 n37
Moses 83, 89 n77, 91, 164, 232–33
mu'ğaza, pl. *mu'ğazāt* (Prophetic miracle) 120, 141, 146, 158, 165
muğāddid 95–96, 128, 144, 158
Muhammad (the Prophet) 39, 51, 72–77, 80, 83–85, 87, 91–92, 94, 95 n103, 115–16, 118, 125, 128–29, 134, 145 n115, 149, 151, 155, 158, 164, 166, 168, 216–18, 224 n342, 234 n444, 247 n546, 285, 294 n23, 306
Muhsin Auliya 13, 173, 322
Mu'in al-Din Chishti 32, 34 n4, 39 n20, 49 n56, 64 n111, 67, 75, 137, 160–61, 175, 216–18, 232–33, 285
Mujaddidiyya 97–98, 102
Mujibur Rahman, Sheikh 151, 161, 168
Munkar and *nakīr* 132, 206 n199, 217
murāqaba 54–56, 100, 103
murīd 13, 16 n41, 22 n75, 23, 25, 28–29, 32, 42–49, 55–64, 69, 87, 89 n76, 90 n80, 95 n103, 96–97, 115, 121, 127, 142–44, 146, 148, 153–54, 156, 159–60, 174–75, 186 n17, 192, 214, 221, 258 n628, 259, 267 n695, 273–74, 275 n6, 282, 300, 306–11, 313–14
muršid 37, 54, 56–57, 72, 87, 100 n118, 102, 104, 127, 143, 162–63, 166, 186–87, 191, 200, 204, 214–15, 225, 229, 243, 246, 253, 255 n609, 256, 258 n628, 261–62, 267 n695, 275, 283 n26, 284, 293 n21, 308, 310, 341
mušāḥida 89, 103

nāḍī / *nāṛī* 257 n624, 259–61, 268, 274–75, 267 n692
nafs 52, 71–72, 80–81, 91, 97, 101, 104, 123, 199–200, 208, 267, 276
Nakīr see Munkar
namāz 24, 50, 52, 79, 138, 296 n29
Naqshbandiyya 17 n50, 54 n79, 97–98, 102
nāsūt 77–78, 90, 128, 258, 261–62, 274–76

nationalism (in Bangladesh) 105 n138f., 296 n27, 312, 329
nirguṇa bhakti 218
nisba 72, 336
Nizam al-Din Awliya 25 n82, 32, 24 n6, 39 n20, 175 n15, 313 n72
Noakhali 19, 22, 113 n25, 166, 175
nubuwwa 81 n48, 91–92, 149, 161, 182
nūr / nūr-i muḥammadī 71–76, 89–90, 110 n14, 116, 129, 164, 197 n128f., 198 n132, 203 n172, 204 n181, 212, 215 n289f., 218, 222, 229 n396, 247 n546, 248 n560, 268, 294 n23, 327 n26, 334, 337

Pabna Mental Hospital 28, 153, 159, 167
pāgal ('crazy', cf. also *mastāna*) 82, 193, 205 n193, 212 n254, 236, 241 n497, 249–53, 333, 340
Pakistan 68 n6, 90, 151 n123, 165, 224
Pakistani Sufi institutions etc. 34 n5, 49 n57, 175, 236 n449, 320 n11
Pakistani period (1947–1971) 2, 46, 170, 311, 316
Pandua 67, 107 n4
Persian (language) 6, 25 n85, 27, 51, 67–68, 71, 88 n70, 96, 107, 108 n4f., 109–12, 127, 139, 145 n115, 163, 169, 174, 182, 186, 190 n59, 227, 235 n446, 328, 335–37
parda 76 n26, 88 n68, 121, 222 n332, 226 n361, 319
Phaẏā (Chittagongian appellation of the Buddha) 222
pīr 33–43, 209–19, and *passim*
pīrī-murīdī 144
Potia 20, 119, 129
prem 69, 71–72, 82, 104 n132f., 193 n85, 207 n210, 208 n218, 209 n224, 213 n262, 215, 228–33, 235 n446, 236 n449, 237 n461f., 238 n474f., 239 n479f., 241 n429, 244 n522, 246 n531f., 247, 250, 265 n667, 270, 280 n22, 281n23, 282 n25, 330, 332–35, 337, 339–41
pūjā 155, 199 n139

Qadam Mubarak Mosque (Anderkilla, Chittagong) 12, 74
Qadiriyya 38, 67, 90, 97–102, 128
qalandar 45
Qalandar, Bu 'Ali 84–85
Qalandariyya 91 n88, 102
qawwālī 175
qibla (except as part of honorific titles) 34, 71, 143, 229
Qur'ān 3, 24, 34 n6, 64 n110, 71–72, 74, 80–87, 93, 102, 115–16, 120, 123–25, 130, 134 n82, 136, 142, 144, 148, 153, 158, 160–66, 180–82, 195, 199, 206–7, 216–17, 220, 223, 227, 267 n696, 286, 302–04, 309, 318, 327, 329 n31

Rabi'a of Basra 161
Rabindranath Tagore 3 n6
rābiṭa 57, 99 n115
Radha 232, 234–35, 240, 243–44, 262 n653, 280–81, 283
Radhakrishnan, Sarvepalli 288 n2
Rahmaniyya Manzil 25 n85, 26–27, 29, 34, 36–37, 39, 42, 45–46, 69, 95–96, 103–04, 135, 143
Rajapuri *see* Aliullah Rajapuri
rakter dhārā 39–40
Ramesh Shil (song writer) 17, 27, 54 n81, 55 n82, 73 n18, 147, 172 n1, 174, 183 n36, 184–85, 187–89, 191–93, 196–201, 203–04, 206–18, 220–33, 236, 238–42, 244–56, 258, 261–69, 271, 274, 276–80, 284–85, 303 n47, 331–32
Rangoon 121 n45, 123
raqs 103, 142
rasūl 72, 215 n285f., 216 n301, 244 n522, 285
rawḍa 33–34, 125, 160
Reagan, Ronald 154
riyāẓa 152, 162
Rokeya Begum (Rokeya Sakhawat Hosain) 111 n18
Roy, Asim 3–5, 21 n70, 37 n13, 67, 72–73, 77, 109, 285 n30, 287 n1, 293, 294 n24, 295 n25, 316, 318 n9, 323–26
Rumi, Jalal al-Din *see* Jalal al-Din Rumi

sādhanā 145, 150–51, 153, 258, 263, 274, 341
šağara 22 n72, 38, 158

sağda 2, 49, 97, 133, 152, 182, 301, 319, 322
saǧǧādanašīn 26, 28 n101, 29, 32, 38, 39 n22, 40, 43, 58, 64, 68–9, 126, 153, 251 n580, 300 n35, 307 n56, 314
saguṇa bhakti 218–19
Saleh Lahori *see* Abu Shahmah Muhammad Saleh Lahori
*samā*ʿ 44, 51–54, 68, 78, 97, 104 n134, 119, 142, 150, 174–76, 179–83, 185 n45, 246 n535, 254 n602, 301, 319, 334
Śaman(a) 203, 206
samanvaẏ(a) 16 n41, 76, 288
sampradāẏ 82, 311
sandhābhāṣā 258–59, 263, 273–74, 277, 279–80
sāqī 211–12
*śariẏatpanthī*s 299, 301, 304
Satyanārāẏaṇ / Satyapīr 12 n22, 108 n7
Schiffauer, Werner 297
Shafiul Bashar Maijbhandari 27 n95f., 28–29, 36–37, 39 n22, 45, 51, 63, 68 n3, 73 n18, 100, 113, 162–67, 169 n22, 185 n46, 187, 188 n54, 191 n63f., 192 n75f., 193 n81f., 196, 197 n128, 200, 203, 211 n241f., 212 n258f., 213–17, 225–27, 229–31, 233, 237–38, 240 n493f., 241–42, 247, 251, 255–56, 265 n677, 266, 268, 307 n55f., 337
Shah Jalal of Aleppo 20
Shah Jalal of Sylhet 13 n31, 32, 38 n16, 43 n33, 107 n3, 109–10, 112, 139, 319, 322, 328 n29
Shah Jalal Tabrizi 107 n4, 108 n4
Shah of Iran (Reza Pahlavi) 154, 168
Shamsher Tabrizi 84
Shirin and Farhad 216 n300, 232
Shiva 234, 261 n642, 318 n8, 335
ṣifa, pl. *ṣifāt* 70, 78–79, 84, 149, 231
silsila 38–39, 80, 135, 139, 148, 153, 276, 306, 308
širk 88, 142, 146
Sitakunda 7, 11 n19, 12, 17, 140, 278
Sufism: Sufi concepts 69–96 (and terms in this index); Sufi orders *see* Qadiriyya, Chishtiyya, naqshbandiyya, Suhrawardiyya, Mujaddidiyya, Maijbhandari *ṭarīqa*; Sufi saints *see walī / awliyā*ʾ
Suhrawardiyya 90, 100, 102
Sultan, Saiyad 255, 278, 285 n30, 316, 324
Śyāma (appelation of Krishna) 240–41, 281
syncretism (syncretic, syncretistic) 3–8, 16 n17, 105 n140, 221 n326, 270 n712, 285 n30, 287–94, 297, 324

tabarruk 64
tağallī 69–70, 78, 117
Tagore *see* Rabindranath Tagore
Tantra / tantric 2, 11, 77, 129 n63, 229 n385f., 248, 254, 258–60, 269, 274, 277–78, 299, 302, 313, 323–25
tanzīlāt 78
ṭarīqa (as mystical path) 71–72, 77, 79–85, 89, 97, 182, 254
ṭarīqa (as Sufi order) 17, 20, 24, 39 n20, 47, 52 n70, 72, 90, 91 n88, 93, 97–102, 161, 216, 299–301, 304, 307, 323
ṭarīqa (Maijbhandari) *see* Maijbhandari *ṭarīqa*
Ṭarīqa al-Muḥammadiyya 316–17
tauhīd-i adyān ('unity of religions') 85–86, 88, 93, 96, 150, 302
Thakurgaon 39 n21, 74 n22, 134 n83, 200 n150
triveṇī / tribeṇī 257, 258 n627, 259–60, 262–63, 274–76
Tukaram 219 n319, 234 n441, 238 n476

*ʿulamā*ʾ, sg. *ʿālim* 19, 41, 45, 67, 80, 81 n49, 83–85, 114, 116, 120, 132, 142, 150, 167–68, 170, 179, 181–82, 325
Urdu (language) 6, 23, 25 n85, 27, 51, 96, 110–12, 114, 127, 132, 155, 163, 169–70, 174, 182, 186, 190, 236, 328 n30
Urdu in Bengali script 212 n249f., 213 n270, 216 n302, 217 n304, 229 n393
ʿurs 13, 15, 27, 28 n98, 43, 45, 51, 53, 61–65, 108, 135, 142, 147–48, 173 n6, 175, 177, 214 n277, 252, 277, 278 n13, 296, 312–14

Uways al-Karani 90, 139, 232–33

Vaishnava(s) 10, 194 n101, 218, 227 n369, 232 n419, 234–35, 240 n487, 244, 253, 270, 273, 281–82, 293 n21, 299, 313, 324, 327 n26
viraha bhakti 192, 195, 214, 227, 231, 233–35, 240 n492f., 243, 255, 282
Viṣṇupurāṇa 282
Vrindavan 214, 217, 220–22, 235, 240, 327, 335

Wahab Manzil 46
waḥdat al-wuǧūd 84, 161
*Wahhābī*s 144, 158, 182 n30, 294, 301, 317, 323
waḥy 151
walī, pl. *awliyāʾ* / āuliẏā 11, 13, 26, 32, 37 n13, 39, 57 n88, 72, 88–90, 94–95, 110 n14, 114, 116, 127, 130, 134, 137, 144–45, 150–51, 154–55, 158, 159 n136, 165, 208, 247, 294 n23
waǧd 142
Waliullah, Shah 72 n15, 320 n11
waqf (in relation to Maijbhandar) 13, 29, 46
Warith ʿAli Shah (Dewa, India) 221 n325, 222 n331, 255 n607, 302 n42
wilāya / *vilāyat* / *belāẏat* 18, 22, 28, 36, 38–39, 58, 61, 76 n28, 81 n48, 88–96, 102, 114 n27, 120–23, 125, 128, 130, 134–35, 144, 149, 151–53, 161, 166, 222 n333, 294 n23, 300, 307, 341

Yama 206, 208 n213, 213
yogī 146, 247–48, 268
yoginī 236, 239, 240
Yusuf 138, 146, 232, 235, 250, 340

ẓāhir 75, 79–82, 85, 114, 143, 161, 168, 308
Ziaul Haq Maijbhandari 16, 21, 26–28, 34 n4, 36, 39 n22, 50, 63, 96, 103, 113, 130 n64, 148, 151–62, 167–70, 187, 197, 204 n182, 238, 247, 284, 312 n71
Zulaykha 232, 235, 250